Gymanfa Ganu
Cleveland
2011

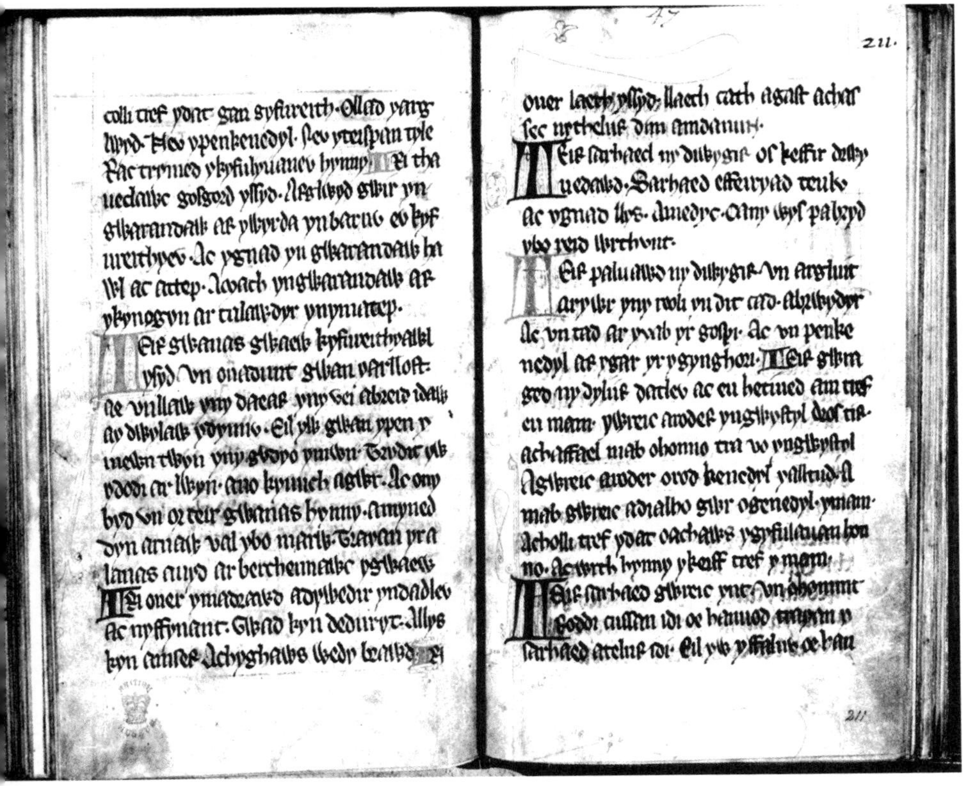

BL Cotton Cleopatra Bv, fols. 210v and 211r. © British Library.

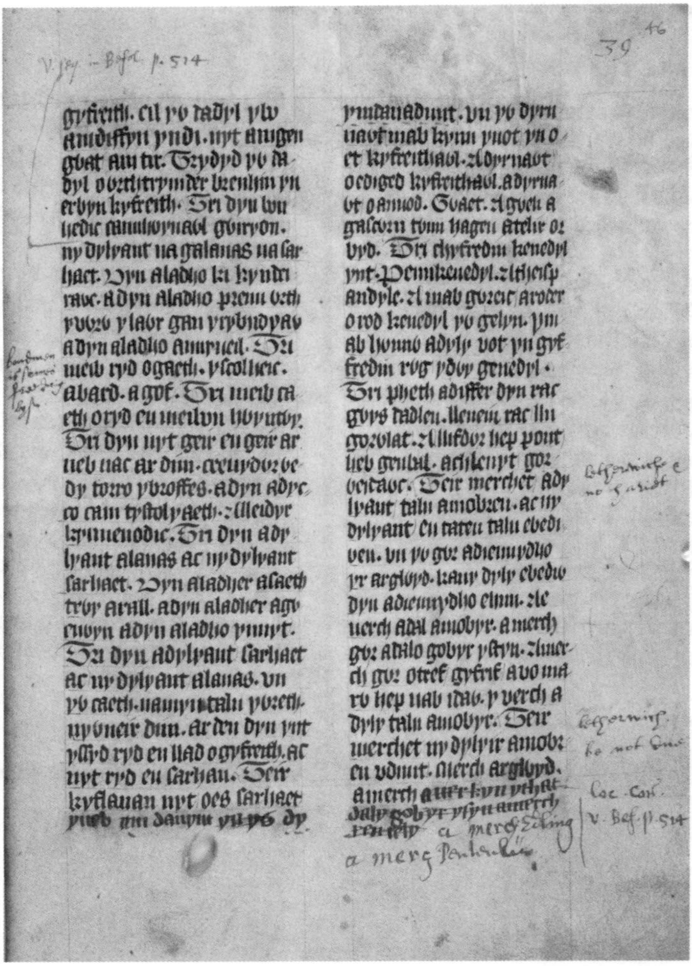

gyfreith. eil yw tadyl yw
a amdiffyn yndi. nyt amgen
gwat am tir. Trydyd yw ta
dyl o wrthtrymder brenhin yn
erbyn kyfreith. Tri dyn lwu
hedic anmilwynawl gwiryon.
ny dylyant na galanas na sar
haet. Dyn a ladho lleidyr
rawc. a dyn a ladho prenn vrth
ywwr y lafur gan ymchwelyaw
a dyn a ladho amwyneil. Tri
meib yssyd o gaeth. ysgolheic.
a bard. a gof. Tri meib ca
eth o ryd eu meibon wyntwy.
Tri dyn nyt geir eu geir ar
neb nac ar dim. ...
dy torro y broffes. a dyn a dyc
co camtystolyaeth. a lleidyr
kymenodic. Tri dyn a dy
lyant galanas ac ny dylyant
sarhaet. Dyn a ladher a gaeth
trwy arall. a dyn a ladher ag
ewyn. a dyn a ladho ymwyt.
Tri dyn a dylyant sarhaet
ac ny dylyant galanas. vn
yw caeth. namyn talu y werth
ny bwrir dim. ar deu dyn ynt
yssyd ryd eu llad o gyfreith. ac
nyt ryd eu sarhau. Teir
kyflauan nyt oes sarhaet
...

ymdanadunt. vn yw dyyn
nawt mab kymu ynot yn o
et kyfreithawl. a dyrnawt
o ediged kyfreithawl. a dyrna
wt o amod. Gwaet. a gwelu a
gasso rn twm haggn atelir or
byd. Tri chyfredin kenedyl
ynt. Penn kenedyl. a theisy
andyle. a mab gwreic a roder
o rod kenedyl yn gelyn. yn
ab lwnnw a dyly vot yn gyf
fredin rwg y dwy genedyl.
Tri pheth a differ dyn rac
gwys dadleu. llenwi rac llu
gorwlat. a llifdwr heb pont
heb geubal. a chlefyt gor
weidawc. Teir merchet a dy
lyant talu amobreu. ac ny
dylyant eu tatu talu ebedi
wen. vn yw gwr a dienydho
yr arglwyd. kany dyly ebediw
dyn a dienydher. ...
merch a dal amobyr. a merch
gwr a dalo gobyr ystyn. a mer
ch gwr o tref gyfrif a vo ma
rw heb mab idaw. y verch a
dyly talu amobyr. Teir
merchet ny dylyir amobr
eu ydunt. merch arglwyd.
a merch ...
a merch Edling
a merch Penkenedl

NLW Wynnstay 36, fol. 39r. National Library of Wales.

THE LEGAL TRIADS OF MEDIEVAL WALES

The Legal Triads
of Medieval Wales

Sara Elin Roberts

UNIVERSITY OF WALES PRESS
CARDIFF
2007

British Library in Cataloguing-in-Publication Data
A catalogue record for this book is available from the British Library.

ISBN 987-0-7083-2107-2

The publishers wish to acknowledge the financial support of the Higher Education
Funding Council for Wales in the publication of this book.

Printed in Great Britain by Antony Rowe Ltd, Chippenham, Wiltshire

I'r tri anhepgor: Mam, Dad a'm gŵr

Contents

Preface

The aim of this edition is to present, as far as that is possible, all of the legal triads found in the Welsh law manuscripts. There are two main types of triads in the lawtexts: triads found on their own as part of a law tractate, often as a supplement or a prologue to a tractate; and triads found in the law manuscripts in the large triad collections.

The main focus of this book is on the triads found in collections, and so a full edition, with notes, will be given for these. For the triads which do not occur in collections, brief notes on the context are given, with references to printed editions in which the triads occur, where relevant.

The triads from two manuscripts – manuscripts X, BL Cotton MS Cleopatra Bv, and Q, NLW Wynnstay 36 – are given in their entirety. These two manuscripts have been chosen as the main triad collections contrast with each other well: the X collection demonstrates the basic Cyfn collection, whereas Q is a fifteenth-century Bleg manuscript with an extended triad collection. The triads are numbered according to the order in which they appear in those manuscripts, and the position of the main triad collection is marked. The triads from these two manuscripts are supplemented by individual triads found in other manuscripts but not in X or Q, numbered according to the same scheme. The conspectuses should be consulted for lists of which triads occur in which manuscripts.

X is used as the base manuscript for the Cyfn triad collection as it best shows the Cyfn triad collection in its basic form, without the Bleg-type additions. Triads which do not occur in the X triad collection but which are found in the collections in other Cyfn manuscripts are also included in the edition. However, Bleg-type triads found in Cyfn triad collections are not included: they will be found in the Bleg section, and listed in the conspectuses. All of those triads are found as part of the triad collection in the Cyfn manuscript from which it is quoted.

The first half of the main triad collection in Q is found as a triad collection in all Bleg manuscripts, although the order of the collection varies slightly – see Conspectuses 6a and 6b.

The manuscripts are followed as closely as possible, and if another manuscript is used, it is noted in the apparatus. The triads are numbered according to my numbering scheme, and the conspectuses share the same numbering. Variant readings from the other Cyfn manuscripts are given (if any) for the X triads, but they *do not necessarily* occur in the same order in those manuscripts. No variant readings are given from Bleg manuscripts for the Cyfn text and vice versa. The conspectuses should be consulted for the corresponding numbers. The triad number is given at the beginning of each triad; following the number, the manuscripts used for variant readings are listed. If the limbs of the triad are in a different order in another manuscript, the order is given in square brackets, also shown following the triad number. Variant readings and any corrections to the text are given in the apparatus. Any emendation of the text is given in square brackets in the text.

Where a triad occurs in another manuscript but is too different for variant readings to be given, it is shown following the main version, but in a narrower paragraph format. Latin D correspondence is also noted for the Q collection – see the conspectus for the order of the triads in that manuscript. Where a triad occurs in Latin in Latin D, the number is not in italic and no variant readings are given. Numbers in square brackets within the text indicate the pagination.

The Notes

The number of the triad as found in X is given first, followed by the number of the triad in any other manuscript in which it may appear, with the siglum of the manuscript noted. In the case of Bleg, if the triad appears in Q, this is noted, but the other Bleg manuscripts are not noted unless the triad does not appear in Q. For notes on the Q triads, the Bleg manuscripts are not noted for the ordinary (rather than additional) triads. In referring to triads, the manuscript sigla is given, followed by the number of the triad. Such numbers given in square brackets indicate different versions of the triad. For triads in Ior and DwC, the paragraph reference is given.

The notes for the triads in the collections will include any significant variations in the triads if they are both found in X and Q; there will be no comment on the Q triad in these notes if the triads are identical, and there will be no notes for the triad in the Q set of notes, to avoid repetition.

Appendix 1

These are triads from the additional collection found in *K, S* and *Tim*, and *Q*. The text is taken from *K*, with variant readings from *S* and *Tim*, but the triads already given in the main *Q* collection are not repeated. See Conspectus 7.

Appendix 2

The triads found in the Latin manuscripts but which are not found in the Welsh manuscripts. Page references to *The Latin Texts of the Welsh Laws* are given in square brackets. A translation has been provided.

Appendix 3

These triads occur in some Bleg manuscripts, but do not occur at all in manuscript *Q*. Triads are numbered according to my scheme. For triads in *S*, references to Christine James's edition are given in square brackets.

Variant readings, if any, and any corrections to the text are given in the apparatus. Any additional material to amend the text is given in square brackets in the text.

Acknowledgements

The list of acknowledgments is extensive, as many people have contributed their time, expertise and support during the creation of this book.

The work began its life as my D.Phil. thesis under the supervision of Professor Thomas Charles-Edwards. I have benefited greatly from his friendly guidance, both during my studies with him and afterwards. I would not consider publishing this work without his support.

My internal examiner was Dr Paul Russell and his comments and corrections have been particularly valuable. Apart from reading the work (on several occasions and in several different forms!) Paul has helped me to change my thesis into its present form, sorted out my dreadful Latin translations, and shared his own, unpublished work with me. Paul and his family have been unstinting in their support and friendship. Thank you, Paul, Fliss and Ben.

I would also like to express my gratitude to Professor Huw Pryce, who has encouraged me from the very start of my academic studies. The friendly staff of the Centre for Advanced Welsh and Celtic Studies assisted me as the book neared completion, and I would like to thank Dr Barry Lewis in particular for translating the list of triads into modern Welsh when the enormity of the task was beyond me. He also checked readings and responded promptly and helpfully to my queries. Dr A. Cynfael Lake proofread the volume – although calling it 'proof reading' is an understatement, as he went above and beyond the call of duty – and with his help this work is far more user-friendly. Various friends helped by reading sections, including Aliki Pantos, Claire Jamset, Louise Bishop and Kate Metzner. I thank you, and apologize!

The staff of the National Library of Wales and the British Library were helpful and patient, and I was also assisted by the staff of *Geiriadur Prifysgol Cymru*.

My thanks also goes to the members of the Board of Celtic Studies and University of Wales Press who helped me through the complicated editorial process, and in particular to Jonathan Wooding, Elin Lewis and Julian Roskams.

Tim Petts, my husband, created the index, and has read the whole of this book several times over. He, my parents and my family have given me the support without which I would never succeed.

Abbreviations and Conventions

AL	*Ancient Laws and Institutes of Wales*, ed. A. Owen (London, 1841). References to Vol. I refer to the Code (DC, GC, VC), with chapter and section, and references to Vol. II refer to book (upper-case roman), chapter (lower-case roman) and section (arabic).
Bleg	Texts of that redaction.
Bleg	The edition of Blegywryd in *Llyfr Blegywryd*, ed. S. J. Williams and J. E. Powell (Cardiff, 1942). References to page and line of the text.
BBCS	*Bulletin of the Board of Celtic Studies.*
CMCS	*Cambrian Medieval Celtic Studies.*
CO	*Culhwch ac Olwen*, ed. R. Bromwich and D. Simon Evans (Cardiff, 1997).
Col	*Llyfr Colan*, ed. D. Jenkins (Cardiff, 1963). References to numbered sentences.
Cyfn	Texts of that redaction.
Cyfn	The edition of Cyfnerth in *Welsh Medieval Law*, ed. A. W. Wade-Evans (Oxford, 1909). References to pages and lines.
DC	Dimentian Code from *AL* (now Blegywryd).
DwC	*Damweiniau Colan*, ed. D. Jenkins (Aberystwyth, 1973). References to numbered sentences.
EIWK	T. Charles-Edwards, *Early Irish and Welsh Kinship* (Oxford, 1993).
GC	Gwentian Code from *AL* (now Cyfnerth).
GPC	*Geiriadur Prifysgol Cymru.*
Ior	Texts of that redaction.
Ior	The edition of Iorwerth in *Llyfr Iorwerth*, ed. A. Rh. Wiliam (Cardiff, 1960). References to numbered sections and unnumbered sentences.
LAL	T. M. Charles-Edwards, M. E. Owen and D. B. Walters (eds), *Lawyers and Laymen* (Cardiff, 1980).

LEEK	*The Laws of the Earliest English Kings*, ed. F. L. Attenborough (Cambridge, 1922).
LTMW	D. Jenkins, *The Law of Hywel Dda* (Llandysul, 1986).
LTWL	*The Latin Texts of the Welsh Laws*, ed. H. D. Emanuel (Cardiff, 1967). References to pages and lines.
NLWJ	*National Library of Wales Journal.*
OED	*Oxford English Dictionary.*
PKM	*Pedeir Keinc y Mabinogi*, ed. I. Williams (Cardiff, 1951).
TCC	T. M. Charles-Edwards and P. Russell, Tair Colofn Cyfraith. *The Three Columns of Law in Medieval Wales: Homicide, Theft, and Fire* (Cardiff, 2007).
THSC	*Transactions of the Honourable Society of the Cymmrodorion.*
TYP	*Trioedd Ynys Prydein: The Welsh Triads* ed. R. Bromwich (Cardiff, 1978).
VC	Venedotian Code from *AL* (now Iowerth).
WHR	*The Welsh History Review.*
WKC	T. M. Charles-Edwards, M. E. Owen and P. Russell, *The Welsh King and his Court* (Cardiff, 2000).
WLW	D. Jenkins and M. E. Owen, *The Welsh Law of Women* (Cardiff, 1980).
WML	*Welsh Medieval Law*, ed. A. W. Wade-Evans (Oxford, 1909). References to pages and lines.

Manuscript Sources and Sigla

Iorwerth Redaction / Llyfr Iorwerth / Venedotian Code

A	NLW Peniarth 29 (The Black Book of Chirk), 13c.
B	BL Cotton Titus D.ii, 13c.
C	BL Cotton Caligula A.iii, *c.*1250.
D	NLW Peniarth 32 (Llyfr Teg), *c.*1380–15c.
E	BL Additional 14931, 13c.
F	NLW Peniarth 34, 15c.
G	NLW Peniarth 35, *c.*1300.
H	NLW Peniarth 164, 14c. NLW Llanstephan 121 and NLW Peniarth 278 are copies of *H*, and a partial copy is in NLW Llanstephan 73.
K	NLW Peniarth 40, 15c.
Col	NLW Peniarth 30 (Llyfr Colan), 13c.
Lew	NLW Peniarth 39, 15c.

Blegywryd Redaction / Llyfr Blegywryd / Dimetian Code

J	Jesus College Oxford 57, *c*.1400.
L	BL Cotton Titus D.ix, 14c. Base text for the Dimetian Code in *AL*.
M	NLW Peniarth 33, 14c.
N	NLW Peniarth 36B, *c*.1300.
P	NLW Peniarth 259A, 15c.
Q	NLW Wynnstay 36, 15c.
R	NLW Peniarth 31, 14c.
T	BL Harley 958, 14c.
Bost	Boston Libr Hist Soc Mass 5, 14c; a facsimile is found as NLW Add. 11125A.
Tim	NLW Llanstephan 116, 15c.
Llan	NLW Llanstephan 29, *c*.1500.
Є	NLW Peniarth 258, 15c.
I	NLW Peniarth 38 (*OTr*-type), 15c.
O	NLW Peniarth 36A (*OTr*-type), *c*.1300.
S	BL Additional 22356 (*OTr*-type), 15c.
Tr	Trinity College Cambridge O.vii.I (*OTr*-type), *c*.1300.

Cyfnerth Redaction / Llyfr Cyfnerth / Gwentian Code

U	NLW Peniarth 37, 14c. Base text for the Gwentian Code in *AL*.
V	BL Harley 4353, 14c.
W	BL Cotton Cleopatra A.xiv, 14c.
X	BL Cotton Cleopatra B.v, 14c.
Y	NLW 20143, 14c.
Z	NLW Peniarth 259B, 16c. but containing an earlier text.
Mk	Bodorgan MS, in private ownership, 14c. NLW Llanstephan 72 is a copy of *Mk*.

The Latin Manuscripts

Lat A	NLW Peniarth 28, 13c.
Lat B	BL Cotton Vespasian E.xi, *c*.1250.
Lat C	BL Harley 1796, 13c.
Lat D	Oxford, Bodley Rawlinson C 821, *c*.1300.
Lat E	Corpus Christi College Cambridge, 454, 15c.

Introduction

Triads and the Lawtexts

Triads, the grouping of ideas or themes in threes, occur throughout medieval Welsh literature. It is difficult to turn to any genre of medieval Welsh literature without coming across a triad.[1] There are triads scattered throughout the prose tales; triads or references to the triads appear in medieval Welsh poetry, and many triads are found in the more functional literature – the laws, the bardic grammars and the medical texts.[2] Furthermore, there are several large collections of triads found in Welsh manuscripts, the best-known being *Trioedd Ynys Prydain* (*TYP*).[3] The triads are not confined to Welsh literature: within the Celtic language group, triads occur in Scottish Gaelic, Breton, Cornish and Irish texts, as well as in Welsh texts.[4] Indeed, it has been noted that triads in general occur in the literatures of many cultures, but rarely do they occur in such great numbers as in the Celtic literatures.[5] There is a large collection of Irish triads, *The Triads of Ireland*, but there are differences between the Welsh and Irish collections, so this makes it less likely that triads are an exclusively Celtic phenomenon; they are probably a literary device which was used in Celtic literature as well as in other literature.[6]

What was the purpose of these triads? The triad form is a well-known mnemonic device, and grouping ideas in threes may have been a useful method for memorizing large amounts of material.[7] Aristotle suggested using visual images as an aid to memory. He proposed that, by grouping ideas in threes, one could begin at a medial position when recalling them, making it easier to

---

[1]   N. Lloyd and M. E. Owen (eds), *Drych yr Oesoedd Canol*, 208.

[2]   Ibid., 76, 151, 208, 211, 215.

[3]   *TYP*.

[4]   F. Kelly, 'Thinking in threes', 1–18.

[5]   Ibid.

[6]   Ibid.

[7]   *TYP*, p. lxx, and for use of numbers as mnemonic aids, M. Carruthers, *The Book of Memory*, 80–106. Numbers were also felt to have particular significance and symbolism; see M. E. Owen, 'Y Cyfreithiau – (2) Ansawdd y Rhyddiaith', 233.

remember those on either side.[8] Since any number greater than twelve is difficult to remember, breaking up a large number into groups of smaller ones makes for easier recollection.[9]

The medieval laws of Wales, which differ from both English common law and canon law, are attributed to King Hywel the Good, who ruled most of Wales in the tenth century.[10] Although there is no evidence to link Hywel to the surviving law manuscripts, he may have been involved in some form of legal activity; linking Hywel to the laws also gave the laws more credibility and authority.[11] There are around forty surviving manuscripts of Welsh law (six of which are in Latin). Aneurin Owen, the editor of *Ancient Laws and Institutes of Wales* (London, 1841), separated the Welsh texts into three groups, with the Latin manuscripts forming a separate group. The groups were named after the areas of Wales with which he believed them to be linked, Gwynedd, Dyfed and Gwent, and so he labelled them the Venedotian, Dimetian and Gwentian Code respectively. Wade-Evans, in his study of the book of Cyfnerth in 1909, suggested less misleading names, based on people named in the prologues to the lawtexts in the manuscripts, and these are the terms that are still used today: Cyfnerth (formerly the Gwentian Code), Blegywryd (Dimetian) and Iorwerth (Venedotian).[12]

The manuscripts are still referred to using the sigla given to them by Aneurin Owen, but as there are more law manuscripts than letters in the Roman alphabet, some manuscripts were given Greek sigla, or if Owen was unaware of them, they have instead been named after their owner, editor, or library in which they were kept.[13]

The Cyfn group probably retains the earliest version of the laws. The manuscripts are all fourteenth-century in date with the exception of Z, which is a sixteenth-century manuscript containing a copy of an older text.[14] The material contained in all of the manuscripts shows signs of being older than the manuscripts, probably late twelfth-century.[15]

The Latin manuscripts form a separate redaction, and are distinct from the three Welsh redactions; the Latin manuscripts are not a text of Bleg, Cyfn or Ior in Latin, but the five versions of the Latin laws are related to each other.

---

[8]   Carruthers, *Book of Memory*, 63. Aristotle, in *De Memoria*, was referring to the technique of using individual visual or verbal associations. See R. Sorabji, *Aristotle on Memory*, 56.

[9]   Carruthers, *Book of Memory*, 107.

[10] A general introduction to Welsh law can be found in D. Jenkins, 'The significance of the law of Hywel', *THSC* (1977), 54–76; the Appendix is particularly useful. See also D. Jenkins, *Cyfraith Hywel*; D. Jenkins, *LTMW*; and T. M. Charles-Edwards, *The Welsh Laws*.

[11] K. Maund, *The Welsh Kings*, 46.

[12] *WML*, pp. vii–xii.

[13] A full list is provided with the list of abbreviations. See also Charles-Edwards, *The Welsh Laws*, 100–2, *Coleg yr Iesu LVII*, pp. xiv–xxii; and on dating see D. Huws, *Medieval Welsh Manuscripts*, 57–64.

[14] M. E. Owen, 'The laws of court from Cyfnerth' in *WKC*, 425.

[15] H. Pryce, 'Lawbooks and literacy', 38–9.

However, there are similarities between the Welsh redactions and the Latin group, in particular with the Cyfn redaction, and the Latin versions of the law draw heavily on early Welsh versions no longer extant. Latin A is no longer considered to be the oldest of the Latin manuscripts, and some sections of it draw on Ior and Cyfn. It is also related to Latin B.[16] Latin B and E are related, but Latin C, which is probably a northern text, survives in an incomplete form, and it is difficult to determine its relationship with the other Latin manuscripts.[17]

The Bleg redaction is largely a translation of Latin D and is closely related to the Latin group. The Bleg group, the largest of the three Welsh groups, itself splits into two types of manuscripts: those called *L*-type, as they are similar in order to manuscript *L*, and those more similar to manuscripts *O* or *Tr*.[18] Cyfn and Bleg are considered to contain 'southern' law, in contrast to Ior, the latest of the three groups, which probably reflects the legal situation in Gwynedd in the reign of Llywelyn the Great (d. 1240). The Ior manuscripts, however, are the oldest in Welsh and date from the thirteenth century.[19]

Each of the lawbooks contains the same basic tractates, or essays, on various topics in laws, but each lawbook is a little different, and the order in which the material occurs varies not only between the groups but also between the individual manuscripts. Most of the manuscripts open with a prologue, giving the story of Hywel Dda and how the laws were created, and then continue with the laws of the court, listing the officers of the royal court and their duties.[20] All of the redactions have a section called the Three Columns of Law, discussing homicide, theft and arson. Other topics include the law of women, land law, suretyship (contract), corn damage and the value of houses and equipment.[21] Some of the fifteenth-century Bleg manuscripts also contain a 'tail' of additional material, often taken from other tractates, appended to the main text of the law.[22]

The medieval Welsh lawyers were a group of learned people similar in many ways to the poets, another group who had large collections of triads. There is very

---

[16] *WKC*, 478–9.

[17] Latin E is discussed more fully in P. Russell, *Vita Griffini Filii Conani*, 17–23. With thanks to Paul Russell for sharing his knowledge on this topic with me.

[18] For an explanation of the *L* and *OTr* Bleg groups, see the introduction to M. Richards, *Coleg yr Iesu LVII*, pp. xvi–xviii, and pp. 17–19, below.

[19] Jenkins, 'Significance of the Law of Hywel', 74–5.

[20] For a fuller study of the laws of court, see *The Welsh King and his Court*.

[21] Charles-Edwards, *The Welsh Laws*, 27–8; for detailed discussions on the law of women and suretyship, see *WLW* and *LAL* respectively. Editions of the laws can be found in *AL*, with translations (albeit antiquated) included, and for an edition and translation of Cyfnerth, see *WML*. Blegywryd can be found in *Llyfr Blegywryd,* and this was translated by M. Richards, *The Laws of Hywel Dda*. An alternative edition of Bleg can be found in Richards, *Coleg yr Iesu LVII*. For the Iorwerth texts, see *Llyfr Iorwerth*, and the translation is *LTMW*. An edition of Col, the 'edited' version of Ior, is available in *Llyfr Colan*.

[22] *Coleg yr Iesu LVII*, pp. xvi–xvii.

little evidence regarding the poets' education in Wales, but there were bardic schools in Ireland, and it is often stated that Wales probably had a similar system.[23] Both countries had families of poets, and Caerwyn Williams suggested that the bardic school was a further development of the bardic family – if a poet had the time or inclination, he could take the sons of other men to train, as well as his own sons, thus creating a school.[24] There is some evidence in Wales for bardic schools in the document known as *Statud Gruffudd ap Cynan*.[25] In the same way, it is possible that there were schools of lawyers in medieval Wales. The Irish evidence again points to the learning being passed from father to son, and the Welsh legal craft was similar to poetry in many ways.[26] A third professional group likely to have had a similar education would have been the mediciners.[27]

The poets and the lawyers would have had to learn a large amount of information in order to be masters of their crafts, and both would have had to apply that material in a practical way – the poets through their poetry, the lawyers in court. It is likely that the poets and the lawyers (and indeed the mediciners) were trained orally, and therefore mnemonic devices would have been used to aid their learning.[28] Several elements of the poets' education are found in triadic form: the *Trioedd Cerdd* (the poets' triads) found in the bardic grammars point to the linguistic and composition skills they needed, and the gnomic triads, often grouped with *TYP* in the manuscripts, were summaries of traditional 'wisdom'.[29] *TYP* was an index to the corpus of historical lore, folk tales and mythology, and the references to triads from *TYP* in medieval poetry and prose may be testimony to their use in this way.[30]

It is interesting that there are written collections of triads, as their original purpose was as mnemonics; mnemonics, by their very nature, would not normally exist in a written form. However, there are several different collections of triads for different purposes, so there must have been a shift in the way the triads were considered – at some point, they became a written form, and manuscript copies of triads from different genres are found in manuscripts from the early thirteenth century onwards. This may be because they were useful; the legal triads are a quick reference to the full texts of the Welsh law, and whole legal concepts are expressed as triads in the later manuscripts. *TYP* also became a

---

[23] S. E. Roberts, 'Addysg Broffesiynol', 7–11; A. Matonis, 'Problems relating to the composition of the Welsh bardic grammars', 287, and J. E. Caerwyn Williams, 'Beirdd y Tywysogion: Arolwg', 37–8.

[24] J. E. Caerwyn Williams, *Traddodiad Llenyddol Iwerddon*, 38; *Gwaith Meilyr Brydydd*, 51.

[25] *Llyfr Iorwerth*, 40/5–6, *Damweiniau Colan*, 77; T. Parry, 'Statud Gruffudd ap Cynan', 28–9.

[26] F. Kelly, *A Guide to Early Irish Law*, 253–8; D. Jenkins, 'A family of Welsh lawyers', 125–9.

[27] M. E. Owen, 'Gwŷr Dysg yr Oesoedd Canol', 60–1.

[28] Ibid., 42, 59–60.

[29] *Gramadegau'r Penceirddiaid*, p. lxxxviii, and M. E. Owen, 'Trioedd hefut y6 yrei hynn', 91, 98.

[30] *TYP*, pp. lxxiii–lxxiv.

written list at one stage, and that collection was also revised and extended as time went on.[31] There may be other traces of legal training in the lawtexts – the *holiadon* (formulaic sentences following the pattern 'Is there any case …? There is: …') in particular seem to have been created for teaching purposes.[32]

There is no overlap between the collections of legal and non-legal triads. *TYP* was not a general collection of triads but consisted of triads of only one type, or genre. It did not include legal triads and it covered a different range from *The Triads of Ireland*. The Irish triads are, however, paralleled in the gnomic triads.[33] Although one kindred might contain both poets and lawyers, individual poet-lawyers were rare in Wales, and so mixed collections of bardic, legal and other triads, such as the Irish collection, would have been unnecessary in medieval Wales.[34] The two traditions may have been similar, law and poetry being parallel branches of native learning, with triads being an important part of that heritage.[35] Apart from *TYP*, there are collections of triads in the bardic grammars (*Trioedd Cerdd*) and the medical texts. There are also the gnomic triads often found in the same manuscript as *TYP*, and the *Trioedd Arbennig* (special/exceptional triads) encompassing learning which was more European in nature.[36] However, there is no link between the *TYP* material and the legal triads, nor is there an overlap in the material.[37]

TYP, like the legal triad collections, probably began life as oral assemblages of triads.[38] Bromwich argues that evidence for an oral origin is offered by the way the triads in *TYP* often occur in groups and contrasting pairs; the same may be said of the gnomic triads, and indeed, the legal triads.[39] The written triad collections, *TYP* and the *trioedd cerdd*, like the written legal triad collections, have a fixed or semi-fixed order. The poets used the triads as a mnemonic aid to the information they had to learn as part of their trade.[40] Similarly, the lawyers probably had, as part of their traditional equipment, their own oral assemblages of specifically legal triads, which the poets would not have used. When the written collections were made, these oral assemblages of legal triads were separate from

[31] *TYP*, pp. cviii–cxxi.

[32] C. James, 'Golygiad o BL Add. 22356', p. xxi. R. C. Stacey, 'Learning to plead in medieval Welsh law', 108–9.

[33] Owen, 'Trioedd hefut y6 yrei hynn', 93–4.

[34] D. Jenkins, 'Iorwerth ap Madog', 165, and also in *Celtic Law Papers*, 121–33. One example may be Einion ap Gwalchmai, who appears to have combined the functions of the court justice and the court poet in the court of Llywelyn ab Iorwerth: D. Stephenson, *The Governance of Gwynedd*, 14.

[35] Ibid.

[36] *Gramadegau'r Penceirddiaid*, pp. lxxxviii–cv; Owen, 'Trioedd hefut y6 yrei hynn', 98; M. E. Owen, 'Y Trioedd Arbennig', 434.

[37] There is however one example of overlap between the legal triads and the gnomic triads: *Tri Chadarn Byd* (The three powerful ones of the world) is found in both collections. Owen, 'Trioedd hefut y6 yrei hynn', 105.

[38] *TYP*, p. lxv.

[39] *TYP*, p. cviii; Owen, 'Trioedd hefut y6 yrei hynn', 90.

[40] *TYP*, p. lxx.

the triads belonging to the poets, and so the subsequent written collections were also distinct. Another reason why *TYP* does not contain legal triads may be that there already was a written collection of legal triads.

The number of triads found in the lawtexts increases with time, but all manuscripts of Welsh law contain triads – they are an accepted part of the law. The tradition of having triads in lawtexts is thus one that may go back a long way. Even the law itself is made into a triad: the triad *Tair rhan yw awdurdod Hywel Dda* (There are three parts to the authority of Hywel Dda) splits the law into three main sections: the law of the court, the law of the country and *arferion cyfraith* (practices of law).[41] There are triads concerning the king and his court, triads relating to *galanas* (the laws of homicide), *sarhaed* (the insult-payments, similar to *wergeld*) and the laws of women. Not only are there triads relating to land, but land law is itself split into three: there are three ways of claiming land (*dadannudd, camweresgyn* and *ach ac edryf*) and then both *dadannudd* and *camweresgyn* are further split into three.[42] This is also true of the *trioedd cerdd*: *cerdd dafod*, for example, is expressed as a triad, and the three individual items in the *cerdd dafod* triad are then given a triad each.[43] By the fifteenth century some lawtexts contained over two hundred triads, and one or more triads might supplement most subjects discussed in the main body of the law. Some tractates are arranged in triadic form, the most obvious example being the three columns of law.[44] Triadic arrangement of this sort should be distinguished from actual triads: a triad normally begins with the numeral three as part of a heading, and lists three items, whether as a short list or a longer section. Therefore, the three columns of law are not counted amongst the triads in Cyfn or Bleg, as nowhere is there a statement listing the three columns – there is no heading. Another example is *dadannudd*, one of the procedures for claiming land: in Bleg, the tractate is not a triad but there are three stages to the procedure; however, in Ior, it is a proper triad.[45] It is therefore difficult to discuss any aspect of the Welsh laws without touching on triads. Triads were thus part of a more general liking for arranging material in threes.

This attachment to the number three is not the only aspect of the law that shows numerical ordering. As well as three, enneads regularly appear: *naw affaith tan* (the nine abetments of arson), *naw tafodiog* (the nine tongued-ones) and *naw cynyweddi teithïog* (the nine lawful unions); as do heptads: *seith escopty Dyfed* (the seven bishop-houses of Dyfed). There are other examples of numerical grouping, for example, twenty-four officers of the court.[46] There is one

[41] *Llyfr Blegywryd*, 126; *The Laws of Hywel Dda*, 116.
[42] *Llyfr Blegywryd*, 78–9; *The Laws of Hywel Dda*, 80.
[43] *Gramadegau'r Penceirddiaid*, 6.
[44] The three columns of law may be based on a medieval visual mnemonic, where the page is divided into three columns, possibly recalling a building. Carruthers, *Book of Memory*, 124–5.
[45] *Llyfr Blegywryd*, 71–3, and *Llyfr Iorwerth*, 84/1.
[46] *Llyfr Blegywryd*, 2, 30. *Llyfr Iorwerth*, 2/2; *Welsh Medieval Law*, 2. Twenty-four is a number

example of a triad of tetrads: *tri phetwar yssyd* (there are three fours).[47] There are further links with the number three: an ennead may be significant because it is three sets of threes as in *Naw affaith galanas* (the nine abetments of homicide), where the punishments for the nine are organized in three groups of three.[48] This may explain why there are so many enneads in law. *Q* has a list of sixteen enneads, but some are land measurements. Pairs of triads are also attested, for example, *O whe fford y gwahan dyn a 'e da* (in six ways a man is separated from his goods), again split into two groups.[49]

The Triad Genre

Within the genre of triads, there are different types of triad. Probably the oldest type of triad in existence, given the original purpose of the triad form as a mnemonic, is the simple, short triad, with a 'heading' and three 'limbs'.

Simple triad (X41)

Teir gormes doeth ynt: meddawt, a dryc annyan, a godinheb.

These are the three oppressors of the wise: drunkenness, and bad temper, and adultery.

The heading is the opening phrase, beginning with *Tri/Teir* (Three) or *O tri* (In three [ways]), and they state the subject of the triad: three things, for example, Q116, *Tri argae g6aet* (Three stays of blood), X27, *Tri ofer llaeth yssyd* (There are three useless milks); or the three types of things, for example, Q102, *Tri ryw tal yssyd* (There are three kinds of payments), or the three ways of doing something, for example, Q141, *O tri mod y kae kyfreith* (In three ways the law is closed). The limbs can be single words, pairs of words, or whole sentences. The limbs can be simple, with no extensions, such as X21, *Tri pheth ny chyfran brenhin a neb* (Three things which a king does not share with anyone), which has a word for each limb, or X26, *Tri ofer ymadra6d* (Three useless statements), where each limb is a short phrase. Although useful as a mnemonic aid, these simple limbs do not, however, explain or expand on the rules contained in them. Therefore, a natural development is an extension to the triad. This can be done in two ways: the triad can be stated and the explanation can follow, or each limb can have an individual extension.

which occurs in other genres, the most significant instance being the twenty-four poetic metres. Heptads are also common in Irish literature, and there is a collection of them. *Corpus Iuris Hibernici*, i. 1–64.

[47] See X22; and *Llyfr Blegywryd,* 109; *WML*, 124.

[48] *Llyfr Blegywryd*, 30; *Llyfr Iorwerth*, 104; *WML*, 37.

[49] *WML*, 118.

Triads with extension following the limbs (X48)

Tri phryf a dyly brenhin ev gwerth pa le bynnac y llader:

[1] llostlydan,
[2] a bele6,
[3] a charlwng;

[Extension] canys ohonunt wy y dylyur wneuthur amarwye6 y dillad y brenhin.

Three animals to whose value the king is entitled wherever they are killed: a beaver, and a sable, and a stoat; because from them the borders of the king's clothes should be made.

Triad where each limb is given an extension (X39)

Tri gwerth kyfureith beichyogi gwreic:

[1] gwaed kyn delwad,

[Extension] wyth a deugein a dal o chollir drwy greulonder.

[2] Eil yw kyn dyuod eneid yndaw,

[Extension] trayan yr alanas a dal.

[3] Y trydyd yw gwedy el eneid yndaw,

[Extension] galanas gwbyl a delir amdanaw o chollir trwy grevlonder.

Three legal values of a woman's foetus: blood before formation, it is worth forty-eight [pence] if it is lost through cruelty. The second is before life enters it, a third of the galanas is paid for it. The third is after life enters it, its full galanas ought to be paid if it is lost through cruelty.

X27, *Tri ofer llaeth* (Three useless milks) has a very short sentence as an extension, and X19, *Teir dir6y brenhin* (Three *dirwy*-fines of a king) has a much longer and fuller explanation. Bromwich notes that in the *TYP* collection, where the 'key epithet', or heading, is obscure, short explanations occur, and in the later manuscripts, Arthurian characters are given as a fourth, better, addition to some triads.[50] For an example of an extension to each limb of a legal triad, see X37, *Tri meib yn tri broder vn vam vn tat* (Three sons being three brothers of the same mother and same father), or the pair of triads in the Cyfn manuscripts *O teir fford y dygir mab / O teir fford y g6edir mab* (In three ways is a son affiliated / In three ways is a son denied).[51] Bromwich notes that expanded triads 'do not ... represent the oldest stratum in *TYP*', and this is also true of the legal triads.[52]

---

[50] R. Bromwich. 'The historical triads', 4–5. For an example of an Arthurian addition, see Bromwich, *TYP*, 20, the White Book version of triad 20.
[51] An edition is given as a variant following X40.
[52] *TYP*, p. cix.

Interestingly, Kelly notes that adding explanatory material to a triad, as in Bromwich's Early Version of *TYP*, is very rare in the *Triads of Ireland* collection.[53] There are fewer triads with long extensions in the Cyfn collections, and many more of them in the *Q* and later Bleg collections, which again suggests that this was a later development. These two schemes, extending each limb and adding an extension at the end of the triad, can be used together, for example, *Tri lle ny dyly dyn rodi ll6 g6eilyd* (Three places where a man is not entitled to swear a fore-oath),[54] which has an addition rather than explanation at the end of the triad. Later manuscripts such as *Q* and *S* both contain examples of the most extreme form of extending triads, with the whole triad being a very detailed exposition of a particular legal point, lasting for three to four pages – these are far removed from simple mnemonics, if they are even capable of being committed to memory without great difficulty.[55]

Several tractates open with a triad in the lawbooks, for example, *Arferion Cyfraith* and the *dirwy* (fines) section in Bleg.[56] Another phenomenon found in the later manuscripts is the practice of having whole sections based around an individual triad. *S* has several long sections within its 'tail' of additional material, and *Q* has one 'anomalous' section, *Llyfr Kynyr vab Kad6ga6n* (the Book of Cynyr ap Cadwgan), which uses a triad as a hook on which to hang some legal theory. The triad behind this section (Mk97) is only found as a separate triad in the *Mk* version of the Cyfn text, but it is an important part of the section in *Q*.[57] Cynyr ap Cadwgan is a figure who occurs in the records as the abbot of Llandinam in Arwystli in the early thirteenth century.[58] He also appears as one of the *sapientes* (wise men) in a land case in mid-Wales.[59] He was a clerical jurist and his sons were declared official jurists in Arwystli by Llywelyn ap Gruffudd in 1281.[60] The Book of Cynyr is a short book which, according to the explanation given in the manuscript, was compiled by Cynyr and passed down through his family and gives guidelines on how to learn to be a jurist. The first line runs thus:

Ac yn gyntaf yd erchis vdynt dysgu tri gr6ndwal doethineb; sef y6 y tri hynny ...[61]

First, he asked them to learn the three foundations of learning; those three are ...

What we have in the Book of Cynyr ap Cadwgan is a study on a triad. The triad as found in *Mk* is set out next, and then there is further justification for each of

---

[53] Kelly, 'Thinking in threes', 13–14.
[54] See Mk48 in the triads from other Cyfnerth manuscripts.
[55] James, 'BL Add. 22356', p. xxi, and Q196.
[56] *Llyfr Blegywryd*, 127, 42.
[57] *AL*, X. x. 1–8, and Mk97. The triad is not included in the collection of triads in *Q*.
[58] H. Pryce, *Native Law and the Church*, 185; D. Stephenson, *Thirteenth Century Welsh Law Courts*, 13–14.
[59] Pryce, *Native Law and the Church*, 34.
[60] Ibid.
[61] *AL*, X. x. 1–8.

the three elements. It thus seems to be a reworking of an earlier triad, only included in the *Mk* triad collection. The remainder of the book is also numerical and mnemonic: *Pymp clo yssyd ar ygneidaeth* (There are five keys to justice-ship). In the same way, another triad from *Mk*, triad 96, is used as a basis for a section in the *Llyfr Cynghawsedd*.[62] The triads used in such sections are often earlier triads from Cyfn, and are rarely included in a separate collection in the same manuscript as the texts in which they are used. This may be evidence that at least some of the Cyfn triads were widely known. A literary parallel to this use of the triadic form as the basis of a text is *Cyfranc Lludd a Llefelys*, which is a tale based on an extended triad.[63]

Triads were mnemonics, and certain devices were used in order to make the process of memorizing large numbers of triads even simpler, but as noted above, these devices could also be seen as stylistic devices. The simple mnemonic triad would usually consist of a heading and three limbs, and often the triad would be similar in form to the proverbs, employing nominal sentences.[64] However, within the individual triads, several features such as alliteration were used, for example, Q22, *Tri gwanas gwayw* (Three thrusts of a spear), or X57, *Tri enw rhingyll ysydd: 'gwaedd gwlad', a 'garw gychwedl gwas y cynghellor', a 'rhingyll'* (There are three names for the *rhingyll*: 'the shriek of the country', and 'bad news the servant of the *cynghellor'*, and *'rhingyll'*). Another device is repetition in each limb, or incremental repetition: for example, X27, *Tri ofer llaeth ysydd: llaeth caseg, a llaeth gast, a llaeth cath* (There are three useless milks: the milk of a mare, and the milk of a bitch, and the milk of a cat). Another feature of the triad collections in particular which suggests an oral source is the occurrence of contrasting pairs.[65] Such pairs occur in most collections, and examples from the legal collections include the long Cyfn triads on affiliating and denying a child.[66] The legal collections also have series of triads each with a similar heading but slightly different: there are several sets of three triads, such as X16, 17 and 18, the *rhwydi* (nets), and Q64, 65 and 66, the *anhepgor* (indispensables), triplets found at the beginning of most of the collections of legal triads, and also the five consecutive triads in Bleg, each starting *Tri lleidr___ ysyd* (There are three ___ thieves).[67] These would have helped whoever was trying to recall the triads, but also contributed to the fixed order of the written triad collections – such triads were unlikely to be separated.[68] As well as being purely legal mnemonics, legal triads also show that the redactors or composers were masters in the craft of writing: they show alliteration, compound words, and repetition or incremental

---

[62] *AL*, VIII. iv–vi.
[63] R. M. Jones 'Tri Mewn Llenyddiaeth', 97; *Cyfranc Lludd a Llefelys*, pp. xvii–xviii.
[64] Owen, 'Trioedd hefut y6 yrei hynn', 98.
[65] *TYP*, p. cviii.
[66] The triads are combined to form one triad in X40, but see the two triads given as a variant.
[67] Owen, 'Gwŷr Dysg', 48; Owen, 'Y Cyfreithiau (2)', 233–4.
[68] E. P. Hamp, 'On the justification of ordering in *TYP'*, 105.

repetition, a device often found in poetry and prose texts to emphasize a point or build up to a climax. These are all aids to remembering complex facts, but, at the same time, decorative devices.[69] Finally, Kelly notes that in the Irish collection, later additions often tend to have a 'punchline', or at least, a climax or anti-climax.[70] Although this is less commonly found in the legal triad collections – perhaps humour would not have been deemed appropriate in a learning environ-ment or within the serious confines of law – there are occasional anti-climaxes, some of which are humorous. Perhaps the best example is X69, *Tri pheth ni thelir kyn coller yn ranty: kyllell, a chledyf, a llawdyr* (Three things which are not paid for if they are lost in a house where someone is lodged: a knife, and a sword, and trousers): admittedly not side-splitting material, but humorous nonetheless.[71]

Triads: Law or Custom?

J. Enoch Powell, when discussing Bleg, developed the theory that if the triads were developed exclusively for teaching purposes, the triads were not part of the original lawtexts for this reason as they were not strictly law:

> Nid cyfreithiau yw trioedd, ond crynodebau o gyfreithiau neu arferion cyfraith, wedi eu llunio ar ddull nodweddiadol modd y cofid hwy'n hawdd.[72]

Powell had two independent premises to his argument about triads. First, he believed that triads in Bleg were 'floating sections' that were added later where relevant. There are, in his opinion, nine groups of later additions, with the order of these groups differing depending on whether the manuscript is from the *L* group or the *OTr* group.[73] Secondly, Powell started from the basis that law consists of rules that have binding force because they enjoy the backing of a sovereign power – statute law being an obvious example. However, triads express and are sustained by the legal tradition, rather than state power, and there-fore triads are not law but mnemonic teaching aids embodying custom.[74] Accordingly, in Powell's opinion, since triads were not found in his hypothetical archetype of the book of Blegywryd, triads were floating sections that had been added at a later date.[75] However, his classification of what is and is not 'law'

---

[69] Owen, 'Y Cyfreithiau (2)', 233.

[70] Kelly, 'Thinking in threes', 10–12.

[71] See also 'Tri enw rhingyll', X57, where the third limb is a sharp contrast to the previous descrip-tions of the *rhingyll*'s position and duties, and also provides humour by stating the obvious.

[72] 'Triads are not laws, but summaries of laws or legal custom, made in a distinctive form so that they would be easily remembered', *Llyfr Blegywryd*, pp. xlii–xliii.

[73] *Llyfr Blegywryd*, p. xlii. For an explanation of the *L* and *OTr* Bleg groups, see the introduction to *Coleg yr Iesu LVII*, pp. xvi–xviii.

[74] J. E. Powell, 'Floating sections in the law of Hywel', 29.

[75] Ibid.

depends too heavily on an *a priori* concept of the nature of law foreign to the Welsh tradition, and on the belief that Hywel Dda promulgated in the tenth century all that counted for law in twelfth- and thirteenth-century Wales.

There are two issues to consider when looking at Powell's theory. First, whether the triad collections were added when Bleg was being compiled or whether they were added later to the 'finished' lawbook; and secondly, whether having a triad collection was part of the 'model lawbook', or Powell's idea of the basic content of the lawbook upon which the surviving manuscripts are based, and to which additions were made.[76]

Although the triad collection changes position depending on whether the manuscript is *OTr* or *L* type, it is highly unlikely that the addition of a triad collection to the law manuscripts was a Bleg phenomenon. Both Cyfn and the Latin manuscripts (including Latin D) contain triad collections, and those redactions predate Bleg. Whether there was a triad collection in the original 'model lawbook' (the basic content of the different versions of the laws) is more uncertain. There may well have been individual triads in the text.[77] The triads from the law tractates are not included in the triad collections. This means that the triad collections have triads which differ from, and are additional to, the triads contained in the tractates. The triad collections therefore complement the lawbooks, but whether they were part of the lawbooks from the beginning, rather than simply being linked to them by subject matter, is uncertain.

A possible starting point to the triad collection, or a way in which it developed, is found in Ior manuscript *A*. Ior manuscripts do not have a large collection of triads, although the triadic form is known and used.[78] However, there is a group of eleven triads, and they are found at the end of the laws of court. If a section of text was made to coincide with one or more quires, it may be called a booklet. *Llyfr Prawf* (Test Book) and the laws of court were booklets, and Ior was made of three main booklets: the laws of court, the laws of country and the *Llyfr Prawf*. If the unit of text did not fill all of the space in the quires assigned to it, the scribe could either leave the space or folios blank, or use them for addenda – the latter was often the case as parchment was expensive. In *A* there is clear evidence for supplementary material being added to fill a quire: the laws of court proper finish on fo. 14v, leaving two folios empty at the end of the second quire.[79] A collection of eleven triads is then found on fo. 15r, followed by miscellaneous sections on the lord, proverbs and the beginning of *Marwnad Llywelyn ab Iorwerth* (Elegy for Llywelyn ab Iorwerth).[80] Not all of the material added to *A* was in the

---

[76] On the theory regarding the 'model lawbook', see Charles-Edwards, *The Welsh Laws*, 32–6.
[77] Examples include *WML*, 2, 3; *Llyfr Blegywryd*, 3, 4; *Llyfr Iorwerth*, 3/3, 3/6.
[78] Pryce, 'Lawbooks and literacy', 40–1.
[79] P. Russell, 'Scribal (in)competence', 133.
[80] Ibid. However, the elegy for Llywelyn ab Iorwerth is in the lower margin and runs over the quire boundary so is thought to be a later addition.

exemplar, but *Breiniau Gwyr Arfon* (The Liberties of the Men of Arfon) was also added to manuscript *E*, a similar manuscript to *A*, and was probably in the exemplar.[81] The proverbs and other material were acquired later.[82]

Looking at the ordering of the laws of court in manuscript *B*, we find the basic text of the laws of court until §41, and §§42–3 appear to be additional material, including the triads which make up the main part of §42.[83] This material is found in all of the complete Ior manuscripts, and so we may deduce that the original laws of court in Ior had systematic legal text pertaining to the laws of court, and also miscellanea which were seen to be an addition, as Ior §42/1 suggests. The triads, then, were probably in the exemplar as they occur in every Ior manuscript (although they are not with the laws of court in manuscript *D*), but *A* added further material to the appendage.[84] The way the proverbs and miscellaneous sections in *A* were used to fill up the blank parchment at the end of a quire is evidence of additional material being added to the text after the existing Ior version of the laws of court, but, as the triads are in the same position in all but one of the Ior manuscripts, their positioning probably predates *A*. Furthermore, the laws of women in Ior, a separate quire in *A*, also has triads added at the end, followed by miscellaneous material, which again contributes to the evidence for triads being added at the end of a tractate.

This may have suggested to the scribes of the other redactions that it was usual to include triads at the end of the laws of court. After all, *L*-type Bleg manuscripts have a large collection of triads after the laws of court, and they start with exactly the same eleven triads that are found in exactly the same position and usually in the same sequence in the Ior manuscripts.

Powell was convinced that there was a legal triad collection separate from the law manuscripts at one stage, which was eventually combined with the (Bleg) manuscripts.[85] If this theory was correct and there was a triad collection separate from the lawbooks, it could help explain the lack of a large triad collection in Ior: as the northern lawyers were memorizing the triads, their tradition was oral and they would not need to include a written triad collection in their manuscripts.[86] Whilst there is no existing twelfth- or thirteenth-century book of legal triads found separately to the law manuscripts, there are some possible candidates.

Manuscript *K* was originally grouped with the Bleg manuscripts by Owen, but is a late fifteenth-century Ior manuscript. It has left out the laws of court, and it has eighty triads, some in a large collection. The collection is also found in the

---

[81] Ibid., 134.
[82] Ibid., 133–4.
[83] *Llyfr Iorwerth*, §§42–3, and also p. xliii.
[84] Ibid., p. xliii.
[85] *Llyfr Blegywryd*, p. xliv.
[86] However, they did codify their teaching material in different ways; for example, *cynghawsedd*, the sections of model pleadings, is mainly found in the Ior manuscripts, and the Ior manuscripts also often contain large collections of *damweiniau*.

tail of manuscripts *S* and *Tim*, and it forms part of the additional collection in manuscript *Q*. This triad collection could point to a separate Ior collection, but it is instead more likely that *K*, as a southern manuscript, was influenced by the Bleg manuscripts. The material is discussed more fully below.[87]

Manuscript *H* could also be earmarked as the Ior collection. *H* is primarily a manuscript of triads, with almost 500 triads. These are mostly in large collections, but there are some sections of non-triadic laws or tractates (essays dealing with various aspects of law) that have triads inserted at relevant points. However, it cannot be said that this triad collection itself supports Powell's theory. It cannot be reconciled with any of the redactions. Whilst the number of triads in the manuscript exceeds the number found in any extant law manuscript, the triads do not include, for example, a Bleg collection in order, even though some recognizable triads from the Bleg and Cyfn collections are found in the manuscript. The triads in *H* are grouped by subject to a large extent, as are the triads in the legal tractates. There is a large group in *H* relating to the laws of the court, but none of these triads is found in any of the redactions. So what was this collection? One option suggested by Owen's classification and Powell's theory is that this is the northern Ior collection of triads not included in the lawbooks because it is in a separate manuscript. Although this is a possibility, it seems odd that there are also law tractates in *H*. Another oddity is that this collection is preserved in only one manuscript. Surely, if this collection was as important as the triad collection included after Powell's main section of law in the Bleg lawbooks, or if it was an appendix or a companion to Ior, it would have been copied more than once? Also, *H* seems too different from the collections in Bleg and Cyfn to be a separate version of any of those triad collections.[88] If it were copied from the Bleg and Cyfn collections, one would expect that all of the triads found in one of those collections would be included in the *H* collection, with other triads added to bring the total to almost 500. This is not the case.

It is possible that this is an oral collection written down for posterity: several points support this hypothesis. First, the manuscript is not written in an organized fashion and does not appear to be part of the copying and recopying system apparent with the three redactions. The material is written down in a tiny hand, filling every spare piece of parchment, and in a court hand which is not usually seen in manuscripts which may have been produced for a library, as it is not a display style.[89] The use of court hand suggests that it was written by a practising lawyer, and this may have been done for practical use.[90] However, the fact that there are so many triads, as well as tractates, in the manuscript, weakens the argument for an oral collection, as it is unlikely that any one person could remember

---

[87] See pp. 32–34.
[88] *Llyfr Blegywryd*, xliii–xliv.
[89] Huws, *Medieval Welsh Manuscripts*, 46.
[90] Pryce, *Native Law and the Church*, 19, n. 8.

the bulk of material contained in *H*. I intend to discuss this collection of triads in greater detail elsewhere.

The Development of the Collection of Legal Triads

The triad collection increases in size moving through the redactions. The largest triad collections found in the Bleg manuscripts, all southern, are later than those in Cyfn. Also, the later the manuscript, the larger the collection. The largest single collection of triads in a Bleg manuscript is in manuscript *Q*, where the basic Bleg collection has an additional 150 triads appended to it. Manuscript *S* also has more triads than most Bleg manuscripts, but they occur in the tail of the manuscript, as shorter collections.

If we accept Powell's theory that the triads were for oral learning only and not part of Welsh law in the strict sense, the inclusion of these triads in the southern texts can be explained by the difference in tradition between north and south Wales. There is evidence for legal training in north Wales, and families of lawyers are attested in the thirteenth century.[91] However, the story is different in south Wales. There seems to be less emphasis on trained lawyers, and there is evidence that men of status could make judgements and act as semi-professional lawmen – *brawdwyr o fraint tir* (justices by virtue of land).[92] These men would be local gentry or landowners and they might not have had rigorous legal training as would the professional men of north Wales. They would not have memorized triads, and therefore would be more likely to need written collections. The Bleg redaction also places emphasis on the use of lawbooks in court – in making a judgement, written law could be decisive, and the lawmen might need to take a lawbook with them to assist judgement or pleading.[93] Manuscripts from the Bleg reduction have a section stating that, when it is claimed that a jurist has made a false judgement, the jurist has to answer to the king, and the claimant wins his case if he can show from a lawbook a better judgement than the one previously given by the jurist.[94] The illustration of the court judge in Peniarth MS 28 is a further piece of evidence: he is pictured with a book in his hand.[95] This emphasis on written law may explain the existence of the triads in the southern lawbooks: quoting a triad from memory would not stand up in court, but pointing to a triad written in a lawbook would be more effective. There would have been a need in south Wales to write down triads to give them authority, whereas in north Wales

[91] R. R. Davies in *LAL, 263.*
[92] Ibid., 264.
[93] *Llyfr Blegywryd,* 101, *The Laws of Hywel Dda,* 96–7, and James, 'BL Add. 22356', p. xxviii. There are examples of triads being quoted in both the model plaints found in *Q*, and a sixteenth-century land case. *AL,* XII. i–x, T. Jones Pierce, 'The law of Wales: the last phase', 369–89.
[94] *Llyfr Blegywryd,* 101; *Laws of Hywel Dda,* 96–7.
[95] D. Huws, *Peniarth 28: Darluniau o Lyfr Cyfraith Hywel Dda.*

they would have been memorized. In addition, as the legal profession was more exclusive in north Wales, fewer people would need the legal triads on parchment.

If this is why collections of triads were written down, where did they originate? We need not worry as to whether they were druidic in origin as was once believed.[96] As noted earlier, Powell thought that there must have been originally a separate manuscript of triads, which then continued as a developing collection and was preserved at various stages of its development in the different manuscripts.[97] However, Brynmor-Jones correctly states that there is no evidence for a separate 'Book of Triads' in any manuscript.[98] Christine James has further shown that there are many problems with Powell's theory and if it is to stand, then we must accept that there were at least three separate collections of triads. Furthermore, it is problematic to see the collection of triads in each manuscript as 'floating sections'.[99] One might perhaps concede that the triads may originally have started as a collection separate from the lawbooks. There are three ways of looking at this material in relation to the lawbooks. First, there may have been oral triadic law as well oral laws which were not in the form of triads. This would mean that legal triads, and non-triadic legal prose, started orally but were written down at later stages of their development.[100] Secondly, even if the non-triadic law was already written down, there may have been unwritten triads which were memorized as a group, making an oral collection of legal triads. Thirdly, there may simply have been written lawbooks with written collections of triads as some kind of companion or supplementary volume. The way the legal material (triadic and non-triadic) is 'edited' and moved around to different positions within different manuscripts by the time of the Bleg redaction suggests that a collection of triads may have existed as a separate booklet or booklets, incorporated at different points, perhaps when fair copies were bound. However, it is difficult, given the nature of the evidence, to agree with Powell that this was *one* collection. The Cyfn redaction suggests, for example, that there was more than one collection, made up mainly of the same triads, but with different ordering. This collection may have been closer to an oral stage. By the time of the Bleg redaction, where the triads have a fixed order and therefore are later than the oral stage if not the Cyfn version, the triads were accepted as part of the law, and any developments in the triad collection would have been made within the legal manuscripts, rather than in a separate collection of triads.

---

[96] D. Brynmor-Jones, 'Foreign elements in Welsh law', 20.
[97] *Llyfr Blegywryd*, pp. xliii–xliv.
[98] Brynmor-Jones, 'Foreign elements', 25.
[99] James, 'BL Add. 22356', p. xlvii.
[100] Pryce, 'Lawbooks and literacy', 37.

Enoch Powell's Classification of the Triads in Bleg

Powell, in the introduction to *Llyfr Blegywryd*, split the triads into nine groups called A-I.[101] These groups can be used to demonstrate the different position of the triad collection in the *OTr*-type Bleg manuscripts and the *L*-type manuscripts (see Table 1).

Table 1. Enoch Powell's Triad Collections

	No. of triads	*Llyfr Blegywryd*	*J* ed. page	Title in *Llyfr Blegywryd* / *J* no. + title
A	6	78.24–80.6	44.7–45.4	*Trioedd Ynghylch Tir* / 44.
B	8	98.28–105.17	45.5–49.24	*Swydd a Braint Brawdwr* / 46.
C	1	105.18–27	22.3–12	*Cyngaws* / 33. *Trioedd*
D	2	105.28–106.17	22.33–23.8	*Cyngaws* / 33. *Trioedd*
E	1	106.18–107.8	49.25–39	*Rhaith Gwlad a Dedfryd Gwlad* / 48.
F	3	107.9–17	85.29–36	*Cynefodau* / 91.
G	103	107.18–124.14	33.3–44.6	*Trioedd* / 44.
H	1	124.15–125.3	22.13–32	*Trioedd* / 33. *Trioedd*
I	6	125.4–126.18	20.13–22.2	*Trioedd* / 33. *Trioedd*

Most of Powell's groups contain so few triads that they can hardly be called a collection – one triad does not make a collection. It is clear that in the Bleg lawbooks there is only one large triad collection, and that is Powell's G. The triad collection is found towards the end of the *OTr*-type manuscripts.

Powell's A is a group of five triads about land, found following the land law section; B, C, D, E and F are found before the main triad collection as parts of short sections of law which are mainly in triadic form; and H and I are similarly in short sections mainly as triads, and follow immediately after G. Whilst this may give the appearance of one large triad collection in *OTr* manuscripts, comprised of B–I, in fact, only G is a triad collection uninterrupted by explanatory sections of text.[102] In *L* manuscripts, the order is different, and mini-collections occur: Aneurin Owen has three sections labelled 'Triads' in his Dimetian Code based on manuscript *L*.[103] In *L* manuscripts, Powell's I, C, H and E (found in that order) follow the laws of court, immediately after the *rhingyll*'s section.[104] G, A, B and E follow the section on *dirwy*, and form the main and largest triad collection. F, labelled *cynefodau* (customs) in the printed version, is before the *arferion cyfraith* (practices of law) towards the end of the manu-

---

[101] *Llyfr Blegywryd*, p. xlii.
[102] Ibid., 98.28–126.18.
[103] *Ancient Laws*, DC I.xxx, II.viii, II.xxxvi.
[104] *Llyfr Blegywryd*, 27.25–29.25 is the *rhingyll*'s section: for the *L* order, see *Coleg yr Iesu LVII*, 19–23.

script.[105] Powell's classification shows that there are set groups of triads, but they are seen as part of a one larger group in *OTr*, and as several groups in *L*.

The order in *L*, where the largest collection of triads is found closer to the laws of court, is likely to be earlier as *OTr* omitted the laws of court; this omission meant that the manuscripts, minus the laws of court, might start with triads.[106] Instead of this, the first group of triads was moved to the end of the manuscript to become one collection.

A Latin D-type manuscript lay behind the Bleg redaction, and Emanuel has proved that Bleg is largely a translation of that Latin original.[107] Looking at Powell's groups of Bleg triads, it is noticeable that C and D, the triads on *cyngaws* (plea), are not found in Latin D, and neither is group H. The triads from Group I are found, but not as a group: the triads are split, with one in the laws of court[108] and the remainder in a section where there are several other triads.[109] These I triads are followed by sections B and E.[110] So, if we accept that Powell's grouping of the triads was accurate for Bleg, it is clear that the triads were not formed into such tidy groups in Latin D. The redactor of Bleg may have brought triads together to make little blocks or, as in the case of *OTr*, brought all the smaller groups together to create one big collection. It is, of course, possible that Latin D split a large group into two, but this is less likely, as the tendency was to bring similar material together, so triads would be placed with other triads. To split a large group into two would be an unusual step for the redactor to take, particularly as there does not seem to be a marked distinction in the subject matter of the two groups.

The triad collection aside, triads are found throughout the main text of Bleg, usually placed at relevant points within the tractates. In Bleg, there are three sections in particular which contain significant numbers of triads that are not found in the triad collections. There are several triads found in the laws of court, but they are not a consecutive collection; the same can be said of the section on *brawdwr a brawd* (judge and judgement) in Bleg which includes Powell's section B.[111] The third section in Bleg is the land law tractate, which has its own collection of six triads relating to land (Powell's section A), and also has four further triads within the tractate.[112]

The first tractate to contain a significant number of triads scattered throughout the text is the laws of the court. The tractate usually includes a triad each relating to the king and the queen's *sarhaed*, a triad stating the three types of men in law,

---

[105] *Coleg yr Iesu LVII*, 85.
[106] James, 'BL Add. 22356', pp. li, lii–liii.
[107] H. D. Emanuel, 'The Book of Blegywryd and MS. Rawlinson 821', 161–70.
[108] *LTWL*, 335.3–14 in the laws of court, and 348.40–349.18.
[109] Ibid., 335.3–14, 348.40–349.18.
[110] Ibid., 349.26–353.5.
[111] Ibid., 349–57.
[112] Ibid., 384–90.

and a triad which fits in the *offeiriad llys* (court priest's) section – his three duties.[113] These triads are a standard fixture in the laws of the court rather than part of a triad collection; they are found in Ior as well as in Bleg, and most of them are in Cyfn and the Latin texts, so they may well be part of the 'model lawbook', or the basic material behind the lawbooks as Powell saw them.[114]

Powell's B is another section of triads that, whilst not consecutive, all relate to the same subject. They are scattered throughout the section on *brawdwr a brawd*. Powell probably considered them to be a small collection of triads as they are close together, although interspersed with sections of ordinary legal text. This is naturally a significant section of the laws, and the triads are again part of the text rather than being a separate collection, since other sentences come between the triads. However, in the *OTr* version of Bleg, this section marks the beginning of the triad collection; a section already containing many is a natural place to add more triads. These triads are not found in Ior and Cyfn as the section on *brawdwr a brawd* is absent.

Powell's A is a small section of consecutive triads which all relate to land law and are inserted following that section in *OTr*, but are at the end of the triad collection (Powell's G) in *L*.[115] The A triads are found in the land law section in Latin D; these triads stay in the same position in Bleg *OTr* manuscripts and nothing is added to this group in any manuscript after Latin D. Christine James argues that these triads were already in the position in which they are found in the extant *OTr* manuscripts from an early stage, and that the large collection of triads, the actual group found under the heading(s) 'Triads' in *Ancient Laws*, was extracted from elsewhere and edited by various scribe-editors.[116] This certainly seems to be the case, because, by the time of Bleg, these triads in the body of the text were more or less fixed, and no more were added (whereas this is not true of the large triad collections). Their position in *OTr* therefore may reflect their position in the original Bleg. This group also occurs (with slight differences in order) in manuscript *V* of the Cyfn redaction,[117] which suggests that the trend of having triads in the land law section was started early on, and may also suggest some connection between the texts: either the branch of the Cyfn manuscripts containing *V* was influenced by Bleg, or vice versa.

[113] *Llyfr Blegywryd*, 13.1–20.
[114] *Llyfr Iorwerth*, §3; *WML*, 2, 3; *Llyfr Blegywryd*, 3, 4.
[115] *Coleg yr Iesu LVII*, 33.3–44.6.
[116] James, 'BL Add. 22356', p. xlviii.
[117] *WML*, 53–4.

The Growth of the Legal Triad Collections in the Redactions

(i) Cyfnerth

One of the faults of Powell's theory about triads is that it was effectively based solely on Bleg. However, Cyfn probably represents the oldest redaction of the laws.[118] There are seven manuscripts in this group, labelled *U–Z*, and *Mk* (a manuscript privately owned by Sir George Meyrick of Bodorgan), which are all fourteenth-century in date (apart from *Z*, which is sixteenth-century) but probably contain a text from the twelfth century.[119] However, some of the Cyfn manuscripts contain material from other tractates, and it is difficult to determine the contents and order of the original Cyfn redaction, including the triad collection.[120]

The *U* manuscript used by Aneurin Owen as his Gwentian Code has fewer triads than the other Cyfn manuscripts, and the order of the triads is very different.[121] Aneurin Owen stated that he used *U* because it was the simplest, and it is also smaller than the other manuscripts of the same redaction.[122] *U* is southern in orthography and vocabulary, but has some northern influence.[123] It contains a collection of forty-nine triads, found at the end of the manuscript.

Mk has a large collection of triads – a total of 115 – but there is a hiatus in the manuscript which occurs in the middle of the triad collection.[124] The hiatus occurs where the collection in *Mk* is very similar to, if not a copy of, *L*, a Bleg manuscript, so it does not appear that there are lost triads. In his description of *Mk*, Wotton stated that it was not greatly different from *L*, but most of the triad collection follows the Cyfn type closer than it does the Bleg type; *Mk* also has the typical Cyfn triads which are not found in the Bleg collections.[125] However, from Mk95 onwards (see Conspectus 3), the only other manuscript in which the triads are found is *W*, and Mk104 onwards is much closer to Bleg, with triads that are not found in the other Cyfn manuscripts: the exceptions are Mk122–5, also found in *V*; Mk127, which is also in *U*; Mk131, which is in *X* and *Z*, and Mk132, which occurs in *U* and *Z* (see Conspectus 3). Mk122–3 are found in both *V* and Bleg as a small collection of triads relating to land and, according to the *V* evidence, they were seen as a short collection following the land law section. They are in the main text of *V* rather than in the triad collection.

Wade-Evans used *V* and *W* for his edition, as the manuscripts are similar and written by the same scribe. The triad collection is found at the end of both

---

[118] Jenkins, *Cyfraith Hywel*, 6; Charles-Edwards, *The Welsh Laws*, 20, 35–6.

[119] Owen, 'The laws of court from Cyfnerth', in *WKC*, 425; Pryce, 'Lawbooks and literacy', 38–9.

[120] Ibid., 40.

[121] See Conspectus 1.

[122] *AL*, p. xxxi.

[123] D. Jenkins, 'Excursus: the lawbooks and their relation', in *WKC*, 13.

[124] See Conspectus 3.

[125] W. Wotton and M. Williams, *Leges Wallicae*, introduction.

manuscripts, and the collection in the Wade-Evans edition has eighty-one triads, forty-eight of which are from V – the remainder are taken from W as V is defective in this section.[126] Eight of the triads are repeated in the printed text merely because there was some overlap when Wade-Evans switched from V to W.[127] Wade-Evans stated that the manuscripts used in his edition (V and W) could actually be called the 'Composite Book of Cyvnerth and Blegywryd' as they resemble the Bleg redaction in some aspects whereas Owen's U may be closer to the original Cyfn text.[128] Wade-Evans's suggestion is not borne out by the triad collection.[129] Many of the Cyfn triads do appear in the Bleg collection, but finding 'runs' of triads following the same order in V, W and Bleg is difficult – the biggest run is of five triads.

X and Z seem to be close to each other, and separate from the other Cyfn manuscripts.[130] X has fewer triads than V, W and Mk, but the collection is not the short collection found in U. The collection in X is very similar in order to that in V, W and Mk up to Mk67, but there are certain triads in the Mk, V and W collection which are not in the X collection, and so there are 'gaps' in the correspondence of the lists of triads.[131] Most of the gaps are also found in Z. It may be that these triads are additions to the collection in Mk, V and W. In both X and Z the triad collection is 'interrupted' by short tractates halfway through, but it continues in a similar way afterwards, with largely the same triads in both manuscripts. X also lacks one triad found in most of the other Cyfn manuscripts, but it appears that that triad was omitted deliberately, because of its subject matter. The triad in question, X49a, is on the three legal cunts, and is not really a legal triad. The triad is censored in W, with the word 'cunt' blacked out each time it occurs in the triad, and in Z where the word has simply been omitted, so the scribe of X is not the only censor in this case. But there is reason to believe that the triad was in his exemplar: the triad is part of the 'core' collection in the other Cyfn manuscripts, and the order of the collection in each of the manuscripts is very similar at this point.[132] In addition, there is other evidence of the scribe of X apparently censoring another triad with a delicate subject matter. X55, on the three thrusts, has a final limb discussing the punishment for a false virgin. The wording is different in X: the words *a bonllost a'i hymrain un waith* (… with a penis and copulates with her once) are omitted, although they occur in every other version of the triad. This censorship may suggest a clerical origin for manuscript X. It is interesting that Bleg, which also had some clerical influence, does not include

[126] *WML*, p. lviii.
[127] Ibid., 132–3.
[128] Ibid., pp. xii–xiii.
[129] Nor is it borne out by the prologues to the lawbooks. H. Pryce, 'The prologues to the Welsh lawbooks', 152.
[130] Owen, 'The laws of court from Cyfnerth', in *WKC*, 431. See also Conspectus 1.
[131] See Conspectus 1.
[132] See Conspectus 1.

X49a, and no version of the three thrusts triad in Bleg (see Q106) includes the detail also omitted in *X*.

Z poses further problems, as it appears to be the only Cyfn manuscript with a 'tail'.[133] *Z* is written in more than one hand. Aneurin Owen stopped using it after the laws of court, as with *Y*.[134] As Gwenogvryn Evans correctly states, the order of this manuscript varies considerably and it contains what seems to be a portion of *Llyfr Cynog*, a lawbook attributed to that author.[135] The triad collection in *Z* is similar to that in *X*, but the 'tail' of *Z* begins immediately after the triad collection, and includes some triads from other sources.[136] Most of the triads in *Z* which are not found in the other Cyfn editions are found in Bleg manuscripts. *Z* has 119 triads in total.

There appears to be a 'core' collection of triads in Cyfn, up to around Mk67, which is found in most of the Cyfn manuscripts except for *U*.[137] *Mk*, *V* and *W* are very close in order up to this point, and *X* and *Z* are also close. *Mk*, *V* and *W* are southern manuscripts, whereas *X* and *Z* are northern, and these links are borne out by other sections of the manuscripts.[138] This core collection is the main triad collection found in *X* (*Z* is more complicated on account of its tail), and so *X* may preserve the earlier form of the Cyfn collection, whereas the collection is extended in *Mk*, *V* and *W*, making it closer to the Bleg collection in content if not in order. *U* seems to stand alone, as it does not appear to have the 'core' Cyfn triad collection. There are several triads in *U* also found in *W*, and some triads which are not found in *X*. The triad collection in *U* does include Cyfn-type triads, which are not found in Bleg (for example, the pair of triads on affiliation and denial of children, Mk46 and 47), and so this is not a separate collection even though it is rooted in the Cyfn tradition. Perhaps the scribe of *U* was copying his triad collection from a different source to the other Cyfn manuscripts, or adapting an existing collection.

Further interesting links are found in the variant readings for the core triad collections. In the core triad collection, *X* and *Z* correspond closely, as they do in other tractates.[139] One of the most significant similarities between these two manuscripts is their treatment of the pair of triads on affiliation and denial of children: both *X* and *Z* combine the triads to create one triad: the heading combines the two headings of MK46 and 47: X40 reads *Teir fford y dygir mab ac y diwedir* (In three ways is a son affiliated and denied), and the two triads are set out as one section, first giving the procedure for affiliating, and then for denying a child.[140]

[133] See Conspectus 4.
[134] *WML*, pp. xvi–xvii.
[135] J. G. Evans, *Report*, 1074–975; A. Rh. Wiliam, *Llyfr Cynog*.
[136] See Conspectus 4.
[137] See Conspectuses 1 and 3.
[138] Jenkins, 'Excursus', in *WKC*, 13, and Owen, 'The laws of court from Cyfnerth', in *WKC*, 428.
[139] Ibid., 13, 428.
[140] See X40.

X and *Z* also appear to have a slightly different, extended, version of Mk26 (X19), and in Mk63 (X54) both manuscripts replace *treis* (violence or rape), the first limb, with *anghyfreith* (unlawfulness). In X53, both *X* and *Z* omit the repetition of *hela* (hunting) found in each limb in the other Cyfn manuscripts, and add a sentence stating that a roebuck is the same value as a goat.

V is the manuscript closest to *Mk*, which is unsurprising as both are considered to be related to Bleg. They both have the group of triads on land law, triads which are not found in any of the other Cyfn manuscripts.[141] The readings of *V* and *Mk* are also very close in the surety tractate.[142] *W* does not seem to be as close to *Mk* as *V* is. *W*, however, shares several significant variants with *U*. As mentioned earlier, the collection in *U* is very different in order from that in the other Cyfn manuscripts, and *U* does not appear to have the same core of triads. This affinity with *W*, then, is surprising. Examples of *U* and *W* agreeing where the other manuscripts have a different reading include Mk43, where *U* and *W* have *a gaffat kyn noc ef* (begotten before him) rather than *y mab kyntaf* (the first son), making it quite clear which son was born first; in both Mk48 and 50, *U* and *W* leave out the sentence of extension to the triad; and in Mk75, rather than *y gwyr brathedic* (the injured men), both *U* and *W* have *y wnia6 g6eliau* (to stitch wounds).[143] In Mk92, *U* and *W* change the order of the limbs. However, there are examples where *U* has a completely different version of a triad, for example, Mk46 and 47, where *U* has different wording to the other manuscripts, and Mk62 where the triad is more concise in *U*.[144] There does appear to be a link between *U* and *W*, but it is not as close as that between *X* and *Z*. The stemma in Figure 1 summarizes the relationship between the triad collections in the Cyfn manuscripts as far as is possible.

The order of the Cyfn triad collection does not appear to follow the order of the triads in their Bleg form, or the Latin collections of triads.[145] The first three triads in the Cyfn collection are found in the same order in the Bleg manuscripts, but they are clearly a natural group of three triads that would hardly be separated as they list the *tair rhwyd* (three nets, metaphors for sources of income), of a king, a nobleman and a bondsman. The first part of the triad collection in Bleg follows the same order and has many of the same triads as the core collection as found in *X*; the *X* collection is not identical to this section of the Bleg triad collection, but the two collections are too similar to be separate collections. The main differences are towards the end of the collection in *X*, but this is true in general; the last ten or so triads in *X* do not correspond as closely to *Z*, for example, as the rest of the collection. This is not surprising, as an obvious place for the addition of stray

---

[141] See Conspectus 3.
[142] M. E. Owen, 'The Cyfnerth Text', in *LAL*, 179.
[143] See the variant readings for X37 and X63.
[144] See the alternative versions of X40 and X51.
[145] See Conspectus 1.

Figure 1 Stemma for Cyfnerth triad collection

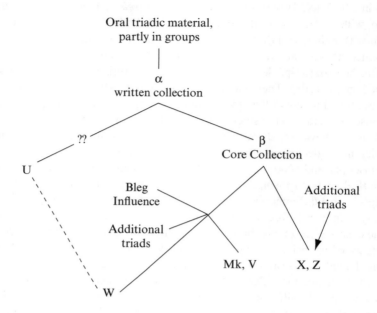

triads is at the end of a collection. So, the core collection of triads found in Cyfn, and in particular in *X*, is a collection which was used for the Bleg collection, via a Latin D-type text, as there is too much overlap between the triads contained in the collections in Cyfn, Latin D and Bleg to allow one to suppose that they are independent.

In summary, the inclusion of triads in the main text of the lawtexts, at points where they were relevant was a habit already begun, and it may be that triads were still being added within the tractates. The Cyfn evidence shows that including a collection of triads at the end of the lawbook was a developing tradition; the fact that there are more triads in *V* and *W*, and more again in *Mk*, suggests that this was popular, and that scribes added triads to their core as they went on. Most of the triads from the Cyfn core are found in Bleg, and the extended collection in *Mk* is comprised mainly of triads which occur later, in Latin D and Bleg.

(ii) Latin A, B and E

The Latin texts of the Welsh law present a similar problem to that of Cyfn. Latin A does not seem to bear much relation to the other Latin texts, but the triad collection in Latin B and Latin E is very close in content and sequence, and is probably

from the same source, or Latin E may be derived from Latin B in this case.[146]
Latin C has survived in an incomplete form and the extant sections do not include
triads, so Latin C can be disregarded in this particular discussion. Each of the
three manuscripts has a triad collection, but both Latin B and Latin E have several
shorter collections, often at relevant points in the tractates, and the triads are in
Latin. One of these mini-collections, triads 5–9 in Latin B and 20–4 in Latin E,
is the same in content and sequence, and occurs in the same place in both manuscripts, in the laws of court.[147] Significantly, this mini collection includes the
three triads on *rhwydi* (nets), also found following the laws of court in Ior, and in
Latin B, Latin E and Ior the next item is the *wyth pynfarch* (eight packhorses).

Some of the triads found in the Latin texts are also found in the Cyfn manuscripts but not in the Bleg triad collections; for example, X59, *O teir ffordd y telir
gwialen arian i'r brenin* (In three ways a silver rod is paid to the king) is found
both in Latin B and the Cyfn versions, as is *Tair aelwyd* (three hearths).[148] Some
of these triads may have come from a common origin but the collection found in
Cyfn is not the same as the collections in the Latin texts.

There are triads on *mechniaeth* (suretyship) following the relevant section in
Latin B, and some triads on the subject of women in the law of women. These
are small groups which are not part of the large collection, and they subsequently
occur in the same position in the Latin D and Bleg group of texts.[149] Latin B and
E have more triads than Latin A and also larger collections; Latin A seems to
avoid including triads. Although most of the triads in Latin A are also in Latin B,
they are not in the same order. All the Latin redactions have many triads in
common with Latin D, but they are not in the same order, and many triads are
unique to Latin A, B and E.[150] As we shall see, the triads in Latin D are written
in both Latin and Welsh; the triads in Latin A, B and E, however, are written in
Latin, with two exceptions: *Teir gorsaf unben* (Three stoppings of a ruler) and
Teir meuylwriaith mechniaith (Three shameful failings of suretyship).[151] These
triads are consecutive; *Teir gorsaf unben* is a short triad, with the keyword and
then three words. This is not in Latin A, D or Cyfn. *Teir meuylwriaith mechniaith*
is found in most of the Welsh redactions, and appears twice in Latin B, with both
versions in Welsh.[152] This triad is also in Welsh in Latin A.[153] 'Keywords', or the
first words of a triad's heading are often (but not always) given in Welsh in both
of the manuscripts, but the triads are written out in full in Latin. This suggests that
the triads were originally Welsh triads, and may have been known or referred to
by their first few words.

---

[146] See Conspectuses 9, 10 and 11.
[147] See Conspectuses 10 and 11.
[148] *WML*, 131, 135, and *LTWL*, 243, 254.
[149] *LTWL*, 217–18. See also *Llyfr Blegywryd*, 40–2.
[150] See Conspectus 6.
[151] *LTWL*, 243.
[152] *LTWL*, 218.
[153] *LTWL*, 125.

(iii) Latin D

A different source was used for Latin D; the Bleg tradition shows a closer relationship to Latin D than to Latin A and B. Emanuel proved that this was so
because the Bleg redaction was to a considerable extent a translation of a Latin
D type manuscript. He also states that Latin D is largely derived from Latin A and
B.[154] The triads in Latin D are not derived from Latin A and B, but the main Bleg
triad collection and the two main triad collections in Latin D are clearly versions
of the same collections. Neither Bleg *OTr* nor *L* is identical with Latin D, as far
as the triads are concerned. Table 2 shows the grouping of triads in Latin D, with
some comparisons with Bleg.

Table 2. The Triads in Latin D

	Latin D	Language*	Comments
1	1–7	Latin (7)	In laws of court
2	8	Latin	Found in Powell's I in Bleg
3	9	Latin	Following *galanas*: *tri dygyngoll cenedl*
4	10–16	Welsh	Inserted at relevant points in *tair colofn cyfraith*
5	17–19	Latin	*Dirwy* triad, and laws of women
6	20–22	Latin	Found in Powell's I in Bleg
7	23–28	Latin	Powell's B in Bleg
8	29–30	Latin	Powell's E in Bleg
9	31–34	Latin (34)	Not in Bleg. Before the triad collection
10	**35–55, 56–64**	**Welsh, Latin**	**Second part of the main collection in Bleg**
11	65–70	Welsh (67, 70)	With relevant sections e.g. *mechniaeth*
12	**71–81**	**Latin**	**71–81 in Ior as a group**
	82–125	**Welsh**	**First part of the collection in Bleg, with**
	126–142	**Latin (130, 138)**	**some missing**
13	143	Latin	Not in Bleg
14	144–148	Latin	*Trioedd ynghylch Tir*, Powell's A
15	149–50	Latin, Welsh	Only 149 is in Bleg
16	151–152	Welsh, Latin	Powell's F, *Cynefodau*
17	153–155	Latin	*Arferion Cyfraith*

* Numbers in ellipses indicate single triads in Welsh in a Latin group, or *vice versa*.

The significant point about Latin D is the treatment of the triad collection. For
a start, it is in two sections, not consecutive (marked in bold in Table 2).[155] The
first large section of triads, no. 10 in the table, begins with three triads in Latin
which are not found in the Bleg manuscripts. It then continues with triads which
are more or less identical in sequence to that of the corresponding triads, numbers
118–43 in Bleg *OTr*, with the odd triad missed out, and ends where Powell's

[154] Emanuel, 'Blegywryd and Rawlinson 821', 164.
[155] See also Conspectus 6.

section G ends. Whereas in Latin D these triads form the first large block of triads, in Bleg *OTr* these triads are found towards the end of the triad collection. The triads are roughly similar in subject – they mainly deal with procedure and the practical side of the law – and they contain the series of triads on thieves that is found exclusively in the Bleg redaction. Also significant is the fact that these triads are not found as a collection or even as part of a collection in most Cyfn manuscripts, although some of them are found in the *Mk* collection. However, it should be remembered that *Mk* has more of an affinity with the Bleg redaction than most of the other Cyfn manuscripts. What we may have in this first block of triads in Latin D are triads which are brought together for the first time as a collection from other sources, or a source that was not previously used by the other redactions. The redactor of Bleg then appended this collection to the end of his main collection of triads (the second group in Latin D), and it remained as a fixed part of the triad collection from then on.

The second block of triads in Latin D (12 in Table 2) follows the section on *mechniaeth* (suretyship) in the lawbook. It corresponds to the beginning of Bleg *OTr*'s triad collection, or Powell's G: triads 44–117, in Bleg, in order, although Latin D contains some additional triads.[156] The section is the only section in Latin D with the title '*De Trinis*' (The Threes/Triads), which suggests that this was recognized as a triad collection. The other section, 10 in Table 2, may be supplementing a section of law as the triads are on a similar subject. Group 10 is more varied in content and subject matter, and most of the triads are also found in Cyfn *V*, *W* and *Mk*, if not *U* and *X*. The collection starts with a group of three triads on *tair rhwyd brenin*, *breyr* and *taeawc*, and the first eleven, written in Latin, are also found in Ior, following the laws of court. These eleven triads may well be the core from which the principal Bleg collection grew over time. In any case, as Bleg was a Welsh version of a Latin D type text, the two groups of triads must have been joined together at the translating/editing stage. Section 10, the first section of triads occurring in Latin D, was probably appended to the *De Trinis* section (12), as section 12 was already recognized as a triad collection whereas the same was not necessarily true of section 10. The *De Trinis* section is very similar to the corresponding section found in Bleg, but it is not identical. There are one or two triads found in the Latin D collection which do not occur in Bleg, and there is one instance of two versions of the same triad in Latin D.[157] The order of the two collections is reversed in Bleg. Christine James suggests that, while editing, the compiler of a lawbook may pass a section then turn back to it, so reversing the order.[158]

[156] See Conspectus 6.
[157] *LTWL*, 374.5–12 (no. 125), 375.20–5 (no. 133). The two versions of this triad, *tri chargychwyn*, are very close together (there are only seven triads separating them) but they are not the same version. No. 133 is the version found in Bleg and in all other versions of the triad; no. 125 only occurs in Latin D.
[158] James, 'BL Add. 22356', pp. li–lii.

The second significant point about Latin D, which is again not matched by
Bleg, is evidence of editing in the three columns of law section. Seven triads are
found in the three columns section of Latin D which are not found in this section
in most other manuscripts – they are section 4 in Table 2, above. In Bleg, these
seven triads are found in the main triad collection, although they are not consecutive there; they are numbers 51, 57, 59, 72, 79, 84 and 99.[159] In the three
columns section of Latin D, these triads occur in the same order, but at relevant
points, following *galanas*, *tân* and *lledrad*. The redactor of Latin D has therefore
moved triads from his triad collection and placed them at relevant points in his
three columns section, so bringing material on the same topic together. The triads
are only taken from section 12, *De Trinis*, which again supports the theory that
section 12 was seen as the main triad collection. This arrangement in Latin D
appears to be an example of editing, paralleled by the actions of the redactor of
manuscript *Q* in the fifteenth century. In *Q* several triads are moved from the triad
collection and inserted at the end of each of the three columns of law; the same
thing appears to have been done in Latin D, and some of the triads moved are
actually the same ones. However, *Q* is not a copy of Latin D, and does not seem
to be derived directly from it, and so this appears to be a coincidence. Editing in
this way, by moving triads from the triad collections and placing them with
similar subject matter, is not surprising. However, the idea of the Bleg redactor
moving triads out of the three columns of law section where they are relevant to
the topic and placing them at random, individually, in the triad collection is
slightly more difficult to accept. If he wanted to move the triads into a collection,
he would presumably do so as a block. The triads do not fit with neighbouring
triads in the triad collection. The only possible explanation is that the reorganization of the three columns material happened at a later stage in Latin D: Bleg
is derived from an earlier form of Latin D than that found in Bodleian MS.
Rawlinson C 821, our earliest surviving text of this redaction.[160] If, as Emanuel
suggests, both Bleg and Rawlinson are one remove from the archetype, we can
accept that the archetype had two blocks of triads, and the redactors treated them
differently – Bleg combined the two large blocks to make one collection, and
Rawlinson 821 kept the two blocks, but moved some triads from the collection
to the three columns section. There does not appear to be any evidence for this
happening elsewhere in Latin D.

Seventy-four of the 155 triads in Latin D are in Latin. Most of the triads in the
body of the text are in Latin, but group 4 (see Table 2) is in Welsh, as are most of
the triads in the two main triad collections: section 10 is in Welsh with the last
nine in Latin. Section 12 starts in Latin with triads also found in Latin A and B,
and these triads form the only triad collection in Ior.[161] This Ior group is clearly

[159] See also Conspectus 6.
[160] Emanuel, 'Blegywryd and Rawlinson 821', 169.
[161] *Llyfr Iorwerth,* 42; *LTWL*, 369–70.

seen as a group of triads which stay together, and it is likely that the large collections found in Latin D and Bleg are comprised of several smaller collections. The language of section 12 then turns to Welsh, before finally reverting to Latin. These switches in language may point to the fact that the compiler was getting his triads from separate sources. It seems certain that the compiler of Latin D was copying an original when it came to his triads, and the original may have been in Welsh. He may also have had a Latin version of the laws to hand, which included some triads; where possible, he wrote the triads in Latin. The fact that all of the triads in Bleg and Latin D follow more or less the same order suggests copying, but Bleg was not copying and translating from Latin D directly – it is more likely that they had a similar or the same exemplar.[162] Emanuel makes this clear: there are too many examples of mistranslating and miscopying in Bleg for all of it to be from a Welsh original, but the extant version of Latin D is not the text Bleg was copying.[163] Emanuel, however, suggests that the copyist of Bleg may have been working from the same original as the manuscript from which our extant Latin D text was taken, or a text very similar to it.[164]

(iv) Blegywryd

The reorganization of the triads was more or less complete by the time of Bleg *L*, the tradition from which most of the later Bleg manuscripts derive. The triads in the main body of the text are in place by this stage and the triads and their position are kept, on the whole, in Bleg manuscripts. The order within the triad collection is also fairly settled by the time of Bleg; it begins with the three triads relating to *rhwyd brenin, breyr* and *taeog* (seen as a group of three early on, in Cyfn, and also in Ior).[165] Another set of triads within the main group discusses thieves and punishments. This group is not found in Cyfn or Latin A and B.

There are some differences between the two groups of manuscripts in the two branches of Bleg: *OTr* and *L*. Of the seventeen manuscripts in the Bleg redaction, thirteen are *L*-type: *L, M, N, R, Bost, T, J, Tim, Llan, Crd, Q, E,* and *P*.[166] There are two main differences between the sets of manuscripts: first, *OTr* manuscripts do not contain the laws of court whereas *L* manuscripts do, and secondly, the triad collection is in a different position in the two groups.[167] The main triad collection in the *L* manuscripts follows the three columns of law, after a section on *dirwy*, whereas in the *OTr* manuscripts the bulk of the triads are found at the end of the manuscript. As stated earlier, it is likely that the *L* group has the original

---

162 See Conspectus 6.
163 *LTWL*, 168.
164 Ibid., 169.
165 See Conspectuses 5 and 7.
166 *Coleg yr Iesu LVII*, p. xvi.
167 Ibid., and see also Conspectus 7.

positioning of triads, after the laws of the court.[168] The actual triads found in the *L* type manuscripts are the same as those in *OTr*. The manuscripts all contain the same triads, apart from the later Bleg manuscripts, including *Q*, which have a tail of additional material. The order within the collection is identical, containing eighty-eight triads and starting with *Teir rhwyd brenhin*. The stemma for the Bleg manuscripts given in *Coleg yr Iesu LVII* can be used for the triad collections, and only one additional point may be made here.[169] It is stated in the introduction to *Coleg yr Iesu LVII* that manuscripts *M* and *Bost* are very similar, but it is impossible to tell, due to the fragmentary nature of those manuscripts, whether they are from the same source.[170] Looking at the triad collection in particular, these manuscripts are almost identical; there is nothing in *M* which is not also in *Bost*. Furthermore, both manuscripts share a significant case of eyeskip, where two similar triads (Q99 and 100) are combined. Another case of eyeskip is found in *M*, where, similarly, Q102 and 103 are combined. This is not found in *Bost*, which suggests that if one manuscript is a copy of the other, *M* is the copy of *Bost*.

The Triads in Manuscript Q

Q is a fifteenth-century version of an *L*-type Bleg text, and both manuscripts *C* and *P* appear to be copies of *Q*; the order of the text is identical in each manuscript.[171] The only difference is that there is a hiatus in *Q* due to loss of a leaf, but the missing section is found in *C*. *Q* has more triads than are found in *OTr* or *L* texts: it has a total of 262 triads, and the main triad collection has almost twice as many triads as expected. In addition to the extended collection, *Q*, as is typical of fifteenth-century Bleg redaction texts, has a tail of material made up either of material from other redactions or of additional material (so-called 'anomalous' material), which includes triads. Unlike *S*, *Q* does not have smaller collections in its tail, but *Q*, *S* and *Tim* share some of the extended triads that give detailed explanations, in contrast to the epigrammatic triads found in the collections.[172] Most of the 'anomalous' material from *Q* was printed in Book X of *Ancient Laws*. The extra triads are printed as a collection of forty-three triads, but there are actually fifty in the additional collection in *Q*.[173] These triads are added at the end of the triad collection, continuing what is found in *Llyfr Blegywryd* and Owen's Dimetian Code, and some are also found in manuscript *S*. There is a note in the

---

[168] Ibid.

[169] Ibid., p. xviii.

[170] Ibid., pp. xvii–xviii.

[171] For a fuller discussion on manuscript *Q*, see S. E. Roberts, 'Creu trefn o anhrefn', 397–420.

[172] James, 'BL Add. 22356', p. xxi.

[173] *AL*, X.vii.1–49.

hand of William Maurice in manuscript *P*, which is derived from *Q*, stating that there are more triads in the *P* collection than in the Bleg manuscript with which he was comparing it: *dyma drioedd ychwaneg nag sydd yn Beta* (here are more triads than there are in Beta).[174] This additional collection is probably itself made of smaller collections, as is the case with the main Bleg collection. The first few triads in the additional collection are found in several sources, often with *holiadon* (interrogatories, a collection of question-and-answer sections), and are usually found in the same order in the other manuscripts.[175] These may be a section of the Book of Cynog; *Q* has sections of this book, but the triads have been moved and placed in the triad collection.[176] Some of the triads occur in other redactions; it is certain that the compiler of *Q* did have access to a Ior manuscript as there is both a large collection of *damweiniau* and actual Ior sections in the tail of the manuscript. There are no triads found in the collection of *damweiniau* included in the tail of *Q*, which is unusual, but many of the triads found in *Damweiniau Colan* are found in the extended collection in *Q*, so, again, the scribe was moving similar sections, triads in particular, closer together. This also indicates that the redactor of *Q* considered that triads and *damweiniau* were two different genres. Looking at the Ior triads found in *Q*, there are two which stand out as they are extended triads. First, the triad found in the *mechniaeth* (surety-ship) section in both *Q* and Ior, *Teir ouer vechni* (Three useless suretyships), Q53, also occurs in *J* and *Tim*, but the variant readings are too different to be included in the edition of the *Q* triad. Secondly, the long triad found in the extended collection in Q196, *Teir bala6c vechni* (Three buckle suretyships), also occurs in *Tim*, and in manuscript *D* of the Ior redaction. Neither *Tim* nor *D* is sufficiently close in reading to *Q* to suggest which branch of Ior is a source for the Ior material in *Q*.[177]

Finally, triads 168–94 in the additional collection in *Q* are very similar in sequence to part of the *K* and *S* collection (see below).[178] Several triads from the *K* and *S* collection are missing in the *Q* extended collection, and some triads occur in *Q* but do not occur in the *K* and *S* collection, so the *Q* text does not contain a direct copy of the collection. However, it is probable that the redactor of *Q* had a version of that triad collection to hand, and copied it selectively, omitting repetition as several of the triads in this collection are expanded versions of triads found in the main Bleg collection.

The collection of triads in *Q* is therefore the Bleg collection with many more triads added. Within the tractates as opposed to the collection, there are again more triads in *Q* than are found in Bleg – in fact, there are more triads in the

---

[174] Peniarth MS 259A, fo. 39. *Beta* is Peniarth MS. 33, *M*.
[175] *AL*, DC III.iii.1–11.
[176] Wiliam, *Llyfr Cynog*, pp. xvii–xviii.
[177] *Coleg yr Iesu LVIII*, pp. xx–xxii.
[178] See Conspectuses 7 and 8.

tractates in Q than in any other Bleg manuscript. The redactor of Q reorganizes his material a little by adding relevant triads and additional material from other sources (often the Ior redaction) at the end of tractates. Some of these triads are also found in S, in the tail of that manuscript. Most tractates have additional Ior material tacked on at the end, and some have material which is unique to Q (and thus found in *Ancient Laws*, Book X). However, this reordering of material is found, most significantly, in the three columns of law tractate in Q. The compiler of the lawbook seems to have started editing the section on the three columns of law by copying the section on *galanas*, then placing additional material directly after it, including triads; he then did the same thing with theft and arson.[179] A similar reordering occurred in Latin D.[180] Some of the other tractates are also edited, with material on the same subject brought together, but the three columns of law and the section on witnesses are the only tractates where triads are moved from the collection as part of the editing process.[181] However, as Christine James explains, this middle section seems to be the only section of the manuscript that is so carefully edited, and the compiler even managed to repeat some of the 'moved' triads in their original position.[182]

These fifteenth-century texts, the last phase of the triad collection, show that triads grew in popularity, as the triads are retained in the manuscripts and more are added. The collection was fairly fluid in the early Cyfn period, but by the time of Latin D and Bleg, a collection had become more or less fixed in order and content. The only change in the later texts was that additional triads were added to the collection. Some of these triads were taken from other sources, and some may have been new compositions. There were legal triads available to add to the manuscripts, as the anomalous tail to Q includes many triads, and this is either material which the redactor had been unable to include at relevant points, or additional material which he chose to commit to parchment, but which was not part of his standard original.

The Triad Collection in Manuscripts K, S *and* Tim

The theory that there were separate collections of triads available for the redactors of the later manuscripts to use is upheld by a collection which is found in manuscripts *K* (a fifteenth-century Ior text), *S* and *Tim*. This is a separate collection from the Bleg collection, although several of the triads appear to be the same in content if not in wording.

---

[179] James, 'BL Add. 22356', pp. lv–lvi.
[180] See above, p. 28.
[181] James, 'BL Add. 22356', pp. lv–lvi.
[182] Ibid., liv, lvi.

K is an interesting fifteenth-century manuscript, in the hand of Lewys Glyn Cothi, and possibly linked with Cefnllys, Radnorshire. The manuscript seems to have several southern features, such as a large collection of triads, beginning on page 126.[183]

S is a large fifteenth-century Bleg redaction manuscript, with a very long tail of material, some unique to this manuscript, and some taken from other redactions, such as the Ior redaction. Christine James's edition of *S* includes a conspectus demonstrating where the material in the manuscript occurs elsewhere. There is a collection of triads, beginning with the *tri dygyngoll cenedl* (three dire losses) triad, found in the tail of *S*.[184] Christine James called this triad collection 'Triads – IV' in the list of the contents of *S*. It comes immediately after a section called *Gwadu mab* (denying a son), corresponding to Ior 100 and 101. Manuscript *J*, which is mainly Bleg but has a Ior 'tail', has two versions of the *dygyngoll* triad: the Bleg version in the *galanas* tractate and the Ior version in the tail of the manuscript, as part of the family law section.[185] *S* initially appears to be the same as *J*, in that it has a Ior section including the triad. However, although the preceding section is from Ior, the triad is not the same as that found in the Ior redactions. Instead, it appears to be a version of the Bleg/Cyfn triad, but expanded. The collection (consisting of forty-eight triads) contains other triads found in the Bleg collections, but in different versions.

The collection in *K* also follows a section on denying a son, as in *S*. It seems that *K* and *S* are copying from a similar source at this point, as the triad collection is almost identical: *K* has nine triads which are not found in *S* (six, if the first three triads in the collection are discounted), and *S* has one triad which is not found in the corresponding *K* collection; but the sequence of the triads is the same in both manuscripts. This collection of triads is significant as it is a collection copied more than once: sections of it are found in *Tim*, written by the scribe of *S*, but there is more than one hiatus in *Tim* at this point. Sections of it also occur in the additional collection in *Q*. Looking at the variant readings, in particular for K51 and K52, it is clear that *S* and *Tim* are linked, and that *K* is independent of them; there is a case of omission in K51, which does not occur in *S*, *Tim* or *Q*. Furthermore, in K52, there is an eyeskip in *S* and *Tim*: *K* and *Q* have the reading *a'r g6yr hynny nit oes nodiat arnunt namyn eu bot yn oreug6yr o'i cenedyl*, and *S* and *Tim* have *a'r g6yr hynny nit oed nodiat arnunt namyn eu bot yn genedyl o'r*. The final line of K52 is wrong: the triad states that a child cannot be affiliated by (*i gan*) the dead, whereas *S*, *Tim* and *Q* have affiliated to (*i/y*) the dead.

This collection of triads is separate from, and different to, the main collection found in most Bleg manuscripts, although it contains different versions of triads found in the Bleg collection. This collection in *K* and *S* appears to be separate;

---

[183] *Llyfr Iorwerth*, p. xxxii.
[184] James, 'BL Add. 22356', 153.
[185] S. E. Roberts, 'Tri Dygyngoll Cenedl', 163–82.

the original compilation could belong to the fifteenth-century and so be later than most Bleg manuscripts. Either way, this is evidence that there was more than one triad collection that was standard in content and sequence. The first three triads found in *K* are a group always found together in the law manuscripts – a group of three triads discussing the *tri anhepcor* (three indispensables) of a king, nobleman and a bondsman. These triads are found at the end of the laws of court in Ior manuscripts, and are labelled 'Regarding the triads which pertain to the king' in red in *K*. They may not be part of the original collection copied by both *K* and *S*, but they are usually found at the beginning of any Bleg triad collection. It may be that the redactor of *K* decided that he wanted to copy the triad collection found in his original, and wanted to begin his collection in the same way as other collections of triads with which he was familiar.

The *dygyngoll* triad in particular is an example of how a triad can develop or change between different redactions of the laws. *S* and *K* have the same version but with different orthography, and as mentioned, the triad is an extended, fuller version of the Bleg and Cyfn triad.

The redactor of *S* copied the Ior section on children into the tail of his manuscript. This section in Ior is followed by the Ior *dygyngoll* triad, but rather than copy the Ior *dygyngoll* triad (which he had already included in the tail of his manuscript, S216), the redactor of *S* copied a triad, with the same heading, which he had in another collection of triads, and followed it with the whole collection. The same thing has happened with *K*, but *K* also copied three more triads at the beginning of his collection. Whether *K* and *S* also have a common source for the Ior section found preceding the triad collection is more difficult to determine; the family law section preceding the collection in *S* and *K* is also found in *Q*, but not with, or close to, the triad collection.

Conclusion

Triads are an integral part of the Welsh laws, and it is unlikely that the large triad collections which form part of most of the lawbooks extant today were ever separate entities. The only exception, perhaps, is the triad collection found in manuscripts *K*, *S* and *Tim* and parts of it incorporated into the extended triad collection in manuscript *Q*. However, it may be telling that one 'separate' collection of legal triads was copied quite naturally into four separate legal manuscripts, and incorporated quite skilfully into one. Even though it may have been a separate collection of legal triads, the redactors of those manuscripts saw it as an obvious part of the material for inclusion in their lawbooks.

Triads were regularly added to the tractates of a lawbook – the main example being the eleven triads on the same subject matter found at the end of the laws of court in Ior. Several tractates in Bleg open with a triad giving the main points, and the triadic division was also an acceptable form for a legal tractate in the Middle Ages (as it is for essays and sermons today). The triads found in the tractates remain as part of the section in most manuscripts, the only exception being manuscript *Q*, where the systematic rearrangement of tractates and triads occurs.

It is possible to follow the development of the triad collection as found in the legal manuscripts. The triad collection may have begun its life as a short collection of around a dozen triads, all discussing the king and his court. This is the short triad collection placed at the end of the laws of court in Ior manuscripts; it may have been put there to fill spare leaves of parchment, and it was probably put in that position as it was discussing similar matters. It is likely, however, that this short collection was the basis for the 'core' collection of triads, and it is this collection, with perhaps some additional triads added at the end of the core

Figure 2 Stemma for the triad collections

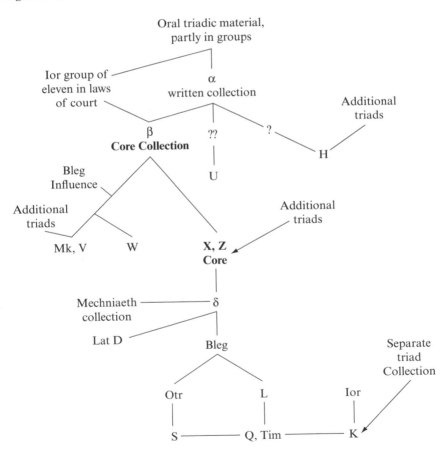

collection, which is found in manuscript *X* of the Cyfn redaction; a very similar collection is found in manuscript *Z*. The other Cyfn manuscripts also have the core collection, but more triads are added to the collection in those manuscripts – in *Mk* and *V*, and probably also in *W*, there is a great deal of Bleg influence, and many of the triads added to the triad collection are Bleg-type triads. Manuscript *U* of the Cyfn redaction stands alone. Although there is evidence that the redactor of *U* copied the core collection, the triads are in a different sequence, and there are fewer triads in the manuscript. This may be deliberate – the redactor may have left out triads according to his (now unknown) scheme, or it may be the case that *U* is the sole witness to a different version of the core triad collection.

The core triad collection contains largely the same triads in more or less the same order, and it occurs as a triad collection in the Latin texts. Latin D, however, has two triad collections – one collection of triads mainly dealing with procedure and suretyship, and the second collection labelled *De Trinis*, containing the core collection, again with most of the same triads in a similar order to the triad collection in *X*. As a version of Latin D was the basis of Bleg, we find both triad collections in Bleg, but with the order reversed – the main Bleg triad collection begins with the triads labelled *De Trinis* in Latin D, that is, the core collection, then is followed by the other large collection in Latin D. The two Latin D collections are combined in Bleg to make one large collection, and all of the Bleg manuscripts have the same collection, although some manuscripts, in particular *Q*, add triads to the main collection. The core triad collection was probably formed from small groups of triads – for example, a group of eleven is found in Ior and in every version of the triad collection thereafter – and the Bleg collection was formed from two shorter collections of triads.

The legal triad collection grows and develops. Although the core collection is more or less preserved, sometimes intact, sometimes adapted, it is usually added to and expanded – the only manuscript which may be different in this respect is manuscript *U*. Although anything up to and even over a hundred triads may be added in some manuscripts, it is surprising how little 'new' material appears. Most of the triads are repeating rules which may be found elsewhere in the law tractates. On the whole, new legal doctrine is not found as triads. Most of the triads in the core collections can be found as separate provisions in the tractates, although some of the triads do not occur at all – obvious example would be *Tri ofer llaeth* (three useless milks), a triad which is not as firmly based in the Welsh laws as, say, a triad on land law would be. The main Bleg collection, itself formed from two shorter collections, is also comprised of triads where the legal provisions would be found elsewhere in the tractates – the core collection remains the same, and the Bleg collection is amplified by adding several triads mainly on the subject of *mechniaeth* and procedures. These triads do not, on the whole, introduce new legal rules and principles, but summarize existing law. There are some examples of one limb being added to create a triad from two basic concepts – the best example perhaps is triad X37, *Tri meib yn tri broder vn mam vn dat* (Three sons being three brothers of the same mother and same father); as demonstrated by Huw Pryce, the third limb of this triad is a later addition (in fact, the third limb occurs as a proverb in an early collection of proverbs found in the Red Book of Hergest).[186] There are examples of sections of tractates containing three similar items being turned into simple triads too – for example, Z56, where the three limbs are found together as part of a tractate in Bleg, although not as a triad proper.

As far as the core triad collection and the larger Bleg triad collection are concerned, the triads are largely summaries of rules and principles already enunciated in non-triadic form in the tractates. In the case of *Q* and the later Bleg manuscripts, however, there are some legal ideas only found as triads, although the triads do tend to be longer, extended triads rather than the original short mnemonic forms found in the core collection. In both *S* and *Q*, there are also long tractates, often newer sections of laws from the fifteenth century based on older triads, but although they may follow the triadic form, these sections are far removed from the original pithy mnemonic triads found in the core collection.

As the triads on the whole tend to be repeating legal ideas in triadic form, it is unlikely that the amplification of the triad collections reflect social or legal changes between the thirteenth and the fifteenth centuries. By the end of this period, it is more likely that triads had become an authoritative genre and a recognized form which lawyers would have used, as well as an acceptable literary form. However, given that fifteenth-century lawbooks often have tails of material which reflects practice in the fifteenth century, and triads usually form part of the material found in those tails, there are some examples of newer triads. On the whole, though, the triads in the collections are conservative – rooted in the earlier legal tradition rather than being an expression of legal changes in the later stages of Welsh legal redaction.

A close textual study of the legal triads is more than a simple study of the genre. Much can be determined from the sequence of the triads within the collections, as well as from the actual wording and form of each individual triad. It is possible to show, as demonstrated above, the development of the collection of triads. We can determine a 'core' collection of triads which was a basic collection which stayed more or less the same throughout the different lawbooks and tractates. This is a valuable contribution to our understanding of medieval Welsh law as it shows the written development of a significant section of the laws. Although not every tractate works in the same way, it is possible to show that there are basic sections of law, quite early in date and short, upon which the tractates were built and the lawbooks compiled. In the case of the triads, this development can be seen very clearly. A close textual study of the triads also gives us a glimpse of the

---

[186] Pryce, *Native Law and the Church*, 100–5.

medieval Welsh lawbook compiler's mind. Although much of his work will remain unclear, it is possible to make some simple assumptions about the way a compiler of the triad collections, if not of the lawbooks in general, went about his work.

The triads in *X*, BL Cotton Cleopatra B.v

X1. Z1, U1, Mk1, V1, W1 [166r]

Tri dyn a wnant sarhaed y'r brenhin: y nep a torro y nawd, a'r neb a ladho y wr yn y wyd,[1] a'r neb a rwystro y wreic.[2]

X2. Z2, U2, Mk2, V2, W2 [1 2 3 = 1 3 2 Z] [166v]

O dri mod y sarheir y brenhines: bann dorrer y nawd, neu ban trawer drwy lid, neu ban dynher peth gan treis o'e llaw; ac yna telir[3] trayan kywerthid sarhaed y brenhin y'r vrenhines,[4] heb eur, heb aryan.[5]

X3. Z3 [174r]

Tri gwassanaeth a wna y brenhin y'r hebogyd y dyd hwnnw: daly y warthauyl tra disgynho, a daly y march tra gyrcho yr adar, a daly y warthauyl tra ysgynho.[6]

X4. U5, Mk8, V4, W4 [188r]

Tri[7] dadanhvd tir y syd:[8] carr, a[9] beich, ac[10] eredic.

[1] + ac yngwydd i wyr pan vo ymarvoll a chymanva rryngtho a phenaeth arall i *Z, Mk, V, W*
[2] + canmu hagen a telir yn sarhaet y brenhin yg ky6eir pob cantref oe teyrnas *U*
[3] − *Mk, U, V, W*
[4] ac yna telir ... vrenhines] ac yna traian syrhaed y brenhin 6yd i syrhaed hithe *Z*
[5] + hagen *U, Mk, V, W*
[6] daly y warthauyl ... ysgynho] daly i march tra ddiscyno a thra achuppo i adar a thra escyno.
[7] + ry6 *Mk, U*
[8] + datanhud *Mk, V, W*
[9] + datanhud *Mk, V, W*
[10] + datanhud *Mk, V, W*

Translation of the triads in *X*, BL Cotton Cleopatra B.v

X1

Three persons who commit *sarhaed* to the king: whoever breaks his protection, and whoever kills his man in his presence, and whoever obstructs his wife.

X2

In three ways *sarhaed* is done to the queen: when her protection is broken, or when she is struck through anger, or when something is taken with force from her hand; and then a third of the *sarhaed* value of the king is to be paid to the queen, without gold, and without silver.

X3

Three services which the king performs for the falconer that day: holding his stirrup as he dismounts, and holding his horse whilst he seeks the birds, and holding his stirrup as he mounts.

X4

There are three kinds of *dadannudd* for land: car, and load, and ploughing.

X5. Z5, U6, Mk9, V5, W5 [188v]

Teir gweith y rennir [tir]: gessefin[11] rwg brodoryon,[12] odyna rwg kefuyndyrw, a'r tryded weith[13] y rwg kyfrderw; gwedy hynny[14] ny byd[15] rann ar dir.

X6. Z68, Mk13, V13, W7 [1 2 3 = 2 3 1 Z] [190r]

Tri pheth ny werth taeawc heb ganhyad y arglwyd: march, a moch, a mel. Os gwrthyd yr arglwyd,[16] gwerthed y'r nep y mynho.[17]

X7. Z69, Mk14, V14, W8 [190r]

Teir keluydyt ny dysc taeawc y vap[18] heb ganhyad y arglwyd: yscolheictod, a bardoni, a gouannaeth; os tiodef[19] arglwyd hagen yny roder corun y'r yscolheic,[20] neu yny el yn gof yn y efueil, a'r bard yny enillo gadeir,[21] ryd uyd pob vn ohonynt yna.[22]

X8. Z70, U4, Mk15, V15, W9 [192r]

O teir mod y telir teithi buwch vawr:[23] nyd amgen,[24] o dec ar hugein aryant, neu vuwch gyhyd y chorn a'e hysgyuarn,[25] neu o blawd.

X9. Z6, Mk18, W12 [1 2 3 = 1 3 2 Mk] [202r]

O dri achaws ny chyll gwreic y hagwedi kyd adawho hi[26] y gwr:[27] nyd[28] amgen, o glafuri, a dryc anadyl,[29] ac eissyev kyd.

---

[11] yn gyntaf *Mk, V, W*
[12] brodvr *Z, U, Mk, V, W*
[13] a'r tryded weith] o ddyna *Z*
[14] gwedy hynny] odyna *U, Mk, V, W*
[15] ny byd] nyt oes pria6t *Mk, V, W*
[16] + gyssefin *Mk, V, W*
[17] y'r nep y mynho] ynte wedi hynny fford y myno *Z;* + g6edy hynny *Mk,V, W*
[18] taeawc y vap] mab taiawg *Z*
[19] os tiodef] kanys or godef *Mk;* o diodef *V, W*
[20] roder … yscolheic] gaffo gorvn *Z*
[21] yny enillo gadeir] 6rth y gerd *Z, Mk, V, W*
[22] ryd uyd … yna] ni ddyly ddim wedi hynny *Z;* ni ellir eu keithiwa6 g6edy hynny *Mk, V, W*
[23] – *Z, U, Mk, V, W*
[24] – *U, Mk, V, W*
[25] o uuch hesp tec *Mk, Z, U, V, W*
[26] – *Z*
[27] hi y gwr] y g6r *Mk, W*
[28] + nyd *X*
[29] dryc anadyl] anadl ddrwc *Z*

X5

Three times land is divided: first between brothers, then between cousins, and the third time between second cousins; after that there is no division of land.

X6

Three things a bondsman may not sell without the permission of his lord: a horse, and swine, and honey. If the lord refuses, let him sell to whoever he wishes.

X7

Three crafts a bondsman may not teach his son without the permission of his lord: clerkhood, and poetry, and smithcraft; if a lord tolerates it however until the cleric be tonsured, or until he becomes a smith in his smithy, and the poet until he wins a chair, each of them will be free after that.

X8

In three ways are the legal characteristics of a fully grown cow valued: namely, by thirty of silver, or cow of the same length in horn and ear, or by flour.

X9

For three reasons a woman does not lose her *agweddi* although she leaves her husband: namely for leprosy, and bad breath, and the want of intercourse.

X10. *Z7, Mk19, W13* [202r]

Tri pheth ny dygir y ar[30] wreic kyd gatter hi[31] am y cham: y chowyll, a'e hargyfure, a'e hwynebwerth.[32]

X11. *Z55, 60, Mk74, W69* [207v]

Teir aelwyd a dyly wneuthur yawn[33] drosd[34] dyn ny bo arglwyd adef idaw a chymell yawn idaw:[35] tad, a[36] brawd,[37] a chwegrwn.[38]

Z60

Tair aelwyd a ddyly gwneuthur bodd dyn kyny bo arglwyđ ef iddaw: vn, i dad; ac vn, i chwegrwn; ac vn, i vrawd hynaf.

X12. [207v]

Teir gosgord brenhinawl ysyd: gosgord brenhin, ac esgob, ac abad, canys llys vreinhawl a dyly pob vn ohonunt.

X13. [207v]

Tri amev brawd ysyd: vn yw bod kynghaws yr hawlwr a'r amdiffynnwr am y urawd a uarnwyd vdunt, ac yna y [208r] mae dosbarth ar y brawdwr. Yr eil yw i bod ymwystlaw y rwng y brawd a'r hawlwr. Trydid yw bod ymwystlaw rwng y brawdwr a'r amdiffynnwr am y vrawd a varnwyd vdunt, ac yna y mae reid dodi y dadyl honno ar awdurdawd y llys ac yneid o le arall.

---

[30] dygir y ar] chyll g6reic *Mk*
[31] gatter hi] adawer *Z*
[32] + pan gyttio gwr a gwraic arall *Z*
[33] + a'e chymryt *Mk, W*
[34] i bob *Z*
[35] a chymell yawn idaw] – *Mk, W*; + vn o *Z*
[36] + vn o *Z*
[37] + hynaf *Mk, W*
[38] a chwegrwn] ac vn i vrawd yr hynaf *Z*

X10

Three things are not taken from a woman although she is left for her offence: her *cowyll*, and her *argyfreu*, and her *wynebwerth*.

X11

Three hearths which should make redress on behalf of a man who has no acknowledged lord and seek redress for him: a father, and a brother, and a father-in-law.

Z60
The three hearths which ought to make satisfaction for a man although he has no lord: one, his father; and one, his father-in-law; and one, his eldest brother.

X12

There are three royal retinues: the retinue of a king, and a bishop, and an abbot, as each of them is entitled to a privileged court.

X13

There are three doubtings of judgement: one is that [of the] the *cyngaws* of the claimant and the defendant about the judgement which was judged to them, and then the decision rests with the justice. The second is that there is mutual pledging between the justice and the defendant. The third is that there is mutual pledging between the justice and the defendant regarding the judgement which was judged to them, and then it is necessary to give that pleading to the authority of the court and justices from another place.

X *Triad Collection*

X14. *Z10, U14, Mk21, V19, W17* [208r]

Tri digingoll kenedyl ynt: vn yw bod mab amheuedic[39] heb dwyn a heb diwad
ynghenedyl,[40] a llad o hwnnw gwr o genedyl arall;[41] talv a dylyir yr alanas
honno, ac odyna y diwad ynteu rac gwneuthur yr eil gyflauan ohonaw. Eil yw
talu galanas oll eithyr keinhyawc a dimei, ac o byd godor am hynny a llad[42] y
dyn[43] hwnnw, nyt oes govyn[44] amdanaw. Trydit yw pan enllipper [208v]
gwiryon am gelein a'e holi, a dodi oed kyfureithyawl o'r dwy genedyl y
dywad, a thorri yr oed hwnnw o'r gwiryon;[45] o lledir dyn o'r genedyl yna, ny
diwygir.[46]

X15. *Z11, U15, Mk22, V20, W18*

Tri oed kyfureith y dial kelein: y rwng dwy genedyl ny anffwynt o vn[47] wlad,
enwinv hawl y dit kyntaf o'r kysseuin wythnos y llader y gelein, ac erbyn pen
y pythefnos ony daw attep, kyfureith[48] yw dial. Eil yw o bydant y dw[y]
genedyl yn vn gantref, enwinv hawl yn y trydit[49] gwedy llader y gelein, ac ony
daw attep kyn y nawvettyd,[50] kyfureith yw[51] dial. Trydit yw os yn vn gymwd
y bydant y dwy genedyl, enwinv [hawl yr ail[52] dyd wedi lladder y gelain],[53]
kyn pen y chwechuettyd[54] dyuod attep, ac ony daw, kyfureithyawl[55] y dial.

---

[39] − *Z, U*

[40] − *V, W*

[41] + heb dylyu dim ida6 *Mk, V*

[42] + or genedl am y godor *Z, U, Mk, V, W*

[43] y dyn] − *Z, U*

[44] dial *Z*

[45] a dodi ... gwiryon] ac nas dywatto yn oed k*yfraith Z*; ac ony diwat erbyn oet kyfreitha6l *U, W*; ac
onys g6atta erbyn oet kyfreith *Mk, V*

[46] ny diwygir] ni thelir amdanaw *Z*; ny dylyir dim ymdana6 *U*; ny dylyir y diu6yn *Mk*; ny dylyir
diu6yn ymdana6 *V, W*

[47] genedyl ... vn] − *Z*

[48] rryddhav *Z, U, Mk, V, W*

[49] trydydd dyd *Z, U, Mk, V, W*

[50] kyn y nawvettyd] − *Z*

[51] yn rydhau *U, Mk, V, W*

[52] trydydyd *U, Mk, V, W*

[53] hawl ... attep] − *X*; from *Z*

[54] wythved dyd *Z*

[55] kyfreith a rydha *U, Mk, V, W*

X *Triad Collection*

X14

These are the three dire losses of a kindred: one is that there be a doubted son without affiliation or denial in a kindred, and that he kills a man from another kindred; that *galanas* ought to be paid, and then he should be denied lest he commits a second crime. The second is paying the whole of a *galanas* except a penny and a halfpenny, and if there is a delay concerning that and that man is killed [for that delay], there is to be no claim for him. The third is when an innocent man is accused of a killing and a claim is made against him, and a legal time is set by the two kindreds in order to deny it, and the innocent man breaks that set legal time; if a man from the kindred is then killed, there should be no compensation.

X15

Three legal periods to avenge a killing: between two kindreds who do not originate from the same country, to send [notice of] the claim on the first day of the first week from when the dead was slain, and if no answer comes by the end of the fortnight, the law allows revenge. The second is if the two kindreds are in the same *cantref*, to send [notice of] the claim on the third day after the dead was slain, and if no answer comes by the end of the ninth day, the law allows revenge. The third is if the two kindreds are in the same commote, to send [notice of] the claim on the second day after the killing has occurred, the answer is to come by the end of the sixth day, and if it does not come, the law allows revenge.

X16. *Z12, U16, Mk23, V21, W19*

Teir rwyd brenhin yw: y teulv; nyd os diwyn am y rwyd honno namyn trugared
     brenhin. Eil rwyd yw y gre;[56] a dhaer ar y gre iiii o'r keinhawc kyfureith a
     [209r] geiff.[57] Y trydet yw gwarthec y vaerdy; kanys o bop eidyon a gaffer[58]
     arnunt iiii o'r keynhyawc kyfureith a geiff.

X17. *Z13, U17, Mk25, V22, W20*

Teir rwyd breyr ynt: gre, a gwarthec,[59] a moch; canys o keffir aniueil[60] yn ev plith
     iiii o'r k*einhawc* kyfureith a geiff o bop vn ohonunt.[61]

X18. *Z14, U18, Mk24, V23, W21*

Teir rwyd taeawc ynt: y warthec, a'e uoch, a'e hendref; o galan Mei hyd pan
     darffo Medi iiii o'r cotta a geiff o bop aniveil[62] or a gaffo yndunt.[63]

X19. *Z15, Mk26, U19, V24, W22 [1 2 3 = 2 3 1 Z, Mk, V, W]*

Teir dirwy brenhin ynt: dirwy ymlad kyuadev, a dirwy treis, a dirwy y ledrad
     anofeis, .i. anobeith.[64] Diwyn dirwy treis yw gwialen aryant yw a arhaedo o'r
     daear hyd yn yad y brenhin pan eistedo yny gadeir, gyrreued ac aranvys[65] a'r
     tri ban ar pob pen y'r wialhen,[66] a ffiol eur a anho llawn diawd y brenhin yndi,
     kyn tewed ac ewin amaeth a amaetho seith mlyned,[67] a chlawr eur a vo kyfuled
     ac wyneb y bren[209v]hin kyn[68] tewed a'r fiol.[69] Diwyn dirwy ymlad[70] yw
     deudeg mvw. Diwyn dirwy ledrad: kysswynaw lledrad ar dyn a diwad
     ohonaw[71] a'y dauawd, a gossod reith a'y ffallv – lleidyr kyvadeu can pallws y

---

[56] + o bob march *Z, U, Mk, V, W*
[57] kyfureith ... geiff] – *Z*; + y brenhin *U, Mk, V*
[58] dalher *Mk, V*
[59] + y vayrdy *Z, Mk, V, W*
[60] ll6dyn *Mk, V*
[61] o bop ... ohonunt] y breyr *U*; y breyr o pop ll6dyn *Mk, V*
[62] ll6dyn *Mk, V*
[63] + a hyny yw pedair keiniawc k. mynac *Z*
[64] anofeis .i. anobeith] anolaith *Z*; – *Mk, V, W*
[65] gyrreued ac aranvys] gyn crassed a'i hir6ys *Z*
[66] yw a arhaedo ... wialhen] – *Mk, V, W*
[67] a anho ... mlyned] – *Mk, V, W*
[68] ac wyneb y brenhin kyn] – *Z*
[69] a vo kyfuled ... a'r fiol] yn y mod y dywesp6yt am y messureu yn difwyn sarhaet brenhin *Mk, W*;
     yn y mod y dywesp6yt yn diu6yn sarhaet brenhin *V*
[70] + kyfadef *V, W*
[71] + yn da *Mk, V, W*

X16

The three nets of a king are: his warband; there is no compensation for that net but the mercy of the king. The second net is his stud; for every horse found in his stud he receives four of the legal pence. The third is the cattle of his home farm; because for every bull found amongst them he receives four of the legal pence.

X17

These are the three nets of a nobleman: his stud, and cattle, and pigs; for if an animal is found amongst them he receives four of the legal pence for each one.

X18

These are the three nets of a bondsman: his cattle, and his pigs, and his winter dwelling; from May Day until the end of September he receives four of the curt [pence] for every animal if it be found amongst them.

X19

These are the three *dirwy*-fines of a king: a *dirwy* for public fighting, and a *dirwy* for rape, and a *dirwy* for a bottomless, that is, hopeless, theft. The payment of the *dirwy* for rape is a silver rod which reaches from the ground to [the crown of] the king's head when he sits in his chair, as thick as his ring finger and with the three knobs on each end of the rod, and a gold cup which holds the king's full draught in it, as thick as the fingernail of a ploughman who has ploughed for seven years, and a gold lid as broad as the king's face and thick as the cup. The payment of the *dirwy* for public fighting is twelve kine. The payment of the *dirwy* for theft: charging a man with theft and he makes a denial by his tongue, and a compurgation is set on him and it fails – he is an admitted thief since his compurgation has failed; he is innocent from his own mouth, with nothing caught in his hand and nothing seized in his possession – a *dirwy* of twelve kine is put upon him.

reith idaw; gwirion o'e ben ehvnan,[72] ny delut dim yn y law ny cheffid dim[73] ganthaw – deudeg muw dirwy a a arnaw.

U19

Teir dirwy bren*hin*: dirwy ymlad kyuadef a dirwy treis; gwialen aryant megys y dywetpwyt yn dechreu dirwy, achos llef k*yfreith* neu waet.

X20. *Z16, Mk27, V25, W23 [1 2 3 = 2 3 1 Z]*

Tri anhepcor brenhin ynt: effeiryad teulv, yngnad llys, a[74] teulv.

X21. *Z17, Mk28, V26, W24*

Tri pheth ny chyfran brenhin a nep: y eurgrawn, a'e hebawc, a'e leidyr.

X22. *Z18, U56, Mk29, V27, W25 [Second iv: 1 2 3 4 = 1 3 4 2 U; Z numbers the items incorrectly]*

Tri phedwar ysyd. Pedwar achaws yd ymchwelir brawd: ovyn gwr cadarn, a chas galon, a charyad kyueillyon, a serch da. Eil pedwar yw y pedeir taryan a a rwg dyn a reith gwlad rac hawl ledrad: vn ohonu*n*t yw cadw gwesti ynghyfureithyawl, nyd amgen no chadw o pryd gorchyuaerwy hyd y bore trannoeth, a dodi y law drostaw teir gweith yn y nos honno a [210r] hynny ty*n*gv ohonaw a dynyon y ty ganthaw; eil[75] taryan yw geni a meithrin: tynghv o'r pe*r*chennawc ar y trydid[76] o wyr vn vreint ac ef gweled geni y aniveil a'e veithrin ar y helw heb vyned teir nos y wrthaw;[77] trydit taryan yw gwarant; pedweryd taryan yw cadw kyn coll: gwneuthur[78] o'r dyn ar y trydit[79] o wyr vn vreint ac ef, bod y da hwn ar y helw[80] kyn colli o'r llall y da.[81] Nyd oes gwarant namyn hyd yn oes teir[82] llaw, [a gwneuthur or drydedd law][83] cadw kyn coll, a hynny

---

[72] + ae taua6t *V*
[73] yn y law ny cheffid dim] – *W*
[74] + veddic *Z*
[75] trydydd *Z*
[76] ar y trydid] a dav *Z*
[77] + cyn colli or holawdyr *U*
[78] a hynny tygu *Mk*, *V*; a hynny guneuthur *W*
[79] deu *W*
[80] bod y da ... helw] – *Z*
[81] + irioed i vod ar i helw ef *Z*
[82] namyn hyd yn oes teir] pellach y tryded *U*
[83] from *Z*; yn y dec llaw a dyly *X*

U19

The three *dirwy*-fines of a king: a *dirwy* for public fighting and a *dirwy* for rape; a golden rod as was said at the beginning on *dirwy*, because of legal cry or blood.

X20

These are the three indispensables of a king: the priest of his warband, his court justice, and his warband.

X21

Three things which a king does not share with anyone: his treasure trove, and his falcon, and his thief.

X22

There are three fours. The four cases where judgement is overturned: for fear of a strong man, and hatred of enemies, and the love of friends, and lust for goods. The second four are the four shields which go between a man and compurgation of the country for a claim of theft: one of them is keeping a guest legally, namely keeping him from the evening meal until the next morning, and putting his hand over him three times that night and those things to be sworn by him together with the men of the house; the second shield is birth and rearing: the owner swearing as one of three men of the same status as him that he saw the birth of the animal and that it was reared in his possession without it leaving him for three nights; the third shield is warranty; the fourth shield is keeping before loss: the man acting as one of three men of the same status as him, that these goods were in his possession before the other one lost the goods. There is no warranty except up to three hands, and the third hand carries through 'keeping before loss', and that saves a man from theft. The third four is the four persons for whom there is no protection from the king neither in court nor church before the king: one of them is a person who breaks the king's protection in one of the three special feasts in the court; the second is a person who is given as a voluntary hostage to the king; the third is the king's supper-giver, if he fails in his duties to him; the fourth is his slave.

a differ dyn rac hawl[84] ledrad.[85] Y trydit pedwar yw y pedwar dyn nyd oes nawd vdunt nac yn llys nac yn llann rac y brenhin:[86] vn o honunt dyn a dorro nawd y brenhin yn vn o'r teir gwyl arbenic yn y llys;[87] eil yw y dyn a wystler o vod y'r brenhin; trydit yw cwynossawc y brenhin, o phalla idaw;[88] pedweryd yw y caeth.

X23. Z19, Mk30, V28, W26

Teir kyfulauan, os gwna dyn yn y wlad, y dyly y vap yntev[89] [210v] colli tref y dat gan gyfureith – o llad y arglwyd, nev y penkenedyl, nev y teispantyle – rac trymed y kyfulyuanev hynny.[90]

X24. Z20, Mk31, V29, W27

Tri thauedawc gosgord[91] yssyd:[92] arglwyd gwir yn gwarandaw ar y wyrda yn barnv ev kyfureithyev, ac yngnad yn gwarandaw hawl ac attep, a mach yn gwarandaw ar y kynogyn[93] a'r[94] talawdyr[95] yn ymatep.

X25. Z21, U49, Mk32, V30, W28

Teir[96] gwanas gwaew kyureithyawl ysyd:[97] vn onadunt gwan y arllost a'e vn llaw yn y daear yny vei abreid idaw a'y dwy law y dynnv. Eil yw gwan y pen y mewn twyn yny gvdyo y mwn. Trydit yw y dodi ar lwyn a uo kyvuch a gwr; ac ony byd yn vn o'r teir gwanas hynny a myned dyn arnaw val y bo marw, trayan yr alanas a uyd ar berchennawc y gwaew.

X26. Z22, Mk33, V31, W29

Tri ouer ymadrawd a dywedir yn dadlev ac ny ffynant: gwad kyn deduryt, a llys kyn amser, a chynghaws wedy brawd.

---

[84] – *V, W*
[85] a hynny … ledrad] – *U*
[86] rac y brenhin] – *Z*
[87] yn y llys] – *Mk, V*
[88] o phalla idaw] y neb a ddyleo i borthi y nos honno ac ai gatto heb vwyd *Z, Mk, V, W*; – *U*
[89] y vap yntev] dyn *Z*
[90] + am hynny y ddyly yntav colli treff i dad *Z*
[91] gorsed *Z, Mk, V, W*
[92] + arglwydd ac ynad a mach *Z*
[93] ha6l6r *Mk, V, W*
[94] kynogyn a'r] – *Z*
[95] amdiffynn6r *Mk, V*
[96] tri *W*
[97] + yn dadlav *Z, U, Mk, V, W*

X23

Three offences for which, if a man commits them in his own country, his son should lose his patrimony by law – killing his lord, or his head of kindred, or his representative – because of the seriousness of those offences.

X24

There are three silent ones of a court: a true lord listening to his nobles judging their laws, and a justice listening to claim and defence, and a surety listening to the claimant and the defendant answering each other.

X25

There are three legal thrusts of a spear in pleadings: one of them is thrusting the shaft with one hand into the ground until it can scarcely be pulled out with his two hands. The second is thrusting the head into a dune until the socket is hidden. The third is placing it on a bush which is as high as a man; and unless it is in one of those three rests and a man goes onto it so that he dies, a third of the *galanas* is charged to the owner of the spear.

X26

Three useless statements which are made in court and they do not avail: a denial before verdict, and an objection before time, and argument after judgement.

X27. *Z23, Mk34, V32, W30 [1 2 3 = 3 2 1 Z, Mk, V; 3 1 2 W]*

Tri [211r] ouer laeth yssyd: llaeth cath, a gast, a chassec; ny thelir dim amdanunt.

X28. *Z24, Mk35, V33, W31*

Teir sarhaed ny diwygir os keffir drwy uedawd: sarhaed effeiryad teulv, ac ygnad llys, a medyc;[98] cany wys pa bryd y bo reid wrthvnt.[99]

X29. *Z25, Mk36, V34, W32*

Teir paluawd ny diwygir: vn argluit ar y wr yn y reoli yn dit cad a brwydyr, ac vn tad ar y vab yr [y] gospi, ac vn penkenedyl ar y gar yr y gynghori.

X30. *Z26, 118, U11, Mk37, V35, W33*

Teir gwraged ny dyliir datlev ac eu hetiued am tref eu mam: y wreic a rodes yngwystyl dros tir a chaffael mab o honno tra vo yngwystyl; a gwreic a roder o rod kenedyl y alltud; a mab gwreic a dialho gwr o genedyl y mam, a cholli tref y dat o achaws y gyfulauan honno, ac wrth hynny y keiff[100] tref y mam.

Z118

Tair merched ni ddyleir dadle ac ev hytivedd am dir o barth ev mam: mab gwraic vonheddic a roddo kenedl i alldvd; a mab gwraic a rodder yngwystl dros genedl, a chayl mab a hi yngwystl dros[tunt]; a mab a ddialo gwr o genedl i vam a cholli tref i dad o achaws y gyflavan hono.

---

[98] + llys *V, W*

[99] cany wys ... wrthvnt] kani ddyly yr vn or rrai hyny vod yn veddw 6yth *Z*; kani wddant na bo rraid ir brenin wrthvnt *Mk, V*; kany dylyant uot yn ued6 byth kany 6dant 6y pa amser y bo reit yr brenhin 6rthunt *W*

[100] y keiff] na ddyleir dadle ac ef am *Z, U, Mk, V, W*

X27

There are three useless milks: the milk of a cat, and a bitch, and a mare; for nothing is paid for them.

X28

Three *sarhaed*s for which there is no redress if they are received whilst drunk: a *sarhaed* to the priest of the warband, and the court justice, and a mediciner; because it is not known when they will be needed.

X29

Three blows for which there is no compensation: that of a lord to his man to control him in a day of battle and fighting, and that of a father to his son to punish him, and that of a head of kindred to his kinsman in order to advise him.

X30

Three women with whose heirs there should not be pleadings concerning the inheritance of their mother: a woman who is given as a hostage on behalf of a territory and she has a son while she is a hostage; and a woman who is given by gift of kin to an alien; and the son of a woman who avenges a man from his mother's kindred, and he loses his patrimony because of that offence, and because of that he receives the inheritance of his mother.

Z118

Three women with whose heirs there should not be pleadings concerning the inheritance of the mother: the son of a noblewoman whom a kindred gives to an alien; and the son of a woman who is given as a hostage on behalf of a kindred, and she has a son whilst she is a hostage on their behalf; and a son who avenges a man from his mother's kindred and loses his patrimony because of that offence.

X31. *Z27, Mk41, V40, W34*

Teir sarhaed gwreic ynt:[101] vn ohonunt roddi cussan idi o'e hanuod; trayan y
sarhaed a telur idi. Eil yw y ffaluv o'e han[211v]vod;[102] a honno yssyd sarhaed
cwbyl idi. Trydyd yw y vod genthi o'e hanuod; a honno a dyrcheif arnei, nyd
amgen no thraean y sarhaed.[103] Os gwryawc[104] uyd, herwyd breint y gwr y telir
idi y sarhaed.[105]

X32. *Z29, Mk39, V38, W36*

Tri chadarn enllip gwreic ynt: vn ohonunt y gweled y gwr a'r wreic o'r llwyn vn
o boparth y'r llwyn, eil yw y caffael dan vn vantell, trydit yw caffael gwr rwng
deu vordwyd y wreic.

X33. *Z28, U20, Mk38, V36, W35*

Tri chewilyd kenedyl ynt ac o chaws gwreic y maent oll tri: vn ohonunt
llathrudaw gwreic o'e hanuod; eil yw dwyn o'r gwr gwreic arall ar y phen y'r
ty[106] a'e gyrrv hitheu allan; trydyd yw y hyspeilyaw, bod yn trech gan y gwr y
hyspeilyaw no bod genthi.

X34. *Z30, U21, W37 [1 2 3 = 2 1 3 U]*

Tri chyffro dial ynt: vn ohonunt diaspedain y caressev, eil yw gweled gelor eu car
yn myned y'r llan,[107] trydyt yw gweled[108] bed ev car[109] heb ymdiwyn.

X35. *Z31, Mk42, V41, W39*

[212r] Teir fford yssyd y lyssv tystyon: vn ohonunt tynghv anudon kyhoedoc am
ledrad, eil yw galanas heb ymdiwyn, trydyd yw bod y vn gan y wreic y gilyd.[110]

---

[101] + 6n a ddyrchaif ac vn a istwng ac vn y sydd syrhaed gwbwl *Z, Mk, V, W*
[102] o'e hanvod] − *Mk, V*
[103] arnei … sarhaed] y trayan *V*
[104] gwrygwc *X*, gwraic *Z*
[105] os gwryawc … sarhaed] − *Mk, V*; + os gweddw vyd herwyd braint i that i telir iddi *Z, W*
[106] y'r ty] oi hanvod *Z, W*
[107] gelor … llan] yr elor *U*
[108] g gweled *X*
[109] + yn y 6ynwent yn newydd *Z, W*
[110] bod y vn … gilyd] gwreicdra *Z*

X31

These are the three insult [payments] for a woman: one of them is giving her a kiss against her will; a third of her *sarhaed* is paid to her. The second is to grope her against her will; and that act is complete *sarhaed* to her. The third is to have intercourse with her against her will; and that act augments for her, namely [by] a third of her *sarhaed*. If she is married, her *sarhaed* is paid to her according to her husband's status.

X32

These are the three confirmed scandals of a woman: one of them is seeing the man and the woman [emerging] from the bush one on either side of the bush, the second is finding them under one blanket, the third is finding the man between the two thighs of the woman.

X33

These are the three shames of a kindred and each of the three is because of a woman: one of them is abducting a woman against her will; the second is the man bringing another woman to the house besides her and sending her [the first woman] out; the third is to despoil her, because he prefers despoiling her to having intercourse with her.

X34

These are the three incitements of revenge: one of them is the wailing of female relatives, the second is seeing the bier of their relative going to the church, the third is seeing the grave of their relative without reparation.

X35

There are three ways to object to witnesses: one of them is to swear a false oath publicly for theft, the second is *galanas* without redress, the third is that one of them has intercourse with the wife of the other.

Mk42. V41 [1 2 3 = 1 3 2 V]

O teir fford y llyssir tyston: o tirdra, a g6reictra, a galanastra.

X36. Z32, Mk40, V39, W38 [1 2 3 = 3 2 1 Mk]

Tri peth a hawl dyn yn lledrat ac ny chynghein lledrad yndaw:[111] adeilad, a diod[112] coed, ac eredic.

X37. Z33, U7, Mk43, V42, W40

Tri meib yn tri broder vn mam vn dat ac ny dylyant gyfuran o dref tad[113] gan ev brawd vn mam vn dat. Vn ohonunt mab llwyn a pherth ac wedy caffael y mab hwnnw,[114] kymryd y wreic honno[115] o rod kenedyl a chaffael mab o'r [vn][116] wreic;[117] gwedy hynny ny dyly hwnnw kyfurannv tir a mab[118] llwyn a pherth. Eil yw kymryd o ysgolheic [wreic] o rod kenedyl a chaffael mab ohonei, ac odyna kymryd vrdev ohonaw effeiryadeth, a chaffael mab o'r vn wreic,[119] ny dyly y mab kyntaf[120] kyfurannv tir a'r diwaethaf,[121] canys [212v] anedvawl y kaffad.[122] Trydyd yw mvd, kany dyly tir ny ateppo drostaw,[123] ac am hynny y dywedir[124] ny roddir gwlad y uud.

X38. Z34, Mk44, V43, W41

Tri dyn a gynnyd ev breint yn vn dyd: tayawctref[125] a gyssegrer[126] o ganyad y brenhin; y dyn o'r tref honno y bore yn taeyawc a'r nos honno yn ryd. Eil yw y dyn rodo brenhin vn o'r pedeir swyd ar hvgein[127] idaw; odyna ryd uyd.[128]

[111] a hawl ... yndaw] ni chyngain hawl ladrad arnvnt kyd holer yn lladrad Z
[112] diosc Z
[113] gyfuran o dref tad] ran o tir Mk, V
[114] caffael y mab hwnnw] g6edy hynny V
[115] kymryd y wreic honno] kymryt or vn g6r yr vn wreic V; or g6r wreic honno W
[116] y X
[117] o'r vn wreic] – Z; ohonei V
[118] + a gaffad kyn noc ef yn Z, U, Mk, V, W
[119] a chaffael mab ohonei] ac ef yn effeiriad kaffel mab Z; a chaffael mab arall or vn wreic U; kaffel or effeirat h6nn6 vab or wreic kynt Mk; kaffel mab or effeirat h6nn6 or wreic kynt V, W
[120] a gad kyn yr vrdde Z; hwnnw U; a gaffat kyn noc ef W
[121] mab a gad gwedi yr vrdde Z; h6nn6 W
[122] canys ... kaffad] – Z; kanys yn erbyn dedyf y kahat Mk, V, W
[123] kany dyly tir ... drostaw] – U
[124] am hynny y dywedir] – Z, U, Mk, V, W
[125] taiawc o dref Z
[126] + eglwys ynddi Z, Mk, V, W
[127] + brenhinawl Z, Mk, V, W
[128] odyna ... uyd] – Z; kyn rodi y s6yd ida6 yn taya6c a gwedy y rodi yn 6r ryd Mk, V, W

Mk42

In three ways witnesses are objected to: for land-feud, and woman-feud, and homicide-feud.

X36

Three things a man may prosecute as theft but they do not constitute theft: building, and removing timber, and ploughing.

X37

Three sons being three brothers of the same mother and same father, and they should not get a share of patrimony from their brother of the same mother and same father as them. One of them is a son of bush and brake and after that son is begotten, the same woman is taken by gift of kin and a son is begotten with her; after that he is not entitled to share land with a son of bush and brake. The second is when a cleric takes a woman by gift of kin and begets a son with her, and after that he takes the orders of priesthood, and has a son by the same wife, the first son is not entitled to share land with the last son, as he was conceived contrary to law. The third is a mute, as no one is entitled to land that they cannot answer for, and because of that it is said that lordship is not given to a mute.

X38

Three men whose status increases in one day: a bond township in which a church is consecrated by the permission of the king; a man of that township would be a bondsman in the morning and that night would be free. The second is a man to whom the king gives one of the twenty-four royal offices; after that he will be free. The third is a cleric the day he is tonsured; in the morning a bondsman and that night a free man.

Trydyd yw ysgolheic y dyd y caffo [corun; y bore][129] yn[130] tauawc a'r nos honno yn wr ryd.

X39. *Z35, Mk45, V44, W42*

Tri gwerth kyfureith beichyogi gwreic:[131] gwaed kyn delwad, wyth a deugein a dal o chollir drwy greulonder.[132] Eil yw kyn dyuod eneid yndaw,[133] trayan yr alanas a dal. Y trydyd yw gwedy el eneid yndaw, galanas gwbyl a delir[134] amdanaw o chollir trwy grevlonder.

X40. *Z36, U51, 52, Mk46, 47, V45, 46, W43, 44*

Teir ford y dygir mab ac y diwedir: vn ohonu*n*t, gwreic lwyn a pherth, o byd beichyawc, ban vo ar[135] y llawfuaeth, dyget attei yr offeiryad[136] a thynghed wrthaw[137] mal hynn: "esgor neidyr y my ar y beichyogi hwnn os crews tad gan vam eithyr y gwr hwnn (a henwi y gwr)"[138] ac y velly y dwc yn gyfureithyawl. Eil yw penkenedyl bieu y dwyn a seith law kenedyl ganthaw. Ac ony byd penkenedyl idaw roddet llw dengwyr a deugeint o genedyl y vam. Mal hynn y diwedir mab: kymryd o'r gwr y mab[139] y rynthaw a'r allawr,[140] a'y law assw ar ben y map, a'e law dehev ar yr allawr a'r creiryev,[141] a thynghed nas crews ef y gan y vam[142] ac nad oes vn dauyn o'e waed yndaw. Ac oni byd byw y tad, penkenedyl bieu y diwad a seith law kenedyl ganthaw. Ac ony byd penkenedyl idaw, llw dengwyr a deugeint o genedyl y tad; ac uelly y diwedir.[143]

---

[129] – *X; from Z*
[130] + vab *Mk, V*
[131] – *Z*
[132] o chollir drwy greulonder] – *Z, V, W*
[133] + o chollir o grevlonder *Z, Mk, V, W*
[134] delur *X*
[135] ar ar *X*
[136] pheriglawr *Z*
[137] yngwyd y periglawr *Z*
[138] a henwi y gwr] yr awr hon *Z*
[139] + a dywetter i vod yn vab iddo *Z*
[140] llawr *Z*
[141] a'r creiryeu] – *Z*
[142] + y mab hwnnw *Z*
[143] o genedyl y tad ac uelly y diwedir] ai dywad *Z*

X39

Three legal values of a woman's foetus: blood before formation, it is worth forty-eight [pence] if it is lost through cruelty. The second is before life enters it, a third of the *galanas* is paid for it. The third is after life enters it, its full *galanas* ought to be paid if it is lost through cruelty.

X40

Three ways a son is affiliated and denied: one of them, a woman of bush and brake, if she is pregnant, when she is nursing, let her take her priest to her and let her swear to him like this: 'let a snake be born to me of this pregnancy if a father created it of a mother except this man (and names the man)' and thus she affiliates him lawfully. The second is the head of kindred has the right to affiliate him and seven men of the kindred with him. And if he has no head of kindred let the oath of fifty men from the mother's kindred be given. This is how a child is denied: the man takes the child between him and the altar, and his left hand on the head of the son, and his right hand on the altar and the relics, and let him swear that he [the man] did not create him with that mother and that there is not one drop of his blood in him. And if the father is not alive, the head of kindred has the right to deny him and seven men from the kindred with him. And if he has no head of kindred, the oath of fifty men from the father's kindred; and thus he is denied.

Mk46. U51, V45, W43

O teir fford y dygir mab y tat: vn yv gvreic llvyn a pherth, or byd beichavc, pan vo ar y llavuaeth, dyget y pheriglavr[144] etti a thyget vrthav "escor neidyr imi y ar y beichogi hvn os crevys tat gan vam[145] onyt y gvr y dygaf idav[146] (a'e enwi)", ac uelly kyfreithavl y dvc. Eil yv, penkenedyl a seith lav kenedyl gantav bieu y[147] dvyn.[148] Trydyd yv, ony byd penkenedyl,[149] llv deg wyr a devgeint o'e genedyl a'e dvc, a'r mab ehunan a tvg o'e blaen, kanyt kyfreithavl llv y vam onyt ar y dygyat vry.[150]

Mk47. U52, V46, W44

O teir fford y gvedir mab o genedyl:[151] vn yv kymryt y mab o'r gvr y dywetter y vot yn vab idav, a'e dodi y rydav a'r allavr,[152] a dodi y llav asseu ar pen y mab, a'r llav deheu ar yr allavr a'r creireu,[153] a thyget nas crevys ef ac nat oes dafyn o'e waet yndav.[154] Eil yv, ony byd byv y tat,[155] penkenedyl bieu y wadu a se[111]ith lav kenedyl gantav. Trydyd yv ony byd penkenedyl idav, llv deg wyr a deu vgeint o'r genedyl a'e gvatta; a'r mab hynhaf y'r gvr yd oed y mab ar y gystlvn bieu tygu yn y blaen.[156]

X41. Z37, U53, Mk49, V48, W45 [1 2 3 = 1 3 2 Z, U, Mk, V, W]

Teir gormes doeth ynt: meddawt, a dryc annyan, a godinheb.

---

[144] hoffeirat pl6yf *U*
[145] uab *U*
[146] onyt y g6r y dygaf ida6] namyn y g6r h6n *U*
[147] + wadu *Mk*
[148] bieu y d6yn] – *U*
[149] ony byd penkenedyl] – *U*
[150] d6c a'r mab ... y dygyat vry] dyget yr g6r *U; * ar mab ehunan ... dygyat vry] – *W*
[151] o genedyl] – *U, W*
[152] y dywetter y vot yn vab ida6, a'e dodi y ryda6 a'r alla6r] – *U*
[153] a'r creireu] gysegyr *U*
[154] + ae diwat *U*
[155] ony byd by6 y tat] – *U*
[156] a'r mab hynhaf ... y blaen] – *U, W*

Mk46

In three ways is a son affiliated to a father: one is a woman of bush and brake, if she is pregnant, when she is nursing, let her bring her confessor to her and let her swear to him "let a snake be born to me by this pregnancy if a father created it in a mother apart from the man to whom I affiliate it (and names him)", and thus legally she affiliates it. The second is, the head of kindred and seven men of the kindred with him have the right to affiliate him. The third is, if there is no head of kindred, the oath of fifty men from the kindred affiliates him, and the son himself swears first, because the oath of the mother is not legal unless it is the above affiliation.

Mk47

In three ways a son is denied from a kindred: one is that the father whose son he is said to be takes him, and puts him between himself and the altar, and places his left hand on the head of the boy, and the right hand on the altar and relics, and let him swear that he did not create him and that there is not a drop of his blood in him. The second is, if the father is not alive, the head of kindred has the right to deny him together with seven men of the kindred. The third is if he has no head of kindred, the oaths of fifty men from the kindred deny him; and the eldest son of the man to whom the child is linked [by naming] has the right to swear first.

X41

These are the three oppressors of the wise: drunkenness, and bad temper, and adultery.

X42. *Z38, U54, Mk50, V49, W46 [1 2 3 = 1 3 2 U, Mk]*

Tri dyn a dyly tafuodyawc drostun [213v] yn dadlev:[157] gwreic, *ac* alltud[158] anghyuyeith, a chryc annyanawl. Vn dyn a dewis y dauodeoc: arglwyd.[159]

X43. *Z39, U55, Mk51, V50, W47*

Tri llwdyn digyfureith y gweithred yssyd:[160] ystalwyn, a tharw trefgord, a baed kenvein.

X44. *Z40, Mk52, V51, W48*

Tri llwdyn nyd oes gwerth kyfureith arnu*n*t: knyw hwch, a bitheiad, a charlwng.[161]

X45. *Z41, Mk53, V52, W49*

Tri gwaed kyfureith[162] ysyd: gwaed[163] crach, a deint, a thrwyn,[164] onyd drwy lid y trewir.[165]

X46. *Z42, 98, U26, Mk54, V53, W50*

Tri than digyfureith ysyd:[166] tan godeith o hanner Mawrth hyd hanner Ebrill, a than eneint trefgord, a than geveil trefgord[167] a uo naw cam y wrth y dref a'e tho o vanadyl arnei neu tywarch.

Z98
   Tri than ni ddiwygir: tan gevail trefgord yn gwnevthvr gwaith y dref; o gwna y tan hwnw ddrwc mewn tref arall, ef a ddiwygir. Tan goddaith Mawrth ynifaith, o gwna hwnw ddrwc ynghyvanedd, ef a ddyleir y ddiwyn, kani ddyly goddaith vod ynghyvanedd. A than enaint trefgordd; ni ddiwygir i ddrwc a wnel yn y dref hono, o gwna y tan hwnw ddrwc mewn tref arall, ef a ddyleir i ddiwygio.

[157] yn dadlev] – *Z*; mywn llys *U*; yn llys *Mk, V, W*
[158] + ac *X, Z*
[159] vn dyn ... arglwyd] – *U, W*
[160] + ar aniveiliaid mvd *Z*; + pob un yny hydref; + yn y hydref ar aniueileit mut *Mk, V, W*
[161] broch *Mk, V, W*
[162] digyfreith *Mk, V, W*
[163] + pen dyn *Z*; + o pen *Mk, V, W*
[164] ffroen *Mk, V*
[165] onyd ... trewir] – *Z*
[166] digyfureith ysyd] ni ddywygir *Z*; digyfreith eu gweithret *U, V, W*
[167] – *Mk, V, W*

X42

Three persons who are entitled to a representative in court on their behalf: a woman, and a foreign-tongued alien, and a congenital stammerer. One man who choses his representative: a lord.

X43

Three animals whose behaviour is not subject to law: a stallion, and a township bull, and a herd boar.

X44

Three animals on whom there is no legal value: a young sow, and a baying-hound, and stoat.

X45

There are three legal bloods: blood from a scab, and a tooth, and the nose, unless a blow is struck in anger.

X46

There are three fires not subject to law: a muirburn fire from mid-March to mid-April, and the fire of a township bathhouse, and the fire of a smithy which is nine paces from townland and has a broom or turf roof upon it.

Z98

Three fires for which there is no redress: the fire of a township smithy doing the work of the homestead; if that fire does damage in another homestead, redress ought to be made for it. The fire of a March muirburn on land which is not settled, if that fire does damage in settled land, redress ought to be made for it, as there ought not be a muirburn in a settled land. And the fire of a township bath; redress is not made for the damage that it does in that town, and if that fire does damage in another town, redress ought to be made.

X47. Z43, U22, Mk55, V54, W51

Tri edyn a dyly brenhin ev gwerth pa le bynnc ev lladher: hebawc,[168] a gwalch,[169] a chicvran; perchennawc y tir y llader arnaw a dyly dec a deugein[170] y gan y nep a'e llatho.

X48. Z44, Mk56, V55, W52

Tri phryf a dyly brenhin ev gwerth pa le bynnac y llader:[171] llostlydan, a belev, a charlwng; canys ohonunt wy[172] y dylyur wneuthur amarwyev[173] [214r] y dillad y brenhin.

X49. Z45, Mk57, V56, W53

Tri pheth ny ad kyfureith y ev damdwng: blawd, a gwenyn, ac aryant; canys kyffelyp a geffir vdunt.[174]

X49a. Text from Z. Z46, U27, Mk58, V57, W54 [1 2 3 = 2 1 3 Mk, V; triad is censored in W and is illegible.]

Tair k[ont] kyfreithiawl y sydd: k[ont] kath, a k[ont] gast, a k[ont][175] gwiwair, kanis attal a allant pan vynont, a gillwng.[176]

X50. Z47, 91, U43, Mk59, V58, W55 [1 2 3 = 1 3 2 Z, V]

Tri phren ysy ryd ev llad[177] y mewn forest:[178] prenn crib eglwys, a gelor,[179] a pheleidyr a el[180] yn reid y brenhin.

Z91

Tri ffren y sydd rydd i ambriodawr i llad ynghoed priodawr heb i genad: paladr arff, a ffren gelor, a bagl ddiowrvd.

[168] eryr *Mk, V*
[169] garan *Mk, V*
[170] arugeint *U*
[171] pa le … llader] – *Z*
[172] ohonunt wy] oc eu cr6yn *Mk, V*
[173] amryw *Z*
[174] a geffir vdvnt] ynt bob vn yw gilid *Z*
[175] k__c *Z*
[176] kanis attal a allant pan vynont, a gillwng] dill6g ac ell6g a allant pan vynhont *Mk, V*; attal a digonant a gellwg pan y mynhont *U*
[177] ev llad] – *U, Mk, V, W*
[178] + y brenin *Z, Mk, V, W*
[179] + gwr a ladder yn rraid y brenin *Z*
[180] wneler *Z*

X47

Three birds to whose value the king is entitled wherever they are killed: a falcon, and a hawk, and a raven; the owner of the land they are killed upon is entitled to fifty [pence] from whoever kills them.

X48

Three animals to whose value the king is entitled wherever they are killed: a beaver, and a sable, and a stoat; because from them the borders of the king's clothes should be made.

X49

Three things of which law does not allow sworn appraisal: flour, and bees, and silver; for similar to them are to be had.

X49a

There are three legal cunts: the cunt of a cat, and a cunt of a bitch, and the cunt of a squirrel; for they can tighten whenever they wish, and release.

X50

There are three free timbers which are free to fell in a forest: the timber for the ridge of a church, and a bier, and shafts that meet the king's needs.

Z91

Three timbers which are free for a non-proprietor to fell in the woods of a proprietor without his permission: the shaft of a weapon, and the timber for a bier, and the staff of an ascetic.

X51. *U42, Mk62, V37, W56, Z48*

Tri chehyryn canhastyr yssyd: vn ohonu*n*t, lledrad, canys ba ford bynnac y del
kyfuran ohonaw, o naw affeith lledrad y byd. Eil yw hyd brenhin o'r cam
ymdanaw. Trydyd yw abo bleid.

Mk62. *V37, W56, Z48*

Tri cheheryn canhastyr yssyd: vn yv lledrat, y[181] fford y kertho ran
ohonav,[182] kanys nav affeith yssyd idav; eil yv hyd brenhin, pvy bynhac
a'e kyllello;[183] trydyd yv abo[184] bleid, y neb a wnel kam ymdanav.[185]

U42

Tri chehyryn canastyr: lledrat, a hyd bren*h*in, ac abo bleid.

X52. *Z49, U28, Mk60, V59, W57*

Tri chorn buelhin y brenhin; punt yw gwerth pob vn ohonu*n*t: corn yved,[186] a
chorn kyweithas, a chorn hely[187] y penkynyd.

X53. *Z50, U47, Mk61, V60, W58 [1 2 3 = 1 3 2 Mk, V; 2 3 1 Z, U]*

Tri hely ryd yssyd ymhob gwlad, canys nyd oes tref tad vdunt: ywrch, a dyfuyrgi,
a chadno. Vn vreint yw ywrch a gafyr.[188]

X54. *Z51, Mk63, V61, W59 [1 2 3 = 2 1 3 Mk, V, W]*

Tri pheth a dyrr ar gyfureith: amod, ac anghuuureith,[189] ac ychenoctid.

---

[181] lledrat y] – *W*
[182] ran ohona6] kyfran ohona6 *V, Z;* kyfran o letrat *W*
[183] a'e kyllello] a wnel kam iddo *Z*
[184] y6 abo] bo *Z*
[185] + sef yw abo blaidd a driblin gweddill dant ac awch ni varn ky. tal eithyr o delediw nac o adriblin ni varn kanis nid adriblin yn dal *Z*
[186] enaid *Z;* kyfedach *U*
[187] + yn llaw *Z, V, W*
[188] Vn vreint ... gafyr] vn werth yw iwrch ac vn arddrychavel a gavyr *Z;* – *U, Mk, V*
[189] treis *Mk, V, W*

X51

There are three muscles of a hundred hands: one of them, theft, because whichever way part of it comes, it will be of the nine abetments of theft. The second is the hart of the king for a wrong concerning it. The third is the prey of a wolf.

Mk62

There are three muscles of a hundred hands: one is theft, the way a share of it travels, for it has nine abetments; the second is the hart of the king, whoever cuts it up it; the third is the prey of a wolf, whoever does wrong concerning it.

U42

Three muscles of a hundred hands: theft, and the hart of a king, and the prey of a wolf.

X52

Three buffalo horns of the king; each one is worth a pound: his drinking horn, and the horn of his retinue, and the chief huntsman's hunting horn.

X53

There are three free hunts in every country, for they have no inherited dwelling: a roebuck, and an otter, and a fox. A roebuck and a goat are of the same value.

X54

Three things that prevail over law: a contract, and unlawfulness, and neediness.

X55. *Z52, U23, Mk66, V64, W60*

Tri hwrd ny diwygir: vn honunt govyn o dyn yawn y elyn am y [214v] car yn tri
datleu ac na chaffei yawn,[190] a chyvaruod y elyn ac ef,[191] a gwan hwrd yndaw
ac gwaew hyd ban vei marw; ny diwygir[192] hwnnw. Eil yw gwneuthur eidiged
o wreic wryoc am y gwr wrth wreic arall,[193] a chyuaruod o'r dw[y] wraged,[194]
a gwan hwrd o'r wryauc yn y llall a'y dwy law yny vo marw; ny diwygir idi.
Trydyd yw rodi morwyn[195] y wr a mach ar y morwyndawd, a gwan hwrd
yndi[196] o'r gwr a'e chaffael yn wreic; yntev a dyly yna galw y[197] neithyorwyr
a golheuav kanhwyllev, a llad y chrys o'r tu dracheuyn yn gyuuch a thal y
ffedrein, ac o'r tu recdi yn gyfuuch a gwarr y chont – kyfureith twyll morwyn
yw hyny – a'e hellwng a'r hwrth hwnnw yndi heb diwyn dim idi.

X56. *Z53, Mk67, V65, W61*

Tri dyn ny dyly brenhin[198] eu gwerthu:[199] lleidyr,[200] a chynllwynwr, a bradwr
arglwyd.

X57. *Z54, Mk64, V62, W62*

Tri henw righill yssyd: 'guaet gwlad', a 'garw gychwetyl[201] gwas y kynghellawr',
a ringhyll.

---

[190] ac na chaffei yawn] heb i gaffel *Z*
[191] + gwedi hynny *Z, U, Mk, V, W*
[192] + ida6 yr h6rd *W*
[193] wrth wreic arall] – *V*
[194] + ygyt *Mk, V, W*
[195] + aeduet *V*
[196] + a bonllost ai hymrain vn weith *Z, U, Mk, V, W*
[197] ai *X*
[198] – *Mk, V, W*
[199] + o gyfreith *Mk*
[200] + kyfadef or byd g6erth pedeir keinha6c kyfreith yn y la6 *Mk, V, W*
[201] garw gychwetyl] garweith ueddel *Z*

X55

Three thrusts for which reparation is not made: one of them is when a man asks for redress from his enemy for his kinsman in three pleadings and he would not receive redress, and he and his enemy meet, and a thrust is made with a weapon into him until he is dead; compensation is not paid for that. The second is [when] a married woman is jealous of another woman because of her husband, and the two women meet, and the married woman makes a thrust into the other with her two hands until she is dead; no recompense is made for her. The third thrust is when a virgin is given to a man with a surety on her virginity, and the man makes a thrust into her and finds her a woman; he is entitled to call his wedding guests and light candles, and cut her shift behind her as high as the top of her buttocks, and in front of her as high as the top of her cunt – that is the law of a false virgin – and he releases her with that thrust in her without any compensation for her.

X56

Three men whom the king is not entitled to sell: a thief, and a conspirator, and a man who betrays a lord.

X57

There are three names for the *rhingyll*: 'the shriek of the country', and 'bad news the servant of the *cynghellor*', and '*rhingyll*'.

Law tractates here in X *and also in* Z

X58. Z9, Mk16, V16, W10 [216r]

Tri lle[202] yd ymdiueichya mach gan gyfure[216v]ith:[203] vn ohonunt[204] talu o'r talawdyr drostaw, a'r eil yw[205] roddi oed o'r kynogyn – oed yn absen y mach – y'r talawdyr,[206] trydit yw[207] dwyn gafvael o'r kynogyn[208] ar y talawdyr in absen[209] y mach; ac yna taled[210] tri buhin camlwrw.[211]

X59. Mk17, V17, W11 [216v]

O teir fford y differis mach a chynnogyn: o clybod corn y brenhin yn mynet yn llwit, ac o hawl treis, a hawl ledrat.[212]

X60. Z61, Mk65, W63 [217r]

O teir ford y telir gwialen y brenhin arnaw a fiol eur a clawr eur arnei: o dwyn treis ar wreic,[213] a thorri tangneved y fford,[214] ac am gynllwyn.[215]

Mk65. [V63]

O teir fford y telir gvyalen aryant y'r brenhin: am treis, ac am torri navd fford ar aghenavc diatlam, ac am sarhaet brenhin.

---

[202] Tri lle] o teir fford *Mk, V, W*
[203] gan gyfureith] – *Mk, V, W*
[204] vn ohonunt] *Mk, V*
[205] a'r eil yw] ac o *Mk*
[206] o'r kynogyn ... y'r talawdyr] i'r talawdr yn absen y mach *Z*; or ha6l6r yr tala6dyr yn a6ssen y mach *Mk, V, W*
[207] trydit yw] ac o *Mk*
[208] o'r kynogyn] – *Z*; ha6l6r *Mk, V, W*
[209] in absen] heb ganhat *Mk, V, W*
[210] tal6 *Z*
[211] + ir arglwyd *Z*; yr brenhin *Mk, V, W*
[212] + kanys aghen yn aghen y6 pop vn or holyon hyn *Mk, V, W*
[213] vorwyn *Z*
[214] tangneved y fford] tangnevedd *Z*; na6d ford ar ychena6c diatlam *W*
[215] sarhaet brenhin *W*

Law tractates here in X *and also in* Z

X58

Three places a surety is released by law: one of them is by the debtor paying on his behalf, and the second is by the claimant giving an appointed time – an appointed time in the absence of the surety – to the debtor, the third is by the claimant distraining the debtor in the absence of the surety; and then let him pay three kine *camlwrw*.

X59

In three ways a surety and debtor are protected: by hearing the horn of the king going to battle, and for a claim for violence, and a claim of theft.

X60

In three ways a silver rod is paid to the king and a gold cup with a gold lid on it: from violence against a woman, and breaking the peace of the road, and for a conspiracy.

Mk65
In three ways a silver rod is paid to the king: for violence, and breaking the protection of the road on a homeless needy person on the road, and for the *sarhaed* of the king.

Triad collection resumes in both X *and* Z

X61. Z62, U34, Mk92, W86 *[1 2 3 = 1 3 2 U, W]* [217v]

Tri ergyd ny thelir dim amdanu*n*t:²¹⁶ vn ohonunt y garw yn yd, ac y ky, ac y hebawc²¹⁷ yn yd.

X62. Z63, Mk131

Tri chyfwrch dirgel a dyly y brenhin y gaffael heb y brawdwr: ygyd a'e effeiryad, a'e wreic, a'e uedic.

Mk131
Tri chyfrvch dirgel a dyly y brenhin eu kaffel heb y vravtvr: gyt a'e wreic, a chyt a'e effeirat, a chyt a'e vedyc.

Z63
Tair kyfrinach a ddyly y brenin i gaffal: i gan i vrowdwr, a'i yffeiriad, a'i veddic.

X63. Z64, U36, Mk75, W70

Teir nodwyd gyfureithyawl yssyd: vn gwenigawl y urenhines, eil yw nodwyd y medyc llys,²¹⁸ trydit yw notwyd y penkynyd;²¹⁹ iiii keynnyauc a tal pob vn onadunt.²²⁰

X64. Z76, U10, Mk76, W71

Teir marw tystyolaeth yssyd ac allant sefuyll yn y datlev yn da:²²¹ vn ohonu*n*t pan vo amrysson ac ymlad²²² rwng deu arglwyd²²³ am tir a thervynev, tervynv hwnnw yn dyledus [218r] yn gwyd pawb,²²⁴ yna meibyon y rei hynny nev eu hwyryon²²⁵ a allant dwyn tystyolaeth gweled teruynv yr amryssonn hwnnw yn dyledus.²²⁶ Eil yw dynnyon bonhedic o boparth, amhinogev tir y gelwir y rei

---

²¹⁶ thelir ... amdanunt] diwygir *U, Mk, W*
²¹⁷ ebawl gwyllt *Z, U, Mk, W*
²¹⁸ medyc llys] meddic yn gwniaw gwelioedd *Z, U, W*; medyc llys y wnia6 y g6yr brathedic *Mk*
²¹⁹ + yn jacha6 kwn brathedic *Z*; y wniaw y cwn rwygedig *U, Mk, W*
²²⁰ iiii ... onadunt] – *Z*; + notwyd g6reic kywrein arall keinha6c kyfreith a tal *Mk*
²²¹ yn y datlev yn da] ym brawt tir *U*; yn lle tyston yn dadleu yn da *Mk*
²²² – *U*
²²³ pleit *U*
²²⁴ + gwedy bo marw y rei hynny oll *U, Mk*; guedy y bo mar6 y niueroed hynny *W*
²²⁵ + neu rei or genedyl *U, Mk, W*
²²⁶ gweled ... dyledus] a glywyssynt gan eu rieni ar rei hynny aelwir gwybydyeit am tir *U*; am y tir h6nn6 a rei hynny a elwir g6ybydyeit am tir *Mk, W*

Triad collection resumes in both X *and* Z

X61

Three blows that are not compensated: one of them to a deer in corn, and to a dog, and to a falcon in corn.

X62

The three private meetings that the king is entitled to have without his justice: with his priest, and his wife, and his mediciner.

Mk131
Three private meetings that the king is entitled to have without his justice: with his wife, and with his priest, and with his mediciner.

Z63
The three secrets which the king is entitled to have: with his justice, with his priest, and his mediciner.

X63

There are three legal needles: one is the needle of the seamstress of the queen, the second is the needle of the court mediciner, the third is the needle of the chief huntsman; each of them is worth four pence.

X64

There are three testimonies regarding the dead and they stand well in pleadings: one of them is when there is a dispute and fighting between two lords for land and borders, that is ended in the way it ought to be in the sight of everybody, then their sons or their grandsons may bring testimony about seeing the ending of that dispute lawfully. The second is noble men from every side, they are called the door posts of land, to confirm a man's lineage and paternity and his entitlement to land and earth. The third is seeing the hearthstone of the father or the grandfather or the great-grandfather, and the position of his barns and the furrows in the land which they ploughed previously.

hynny, y dwyn dyn ar uonhed[227] a dylyet ar dir a daear.[228] Trydyd yw gweled pentan[229] y dat neu y hendat nev y horhendat,[230] a lle y[231] ysguboryeu a rychev y tir a ardassant gynt.[232]

Z76

Tair marwdysdioleth y sydd: vn yw o dervydd bod dadlav y rwng dav ddyn am dir a dayar, a rroddi o'r naill o naddvnt ymhen gwybyddiaid, a dwydvd or gwybyddiaid rry adaw o'i rieni ganthvnt bod yn wir y dysdioleth, hono y sydd varw dysdioleth. Ail yw pan vo dadl ymdervynv, i gadw o aminiogav tir o ach ac edryf. Trydyd yw o hawl dyn dyr a dayar a dan gof pentanv i dad nev i hendad nev i orhendad, a lleoedd ydeilad odvn, ac ysgvbawr; hono y sydd varw dysdyoleth ac a seif ynghyfraith.

X65. *U31, Mk82, W72*

Teir kyfurinach yssyd gwell ev hadev[233] noc eu kelv: vn ohonu*n*t colledeu y brenhin,[234] a chynllwyn, a llad o dyn y tad.[235]

X66. *U29, Mk83, W73 [1 2 3 = 2 1 3 Mk]*

Tri aniueil vn troedyawc yssyd: march,[236] a hebawc, a gellgi.[237]

X67. *W16*

Pob adeilwr maestir a dyly caffael tri ph[r]en y gan y neb bieuffo y coed:[238] nenbren, a dwy nenforch. Pwybynnac a uo goruodawc oed vn dit a blwydyn a dyly.

---

[227] − *U, Mk*; y dwyn dyn ar uonhed] − *W*
[228] ar dir a daear] ac y dosparth iawn ac y edrych *U*; y dosparth ia6n tr6y ach ac etruryt a chadarnhau gan dyn a allant y d6yn tystolyaeth y achwanegu dylyet dyn o tir a dayar *Mk, W*
[229] + neu esgynuaen *U*; pentanuaen *Mk*
[230] + neu wr or genedyl un dylyet ac ef *U, Mk, W*
[231] + tei ar *U, Mk, W*
[232] + pob un or rei hynny a dygant tystollaeth ydyn ar ydylyet *U*; + a ffinyeu yr erwyd pop vn or rei hynny a rodant tystolyaeth y dyn ar y dylyet *Mk, W*
[233] dywedut *U*
[234] arglwyd *U, Mk, W*
[235] + ot adeuir yg kyfrinach *U, Mk, W*
[236] amws *U*
[237] milgi *Mk*; + p6y bynhac a torho troet un ohonunt talet y werth yn holla6l *W*
[238] + mynho na mynho y coet6r *W*

Z76

There are three dead testimonies: one is if it happens that there are pleadings between two men for land and earth, and one of them puts [the issue] before knowers, and the knowers mentioned above state that their parents say that the testimony is true, that one is dead testimony. The second is when there is a case about [mutually] fixing a boundary, the door posts of land should keep through lineage and paternity. The third is if a man claims land and earth through the memory of a making of a hearth by his father or his grandfather or his great-grandfather, and the building places of the kiln, and a barn; that one is dead testimony and stands in law.

X65

Three secrets that are better confessed than concealed: one of them the losses of the king, and a secret killing, and a person killing his father.

X66

There are three one-footed animals: a horse, and a falcon, and a greyhound.

X67

Every builder of open land is entitled to get three timbers from whoever owns the woods: a ridge-piece and two crucks. Whoever may be a guarantor is entitled to a set lawful period of a year and a day.

X68

Tri lle y ran kyfureith: vn ohonunt y da a dyccer o anghyfureith y gyfureith, eil [218v] yw rwng byw a marw, trydyt yw o byd amrysson am dev teruyn a thyngv o bawb y teruyn a uo y rwng y dev, ymrysson a rennir in deu hanner.

X69. *Mk84, W74*

Tri pheth ny thelir kyd koller yn y randy: kyllell, a cledyf, a llawdyr.[239]

Brawdyr a dyly gwarandaw yn llwyr, a chadw yn gofuyawdyr, a dysgu yn graff, a datkannv yn war, a barnv yn trugarauc.

X70. *U39, Mk86, W75*

Teir sarhaed kelein yw: y llath,[240] a'e hyspeilyaw,[241] a gwan gwth troed yndaw.[242]

X71. *Z73, U41, Mk70, W76*

Teir gwarthrud kelein[243] yw: gofuyn 'pwy a ladawd hwnn?', a 'phiev yr elor?',[244] a gofuyn 'piev y beth newyd[245] hwnn?'[246]

X72. *Z74, U40, Mk85, W78*

Teir gauael[247] nyd atuerir: vn onadunt[248] dros ledrat, a mach,[249] a galanas.[250]

---

[239] + kanys y neb bieiffont a dyly eu kad6 *Mk, W*
[240] pan ladher *U, Mk, W*
[241] pan yspeilher *U, Mk, W*
[242] gwan ... yndaw] a phan ythyer yny gorwed *U, Mk*; pan uyrhyer yn y orwed *W*
[243] kenedl *Z*
[244] phiev ... elor] govvn pa elor yw hon *Z*
[245] – *U, Mk, W*
[246] piev ... hwnn] pa vedd yw hwn *Z*
[247] ytavel *Z*
[248] a ddyker *Z*
[249] a mach] ac vn a ddyker ar vach pan vo negyf o gymell *Z*; ac ar uach ny chymhello iawn *U*; a thros vach ny chymhello *Mk, W*
[250] ytavel a ddyker dros alanas *Z*

X68

Three places the law divides: one of them is for goods taken from being illegal to being legal, the second is between living and dead, the third is if there is a dispute about two boundaries and everyone swears to the boundary which is between the two, the [land subject to] dispute is divided in two halves.

X69

Three things which are not paid though they are lost in a house where someone is lodged: a knife, and a sword, and trousers.

A justice should listen fully, and preserve [records] as a remembrancer, and learn diligently, and state courteously, and judge mercifully.

X70

The three shames of a corpse are: striking it, and despoiling it, and giving it a shove with a foot.

X71

The three shames of a corpse are: asking 'who killed this one?', and 'whose is this bier?', and asking 'whose is this fresh grave?'

X72

Three distraints that are not restored: one of them for theft, and for a surety, and for *galanas*.

X73

Tri edyn ar dyr dyn arall heb ganyad: eryr, a garan, a chigfuran. Pwybynnac ac
ev lladho, taled dec a devgein y berchennawc y tir.

X74. *Z65, U33, Mk87, W79 [1 2 3 = 2 1 3 Z]*

Tri peth or keffir ar ford ryd ynt y'r neb a'y caffo:[251] [219r] petol, a notwyd, a
cheinyawc.

X75. *Mk88, W80*

Tri dyn a dyly gweli dauawt:[252] y brenhin,[253] a brawdwr yni medylyav am y
varn,[254] a'e effeiriad yn y wisc[255] yn y teir gwyl arbennic,[256] nev yn darllein
ysgriuen[257] rac y vron y brenhin nev yn y gwneuthur.

End of X *Triad Collection*

X76. *U8, Mk12, V12, W6* [221v]

Tri gwybyteid yssyd am dir: henadvreid gwlad y wybod ach ac edrif, eil yw
aminhogev y dwyn y'r tir, trydyd yw meiri a chyghelloryon y dangos teruynev.

Mk12. *U8, V12, W6*

Tri gvybydyeit yssyd am tir: henaduryeit gvlat y vybot ach ac eturyt y dvyn
dyn ar dylyet o tir a dayar; eil yv gvr o pop rantir o'r tref honno yv
amhinogyon tir, y vybot kyfran rvg kenedyl a charant; trydyd yv pan vo
amrysson rvg dvy tref,[258] meiri a chyghelloryon a righylleit bieu[259] kadv
teruyneu kanys brenhin bieu teruynu.[260]

---

[251] ryd ... caffo] ni roddir atteb amdan6nt *Z*; ny wrtheb y neb perchennawc ohonw *U*; nyt reit atteb y
eu perchenna6c o honunt *Mk, W*
[252] dyly gweli dauawt] telir g6eli taua6t udunt *Mk*
[253] argl6yd *Mk*
[254] yni medylyav ... varn] pan amheuer am y varn *Mk*
[255] offerwisc uch pen y alla6r *Mk*
[256] + uch y alla6r *W*
[257] llythyr *Mk, W*
[258] + vn vreint *V*
[259] y 6ybot *U*
[260] kanys ... teruynu] – *U*

X73

Three birds on another man's land without permission: a eagle, and a heron, and a raven. Whoever kills them, let him pay fifty pence to the owner of the land.

X74

Three things which, if they are found on the road, are free to the person who finds them: a horseshoe, and a needle, and a penny.

X75

Three men who are entitled to a tongue-wound: to the king, and the judge when his judgement is doubted, and his priest in his vestments in the three special feasts, or reading a letter before the king, or composing it.

End of X *Triad Collection*

X76

There are three knowers for land: the elders of the country to know kin and descent, the second is the borderers to bring him to the land, the third are the *meiri* and the *cyngellorion* to show the borders.

Mk12

There are three knowers for land: the elders of the country to know the lineage and descent to bring a man upon his entitlement of land and earth; the second is a man from each division of that township, that is the door posts of land, to know the division between kin and relatives; the third is when there is a dispute between two townships, the *meiri* and the *cyngellorion* and the *rhingylliaid* have the right to keep the borders as the king has [the right] to settle boundaries.

Triads in other Cyfnerth manuscripts which are not found in *X* or *Q*

From the main texts of the manuscripts

U3. V3, W3, Z4. [52]

Teir creith gogyuarch yssyd ar dyn: creith ar y vyneb,[261] vheugeint a tal; creith ar geuyn y lav deheu,[262] trugeint a tal; creith ar geuyn y troet deheu,[263] dec arugeint a tal.

Z4

Tair kraith gogyvarch ysyd: vn ar wyneb dehav cxx a dal, vn ar law dehav lx a dal, vn ar droed devat xxx a dal.

U9. [94]

Tri lle y rann k*yfreith*: un ohonunt, or tyf kynhen rvg dvy tref am tir a theruyn ac wynteu yn un ureint, gwyrda bren*hin* bieu teruynu hvnnv os medrant; or byd pedrus dyledogyon y tir, pavb bieu tygu y teruyn, odyna rannent yn deu hanher rvg y dvy tref y hamrysson; ket teruyno tref ar arall, ny dyly dvyn randir y vrthi. Hanher punt a dav y'r bren*hin* pan teruynher, a phedeir ar ugeint a dav y'r bravdvr. Eil yv rvg gvr a gvreic pan uo marv y lleill. Trydyd yv pan dyker anyueil o'r lle ny aller y caffel vrth k*yfreith*, nyt amgen o aghyfreith y kyureith.

---

[261] y 6yneb] 6yneb dyn *V, W*
[262] – *W*
[263] – *W*

Translation of the triads in other Cyfnerth manuscripts which are not found in *X* or *Q*

From the main texts of the manuscripts

U3

There are three conspicuous scars on a man: a scar on his face, it is worth a hundred and twenty [pence]; a scar on the back of his right hand, it is worth sixty [pence]; a scar on the back of his right foot, it is worth thirty [pence].

Z4

There are three conspicuous scars: one on the right face it is worth a hundred and twenty [pence], one on the right hand it is worth sixty [pence], one on the ?right foot it is worth thirty [pence].

U9

Three places the law divides: one of them, if a dispute grows between two townships for land and bordering and they are of the same status, the nobles of the king have the right to settle the border in that case if they are able to; if it is doubtful who is entitled to the land, everyone has the right to swear to the border, and then they divide in two halves between the two townships of the dispute; although a township borders on another, territory ought not be taken from it. The king receives half of a pound when the borders are settled, and twenty-four come to the justice. The second is between a husband and wife when the other one dies. The third is when an animal is taken from the place where it cannot be got by law, namely from unlawfulness to lawfulness.

W15. *U12* [91v]

Tri argae teruyn yssyd: breint, a phriodolder, a chygwarchadv. Ny dyly dyn a uo
is y ureint no'e rei hynny teruynu arnunt.[264]

Triads from the triad collections in the manuscripts

Mk48. *U44, V47, W95* [111]

Tri lle ny dyly dyn rodi llv gveilyd: vn yv ar pont vn pren heb ganllav; eil yv ar
porth y vynwent, kanys kanu y pater a dyly yna rac eneiteu Cristonogyon y
byt; trydyd yv ar drvs yr eglvys, kanys canu y pater a dyly yna rac bron y groc.
Hyn o dynyon a dieinc rac llv gveilyd: arglvyd, ac escob, a mut, a bydar, ac
anghyfyeithus, a gvreic veichavc.[265]

Mk69. *U30, W65* [114]

Tri chyffredin gvlat: lluyd, a dadleu, ac eglvys.[266]

Mk71. *U46, W67, Z58* [115]

[115] Tri argae gvaet: mynwes, a gvregys per*u*ed, a gvregys llavdvr.

Mk73. *U32, W68* [115]

Tri divyneb gvlat yssyd ac ny ellir bot hebdunt:[267] arglvyd, ac effeirat, a chyfreith.

---

[264] ny dyly ... arnunt] – *U*
[265] Hyn o dynyon ... veicha6c] – *U, W*
[266] + kanys guys a uyd ar pa6b vdunt *W*
[267] + mal kynt *U*

W15

There are three stays of a boundary: privilege, entitlement, and original possession. A man whose status is lower than those ones ought not border on them.

Triads from the triad collections in the manuscripts

Mk48

Three places where a man is not entitled to swear a fore-oath: one is on a bridge with one plank without a handrail; the second is at the gateway of the graveyard, as the *pater noster* should be sung there on behalf of the souls of the Christians of the world; the third is at the church door, as the *pater noster* should be sung there before the crucifix. These people are exempt from making a fore-oath: a lord, and a bishop, and a mute, and a deaf person, and a foreign-tongued man, and a pregnant woman.

Mk69

Three things common to a country: a hosting, and pleadings, and a church.

Mk71

Three stays of blood: a chest, and a middle-girdle, and a trouser-band.

Mk73

There are three without shame in a country and it is not possible to be without them: a lord, and a priest, and law.

Mk79. U25 [1 2 3 = 1 3 2 U] [116]

Tri dyn yssyd ryd udunt kerdet fford a heb[268] ford dyd a nos:[269] effeirat,[270] a medyc,[271] a righyll.[272]

Mk81. U48 [117]

Tri anhebcor kenedyl: penkenedyl,[273] a'e dialvr,[274] a'e hardadlvr.[275]

Mk89. W81 [1 2 3 = 3 2 1 W] [117]

Tri lle yg kyfreith Hywel y mae pravf: vn yv proui bugeilgi, eil yv havlvr[276] bieu profi vch pen bed y mach y vot yn vach,[277] trydyd yv gvreic bieu profi treis ar vr.

Mk93. W90 [118]

Tri dyn kas kenedyl: lleidyr, a thvyllvr, kany ellir ymdiret udunt; a dyn a latho dyn o'e genedyl ehunan, kany dylyir llad y kar byv yr y kar marv. Kas vyd ynteu gan pavb.[278]

Mk94. U37, W92 [1 2 3 = 2 3 1 U, W] [118]

Tri mefyluethyant gvr: bot yn vr arglvyd drvc, a bot yn dryc karvr, a bot yn llib-invr yn dadleu.

Mk96. [118]

Tri pheth a dyly dyn colli y dadyl, yr dahet vo y defnyd: llys kyn amser, a thyst ar vach, a chadv gvedy gvrthot.

---

[268] dieithyr *U*
[269] dyd a nos] – *U*
[270] + y ou6y claf y gyt ae gennat *U*
[271] + gyt a chennat y claf *U*
[272] yn negesseu y argl6yd *U*
[273] teispantyly *U*
[274] + kenedyl *U*
[275] hardel6r *U*
[276] kynnogyn *W*
[277] + ac na diwyg6yt drosta6 y uechniaeth tra uu uy6 *W*
[278] + y welet ynteu *W*

Mk79

Three men who are free to walk on the roads and off the roads day and night: a priest, and a mediciner, and a *rhingyll*.

Mk81

Three things essential to a kindred: the head of kindred, and its avenger, and its pleader.

Mk89

Three places in the law of Hywel where there is proof: one is to test a herd-dog, the second is that it is the claimant's right to prove over the grave of the surety that he was a surety, the third is that it is a woman's right to prove rape against a man.

Mk93

Three hated men of a kindred: a thief, and a deceiver, for they cannot be trusted; and a man who kills a man from his own kindred, for the living kin should not be killed for the dead kin. He will be hated by everybody.

Mk94

Three shameful failings of a man: being the man of a bad lord, and being a bad lover, and being feeble in a [legal] case.

Mk96

Three things a man should lose in a case, however good his substance: an objection before time, and a witness on a surety, and keeping after refusal.

Mk97. [118]

Tri grvndwal doethinab: mabavl ieuenctit y dyscu, a chof [119] y gadv y dysc, a synhvyr oet y datcanu.

Mk99. [119]

Teir kyfnewit a doant trachefyn: dinewyt clafvr, a lledrat, a'r tri pheth ny at kyfreith y tayavc eu gverthu heb ganhat y arglvyd.

Mk102. [119]

O teir fford ny ellir gvadu mab o genedyl: vn yv y eni yn y gvely kyfreithavl a'e vagu vn dyd a blvydyn o da y tat heb y wadu. Eil yv o rodir gverth yr y vagu, kyn bo mab llvyn a pherth vo. Trydyd yv or kymerir ar ostec neu or dygir yn gyfreithavl.

Mk103. Z75 [119]

Tri gorsaf aryf yssyd: ym porth y vynwent dan amdiffyn Duv a'r sant, ac yn y dadleu dan amdiffyn y brenhin, ac arueu gvestei yn y [120] lety dan amdiffyn Duv a'r brenhin. Beth bynhac a wnelher a'r arueu hynny gvedy dotter uelly, ryd uyd eu perchennavc.

Z75

> Tair gorsedd arf: drws y vynwent, a dadle arglwydd, a'r lle ydd atverer. A chyd gwnel arall gam a'r arvav yn y lleoedd hyny, ni syrth ar yr arvav dim.

U35. W77 [113]

Tri gvg ny diwygir: gvg gvr vrth wreic a rodit rith morvyn idav[279] a hitheu yn wreic. A'r eil yv difetha dyn o *kyfreith* a gvneuthur o'e genedyl[280] gvg vrth y neb a diffethaei.[281] Trydyd yv gwg gvr[282] vrth ki yn y gyrchu ac ef yn y welet.[283]

[279] a rodit rith mor6yn ida6] a gymerho ar ureint mor6yn *W*
[280] a g6neuthur o'e genedyl] a dyn oe genedyl yn g6neuthur *W*
[281] 6rth y neb a diffethaei] am hynny *W*
[282] dyn *W*
[283] gyrchu ac ef yn y welet] ruthra6 *W*

Mk97

Three foundations of learning: adolescence and youth to learn, and a memory to preserve the learning, and the sense of age to declare [the learning].

Mk99

Three exchanges which return afterwards: calves of a leper, and theft, and the three things that the law does not allow a bondsman to sell without the permission of his lord.

Mk102

In three ways a child may not be denied from a kindred: one is that he is born in the legitimate bed and reared for a year and a day on the father's goods without rejection. The second is if payment is given for rearing him, even if he may be a son of bush and brake. The third is if he is accepted by not saying anything or if he is affiliated legally.

Mk103

There are three rests of a weapon: in the gateway of a church under the protection of God and the saint, and in the law court under the protection of the king, and the weapons of a guest in his lodging under the protection of God and the king. Whatever is done with those weapons after they have been placed in that way, their owner shall be free.

Z75

The three rests of a spear: the door of the cemetery, and the pleadings of the lord, and the place where it is repaired. And if someone else does wrong with weapons in those places, no liability falls on the weapons.

U35

Three injuries for which there is no compensation: the injury of a man to a woman who is given in the guise of a virgin to him and she is a woman. And the second is to ruin a man by law and his kindred injure whoever ruined him. The third is the injury of a man to a dog attacking him and he can see it.

U38. W94 [114]

Tri chyuanhed gvlat: meibon bychein, a chvn, a cheilogeu.

W82. [103v]

Teir pla kenedyl: magu mab arglvyd, a dvyn mab y genedyl yg kam, a guarchadv
penreith.

W87. [104r]

Tri dyn a wna gulat yn tlavt: arglvyd deu eiravc, ac ygnat camwedavc, a maer
cuhudyat.

W89. [104r]

Tri aniueil yssyd un werth eu llosgyrneu ac eu llygeit ac eu heneit: llo, ac eboles
tom, a chath; eithyr cath a warchatwo yscubavr brenhin.

Z56. [37vb] *This triad is from the triad collection in the Cyfn section*
rather than the tail of the manuscript

Tri dyn a ddylant vod yn anrraith odde o ky*fraith* ac ni ddylant ev divetha ev
hvnain. Dyn a wrthott ky*fraith* lys, a dyn a vo fflemawr rrwng dwy wlad, a
llawruđ a laddo kelain yngwlad y brenin; a gaffer o dda iddaw o'r pryd bigiliđ
y brenin biav oll.

U38

The three [signs of] inhabitation of a country: young children, and dogs, and cocks.

W82

The three plagues of a kindred: rearing a lord's son, and affiliating a child wrongly to a kindred, and guarding the chief compurgator.

W87

The three men who impoverish a country: a double-tongued lord, and an unjust justice, and a *maer* who is an accuser.

W89

The three animals whose tails and eyes and lives are of the same value: a calf, and a dunghill filly, and a cat; except for a cat which guards the king's barn.

Z56. This triad is from the triad collection in the Cyfn section rather than the tail of the manuscript

The three men who ought to have their moveable goods confiscated by law and who are not entitled to dispossess themselves. A man who refuses the law of a court, and a man who is a fugitive between two countries, and a homicide who commits a killing in the king's land; whatever comes to him as goods from one day to the next the king owns it all.

The triads in *Q*, NLW Wynnstay 36

Q1. *I1, J1, L1, M1, Bost1, O1, P1, R1, S1, T1, Tr1, €1,* LatD1

[1va.30] Teir sarhaet brenhin ynt: vn y6 torri y na6d, llad dyn ar na6d y brenhin; eil y6 pan del deu vrenhin ar eu keffinyd y vynnu[1] ymaruoll, or lledir dyn yn eu g6yd, sarhaet brenhin y6; trydyd y6 kamaruer o'e 6reic.[2]

Q2. *I2, J2, L2, M2, Bost2, O2, P2, R2, S2, [221], T2, Tr2, €2,* LatD2

[1vb.5] Tri ry6 sarhaet yssyd y pop g6r g6reiga6c: vn y6 y tar[a]6 ar y gorff, eil y6 bot arall yg kamaruer o'e 6reic, trydyd y6 torri na6d [dyn] a allo rodi na6d y arall tr6y gyfreith.

Q3. *I3, J3, L3, M3, Bost3, O3, P3, R3, S3, T3, Tr3, €3,* LatD3

[2ra.7] O tri mod y serheir y vrenhines: pan torher y na6d, neu pan tra6er tr6y lit, neu pan tynher peth gan treis o'e la6.

Q4. *I4, J4, L4, M4, Bost4, O4, P4, R4, S4, T4, Tr4, €4,* LatD4 *[1 2 3 = 2 1 3 S]*

[2rb.19] Tri ry6 dyn[3] yssyd: brenhin, a breyr, a bilaen ac eu haelodeu.

---

[1]   y vynnu] *– I, S*
[2]   + sef y6 hynny bot genthi *J*
[3]   *– M, Bost*

Translation of the triads in *Q*, NLW Wynnstay 36

Q1

These are the three *sarhaeds* of the king: one is breaking his protection, killing a man under the protection of the king; the second is when two kings come to their boundaries wishing to negotiate, if a man is killed in their presence, it is a *sarhaed* of the king; the third is misusing his wife.

Q2

Three kinds of *sarhaed* pertain to every married man: one is to strike him on his body, the second is that another misuses his wife, the third is breaking the protection of one who is able to give protection to another by law.

Q3

In three ways *sarhaed* is done to the queen: when her protection is broken, or when she is struck through anger, or when something is taken from her hand by force.

Q4

There are three kinds of person: a king, a nobleman, and a bondsman and their members.

Q5. J5, L5, M5, P5, R5, S170, T5, €5, LatD5

[4vb.3] Tri ry6 6assanaeth a 6na⁴ offeirat llys yn y⁵ dadleuoed: dileu pob dadyl a darffo y theruynu o'r rol,⁶ eil y6 cad6 yn yscriuendic hyt varn pop dadyl ny theruyn6yt,⁷ trydyd y6 bot yn para6t ac yn diued6⁸ 6rth reit⁹ y brenhin y 6neuthur llythyreu ac y¹⁰ darllein.¹¹

Q6. J6, L6, M6, P6, R6, €6

[4vb.15] Tri g6assanaeth a 6na¹² y brenhin¹³ y'r hebogyd y dyd y kaffo 6hibon- ogyl vynyd, neu grychyd, neu b6n o'e hebogydyaeth: nyt amgen, daly y 6arthafyl pan disgynho, a dala y varch tra gymhero y heba6c ar ederyn,¹⁴ a daly y 6arthafyl 6rth escynnu.

Q7. I25, J7, L7, M7, Bost5, N1, P7, R7, S25, Tr25, Y27, €7, LatD6

[6ra.1] Tri pheth a perthyn y¹⁵ vra6d6r: vn y6 dill6g kyfarcheu 6rth reit y brenhin, eil y6 datcanu a dosparth kynheneu¹⁶ y my6n llys, trydyd y6 yr hyn a dospartho tr6y varn, y gatarnhav tr6y 6ystyl a bra6tlyfyr,¹⁷ ot ym6ystlir ac ef, neu os gouyn ida6 y brenhin heb ym6ystla6.¹⁸

Q8. I26, J8, L8, M8, Bost6, N2, P8, R8, S26, Tr26, Y28, €8, LatD7

[6rb.2] Tri amheu bra6t yssyd: vn y6 bot amrysson r6g ha6l6r ac amdiffynn6r am y varn a rodet vdunt, ac yna y mae¹⁹ y dosparth ar y bra6d6r a'e²⁰ rodassei.²¹ Eil y6 bot amrysson r6g ha6l6r a'r²² bra6d6r ac ym6ystla6 am y varn.²³ Trydyd

---

⁴ a 6na] yssyd y *J, L, M, R, T;* yssyd ar *S*

⁵ yn *J, L*

⁶ a darffo y theruynu o'r rol] or llyfreu ar a vo tervyn kyfya6l arnynt *S*

⁷ ny theruyn6yt] kyñu vo tervyn k'a6l arnynt *S;* yny deruyner *J, M;* hynny teruynner *L*

⁸ ac yn diued6] – *S*

⁹ *hiatus in T*

¹⁰ + eu *Q;* eu *J, L, M, R*

¹¹ 6rth reit … darllein] 6rth arch y gorsseda6c *S*

¹² dyly *J, L, M, R*

¹³ + eu g6nneuthur *J, L, M, R*

¹⁴ edern *Q, €*

¹⁵ a perthyn y] – *I;* a berthyn 6rth *J, L, M, Bost, R, S, Tr, Y*

¹⁶ + trwy 6ystl a bra6dlyfr *P*

¹⁷ bratlyfyr *Q*

¹⁸ neu os … ym6ystla6] – *Y;* + ac ef *I, S*

¹⁹ y mae] – *I, S*

²⁰ ar y bra6d6r a'e] a *I*

²¹ + y varn *I, S*

²² a *J, L, N, Tr*

²³ am y varn] am varn *I;* – *S,*

Q5

Three kinds of services the court priest performs in pleadings: to delete every pleading which has been settled from the roll, the second is to keep a written record for every pleading which is not completed until judgement, the third is to be ready and sober at the king's need to write letters and to read them.

Q6

Three services the king performs for the falconer the day he catches a curlew, or a heron, or a bittern by his falconry: namely, holding his stirrup as he dismounts, and holding his horse whilst his falcon takes a bird, and holding his stirrup as he mounts.

Q7

Three things pertain to a justice: one is to issue pronouncements at the king's need, the second is to set forth and settle disputes in court, the third is that which he may determine by judgement, he should confirm by a pledge and a lawbook, if pledges are exchanged with him, or if the king asks him without pledging.

Q8

There are three doubtings of judgement: one is that there is a dispute between a claimant and a defendant about the judgement given to them, and then the decision rests with the justice who gave it. The second is that there is a dispute between a claimant and the justice, and there is mutual pledging regarding his judgement. The third is that there is mutual pledging between the defendant and the justice about his judgement; and in respect of the two pledgings the decision rests on written authority, because [written] authority is universally unbiased, that is, a judgement book.

y6 bot ym6ystla6 r6g amdiffynn6r a bra6d6r am y vra6t; ac am y deu ym6ystla6 yt uyd[24] y dosparth ar a6durda6t lythyra6l, canys diledyf gyffredin vyd yr a6durda6t, sef y6 hynny, bra6tlyfyr.[25]

Q9. 1140, J9, L9, N3, P9, R9, S139, T6, Tr65, Y149, €9, LatD20

[9rb.4] O tri mod y kedernheir g6ys: o tyston, a mechniaeth, neu auael.

Q10. 1141, J10, L10, N4, P10, R10, S140, T7, Tr66, Y150, €10, LatD21

Teir g6ys a[26] ellir eu g6adu kyn amser tyston: g6ys gan tyston[27] ny 6neir onyt am[28] tir a ofynher[29] o ach ac eturyt tr6y na6uet dydyeu Mei neu galan gayaf.[30] O gofynir tir yn amgen no hynny, neu peth arall, a[31] g6adu vn 6ys tr6y t6g[32] ymdana6, tr6y uechni y dylyir kadarnhau[33] g6ys ar y neb a'e g6atto. Y lle y pallo mechni vn 6eith, gaffel[34] a dylyir y gymryt yno, ac os tir a ouynnir, tir a eueylir. Pallu mechniaeth y6 na rother mach yny dylyher, neu y rodi a'e termygu. Tremyc g6ys neu uechniaeth y6 na del dyn yn dyd gal6 y lys ossodedic y atteb, neu y amdiffyn rac atteb.

Q11. 1142, J11, L11, N5, P11, R11, S141, Tr67, Y151, €11, LatD22

Tri dyn ny dylyir eu g6ysya6: tyst, a g6arant, a g6eithreda6l kyss6yn neu gyfadef; mechni a dylyir ar h6nn6.[35]

Q12. 1143, J12, L12, N6, P12, R12, S142, Tr68, Y152, €12, LatD8

[9rb.27] Tri ry6 6adu yssyd: g6adu oll y dadyl a dotter ar dyn, a h6nn6 a 6edir tr6y reith ossodedic heb na m6y na llei. Eil y6 adef ran o dadyl [9va.1] dryc 6eithret, a g6adu y c6bl 6eithret; ac yna y g6edir gan ach6enegu reith

---

[24] yt uyd] ytu6yd *€*
[25] + yn y mod racdywededic *J*
[26] ny *L*
[27] dystu *J;* + a d6yn *S*
[28] – *Q, P, €*
[29] a ofynher] – *N*
[30] galan gayaf] racuyr *I, S, Y;* galan racvyr *P*
[31] *hiatus in T*
[32] l6 *P; – €*
[33] + yr eil *S*
[34] gafaelu *I;* gauel *J, N, P;* gafael *R, S, Y*
[35] mechni a dylyir ar h6nn6] – *Tr*

Q9

In three ways a summons is confirmed: by witnesses, and suretyship, or distraint.

Q10

Three summonses which can be denied before the time for witnesses: a summons by witnesses is not made unless land is claimed by lineage and paternity through the ninth days of May or the Winter Calends. If land is claimed by another way, or something else [is claimed], and one summons is denied by an oath about it, the summons should be confirmed by suretyship against whoever denies it. Where suretyship fails once, distraint should be taken there, and if land is claimed, land is distrained. The failure of suretyship is that surety is not given where it ought to be, or it is given and contempt is made for it. Despising a summons or suretyship is that a man does not appear on the day he is called to a set court to answer, or to defend himself against an answer.

Q11

Three men who ought not be summoned: a witness, and a guarantor, and an alleged or acknowledged confederate; suretyship ought to be adopted against such a person.

Q12

There are three kinds of denial: denying all of the case that is brought against a person, and that is denied by a set *rhaith* without either more or less. The second is to acknowledge part of a case [brought] on account of a bad deed, but to deny the whole deed; and then it is denied by increasing the set *rhaith*, as it is in the columns of law for homicide: where fifty men swear, denying homicide and all of its abetments, then one hundred or two hundred or three hundred men should swear, denying homicide and acknowledging the abetment. The third is denying part and acknowledging another part of a case without a deed being involved; and then it is denied by decreasing the set *rhaith* as in suretyship: where the surety swears as one of seven denying all of his suretyship, then he swears himself to deny a part and acknowledge another part of his suretyship.

ossodedic, megys y mae yg colofneu kyfreith am la6rudyaeth:[36] yn y lle y
tygyei deg 6yr a deu vgeint, gan 6adu lla6rudyaeth a'e haffeitheu[37] oll, yno y
t6g cant neu deu cant neu tri chant, gan 6adu llofrudyaeth ac adef affeith.
Trydyd y6 g6adu y ran ac adef ran arall o dadyl heb 6eithret yndi; ac yna gan
leihau reith ossodedic y g6edir megys y me6n[38] mechni: lle y tygei y mach ar
y seithuet gan 6adu y vachniaeth oll,[39] yno y t6g ehunan gan[40] 6adu ran ac adef
ran arall o'e vechni.

Q13. I144, J13, L13, M9, N7, P13, R13, S143, Tim106, Tr69, €13

[9va.19] Tri mach yssyd ny cheiff vn ohonunt d6yn y vechni ar y l6 ehunan kyn
g6atto ran ac adef ran arall[41] o'e uechni: nyt amgen no dyn a el yn vach yg
g6yd llys, a mach diebredic, a mach kynnogyn.[42] Beth bynnac a tygho[43] y
kyntaf, y llys a dyly tygu gyt ac ef neu yn y erbyn. Yr eil neu y trydyd, beth
bynnac a tygho[44] ar y seithuet o'e gyfnesseiueit y t6g, canys tala6dyr o
gyf[9vb.1]reith uyd pop vn ohonunt.[45]

Q14. I145, J14, L14, M10, N8, P14, R14, S144, Tr70, Y153, €14

[9vb.1] Tri ry6 t6g yssyd: kadarnhau g6ir gan tygu tr6yda6 perued, eil y6 g6adu
geu gan tygu tr6yda6 perued, trydyd y6 tygu peth petrus her6yd kyt6ybot[46] –
yr hyn ny 6ypper yn dieu[47] beth vo, ae g6ir ae geu.

Q15. I28, I38, J15, L15, M11, N9, O32, P15, R15, S28, Tr33, Y35, €15

[9vb.8] O teir fford y dosperthir bra6t gygha6s: kyntaf y6 tr6y odef, canys godef
a tyrr pop kygha6s. Os bra6d6r a odef g6ystyl yn erbyn y varn yn tagneuedus
heb rodi g6ystyl,[48] yna[49] dyg6ydedic uyd y varn. Eil y6 bra6tlyfyr y r6g deu

---

[36] + ae haffeitheu oll *I, S, Y*

[37] a'e haffeitheu] – *Tr*

[38] m6m *Q*

[39] gan 6adu y vachniaeth oll] – *I, S;* 6adu *Y*

[40] yno y t6g ehunan gan] – *Y*

[41] all *Q*

[42] yg g6yd … mach kynnogyn] – *M*

[43] 6atto *S*

[44] y kyntaf … a tygho] pob vn *I*; beth bynnac a tygho] – *S*

[45] or deu *S;* + yn amser kynnocnaeth *Tim*

[46] + sef y6 peth petrus *S*

[47] yn dieu] – *I, S, Tr, Y*

[48] g6rthg6ystyl *J, L, M, O*

[49] + y gatarnhau y vra6t *I28, S;* y chadarnhau *I138*

Q13

There are three sureties none of whom shall discharge his suretyship by his own oath although he may deny part and acknowledge another part of his suretyship: namely a man who becomes a surety in the presence of the court, and a with-holding surety, and a debtor surety. Whatever the first may swear, the court should swear with him or against him. The second or the third, whatever he may swear he should swear as one of seven of his next of kin, because every one of them will be liable to pay by law.

Q14

There are three kinds of oath: confirming the truth by swearing through and through, the second is denying falsehood by swearing through and through, the third is swearing a doubtful thing according to conscience – that which is not known definitely what it may be, whether true or false.

Q15

In three ways a plea concerning judgement is determined: the first is by suffer-ance, because sufferance overrides every plea. If a justice suffers a pledge against his judgement peacefully without giving a [counter] pledge, then his judgement is void. The second is a lawbook between two pledges; that is, a pledge given against a judgement, and another pledge given with that judgement. This is the third way: a justice has the right to decide between two men pleading about the judgement he had given to them without exchange of pledges with him.

6ystyl;[50] sef y6 hynny, g6ystyl a rother yn erbyn barn, a g6ystyl arall a rother gyt a'r uarn honno.[51] Tryded fford y6: bra6t6r bieu dosparth y r6g deu dyn yn kygha6s am y varn a rodassei udunt, heb ym6ystla6 ac ef.[52]

Q16. I139, J16, L16, M12, N10, P16, R16, S138, Tr64, Y11, €16

[9vb.22] Tri ry6 vanac yssyd, ac am pop vn ohonunt y gossodir reith g6lat ar dyn[53] am letrat: vn y6 dyfot[54] colledic a manac6r gyt ac ef a tygho yn erbyn arall clybot a g6ybot arna6 y lletrat. Eil y6 tygu o'r manag6r g6elet a g6ybot arna6 y lletrat, a h6nn6 a el6ir lli6. Trydyd y6 lludya6 rac [10ra.1] dyn geissa6 da a gollyssei[55] yn y lle y typpei y vot.

Q17. J17, L17, M13, N11, O33, P17, R17, Tr34, €17 [1 2 3 = 2 1 3 J, L, M, R, Tr]

[10ra.19] Tri pheth a dyly bra6d6r eu datganu pan varnho: atteb, ha6l, a barn.

Q18. J18, L18, M14, N12, O34, P18, R18, S137, Tr35, Y37, €18

[10ra.21] O tri mod y kyll bra6d6r gaml6r6 o varnu, ac ny chyll g6erth y taua6t: vn pan diuarno kyfry6 ac a varnassei gynt tr6y gyffelybyon ach6ysson. Eil y6 pan el ar gyfeilorn yn datganu dadyl, or cadarnha m6y neu lei yn y dadyl noc a uu o eireu grym. Trydyd y6 na rotho g6ystyl gyt a'e varn pan rother g6ystyl arall [10rb.1] yn y herbyn. O'r mod kyntaf y varn gamhaf[56] a dileir. O'r eil y datganu a ia6nheir. O'r trydyd y varn heuyt a dileir[57] yna, kyt boet ia6n, canys kadarnha6ys y bra6d6r hi[58] yn amsera6l tr6y 6ystyl.

---

[50] y r6g deu 6ystyl] – *J*
[51] honno] – *I;* g6ystyl a rother yn erbyn … uarn honno] priodolder y gyfreith deilyngaf r6ng g6ystyl a g6rth6ystyl rodedic yn lla6 gorseda6c o law bra6d6r ac o la6 pleit defnyd kynnen am varn *J*
[52] ym6ystla6 ac ef] y hameu tr6y wystyl *J;* ym6ystla6 *L*
[53] ar dyn] – *Tr, Y*
[54] + y *M, S, Tr, Y, €*
[55] a gollyssei] – *I, S, Y*
[56] gyntaf *J*
[57] dyleir *Q*
[58] y bra6d6r hi] – *O, Tr, Y*

Q16

There are three kinds of information, and for each of them the compurgation of the country is imposed upon a man for theft: one is when the person who has suffered loss together with the informant come and swear against another person that he was heard and known to be guilty of the theft. The second is the informant swearing that he was observed and known to be guilty of the theft, and that is called an accusation. The third is preventing a man seeking the property he lost in the place he had thought it might be.

Q17

Three things a justice ought to sum up when he judges: answer, claim, and judgement.

Q18

In three ways the justice loses a *camlwrw* through judging, and he does not lose the value of his tongue: one is when he retracts whatever he judged previously in similar cases. The second is when he strays from the point when summing up a case, if he confirms more or less in the case than there were of crucial terms. The third is that he does not give a pledge with his judgement when another pledge is given against it. In the first case the most wrongful judgement is annulled. In the second the summing up is corrected. In the third the judgement also is annulled, although it is right, as the justice did not confirm it at the correct time with a pledge.

Q19. I5, J19, L19, M15, N13, O5, P19, R19, S5, [216], 277, Tr5, Y4, €19, LatD9

[11va.23] Tri dygyngoll kenedyl ynt. Vn y6 dechreu o 6elygord talu galanas dyn a lather ac na thal6yt[59] c6byl, ac am hynny llad dyn[60] o'r 6elygord honno;[61] ny thelir galanas h6nn6, ac nyt atuerir dim or a tal6yt dros y kyntaf. Eil y6 bot kyss6ynvab ymy6n kenedyl heb y d6yn a heb y di6at, a llad dyn o h6nn6; talu yr alanas oll a uyd reit y'r genedyl honno drosta6,[62] ac os g6atant g6edy hynny, dygyngoll y6. Trydyd y6 pan enllippyer g6iryon am[63] gelein ac na 6nel ia6n am hynny namyn tremyc; or lledir dyn am h6nn6 ny thelir dim drosta6, kyn bo g6iryon, kany eill kenedyl g6adu yn y var6 yr hyn ny 6ada6d ef yn y vy6yt.

S277

Tri dygy[n]goll kenedyl: vn y6, o dervyd y vab ameu 6neuth*ur* kyflafan, ac am y gyflafan keissa6 y 6ady, ac nas g6adysynt gynt ef, ni ad k*yfreith* y 6ady hynny di6ikio y'r genedyl y gyflafan drosta6. Eil y6, o dervyd llad mab ameu diodefedic ac na ry gymerer, ny thelir y alanas; sef achos na thelir, kan*ny* chymerassant h6y efo yn*n* gyfr*eith*ol yn*n* y vo6yd ny varn k*yfreith* gaffel da ohonynt h6ynteu o'e ageu ef. Trydyd y6, o dervyd y dyn lad arall, [ac] yn*n* ol y llad h6nn6 dyg6yda6 galanas a meichieu o'r genedyl a[c] ohona6 ynteu ar yr alanas, a chyn dyfod oed y tal y d6yn o'e vam y dad arall, sef a d6eid k*yfreith*, y dylyant taly galanas euthur y ran ef, ac o hynny y de6edir "tal6ys a vechni6ys".

Q20. I36, J40, L40, M36, Bost26, N34, O52, P20, R40, S36, T27, Y43, €20, LatD11

[12ra.7] Tri oet kyfraith y dial kelein r6g d6y genedyl ny hanffont o vn 6lat: enuynu ha6l yn y dyd kyntaf o'r 6ythnos nessaf[64] g6edy llather y gelein, ac erbyn pen y pythe6nos ony da6[65] atteb kyfreith yn rydhau dial. Eil y6 enuynu ha6l yn y trydyd dyd g6edy llather y gelein[66] or bydant y d6y genedyl yn vn

---

[59] Tha6yt *Q*, thalont *Y*
[60] Vn *J, L, N, O, R, Tr; Y*
[61] hynno *Q*
[62] uyd reit y'r genedyl honno drosta6] dylyir drosta6 *I;* uyd reit *S*
[63] + lad *P, S*
[64] gyntaf *I, S; – P, €*
[65] + y *€*
[66] gein *Q*

Q19

These are the three dire losses of a kindred. One is when the kin starts to pay the *galanas* of a killed man and the whole was not paid, and because of that a man from that kindred is killed; that person's *galanas* is not paid, and nothing is returned of that which was paid for the first. The second is that there is a doubted son in a kindred not having been affiliated or denied, and he kills a man; all of the *galanas* should be paid to that kindred on his behalf, and if they deny after that, it is a dire loss. The third is when an innocent man is accused in respect of a corpse and he does not make reparation for that but makes a contempt for it; if someone is killed because of that nothing is paid for him, although he is innocent, as a kindred cannot deny after his death that which he did not deny whilst alive.

S227

Three dire losses of a kindred: one is, if it happens that a doubted son commits an offence, and for that offence it is attempted to deny him, and they did not deny him previously, the law does not allow him to be denied until reparation has been made to the kindred for the offence on his behalf. The second is, if it happens that a doubted son by sufferance is killed and he is not affiliated, his *galanas* is not paid; the reason it is not paid, because as they did not affiliate him legally in his lifetime the law does not judge them [entitled] to receive goods because of his death. The third is, if it happens that a man kills another, and after that killing *galanas* is offered and sureties from the kindred and also from him for the *galanas*, and before the appointed time for paying he is affiliated by his mother to another father, this is what the law says, they should pay the *galanas* apart from his share, and because of that it is said 'he who has given a surety has paid'.

Q20

Three legal periods to avenge a killing between two kindreds that do not come from the same country: to send [notice of] the claim on the first day of the next week after the dead person was slain, and if no answer comes by the end of the fortnight the law allows revenge. The second is to send [notice of] the claim in the third day after the dead person was slain if the two kindreds are in the same cantref, and unless an answer comes by the end of the fortnight law the law allows revenge. The third is, if they are in the same commote, to send [notice of] the claim in the third day after he is killed and unless an answer comes by the sixth day law allows revenge.

gantref, ac ony da6 atteb erbyn pen y pethe6nos[67] kyfreith yn rydhau dial. Trydyd y6, os yn vn gym6t y bydant, enuynu ha6l yn y trydyd dyd g6edy llather[68] ac ony da6 atteb erbyn y ch6echet dyd kyfreith yn rydhau dial.[69]

Q21. *I51, J41, L41, M37, Bost27, N35, O53, P21, R41, S50, [239], T28, Y58, €21, LatD83*

[12ra.24] Tri tha6eda6c gorsed: argl6yd g6ir yn g6aranda6 ar y 6yrda[70] yn barnu eu kyfreitheu, ac ygnat yn g6aranda6 ha6l6r ac[71] amdiffynn6r yn ymatteb,[72] a mach yn g6aranda6 y kynnogyon[73] a'r tala6dyr yn ymatteb.

Q22. *I52, J42, L42, M38, Bost28, N36, P22, R42, S51, T29, Y59, €22, LatD12*

Tri [12rb.1] g6anas g6ay6 kyfreitha6l yn dadleu yssyd: g6an y arllost[74] yn y dayar ac vn lla6 hyny uo abreid y tynnu a d6y la6, a g6an y pen y my6n t6yn hynny gudyo y m6n, a'e dodi ar l6yn a vo kyfuch a g6r; ac ony byd ar[75] vn o'r teir g6anas hynny, ot a dyn arna6 mal y bo mar6,[76] trayan yr alanas a a[77] ar[78] perchena6c y g6ay6.

Q23. *I55, J45, L45, M41, Bost31, N39, P23, R45, S54, T32, Y61, €23, LatD86*

[12rb.17] Teir sarhaet ny di6gir or keffeir tr6y ueda6t: sarhaet y'r offeirat teulu, a'r ygnat llys, a'r medic llys;[79] kany dyly vn o'r tri hynny[80] bot yn ved6 byth kany 6dant py amser y bo reit y'r brenhin 6rthunt.[81]

Q24. *I58, J48, L48, M44, Bost34, N42, P24, R48, S57, T35, Y64, €24, LatD88*

[12rb.17] Teir sarhaet g6reic ynt, vn a drycheif, ac vn a ost6g, ac vn ysyd sarhaet g6byl:[82] kyntaf y6 bot genthi o'e hanuod, a honno gan vn drychafel y telir

---

67 na6uettyd *J, L, M, Bost, O, R, T, Y, LatD*
68 + y gelain *I, J, L, M, Bost, O, P, Y*
69 + oher6yd na deyth atteb *S*
70 ar y 6yrda] y yneit *O*
71 *hiatus in O*
72 ha6l6r ac amdiffynn6r yn ymatteb] hawl ac attep *LatD*
73 kynnogyon] ha6l6r *I, S*
74 + y g6ay6 *M, Bost*
75 y g6ay6 yn *I, S*
76 mal y bo mar6] ae var6 *S*
77 dyg6yd *I, S, Y*
78 – *M, Bost*
79 – *M;* teulu *S, Y, LatD*
80 dyly ... hynny] dylyant *M, Bost*
81 kany 6dant ... 6rthunt] – *J*
82 g6byl] hep ostwg a hep dyrchauael *LatD*

Q21

Three silent ones of a court: a just lord listening to his nobles judging their laws, and a justice listening to the claimant and the defendant answering each other, and a surety hearing the debtors and the debtor (*sic*) answering each other.

Q22

There are three legal thrusts of a spear in sessions: to thrust the shaft in the ground with one hand until it is difficult to pull it out with two hands, and to thrust the head into a dune until the socket is hidden, and to place it on a bush which is as high as a man; and unless it is on one of those three rests, if a man encounters it so that he dies, a third of the *galanas* is charged to the owner of the spear.

Q23

Three *sarhaeds* which are not compensated if they are received whilst drunk: a *sarhaed* to the priest of the household, and the court justice, and the court mediciner; as not one of those three is entitled to be drunk because they do not know when the king may have need of them.

Q24

These are the three *sarhaeds* of a woman, one which is augmented, one which is decreased, and one which is complete *sarhaed*: the first is to have intercourse with her against her will, and that is paid to her with one augmentation. The second is to give her a kiss against her will, and that is decreased, a third is lacking from it. The third is to grope her against her will, and that is complete *sarhaed* to her; and if she is married, it is paid to her according to the status of her husband.

idi.[83] Yr eil y6 rodi cussan idi o'e hanuod, a honno[84] a ost6g, y[85] trayan a vyd eisseu idi. Trydyd y6 y phaluu o'e hanuod, a honno yssyd[86] sarhaet[87] g6byl idi; ac os g6rya6c vyd, her6yd breint y g6r y telir idi.[88]

Q25. 162, J51, L51, M47, Bost37, N45, O55, P25, R51, S61, T38, Y67, €25, LatD91

[12rb.29] Tri chyffro dial yssyd: diaspedein karesseu, a g6elet elor eu kar, a g6elet [12va.1] bed eu kar[89] heb ymdiu6yn.

Q26. 165, J55, L55, M51, Bost41, N49, O59, P26, R55, S64, T42, Y71, €26, LatD13

[12va.2] Tri g6erth kyfreith beichogi g6reic: vn y6 g6aet kyn del6at, 6yth a deu vgeint a tal or collir tr6y greulonder.[90] Eil y6 kyn dyuot eneit ynda6, or collir tr6y greulonder[91] trayan galanas a telir ymdana6. Trydyd y6 g6edy yd el eneit ynda6, talu c6byl o'e alanas a dylyir[92] or collir tr6y greulonder.[93]

Q27. 172, J62, L62, M58, Bost48, N56, P27, R62, S71, T49, Tim1, Y78, €27, LatD14

[15ra.30] Tri than digyfreith a dotto dyn yn y tir ehunan:[94] tan [15rb.1] gotheith o hanher Ma6rth[95] hyt hanher Ebrill, a than odyn trefgord, a than gefeil trefgord a vo na6 cam y 6rth y tref a tho banadyl neu ty6arch arnei.

Q28. O101, P28, €28 Also 121 in Q

[15rb.5] Tri gol6c a dygir yghyfreith: gol6c tyst o'e tystolyaeth, a gol6c managyat o'e vanac, a gol6c llygatrud kylus am lad neu losc neu letrat.

[83] y telir idi] – *I, L*; y telir *M, R, S, Y, LatD;* + ac os g6rya6c vyd her6yd breint y g6r y telir idi *I, J, L, M, Bost, R, S, T, Y, LatD*
[84] *eyeskip in T;* + gan vn ardyrchauel y telir ac os g6ria6c uyd herwyd breint y g6r y telir idi yr eil y6 rodi cussan idi oe hanuod *T*
[85] y] nid amgen nor *LatD*
[86] honno yssyd] – *LatD*
[87] + yw honno hep ostwg, hep dyrchauael *LatD*
[88] ac os g6rya6c ... telir idi] – *I, J, L, M, Bost, R, S, T, Y, LatD*
[89] + yn newyt *LatD*
[90] or collir tr6y greulonder] – *LatD*
[91] tr6y greulonder] – *LatD*
[92] talu c6byl ... a dylyir] – *I, S;* + amdana6 *J; hiatus in O*
[93] + y alanas oll a telir yna *O;* y alanas oll a telir *S*
[94] dyn yn y tir ehunan] – *LatD;* + yssyd *J, L, M, Bost, R, T, Tim, LatD*
[95] + a dotto dyn eu y tir ehunan *LatD*

Q25

There are three incitements to revenge: the wailing of female relatives, and seeing the bier of their relative, and seeing the grave of their relative without compensation.

Q26

Three legal values of a woman's foetus: one is blood before formation; if it is lost through cruelty it is worth forty-eight [pence]. The second is before life enters it, if it is lost through cruelty a third of the *galanas* is paid for it. The third is after life enters it, its full *galanas* ought to be paid if it is lost through cruelty.

Q27

Three fires not subject to law which a man starts in his own land: a muirburn fire from mid-March to mid-April, and the fire of a township kiln, and the fire of a hamlet smithy which is nine paces from the township and has a broom or sod roof upon it.

Q28

Three sights that are accepted in law: a witness's sight in respect of his evidence, and an informant's sight in respect of his information, and the sight of a guilty red-eyed person for homicide or arson or theft.

Q29. P29, C29 Also 122 in Q

[15rb.10] Tri geir kylus yssyd: geir y bo g6eli taua6t, a g6alla6geir yn llys, a thaua6trudyaeth am lad neu losc neu letrat.

Q30. I49, J38, L38, M34, Bost24, N32, O50, P30, R38, S48, T25, Y56, C30, LatD81, 92

[16rb.13] Tri peth ny chyfran brenhin a neb: y eurgra6n, a'e heba6c, a'e leidyr.

Q31. I63, J52, L52, M48, Bost38, N46, O56, P31, R52, S62, T39, Y68, C31

[16rb.16] Tri peth a ha6l dyn yn lletrat ac ny chygein lletrat yndunt: adeilat,[96] a diot coet, ac eredic.

Q32. I146, J116, L116, M110, Bost101, N110, O90,
P32, S145, T103, Tim55, Tr50, Y141, C32, LatD51

[16rb.19] Tri lleidyr camlyryus yssyd: lleidyr ki, a lleidyr llyssyeu yny tyfhont o'r dayar, a lleidyr a tyster[97] arna6 yn g6adu lletrat onys llyssa.

Q33. I147, J117, L117, M111, Bost102, N111, O91, P33, S146,
T104, Tim56, Tr51, Y142, C33, LatD52 [1 2 3 = 1 3 2 I, S]

[16rb.24] Tri lleidyr dir6yus yssyd: lleidyr hyd brenhin g6edy as llatho y g6n, a lleidyr y pallo y reith ida6, a lleidyr a latho ll6dyn y dyn arall yn y ty neu yn y vuarth yn lletrat.[98]

Q34. I148, J118, L118, M112, Bost103, N112, O92,
P34, S147, T105, Tim57, Tr52, Y143, C34, LatD53

[16rb.30] Tri lleidyr g6erth yssyd: lleidyr y kaffer dogyn [16va.1] vanac arna6 tr6y egl6ys, a chytleidyr lleidyr a groccer am letrat, a lleidyr a dalher g6erth pedeir keinha6c ganta6 neu lei[99] o da mar6a6l yn lletrat.

---

[96] – *Y*
[97] a tyster] – *J*
[98] yn lletrat] – *M, Bost*
[99] neu lei] – *O*

Q29

There are three guilty words: a word through which there may be a tongue-wound, and a false word in court, and a guilty red-tongued person for homicide or arson or theft.

Q30

Three things a king does not share with anyone: his treasure trove, and his falcon, and his thief.

Q31

Three things a man prosecutes as theft but they do not constitute theft: building, and removing timber, and ploughing.

Q32

There are three thieves liable to *camlwrw*: a dog-thief, and the thief of herbs where they grow in the earth, and a thief who is testified against while denying theft unless he objects to him [the witness].

Q33

There are three thieves liable to *dirwy*: the thief of a king's hart after his hounds kill it, and a thief whose compurgation fails him, and a thief who kills another person's animal secretly in his house or in his yard.

Q34

There are three thieves liable to be sold: a thief against whom sufficient information has been given by means of a church, and the fellow-thief of a thief hanged for theft, and a thief who is caught with the value of four legal pence or less of goods other than livestock on him as theft.

Q35. *I149, J119, L119, M113, Bost104, N113, O93,*
P35, S148, T106, Tim58, Tr53, Y144, C35, LatD54

[16va.6] Tri lleidyr crogad6y yssyd: lleidyr da by6a6l a dalher vn ll6dyn[100] ar y li6 ganta6, a lleidyr da mar6a6l a dalher g6erth pedeir keinha6c kyfreith ganta6 neu a uo m6y, a lleidyr da by6a6l a dalher croen ar y li6 ganta6, ac ny diheurer am y ll6dyn o g6byl.

Q36. *I150, J120, L120, M114, Bost105, N114, O94,*
P36, S149, T107, Tim59, Tr54, Y145, C36, LatD55

[16va.14] Tri lleidyr a dieinc o letrat kyfadef: reudus a gr6yttro teir tref a na6 tei ym pop tref heb gaffel[101] nac alussen a'e g6areto[102] nac g6estua; kyt dalher a lletrat ymborth,[103] ryd vyd o gyfreith. A g6reic o gyt letrat a'e g6r pria6t.[104] A lleidyr[105] edyn:[106] kyfreith a'e rydha[107] eithyr talu g6erth kyfreith yr edyn a duc[108] o'e perchenna6c.[109]

Q37. *I35, J142, L142, M136, Bost127, O13, P37,*
R20, S35, T129, Tim81, Tr13, C37, LatD30

[16vb.27] Tri pheth a dyly g6arant diball eu g6neuthur: vn y6 g6rtheb[110] yn diohir drosta6 ehun a thros y da kynhennus a thros amdiffynn6r y da.[111] Eil y6 se[17ra.1]uyll 6rth gyfreith a barn dros yr holl dadyl tr6y deturyt g6lat. Trydyd y6 g6neuthur c6byl dros yr holl dadyl val y barnher ida6.

Q38. *I10, 20, J20, L20, M16, Bost7, N14, O6, P38, S20, Tr6, C38*

[22va.30] Tri acha6s yssyd y lyssu tyston: vn y6 galanas heb ym[22vb.1] diu6yn,[112] eil y6 o vot dadyl am tir y rydunt heb teruynu, trydyd y6 kamarueru o vn o 6reic y llall; os eu llyssu a ellir, palledic bydant. Ony ellir,[113] tyston diball vydant.

---

[100] – *Y*
[101] + na charda6t *N*
[102] a'e g6areto] – *M, Bost*
[103] + ganta6 *I, J, M, O, P, S, T, Tr, Y, LatD*
[104] a g6reic ... pria6t] – *S*
[105] – *Y*
[106] + dof *S*
[107] kyfreith a'e rydha] – *I, O, S, Tr, Y*
[108] yr edyn a duc o'e] o'e *I, O, S;* yr edyn *Tr;* y *Y*
[109] + am hynny *M;* + y kyfatef *LatD*
[110] atteb *I, O, Tr*
[111] kynhennus ... y da] – *M*
[112] amdiffyn *J*
[113] +eu llyssu *J, O*

Q35

There are three thieves liable to be hanged: the thief of livestock who is caught with one animal on him upon accusation, and the thief of goods other than livestock who is caught with the value of four legal pence or more on him, and the thief of livestock who is caught with a skin on him upon accusation, and no justification is made for the theft at all.

Q36

Three thieves who escape in spite of an acknowledged theft: a needy person who has travelled three townships and nine houses in each township without obtaining either alms to relieve him or a place offering hospitality; though he may be caught with stolen eatables, he is free by law. And a woman for stealing jointly with her husband. And the stealer of a bird: the law releases him except that he pays the legal worth of the bird which he took from its owner.

Q37

Three things which an efficient guarantor ought to do: one is to answer without delay for himself and for the disputed property and for the defendant of the property. The second is to stand to law and judgement for the whole case through verdict of the country. The third is to do everything for the whole case as he may be adjudged to do.

Q38

There are three reasons to object to witnesses: one is *galanas* without compensation, the second is that there is a case concerning land between them which has not been terminated, the third is one of them misusing the other one's wife; if they can be objected to, they are failed; if objection can be made, they are unfailing witnesses.

Q39. P39, €39 *Also 129 in Q*

[23rb.29] Teir tystolyaeth dilys yssyd: tystolyaeth llys yn d6yn cof; a thystolyaeth [23va.1] g6ybydyeit[114] a gredir pob vn ygkyfreith, megys tat r6ng y deu vab, neu yn lluoessa6c am tir; a thystolyaeth y g6rthtyston.

Q40. P40, €40 *Also 130 in Q*

[23va.5] Tri lle y ty6ys cof llys: am gyfundeb d6y pleit; ac am teruyn dadyl, or da6 kygha6s vn yn dy6edut y theruynu, ac arall yn dy6edut na theruyn6yt; ac am aghyfreith a 6nel argl6yd a'e dyn yn y lys.

Q41. P41, €41 *Also 131 in Q*

[23va.12] Teir tystolyaeth mar6a6l yssyd: tystu ar dyn kyn y holi o'r hyn y tyster, neu tystu ar dyn na 6ad6ys ac nat amdiffyn6ys yr hyn a[115] daroed ida6 y 6adu neu y amdiffyn, neu tystu ar dyn dy6edut yr hyn ny dy6a6t; g6yr llys a[116] bra6t6yr a'e cly6ho a dyly eu d6yn yn var6a6l tr6y arch yr amdiffynn6r, os coffa. A llyna y tri lle y mae trech g6ybydyeit no thyston.

Q42. P42, €42 *Also 132 in Q*

[23va.25] Tri g6ahan yssyd r6g g6ybydyeit a thyston. G6ybydyeit am a vu kyn ymhya6l y dygant tystolyaeth, ac nyt ef y d6c tyston. Eil y6 g6ybydyeit [23vb.1] bieu deturyt eu g6ybot ygkyfreith tyston kyny rytyster[117] udunt, ac nys pieu tyston. Trydyd y6 g6ybydyeit bieu d6yn tystolyaeth yn erbyn g6at ac amdiffyn; sef y6 hynny, g6ybydyeit bieu proui g6ir g6edy geu, ac nys pieu tyston.

---

[114] g6ybyeit *Q*
[115] ar *Q*
[116] ar *P*
[117] thyster *P*

Q39

There are three testimonies which cannot be impugned: the testimony of a court bringing to remembrance; and the testimony of knowers who are believed on their own in law, as that of a father between his two sons, or many for land; and the testimony of the counter-witnesses.

Q40

Three places where the record of the court offers guidance: about an agreement between two parties, and about the conclusion of a case, if the *cyngaws* of one party comes and says that it was concluded, the other saying that it was not concluded; and about an illegality that a lord committed against his man in his court.

Q41

There are three dead testimonies: testifying against a person before claim is made against him in respect of what is testified, or testifying against a person that he neither denied nor defended that which he had already denied or defended, or testifying against a person that he said something which he did not say; the men of the court and the judges that hear them should adjudge them as dead at the request of the defendant, if it [the court] recalls it. And those are the three places where knowers are better than witnesses.

Q42

There are three differences between knowers and witnesses: knowers bring evidence about that which was before accusation, and that is not what witnesses bring. The second is that it is the right of knowers to state their knowledge in the law of witnesses before they are testified against, and it is not the right of witnesses; the third is that it is the right of knowers to bring evidence against denial and defence; that is, knowers have the right to prove truth after falsehood, and it is not the right of witnesses.

Q43. P43, €43 Also 133 in Q

[23vb.8] Teir ford y mae kadarnach g6ybydyeit no thyston: vn y6 gallu d6yn llia6s o 6ybydyeit am vn peth ygkyfreith neu vn g6ybydyat megys mach, ac ny ellir d6yn na m6y na llei no deu o tyston; eil y6 gallu dir6y dyn neu y 6erthu tr6y 6ybydyeit, ac ny ellir tr6y tyston o gyfreith; trydyd y6 gallu ohonu*n*t profi yn erbyn g6at neu amdiffyn, ac nys dicha6n tyston. Pan tysto tyst yn y tystolyaeth peth yn gyfreitha6l y ereill yn erbyn amdiffynn6r, neu amdiffynn6r pan tysto ynteu peth yn gyfreitha6l yn erbyn tyston, yr rei hynny a el6ir g6rthtyston ygkyfreith, ac ny dylyir eu llussu.

Q44. P44, €44 Also 134 in Q

[23vb.28] Teir tystolyaeth yssyd ar eir, ac ny dygir y greir: tystolyaeth lleidyr ar y gytleidyr 6rth y groc, a thy[24ra.1]stolyaeth nyt elher yn y herbyn pan dyccer ar eir, a thystolyaeth g6rthtyston. G6ybydyeit ym pop dadyl grym tyston a gynhalyant a chystal allant ac a diga6n[118] tyston[119] ym pop acha6s.

Q45. I6, J21, L21, M17, Bost8, N15, O7, P45, R21, S6, T8, Tr7, Y12, €45, LatD68

[24va.13] Teir[120] fford y byd ryd mach am dylyet kyfadef: vn y6 am rodi oet heb y ganhat[121] dros yr oet kyntaf, eil y6 o talu y dylyet, trydyd y6 d6yn gauel am y dylyet[122] heb genat y mach.[123]

Q46. I7, J22, L22, M18, Bost9, N16, O8, P46, R22, S7, T9, Tr8, Y13, €46, LatD69

[24vb.20] O teir fford yd oedir mach a chynnogyn: o glybot corn y brenhin yn mynet yn lluyd, ac o ha6l[124] treis, ac o ha6l letrat.

---

[118] a diga6n] ac y dicha6n *P, €*
[119] – *P*
[120] O teir *I, J, L, M, Bost, O, S, Tr, Y*
[121] heb y ganhat] or ha6l6r yr tala6dyr *I;* + y mach *Y*
[122] y gahat … am y dylyet] – *S*
[123] heb genat y mach] – *J, L, M, Bost, N, R, T, Tr*
[124] acha6s *L*

Q43

Three ways knowers are stronger than witnesses. One [of them] is the ability to bring many knowers for one thing in law, or one knower such as a surety, and no more nor less than two witnesses can be brought. The second is the ability to impose a *dirwy*-fine on a man or sell him by knowers, and by law this cannot be done through witnesses. The third is that [knowers] are able to prove against denial and defence, and witnesses may not. When a witness testifies in his testimony to something legally to others against a defendant, or a defendant when he testifies to something legally against witnesses, those ones are called counter-witnesses in law, and they may not be objected to.

Q44

There are three testimonies accepted at their word, and which are not taken to relics: the testimony of a thief on his fellow-thief at the gallows, and a testimony which is not disagreed with when it is stated by word of mouth, and the testimony of counter-witnesses. Knowers have the force of witnesses in every case and they can do as well as a witness can in every case.

Q45

Three ways a surety is released in respect of an acknowledged debt: one is by [his principal] giving a set time without his permission after the original set time, the second is if the debt is paid, the third is that distraint is taken for the debt without the surety's permission.

Q46

In three ways is a [case for] surety and a debtor delayed: by hearing the king's horn going on a hosting, and by a claim for violence, and by a claim for theft.

Q47. J23, L23, M19, Bost10, N17, O9, P47, R23, T10, Tr9, €47, LatD70

[24vb.24] Teir mefel6ryaeth mach yssyd: g6adu y vechni ac ef yn vach, ac adef y vechni ac na allo y chymell, a diebryt y mach g6edy rother.[125]

Q48. P48, S185, Y17, €48

[25va.4] Tri pheth ny dylyir[126] na6d racdunt o bydant adeuedic:[127] goruodogaeth, a mechniaeth, a goresgyn.[128]

Q49. P49, S164, Y16, €49

[25va.29] Tri mach yssyd ny cheiff vn ohonunt d6yn y vechni ar y l6 ehun kyt g6atto [25vb.1] ran ac adef ran arall o'y vechni: vn y6 dyn a el yn vach yn g6yd llys, a mach diebredic, a mach kynnogyn.[129] Beth bynnac a dygo y kyntaf, y llys a dyly tynghu y gyt ac ef neu yn y erbyn. Yr eil y6 neu y trydyd, beth bynnac a tyngon, ar y seithuet o'y gyfnesseiuet o 6yr[130] y t6ng, kanys tala6dyr o gyfreith vyd pop vn ohonunt yn amser kynhognaeth.

Q50. P50, S162, Tim104, €50

[26ra.31] Tri lle ysyd o rodir [26rb.1] meicheu, ny ellir eu g6adu. Vn y6 yg6yd[131] pl6yf, eil y6 y gorssed gyfreitha6l, trydyd y6 yghydrycholder argl6yd, 6rth vot y tri lle hynny yn tri chyhoed kyfreith, ac nat [oes][132] dim a 6neler yghyoed a aller o gyfreith y 6adu. A chyn na dlyo yr amdiffynn6r g6adu y meiche, nyt ydi6 kyfreith yno yn kayu[133] hyt na dylyo y mach g6adu y vynet[134] yn erbyn gyr y rigill. Kanys kyfreith a dy6eit pan 6atto mach y vachniaeth yn erbyn gyr y rigill, rodet y l6 ar y h6echet o 6yr vn vreint ac ef, kany dyly g6rtht6g vot eithyr ar vach am y gyndlyeit, eithyr [mach][135] a el yghyoed, g6adet tr6y deturyt g6lat, eithyr y lle y perthyno cof llys.

---

[125] + yn vach *P*
[126] ny dylyir] nid oes *S*
[127] o bydant adeuedic] gan eu bot yn gyuadefuedic *Y; – S*
[128] + y ran6yr a dyliyr y kredy am pob peth ac aranont kyno hyny *S*
[129] talu *P*
[130] o'y gyfnesseiuet o 6yr] or dynyon nessaf y 6erth *Y*
[131] yghyhoed *S; ynghoed Tim*
[132] *from S, Tim*
[133] katarnhay *Tim*
[134] + yn vach *Tim*
[135] *from S, Tim*

Q47

There are three shames of a surety: denying his surety when he is a surety, acknowledging his surety but he cannot enforce it, and the surety holding back after he has been given.

Q48

Three things against which there ought not to be protection if they are acknowledged: bail, and suretyship, and gaining possession.

Q49

There are three sureties none of whom shall perform his suretyship by his own oath although he should deny part and acknowledge another part of his suretyship: one is a man who becomes a surety in the presence of the court, and a rejected surety, and a debtor surety. Whatever the first swears, the court should swear with him or against him. The second or the third, whatever they swear, he should swear as one of seven of his next of kin, because every one of them shall be a debtor by law at the time when there is liability for debts.

Q50

There are three places where if sureties are given, they cannot be denied. One is before a parish, the second is in a lawful session, the third is in the presence of a lord, because those three places are the three publicities of law, and nothing that is done publicly can be denied by law. And although the defendant is not entitled to deny his suretyship, law there does not close until the surety is not entitled to deny going against the prosecution of the *rhingyll*. For the law states that when a surety denies his suretyship against the prosecution of the *rhingyll*, let him give his oath as one of six men of the same status as himself, because there should not be a counter-oath apart from on a surety for his original obligation, apart from a surety who becomes public, let him make his denial by means of a verdict of the country, except for where the memory of the court is involved.

Q51. I8, J24, L24, M20, Bost11, N18, O10, P51, R24, S8, T11, Tr10, Y14, €51, LatD121

[26va.2] Tri lle yd ymdiueicha mach kyfadef am dylyet aghyvadef: vn y6 o di6at o'r tala6dyr[136] y mach, eil y6 o gaffel tystolyaeth o vn o'r kynnygyn[137] ar y gilyd tr6y ymhya6l yn llys, trydyd y6 o lyssu o vn tyston[138] y llall yn y llys.[139]

Q52. I9, J25, L25, M21, Bost12, N19, O11, P52, R25, S9, T12, Tr11, Y15, €52, LatD122

[26va.9] Tri pheth ny henynt o vechni: agheu,[140] a chleuyt, a charchar.

Q53. [J167], P53, Tim119, €53

[28rb.13] Teir ouer vechni ysyd: vn y6 pan brynho dyn [beth] y gan arall yr aryant, a bot yn ediuar gan berchenna6c yr aryant y gyfne6it.[141] Kany mynn m6ynhau y mach yssyd ida6 ar y peth a brynna6d,[142] ac nat oes vach y'r llall[143] a gymhello ida6 y gyfne6it, 6rth hynny y mae ouer[144] o'r neilltu kany mynn y perchenna6c ef. Yr eil y6 o deruyd y dyn rodi mach y arall ar peth anylys yn rith peth[145] dilys a dyuot perchenna6c y da o'y anylyssu. Ia6n y6 caffael o perchenna6c y da yr eida6, kyt roder mach arna6, cany dylyit y rodi, ac ny dyleir y kych6yn[146] o'r lla6 y mae y[28va.1]ny del ar6ystyl kystal[147] ac ef y'r ar6aessaf. O deruyd y'r ar6aessaf dy6edut ny dyly talu namyn kymeint ac a gauas yr y peth, pa ry6 peth bynnac vo, y kyfreith a dy6eit dyly ohona6 ef [talu] 6erth kyfreith y peth,[148] pa ry6 peth bynnac vo. Ac 6rth na eill kynnal y vechni y mach yd aeth yn vach arnei y gel6ir yn ouer vach. Y da anilys a dy6edyssam ni vchot, p6y bynnac a dyg6ydo[149] am y vechniaeth[150] bit yr argl6yd yn y ol. Trydyd y6 nyt mach mach g6reic. Sef y6 hynny, ny dyly g6reic vot yn vach, cany dyly g6raged g6adu mach, ac ny dyly hitheu reith o 6yr o'e

---

[136] kynnogyn *LatD*
[137] kynnogyn *Q*
[138] tystolaeth *P*
[139] yn y llys] – *I, S, LatD;* y my6n llys *J, O, R T, Tr, Y*
[140] + a ball *LatD*
[141] a bot yn ediuar … gyfne6it] achymryd mach ar y peth ac nachymerer ar yr ariant a bod yn eida6 gan y perchena6c yr ariant kyfne6id *Tim*
[142] kymerth *Tim*
[143] + ar yr aryant *Tim*
[144] + y vach *Tim*
[145] yn rith peth] y 6rth *Tim*
[146] kynogyn *Tim*
[147] kystal] – *Tim*
[148] ny dyly talu namyn … kyfreith y peth] – *Tim*
[149] + yngham *Tim*
[150] kych6nad *Tim*

Q51

Three places an acknowledged surety becomes free of suretyship for an un-acknowledged debt: one is by the creditor denying the surety, the second is by receiving testimony from one of the debtors on the other through accusation in court, the third is by one person objecting to the witness of the other in the court.

Q52

Three things which do not pertain to suretyship: death, and sickness, and imprisonment.

Q53

There are three useless suretyships: one is when someone buys [something] from another for money, and the owner of the money changes his mind about the exchange. Since he does not wish to make use of the surety that he has for the thing that he bought, and the other party has no surety who can enforce the exchange for him, as a consequence the surety from the one side is useless since the owner does not want [to use] him. The second is if it happens that a man gives a surety to another for something which does not belong to him on the basis that it is his and the owner of the goods comes to reclaim it. It is right that the owner should get what is his, though a surety be given for it, since there was no obligation to give it, and it is not right that it should leave the hand in which it is until there comes a substitute of equal value to it to the warrantor. If it happens that the warrantor says that he should only pay as much as he got for the thing, whatever kind of thing it may be, the law says he ought to pay the lawful value of the thing, whatever thing it may be. And as he cannot sustain his suretyship for which he became a surety he is called a useless surety. The goods that he did not own which we mentioned above, let the lord pursue whoever should be found to be at fault concerning their change of possession. The third is that a woman's surety is not a surety. That is, a woman is not entitled to be a surety, since women are not enti-tled to deny a surety, and she is not entitled to have men as compurgators to deny it. The law says that the surety that a woman gives is a surety, because whoever can reclaim ownership of goods, the law says that it is lawful for him to transfer [ownership which is immune from claim]. Since a woman can reclaim goods, the law says that it is necessary to have from her a surety as to immunity from claim, and since it is a man that she is denying, she is entitled to have men along with her to deny a surety.

6adu[151] hi. Y kyfreith a dy6eit bot yn vach y mach a rodo g6reic, canys p6y bynnac a allo anylyssu da, kyfreith a dy6eit bot yn ia6n yda6 y dylyssu.[152] A chanys g6reic a eill anylyssu da, y kyfreith a dy6eit vot yn reit [mach] ar dilysr6yd y genthi hitheu, canys g6r a 6atta hy, g6yr a dyly y gyt a hi y 6adu mach.[153]

Q54. P54, S204, €54

[31rb.16] Tri peth y kyll dyn y ha6l,[154] er daet vo y defnyd:[155] llys kynn amser, a thyst ar vach, a chad6 g6edy g6rtheb.

Q55. I37, J26, L26, M22, Bost13, N20, O12, P55, R26, S37, [247], T13, [Tim128], Tr12, Y44, €55,
LatD17

[32vb.6] Tri ry6 dir6y yssyd: vn o ymlad, ac arall o treis,[156] tryded o[157] letrat.

S37
Teir dir6y brenhin ynt: dir6y ymlad kyfadef, a dir6y treis, a dir6y lledrat. Dif6yn dir6y ymlad, deudec mu. Dif6yn dir6y treis mor6ynn y6 g6yalen aryant a ffiol eur a chla6r eur val y dy6esp6yt am eu messureu yn dif6yn sarhaet y brenhin. Dif6yn dir6y letrat y6 kyss6ynna6 lletrat ar y dyn, a g6ady ohona6 yn da ar y tafa6t, a gossot reith arna6 a'e phallu – lleidyr kyfadef kan pall6ys y reith g6iryon o'e pen ehunan a'e tafa6t, ny delit yn y la6, ny chaffat[158] dim ganta6 – deudec mu dir6y arna6.

---

[151] o'e 6adu] ygyd a *Tim*
[152] anilyssu *P*
[153] canys g6r … 6adu mach] kanys g6yr a 6atta machniaeth y gyd a hytheu *Tim*
[154] y kyll dyn y ha6l] yssyd y dychon y dyn golli y dadyl ohonynt *S*
[155] + o 6ir a chyf' sef ynt y tri hynny *S*
[156] ac arall o treis] a dir6y treis *P*
[157] tryded o] a dir6y *P*
[158] chanhat *S*

Q54

Three things for which a man loses his claim, however good his substance: an objection before time, and a witness on a surety, and keeping after refusal.

Q55

There are three kinds of *dirwy*: one for fighting, and another for violence, a third for theft.

S37

There are three fines of a king: a fine for public fighting, and a fine for violence, and a fine for theft. The payment for the fine for fighting, twelve kine. The payment for the fine for raping a maiden is a silver rod and a gold cup and a gold lid as was said regarding the measures for the expiation of the *sarhaed* of a king. The payment for the fine for theft arises from swearing theft on a man, and he makes a good denial by his tongue, and a compurgation is set on him and it fails – [he is] an admitted thief since his compurgation has failed [but] an innocent from his own mouth and his tongue, with nothing caught in his hand, and nothing received from him – a fine of twelve kine upon him.

Q *Triad Collection*

Q56. *I38, J27, L27, M23, N21, O39, P56, R27, S38, [235], T14, Tr40, Y45, €56,* LatD71

[35rb.6] Teir r6yt brenhin ynt: y teulu, ac all6est y veirch, a'e preidoed[159] g6arthec; pedeir keina6c kyfreith a geiff y brenhin o pop[160] eidon a gaffer ym plith y[161] 6arthec,[162] ac velly o pop march a gaffer ym plith[163] y veirch.[164]

Q57. *I39, J28, L28, M24, Bost14, N22, O40, P57, R28, S39, [236], T15, Tr41, Y46, €57,* LatD72

[33rb.15] Teir r6yt breyr ynt: all6est y veirch, a'e preid 6arthec, a'e genuein voch; o pop ll6dyn a gaffer yn eu plith oc eu kyfry6, pedeir keinha6c kyfreith a geiff y breyr.

Q58. *I40, J29, L29, M25, Bost15, N23, O41, P58, R29, S40, [237], T16, Tr42, Y47, €58,* LatD73

Teir r6yt taya6c ynt: y 6arthec, a'e voch, a'e hentref; o pop ll6dyn a gaffer yn eu plith o galan Mei[165] hyt amser medi, pedeir keina6c[166] a geiff y taya6c.

Q59. *I41, J30, L30, M26, Bost16, N24, O42, P59, R30, S41, T17, Tr43, Y48, €59,* LatD74

Tri chorn buelyn y brenhin: y gorn kyfed, a'y gorn ke6eithias, a'y gorn hely yn [33va.1] lla6 y penkynyd; punt a tal pop vn ohonunt.

Q60. *I42, J31, L31, M27, Bost17, N25, O43, P60, R31, S42, T18, Tr44, Y49, €60,* LatD75

Teir telyn kyfreitha6l yssyd: telyn brenhin, a thelyn penkerd, 6heugeint a tal pop vn o'r d6y hynny, [kyweirgorn pob vn deudec keinya6c a dal];[167] a thelyn vchel6r, trugeint a tal, a'e chy6eirgorn, pedeir keinha6c kyfreith a tal.[168]

---

[159] Preid *I, O, Tr, Y*
[160] + march ac *I, S*
[161] + veirch ae *S*
[162] 6arthec] veirch *T*
[163] y 6arthec ... ym plith] – *I, T*
[164] ac velly ... veirch] + ae 6arthec *I;* – *T, S*
[165] gayaf *Y*
[166] + cotta *I, S*
[167] – *Q, €, P*
[168] – *I, M, Bost*

Q *Triad Collection*

Q56

These are the three nets of a king: his warband, and his stud, and his herds of cattle; the king receives four legal pennies for every bovine found amongst his cattle, and the same for every horse found amongst his stud.

Q57

These are the three nets of a nobleman: his stud, and his herd of cattle, and his herd of pigs: for every similar animal found amongst them, the nobleman receives four legal pennies.

Q58

These are the three nets of a bondsman: his cattle, and his pigs, and his winter dwelling; for every animal found amongst them from May Day until the time of harvesting, the bondsman receives four pennies.

Q59

Three buffalo horns of the king: his drinking horn, and the horn of his retinue, and his hunting horn in the hand of the chief huntsman; each one is worth a pound.

Q60

There are three legal harps: the harp of a king, and the harp of a chief poet, each one is worth 120 pence, and the tuning-horn of each one is worth twelve pence; and the harp of a nobleman, it is worth sixty [pence], and its tuning-horn, it is worth four legal pennies.

Q61. I43, J32, L32, M28, Bost18, N26, O44, P61, R32, S43, T19, Tr45, Y50, €61, LatD76

Tri pheth nyt ryd y vilaen eu g6erthu heb gynnat y argl6yd: march, a moch, a mel; os g6rthyt yr argl6yd gyssefin, g6erthet ynteu[169] y'r neb y mynno.

Q62. I44, J33, L33, M29, Bost19, N27, O45, P62, R33, S44, [253],
T20, Tim134, Tr46, Y51, €62, LatD77 *[1 2 3 = 1 3 2 I, S, Y]*

Teir keluydyt ny eill[170] taya6c eu dyscu y vab heb ganhat y argl6yd: yscolheicta6t, a gofanyaeth, a bardoniaeth; canys o diodef yr argl6yd hyt pan rother corun y'r yscolheic, neu yny el gof yn y eueil, neu vard 6rth y gerd, ny dicha6n eu keithi6a6 g6edy hynny.

Q63. I45, J34, L34, M30, Bost20, N28, O46, P63, R34, T21, Tr47, Y52, €63, LatD10 [1 2 3 = 1 3 2 Y]

Teir kyflauan, os g6na dyn yn y 6lat, y dyly y vab colli tref y tat o'e hacha6s o gyfreith: llad y argl6yd,[171] a llad y penkenedyl, a llad y teispantyle, rac trymhet y kyflaua[33vb.1]neu hynny.

Q64. I46, J35, L35, M31, Bost21, N29, O47, P64, R35, S45, [222], T22, Y53, €64, LatD78

Tri anhepcor brenhin ynt: yffeirat y ganu offeren ac y vendiga6 y v6yt a'e lyn, a'e vra6t6r llys[172] y varnu brodyeu ac y rodi kyghoreu, a'e teulu 6rth 6neuthur negesseu y brenhin.[173]

Q65. I47, J36, L36, M32, Bost22, N30, O48, P65, R36, S46, T23, Y54, €65, LatD79

Tri anhebcor breyr:[174] y telyn,[175] a'e vryccan, a'e galla6r.[176]

Q66. I48, J37, L37, M33, Bost23, N31, O49, P66, R37, S47, T24, Y55, €66, LatD80

Tri anhebccor taya6c:[177] y gafyn, a'e trothy6, a'e talbren.

---

[169] − *I, J, O, Y*
[170] ny eill taya6c eu dyscu] nys dysc taya6c *I, S, Y*
[171] *Hiatus here in Tr*
[172] − *M*
[173] negesseu y brenhin] negesseu *I; − S;* negesseu yr argl6yd *Y*
[174] + ynt *I, J, M, O, S, Y*
[175] teulu *Q;* teulyn *M, O*
[176] ta6lbord *I, S*
[177] + ynt *I, J, M, Bost, O, S*

Q61

Three things a bondsman is not free to sell without the permission of his lord: a horse, and pigs, and honey; if the lord refuses [to buy them] first of all, let him [the bondsman] sell them to whomsoever he wishes.

Q62

Three crafts a bondsman may not teach his son without the permission of his lord: clerkship, and smithcraft, and poetry; for if the lord allows it until a clerk is tonsured, or until a blacksmith enters his smithy, or a poet [enters upon] poetry, it is not possible to reduce them to bondage after that.

Q63

Three offences for which, if a person commits them in his own country, his son should lose his patrimony because of them by law: killing his lord, and killing the head of kindred, and killing the representative, because of the seriousness of those offences.

Q64

These are the three indispensables of a king: a priest to sing mass and to bless his food and drink, and his court judge to judge judgements and to give advice, and his warband carrying out the requirements of the king.

Q65

Three indispensables of a nobleman: his harp, and his blanket, and his cooking pot.

Q66

Three indispensables of a bondsman: his trough, and his threshold, and his hearth-log.

Q67. I53, J43, L43, M39, Bost29, N37, P67, R43, S52, T30, Y60, €67, LatD84

Tri ofer ymadra6d a dy6edir[178] ac ny ffynyant: g6at kyn deturyt, a llys kyn amser, cof[179] a chygha6s g6edy bra6t.

Q68. I54, J44, L44, M40, Bost30, N38, P68, R44, S53, T31, €68, LatD85

Tri over llaeth yssyd: llaeth kath, a llaeth gast, a llaeth kassec; cany di6gir dim ymdanunt.

Q69. I50, J39, L39, M35, Bost25, N33, O51, P69, R39, S49, T26, Y57, €69, LatD82 [1 2 3 = 3 2 1 I; 2 1 3 S; also, the second sentence of the second limb is found as the fourth sentence of the second limb in S and I]

Tri phet6ar yssyd. Kyntaf ynt; pet6ar acha6s yd ymchoelir bra6t: o ofyn g6yr kadarn, a chas galon, a charyat kyfeillon, a serch da. Eil y6 pedeir taryan a a r6g dyn a reith g6lat rac ha6l letrat: vn y6 cad6 g6estei yn gyfreitha6l, nyt amgen no'e gad6 o pryt gorchyfaer6y hyt y bore, a dodi y la6 drosta6 o'e gy6e[34ra.1]ly teir g6eith y nos honno a hynny tygu ohona6 a dynyon y ty[180] yn reith.[181] Eil y6 geni a meithrin: tygu o'r perchenna6c ar y trydyd o 6yr vn vreint ac ef g6elet geny yr aneueil a'e veithrin ar y hel6 heb y vynet y 6rth[182] teir nos nac o rod nac o 6erth. Trydyd y6 g6arant. Pet6ryd y6 kad6 kyn coll, a hynny g6neuthur o'r dyn ar y trydyd o 6yr vn vreint ac ef kyn colli o'r llall y da bot y da h6nn6 ar y hel6 ef. Nyt oes 6arant namyn hyt[183] ar teir lla6, ac yna amdiffynnet y tryded tr6y gyfreith. Trydyd pet6ar y6 pet6ar dyn nyt oes udunt nawd[184] nac yn llys nac yn llan rac brenhin: dyn a torro na6d brenhin yn vn o'r teir g6yl arbennyc yn y llys; eil y6 dyn a 6ystler o'e vod y'r brenhin; trydyd y6 y g6ynossa6c,[185] y neb a dylyo y borthi y nos honno ac nys portho;[186] pet6ryd y6 y gaeth.[187]

---

[178] + yn llys *I, J, L,R, S;* + yn datleu *LatD*
[179] – *I, O, S, Y*
[180] + honno *M;* + ohonaw *LatD*
[181] yn reith] ganta6 *I, S, Y;* ganta6 yny reith *O;* + honno *M, Bost*
[182] y 6rth] y 6rtha6 *N, P, €;* – *R, Y*
[183] llyt *Q*
[184] *Later gloss in Q*
[185] + brenhin *LatD*
[186] ac nys portho] – *Y*
[187] pet6ryd y6 y gaeth] – *I*

Q67

Three useless statements which are made and which do not succeed: a denial before verdict, and an objection before time, record and argument after judgement.

Q68

There are three useless milks: the milk of a cat, and the milk of a bitch, and the milk of a mare; for there is no compensation for any of them.

Q69

There are three fours. These are the first; the four cases where judgement is overturned: for the fear of strong men, and hatred of enemies, and the love of friends, and lust for goods. The second is the four shields which come between a man and compurgation of the country for a claim of theft: one is keeping a guest legally, namely keeping him from the evening meal until the morning, and his bedfellow putting his hand over him three times that night and those things to be sworn by him with the men of the house as a body of compurgators. The second is birth and rearing: the owner swearing as one of three men of the same status as himself that he saw the birth of the animal and that it was reared in his possession without it leaving him for three nights neither by gift nor selling. The third is warranty. The fourth is keeping before loss, that is swearing by the man as one of three men of the same status as him that before the other one lost the goods those goods were in his possession. There is no warranty except up to three hands, and then let the third defend by means of law. The third four are the four persons for whom there is no protection from the king either in court nor church: a person who breaks the king's protection in one of the three special feasts in the court; the second is a person who is given as a voluntary hostage to the king; the third is his [the king's] supper-giver, the person who ought to feed him that night and who does not feed him; the fourth is his slave.

Q70. *I56, J46, L46, M42, Bost32, N40, P70, R46, S55, T33, Y62, €70, LatD87 [1 2 3 = 1 3 2 1, S, Y]*

Teir palua6t ny di6ygir: vn argl6yd ar y 6r yn y ryoli yn[188] dyd kat ac br6ydyr, ac
vn tat ar y vab yr y gosbi, ac vn [34rb.1] penkenedyl ar y gar yn y gyghori.

Q71. *I57, J47, L47, M43, Bost33, N41, O106, P71, R47, S56, T34, Y63, €71 [1 2 3 = 1 3 2 N]*

[34rb2–13] Teir g6raged a dyly eu meibon tref eu mam: g6reic a rother tros y that
yng g6ystyl, a chaffel mab ohonei yn y g6ystyloryaeth; a g6reic a rother o rod
kenedyl y alltut; a g6reic a lather[189] g6r o'e chenedyl, a dial o'e mab[190]
h6nn6,[191] ny dylyir y oedi am tref y vam, nac aros nauetdyd yn y erbyn.

Q72. *I60, J49, L49, M45, Bost35, N44, P72, R49, S59, T36, Y65, €72, LatD89*

Tri che6ylid kenedyl ynt ac o acha6s g6reic y maent:[192] llathrudra6[193] o'e hanuod;
eil y6 d6yn o'r g6r 6reic[194] arall ar y pen y'r ty; trydyd y6 y hyspeila6.

Q73. *I61, J50, L50, M46, Bost36, N44, O54, P73, R50, S60, T37, Y66, €73, LatD90*

Tri chadarn enllip g6reic ynt: vn y6 g6elet y g6r a'r 6reic yn dyuot o'r vn ll6yn
vn o pop parth y'r ll6yn,[195] eil y6 eu kaffel ell deu dan vn vantell, trydyd y6
g6elet y g6r[196] r6g deu uord6yt y 6reic.

Q74. *I64, J53, L53, M49, Bost39, N47, O57, 99, P74, R53, S63, I66, 205, T40, Y69, €74*

[34rb.25] Tri meib yssyd ny dylyant gyfran o dir y gan eu brodyr vn uam vn tat
ac 6ynt: mab a gaffer yn ll6yn ac ym perth ac yn anedua6l, a g6edy hy*n*ny

---

[188] di6ygir ... ryoli yn] – *M*
[189] a lather] – *M, Bost*
[190] hitheu *J*
[191] *Hiatus in O*
[192] + ell tri vn y6 *I, Y;* + eill tri *S*
[193] + g6reic *I, J, L, N, Bost, T, Y, LatD*
[194] o'r g6r 6reic] or g6r 6r6eic *Q;* – *I, S*
[195] ida6 *I, M, Bost*
[196] g6elet y g6r] – *Bost*

Q70

Three blows for which there is no compensation: that of a lord to his man to control him in a day of battle and fighting, and that of a father to his son to punish him, and that of a head of kindred to his kinsman whilst advising him.

Q71

Three women whose sons are entitled to the inheritance of their mother: a woman who is given as a hostage on behalf of her father, and she has a son during that hostageship; and a woman who is given by gift of kin to an alien; and a woman from whose kindred a man is killed, and her son avenges him, there should be no delaying him concerning the inheritance of his mother, nor waiting until the ninth day to receive it.

Q72

These are the three shames of a kindred and they are because of a woman: abducting her against her will; the second is if her husband brings another woman to the house to encounter her; the third is to despoil her.

Q73

These are the three strong scandals of a woman: one is seeing the man and the woman emerging from the same bush one on either side of the bush, the second is finding them both under one blanket, the third is seeing the man between the two thighs of the woman.

Q74

There are three sons who are not entitled to a share of land from their brothers of the same mother and same father as them: a son who is begotten by bush and

kymryt y vam[197] o rod kene[34va.1]dyl a chaffel[198] mab arall;[199] ny dyly h6nn6
kyffranu tir a'r mab a gahat kyn noc ef yn ll6yn ac ym perth. Yr eil y6 kymryt
o yscolheic 6reic[200] o rod kenedyl[201] a chaffel mab oho*n*ei,[202] ac odyna kymryt
o'r yscolheic urdeu[203] offeiriadaeth,[204] ac odyna kaffel mab[205] o'r vn[206] 6reic o'r
offeirat;[207] ny dyly y mab a gahat kyn noc ef[208] kyfranu tir a h6nn6, canys yn
erbyn dedyf y kahat.[209] Trydyd y6 mut kany dyly tir[210] nyt atteppo drosta6,[211]
kany[212] rodir g6lat y vut.[213]

S166

Tri meib yssyd ni dylyant gaffel ran o deref eu tadeu her6yd k*yfreith*, nid
amgen: mab effeirad a eniller g6edy ymr6yma6 mewn vrdeu effeiriadaeth.
Eil y6 mab claf6r a eniller g6edy g6ahaner y 6rth y bobyl o blegid clefri.
Trydyd y6 mab a dalo y dat y dir dros gelein yn*n* waettir er hed6ch y'r mab
val y'r tad.

S205

Tri brodyr y dyly vn o honynt dref y dad ac nis dyly y deu ereill, ac yn*n* vn
vam ac yn*n* vn dad, o'r vn g6r priod ac o'r vn 6reic briod: sef y6 yr vn a'e
keiff, dianaf; sef y6 vn o'r deu ereill, myd; arall y6 klaf g6an; seff fford y
difer[n]ir y klaf g6ahan, am na hein6 or byd; trydyd y6 myd kan*n*s
agh6byl y6 o dafa6d, ac ny dyly ynteu vod yn vra6d6r, kans ni ellir c6byl
o agh6byl, ac 6rth hynny nid dyn ynteu, ac am nad dyn ef, ny dyly vod
yn*n* vra6d6r.

---

[197] + y mab or g6r *I*
[198] + y *Q, C, N*
[199] + ohonunt *I, S*
[200] – *P*
[201] kenedyli *Q*
[202] n *in later hand Q*
[203] – *Y*
[204] ac odyna … offeiriadaeth] – *O57*
[205] + arall *O99;* ohona6 *M, Bost*
[206] – *O99*
[207] mab o'r … offeirat] – *I;* mab ohonaw or vn 6reic *M*
[208] a gahat kyn noc ef] – *M, Bost*
[209] canys … kahat] – *I, S*
[210] dyly tir] rodir y neb *O99*
[211] kany dyly … drosta6] – *M*
[212] ac ny *O99*
[213] kany … vut] – *I, S*

brake and illegally, and after that his mother is taken by gift of kin and has another son; that one is not entitled to share land with the son that was begotten before him in bush and brake. The second is when a cleric takes a woman by gift of kin and has a son by her, and after that the cleric takes the orders of priesthood, and after that the priest has a son by the same woman; the son that was begotten before him should not have to share land with the other, because he was conceived contrary to law. The third is a mute as no one is entitled to land that they cannot answer for, since lordship is not given to a mute.

S166

There are three sons who are not entitled to a share of their fathers' land according to law, namely: the son of a priest whom he begets after binding himself to the orders of priesthood. The second is the son of a leper who is begotten after he is separated from his people because of leprosy. The third is a son whose father pays his land for a killing as blood land to obtain peace for the son as for the father.

S205

Three brothers one of whom is entitled to his father's land and the others are not entitled, and they are from one father one mother, by the same married man and by the same married woman: this is what the one who gets it is, the unblemished one; this is what one of the other two is, a mute; another is a separated leper; this is why the separated leper is deprived by a judgement, as he is not of this world; the third is a mute because he is incomplete of speech, and he also should not be a judge, as complete cannot be obtained from incomplete, and because of that also he is not a full person, and as he is not a full person, he is not entitled to be a judge.

Q75. I59, J54, L54, M50, [Bost40], N48, O58, P75, R54, S58, T41, Y70, €75, LatD93

Tri dyn a gynnyd eu breint yn vn dyd: taya6ctref y kyssegrer egl6ys yndi gan ganhat y brenhin; dyn o'r tref honno a uei y bore yn taya6c a'r nos honno yn 6r ryd. Eil y6 dyn y rodo y brenhin vn o'r pedeir s6yd ar hugeint llys brenhinya6l ida6: kyn rodi y s6yd ida6, yn taya6c, ac g6edy y rodi yn 6r ryd. Trydyd y6 yscolheic: y dyd y[214] kaffo corun, yn vab taya6c, a'r nos honno, yn 6r ryd.

Q76. I66, J56, L56, M52, [Bost42], N50, P76, R56, S65, T43, Y72, €76, LatD104

[34va.30] O tri mod y g6edir kyss6ynplant o genedyl. [34vb.1] Vn y6, y neb a dy6etter y vot yn tat ida6, o byd by6 ef, a eill y 6adu ar y l6 ehunan. Ony byd by6 y tat, penkenedyl [a seith law kenedyl][215] ganta6 a'e g6atta. Ony byd penkenedyl, ll6 deg6yr a deugeint o'r genedyl a'e g6atta.[216] Ac velly mam neu genedyl mam a dicha6n d6yn y kyfry6 etiued h6nn6 y genedyl gan y odef udunt. Ny dyly pra6f vot o pleit etiued kyss6yn yn erbyn g6at c6byl o'r parth arall, namyn pra6f a dyly bot gan y odef o'r pleit arall, canys godef ym pop peth a tyrr y gygha6s. Os g6reic a'e d6c ef, tyget ar alla6r gyssegredic, ony chredir heb y th6g, neu ony 6edir c6byl yn y herbyn.

Q77. I67, J57, L57, M53, Bost43, N51, P77, R57, S66, T44, Y73, €77, LatD96

Teir gormes doeth ynt: medda6t, a godineb, a dryc anyan.

Q78. I68, J58, L58, M54, Bost44, N52, P78, R58, S67, T45, Y74, €78, LatD31, 97

Tri dyn a dyly tauodya6c yn llys y gan y brenhin:[217] g6reic, ac alltut agyfyeithus, a chryc anyana6l. Vn dyn a dyly de6is y tafodya6c: argl6yd.[218]

---

[214] kynn *J, L*
[215] a seith law kenedyl] – *Q, €*
[216] Ony byd ... g6atta] – *M*
[217] y gan y brenhin] drostunt *I, S, LatD*; – *L, N*
[218] + ac ef a dyly kymell yr rei ereill tauodogyon *J*

Q75

Three men whose status increases in one day: a bond township in which a church is consecrated by the permission of the king; a man of that township may be a bondsman in the morning and that evening may be a free man. The second is a man to whom the king gives one of the twenty-four royal court offices: before being given the office, he is a bondsman, and after being given it a free man. The third is a cleric: the day he is tonsured, the son of a bondsman, and that evening, a free man.

Q76

In three ways assigned children are denied by a kindred. One is, the one who is said to be his father, if that person be alive, may deny the child by his own oath. Unless the father is alive, the head of kindred and seven hands of the kindred with him deny him. Unless there is a head of kindred, the oath of fifty men from the kindred shall deny him. And thus a mother or a mother's kindred may affiliate such an heir as that one to his kindred by their suffering him. There is no entitlement to offer proof on the part of a reputed heir against a complete denial from the other side, but a proof is entitled to be given if he was suffered by the other side, as suffering in everything overrides the plea. If a woman affiliates him, let her swear on a consecrated altar, unless she is believed without her oath, or unless the whole case is denied against her.

Q77

These are the three oppressors of the wise: drunkenness, and adultery, and bad temper.

Q78

Three persons who are entitled to a representative on their behalf in court from the king: a woman, and an alien of foreign speech, and a congenital stammerer. One man is entitled to choose the representative: a lord.

Q79. 169, J59, L59, M55, Bost45, N53, P79, R59, S68, T46, Y75, €79, LatD98 [1 2 3 = 1 3 2 P]

Tri ll6dyn digyfreith eu g6eithret[219] ar[220] aniueileit mut:[221] ystal6yn, a thar6 trefgord, a baed ken[35ra.1]uein. Digyfreith heuyt y6 g6eithret tar6 tra geisso[222] g6arthec g6assa6t o galan Mei hyt galan gayaf,[223] ac ystal6yn tra geisso kessyc g6ynhed, a baed tra uo llodigr6yd ar y moch y bo arnunt; ny di6ygant a 6nelh6ynt yna.

Q80. 170, J60, L60, M56, Bost46, N54, P80, R60, S69, T47, Y76, €80, LatD99

Tri ll6dyn nyt oes 6erth kyfreith arnunt: kny6 h6ch, a bitheiat, a charl6nc.

Q81. 171, J61, L61, M57, Bost47, N55, P81, R61, S70, [219], T48, Y77, €81, LatD100

Tri g6aet digyfreith yssyd: g6aet o pen[224] crach, a g6aet deint,[225] a g6aet tr6yn, onyt tr6y lit y gollygir.[226]

Q82. 173, J63, L63, M59, Bost49, N57, P82, R63, S72, T50, Tim2, Y79, €82, LatD101

Tri edyn y dyly y brenhin eu g6erth py tu bynnac y llather: heba6c, a g6alch, a chicuran; perchenna6c y tir y llather arna6 a dyly dec a deugeint y gan y neb a'e llatho.

Q83. 174, J64, L64, M60, Bost50, N58, O60, P83, R64, S73, T51, Tim3, Y80, €83, LatD102

Tri phryf[227] y dyly y brenhin eu g6erth py tu bynnac y llather: llostlydan, a beleu, a charl6nc;[228] canys oc eu cr6yn[229] y g6neir amaer6yeu[230] y dillat y brenhin.

---

[219] eu g6eithret] – *I, Y*
[220] or *Q, €, P, Y*
[221] + yssyt *M, Bost*
[222] tra geissio] trae *P*
[223] Digyureith....gaeaf] Kanys ryd vyd y tar6 o galan mei hyt galan gayaf tra vo yn keissa6 g6arthec g6assa6t *I, S*
[224] + dyn *LatD*
[225] a g6aet deint] – *S*
[226] onyt tr6y lit y gollygir] ony thre6ir tr6y lit *I, Y*
[227] tri phryf] triffeth y *Y*
[228] char *L, Tim*
[229] oc eu cr6yn] ohonunt *J, L, M, R, T, Tim, Y, LatD;* oc eu dillat *O*
[230] amaer6yeu] amry6 *S (but corrected in margin)*

Q79

Three animals whose behaviour towards mute animals is not subject to law: a stallion, and a township bull, and a herd boar. Neither is the behaviour of a bull whilst it seeks cows in heat from May Day until Halloween, and a stallion whilst it seeks mares in heat, and a boar whilst the sows over whom he presides are in heat subject to law; there is no compensation for what they do in those cases.

Q80

Three animals that do not have a legal value: a young sow, and a baying-hound, and a stoat.

Q81

There are three bloods not subject to law: blood from the head of a scab, and blood from a tooth, and blood from the nose, unless they are lost through anger.

Q82

Three birds to whose value the king is entitled wherever they are killed: a falcon, and a hawk, and a raven; the owner of the land on which they are killed is entitled to fifty [pence] from whoever kills them.

Q83

Three animals to whose value the king is entitled wherever they are killed: a beaver, and a marten, and a stoat; because from their skins the borders for the king's clothes are made.

Q84. I75, J65, L65, M61, Bost51, N59, O61, P84, R65, S74, T53, Tim4, Y81, €84, LatD103

Tri pheth ny at kyfreith eu damd6ng: bla6t, a g6enyn, ac aryant;[231] canys kyffelyp [35rb.1] a geffir udunt.

Q85. I76, J66, L66, M62, Bost52, N60, O62, P85, R66, S75, T52, Tim5, Y83, €85, LatD105

Tri phren yssyd ryd eu llad[232] yn fforest y brenhin:[233] pren crip egl6ys, a phren peleidyr a 6neler reit y brenhin ohonunt, a phren elor.

Q86. I77, J67, L67, M63, Bost53, N61, O63, P86, R67, S76, T54, Tim6, Y84, €86, LatD15

Tri chehyryn canastyr yssyd: vn y6 lletrat, y fford y kerdo[234] kyfran ohona6, canys na6 affeith yssyd ida6; eil y6 hyd brenhin, p6y bynnac a 6nel cam ymdana6;[235] trydyd y6 abo bleid, y neb a 6nel cam ymdana6.[236]

Q87. I78, J68, L68, M64, Bost54, N62, O64, P87, R68, S77, T55, Tim7, Y85, €87, LatD106

Tri pheth a tyrr ar gyfreith: amot,[237] a defa6t gyfya6n, ac agheu.[238]

Q88. I79, J69, L69, M65, Bost55, N63, O65, P88, R69, S78, T56, Tim8, Y86, €88, LatD107

Tri edyn ny dylyir eu llad ar tir dyn arall heb ganhat: eryr, a garan, a chicuran; y neb a'e llatho,[239] talet dec a deugeint aryant[240] y perchenna6c y tir.

Q89. I80, J70, L70, M66, Bost56, N64, P89, R70, S79, [257], T57, Tim9, 138, Y87, €89, LatD108

Tri pheth, or keffir ar fford, nyt reit atteb y neb ohonunt: pedol, a not6yd, a cheinha6c.

---

[231] + bath *J, M, P, R, T, Tim, LatD*
[232] ryd eu llad] – *P*; ryd *I, S, Y*
[233] + yn ryd eu llad *P*
[234] + ran a *O*
[235] p6y ... ymdana6] y neb ae kyllello *I, S*
[236] + tri kyureithawl ynt *LatD*
[237] am *Y*
[238] aghen *T, L*
[239] + vn ohonunt *I, S*
[240] – *I, S, LatD*

Q84

Three things on which law does not allow sworn appraisal: flour, and bees, and silver; for similar to them are to be had.

Q85

Three timbers which are free to be felled in the king's forest: the timber for the ridge of a church, and the timber for shafts by which the king's need is met, and the timber of a bier.

Q86

There are three muscles of a hundred hands: one is theft, the way sharing it travels, for there are nine abetments for it; the second is the hart of the king, whoever does wrong concerning it; the third is the prey of a wolf, whoever does wrong concerning it.

Q87

Three things that override law: contract, and a just custom, and death.

Q88

Three birds that ought not be killed on another man's land without permission: an eagle, and a heron, and a raven; whoever may kill them, let him pay fifty pieces of silver to the owner of the land.

Q89

Three things for which, if they are found on the road, no one need answer: a horseshoe, and a needle, and a penny.

Q90. I81, J71, L71, M67, Bost57, N65, P90, R71, S80, 176, T58, Tim10, Y88, €90, LatD110

Tri dyn[241] ny dyly y brenhin[242] eu g6erthu: lleidyr g6edy y barner y'r groc,[243] a chynll6yn6r,[244] a brad6r argl6yd.

Q91. I82, J72, L72, M68, Bost58, N66, P91, R72, S81, T59, Tim11, Y89, €91, LatD111

[35va.1] Tri en6 righyll yssyd: 'g6aed[245] g6lat', a 'gar6 gych6edyl g6as y kyghella6r', a righyll.

Q92. I83, J73, L73, M69, Bost59, N67, P92, R73, S82, T60, Tim12, Y90, €92, LatD112 [1 2 3 = 1 3 2 M, Bost]

Tri ergyt ny thelir dim ymdanunt:[246] y gar6 yn yt, ac y gi yn yt, ac y eba6l g6yllt yn yt.[247]

Q93. I84, J74, L74, M70, Bost60, N68, P93, R74, S83, T61, Tim13, Y91, €93, LatD113 [1 2 3 = 2 1 3 L, Tim]

Tri chyfr6ch dirgel a dyly y brenhin y gaffel heb y ygnat: gyt a'e offeirat, a chyt a'e 6reic, a chyt a'e uedic.

Q94. I85, J75, L75, M71, Bost61, N69, P94, R75, S84, T62, Tim14, Y92, €94, LatD114 [1 2 3 = 1 3 2 I, J, L, R, S, T, Tim, Y, LatD; 3 2 M, Bost]

Teir not6yd kyfreitha6l yssyd: not6yd g6enia6l y vrenhines,[248] a not6yd y penkynyd y 6nia6[249] y k6n r6ygedic, a not6yd y medic y 6nia6 g6elioed. G6erth pop vn o'r rei hynny:[250] pedeir keina6c kyfreith.[251] Not6yd g6reic ky6rein arall keinha6c kyfreith a tal.[252]

---

[241] ffeth *Y*
[242] dyly y brenhin] ny myn kyfreith *S176*
[243] g6edy y barner y'r groc] or byd g6erth pedeir ke. k. yny la6 yn gyfadef *S176*
[244] + y veistir *S176*
[245] gwaet *O*
[246] thelir dim ymdanunt] di6ygir *I, Y*
[247] y gi … yn yt] – *T*
[248] not6yd … vrenhines] – *M*
[249] iachau *LatD*
[250] G6erth … hynny] – *I, S*
[251] + a tal pop vn o hynny *I, S*
[252] Not6yd … a tal] *Found as a gloss in red at the bottom of the page in L*

Q90

Three men whom the king is not entitled to sell: a thief after he is condemned to the gallows, and a murderer, and a traitor of the lord.

Q91

There are three names for the *rhingyll*: 'the shriek of the country', and 'bad news the servant of the *cynghellor*', and *rhingyll*.

Q92

Three blows for which nothing is paid: to a deer in corn, to a dog in corn, and to a wild foal in corn.

Q93

Three private meetings that the king is entitled to have without his justice: with his priest, and with his wife, and with his mediciner.

Q94

There are three legal needles: the needle of the queen's seamstress, and the needle of the chief huntsman to stitch the torn dogs, and the needle of the mediciner to stitch wounds. The value of each of those ones: four legal pence. The needle of another skilled woman is worth a legal penny.

Q95. I86, J76, L76, M72, Bost62, N70, P95, R76, S85, T63, Tim15, Y93, €95, LatD115

Teir kyfrinach yssyd 6ell y hadef noc eu kelu: brat argl6yd a'e golledeu, a chynll6yn, a llad o dyn y tat,[253] ot adefir yghyfrinach.

Q96. I89, J77, L77, M73, Bost63, N71, P96, R77, S88, T64,
Tim16, Y94, €96, LatD116 [1 2 3 = 1 3 2 I, J, S]

Tri aneueil vn troeda6c yssyd: march, a heba6c, a milgi; y neb[254] a torro troet[255] vn [o]honunt, talet [35vb.1] y 6erth yn g6byl.[256]

Q97. I90, J78, L78, M74, Bost64, N72, P97, R78, S89, T65, Tim17, Y95, €97, LatD67, 117

Tri phren a dyly[257] pop adeil6r maestir y gaffel y gan y neb pieiffo y coet, mynho na vynho[258] y coet6r: nenpren a d6y nenfforch.[259]

Q98. I91, J79, L79, M75, Bost65, N73, O66, P98, R79, S90, T66, Tim18, Y96, €98, LatD118

Tri pheth ny thelir kyn koller yn ranty: kyllell, a chledyf, a lla6d6r.

Q99. I87, J81, L80, N74, O67, P99, R80, S86, T67, Tim19, Y97, €99, LatD119 [1 2 3 = 2 1 3 R]

Teir sarhaet kelein ynt: pan lather, pan yspeilier, pan ythyer hynny dyg6ydo.[260]

Q100. I88, J80, L81, M76, Bost66, N75, O68, P100, R81, S87, [217],
276, T68, Tim20, Y98, €100, LatD120 [1 2 3 = 1 3 2 O]

Teir g6arthrud[261] kelein ynt: gofyn 'p6y a lada6d h6n?', 'pieu yr elor honn?', 'pieu y bed[262] h6n?'.

---

[253] o dyn y tat] y tat neu y uam *LatD*

[254] y neb] – *I, S*; pwy bynnac *LatD*

[255] – *J*

[256] talet … g6byl] y 6erth oll a tal *I, S*; talet y 6erth yn holla6l *J, L, M, Bost, R, T, Tim, Y*

[257] a dyly] ryd y *I, S*

[258] mynho na vynho] bo drwc bo da gan *Y*

[259] + os prenneu ereill a trychir eithir y rei hynny heb gannyad keinawc o lwyth pop deu ychen a tal y neb a gaffer yn gyfatef arnaw a thri buhyn camlwrw yr arglwyd os diwad a wna diwad lledrad a a arnaw *LatD67*

[260] hynny dyg6ydo] yny or6ed oe sefyll *I, S*; yny gorwed *O, Y*

[261] sarhaet *M, Bost*

[262] + ne6yd *I, J, L, R, S, T, Tim, LatD*

Q95

Three secrets which are better confessed than hidden: the betrayal of a lord and his losses, and a murder, and a man killing his father, if it is confessed in secret.

Q96

There are three one-footed animals: a horse, and a hawk, and a greyhound; whoever may break the foot of one of them, let him pay its value in full.

Q97

Three timbers that every builder in open country should get from whoever owns the wood, whether the woodman wishes or not: a ridgepiece and two crucks.

Q98

Three things which are not paid for although they may be lost in a house where someone is lodged: a knife, and a sword, and trousers.

Q99

These are the three shames of a corpse: when it is struck, when it is despoiled, and when it is pushed until it falls.

Q100

These are the three shames of a corpse: asking 'Who killed this one?', 'Whose is this bier?', 'Whose is this grave?'

S276

Tri g6arthryd kelein: vn o nodynt pan lader kelein, drychaf a gossod erni; a'r
eil, ysbeilia6 kelein; a'r trydyd, y g6an a throed pan ofyner 'p6y hon?';
a'r hei hynny yssyd kymeint a sarhaed, euth*ur*[263] na drychefir erni: ereill
a'e geil6 teir sarhaed kelein.

Q101. I92, J82, L82, M77, Bost67, N76, O69, P101, R82, S91, T69, Tim21, Y99, €101, LatD16

Teir gauael nyt atuerir: vn a dyccer[264] dros letrat, ac vn ar[265] vach ny chymhello,[266]
a thros alanas.

Q102. I93, J83, L83, M78, Bost68, N77, O70, P102, R83, S92, T70, Tim22, Y100, €102, LatD123

Tri ry6 tal yssyd y g6yn6r:[267] geud6g,[268] neu at6erth, neu eturyt.[269]

Q103. I94, J84, L84, Bost69, N78, O71, P103, R84, S93, T71, Tim23, Y101, €103, LatD124

Tri ymdill6g o r6ym ha6l yssyd:[270] g6ir t6g, neu 6aessaf, neu ynuytr6yd.

Q104. I95, J85, L85, M79, Bost70, N79, O72, P104, R85, S94, [233],
T72, Tim24, 126, Y102, €104, LatD [125], 133 [1 2 3 = 1 3 2 L, Tim]

[35vb.23] Tri chargych6yn[271] heb attych6el: vn y6 g6reic g6edy yd yscarho
a'e g6r yn gyfreitha6l, a chyss6ynuab g6edy g6atter o genedyl y tat[272] yn
gyfreitha6l, a threftada6c pan del[273] y dilis g6edy y bo yn [36ra.1] argl6ydiaeth
arall; o ia6nder nyt ymchoel trachefyn.

---

[263] euthur euthur *S*
[264] vn a dyccer] – *I, S*
[265] ar] a dyccer dros *Y*
[266] + y vechni *L, Tim*; y vechniaeth *J, T*
[267] yssyd y g6yn6r] – *J;* yssyt y cwynawdyr *LatD*
[268] g6irt6g *O*
[269] geud6g ... eturyt] – *M*
[270] Tri ... yssyd] – *M*
[271] chargych6el *S*
[272] y tat] – *I, M, Bost, S*
[273] el *J, L, M, Tim*

S276

Three shames of a corpse: one of them is when a corpse is struck, [namely] as assault upon it; and the second, despoiling a corpse; and the third, striking it with a foot when it is asked 'Who is this?'; and those ones are equal to *sarhaed*, except there is no augmentation on it: others call them *teir sarhaed kelein*.

Q101

Three distraints that are not restored: one which is taken for theft, and one on a surety who does not enforce, and for *galanas*.

Q102

There are three kinds of payments for a complainant: perjury, reparation, or restoration.

Q103

There are three releases from a binding claim: true swearing, or vouching to warranty, or madness.

Q104

Three car-startings without return: one is a woman after she has separated from her husband legally, and a putative son after he has been denied from the father's kindred legally, and a patrimonial when he comes to his rightful place after he has been in another lordship; rightfully he should not return afterwards.

Q105. I96, J86, L86, M80, Bost71, N80, O73, P105, R86 (largely illegible), S95, T73, Tim25,
Y103, €105, LatD127

O²⁷⁴ tri acha6s y gossodet kyfreith: vn²⁷⁵ y6 y geissa6 dysc rac g6neuthur
aghyfreith, eil y6 yr gwaret aghyfreith or darffei y g6neuthur,²⁷⁶ trydyd y6 y
gospi y neb a'e g6nelei aghyfreith²⁷⁷ tr6y dir6y a chaml6r6 a'r kyfry6 a dylyei.

Q106. I98, J87, L87, M81, Bost72, N81, P106, R87 (largely illegible),
S97, T74, Tim26, Y104, €106, LatD128

Tri h6rd ny di6ygir: vn y6 h6rd g6r ac aryf yn y elyn am y gar g6edy ys gofynho
yn tri dadleu, a heb gaffel ia6n; kyt as llado, nys di6c. Eil y6 h6rd g6reic 6rya6c
yn y chy6yres a'e d6y la6 yny kyfarffont; kyt bo mar6, ny di6ygir. Trydyd y6
o rodir t6ylluor6yn y 6r, a g6edy y phroui y chaffel yn t6ylluor6yn, a²⁷⁸ mach
ar y mor6ynda6t; kyt as g6anho²⁷⁹ a'e la6 neu a'e troet dros y g6ely²⁸⁰ ac nas
llado, nys di6c. Yr h6rd heuyt a 6anho a bonllost yndi ny di6ygir idi; llather y
chrys, hagen,²⁸¹ yn [36rb.1] gyfu6ch a thal y phedrein,²⁸² a'r tu racdi yn
gyfu6ch a g6arr y chont, a'e gell6g a'r h6rd h6nn6 yndi heb y diu6yn idi.²⁸³ A
hynny y6 kyfreith t6ylluor6yn.

Q107. I97, J88, L88, M82, Bost73, N82, P107, S96, 180, [231],
T75, Tim27, 124, Y105, €107, LatD129

Tri da nyt reit mach arnunt: da a rotho argl6yd y dyn, a chymyn a gymero²⁸⁴
[offeirat]²⁸⁵ gan y mar6, a da a gymero²⁸⁶ medic y gan y neb a²⁸⁷
vedeginyaetho.²⁸⁸

---

²⁷⁴ – *J, N, R, Tim*
²⁷⁵ kyntaf *I, J, L, M, N, O, R, T, Tim, Y*
²⁷⁶ *hiatus in O*
²⁷⁷ + y *Q*
²⁷⁸ + g6edy rodi *I, S*
²⁷⁹ g6ahanho *Q, €*
²⁸⁰ y g6ely] yr erch6yn *N*
²⁸¹ + trachefyn *I, J, S*
²⁸² + dracheuen *L, T, Tim, Y*
²⁸³ llather y chrys … diu6yn idi] – *M, Bost*
²⁸⁴ a gymero] a del y *I, S*
²⁸⁵ – *Q, €*
²⁸⁶ del y *I, S*
²⁸⁷ ad a *L, Tim*
²⁸⁸ neb … vedeginyaetho] claf *I;* vedic y gan y klaf *S;* nep y gwnel meteginnyaeth urthaw *LatD*

Q105

For three reasons law is decreed: one is to seek learning lest illegality be committed, the second is to be rid of an illegality if it happens to be committed, the third is to punish whoever commits an illegality through *dirwy*-fine and *camlwrw*-fine and the equivalent of what he owes.

Q106

Three thrusts for which reparation is not made: one is the thrust of a man with a weapon into his enemy [in revenge] for his relative after he has asked [for redress] in three sessions, without receiving redress; although he may kill him, he does not pay compensation. The second is a thrust of a married woman at her [husband's] concubine with her two hands when they meet; although she may die, compensation is not paid. The third is if a false virgin is given to a man, and after testing her she is found to be a false virgin, with surety on her virginity; although he shoves her with his hand or his foot over the bed and does not kill her, he does not pay compensation. Also there is no redress to her for the thrust he made into her with his penis; however, let her shift be cut as high as the top of her buttocks, and in front as high as the top of her cunt, and she is released with that thrust in her without compensating her for it. And that is the law of a false virgin.

Q107

Three goods which do not need surety on them: goods which a lord may give to his man, and the bequest the priest receives from the dead, and the goods the mediciner takes from someone he treats.

S180

Tri da dilis divach yssyd: vn y6, da a rodo argl6yd y 6r ida6, y da a dylyeu ef y arall dr6y g*yfreith*. Eil y6 da a gaffeu 6reic gan y g6r yn y h6yneb6arth pan kytio ynteu a g6reic arall. Trydyd y6 da a dycker neu a gaffer yn*n* ryfel deu argl6yd.

Q108. *I99, J89, L89, M83, Bost74, N83, P108, S98, [259], T76, Tim28, 140, Y106, €108,* LatD130

Teir mar6 tystolyaeth yssyd am tir ac a safant yg kyfreith a barn: vn y6 or kyfroir dadyl am tir yn llys a'e theruynu yg6yd g6yr y llys, g6edy y bo mar6 y rei hynny oll tystolyaeth eu hetiuedyon hyt y gor6yron neu ach6anec a gredir am yr hynn a[289] gly6ssant y gan eu ryeni o'r dadyl honno, a rei hynny a el6ir g6ybydyeit am tir. Eil y6 henaduryeit g6lat y 6ybot ach ac etryt r6g kenedyl a charant y dyn a ofynho tir dr6y ach ac etryt, a na6uetdyeu kalan[290] Mei neu [36va.1] galan gayaf.[291] Trydyd y6 pan 6eler pentanuaen tat y dyn a ofynho tir, neu y hentat neu orhentat neu ereill o'e genedyl, neu le adeil, neu ar tir[292] y ryeni;[293] y rei hynny oll a safant yn lle tyston ida6 ar y dylyet.

Q109. *I100, J90, L90, M84, Bost75, N84, P109, S99, T77, Tim29, Y107, €109,* LatD131

Tri thorll6yth vn 6erth ac eu mam yssyd nac vn a vo na lla6er[294] or dygir yn lletrat: torll6yth gellast, a thorll6yth h6ch ar y thyle, a nyth[295] heba6c.

Q110. *I101, J91, L91, M85, [Bost76] N85, P110, S100, T78, Tim30, Y108, €110,* LatD132

Tri ll6dyn vn 6erth yssyd yn y genuein pop amser; dec ar hugeint y6 g6erth pop vn ohonunt:[296] baed kenuein, ac arbenhic y genuein,[297] a h6ch a gat6er yg kyfeir yr argl6yd.[298]

[289] + vu gynt ac a *S*
[290] – *I, S*
[291] galan gayaf] racuyr *I, S*
[292] neu y tir ar *Q*; neu tir *I, S;* ar tir ar *M;* ar tir *P;* neu dir *Y;* – *J, Tim*
[293] + ar y dir *J;* ar tir *Tim*
[294] llia6s *I, J, L, Bost, S, T, Tim;* lhast *M;* + y b6ynt *J, L, T, Tim*
[295] nythl6yth *J, L, M, Bost, T, Tim*
[296] dec ... ohonunt] – *I, S*
[297] moch *I, S;* moch ar genvaint *P*
[298] a gat6er yg kyfeir yr argl6yd] a gat6er yg kyfeir g6estfa arglwyd *I, S;* yng kyueir gwestua y brenhin *J, M, Tim;* a gat6er yg kyfeir g6estfa y brenhin *L;* a gat6er yg kyfeir g6estfa brenhin *T;* a gat6er y 6estfa y brenhin *Y*

S180

There are three valid unsuretied goods: one is, goods a lord gives to a man of his, the goods which he owed to another by law. The second is goods a woman receives from her husband as her *wynebwerth* when he has intercourse with another woman. The third is goods that are taken or gained in a war between two lords.

Q108

There are three testimonies regarding the dead for land and they stand in law and judgement: one is if a dispute for land is initiated in court and is terminated in the presence of the men of the court, after all of those people are dead the evidence of their heirs as far as the great-grandsons or more is believed regarding what they heard of that case from their forebears, and those ones are called knowers for land. The second that a country's elders witness lineage and descent between kin and relatives of a man who claims land by lineage and descent, on the ninth days from May Day or from 1 November. The third is when the hearthstone of the father of the man who claims land is seen, or his grandfather's or his great-grandfather's or others from his kindred, or a place for a building, or on the land of his ancestors; all of those ones stand in place of witnesses for him regarding his entitlement.

Q109

There are three litters of the same value as their mother whether [the litter] be one or many if they are taken in theft: the litter of a staghound-bitch, and the litter of a sow on her bed, and the nest [load] of a hawk.

Q110

There are three animals of the same value in the litter at all times; each of them is worth thirty [pence]: a herd pig, and the champion of the pigs, and a sow which is kept for the lord.

Q111. I103, J92, L92, M86, [Bost77], N86, P111, S101, T79, Tim31, Y109, €111, LatD134

Teir fford y de6edir g6ybydyeit am tir:[299] vn y6 henuryeit g6lat y 6ybot ach ac etryt y d6yn dyn ar dylyet tir y gyt a'e garant. Eil y6 amhinogeu[300] tir, nyt amgen g6r o pop rantir o'r tref honno y 6ybot ranneu a finyeu r6g y 6elygord. Trydyd y6 meiri a chyghello[36vb.1]ryon[301] y gad6 teruyneu y kymhydeu, canys brenhin bieu y teruyneu.[302]

Q112. I102, J94, L93, M87, [Bost78], N87, P112, S102, T80, Tim32, Y110, €112, LatD135

Tri pheth a geid6 cof ac a seif[303] yn lle tyston y dyn ar y dylyet o tir: lle hen odyn, neu pentanuaen, neu escynuaen.

Q113. I104, J93, L94, M88, [Bost79], N88, P113, S103, T81, Tim33, Y111, €113, LatD136

Y tri dyn y telir g6eli taua6t:[304] y vrenhin pan dy6eter geir hagyr[305] 6rtha6, ac y vra6d6r pan 6ystler yn y erbyn[306] am ia6n varn os ef a'e katarnha,[307] ac y offeirat yn y egl6ys yn y teir g6yl arbenhic, neu rac bron y brenhin yn darllein llythyr, neu yn y yscriuennu.[308]

Q114. I105, J95, L95, M89, [Bost80], N89, P114, S104, T82, Tim34, 159, Y112, €114, LatD137

Tri cho6ylla6c llys yssyd: ker6yn ved, a braga6t,[309] a chathyl kyn y dangos y'r brenhin.

Tim159
Tri cho6ylla6c llys: ygnad, a bard, a medic.

---

[299] Teir ... am tir] Tri ry6 6ybydieit yssyd am tir *I, S, Y*
[300] amhinogyon *N, S*
[301] + a rigyllyeit *I, Y*
[302] + hynny *J, L, M, S, T, Tim, Y*
[303] seiff *Q*
[304] + udunt *I, J, L, M, S, Tim*
[305] gar6 *J, L, Tim*
[306] 6ystler yn y erbyn] ym6ystler ac ef *I, S, Y*
[307] os ef a'e katarnha] – *I, S*
[308] 6neuthur *I, M, S*
[309] bra6t *L, Tim,Y*

Q111

In three ways people are called knowers for land: one is the elders of a country to know the lineage and descent to establish a man on his entitlement to land along with his relatives. The second is the land borderers, namely a man from every *rhandir* of that township to know the divisions and boundaries between the kin-group. The third is the *meiri* and the *cyngellorion* to maintain the boundaries of the commotes, because the king owns the boundaries.

Q112

Three things that preserve memory and serve in place of witnesses for a man's entitlement of land: the place of an old kiln, or a hearthstone, or a mounting-block.

Q113

The three men to whom tongue-wound is paid: to a king when an ugly word is said to him, and to a judge when a pledge is given against him for a true judgement if he confirms it, and to the priest in his church at the three special feasts, or reading a letter before the king, or composing it.

Q114

There are three cowled ones in a court: a barrel of mead, and one of bragget, and a song before it is shown to the king.

Tim159
Three cowled ones of a court: a justice, and a poet, and a mediciner.

Q115. *I106, J96, L96, M90, [Bost81], N90, P115, S105, T83,*
Tim35, Y113, €115, LatD138 *[1 2 3 = 1 3 2 M, N, Y]*

Tri dyn a geid6 breint llys yn a6ssen y brenhin: offeirat teulu, a distein, a bra6d6r llys; py le bynnac y bont[310] yghyt, yno y byd breint llys.

Q116. *I109, J97, L97, M91, [Bost82], N91, P116, S108, [218],*
T84, Tim36, Y114, €116, LatD109, 139

Tri argae[311] g6aet yssyd: g6aet o pen hyt g6ll, g6aet o g6ll hyt 6regys, g6aet o 6regys hyt la6r. [Ac os o benn hyt la6r][312] [37ra.1] y gellygir, dogyn 6aet y gel6ir. G6erth g6aet pop dyn y6 pedeir ar hugeint.[313] Or g6edir y g6aet kyntaf, tr6y l6 na6 nyn y g6edir, yr eil[314] tr6y l6 6he dyn, y trydyd[315] tr6y l6 tri dyn. Ny dylyir na lleihau na m6yhau g6erth g6aet o pedeir ar hugeint,[316] py gyfeir bynnac o gna6t dyn y gellygir, kyt symuter reitheu o her6yd yr argayeu.

LatD109
Tri argae gwaed yssyt: mynwes, a gwregys peruet, a gwregys llawdwr.

Q117. *I107, J98, L98, M92, [Bost83], N92, P117, S106, [241], T85, Tim37, Y115, €117,* LatD140

Teir hela ryd yssyd y pop dyn[317] ar tir dyn arall: hela i6rch, a hely kadno, a hely dyfyrgi.

---

[310] y bont] – *N;* + ell tri *S*
[311] datssaf *J, L, M, T, Tim*
[312] ac os o benn hyt la6r] – *Q, €;* + os o 6regys hyt la6r *P;* os o pen y gellygir hyt lawr *I, S*
[313] G6erth … hugeint] – *I, S, Y*
[314] + g6aet *J, L, Tim*
[315] tr6y l6 6he … trydyd] – *€*
[316] Ny dylyir…hugeint] ny byd na m6y na llei g6erth g6aet pop ry6 dyn no phedeir ar hugeint *I, S, Y*
[317] y pop dyn] ym pop g6lat *I, S, Y*

Q115

Three men who maintain the status of the court in the absence of the king: the priest of the warband, and the steward, and the court judge; wherever they are all together, the status of a court is there.

Q116

There are three stays of blood: blood from the head to the chest, blood from the chest to the belt, and blood from the belt to the floor. And if it is spilt from the head to the floor, it is called complete [shedding of] blood. The value of the blood of every person is twenty-four [pence]. If the first blood is denied, it is denied by the oath of nine men, the second by the oath of six men, the third by the oath of three men. The value of blood should not be decreased or increased from twenty-four [pence], from whichever part of someone's flesh it is shed, although the bodies of compurgators are changed on account of the stays.

LatD109
There are three stays of blood: a chest, and a middle girdle, and a trouser belt.

Q117

There are three free huntings for every man on the land of another man: hunting a roebuck, and hunting a fox, and hunting an otter.

Q118. *I108, J99, L99, M93, [Bost84], N93, O74, P118,*
S107, T86, Tim38, Y116, €118, LatD19, 141

Tri chy6ilyd mor6yn yssyd: vn y6 dy6edut o'e that 6rthi 'mi a'th rodeis[318] y 6r';
eil y6 pan el gyntaf y g6ely[319] y g6r; trydyd y6 pan el[320] gyntaf o'r g6ely ym
plith dynyon.[321] Dros y kyntaf[322] y rodir y hamobyr y'r argl6yd;[323] dros yr eil[324]
y rodir y chy6yll idi hitheu; dros y trydyd y dyry tat y[325] heg6edi y'r g6r.

Q119. *I110, J100, L100, M94, Bost85, N94, O75, P119, S109, T87, Tim39, Y117, €119,* LatD142

Tri pheth ny ellir y d6yn rac g6reic kyt g6ahaner a hi am y cham: y cho6yll, a'e
hargy[37rb.1]freu, a'e h6yneb6erth, os rygafas kyn hynny o[326] gymryt o'e g6r
6reic arall yn y herbyn.[327]

Q120. *I111, J101, L101, M95, Bost86, N95, O76, 100, P120, S110,*
T88, Tim40, Y118, €120, LatD35 *[1 2 3 = 1 3 2 Y; 2 1 3 0100]*

Tri defnyd ha6l yssyd: gol6c, a geir, a g6eithret.

Q121. *I112, J102, L102, M96, Bost87, N96, O77, 101, P121, S111, T89, Tim41, Y119, €121, LatD36*

Tri gol6c a dygir ygkyfreith: gol6c tyst o'e tystolyaeth, a gol6c managyat[328] o'e
vanac, a gol6c llyga[t]rud kylus[329] am lad neu losc neu letrat.

Q122. *I113, J103, L103, M97, Bost88, N97, O102, P122, S112, T90, Tim42, Y120, €122, LatD37*

Tri geir kylus yssyd: geir y[330] bo g6eli[331] taua6t [ymdana6],[332] a g6alla6geir yn
llys, a thaua6trudyaeth am lad neu losc neu letrat.

[318] + vor6yn *I, N, S, Y*
[319] y g6ely] – *N;* + at *S, Y*
[320] del *J, L, S, Tim, Y; O resumes here*
[321] ym plith dynyon] – *S*
[322] eil *T*
[323] *From* O; tat *Q, J, L, M, N, P, S, T, Tim, €;* – *Y*
[324] kyntaf *T*
[325] dyry tat y] – *L*
[326] oe *Q, L, N, P, S, T, Tim, Y, €*
[327] yn y herbyn] – *O*
[328] manac6r *J, M, Bost, O, Tim;* myneigyad *LatD*
[329] a gol6c llygatrud kylus] – *O*
[330] a *Q*
[331] bo g6eli] gweilyd *O*
[332] *I, L, S, Tim;* ynda6 *P*

Q118

There are three shames of a maiden: one is when her father tells her 'I have given you to a man'; the second is when she goes for the first time to her husband's bed; the third is when she goes for the first time from the bed amongst men. For the first her *amobr* is given to the lord; for the second her *cowyll* is given to her; for the third the father gives her *agweddi* to the husband.

Q119

Three things that cannot be taken from a woman though separation from her is caused by her misdeed: her *cowyll*, and her *argyfrau*, and her *wynebwerth*, if she had received them before then because her husband took another woman in opposition to her.

Q120

There are three substances of a claim: sight, and word, and deed.

Q121

Three sights that are accepted in law: a witness's sight in respect of his evidence, and an informant's sight in respect of his information, and the sight of a guilty onlooker for homicide or arson or theft.

Q122

There are three kinds of guilty words: a word in which there may be a tongue-wound, and a false word in court, and [the word of] a guilty-tongue for homicide or arson or theft.

Q123. I114, J104, L104, M98, Bost89, N98, O78, 103,
P123, S113, T91, Tim43, Y121, C123, LatD39

Tri ry6 6alla6geir yssyd: geir g6all yn holi o r6y[333] neu eisseu, a geir g6all yn amdiffyn o r6y[334] neu eisseu, a geir g6all yn g6adu. O'r kyntaf y kyll ha6l6r y ha6l or perthyno 6rth y geir, or dygir tyston yn y erbyn[335] – ac ny chyll caml6r6, kanyt oes kamg6yn kylus ygkyfreith[336] eithyr tri. O'r eil neu o'r trydyd y kyll amdiffynn6r[337] cam[37va.1]l6r6 a diu6yn[338] yr ha6l o'r a perthyno 6rth y geir y tyst6yt o'e 6all.

Q124. I115, J105, L105, M100, Bost91, N99, O79, P124, S114, T92, Tim44, Y122, C124, LatD40

Tri theruyn ha6l yssyd: g6adu, neu profi, neu lyssu tyston.

Q125. I116, J106, L106, M99, Bost90, N100, O80, P125, S115, T93, Tim45, Y123, C125, LatD41

Tri pheth ny chygein ygkyfreith: pra6f ar 6eithret eithyr tri, a g6at dros 6aessaf, a chof g6edy bra6t.

Q126. I117, J107, L107, M101, Bost92, N101, O81, P126, S116, T94, Tim46, Y124, C126, LatD42

Tri g6eithret yssyd ar pra6f: llafur kyfreitha6l neu aghyfreitha6l ar tir, megys torri ffin neu 6neuthur ffin, neu lafur arall. A g6eithret ll6dyn yn llad y llall yg g6yd bugeil trefgord: tystolyaeth y bugeil[339] yn 6ybydyat a seif am hynny, tystolyaeth g6yby[dy]eit a seif am tir heuyt.[340] A g6eithret kytleidyr lleidyr a grocker am letrat, tystolyaeth h6nn6 ar y gytleidyr a seif.

Q127. I118, J108, L108, M102, Bost93, N102, O82, P127, S117, T95, Tim47, Y125, C127, LatD43

Tri g6aessaf yssyd: ardel6, neu 6arant, neu amdiffyn heb 6arant.

---

[333] r6yf *P*
[334] r6yf *P*
[335] or dygir tyston yn y erbyn] – *J;* or dygir tystyon arnaw *LatD*
[336] – *O78, O103;* namyn *M*
[337] amdifnn6r *Q*
[338] d6yn *O101*
[339] h6nn6 *M, Bost*
[340] tir heuyt] hynny *S;* tir *J, L, Tim*

Q123

There are three erroneous words: an erroneous word claiming too much or too little, an erroneous word defending too much or too little, and an erroneous word denying. For the first the claimant loses his claim if it depends on the word, if witnesses are brought against him – and he does not lose a *camlwrw*, because there are no guilty words in law apart from three. For the second or the third the defendant loses *camlwrw* and settles the claim insofar as it may depend on the word by which testimony was given regarding his error.

Q124

There are three terminations of a claim: denial, or proving, or objecting to witnesses.

Q125

Three things for which there is no place in law: proof in respect of a deed apart from three, and a denial in spite of a guarantee, and record after a judgement.

Q126

There are three deeds which go towards a proof: legal or illegal work on a land, such as breaking a boundary or making a boundary, or other work. And the deed of an animal killing another in the presence of a township herdsman: the evidence of the herdsman as a knower stands for that, and the evidence of knowers stand for land as well. And the deed of a co-thief of a thief who is hanged for theft, the evidence of that one on his co-thief stands.

Q127

There are three supports [of a defendant]: a plea, warrantor, or defence without a warrantor.

Q128. I119, J109, L109, M103, Bost94, N103, O83, 104,
P128, S118, T96, Tim48, Y126, €128, LatD44

Tri chof g6edy bra6t yssyd: godef o vra6d6r rodi[341] g6ystyl yrbyn[342] y vra6t heb [37vb.1] rodi g6ystyl yna,[343] ac g6edy hynny kynnic g6ystyl y'6 gadarnhau;[344] ny dylyir y erbynnya6 o gyfreith ony byd bra6t tremyc. Neu gynnic[345] g6ystyl yn erbyn bra6t g6edy y godef.[346] Neu ada6 ymadra6d yn 6allus ar gyfreith a barn a g6edy barn keissia6 g6aret y g6all nys dyly.

Q129. I121, J110, L110, M104, Bost95, N104, O84, 101, P129, S120, T97, Tim49, Y128, €129,
LatD45

Teir tystolyaeth dilis yssyd: tystolyaeth llys yn d6yn cof; a thystolyaeth g6ybydyeit a gredir pop vn ygkyfreith, megys tat r6g y deu uab, neu yn lluossa6c am tir; a thystolyaeth y g6rthtyston.

Q130. I120, J111, L111, M105, Bost96, N105, O85, P130, S119, T98, Tim50, Y127, €130, LatD46

Tri lle y ty6ys cof llys: am gyfundeb[347] d6y pleit;[348] ac am teruyn dadyl[349] or da6 kygha6s vn yn dy6edut y theruynu, ac arall yn dy6edut na theruyn6yt; ac am aghyfreith a 6nel argl6yd a'e dyn yn y lys.

Q131. I122, J112, L112, M106, Bost97, N106, O86, P131, S121,
T99, Tim51, Y129, €131, LatD47 *[1 2 3 = 1 3 2 LatD]*

Teir tystolyaeth mar6a6l yssyd: tystu ar dyn kyn y[350] holi o'r hyn y tyster, neu tystu ar dyn[351] na [39ra.1] 6ad6ys ac nat amdiffynn6ys[352] yr hyn ar daroed ida6 y 6adu[353] neu y amdiffyn, neu tystu ar dyn dy6edut yr hyn ny dy6a6t; g6yr[354]

---

[341] *– L, M, Bost, T*
[342] yn erbyn *N, O83;* yny erbyn *Tim*
[343] y chadarnhau *I, Y*
[344] y'6 gadarnhau] *– I, S, Y;* + y vra6t *O104*
[345] rodi *I, S*
[346] + yn gyntaf *O83*
[347] + dylyet *Bost*
[348] d6y pleit] pleideu *I, S, Y*
[349] *– Bost*
[350] kyn y] kyny y *Q, €*
[351] ar dyn] *– O86*
[352] ac nat amdiffyn6ys] *– O105*
[353] y 6adu] *– M, Bost*
[354] *– M, Bost, O86*
[355] g6yr llys a bra6t6yr] bra6t6yr y llys *J, L, Tim;* llys a bra6tlyfyr *O103*
[356] kadarnach *O86*
[357] a llyna … thyston] *– J, M, O105; rubricated in L*

Q128

There are three records after a judgement: a justice suffering a pledge given against his judgement without then giving a pledge, and after that he offers a pledge to confirm it; this should not be accepted by law unless it is a neglectful judgement. Or offering a pledge against a judgement after suffering it. Or allowing an erroneous statement in law and judgement and after the judgement he is not entitled to attempt to be rid of the error.

Q129

There are three valid testimonies: the testimony of a court introducing a record; and the testimony of knowers each one of whom are believed in law, as that of a father between his two sons, or many [who are believed] for land; and the testimony of the counter-witnesses.

Q130

Three places where the record of the court offers guidance: about an agreement between two parties; and about the conclusion of a case if the *cyngaws* of one party comes and says that it was concluded, the other saying that it was not concluded; and about an illegality that a lord committed against his man in his court.

Q131

There are three dead testimonies: testifying against a person before claim is made against him in respect of what is testified, or testifying against a person that he neither denied nor defended that which he had already denied or defended, or testifying against a person that he said something which he did not say; the men of the court and the justices that hear them should adjudge them as dead at the request of the defendant, if it [the court] recalls it. And those are the three places where knowers are stronger than witnesses.

llys a bra6t6yr[355] a'e cly6ho a dyly eu d6yn yn var6a6l tr6y arch yr amdiffynn6r, os coffa. A llyna y tri lle y mae trech[356] g6ybydyeit no thyston.[357]

Q132. I123, J113, L113, M107, Bost98, N107, O87, P132, S122, T100, Tim52, Y130, €132, LatD48

Tri g6ahan yssyd r6g g6ybydyeit a thyston: g6ybydyeit am[358] a vu kyn ymhya6l[359] a dygant tystolyaeth, ac nyt ef y d6c tyston. Eil y6 g6ybydyeit bieu deturyt eu g6ybot ygkyfreith tyston kyny ry tyster udunt, ac nys pieu tyston.[360] Trydyd y6 g6ybydyeit bieu d6yn tystolyaeth yn erbyn g6at ac amdiffyn; sef y6 hynny, g6ybydyeit bieu proui g6ir g6edy geu, ac nys pieu tyston.

Q133. I124, J114, L114, M108, Bost99, N108, O88, P133,
S123, T101, Tim53, Tr48, Y131, €133, LatD49

Teir[361] fford y mae kadarnach g6ybydyeit no thyston: vn y6 gallu d6yn llia6s o 6ybydyeit am vn peth yg kyfreith neu vn g6ybydy[38rb.2]at megys mach, ac ny ellir d6yn na m6y na llei no deu o tyston;[362] eil y6 gallu dir6y[363] dyn neu y 6erthu[364] tr6y 6ybydyeit,[365] ac ny ellir tr6y tyston o gyfreith; trydyd y6 gallu ohonunt profi yn erbyn g6at neu amdiffyn, ac nys dicha6n tyston. Pan tysto tyst yny tystolyaeth peth yn gyfreitha6l y ereill yn erbyn amdiffynn6r, neu amdiffynn6r pan tysto ynteu peth yn gyfreitha6l[366] yn erbyn tyston, y rei hynny a el6ir g6rthtyston ygkyfreith, ac ny dylyir eu llussu.[367]

Q134. I125, J115, L115, M109, Bost100, N109, O89,
P134, S124, T102, Tim54, Tr49, €134, LatD50

Teir tystolyaeth yssyd ar eir ac ny dygir y greir: tystolyaeth lleidyr ar y gytleidyr 6rth y groc, a thystolyaeth nyt elher yn y herbyn pan dyccer ar[368] eir, a thystolyaeth g6rthtyston.

---

[358] + yr hyn *I, S*
[359] + yn llys *I, S*
[360] kyny ... tyston] – *T*
[361] O teir *I, S, Y*
[362] – *J*
[363] dir6ya6 *L, M, N, O, P, S, T, Y, LatD*
[364] + o kyfraith *LatD*
[365] *Tr resumes here*
[366] y ereill yn erbyn ... yn gyfreitha6l] – *Tr, Y*
[367] Pan tysto tyst ... ny dylyir eu llussu] – *LatD*
[368] – *Q*

Q132

There are three differences between knowers and witnesses: knowers bring evidence about that which was before examination, and that is not what witnesses bring. The second is that it is the right of knowers to state their knowledge in the law of witnesses before they are testified against, and it is not the right of witnesses; the third is that it is the right of knowers to bring evidence against denial and defence; that is, knowers have the right to prove truth after falsehood, and it is not the right of witnesses.

Q133

In three ways knowers are stronger than witnesses: one of them is the ability to bring many knowers for one thing in law or one knower such as a surety, and no more nor less than two witnesses can be brought; the second is the ability to fine a man or sell him by knowers, and by law this cannot be done through witnesses; the third is that they are able to prove against denial and defence, and witnesses cannot. When a witness testifies something legally to others against a defendant, or a defendant when he testifies something legally against witnesses, those are called counter-witnesses in law, and no one is entitled to object to them.

Q134

Three testimonies accepted as a [mere] statement and which are not taken to relics: the testimony of a thief on his fellow-thief at the gallows, and a testimony which is not disagreed with when it is stated by mouth, and testimony of counter-witnesses.

Q135. I126, J121, L121, M115, Bost106, N115, O95, P135, S125,
T108, Tim60, Tr55, Y132, €135, LatD56 *[1 2 3 = 2 1 3 I, S]*

O tri mod y telir dir6y treis: vn y6 pan pallo y reith y dyn yn g6adu treis; eil y6
pan pallo y amdiffyn y'r amdiffyn[38va.1]n6r yn erbyn dyn; trydyd y6 pan
pallo y 6arant y dyn a'e gal6o yn dadyl treis.

Q136. I127, J122, L122, M116, Bost107, N116, O96, P136,
S126, T109, Tim61, Tr56, Y133, €136, LatD57

O tri mod y kyll dadyl treis y breint m6yaf: o pallu[369] teithi treis, ac o tystolyaeth
v6ya6l yn dadyl treis, ac o g6yna6 o'r ha6l6r d6yn o'e eida6 ef yr hyn a
ducp6yt y treis rac arall, ac nyt y ganta6 ef; nyt m6y hagen y reith yn y tri
ph6nc hyn no ll6 tri[370] dyn, ac nyt m6y y dial no thri buhyn[371] caml6r6,[372] ony
ellir[373] y[374] 6adu yn g6byl[375] neu y amdiffyn.[376]

Q137. I128, J123, L123, M117, Bost108, N117, O97, P137,
S127, T110, Tim62, Tr57, Y134, €137, LatD58

Vn o'r tri a gyll y neb a treisser: ae y dyn, ae tir neu da arall kych6yna6l,[377] ae y
vreint.

Q138. I129, J124, L124, M118, Bost109, N118, O98, P138,
S128, T111, Tim63, Tr58, Y135, €138, LatD59

Tri ry6 amdiffyn yssyd:[378] vn y6 na 6rtheper[379] yn amsera6l[380] y'r gofyn, eil y6
amdiffyn[381] hyt nat attepper byth yr ha6l,[382] trydyd y6 amdiffyn gan atteb
mal[383] na choller dim y'r ha6l.[384]

[369] o pallu] oc na 6neler *I, O, Tr*
[370] *gloss in Q*
[371] bu *L, M, O, T, Tr*
[372] + yr brenhin *I*
[373] eullir *Q*
[374] ony eullir y] – *N (manuscript is torn)*
[375] yn g6byl] – *I, P*
[376] + yn g6byl *P*
[377] neu da arall kych6yna6l] – *Y*
[378] *Hiatus in O*
[379] atepper *S*
[380] anamsera6l *S, Tim, Tr*
[381] atteb *I*
[382] gofyn *I, S, T, Tr*
[383] hyt *M, Bost*
[384] govyn ar atteb *Y*

Q135

In three ways a *dirwy* fine for violence is paid: one is when someone's compurgation denying violence fails; the second is when the defendant's defence fails against a man; the third is when his warrantor fails for a man who invokes him in a case for violence.

Q136

In three ways pleading for violence loses the highest status: if the characteristics of violence are not carried out, and because of living testimony in the case for violence, and if the claimant complains that something was taken from his possession which was actually taken violently from another, and not from him; his compurgation then is not more on these three issues than the oath of three men, and the punishment is not more than three kine *camlwrw*, unless it can be denied completely or defended.

Q137

The person who suffers violent dispossession loses one of three things: either his person, or his land or other moveable goods, or his status.

Q138

There are three defences: one is that a timely answer to the claim is not given, the second is defending so that the claim is never answered, the third is defending so that nothing is lost to the claim.

Q139. I130, J125, L125, M119, Bost110, N119, P139,
S129, T112, Tim64, Tr59, Y136, €139, LatD60

Tri pheth nyt reit atteb y neb ohonunt: vn y6 peth ny bo diebredic yn erbyn kyfre[38vb.1]ith; eil y6 g6eithret y galler dangos yr argy6ed or g6neir,[385] ac ny dangosser; trydyd y6 collet ny 6yppo g6lat o neb ry6 hyspyssr6yd y'r ha6l6r y golli.

Q140. I131, J126, L126, M120, Bost111, N120, P140, S130, T113, Tim65, Tr60, Y137, €140,
LatD61 [1 2 3 = 2 1 3 I, J, L, M, Bost, N, S, T, Tim, Tr, Y ; third item is misplaced and at the bottom
of the page in Q]

Tri ry6 diebryt yssyd: vn y6 ada6 argy6ed ar dyn neu ar yr eidia6 heb 6neuthur ia6n[386] na heduchu ymdana6, eil y6 d6yn peth rac dyn[387] ac nat atuerer dracheuen, trydyd y6 diebryt dyn o'e dylyet dros amser y talu.[388]

Q141. I132, J127, L127, M121, Bost112, N121, P141, S131,
T114, Tim66, Tr61, Y138, €141, LatD62

O tri mod y kae kyfreith r6g ha6l6r ac amdiffynn6r: vn y6 colli y amser, a h6nn6 a dam6eina o la6er mod; eil y6 ha6l hep perchen; trydyd y6 teruynu y dadyl[389] kyn no hynny.

Q142. I133, J128, L128, M122, Bost113, N122, P142,
S132, T115, Tim67, Tr62, Y139, €142, LatD63

Tri theruyn kyfreitha6l yssyd: vn y6 teruyn o gyfundeb pleideu, eil y6 teruyn gossodedic tr6y gymroded6yr r6g pleideu,[390] trydyd y6 teruyn tr6y varn.

Q143. I134, J129, L129, M123, Bost114, N123, P143,
S133, T116, Tim68, Tr63, Y140, €143, LatD64

Teir dadyl a dylyant eu iacha6 ac eu barnu tr6y deturyt g6lat yn erbyn haerllugr6yd: vn y6 dadyl am venffyc neu 6ystyl, neu auael yssyd vn [39ra.1] gyfreith; eil y6

---

[385] or g6neir] o gyfreith *M*
[386] heb 6neuthur ia6n] – *N (manuscript is torn)*
[387] rac dyn] – *J, L, M, N, Tr, Y*
[388] etryt *S*
[389] ha6l *S*
[390] r6g pleideu] – *S, Tr*

Q139

Three things for which no one need answer: one is a thing that is not withheld against law; the second is a deed which causes an injury that can be shown if it is committed, and it is not shown; the third is a loss which the country is not aware by any kind of publicity that the claimant lost.

Q140

There are three kinds of detention: one is leaving an injury to a man or to the property without making satisfaction or settlement concerning it, the second is taking a thing and not restoring it, the third is detaining his right from a person beyond the time for paying it.

Q141

In three ways law is closed between a claimant and a defendant: one is through loss of his time, and that happens in many ways; the second is for a claim without an owner; the third is concluding the dispute legally previously.

Q142

There are three legal conclusions: one is a conclusion by reconciliation of the parties; the second is a conclusion by arbitrators between the parties, the third is a conclusion by judgement.

Q143

Three cases that are entitled to be heard and judged by the judgement of a country against arrogance: one is a case for a loan, or a pledge, or a distraint, which is the same law; the second is a case in which there is defence, namely a denial concerning land; the third is a case arising from oppression by a king against law.

dadyl y bo amdiffyn yndi, nyt amgen[391] g6at am tir;[392] trydyd y6 dadyl o 6rthtrymder brenhin yn erbyn kyfreith.

Q *extended triad collection*

Q144. J159, 162, L159, Bost136, P144, S270, Tim151, Y9, €144

[39ra.5–11] Tri dyn bonhedic cannh6yna6l g6iryon, ny dylyant na galanas na sarhaet:[393] dyn a ladho ki kyndeira6c; a dyn a ladho prenn 6rth y v6r6 y la6r,[394] gan y rybudya6; a dyn a ladho annyueil.

J159. L159, Bost136, S270, Tim151

Tri dyn ny dylyant na galanas na sarhaet kyt llader:[395] vn yw dyn a ladho anieuil, a dyn a gaffer yn rodyaw ystauell y brenhin hyt nos heb na than na goleuat yn y law, a dyn a lader a phrenn yn y vwrw[396] gan y rybudyaw.

Q145. P145, S177, Y161, €145

[39ra.11–13] Tri meib ryd o gaeth: yscolheic, a bard, a gof.

Q146. P146, S178, Y162, €146

[39ra.13–15] Tri meib[397] caeth o ryd: eu meibon h6ynt6y.

Q147. J163, P147, S194, Tim113, €147 [1 2 3 = 3 2 1 J, L, S, Tim]

[39ra.15–19] Tri dyn nyt geir eu geir ar neb[398] nac ar dim:[399] creuyd6r 6edy torro y broffes, a dyn a dycco cam tystolyaeth, a lleidyr kynneuodic.

---

[391] nyt amgen] neu yn amgen *J, L, Tim;* neu y6 amgen *M*
[392] *End of N*
[393] + vn y6 *Y*
[394] 6rth y v6r6 y la6r] – *Y;* 6rth y v6r6 *J*
[395] + h6ynt *S, Tim*
[396] + y la6r *S, Tim*
[397] – *S, Y*
[398] dyn *J*
[399] nac ar dim] – *J, S, Tim*

Q *extended triad collection*

Q144

Three innocent innate noblemen, who are entitled to neither *galanas* nor *sarhaed*: the man whom a mad dog kills; and a man whom a tree kills whilst being felled, despite his being warned; and the man whom an animal kills.

> *J159*
> Three men who are entitled to neither *galanas* nor *sarhaed* although they be killed: one is a man whom an animal kills, and a man who is found walking in the king's chamber at night without either a fire or a light in his hand, and a man who is killed by falling timber despite his being warned.

Q145

Three free sons from slave [fathers]: a cleric, a poet, and a blacksmith.

Q146

Three slave sons from free [fathers]: their sons.

Q147

Three men whose word is not to be accepted against anybody or on anything: a person under vows after he has broken his vows, a man who gives false testimony, and a habitual thief.

Q148. J158, L158, Bost135, P148, S269, Tim150, Y8, €148 [1 2 3 = 3 2 1 Bost]

[39ra.19] Tri dyn a dylyant alanas ac ny dylyant sarhaet:[400] dyn a ladher a saeth tr6y[401] arall, a dyn a ladher a g6en6yn, a dyn a ladho[402] ynuyt.

Q149. J157, L157, Bost134, P149, S268, Tim149, Y10, €149

[39ra.24] Tri dyn a dylyant sarhaet ac ny dylyant alanas: vn y6 caeth, namyn talu y 6erth[403] ny 6neir dim; a'r deu dyn ynt yssyd ryd eu llad o gyfreith, ac nyt ryd eu sarhau.

J157. L157, Bost134, S268, Tim149, Y10

Tri dyn a dylyant sarhaet ac ny dylyant alanas: vn y6 or deruyd tybya6 ar dyn lad y llall,[404] ac nas g6atto, kyt boet g6iryon, ac am hynny y sarhau; ef a dyly taly sarhaet a phei lledit ny chaffei dim. Eil y6 or deruyd y dyn talu c6byl o alanas namyn un geinya6c, ac am hynny[405] y sarhau, ef a dyly taly sarhaet, a phei lledit ny chaffei[406] dim. Trydyd y6 caeth; nyt oes alanas ida6 namyn talu y werth o'e argl6yd ual g6erth ll6dyn.[407]

Q150. P150, S210, €150

[39ra.29] Teir kyflauan nyt oes sarhaet [39rb.1] amdanunt:[408] vn y6 dyrna6t mab kynn y uot yn[409] oet kyfreitha6l, a dyrna6t o e[i]diged kyfreitha6l, a dyrna6t o anuod.[410] G6aet a g6eli[411] ag asc6rn t6nn, hagen, a telir[412] or byd.

---

[400] + vn y6 *J, L,Bost, Y*
[401] + dyn *Y*
[402] a dyn a ladho] – *J, L, Bost, S, Tim, Y*
[403] 6reth *Q*
[404] y llall] arall *S, Tim, Y*
[405] honno *Y*
[406] chau *S, Tim*
[407] nyt oes … ll6dynn] – *Y*
[408] amdanunt] ymdanadunt *Q*
[409] uot yn] – *S*
[410] añvodeu *S*
[411] + a dylyr *S*
[412] hagen, a telir] – *S*

Q148

Three men who are entitled to *galanas* but are not entitled to *sarhaed*: the man who is killed by an arrow through another, and a man who is killed by poison, and a man who is killed by an idiot.

Q149

Three men who are entitled to *sarhaed* but are not entitled to *galanas*: one is a slave, apart from paying his value nothing is done; and the others are the two men whom it is free for them to be killed by law, but it is not free to insult them.

J157

Three men who are entitled to *sarhaed* and are not entitled to *galanas*: one is if it happens that a man is suspected of killing another, and he does not deny it, although he is innocent, and for that he is insulted; he is entitled to be paid *sarhaed* and if he is killed nothing is received. The second is if it happens that a man pays the whole of *galanas* apart from one penny, and because of that he is insulted, he is entitled to be paid *sarhaed*, and if he were killed nothing would be received. The third is a slave; there is no *galanas* for him apart from paying his value to his lord like the value of an animal.

Q150

Three offences for which there is no *sarhaed*: one is the blow of a son before he is of legal age, and a blow from lawful jealousy, and an unintentional blow. Blood and wounds and broken bones, however, shall be paid for if they occur.

Q151. P151, E151

[39rb.7] Tri chyfredin kenedyl ynt: pennkenedyl, a theispandyle, a mab g6reic a roder o rod kenedyl y'6 gelyn; y mab h6nn6 a dyly vot yn gyffredin r6g y d6y genedyl.

Q152. P152, E152

[39rb.13] Tri pheth a differ dyn rac g6ys dadleu: lleuein rac llu gor6lat, a llifd6r hep pont heb geubal, a chleuyt gor6eida6c.

Q153. J160, L160, Bost137, P153, S271, Tim152, E153

[39rb.17] Teir merchet a dylyant talu amobreu, ac ny dylyant eu tateu talu ebedi6eu: vn y6 g6r a diennydho[413] yr argl6yd,[414] kany dyly[415] ebedi6 dyn a diennydho[416] e hun, a'e uerch a dal amobyr; a merch g6r a dalo gobyr ystyn; a merch g6r o tref gyfrif a vo mar6 hep uab ida6: y verch a dyly talu amobyr.

Q154. P154, E154

[39rb.27] Teir merchet ny dylyir amobreu vdunt: merch argl6yd, a merch etlig, a merch pen[39va.1]teulu. Sef achos: na dylyir 6rth[417] ebedi6eu y tateu, namyn eu hemys a milg6n a'e harueu a'e hebogeu; merch argl6yd ny dylyir amobyr idi, kanyt oes a'e gouyno; ny dyly ynteu e hun amobyr y verch.

Q155. P155, S272, Tim107, 153, E155

[39va.8] Tri chadarn byt ynt: argl6yd, a drut, a didym.[418] Sef achos y6 hyny,[419] maen dros iaen y6 argl6yd. Sef y6 drut,[420] ynvyt; sef y6[421] ynuyt, dyn[422] na aller

---

[413] ymdihenydyo *J;* defnydio *S*
[414] – *J*
[415] + argl6yd *S, Tim*
[416] ymdihenydyo *J;* defnydyo *S*
[417] – *P*
[418] *End of Tim160*
[419] – *S, Tim151*
[420] + dyn *Tim151*
[421] sef y6] ac *S, Tim151*
[422] – *S, Tim151*

Q151

These are the three things common to a kindred: a head of kindred, a representative, and a son of a woman given by gift of a kin to its enemy; that son should be common to the two kindreds.

Q152

Three things that protect a man from a summons to sessions: a cry regarding the host of a neighbouring country, and floodwater without a bridge or a ferry-boat, and bed-sickness.

Q153

Three daughters who are obliged to pay *amobrau*, and their fathers are not obliged to pay *ebediw*: one is a man whom the lord executes, for he is not entitled to the *ebediw* of a man whom he executes himself, and his daughter shall pay *amobr*; and the daughter of a man who pays a fee for [gift and] handing over; and the daughter of a man from a bond township who dies without a son: his daughter is obliged to pay *amobr*.

Q154

Three daughters for whom *amobr* is not due: the daughter of a lord, and the daughter of an *edling,* and the daughter of a chief of the warband. This is the reason: that there is nothing due in respect of the *ebediwau* of their fathers, apart from their steeds and greyhounds and their weapons and their hawks; *amobr* is not due for the daughter of a lord, because there is no one who can ask it; he himself is not entitled to the *amobr* of his daughter.

Q155

These are the three powerful ones of the world: a lord, and a fool, and a have-not. This is why, a lord is a stone across a piece of ice. This is what a fool is, an idiot; this what is an idiot is, a man upon whom nothing can be forced unless it is his own will; a have-not [is] a man without any goods, and because of that [handing over of] goods cannot be compelled where there are none.

kymell dim arna6 onyt y e6yllys; dyn didim[423] dyn hep da ida6,[424] ac 6rth hynny ny ellir kymell da yn y lle ny bo.

Q156. P156, Y7, €156

[39va.18] Tri dyn a dyly kenedyl y[425] vam eu gouyn, hep genedyl y tat: mab g6reic vonhedic a rother y alltut, a mab g6reic ny 6ypo p6y uo[426] y tat, a mab g6reic a 6atter o genedyl y tat. Sef achos y dyly kenedyl[427] y vam caffel yr alanas: 6rth dylyu ohonunt 6y 6neuthur ya6n drostunt, ac nat oes genedyl [39vb.1] tat vdunt. Rei a dy6eit dylyu o genedyl eu mam talu g6arthec diuach tros pop vn o rei hynny; kyfreith a dy6eit na dylyir, namyn dros mab alltut.

Q157. P157, S167, €157

[39vb.6] Tri ry6 6rogaeth yssyd: cletrenn g6ayssaf6r, ac ass6yn6r, ac atlam6r.

Q158. P158, S212, €158

[39vb.9] Tri pheth a dyly pop dyn[428] y gymryt hep gannyat arall:[429] dyf6r hep y uot yn llestyr, a maen heb y uot y[430] g6eith, a than o geubren.

Q159. P159, Tim158, €159

[39vb.14] Tri dyn y degemir udunt: offeirat, ac ygnat, a manag6r. Sef achos y6 hynny:[431] ygnat a dyly y decuet geina6c or a varnho eithyr am tir, a lletrat, a llad kelein;[432] ac am bop vn or rei[433] hynny pedeir ar ugeint a dyly. Manag6r a dyly y decuet geinha6c o'r a vanacko. Offeirat a dyly deg6m Crist.

---

[423] + sef y6 h6nn6 *Tim151*
[424] gantta6 *S, Tim151*
[425] – *P, Y*
[426] – *Y*
[427] dyly kenedyl] *from Y;* dylyant *Q*
[428] pop dyn] – *S*
[429] gannyat arall] gennad *S*
[430] me6n *S*
[431] – *Q; from Tim*
[432] llad kelein] ymlad *Tim*
[433] or rei] – *Tim*

Q156

Three persons to whose compensation payment the mother's kindred is entitled, excluding the father's kindred: the son of a noblewoman who is given to an alien, and the son of a woman who does not know who his father is, and the son of a woman who is denied by his father's kindred. This is the reason the mother's kindred are entitled to the *galanas*: because they ought to make redress on their behalf, and they have no father's kindred. Some say that the mother's kindred ought to pay cattle without surety for each of those ones; the law says that it is not due, except for an alien son.

Q157

There are three kinds of homage: the pale of a warrantor, and an *aswynwr*, and a resident.

Q158

Three things that every man is entitled to take without the permission of another: water that is not in a vessel, a stone that is not in use, and a fire from a hollow tree.

Q159

Three men to whom tithe is paid: a priest, and a justice, and an informant. This is the reason for that: a justice is entitled to the tenth penny from that which he judges apart from land, theft and a killing; and for every one of those he is entitled to twenty-four. An informant is entitled to the tenth penny of that on which he informs. The priest is entitled to the tithe of Christ.

Q160. P160, E160

[39vb.24] Tri dadleu ny dylyir eu g6enuthur namyn rac bron ygnat, neu rac bron
y neb a vo yn y le yn g6neuthur y dad[40ra.1]leu hynny yn enn6edic, ac a allo
tragy6ydoli y dadleu h6nn6 yn oes yr argl6yd h6nn6: kyntaf y6 kymryt dyn y
genedyl neu y 6rthlad o genedyl. Eil y6 dadleu tir a dayar. Trydyd y6
tagnouedu kenedyloed am alanassoed, neu am ymlad, 6rth na dylyir
tragy6ydoli y dadleu hynny onyt argl6yd, neu y neb a dotto ef yn y le.

Q161. P161, E161

[40ra.12] Tri thauodya6c:⁴³⁴ argl6yd, ac ygnat, a mach.

Q162. P162, Y5, E162

[40ra.14] Tri dyn a dylyant talu galanas ac ny dylyant rann o alanas:⁴³⁵ g6reic, ac
yscolheic, a dyn a talho keina6c paladyr.

Q163. P163, Y6, E163

[40ra.18] Tri dyn a gaffant rann o alanas ac nys talant: argl6yd, ac ygnat, a righill.
Argl6yd a dyly trayan pob galanas o'r a gymhello;⁴³⁶ ygnat a dyly rann yr
alanas;⁴³⁷ a righill⁴³⁸ a dyly cymhell⁴³⁹ y chynnull, a phedeir keina6c ida6 ynteu
yr hynny.⁴⁴⁰

Q164. P164, E164

[40ra.27] Tri pheth ny dyly ygnat y g6randa6 rac y [40rb.1] vron: kygha6ssed
6edy bra6t, llys kyn deturyt, g6at g6edy kyfreith.

Q165. P165, E165

[40rb.3] Tri dyn a dylyir eu cad6 rac arueu: caeth, a mab ny bo pedeir bl6yd ar
dec, ac ynvyt kyhoeda6c. A'e kenedyl a dyly cad6 yr ynvydyon rac g6neuthur
cam ohonunt. Ac velly y dyly tat cad6 y vab, hyt ym pen pedeir blyned ar dec,

---

⁴³⁴ tha6edawc *P*
⁴³⁵ o alanas] oheni *Y*
⁴³⁶ pob galanas or a gymhello] yr kymhell *Y*
⁴³⁷ rann yr alanas] pedeir ar ugeint yr rannu *Y*
⁴³⁸ rigydd *Y*
⁴³⁹ cymhell] *from P;* y chymhell *Q*
⁴⁴⁰ y chymhell ... yr hynny] pedeir keinha6c yr kynnull *Y*

Q160

Three cases which should not be advanced apart from before a justice, or before whoever is in his place especially for hearing those cases, and who can conclude those cases in the lifetime of that lord: the first is affiliating a man into a kindred or ejecting him from the kindred. The second is a case for land and earth. The third is making peace between kindreds for homicides, or for fighting, as those cases are not entitled to be concluded unless by a lord, or whoever he puts in his place.

Q161

Three tongued-ones: a lord, and a justice, and a surety.

Q162

Three persons who are entitled to pay *galanas* and who are not entitled to a share of *galanas*: a woman, and a cleric, and a man who pays a shaft penny.

Q163

Three persons who receive a share of *galanas* but do not pay it: a lord, and a justice, and a *rhingyll*. The lord is entitled to a third of every *galanas* he enforces; the justice is entitled to a share of the *galanas*; and the *rhingyll* ought to enforce its collection, and four pence to him for that.

Q164

Three things a justice is not entitled to hear [argued] before him: pleading after a judgement, an objection before a verdict, and a denial after law.

Q165

Three men who ought to be kept from arms: a slave, and a son who is not 14 years old, and a known idiot. And their kindred should keep the idiots to prevent them from doing wrong. And so a father should keep his son, up to the age of 14, from

rac arueu; kanys ef bieu talu drosta6 yn yr oet h6nn6. Ac velly y dyly argl6yd cad6 y gaeth byth rac arueu; onys keid6, talet gaeth arall dros y arueu, a'r caeth yn eneit uadeu dros y llofrydyaeth.

Q166. *P166, E166 [See also Q246, and J168, Tim161] Additions from Tim.*

[40rb.20] Tri pheth ny drycheuir arnunt: 6yneb6erth,[441] a[442] sarhaet alltut, [a g6arthryd kelein, kanyd kymeint g6arad6yd 6yneb6arth a sarhaed, ac nyd kymeint sarhaed alltyd a bonhedic breiniol,][443] canyt kymeint y anryded na[444] breint dyn mar6 a dyn by6; 6rth hynny nyt ardrycheuir ar vn o'r tri hynny.[445]

Q167. *P167, S187, 199, Tim117, E167*

[40va.1] Tri pheth yssyd vch no chyfreith, ac a tyrr ar[446] kyfreith pan gyuarff6ynt a hi: argl6yd yn lle g6nel 6ell no chyfreith yn dilyt g6irioned, neu yn g6neuthur trugared; a breint yny galler y broui;[447] ac amot adeuedic.

S199. *Tim117*

Tri pheth yssyd voy no chyfreith. Sef y6 y tri hynny, g6ir brid ar dir yn lle y galer y brofi ac ni aller myned ynny erbyn; ac argl6yd yn erlid g6irio[n]ed r6g deu 6r; a hir odef g6lad a vo yn lle k*yfreith*. Ac yn tri lle hynny ny dyly bra6d6r varnu, kany henyd o *gyfreith*, ac na dyly ynteu varanu namyn k*yfreith*; g6lad ac argl6yd, hagen,[448] a dyly barnu ynna.

Q168. *P168, [S223], E168*

[40va.9] Tri meib ny dylyant tref tat: nyt amgen, mab offeirat, a mab claf6r, a mab g6r a dalei tref y tat yn 6aetir. A llyna yr achos nas dyly mab claf6r: 6rth daruot y Du6 y deol [y] 6rth yach uyda6l, a'e 6ahanu. A sef y6 hynny mab a gaffo

---

[441] 6yneb6yerth *Q*

[442] ar *Q*

[443] ac ar y lyas neu y alanas *Q*; a bonhedic breinhawl *J*

[444] na] *from J*; a hynny a *Q;* nay *Tim*

[445] vn o'r tri hynny] yr un or petheu hynny *J*

[446] ar *gloss in Q*

[447] + yn y erbyn *S*

[448] *Tim;* aghen *S*

arms, because it is his duty to pay on his behalf during that time. And so a lord should keep his slave from taking arms ever; if he does not prevent him, let another slave be paid for his arms, and the first slave condemned for the homicide.

Q166

Three things which are not augmented: *wynebwerth*, and the *sarhaed* of an alien, and the shame of a corpse, as the disgrace of *wynebwerth* is not as great as that of *sarhaed*, and the *sarhaed* of an alien is not as great as that of a privileged noble, and that neither the honour nor the status of a dead man is as great as that of a living man; and because of that there is no augmentation on any of those three things.

Q167

Three things which are superior to the law, and which override law when they encounter it: a lord when he is doing better than the law whilst seeking justice, or whilst being merciful; and a special privilege until it is proven; and an acknowledged contract.

S199

Three things which are higher than law. Those three things are, true purchase on land where it can be proved and it is not possible to go against it; and a lord seeking the truth between two men; and long suffering by a country of that which is in place of law. And in those three places a judge is not entitled to judge, as they do not derive from law, and he is not entitled to judge anything but law; the country and a lord, however, are entitled to judge there.

Q168

Three sons who are not entitled to patrimony: namely, the son of a priest, and the son of a leper, and the son of a man who paid his patrimony as blood land. And this is the reason why the son of a leper is not entitled to it: because God exiled

claf6r 6edy bo barnnedic y glafty;[449] a mab a gaffo offeirat 6edy y del yn vrdeu offeiradaeth; a'r trydyd nyt oes tref tat ida6 her6yd daruot y dat y diuetha kyn noc ef tr6y gyfreith.

Q169. *P169, [S226], €169*

[40va.25] Teir g6raged a dyly eu meibon tir o vam6ys: g6reic vonhedic a rodher o rod kenedyl y alltut, a bot meibon idi ohona6 ac ef yn alltut; y rei [40vb.1] hynny a dyly rann o tir gyt a[450] brodyr eu mam, eithyr hyt y bei breint neu teilygda6t ymdana6; o h6nn6 hagen ny dylyant dim o rann hyt ym pen y pet6areg6r,[451] gan vot neb o bleit tad6ys a'e dylyo, ony bei eu bot yn veibon y bennaeth alltut. Eil y6 bei dam6einhei vot mor6yn, ar vreint[452] brodyr a'e chenedyl, a'e threissa6 o alltut: os mab a uei idi ar yr hynt honno, h6nn6 a dyly rann o tir gyt a brodyr y vam. Trydyd y6 bei dam6einei[453] rodi g6reic vonhedic yg6ystyl y alltuded, ac yno caffel beichogi ohonei a bot mab idi, h6nn6 a dyly rann o tir y gyt a'e brodyr hi. A llyna y dyly plant y 6reic kyntaf: kanys y brodyr hi a alltuda6d y phlant pan y rodyssant hi y alltut; ac 6rth hynny, her6yd na dylyynt rodi y ch6aer namyn y'r lle y caffei y phlant hitheu tir, y dyly y phla*n*t hitheu tir o vam6ys. A llyna yr achos[454] y dyly plant [41ra.1] yr eil 6reic vam6ys: kanys[455] vei hi ar vreint y brodyr a'e chenedyl, h6ynt a dylyant y chad6 hitheu rac pop cam; ac 6rth gaffel honei hi y cam h6nn6 ar y hardel6 h6y, y dyly y meibon hitheu vam6ys. A llyma yr achos y dyly plant y tryded 6reic vam6ys: canys a hi ar eu g6ystloryaeth h6y y cauas hi y dam6ein h6n*n*6; 6rth hynny y dyly y phlant hitheu vam6ys.

Q170. *P170, [S227, Tim120], €170*

[41ra.13] Teir gorssed gyfreitha6l yssyd: gorssed argl6yd, gorssed escob, gorssed abbat. A'r teir hynny a dylyant g6rogaeth g6yr; ac ny dyly g6r yr vn ohonunt g6neuthur ya6n namyn yn y orssed e hun, ony bei dam6eina6 y 6r yr escob neu 6r yr abat yn vn o'r d6y ereill, neu vn o'r d6y ereill yg gorssed yr abat. Pop vn o'r rei hynny g6naet ya6n yn y lle y g6nel y cam.

---

[449] *From P*; glady *Q, S, €,*

[450] ae *Q*

[451] pet6arg6r *Q*

[452] + y that ae *P*

[453] bei dam6einei] bani6eniai *P*

[454] yr achos] y lle *P*

[455] + tra *P*

him from the healthy living people, and separated him. And that one is the son had by a leper after he was judged to a lazar house; and the son begotten by a priest after he has taken holy orders; and the third does not have a patrimony because his father ruined it before him by law.

Q169

Three women whose sons are entitled to land through mother-right: a noblewoman who may be given by gift of kin to an alien, and who has children by him, and he an alien; they are entitled to a share of land with their mother's brothers, as long as there may be no privilege or special status concerning it; and of that however they are not entitled to any share until the fourth man, as there is someone on the patrimonial side who is entitled to it, unless they are the sons of an exiled chief. The second is if it chanced that a maiden, dependent on the status of her brothers and her kindred, is raped by an alien: if a son were born to her as a result of that event, that one is entitled to a share of land with his mother's brothers. The third is if it happened that a noblewoman is given as a hostage into exile, and there she becomes pregnant and has a son, he is entitled to a share of land with her brothers. And that is the reason why the children of the first woman are entitled: because her brothers exiled her children when they gave her to an alien; and because of that, since they ought not to give their sister except to the place where her children would get land, her children are entitled to inherit land though mother-right. And that is the reason why the children of the second woman are entitled to mother-right: because she was dependent on the status of her brothers and her kindred, they should have kept her from every harm; and because she received that wrong whilst she was attached to them, her sons are entitled to mother-right. And this is the reason why the children of the third woman are entitled to mother-right: since she was under their hostageship when she met with that accident; for that reason her children are entitled to mother-right.

Q170

There are three lawful sessions: the session of a lord, the session of a bishop, and the session of an abbot. And those three are entitled to the homage of men; and no man of any of them is obliged to make redress save in his own session, unless it happened to be the man of the bishop or the man of the abbot in either of the other two [sessions], or one of the other two in the session of the abbot. Let each one of those make redress in the place he does wrong.

Q171. *P171, [S228, Tim121], E171*

[41ra.26] Tri g6anas g6ystyl ynt: lla6, a breich, ac ysg6yd. Sef achos y gel6ir yr rei hynny yn 6anasseu g6ystyl: cany dylyir rodi yg6ystyl⁴⁵⁶ ny aller y ar6ein yn vn o'r [tri] lle hynny, [41rb.1] onyt yr ha6l6r a'e mynn, onyt na aller g6ystla6 namyn peth ma6r. Sef achos y6 hynny 6rth na dylyir g6ystla6 peth aghyuodedyn am dylyet a aller y gych6yn.

Q172. *P172, [S229, Tim122], E172*

[41rb.7] Tri g6ystyl gogymreint ynt: g6ystyl o la6 mach, ac o la6 kynnogyn, ac o la6 argl6yd neu y 6assanaeth6r am⁴⁵⁷ dylyet adeuedic heb uach arna6, a heb gadarn6ch,⁴⁵⁸ ac eissoes y vot yn adeuedic.

Q173. *P173, [S230, Tim123], E173*

[41rb.14] Tri g6ystyl nyt reit meicheu ar eu dilysr6yd: vn o la6 vach, ac vn a dycco ha6l6r y ar y mach or na mynnei 6assanaethu y vechni, ac vn o la6 argl6yd neu y 6ass[an]aeth6r. Sef achos nat reit mach ar dilysr6yd g6ystyl o la6 mach neu o la6 argl6yd, canys hynny o dynyon ny 6atta ry6ystla6 o'e lla6 h6y, nac yr h6ant da, nac yr peth arall. A llyna yr achos nat reit mach ar dilysr6yd g6ystyl a dyccer ar vach, canys o'e anuod y dygir; ac os ryd ynteu o'e [41va.1] uod, kymeret y ha6l6r vach y ganta6 ar dilysr6yd, rac g6adu ohona6 yr eil6eith nas rodes.

Q174. *P174, E174*

[41va.4] Tri meich ny dylyir eu g6adu: mach ar obyr ygnat, a mach o'r argl6yd, neu o'e 6assanaeth6yr.

Q175. *P175, E175*

[41va.8] Tri lle y rodir mach yndun, ny dyly y 6adu: kyhoedogr6yd pl6yf, a gorsed gyfreitha6l, neu rac bron argl6yd, 6rth vot y tri lle hynny yn tri kyhoedogr6yd kyfreitha6l, ac nat oes dim a 6neler yg kyhoedogr6yd a dylyir y 6adu.

---

⁴⁵⁶ + peth *P*
⁴⁵⁷ + y *Q*
⁴⁵⁸ gadernyt *P*

Q171

These are the three supports of a gage: a hand, and an arm, and a shoulder. The reason these are called supports of gages: because a thing which cannot be led by one of those things is not entitled to be given as a gage, unless the claimant wishes it, unless it is impossible to gage anything but a large thing. The reason for that is that an immovable thing ought not to be gaged for a moveable due.

Q172

These are the three equal gages: a gage from the hand of a surety, and from the hand of a debtor, and from the hand of a lord or his assistant for an acknowledged debt without a surety on it, and without security, but which is already acknowledged.

Q173

Three gages which do not need sureties on their validity: one from the hand of a surety, and one which the claimant took from the surety who did not wish to serve his suretyship, and one from the hand of a lord or his assistant. This is the reason that a surety is not needed on the validity of a gage from the hand of a surety or a lord, because those men do not deny giving a gage from their hands, neither on account of the lust for goods, nor anything else. And that is the reason why no surety is needed for the validity of a gage taken from a surety, because it is taken against his will; and if he give one willingly, let the claimant take surety from him on its validity, so that he does not deny a second time that he gave it.

Q174

Three sureties which are not entitled to be denied: a surety for the justice's fee, and a surety from the lord, or from his assistants.

Q175

Three places where if surety is given, it ought not to be denied: [in] the publicity of a parish, and [in] a lawful session, or before a lord, as those three places are the three lawful public places, and nothing done publicly is entitled to be denied.

Q176. *P176, [S234], €176*

[41va.18] Tri gorsaf g6reic ynt: kyntaf y6 y lle y kyscer genti; hi a dyly vot yno hyt ym pen y na6uetyd y edrych a vu gyfreitha6l yd ysgar6ys y g6r a hi. Eil y6 y lle yd yscaro a'e g6r;[459] hi a dyly vot yno hyt ympen y na6uettyd y edrych a vu gyfreitha6l yd yscar6ys a'e g6r; ac o bu aet yna ar ol y[460] geina6c di6ethaf o'r eidi. Y [41vb.1] trydyd y6 g6reic a uo mar6 y g6r; hi a dyly vot uch penn y hael6yt hyt ym penn[461] na6uettyd, ac yna aet ar ol y[462] geina6c di6ethaf o'r heidi.

Q177. *P177, [S238], €177*

[41vb.6] Tri chyghyaua6c[463] kyfreith: rannyat galanas, a g6erth tei a dotrefyn,[464] a dadyl mach a chynogyn. Sef achos y gel6ir h6y velly: rac anha6sset eu d6yn ar gof ac ar ethrylith.

Q178. *P178, [S243], €178*

[41vb.13] Tri aneueil yssyd gymeint g6erth y troet pop vn ohonunt a'e eneit: march, a milgi, a heba6c. Sef achos y6 hynny canys budyr y6 pop vn o'r tri anyueil hynny,[465] ac anyueil dif6yn annolo vyd 6edy na aller aruer ohona6, ac aruer pop vn onadunt yssyd o'e troet o'r tri hynny, a g6erth y eneit.

Q179. *P179, [S244], €179*

[41vb.24] Teir sarhaet ny di6ygir: sarhaet a gaffo mab y gan y dat ac ef ar y vreint, a g6reic gan y g6r am vn o'r tri acha6s kyfreitha6l, a sarhaet g6r gan y argl6yd.

Q180. *P180, [S245], €180*

Tri achos y [42ra.1] dyly g6r maedu y 6reic: am vna6 meuyl ar y uaryf, ac am gyfulauann arna6, ac am gaffel g6r arall genti. Os maed ynteu am vn o'r tri hynny, ny dyly caffel amgen ia6n no h6nn6, kans kyfreith[466] y dif6yn ida6 e hun; ny dyly caffel vn ia6n 6edy.

---

[459] + a hi *P*

[460] ar ol y] *from P;* a'r holl *Q*

[461] pem *Q*

[462] ar ol y] *P*; a'r holl *Q*

[463] chynhauawc *P*

[464] dotrefyn *Q*

[465] y6 pop vn o'r tri anyueil hynny] ynt eu kic *P*

[466] kans kyfreith] kanys *P*

Q176

These are the three stoppings of a woman: the first is the place where she is slept with; she ought to be there until the end of the ninth day to see whether her husband parted from her legally. The second is the place where she parted from her husband; she ought to be there until the end of the ninth day, to see whether she parted from her husband legally, and if she did, let her leave with every last penny of her possessions. The third is a woman whose husband has died; she should be on her hearth until the end of the ninth day, and then let her leave with every last penny of her possessions.

Q177

Three complexities of law: the division of *galanas*, and the value of houses and equipment, and a case for surety and debtor. This is the reason that they are so called: because it is difficult to commit them to memory and skill.

Q178

Three animals that have a foot value as great as their life value: a horse, and a greyhound, and a hawk. The reason for that is that those three animals are unclean, and it is a spoiled and useless animal when it cannot be used, and the use of each of these three depends on its feet, and the value of its life.

Q179

Three injuries which are not compensated: the injury a son receives from his father when he is dependent on his status, and [that of] a woman from her husband for one of the three legal reasons, and the injury of a man by his lord.

Q180

Three causes for which a man is entitled to beat his wife: for wishing a blemish on his beard, and for an offence against him, and for her taking another man. If he beats her for one of those three reasons, he is not entitled to any other redress than that, because [according to] law he made redress for it himself; is not entitled to any other redress afterwards.

Q181. P181, [S246], €181

Tri lle y rann kyfreith yn deu hanner: kyntaf y6 or dam6einia[467] bot dylyet a mach arna6, ac ada6 o'r kynogyn y 6lat, neu amgen y dlodi ar dim hyt na allo talu, ac ef yn vn 6lat ac ef; y mach yna a dyly talu hanner y dylyet, kyt bo g6irion, am beri ohona6 y'r ha6l6r y gredu. Eil y6 or dam6eina[468] bot amrysson am teruynu ar 6yr, a hynny yn vn ry6 priodoryon o vreint a g6archad6, ac na 6ypei henuryeit y 6lat y ya6n teruynu y rygtunt. Trydyd y6 or dam6eina bot ynys r6g y d6y auon ac na bei nes yr un no'e gilyd; rannu deu hanner a dylyir am pop peth kyhyded, ac [42rb.1] uelly y6 honn. A sef y6 kyhyded:[469] pop dadyl a hebryger yn gyhyt ac yn gystal.

Q182. P182, [S248, Tim129], €182

[42rb.4] Teir ouer groes ysyd: croes a 6ahardo ll6ybyr a lyccro y yt, a chroes ar risgyl prenn yn y or6ed neu yn y seuyll, a chroes ny hebryger a ll6. Am pop vn o'r teir hynny ny dylyir na dif6yn[470] na dial.

Q183. P183, [S249, Tim130], Y154, €183

[42rb.12] Tri mod y telir amobyr y 6reic: o gy6elogach kyhoeda6c kynny bo na rod nac ystynn, ac o veichogi, ac o rod ac ystyn, kynny bo na chy6elogach na beichogi. Ac o lathrutra heuyt ef a dylyir amobyr, ac eissoes ny heny6 o'r tri achos. A sef paham: 6rth y hanuot o pop un o'r deu, o rod ac o gy6elogach; canys pan aeth hi gan y g6r yn llathrut, yna yd ymrodes hi e hun y'r g6r, ac bu rodyat hi e hun ida6. O hynny yd heny6 llathruta, o rod ac ystyn, o gy6elogach kyhoeda6c y pan hen[42va.1]y6, kanys kyfreith a varn kynny chysco g6r gan 6reic a dycco yn llathrut, ony chymer g6r y ty mach ar y hamobyr, talet e hun yr amobyr.

Y154

Teir fford y telir amobyr: o rod ac ystyn kyny bo kywelogaeth, ac o gywelogaeth kyhoeda6c kynny bo rod, noc o veichogi.

---

[467] damdam6einia *Q*
[468] deruyd *P*
[469] ac uelly y6 honn … kyhyded] – *P*
[470] dir6y *P*

Q181

Three places law divides in two halves: the first is if it happens that there is a debt with a surety upon it, and the debtor leaves his country, or otherwise he becomes so poor that he cannot pay, and he is in the same country as him; the surety then ought to pay half of the debt, although he is innocent, for causing the claimant to believe him. The second is if it happens that there is a dispute for setting land boundaries between men, and they are the same type of proprietors by status and guardianship, and the elders of the country do not rightly know how to set the boundaries between them. The third is if it happens that there is an island between the two rivers and neither is closer than the other; every thing of equality ought to be divided in half, and thus here. And this is equality: every case that is brought for as long and equally well.

Q182

There are three vain crosses: a cross which prevents a passage that may cause damage to corn, and a cross on the bark of a tree lying or standing, and a cross which is not accompanied by an oath. For each of these three there ought not to be compensation or penalty.

Q183

Three ways *amobr* is paid for a woman: for open bedsharing although there is neither gift nor handing over, and for pregnancy, and for gift and handing over, although there is neither bedsharing nor pregnancy. And from abduction too *amobr* is due, although it does not arise from the three cases. And this is why: because it arises from each of the two, from gift and from bedsharing; because when she went with her abductor, she gave herself to the man, and she became her own giver to him. Abduction derives from that, from gift and handing over, and from open bedsharing, because the law judges that although a man may not sleep with a woman he takes secretly, unless the man of the house takes surety on her *amobr*, let he himself pay her *amobr*.

Y154

Three ways *amobr* is paid: by gift and handing over although there is no bedsharing, and by open bedsharing although there is no gift, or by pregnancy.

Q184. P184, [S250, Tim131], €184

[42va.6] Tri dyn a dyly talu amobyr: y neb a vo rodyat arnei, a hitheu e hun, a'r vn a dy6edassam ni vchot.

Q185. P185, [S251, Tim132], €185

[42va.9] Tri dygyat a vyd ar vab: vn y6 y vam arna6 ar y llog6yd, a dygyat y tat neu y genedyl yn y vam egl6ys, a'r trydyd[471] y6 e hun, ony odi6ed y vam bei by6. O gordi6edassei y vam ynteu y d6yn a'e bot yn vy6, kyhyt ac y gallei y d6yn, a'e vot ynteu yn amheuedic, kyfreith a dy6eit na dyly ef[472] d6yn, na chenedyl y gymryt vyth, canys kyfreith a gyssynna6d g6ybot ohonei nat oed vab y mab h6nn6 y'r tat y tebygei ef y uot, canys duc ida6 a hi yn g6elet y vot yn hamheuedic.

Q186. [S252, Tim133], €186

[42va.27] Tri chymeryat a vyd[473] ar vab: ac vn taua6t a'e g6atta ac a'e kymer, y tat [42vb.1] e hun y6 h6nn6. Yr eil y6, ony byd by6 y tat, penkenedyl, a seith6yr yn lle tat y gyt ac ef o'r genedyl. A trydyd y6 ony bei na that ida6 na phenkenedyl, vn g6r ar hugeint a'e g6atta ac a'e kymer: seith yn [lle] tat ida6, a seith yn lle y benkenedyl, a seith y gyt a'r penkenedyl. A sef val y mae y gymryt: y gymryt o'r penkenedyl yn y la6 a'e rodi yn lla6 y g6r hynaf o'r seith6yr, ac uelly o hynaf y hynaf, hyt ym pen y seithuet g6r. A'r g6yr hynny nyt oes nodyat arnunt, namyn y bot yn oreug6yr o'r genedyl, ac[474] ny dylyont ranny[475] tir a dayar ac ef; ac yn vn ansa6d a hynny y kymerir. A'r ygnat a dyly bot vrth varnny, yr hynn a 6neler na'e 6adu na'e gymryt, ac uelly mae kymryt mab neu 6adu. Or darffei vot mab ar ardel6 tat yn vab diodef, ac ym[y]6yt y tat h6nn6 nas dyckei y vam ida6, kyfreith a dy6eit [43ra.1] na ellir d6yn mab y 6r mar6, namyn y vot ymreint mab a 6attei y tat; eithyr gal6 o'e vam y d6yn y tat arall os mynn, kanys duc y h6nn6. O dyckei hitheu h6n6, na dr6c na da vei y tat, kyfreith a dy6eit na dyly ef vyth caffel tat namyn h6nn6, ac am hynny y dy6eit kyfreith na ellir d6yn mab y[476] var6.

---

[471] *P ends here*
[472] + y *Q*
[473] a vyd a uyd *Q*
[474] ar *Q*
[475] *badly smudged Q*
[476] + gan *Q*

Q184

Three men who are obliged to pay *amobr*: whoever may be her giver, and she herself, and the one we mentioned above.

Q185

There are three affiliators of a son: one is his mother on her deathbed, and the affiliation of his father or his kindred in his mother church, and the third is he himself, unless his mother should achieve this were she alive. If his mother had succeeded in affiliating him when she was alive, as far as she was able to affiliate him, and he was doubted [still], the law says that he is not entitled to affiliate, nor his kindred accept him ever, because the law agreed that she knew that that son was not the son of the supposed father, as she did not affiliate him to him when she saw that he was doubted.

Q186

There are three acceptors of a son: the one tongue denies him and accepts him, that is the father himself. The second is, unless the father is alive, the head of kindred, and seven men from the kindred with him in place of the father. And the third is if he has neither a father or a head of kindred, twenty-one men can deny him and accept him: seven in place of his father, and seven in place of his head of kindred, and seven with the head of kindred. And this is how he is affiliated: he is taken by the head of kindred by the hand and placed in the hand of the eldest of the seven men, and so from eldest to [next] eldest, until the seventh man. And of those men none is designated, except that they are the best men from the kindred, and that they may not be entitled to share land and earth with him; and he is affiliated in that fashion. And the justice should be present to judge, whichever is done whether he is denied or accepted, and thus a son is affiliated or denied. If it should happen that a son is a son by sufferance taken as related to a father, and that in the father's lifetime the mother should not have affiliated him to him, the law says that a son cannot be affiliated to a dead man, but that he is of the status of a son whom the father would deny; but his mother could have affiliated him to another father if she wished, since she did not affiliate him to that man. If she affiliated him, whether the father be good or bad, the law says that he is never entitled to have a father apart from him, and because of that the law says that a son cannot be affiliated to the dead.

Q187. S215, [256], Tim137, E187

[43ra.13] Tri dyn a dieinc rac dihenyd[477] kyfadef: yscolheic coruna6c,[478] a mab hyt tra uo ar vreint y tat; na dylyir arna6 na dir6y na dihenyd hyt ym penn y pedeir blyned ar dec, kanyt ydi6[479] yn oet y dyly kyfreith argl6yd vot arna6; y tat hagen a dyly g6neuthur ia6n drosta6 y'r argl6yd ac y'r colledic[480] – a[481] dyn anghyuieith[482] a vyrryer o log y tir, hyt ym penn teir nos a thri dieu – yny wypynt[483] kyfreith y 6lat.[484] Ny dylyir arnunt amgen noc etryt y'r colledic yr eida6. Yscolheic coruna6c ny dylyir arna6 na dir6y na dihe[43vb.1]nyd am y lletrat kyntaf, namyn y diurda6 a'e ada6 ar vreint lleyc.[485]

Q188. S189, Tim108, E188

[43rb.3] Tri pheth ny dylyir eu rannv namyn her6yd y ffr6ytheu:[486] melin, a choret, a pherllan.

Q189. [S261, Tim142], E189

[43rb.7] Tri pheth a a r6g dyn a daly a damt6g: cad6 kyn coll, a geni a meithrin, ac ar6aessaf.

Q190. [S260, Tim141], E190

[43rb.10] Tri llyssyat yssyd ar tir: galanastra, dirtra, a g6reictra. P6y bynnac a vynno llussu o vot galanastra y rygta6 ac ef, ef a dyly en6i y deu car, yr h6nn a las, a'r h6n a'e llada6d. P6y bynnac a vynno llyssu tyst o gerenyd nes, ef a dyly d6yn tyston kyt genedyl, kany dyly estra6n d6yn car y neb, ac ef heuyt a dyly d6yn y gerenyd.

---

[477] rac dihenyd] hep vod ynn eneid vadeu am ledrad ny *S*
[478] + ni dylir am y ledrat kyntaf namyn y diurda6 a'e ell6g ynn llyt *S*
[479] ydydi6 *Q*
[480] a mab ... colledic] Eil y6 mab kyn y vyned yn bedeir bl6yd ar dec *S*
[481] trydyd y6 *S*
[482] agkyfreithus *Q, E,*
[483] b6ynt *Q, E,*
[484] a vyrryer ... 6lat] ny 6ypo kyfreith y 6lat ae defod hyd ymhen tri dieu a their nos *S*
[485] Ny dylyir ... lleyc] – *S*
[486] + nyt amgen *Tim*

Q187

Three men who escape an acknowledged execution: a tonsured cleric, and a son whilst he is under the legal control of his father; it is not right that he should suffer either a *dirwy* fine or execution until the end of the fourteen years, because he is not of the age when he ought to be subject to a lord's law; the father however should do justice on his behalf to the lord and to the person who suffered loss – and a person of foreign speech who is cast ashore from a ship, until the end of three nights and three days – until they know the law of the country. They are not obliged to do anything apart from returning the loser's property. A tonsured cleric is not liable either to a fine or execution for the first theft, but he should be defrocked and left with the status of a layman.

Q188

Three things which ought not to be shared except by their fruits: a mill, and a weir, and an orchard.

Q189

Three things that stand between a man and attachment and swearing: custody before loss, and birth and nurture, and voucher to warranty.

Q190

There are three objections as to land: *galanas*-feud, land-feud, and woman-feud. Whoever wishes to object because there is *galanas*-feud between them, he should name the two relatives, the one who was killed, and the one who killed him. Whoever wishes to object to a witness on the grounds of closer kinship, he should bring witnesses of the same kindred, as a stranger is not entitled to connect a relative to anyone, and he is also entitled to set out his kinship.

Q191. *[S262, Tim143], €191*

[43rb.23] Tri pheth ny dylyir eu damt6g: kic hep croen, ac aryant heb lester, ac yt or pan el ar y yscub. Sef val y mae hynny: or collei y dyn anyueil by6, ac na o*r*di6ededei yn lle bei tyb, namyn y kic [43va.1] hep penn, hep croen, hep traet, kyfreith a dy6eit na dyly ef y damt6g, kany dyly dyn damt6g ar ny 6elo. Yr eil y6 aryant heb y llester, a gollo dyn; ny dyly y damt6g kanys vn ry6 vyd pop aryant a'e gilyd; os collei ynteu yn y llester, her6yd breint y llestyr y dyly damt6g. Trydyd y6 pei collei dyn yt ar y galaf; kyfreith a dy6eit na dyly ef y damt6g, kany dyly dyn damt6g namyn kyfry6 ac a gollo.

Q192. *[S263, Tim144], €192*

[43va.17] Tri g6ystyl ny dyg6ydant vyth: telyn, a phayol y6, a ffl6. Os rodei dyn o'e uod vn o'r tri hynny, ef a dygg6ydei mal g6ystyl arall, kanys e hun a lygra6d y vreint pan y g6ystla6d. Os dyckei y mach y arna6 o'e anuod, ny dyg6yd hyt ympenn vn dyd a bl6ydyn; 6ynt a dyg6ydant yna y'r ha6l6r hagen ympenn y na6uettyd, ka[43vb.1]nys ef a dyly y'r mach 6ystyl kyfreith; y mach a dyg6yd y'r kynnogyn y k6byl.[487]

Q193. *€193*

[43vb.4] Tri gorsseda6c a allant 6neuthur y cabit6l tr6y eu kyfreith e hun, yn y lle na lesteiront gyfreith y brenhin: sef ynt escob, ac abbat, a meistyr ys6yd6r.

Q194. *S275, Tim156, €194*

[43vb.9] Tri thlos kenedyl ynt, ac y gel6ir:[488] melyn, a choret, a pherllann. A rei hynny ny dylyir y rannu na'e kych6ynn6, namyn rannv eu ffr6ytheu y'r neb a'e dylyo.[489]

---

[487] o g6byl *Q*
[488] ynt, ac y gel6ir] – *S, Tim*
[489] A rei hynny … dylyo] Sef achos y gel6ir yn dri thl6s kenedyl 6rth adtel o ba6p or genedyl bot yn gyd am danynt. G6erth kored y6 punt. G6erth melin y6 punt. G6erth k. yssyd ar bop afallen or perllan. *S, Tim*

Q191

Three things that ought not to be sworn to: meat without skin, and money without a vessel, and corn that has gone from the sheaf. This is why this is so: if a man loses a live animal, and he does not overtake it in the place he may suspect it to be, but only the meat without a head, without skin, without feet, the law says that he is not entitled to swear to it, because a man is not entitled to swear to that which he cannot see. The second is money without the vessel, which a man loses; he is not entitled to swear because all money is of the same kind as the next; if he lost it in the vessel, he is entitled to swear for the [legal] status of the vessel. The third is if a man loses corn in straw; the law says he is not entitled to swear, because a man is not entitled to swear apart from the same kind of thing as he has lost.

Q192

Three gages that never lapse: a harp, and a yew pail, and a plume. If a man willingly gives one of those three, it will lapse like another gage, because he himself degraded its value when he gaged it. If a surety takes them from him against his will, they will not lapse until the end of a year and a day; they lapse then to the claimant at the end of the ninth day, because he is entitled to a legal gage from the surety; the surety is wholly liable to the debtor.

Q193

Three enthroned ones who can conduct their chapter by their own law, where they do not hinder the king's law: those are a bishop, and an abbot, and a master of hospitallers.

Q194

These are the three precious things of a kindred, and they are so called: a mill, and a weir, and an orchard. And those ought not to be divided or alienated, but their fruits should be shared among whoever may be entitled to them.

Q195. €195

[43vb.15] Tri corfflann ny dylyir y rannu her6yd tydynneu, namyn her6yd gardeu. Ac o byd tei arna6, nys dyly y mab jeuaf m6y no'r hynaf, namyn y rannu yn deu hanner her6yd estefyll.

Q196. Tim162, €196

[43vb.22] Teir bala6c vechni yssyd: deua6t bala6c vechni y6 bot yn neill penn ydi yn r6ym, a'r llall yn agoret ac yn ryd.[490] Kyntaf y6 ohonunt or pryn dyn dim y gan arall, ac erchi ohona6 mach ar y da y gan y neb a'e g6er[44ra.1]tha6d, a'e rodi ohona6,[491] a dodi y la6 yn lla6 y mach, ac na[492] del y dyn a erchis y vechni y'6[493] gymryt o la6 y mach ac y dodi y la6 yn lla6 y mach,[494] namyn ystynnv y la6 parth ac at y[495] mach, a'r mach parth ac atta6 ynteu, a thebygu[496] ohona6 bot yn diga6n hynny. Kyfreith a dy6eit nat r6ym[497] y vechni honno yn y dyd y bo reit 6rthi, kanny medra6d y chymryt yn gyfreitha6l.[498] Kyt boet mach y gan y neb[499] a'e rodes o vynet y lla6 yn y gilyd udunt h6y, nyt mach y'r neb nys kymerth a'r lla6 yn y gilyd;[500] 6rth hynny y mae bala6c vechni honno.

Yr eil y6[501] or deruyd y dyn prynu da y gan arall ac erchi mach ar y da h6nn6, a dy6edut o'r dyn[502] 'mi a'e rodaf',[503] ac ystynnv y la6 parth a'r h6nn a rodo yn vach,[504] a h6nn6[505] atta6 ynteu,[506] hep rodi o'r vn y[507] la6 yn lla6 y gilyd.[508] A g6edy hynny rodi o'r mach y la6 yn lla6 y neb a bryna[44rb.1]6d y da, a mynet yn vach ida6. Kyfreith a dy6eit yna y vot ef yn vach y'r h6n a'e kymerth yn gyfreitha6l, ac nyt mach y'r h6nn a'e rodes yn agkyfreitha6l;[509] a channyt oes le ida6 y gymell y vechni, dyg6ydet e hun yn y gouyt a del o'r vechni honno.

---

[490] deua6t bala6c … yn ryd] – *Tim*
[491] ae rodi ohona6] mi ay rodaf heb y dyn *Tim*
[492] yna *€*
[493] a erchis y vechni y'6] ae kymero y vechni oe *Tim*
[494] ac y dodi … y mach] – *Tim*
[495] ac at y] ar *Tim*
[496] thebugu *Q*
[497] nat r6ym] na grymha *Tim*
[498] y chymryt yn gyfreitha6l] – *Tim*
[499] y neb] – *Tim*
[500] nys kymerth a'r lla6 yn y gilyd] ae kymerth kanyd aeth y lla6 yny gylyd a *Tim*
[501] + bala6c vechni *Tim*
[502] + a bryno y peth *Tim*
[503] + vach *Tim*
[504] h6nn a rodo yn vach] mach *Tim*
[505] a h6nn6] ac estyny or mach parth ac *Tim*
[506] + y la6 a *Tim*
[507] y6 *Q*
[508] + eissoes *Tim*
[509] a'e rodes yn agkyfreitha6l] nys rodes yn gyf;a6l *Tim*

Q195

It is not right to share enclosures by tofts, but by quillets. And if there are buildings on it, the youngest son is no more entitled to them than the eldest, but they are shared in two by chambers.

Q196

There are three buckle suretyships: the nature of a buckle suretyship is that one end of it is bound, and the other is open and free. The first of them is if a person buys anything from another, and asks for a surety on the goods from whoever sold them, and he gives it, and puts his hand in the hand of the surety, and the man who asked for suretyship does not come to take it from the hand of the surety and to put his hand in the hand of the surety, but only extends his hand towards the surety, and the surety towards him, and he supposes that that is sufficient. The law says that that suretyship does not bind on the day it is needed, because they did not manage to take it legally. Although there was a surety given by the person who gave him by the hand of one being put into that of the other, there was no surety on the part of the person who did not take him by putting one hand into the other; therefore that is a buckle suretyship.

The second is if it happens that a person buys goods from another and asks for a surety on those goods, and the man says 'I will give it', and extends his hand towards the person he gave as surety, and he to him, without either of them putting their hand in the hand of the other. And after that the surety puts his hand in the hand of the person who bought the goods, and becomes a surety to him. The law says then that he is a surety for the one who took him legally, and is not a surety for the person who gave him illegally; and as there is nowhere he can enforce his suretyship, let him be liable for the trouble that may come from that suretyship.

Trydyd[510] y6 or deruyd y dyn kymryt mach ar da[511] yn absen y dylya6dyr,[512] a
dyuot roda6dyr y mach, a rodi y vechni o'e la6[513] yn lla6 y mach, ac en6i y dyn
nyt ydi6 yn y lle,[514] a dyuot y mach at[515] yr h6nn yssyd yn y lle yn y gymryt
yn vach ida6,[516] a'r[517] lla6 yn y gilyd udunt, ac en6i o'r mach heuyt yr h6nn nyt
ydi6 yn y lle.[518] Kyfreith a dy6eit na rymha y vechni honno, yr mynet y lla6 yn
y gilyd y bop vn o'r tri y buant, canyt ydoed yr h6nn a dylyei her6yd rodi y
mach dros y da yn y lle.[519]

Sef achos y gel6ir y rei [44va.1] hynny yn teir bala6c:[520] achos[521] r6yma6 yn
gadarn yn y g6rth6yneper ida6, a phan r6ymher bala6c yny g6rth6ynep ell6g
y r6ym a 6na, ac 6rth hynny nyt dichleis[522] y r6ymat. Ac yn y lle y bo[523] y
mechniaetheu hynny, or g6rth6ynebir vdunt, ny sauant ac ny r6ymant.

Y neb a vo mach dros dyn, onys tal y tala6dyr yn oet dyd, oet pymthec ni6arna6t
a geiff y mach yna, os ar da mar6a6l y byd yn vach. Ac ony thal y tala6dyr yna,
oet dec ni6arna6t ar ugeint a geiff y mach yna. Ac ony thal y tala6dyr yna, oet
deg ni6arna6t a deugeint a geiff y mach yna. Ac ony thal y tala6dyr yna talet
y mach e hunan. Os ar da by6a6l y byd mach ac na thalo y tala6dyr yn oet y
dyd, oet pymthec ni6arna6t a geiff y mach yna. Ac ony thal y tala6dyr yna, oet
deg ni6arna6t a geiff y mach yna. [44vb.1] Ac ony thal y tala6dyr yna, oet
pump di6arna6t a geiff y mach yna. Ac ony thal y tala6dyr yna, talet y mach e
hunan. A phan gyfarfo y mach a'r tala6dyr, yspeilet ef oc a vo ymdana6 o dillat
eithyr y pilin nessaf ida6. Ac velly g6naet byth, yny[524] gaffo tal c6byl y ganta6.

Y neb a adefo dylyu da ida6, talet yn diohir, eithir yn y teir g6yl arbennic, y
Nadolic, a'r Pasc, a'r Sulg6yn: nyt amgen, o Nos Nadolic g6edy gosper hyt

[510] trydyd] ar trydyd bala6c vechni *Tim*

[511] – *Tim*

[512] y dylya6dyr] ar beth *Tim*

[513] o'e lla6] – *Tim*

[514] + a rodi y la6 yn lla6 y mach val ydoed k;a6l *Tim*

[515] + y procurator *Tim*

[516] yn y gymryt yn vach ida6] y dyn y kymer6yd y vechni yda6 *Tim*

[517] a'r] a rodi y vechni yda6 ar *Tim*

[518] + hefyd y vod ef yn vach *Tim*

[519] yr mynet y lla6 ... da yn y lle] sef acha6s y6 kyd el y lla6 yn y gylyd y pob vn or tri dyn y byant
a y vechni nyd amgen hy yr procurator yr hyn a kymerth 6rth hyny ny dyly h6nn6 nar vechni nar
ha6l bey re en6eu y mach y h6nn6 y vechni reid vydeu yda6 ehyn daly y tal y g6r re en6yd yda6
y vechni ac nid oed yn y lle nys dyly kany chymerth y vechni o la6 y mach val y dylyeu ac 6rth
hynny na grymha hytheu ac 6rth hynny gel6ir yr hei hynny yn deir bala6c vechni *Tim*

[520] y rei hynny yn teir bala6c] h6y velly *Tim*

[521] achos] ann6yd bala6c y6 *Tim*

[522] dyffleys *Tim*

[523] ac yn y lle y bo] ac velly y mae *Tim*

[524] hynny *Q*

The third is if it happens that a man takes a surety on goods in the absence of the debtor, and the giver of the surety comes, and gives his suretyship from his hand into the hand of the surety, and names the man who is not present, and the surety comes to the person present who is taking him as a surety, and [they put] their hands in each other's hand, and the surety also names the person who is not present. The law says that that surety will not bind, although the hands of the three were joined together, because the person who was entitled [to payment] on account of the surety being given was not present.

This is the reason these are called the three buckle [suretyships]: because it binds strongly until it is opposed, and when a buckle is bound in the opposite direction it releases the bond, and because of that the bond is not secure. And where those suretyships are, if they are opposed, they do not stand and they do not bind.

Whoever may be surety for another, unless the debtor pay his debt on the set day, then the surety shall have a set time of fifteen days, if he be surety for dead stock. And if the debtor does not pay then, the surety shall have a set time of thirty days. And if the debtor does not pay then, the surety has a set time of fifty days. And if the debtor does not pay then, let the surety himself pay. If he be surety on live stock and the debtor does not pay on the set day, the surety shall have a set time of fifteen days. And if the debtor does not pay then, the surety shall have a set time of ten days. And if the debtor does not pay then, the surety shall have a set time of five days. And if the debtor does not pay then, let the surety himself pay. And when the surety and the debtor meet, let him take from him whatever clothes he has about him save the garment next to him. And let him do thus until he has received complete payment from him.

Whoever admits that goods are due from him, let him pay without delay, save on the three special feasts: Christmas, Easter and Whitsun: namely, from Christmas Eve after the vespers until New Year's Day after mass; from the night of Easter Saturday after the resurrection, until Low Sunday after mass; from the night of Whit Saturday after vespers until Trinity Sunday after mass. For no one should make a demand of another during those days.

Du6 Kalan g6edy offeren; o nos Pasc g6edy dat6yrein, hyt Du6 Pasc[525] Bychan g6edy offeren; o nos Sad6rn Sulg6yn g6edy gosper hyt du6 Sul y Drinda6t g6edy offeren. Kany dyly neb gofyn y gilyd yn y die6ed hynny.

Or canhatta y tala6dyr y'r mach rodi ky6erthyt punt yg g6ystyl keina6c a chyn yr oet y golli, ny dyly y tala6dyr trachefyn namyn [45ra.1] dimei, kanys hynny y6 trayan keinha6c kyfreith,[526] ac ynteu a lygr6ys breint y 6ystyl. Or dyry mach peth ma6r yg g6ystyl peth bychan, yr ha6l6r a dyly y gymryt; a chyn coller kyn yr oet, ny di6c yr ha6l6r y'r mach trachefyn namyn trayan y dylyet. Y mach hagen a'e di6c y'r tala6dyr yn g6byl, canys yn anghyfreitha6l y d6c. Or dyry tala6dyr ky6erthyt punt yg g6ystyl keina6c a'e dyg6yda6, ny di6ygir dim drosta6. Argl6yd a vyd mach ar pop da adefedic diuach.

Q197. €197

[45ra.16] Tri aniueil a drycheif eu g6erth teir g6eith yn vn dyd: milgi, a gellgi, a chol6yn, her6yd symuda6 eu perchenogaeth y gan vab eillt y uchel6r a brenhin.

Q198. €198

[45ra.22] Tri pheth yssyd gymeint g6erth eu hanaf ac eu heneit: march, a milgi, a heba6c.

Q199. €199

[45ra.25] Tri aniueil a a g6erth kyfreith kyn eu bl6yd: kosta6c tom, a dauat, a gafar.

Q200. €200

[45ra.28] Tri lle y dyly ynat kym6t varnu yn rat: o keinia6c hyt ym pedeir, ac ebedi6, a chaml6r6.

Q201. €201

[45rb.1] Tri lle y gallei dyn g6neuthur ky6erthyt dec punt o gollet y arall heb y 6adu a heb y talu. Kyntaf y6 pan atalo kyttiria6c d6fyr y velin y llall o negydyaeth kytundeb neu o aghym6ynas y gan berchena6c y velin, gan allu ohona6 atal y d6fyr yn y eida6 e hun. Eil y6 o symut[527] dyn y yt o'r souyl hyt y g6ynd6n, ac

---

[525] pasc pasc *Q*
[526] keinha6c kyfreith] dimei *Q*
[527] sumut *Q*

If the debtor allows the surety to give the equivalent of a pound as a gage on a penny and before the set time it is lost, the debtor is not entitled to anything afterwards apart from a halfpenny, because that is a third of a legal penny, for he debased the status of his gage. If a surety gives a big object as a gage for a small object, the claimant should take it; and though it be lost before the set time, the claimant does not recompense the surety afterwards, apart from a third of the debt. The surety however repays it to the debtor in full, since he took it illegally. If the debtor gives the equivalent of a pound as a gage for a penny and it is forfeit, nothing is repaid for it. The lord shall be a surety on all known unsuretied goods.

Q197

Three animals whose value is augmented three times in one day: a greyhound, and a staghound, and a pet dog, because their ownership is moved from that of a villein to that of a nobleman and a king.

Q198

Three things whose injury and life is equal in value: a horse, and a greyhound, and a falcon.

Q199

Three animals that reach their full legal value before their first birthday: a dunghill cur, and a sheep, and a goat.

Q200

Three cases where a commote justice should judge freely: from a penny up to four, and *ebediw*, and *camlwrw*.

Q201

Three cases where a man could incur a loss of ten pounds to another without denying it and without paying it. The first is when the owner of bordering land holds back the water of another's mill because of a refusal to agree or unfriendliness on the part of the owner of the mill, he being able to hold back the water on his own property. The second is if a man moves his corn from the stubble to the fallow land, and it is ruined there, it ought not to be compensated to him by law. The third is if it happens that a man does not close his barn in the time he

yno y lygru, ny dyly o gyfreith y di6c ida6. Trydyd y6 o deruyd na chayo dyn y yscuba6r yn yr amser y dylyo o gyfreith; kyt lyckrer y yt ny di6ygir ida6, kany dyly kyfreith ar nys g6nel.

Q202. S10, €202

[45rb.22] Teir g6eith y drycheif ar sarhaet g6r a vyder gan y 6reic y dreis,[528] neu a dyckyr y 6rtha6.

Q203. Tim124, €203

[45rb.25] Tri pheth nyt reit mach ar dilysr6yd drostunt: kynysgaeth gan vreic, ac enill medic gan glaf, a chyfar6s g6r gan y argl6yd.

Q204. €204

[45va.1] Tri meich ny dylyir eu g6adu: mach ar obyr ynat, a mach ar kyfreith, a mach o'r argl6yd neu y 6assanaeth6yr.

Q205. [S254, Tim135], €205

[45va.5] Tri pheth ny dyly taya6c y g6erthu heb ganyat y argl6yd: mel, a moch, a march keilla6c. Rei a dy6eit, os g6erth, dylyu o'r ne6it dyfuot drachefyn, canyt oed kyfreitha6l y g6erth6yt, ac nat oed ellygedic dim or a 6neler yn anghyfreitha6l. Ac eissoes y kyfreith a dy6eit na dyly dyuot drachefyn; namyn o g6naeth y mab eillt cam, dialei y argl6yd arna6 os mynei.

Q206. €206

[45va.19] Tri dyn a dyly kenedyl y vam eu gouyn,[529] heb[530] genedyl y tat: mab g6reic vonhedic a roder y alltut, a mab g6reic ny 6yppo p6y uo y tat, a mab g6reic a 6atter o genedyl y tat. Sef acha6s y dylyant kenedyl y vam caffel yr alanas: 6rth dylyu ohonunt 6ynteu g6neuthur ia6n drostunt, ac nat oes kenedyl tat udynt. Rei a dy6eit dylyu o genedyl eu mam talu g6arthec diuach dros pop un o'r rei hynny; kyfreith a dy6eit na dylyir onyt dros vab alltut.

---

[528] a vyder ... dreis] ymreher y 6reic o dreis *S*
[529] eu gouyn] eu y gouyn *Q*, eu go6yn *€*
[530] neb *Q*

ought to according to law; although his corn be damaged he will not be compensated, because he who does not fulfil law is not entitled to it.

Q202

There are three augmentations on the *sarhaed* of a man when someone copulates with his wife by violence, or whose wife is taken from him.

Q203

Three things that do not need surety in respect of their freedom from any claim: a portion with a wife, and the earnings of the mediciner from the sick, and the gift to a man from his lord.

Q204

Three sureties which are not entitled to be denied: a surety for the fee of a justice, and a surety for law, and a surety from the lord or his servants.

Q205

Three things a bondsman is not entitled to sell without the permission of his lord: honey, and swine, and a stallion. Some say, if he sells them, that the exchange should be rescinded afterwards, because they were not sold legally, and that nothing that is done illegally has been released. But nevertheless the law says that it should not be reversed; but if the bondsman did wrong, his lord might punish him if he wished.

Q206

Three persons to whom the mother's kindred are entitled to their compensation payment, excluding the father's kindred: the son of a noblewoman who is given to an alien, and the son of a woman who does not know who his father is, and the son of a woman who is denied by his father's kindred. This is the reason the mother's kindred are entitled to the *galanas*: because they ought to make redress on their behalf, and they have no father's kindred. Some say that the mother's kindred ought to pay cattle without surety for each of them; the law says that they are not due, except for the son of an alien.

End of Q *triad collection*

Q207. *I34, J141, L141, M135, Bost126, O35, S34, T128, Tim80, Tr36, Y36, €207,* LatD29

[45vb.8] Tri g6rtheb⁵³¹ yssyd: adef, neu 6at, neu amdiffyn.

Q208. *I27, J135, L135, M129, Bost120, S27, T122, Tim74, Tr27, Y29, €208,* LatD23 [143]

[46vb.9] Tri ry6 vra6d6yr yssyd ygkymru her6yd kyfreith⁵³² Hy6el:⁵³³ bra6d6r
llys penydya6l⁵³⁴ her6yd s6yd, gyt a brenhin Dinef6r ac Aberffra6 yn 6astat; ac
vn bra6t6r kym6t neu cantref her6yd s6yd, ym pop llys o dadleueu G6yned a
Pho6ys; a bra6d6r o vreint y tir ym pop llys kym6t neu cantref o Deheubarth,
nyt amgen, pop perchena6c tir.

Q209. *I29, J136, L136, M130, Bost121, O27, S29, I83, T123, Tim75, Tr28, Y30, €209,* LatD24

[48va.1] Tri dyn ny allant ym6ystla6 yn erbyn bra6t tr6y gyfreith: vn y6 brenhin,
y lle ny allo, her6yd kyfreith,⁵³⁵ sefyll ymy6n dadyl geir bron bra6t6r y holi neu
y atteb tr6y vreint any*ana*6l, neu tr6y vreint y dir, mal breyr neu arall. Eil y6
dyn egl6yssic r6ymedic yn vrdeu kyssegredic. Trydyd y6 dyn egl6yssic
r6ymedic⁵³⁶ ygkreuyd,⁵³⁷ cany dicha6n neb, her6yd kyfreith, rodi g6ystyl yn
erbyn bra6t onyt dan berigil g6erth y daua6t, ac nyt oes 6erth gossodedic
yghyfreith Hy6el Da⁵³⁸ ar aela6t a g6aet a sarhaet dyn egl6yssic;⁵³⁹ ac 6rth
hynny ny eill neb ohonunt 6y rodi g6ystyl yn erbyn bra6t na chyta bra6t. Holl
argy6ed segyrffyc⁵⁴⁰ a 6neler y'r egl6ys6yr⁵⁴¹ a dylyir y mendau⁵⁴² udunt yn y
sened her6yd kyfreith egl6yssic.

S183

Tri dyn ny dyly vn ohonynt sefyll me6n barn: vn o nodynt y6 dyn
gorff6ylla6c o envydr6yd ac a orffo yr r6ymo neu gado 6eutheu; eil y6
dyn a ambryno o ledrad kyfadef vn 6eith, neu a ordi6eder yn*n* lleidir ar

---

⁵³¹ g6rth6yneb *L, M, Bost,*
⁵³² – *M, Bost*
⁵³³ + da ae gyureith *M, Bost;* da *J, L, S, T, Tim, Tr*
⁵³⁴ pennadur *J, L, Tim;* beunadur *M, Bost;* penad6r *T*
⁵³⁵ y lle ny allo her6yd kyfreith] kani dicha6n o gyfreith *O, S*
⁵³⁶ *Interlinear addition in Q by scribe.*
⁵³⁷ yghyfreith *Y*
⁵³⁸ – *L, O, S, T, Y*
⁵³⁹ dyn egl6yssic] – *O*
⁵⁴⁰ segyr ffyc] segyrllyt *I, O, S, T, Tim, Tr, Y;* segyr ffyt *€;* + a dylyir *Q*
⁵⁴¹ yr egl6ys6yr] y dyn egl6yssic *I, S, Y*

End of Q *triad collection*

Q207

There are three answers: acknowledgement, or denial, or defence.

Q208

There are three kinds of judges in Wales according to the law of Hywel: the judge of the daily court by virtue of office, continually with the king of Dinefwr and Aberffraw; and one judge of commote or *cantref* by virtue of office, in every court of pleading in Gwynedd and Powys; and a judge by privilege of land in every court of a commote or *cantref* in the Deheubarth, namely, every owner of land.

Q209

Three persons who cannot pledge against a judgement by law: one is a king, for he cannot, according to law, stand in pleadings before a judge to claim or to answer by virtue of natural privilege, or by the privilege of his land, like a nobleman or another. The second is a cleric bound to holy orders. The third is a cleric bound to religion, as no one can, by law, give a pledge against a judgement except under the risk of the worth of his tongue, and there is no established worth in the law of Hywel Dda for the limb and the blood and the *sarhaed* of an ecclesiastic; and therefore not one of them is able to give a pledge against a judgement or with a judgement. Every sacrilegious injury which may be done to the clergy is to be repaired to them in the synod according to ecclesiastical law.

S183

Three men not one of whom is entitled to stand in judgement: one of them is an insane man of madness who needs to be bound or restrained sometimes; the second is a man who ransoms himself from an acknowledged

gyhoed hed6ch; trydyd y6 dyn a dyg6ydo yg6erth y dafa6d vn 6eith
obl[e]gid kam vra6d a rodassay kyn no hynny.

Q210. *I30, J137, L137, M131, Bost122, O28, S30, T124, Tim76, Tr29, Y31, E210,* LatD25

[48va.29] Tri pheth a dyly pop bra6t6r y 6aranda6 y gan y kynhen6yr[543] kyn
[48vb.1] barnu y neb ohonunt yn ennill nac yn gollet: nyt amgen, k6yn, a
deissyf,[544] ac atteb.

Q211. *I31, J138, L138, M132, Bost123, O29, S31, T125, Tim77, Tr30, Y32, E211,* LatD26

[49ra.5] Tri ry6 varn tremyc yssyd: vn y6 barn a roder yn erbyn dyn nys cly6o
pan datkaner gyntaf my6n y llys, nac ympell nac yn agos y bei. Os yn agos y
bei,[545] y ringill a dylyei y al6 megis y cly6ei y varn a rodit ida6 neu[546] arna6.[547]
Os ympell y bei, y aros[548] a dylyit hyt pan ymdangossei yn y llys, o'r gellit y
gaffel 6rth gyfreith yn amsera6l. Eil y6 bra6t a roder ar dyn kyndrycha6l tr6y
orthrymder o bleit y brenhin neu y bra6d6r neu 6yr y llys. Trydyd y6 barn
bra6t6r anheil6ng.

Q212. *I32, J139, L139, M133, Bost124, O30, S32, T126, Tim78, Tr31, Y33, E212,* LatD27

[49ra.22] Tri dyn yssyd ny dicha6n vn ohonunt bot yn vra6d6r teil6ng tr6y
gyfreith: vn ohonunt y6 dyn anafus, megys bydar, neu dall,[549] neu glaf6r, neu
dyn gorff6ylla6c[550] a orffo y r6yma6 vn 6eith[551] am y ynuytr6yd, neu dyn ny[552]
allo dy6edut yn ia6n,[553] [49rb.1] megys cryc anyana6l. Eil y6 dyn egl6yssic
r6ymedic 6rth urdeu kyssegredic, neu 6rth greuyd. Trydyd y6 lleyc heb allu
ohona6 varnu o gyfreith o vreint tir[554] nac o vreint s6yd.

---

[542] talu *I, S,* emendau *J;* emendenhau *L, T, Tim;* enendenhau *M, Bost;* ia6nhau *O, Tr;* emendanu *Y*
[543] dadleu6yr *I, S, Y*
[544] defnyd *S*
[545] y bei] – *M, Bost, T, Tim, Tr*
[546] ida6 neu] – *I, M, Bost, O, T, Tim, Y*
[547] os yn agos … ida6 neu arna6] – *Tr*
[548] – *Y*
[549] neu dall] – *Y*
[550] + sef y6 h6nn6 *I;* sef y6 h6nn6 dyn *M, O, S, Y;* + dyn *L, T, Tim, Tr*
[551] + beunyd *Tr*
[552] – *M, Bost*
[553] yn ia6n] – *O*
[554] – *J, Q*

theft once, or who is overtaken as a thief on the public peace; the third is a man who forfeits the worth of his tongue once because of a wrong judgement which he had given previously.

Q210

Three things to which every judge ought to listen from the litigants before deciding for either of them to gain or lose: namely, a plaint, and a request, and an answer.

Q211

There are three kinds of judgement of contempt: one is a judgement which may be given against a person who may not hear it when it is first pronounced in the court, whether he should be far or near. If he should be near, the *rhingyll* ought to call him so that he can hear the judgement given to him or against him. If he should be far, he should have been awaited until he might appear in the court, if he could be found by law in time. The second is a judgement pronounced against a present person through oppression on the part of the king or the judge or the men of the court. The third is the judgement of an unfit judge.

Q212

There are three persons not one of whom can be a qualified justice by law: one of them is a person with a defect, such as a deaf man, or blind, or a leper, or a madman who may be forced to be bound once for his madness, or a man who cannot speak properly, such as a congenital stammerer. The second is an ecclesiastical man bound to holy orders, or to religion. The third is a layman who is unable to judge in law by the privilege of land or the privilege of office.

Q213. I33, J140, L140, M134, Bost125, O31, S33, T127, Tim79, Tr32, Y34, €213, LatD28

[49rb.7] Teir fford y gellir g6rthneu bra6t6r teil6g: vn y6 o'e vot yn anghyffredin yn y dadyl kynn barnu⁵⁵⁵ r6ng kynhenusson yn llys.⁵⁵⁶ Eil y6 y vot yn gyfrana6c ar⁵⁵⁷ yr hynn y bo y dadyl ohona6, pei gellit y hennill dr6y varn. Trydyd y6 kymryt gobyr yn y dadyl ar ny bo gossodedic y vra6t6r y my6n kyfreith.⁵⁵⁸

Q214. J169, €214

[49va.16] Tri pheth a dyly bra6t6r o vreint tir y 6neuthur kyn barnho dim: nyt amgen, g6aranda6 y dadleu6yr bob eil6ers hyt pan darffo argaeu ar y dadyl6ryaeth, a deissyf o bob parth. Eil y6 g6aranda6 ar y pleideu yn g6rthneu bra6t6yr neu yn y llussu, kanys reit y6 y'r bra6t6yr godefedic adnabot a vo y neb a lysser neu a 6rthneuer yn yr achos a danotter yn y herbyn, ac oni bydant, dycker h6ynt [49vb.1] drachefyn y bra6dle. Trydyd y6 kyfarch devndeb y holl vra6t6yr kydrycholyon kany chynhelir yn lle g6eithret anuvndeb.

Q215. S175, €215

[50ra.5] Teir dadyl nyt oes oet y vra6t6r am eu barnu: vn y6 dadyl y bo ymtystu yndi, eil y6 dill6ng kyfarcheu 6rth reit y brenhin, trydyd y6 barnu dadanhyd⁵⁵⁹ y dyn a'e dylyo o gyfreith.

Q216. S156, Tim98, €216 Found in J as triadic material.

[50va.24] Tri ry6 tremyc absen yssyd: nyt amgen, pei dam6einei diuedyanv dyn o'y tir tr6y varn kyn bot yn amser aeduet kyfreith, canys hyt yna y dylyr y aros ef her6yd kyfreith. Eil dyall tremyc absen [50vb.1] y6 rodi barn ar dyn yn ll6r6 collet neu enill kyn cadeira6 dadyl. Y tremyc⁵⁶⁰ kyntaf o'r deu a dyellir o anamserolder kymesgedic kyny aller ameu y varn o anyan a defnyd o g6byl odieithyr kyflad ar amser. Bei g6edy cadeira6 dadyl y rodit barn ar amdiffynbleit ny bydei varn absen achos y deissyf a gofay y gydrycholder ef. Trydyd tremyc absen y6 rodi barn ar dyn heb y al6 o'r rigil y'r lle y glybot y cof a'r varn pan

---

⁵⁵⁵ yn y dadyl kynn barnu] – *Y*
⁵⁵⁶ yn y dadyl … kynhenusson yn llys] r6g y pleideu yn llys kyn barnu *I;* yn y dadyl r6g y kynhenusson yny llys kyn y varn *O;* r6g y pleideu yn llys *S*
⁵⁵⁷ + dadyl neu *Tim*
⁵⁵⁸ y vra6t6r y my6n kyfreith] or bra6t6r *I;* yn y gyfreith or bra6d6r *S;* y vra6t6r ynny kyfreith *Y*
⁵⁵⁹ *From S;* datkanu *Q*
⁵⁶⁰ trmyc *Q*

Q213

Three ways a qualified judge may be rejected: one is because he is partial in the case before judging between the litigants in the court. The second is that he is an interested party in what the case is about, if it could be won through a judgement. The third is taking a fee for the case that is not allocated to a judge in law.

Q214

Three things which a judge by privilege of land ought to do before he judges anything: namely, to listen to the litigants each in turn until there is an end on the pleading and a request from both parties. The second is to listen to the parties rejecting justices or objecting to them, as the judges who are accepted must recognize who the one may be who is being objected to or rejected in the case which is put against them, and if they are not, let them be brought back to the place of judgement. The third is to recommend the unity of all the judges present as it cannot be held where there is an act of disunity.

Q215

Three pleadings for which there is no appointed time for a justice to judge them: one is a pleading in which there is witnessing on both sides, the second is to issue greetings at the king's need, the third is to judge *dadannudd* to a man who is entitled to it by law.

Q216

There are three kinds of contempt in absence: namely, if it happens that a man is dispossessed of his land before the time in law is mature, because until then one should wait for him according to law. The second meaning of contempt in absence is to give a judgement on a man regarding loss or gain before the case is begun. The first contempt of the two is understood to be of various untimelinesses although it is not possible to doubt the judgement by the nature and substance of the matter at all apart from the issue of time. If it be that after a case is started the judgement is given to the defending party, it would not be a judgement in absence because of the petition which would certify his presence. The third contempt in absence is to give a judgement to a man without the *rhingyll* calling him to the place to hear the record and the judgement as it was proclaimed if he was close to that place, for example within the area of the court. If he were

datkenit os yn agos y bei yno,[561] megys o vy6n plas yr orsed. Os ympell y bei y aros a dylyr hyt pan 6ypper a aller y gaffel yn amsera6l, megis bei rodit barn ar dyn o vy6n yr amser y dylyir y aros y 6ybot a del yn amsera6l, a'r tremyc h6nn6 heuyt o anamserolder y dyellir.

S156. *Tim98*

Tri ry6 dremic kydrycha6l yssyd: vn y6 rodi barn ar dyn y perthyno idav ysbeid vn dyd a bl6ydyn o'e hameu; sef y6 hynny llydyas o 6yr y llys neu y bra6d6yr neu ereill y dyn rodi g6ystul diohir, neu ballu o bleid y brenhin neu'r argll6yd bieiffeu y llys o erbynia6 g6ystyl, ac 6rth hynny ny chyll ef y amser hyd pan*n* vo llithiredic vn dyd a bl6ydyn o'r pan ganattaer k*y*fraith gyntaf ida6, ac ef a gygheinieu vod y varn yn*n* da ac yn briodawl yn*n*y defn*n*yd her6yd dadyl6ryaeth y dadyl. Eil tremyc kydrychol y6 barnu r6ym amherthyna6l ar amdiffyn*n*bleid ky6lad y 6randa6 kof a barn g6edy kadeiria6 dadyl yn ol deisif o bop parth, a'r tremic h6nn6 yssud yn p6ysso ar yr ha6l o bleid, kans o g*y*freith amser bra6d6r barn g6edy deissif o bop parth. Trydyd tremic kydrycha6l y6 roi barn yn*n* erbyn dyn yn ll6r6 colled neu enill kyn kadeiria6 dadyl.

Q217. *S154, Tim96, C217*

[50vb.25] Tri ry6 gamdosparth yssyd y keffir am6aret[562] amdanunt her6yd kyfreith Hy6el[563] heb uot yn reit nac yn berthyna6l ym6ystla6 a bra6t6r, ac ny chyll amser y gyfreith y hameu y dosparth [51ra.1] o bleit godef hyt pan vo llithredic vn dyd a bl6ydyn o dyd y dosparth,[564] nac yn erbyn y etiued os am dir y tyf y gynnen. Ac o dam6einia carcharu kyfreith o bleit argl6yd, yr hyt y bo heb ia6n ny chyll amser y gyfreith, onys[565] gan 6allocau canlyn g6edy cannattaer kyfreith ida6 hyt pan lithro vn dyd a bl6ydyn; ac ny chyll amser y gyfreith heuyt y'r neb a dechreuo canhebr6ng dadyl o'r dam6eina ryuel kyn teruynu y gynnen, onyt dan ebregoui vn dyd a bl6ydyn g6edy g6astattaer hed6ch ac adnabot yr argl6yd a 6ledycho.

Ac, odyna,[566] kyntaf dosparth[567] y6 rodi barn o dyn yn erbyn pleit heb allu yda6 y varnu o vreint tir neu o vreint s6yd, neu dyn r6ymedic y vrdeu

---

[561] y bo *C*
[562] ymod6ared *S, Tim*
[563] – *S*
[564] kam dosbarth *S*
[565] onys] o hameu onyd *S*, onyt *C*
[566] ac odyna] – *S*
[567] – *S, Tim*

afar he should be awaited until it was known whether he could be got in time, for example if a judgement was given to a man within the time he should be waited for to know whether he would come in time, and that contempt is also explained through untimeliness.

S156

There are three contempts in presence: one is to give a judgement to a man to whom pertains a pause of one year and a day in order to doubt it; that is the men of the court or the justices or others prevent the man from giving a pledge without delay, or a failure on the part of the king or the lord to whom the session belongs to receive a pledge, and because of that he does not lose time until one year and a day have elapsed since law was first permitted to him, and he agreed that the judgement was good and appropriate in substance according to the pleading of the case. The second contempt in presence is to judge an inappropriate restriction on a defending party of a neighbouring country to listen to record and judgement after starting the pleading according to a request from each side, and that contempt pressurizes the claiming party, because by law the time for the justice to judge is after a request by both sides. The third contempt in presence is to give a judgement against a man regarding loss or gain before starting the case.

Q217

There are three kinds of wrong decision from which relief is to be had according to the law of Hywel without it being necessary or appropriate to exchange pledges with the judge, and there is no loss of time for doubting the judgement because of suffering it until one year and a day have elapsed from the day of the decision, nor against the heir if the dispute arises regarding land. And if it happens that law is restricted on behalf of the lord, as long as he is without compensation he does not lose time for law, unless he neglects to proceed after law has been permitted for him until one year and a day should pass; and whoever starts prosecuting a case does not lose time for law if war happens before the dispute ends, unless it is through forgetfulness for one year and a day after peace is established and the lord who rules acknowledged.

And the first decision, then, is for a person to give a judgement against a party where he is not able to judge by virtue of land or virtue of office, or is a man bound in holy orders, or to religion, or a disabled man, or a faulty man, or a man with a natural disease, and those points divest them by law of the qualifications of a judge; or judges against whom a legal objection or legal refusal is stated without settling what is at issue in the case, or he gives a judgement after he has been involved in the case; or a judge gives a judgement before the conclusion of the case and requesting by each side; or before it [the issue] is put on behalf of

kyssegredic, neu y greuyd,[568] neu dyn anafys,[569] neu dyn beius, neu dyn o gleuyt anyana6l, a dehor y pynkeu hynny racdu o gyfreith[570] teilygda6t[571] bra6t6r; neu vra6t[51rb.1]6yr a dottit yn [y] erbyn llyssyant kyfreitha6l neu 6rthneuat kyfreitha6l heb teruynu a vei yn yr achos, neu g6edy darffei y uot yn yr acha6s rodi barn; neu rodi barn o vra6t6r[572] kyn argau ar y dadyl a deissyf o bob parth; neu kyn dodi o bleit yr argl6yd yn ol deissyf o pob parth; neu rodi barn o vra6t6r yn deissyueit kyn kyuarch duundeb y gyt vra6t6yr; neu rodi barn o vra6t6r ar dyn yn erbyn[573] kyfreith dr6y gymhell o bleit argl6yd; neu geissio m6ynant o dosparth yn llunyaeth barn, neu gymroded am berchnogaeth tir a dosperthit odieithyr g6eithret[574] gorsed gyfreitha6l, onyt yn y lle y dam6einei y argl6yd o'e dir ehun ystunv perchennogaeth y 6r yda6, ae yghyuar6s ae yn rebuchet arall; a llyna yr vn lle y gellir cadarnhau perchnogaeth y dyn ar dir a dayar odieithyr [51va.1]g6eithret gorssed gyfreitha6l.

Eil dosparth y6 gally rodi yn erbyn bra6t6r neu rei o'y gyt vra6t6yr vn o'r pet6ar achos yd ymhoelir barn, nyt amgen, kas o bleit gelynyaeth; sef y6 hynny, gallu provi ar vra6t6r rodi cam varn neu gadarnhau kel6yd, ae ef ae rei o'e gyt vra6t6yr, my6n cof neu detryt yn erbyn dyn, a hynny o gas achos gelynyaeth; neu broui ar vra6t6r o vreint tir neu rei o'e gyt vra6t6yr erbynnya6 g6erth neu obyr neu ede6it arna6 neu vra6t6r s6yda6c eithyr yr hynn a ossodet ygyfreith ida6 dros varnu, ac o'r acha6s h6nn6 barnu cam varn neu gadarnhau geu tr6y gof neu detryt yn erbyn pleit, a hynny o serch da; neu allu dodi yn erbyn bra6t6r neu [51vb.1] rei o'y gyt vra6t6yr duundeb tr6y r6ym ac ede6it, nyt amgen rodi ehofynder y bleit tr6y gedernit pa dadyl bynnac yd amdangosso yn ha6l6r neu yn amdiffynn6r, yny godeuit yn vra6t6r kydyrnhay y e6yllys yda6 yn y[575] dosparth, a'r p6nc h6nn6 a eil6 kyfreith yn garyat[576] kyueillon; neu allu proui yn erbyn bra6t6r neu rei o'e gyt vra6d6yr gossot byg6th arnadunt megys argy6edu corff dyn neu y eida6 hyt na lyuassei[577] rodi ia6n deruyn, a'r p6nc h6nn6 a dyalla kyfreith yn ofyn kedyrn: sef mod y dylyir proui yr ach6ysson[578] hynny dr6y detryt g6lat, eithyr lle y dam6einia perthynu y orche6iro y gof llys. P6y bynnac a gynhebrygho yghyfreith gorssed ar vra6t6r y golledu tr6y ry6 vn o'r pynkeu a dy6esp6yt [52ra.1] vchot, ef a dyly caffel cof neu detryt yn diohir y rygta6 a'r bra6t6r neu rei[579] o'e gyt vra6t6yr y gossotter yr acha6s yn y herbyn,

[568] neu y greuyd] – *S*
[569] neu dyn anafys] – *Tim*
[570] racdu o gyfreith] – *S*
[571] + y vod yn vra6d6r o gyf; *S*
[572] vrat6r *Q*
[573] – *S*
[574] – *Tim*
[575] neu *S, Tim*
[576] yn garyat] angaryat *C*
[577] kafassei *S;* lassai *Tim*
[578] yr ach6ysson] – *S, Tim*
[579] *From Tim*; rodi *Q*

the lord after a request from each side; or a judgement is given by judges precipitantly before seeking the agreement of his fellow judges; or a judgement is given by a judge on someone against the law by the use of force on behalf of a lord; or he seeks profit from a decision constituting judgement, or arbitration about the ownership of land which is decided in another way than by the act of a lawful session, unless where it happens that a lord grants ownership of his own land to his man, either as a gift or another kind of favour; and that is the one place where someone's ownership of land and earth can be confirmed other than by the act of a lawful session.

The second decision is to be able to bring against a judge or some of his fellow judges one of the four cases where judgement is reversed, namely, animosity on the part of enmity; that is, being able to prove that a judge gave a wrong judgement or confirmed falsehood, either himself or some of his fellow judges, in record or verdict against a man, and that because of animosity through enmity; or proving that a judge by virtue of land or some of his fellow judges received payment or fee or promise on it or a judge by office except for what is appointed in law that he be allocated for judging, and for that reason he judged a wrong judgement or confirmed falsehood through record or verdict against a party, and that because of love of goods; or to be able to bring against a judge or some of his fellow judges an agreement through a bond and a promise, namely giving confidence to a party through confirming that whichever case he would appear in as a claimant or a defendant, as long as he was suffered to be a judge he would further his will in the decision, and that point the law calls love of friends; or being able to prove against a judge or some of his fellow judges that a threat was made to them such as injuring a man's body or his property until he dared not give a correct conclusion, and that point the law explains as fear of strong men: the way those cases should be proved is through a verdict of the country, except in the place where it happens that rectifying pertains to the record of a court. Whoever brings a case in the law of a session against a judge on the grounds that he has caused him a loss through any of the causes mentioned above, he should have record or judgement without delay between him and the judge or some of his fellow judges against whom the case was set, and if record or judgement makes it clear that it is true what was said by whoever is bringing a proof against the judge or his fellow judges, let whoever was found guilty of illegality be punished in the way the law states, and let a new termination be given for the dispute by law and judge.

ac os cof neu detryt a amlyca vot yn 6ir a dy6eit y neb yssyd yn proui yn erbyn bra6t6r neu y gyt vra6t6yr, cosper y neb a ordi6eder yn ach6yssa6l yn yr aghyfreith yn y mod y dy6etto kyfreith, a g6neler teruyn o ne6yd am y gynnen tr6y gyfreith a chyfya6nder.

Trydyd y6 lle y gorffo ac[580] y perthyno ar6ein kynnen ymrysson rac bron canon6yr, nyt amgen pan vo d6y gyfreith ysgriuenedic[581] erbyn yn erbyn yn dosparth yr vn peth, ac nat adnappo y bra6t6r o'r d6y gyfreith p6y deilygaf onadunt; neu ot amheu ha6l6r neu amdiffyn6r y dosparth a 6nel y bra6t6r kyfr6g y d6y gyfreith hynny; neu or [52rb.1] deruyd y ha6l6r neu y amdiffynn6r amheu y dosparth a 6nel g6yra6dur a v6ynt al6edigion o bleit y brenhin y dosparth y kynneneu amrysson kyfr6ng g6ystyl a g6rth6ystyl erbyn yn erbyn a roder o achos barn[582] yn lla6 y brenhin neu argl6ydiaeth[583] – barn a roder ar dyn ny allo, her6yd kyfreith, rodi g6ystyl yn erbyn barn: yna y dyly y brenhin ar6ein y gynnen a'e chadeira6 yn r6ymedic yn oet dyd gossodedic yghyfreith geir bron y canhon6yr y 6neuthur diledyf teruyn dragy6yda6l dr6y dyall y canhon6yr, a chyt g6nel pleit ameu[584] dosparth a 6nel y canhon6yr, nys erbynnir ac nys g6arande6ir her6yd kyfreith: canys Hy6el Da, vrenhin Kymry, o gyghor y doethon ac a6durdot6yr a ossodes [52va.1] yn y gyfreith ef goruot a pherthynu erbynnya6 dyall canhon6yr y dosparth perigl a phetruster yr amryssoneu dy6edigion[585] her6yd syn6yr canon diledyf, a hynny lle nyt adnepit gallu o'e a6durda6t6yr ef[586] 6neuthur teruyn teil6g dylyedus her6yd y kyfreith ef yn y lleoed dy6ededigion tra6gy6edolyon.

Q218. S161, Tim103, €218. LatD32.

[52va.12] Tri chamg6yn kelus yssyd yghyfreith: nyt amgen, yn gyntaf onadunt y neb a rodo g6ystyl yn erbyn barn ac a gaffer a6durda6t yn yscriuenedic yn y erbyn; h6nn6 a dylir y poyni o 6erth y daua6t. Eil y6 y neb a rodo g6ystyl yn erbyn barn a roder ar arall ac nat arna6 ehun y roder, h6nn6 o gaml6r6 y dylyir y poeni. Trydyd y6 p6y bynnac ny bo ida6 vreint y ym6ystlo megis g6r egl6yssic; kenetaedic y6 ida6 vynet yn erbyn barn [52vb.1] tr6y a6durda6t a chyfreith; ac os velly[587] a phallu y a6durda6t ida6, caml6r6 a gyll.

[580] ac] ar y neb *S, Tim*
[581] ysgiuenedic *Q*
[582] o achos barn] – *S*
[583] al6edigaeth *S, Tim*
[584] + a gal6 ar *Q*
[585] yr amryssoneu dy6edigion] – *S;* de6ededigion *Tim*
[586] et *Q*
[587] + y erbyn dy6eeit *Q*

The third is where it is required and appropriate for a dispute to be brought before canonists, namely when two written laws are opposed one against the other giving a verdict on the same thing, and the judge does not know which of the two laws is the most worthy; or if a claimant or a defendant doubt the decision that the judge should make between those two laws; or if it happens that the claimant or the defendant doubt the decision that the authorized men who are called on behalf of the king to decide the various disputes between pledge and counter-pledge one against the other which are given on account of a judgement in the hand of the king or the lordship – a judgement which is given against a person who cannot, according to law, give a pledge against a judgement: then the king ought to bring forward the dispute and set it in an obligatory manner on the appointed day in law before the canonists so that through the understanding of the canonists they may make an unbiased permanent termination, and although a party doubts the decision made by the canonists, it is not opposed and not listened to according to law: because Hywel Dda, King of Wales, by the counsel of his wise men and authorities established in his law the requirement and appropriateness of receiving the interpretations of canonists to decide the risky issues and doubt in the said disputes according to the sense of unbiased canon law, and that is the place where his authorities were not recognized as being able to make a proper rightful termination according to his law in those aforesaid transferred circumstances.

Q218

There are three guilty wrong plaints in law: namely, the first of them is whoever gives a pledge against a judgement and written authority is obtained against him; that one ought to be punished by the value of his tongue. The second is whoever gives a pledge against a judgement given on another and not upon himself, that one should be punished by a *camlwrw*. The third is whoever does not have the privilege to pledge such as a cleric it is permissible for him to challenge the judgement by authority and law and if this happens and his authority fails him, he loses a *camlwrw*.

S161. Tim103, LatD32

Tri ch6yna6dyr kelus yssyd a dylir y poyni[588] am eu k6yneu h6y eu hynein. Kyntaf y6 dyn a rodo g6ystyl yn*n* erbyn barn a aller y chadarnhau o 6rth6ystyl dr6y a6dyrda6d ysgrifenedic o gy*freith*: h6nn6 a gyll g6erth y dafa6d. Eil y6 dyn a rodo g6ystyl yn*n* erbyn g6ystyl a roder ar dyn*n* arall amgen[589] noc arna6 ef y hyn: a h6nn6 a dylir y boini dr6y gaml6r6. Trydyd y6 dyn a rodo g6ystyl yn*n* erbyn barn ac na bo breint ida6 ym6ystla6 a barn, megis yffeirad neu dun arall krefydus;[590] kenattedic hagen y6 y'r kyffelyp dyn h6nn6 g6rth6ynebu y'r varn dr6y a6dyrda6d o gy*freith*, ac os yr ardyrda6d a balla yda6, kaml6r6 a gyll. Ni chyll neb m6y no chaml6r6 y lle ni bo ym6ystla6 dr6y rod g6ystyl a g6rth6ystyl.

Q219. S155, Tim97, *C219*

[54vb.23] Teir gorsed dygunull a ossodet ygkyfreith Ho6el,[591] val na bei neb ry6 diffic yn y gyfreith, na neb ry6 eiseu o deilygda6t a chyfya6nder. Ac ny rodet breint [55ra.1] bra6t6r y neb o'r g6yr dygunull, her6ed na breint tir na breint s6yd. Canys, pan darffei y 6yr y llys honno racreitha6 y cof a chadarnhav y dull tr6y d6ng[592] am yr hynn a ossodit arnadunt, yno y dyly bra6d6r a ossotter o pleit y brenhin rodi barn r6g y kennenusson her6yd dull g6yr y llys honno, o rei a v6ynt odeuedigion o pob parth, heb na'y lyssu na'e g6rthne yn gyfreitha6l.[593] Sef y6 hynny yny dam6eino bot amrysson am dir kyfr6ng amryfaelyon argl6ydiaetheu, megis kymydeu neu cantrefoed, na brenhin[594] e hunan bieiffynt nac argl6ydi ereill, lleyga6l neu egl6ysic, y rei a gynnelynt eu argl6ydiaetheu dan argl6ydiaeth y brenhin,[595] canys 6rth vreint y brenhin y gossodet yn digyffro y ry6 orsed[596] honno her6yd kyfreith. Sef ford y6 hynny: argl6yd y6 ef ar ba6b o'y deyrnas,[597] ac nyt argl6yd neb o'r argl6ydi ereill ar y gilyd; ac 6rth hynny y dyall6yt her6yd y gyfreith na allei neb gyn[55rb.1]nal y ry6 lys honno eithyr y brenhin. Ac 6rth hynny y dylyir, o pleit y brenhin, kymell o 6ys y rybyd hena6duryeit,[598] o doethyon o'r kyghelloryaetheu o pop parth, o rei kymennaf,

[588] poni *S*
[589] angen *S*
[590] – *Tim*
[591] + da *S, Tim*
[592] d6ng] d6g henyrieid *S*
[593] yn gyfreitha6l] – *S*
[594] bar6niaid *S, Tim*
[595] + y ry6 orssed honno a gynhelir oblegid y brenhin *S, Tim*
[596] lys *S*
[597] dyernas *Q*
[598] rybyd hena6duryeit] rybydia6 a6duryeit *C*

S161

There are three guilty complainants who ought to be punished for their own plaints. The first is a man who gives a pledge against a judgement which can be confirmed by a counter-pledge through written authority by law: that one loses the value of his tongue. The second is a man who gives a pledge against a pledge which is put upon another man other than he himself: and that one should be punished by a *camlwrw*. The third is a man who gives a pledge against a judgement and he does not have the privilege to pledge against a judgement, such as a priest or another religious man; however, it is permitted for such a man as that to object to the judgement by authority of law, and if the authority fails him, he loses a *camlwrw*. No one loses more than a *camlwrw* where there is no pledging through the giving of pledge and counter-pledge.

Q219

Three specially convened courts were appointed in the law of Hywel, so that there might not be any kind of deficiency in the law, nor any kind of lack of worthiness and justice. And the status of a judge was not given to any of the specially convened men, neither according to privilege of land nor according to privilege of office. For, when the men of that court have recited their record and confirm with an oath their verdict on that which has been put before them, then the judge who is appointed on behalf of the king should give a judgement between the disputants according to the verdict of the men of that court, [given] of those who might be accepted by all sides, without either having been objected to nor lawfully opposed. That applies when it may happen that there be a dispute concerning land between various lordships, such as commotes or *cantrefoedd*, whether the king himself owns them or other lords, lay or ecclesiastical, who maintained their lordships under the lordship of the king, since it is to the status of the king that that kind of court was indisputably assigned according to law. This is the way that is so: he is lord over everybody within his kingdom, and none of the other lords is a lord over the other; and for that reason it was understood that according to the law no one could maintain such a court as that except the king. And therefore, on behalf of the king, elders, consisting of wise men from the *cynghellor*-ships on every side, of those who are most accomplished, should be required under a summons to warn them to [come to] the place for setting disputes; and that is to be within the law's [appointed] days and its fixed time-limits, as has been made clear in relation to a contention of dispute between court and church and *cantrefoedd*.

y'r lle amryssona6l; a hynny yn nydyeu y gyfreith a'y hoedeu, megis yd ymlykeit my6n kynnen amrysson kyfr6ng llys a llan a⁵⁹⁹ chantrefoed.

Neu, nebun yn kynnal tir tr6y 6eithret y gan y brenhin, ay ida6 e hun ay y vn o'y rieni, a dyuot nebun arall y ganlyn am tir h6nn6, gan dy6edut, pan 6ahan6yt y tir h6nn6⁶⁰⁰ nac ac ef y dy6etto nac ac vn o'y rieni, mae o 6rthrymder y g6ahan6yt, ac aghyfreith. Neu dyfot vn y ofyn tir o pleit g6eithret a geffit y gan argl6yd y tir, ae y'r neb a vei yn canlyn ae vn o'y rieni y caffei y tir, ac y tyuei ia6n ida6 ynteu o'y blegyt, a bot nebun yn kynnal y tir h6nn6 dr6y 6rescyn o ry6⁶⁰¹ vod a[55va.1]rall. A'r deu le⁶⁰² hynny heuyt a dylyir eu kynnal yn llys dygunull, ac eu teruynv, cany ossodet y neb ac a vei yn kynnal tir dr6y 6eithret o bleit ia6n argl6yd, y ba uod bynnac y keffit, ay ar 6erth ay yghyuar6s ay yn rybuchet arall, atteb yn llys⁶⁰³ kym6t neu cantref, dr6y na chof na detryt, megys breyr neu arall, cany ossodet yghyfreith Hy6el teruynv ia6n argl6yd yn y ry6 lys honno.

Os y llys dygynull a ymlakaa g6neuthur gorthrymder, megys y dy6esp6yt,⁶⁰⁴ y brenhin a dyly yn dioir g6aret y aghyfreith, cany dlyir⁶⁰⁵ her6yd kyfreith kynnal g6eithret ny ellit y 6neuthur yn gyfreitha6l.⁶⁰⁶ Or deruyd na allo g6rescynn6r aghyfreitholi y g6eithret nac ameu ia6n yr argl6yd y cahat y tir y ganta6, y bra6d6r a dyly barnv y tir y berch[55vb.1]en y g6eithret, val y dy6etto y 6eithret oreu; ac o ordi6edo ar y tir o da kyffro ef a bieuyd yn dilys.

Eil y6: ny ellir canlyn k6yn galanas eithyr ger⁶⁰⁷ bro*n* brenhin neu y neb a gynnalo yn lle y brenhin; cany ossodet gallu⁶⁰⁸ y gymell k6b6l dal dros alanas eithyr y neb a vei argl6yd ar pa6b, sef y6 h6nn6⁶⁰⁹ y brenhin; cany chygein o gyfreith k6yno o orsed y orsed y ganlyn am yr vn defnyd. Am hynny y gynnen honno yn llys dygunull y gossodet. [Gosodet] y'r brenhin trayan o bob galanas or a gymhello, yn lle cosp, dros kymell y ran arall y'r genedyl, megys y ran kyfreith y rygtu.

Trydyd orsed dygunull y6 lle y dam6eino ymrysson kyfr6ng a6dur6yr⁶¹⁰ am dyall d6y gyfreith erbyn yn erbyn y dosparth y'r vn p6nc,⁶¹¹ heb uot vn ohonunt yn coylo dyall y gilyd, neu na 6ypynt p6y deilygaf o'r d6y gyfreith hynny. Yna y [56ra.1] dylyir o bleit y brenhin kymell o 6ys rybydya6l

⁵⁹⁹ llys a llan a] – *Tim;* + chymydeu a *S*
⁶⁰⁰ gan dy6edut pan 6ahan6yt y tir h6nn6] – *S, Tim*
⁶⁰¹ o ry6] or ry6 *Q*
⁶⁰² a'r deu le] y delei *Tim*
⁶⁰³ + a dadleu *S, Tim*
⁶⁰⁴ + vry *S*
⁶⁰⁵ + neb *S*
⁶⁰⁶ ny ellit y 6neuthur yn gyfreitha6l] a 6nelid yn aghyfreitha6l *S, Tim*
⁶⁰⁷ geir *Q*
⁶⁰⁸ + o neb *Tim*
⁶⁰⁹ + ~ *C*
⁶¹⁰ a6dyrda6d6yr *Tim*
⁶¹¹ p6n6c *Q;* peth *S, Tim*

Alternatively, someone is holding land by means of a [written] deed by the king, either in favour of himself [the beneficiary] or of one of his forebears, and someone else comes to claim that land, by saying, when that land was removed from either him or one of his forebears, that it was by means of oppression that it was removed, and by illegality. Or someone comes to claim land by virtue of a deed that was obtained from the lord of the land, either in favour of the one who is claiming or in favour of one of his forebears by whom he might receive the land, and that a right extended to him through them, and that someone was holding that land by having gained possession in some other way. And those two issues also should be dealt with in a specially convened court, and should be settled, since it was not settled that anyone who might be holding land through a deed on the part of a just lord, in whatever way it was obtained, whether for a price or as a gift or as some other favour, should answer in the court of a commote or cantref, whether through record or verdict, as [would] a nobleman or another, since it was not appointed in the law of Hywel that the right of a lord should be settled in such a court as that.

If a specially convened court confirms that an act of oppression has occurred, as has been said, the king should without delay remedy the injustice, since according to law it is not right to maintain an act that cannot be performed legally. If it happens that one who has taken possession is unable to demonstrate the illegality of the (written) deed nor to cast doubt on the justice of the lord from whom the land was received, the judge should adjudge the land to the owner of the deed, as his deed may best prescribe; and whatever in the way of moveable goods he may find on the land he shall possess without counter-claim.

The second is: it is not possible to pursue a claim for *galanas* except before a king or someone who may maintain [a court] in place of the king; since it is not prescribed that anyone can compel full payment in respect of *galanas* except the person who may be lord over everybody, namely, the king; for there is no room in law for making a plaint from court to court to bring a prosecution for the same matter. For that reason that dispute is settled in a specially convened court. The king was assigned, in place of a punishment, a third out of every *galanas* from whatever he may enforce, in exchange for enforcing [payment of] the other part to the kindred, as the law divides between them.

The third specially convened court is where a dispute may occur between authorities concerning considering two laws as being opposed to one another in their judgement on the one issue, without either of them appearing likely to embrace the other, or [when] they may not know which of those two laws is the most worthy. Then on behalf of the king a warning summons should compel

kanhon6yr, na g6yr o greuyd v6ynt nac egl6ys6yr ereill, y deruynv y gynnen tr6y dyall canon diledyf, gan gatarnhau[612] y dull[613] dr6y d6ng, or byd a'y typpyo. Ac yna y dyly bra6t6r o pleit y brenhin rodi barn her6yd dull y canon6yr.[614]

Neu ga*n*lyn o vn dyn tr6y g6yn rac kyffredin neu[615] gyffredin rac vn dyn, neu vn dyn rac arall lle ny ellit kael bra6t6r teil6g heb y vot y bleit y'r gynnen. Y tri lle hynny heuyt yn llys dygunull y kynhelir.

Neu, ganlyn o argl6yd ar argl6yd arall, a gynhalont eu argl6ydiaeth dan y brenhin; neu ganlyn o 6r argl6yd am aghyfreith a 6nelei ac ef; neu dagnouedu galanas kyfr6g d6y genedyl; y kynhenneu hyny a ossodet y teruynv yno, rac dam6eina6 bot kenedyl y llofrud[616] neu y lladedic yn amryfael argl6ydiaetheu, [56rb.1] kany ellir kanlyn c6yn galanas eithyr rac bron y brenhin neu y neb a vo yn lle y brenhin; cany ossodet gallu y gymell c6byl dros alanas eithyr y neb a vei argl6yd ar ba6b, sef y6 y brenhin; cany chygeinei g6yna6 o orsed y orsed am yr vn defnyd, ac am hynny y trosset y gynnen honn y'r llys dygynull. Ac 6rth hynny y gossodet y'r brenhin trayan galanas, dros gymell y ran arall y'r[617] genedyl megys y ran kyfreith vdunt.

Eil datleu dygynull y6 dam6eina6 y ha6l6r neu amdiffynn6r ameu dosparth a 6nel a6durda6t6yr a v6ynt al6edigion o bleit y brenhin, megis y dy6edir yn y cam dosparth, ac vn onadunt neu[618] m6y yn vn o'r pet6ar acha6s yd ymhoylir bra6t, neu vot yn amprioda6l y dosparth her6yd kyfreith a 6nelynt, kyn na all[56va.1]er her6yd kyfreith y ameu onyt gan gyflad ac vn o'r pet6ar acha6s neu u6y. Os h6ynteu a 6atta nat ynt ach6yssa6l o rei a d6etter arnadunt, yna y dylyir, o bleit y brenhin, kymell doethion o'i kygelloryaetheu o pop parth y adnabot beth a dy6edynt y dosparth6yr ae g6ir ae geu, a hynny o rei a odefir o pob parth. Os yn ach6yssa6l y hardi6edir, neu vot yn amprioda6l y dosporth yn y gyfreith, bit difodedic heb amgen gosp; cany ossodet yn y gyfreith ym6ystla6 yn erbyn dosparth6yr. Canyt oes vreint bra6t6r y ry6 dosparth h6nn6, onyt gan y odef, heb 6neuthur ameu, val y dy6etp6yt o'r blaen. Ac yna y dyly y brenhin gossot bra6t6r penyadur y 6neuthur tervyn tragy6yd am y gynnen tr6y varn. Nyt oes vn gynnen a dlyo y gyfreith y theruynu tr6y varn y bra6t6r pennaf a ymhoylo y lys na chym6t na chan[56vb.1]tref drachefyn, ony bei ida6 c6yno o ne6yd.

---

[612] gatrnhau *Q*
[613] y dull] – *S, Tim*
[614] *S, Tim end here.*
[615] neu neu *Q*
[616] lloffryd *Q*
[617] y'r] y'r y *Q*
[618] na *Q, C*

canonists, whether they be men in religion or other churchmen, to settle the dispute through taking into consideration an impartial canon, and confirming their verdict by means of an oath, if there be anyone who may doubt it. And then a judge should give a judgement on behalf of the king, in accordance with the verdict of the canonists.

Or a single person brings a prosecution by making a plaint against the common people or the common people against a single person, or a single person against another where it is impossible to obtain a worthy judge without him being party to the dispute. Those three cases are also held in a specially convened court.

Alternatively, a lord brings a prosecution against another lord, [the two of them] holding their lordship under the king; or a man of a lord brings a prosecution concerning an injustice which he [the lord?] might have committed against him [the man?]; or peace is made between two kindreds concerning *galanas*; it was prescribed that those disputes should be settled there, lest it should happen that the homicide's kindred or the slain person's kindred are in different lordships, for it is not possible to prosecute a plaint of *galanas* except before the king or before someone who is in the place of the king; since it was not prescribed that a complete [compensation] could be enforced for *galanas* except by the person who is lord over everyone, namely the king; for it was not possible to bring a plaint from court to court concerning the same matter, and for that reason that dispute was transferred to the specially convened court. And therefore a third of a *galanas* was assigned to the king, in exchange for enforcing [payment of] the other part to the kindred as law divides it among them.

A second [kind of] specially convened pleadings occurs when it happens that a claimant or a defendant doubts the verdict made by authorities who may be called on behalf of the king, as it said in relation to a false verdict, and [when] one or more of them is one of the four reasons why judgement is overturned, or [when] the verdict they produce is improper according to law, although by law it is not possible to doubt it unless by connecting it with one or more of the four reasons. If they deny that they are responsible for those things which are attributed to them, then, on behalf of the king, wise men should be required [to come] from their *cynghellor*-ships on every side to make a recognition as to whether what they may say is true or false, and those [wise men] are to consist of persons accepted on each side. If they are found to be responsible, or that the verdict is improper in law, let it be extinguished without any further penalty; for mutual pledging against *dosparthwyr* was not established in the law. For such a verdict as that does not enjoy the status of a judge, unless it has been accepted, without doubt being expressed, as has been said previously. And then the king should set a chief judge to make a final termination of the dispute through judgement. No dispute which the law should settle by the judgement of the chief judge may be overturned in the court of a commote or *cantref*, unless he should have a new plaint.

Q220. I15, J130, L130, M124, Bost115, [N114], O21, S15, T117, Tim69, Tr20, Y22, €220, LatD144

[56vb.3] O tri mod yd holir tir: o gamoresgyn, ac o datannud tr6y vedyant tat neu vam hyt angeu,[619] ac o ach ac eturyt; kyn ny thyckyo gouyn tir o'r mod kyntaf nac o'r eil, ny byd h6yrach no chynt y keffir o'r trydyd.

Q221. I16, J131, L131, M125, Bost116, [N115], O22, S16, T118, Tim70, Tr21, Y23, €221, LatD145

[56vb.12] Tri chamoresgyn yssyd: goresgyn yn erbyn perchenna6c o'e anuod heb vra6t, neu oresgyn tr6y y perchen ac yn erbyn etived o'e anuod a heb vra6t, neu oresgyn tr6y orcheit6at ac yn erbyn ia6n dylyeta6c o'y anuod a heb vra6t.[620]

Q222. I17, J132, L132, M126, Bost117, O23, S17, T119, Tim71, Tr22, Y24, €222, LatD146

[56vb.26] O tri mod y dosperthir dadyl datannud r6ng etiuedyon, nyt amgen tr6y dri breint anyana6l: kyntaf y6 breint oet y r6g hynaf a ieuaf; eil y6 breint priod[57ra.1]a6l[621] r6ng etiued kyfreitha6l ac vn anghyfreitha6l, canys y kyfreitha6l a'e keiff oll; trydyd y6 breint dylyet r6ng dylyeda6c[622] ac andylyeda6c.

Q223. I18, J133, L133, M127, Bost118, O24, S18, T120, Tim72, Tr23, Y25, €223, LatD147 *[1 2 3 = 1 3 2 1, S, 2 1 3 Y]*

[57rb.1] Tri ry6 vreint yssyd: breint anyana6l, a breint s6yd, a breint tir.

Q224. I19, J134, L134, M128, Bost119, O25, S19, T121, Tim73, Tr24, Y26, €224, LatD126, 148

[57rb.3] Tri phriodolder yssyd:[623] ry6, a breint ac etiuedyaeth; etiuedyaeth hagen her6yd breint, breint her6yd ry6, ry6 her6yd y g6ahan a vyd r6ng dynyon her6yd kyfreith, megis g6ahan brenhin y gan uchel6r,[624] g6r a g6reic,[625] hynaf a jeuaf, breyr a bilaen.[626]

---

[619] hyt angeu] – *S*
[620] neu oresgyn tr6y ... a heb vra6t] – *J*
[621] priodas *I, O, T, Tim, Y*; priodaf *L, M, Bost*
[622] dylyet *L*
[623] + y bob dyn *I, M, S, T, Tim, Y*
[624] y gan uchel6r] a breyr *I, S, Y;* + a *M*
[625] g6r a g6reic] – *I*
[626] bilael *Q*; breyr a bilaen] – *I, S*

Q220

In three ways land is claimed: through wrongful taking of possession, and by *dadannudd* through the possession of a father or mother until death, and by lineage and paternity; though a claim for land may not succeed by the first method or the second, it is no less likely that it will be obtained by the third.

Q221

There are three wrongful takings of possession: taking possession in opposition to the owner against his will and without judgement, or taking possession through the owner and in opposition to the heir against his will and without judgement, or taking possession though an occupier and in opposition to the rightful proprietor against his will and without judgement.

Q222

In three ways a pleading for *dadannudd* is to be settled between heirs, namely through three natural privileges: the first is the privilege of age distinguishing the eldest from the youngest; the second is the proper privilege between a lawful heir and an unlawful one, for the lawful one has it all; the third is a privilege of entitlement between an entitled person and a non-entitled person.

Q223

There are three privileges: privilege according to birth, privilege according to office, and privilege according to land.

Q224

There are three essential characteristics: kind [of person], and status, and inheritance; inheritance however is according to status, status according to kind, kind because of the difference there is between persons according to law, such as the difference between a king and a nobleman, man and woman, eldest and youngest, nobleman and bondsman.

Q225. I11, J146, L146, M140, O17, S11, T133, Tim85, Y18, €225

[57va.26] Tri lle y rann kyfreith:[627] a'r honn[628] dy6ededic y6'r gyntaf; yr eil y6 pan ranner eu da r6ng g6r a'e 6reic o var6ola[57vb.1]eth y neill ohonunt; trydyd y6 pan dycker ll6dyn neu beth arall[629] y 6rth anghyfreith y gyfreith.

Q226. I12, J147, L148, M141, Bost131, O18, S12, T134, Tim86, Tr17, Y19, €226, LatD149

[58vb.19] Teir etiuedyaeth kyfreitha6l yssyd ac a[630] drigyant yn dilis y'r[631] etiuedyon: vn y6 etiuedyaeth tr6y dylyet o bleit rieni,[632] eil y6 etiuedyaeth a gaffer tr6y amot kyfreitha6l y gan y perchen yr g6erth, trydyd y6 etiuediuyaeth a gaffer tr6y amot kyfreitha6l o vod y perchen heb 6erth.

Q227. I13, J148, L149, M142, Bost132, O19, S13, [258], T135, Tim87, [139], Tr18, Y20, €227

[59ra.27] Teir g6eith y rennir yr vn tref tat r6ng teir grad kenedyl:[633] yn gyntaf r6g brodyr, eil 6eith r6ng keuender6, tryded 6eith r6ng kyuer[59rb.1]der6; odyna nyt oes pria6t[634] rann ar tir.

Q228. I14, J149, L150, M143, O20, S14, T136, Tim88, Tr19, Y21, €228

[60va.8] Tri ry6 prit yssyd ar tir: vn y6 gobyr g6archad6, eil y6 yr hyn a roder yr ach6aneckau tir neu y vreint, trydyd y6 llafur kyfreitha6l a 6neler ar dir y bo g6ell y tir[635] ohona6.

Q229. J164, [S232], [Tim125], 174, €229 [1 2 3 = 1 3 2 Tim124]

[66va.23] Tri ry6 datannud yssyd a'r datannudeu hynny sef ynt: datannud ar ac eredic, a datannud carr, a datannud b6rn a beich.

---

[627] + yn deu hanher *O, S, Tim*
[628] vn rac *I, M, O, S, T, Tim*
[629] + colledic *O, S, T*
[630] a *Q*
[631] yn *Q, €*
[632] + tr6y ach ac edryd *Tim*
[633] r6g teir … kenedyl] – *M*
[634] – *Bost*
[635] y tir] – *M, O*

Q225

Three places in which the law divides: the first is the aforesaid; the second is when their goods are divided between a husband and a wife on the death of one of them; the third is when an animal or another lost thing is changed from being an illegal situation to being a legal one.

Q226

There are three lawful inheritances and they remain secure to the heirs: one is an inheritance by title derived from parents, the second is an inheritance obtained by a lawful contract from the owner for a price, the third is an inheritance obtained by a lawful contract by the will of the owner without payment.

Q227

Three times shall the same patrimony be shared between the three grades of a kindred: first between brothers, a second time between first cousins, a third time between second cousins; after that there is no proprietary share of land.

Q228

There are three kinds of *prid* of land: one is a fee for protection, the second is what shall be given towards adding to land or its status, the third is lawful labour applied to the land by which the land is improved.

Q229

There are three kinds of *dadannudd* and those *dadannudds* are as follows: *dadannudd* of ploughing, and *dadannudd* of cart, and *dadannudd* of bale and burden.

Q230. J165, Є230

[67rb.22] Teir g6raged her6yd kyfreith a dyly eu meibion eu dylyet o vam6ys: vn ohonunt g6reic a rodo kenedyl yn gyfreith*a6l* y alltut. Eil y6 g6reic a dycko alltut y treis arnei yn honneit, ac o'r treis h6nn6 caffel mab; y gyfreith a dy6eit cany [67va.1] cholles hi y breint, na chyll y mab hitheu y dylyet o vam6ys. Trydyd y6 g6reic a rodo kenedyl yng6ystloryaeth alltuded, ac yn y g6ystloryaeth h6nn6 caffel mab ohonei o alltut; y mab h6nn6 a dyly mamm6ys.

Two triads from the hiatus in Q taken from Є

Q230a

Tri lle her6yd kyfreith ny pherthyn y 6r dyuot bot yn bleit o dadyl tir a dayar kyt en6o yr ha6l6r ia6n ida6 o bleit rieni: nyt amgen, bei dam6einei y dyn g6yna6 rac arall, ac ar6ein ia6n ida6 o bleit mam6ys, megis vn o tri dyn a dylyant caffel kyfran o dir y gan e6ythyr; o dam6heineu y h6nn6 abergofi kanlyn ar yr ia6n yn amser perchnogaeth y gytuaeth, megis pei dam6heineu [mynet] y maes o perchnogaeth y le estrona6l, nyt amgen y 6erthu ne6 y rodi y arall, ny dyly g6r dyuot bot yn pleit y'r ha6l6r, kanyt oes ido ef vn ia6n ar y defnyd h6nn6 euthyr ar y gyt vaeth. Eil y6 bei k6yneu vn rac arall am tir, a g6neuthur ha6l gan ar6ein dylyet o bleit ach ac etryt a'r g6r dyuot, ny 6rthebir y'r ha6l a'r defnyd h6nn6, cany dicha6n h6nn6 ar6ein ia6n o bleit yr un gyfreith kynhala6dyr; ac 6rth hynny y[636] byd pleit yn estron y'r ha6l honno. Trydyd y6 bei k6nei dyn rac arall o dadyl o pleit ia6n ar adran a g6allo [148] ran ohona6 gan hebr6ng yr ia6n hyt pan vei lithredic o'e perchenogaeth y le estrona6l, ny dyly y g6r dyuot atteb na bot yn pleit y'r ha6l honno, canyt oes y neb ar6ein ha6l ar y dyfnyd h6nn6 onyt kytetiued ar g6bled.

---

[636] Ny Є

Q230

Three women whose sons ought to get their entitlement through maternity according to the law: one is a woman whose kindred gives her legally to an alien. The second is a woman who is openly raped by an alien, and from that rape she has a son; the law states that as she did not lose her status, her son also does not lose his entitlement through maternity. The third is a woman who is given by her kindred into hostageship in exile, and from that hostageship she has a son by an alien; that son is entitled to maternity.

Two triads from the hiatus in Q *taken from* Є

Q230a

Three cases according to law where it is not appropriate for an incomer to be a party in a case for land and earth although the claimant names a right belonging to him in relation to his parents: namely, if it happens that a man brings a plaint about another, and derives his right from the mother's side, such as one of the three men who are entitled to have a share of land from their uncles; [and] if it happens that a person forgets to pursue his right during the period when one who was reared with him has ownership, for example, if it should pass from his ownership to a foreign place [an unrelated person], namely selling it or giving it to another, an incomer is not entitled to be a party together with the claimant, because he does not have any right to that matter except against the person in joint fosterage with him. The second is if one brings a plaint about another for land, and a claim is made by deriving the entitlement through lineage and descent down to the incomer, no reply shall be made to the claim and the substance [of the claim], because it was not possible for him to derive his claim from the same supporting law, and because of that a foreigner will be a party to that claim. The third is if a man brings a plaint against another by means of a case arising from a party in the right, and a section of it [the party in the right] fails to pursue the right until it slips from their ownership and passes to a foreign place, the incomer is not entitled to answer or be a party to that claim, because no one is [entitled] to pursue a claim on that issue apart from joint-heirs on an entirety.

Q230b. *S158, Tim100 [AL XI.I.1]*

Tri dyn a gynnal[637] tir ac a'e herbyn o vy6n llys k6m6t neu gantref ac ny dylyant vot yn bleideu y atteb y neb o'r tired yn ll6r6 c6yneu, na bot yn vra6t6r – ygnat o vreint tir, megis brehyryon: nyt amgen, g6r[638] egl6yssic a rodo yr brenhin tir ida6 tr6y 6eithret, a hynny o dir dilis y brenhin.[639] Eil y6 lleyc y rotho y brenhin tir ida6, ae ynghyfar6s, ae yn rybuchet arall yn y kyffelybyon vod. Trydyd y6 dyn a gynhalyo perchnogaeth o daya6ctir dan y brenhin. Y kyntaf a'r eil, rac bron y bra6t6r pennaf y dylyant atteb or byd a'e govynno, ac nyt yn llys vrenhina6l. Y trydyd yghyfreith[640] y daya6ctref y dyly atteb or byd a'e gouynno,[641] ac nyt yn y llys vrehyrya6l.[642]

Q231. *J166, S157, Tim99, €231*

[68vb.1] Tri[643] ry6 argaedigaeth dadyl ynt: vn onadunt y6 pei damch6einei y dyn gouyn tir y arall tr6y g6yn a ha6l, gan ar6ein ia6n disgynedic hyt[644] ar nebun o'e rieni, neu ystlys ia6n o blegyt kytetiued, kyny hanffei y tir o ia6n rieni; a gallu o'r atteb6r dodi yn y erbyn[645] g6ahanu yr ia6n ac 6ynt tr6y gyfreith dilis,[646] a'e dyuot, tr6y gyfreith dilis,[647] y vn o'e rieni y gallo ynteu ar6ein ia6n[648] diffodedic hyt atta6 neu y gytetiued ida6, kyt bei g6r dyuot, neu ida6 e hun, neu y estra6n y caffei y tir y gantha6, megys y gallei dadleu yn eu ia6n; neu amser ym6ystla6 am varn.

Eil argaedigaeth y6: gallu o atteb6r dodi yn erbyn ha6l6r a ar6edo[649] ia6n o bleit rieni, neu gytetiued,[650] neu o'e ansa6d e hun, neu[651] pa vn bynnac arall vo, diffodi[652] yr ia6n tr6y dadyl6ryaeth did6yll anyana6l [a] barn ym person y neb y har6edo [69ra.1] ia6n o'e bleit, neu y etiued,[653] tr6y ordi6es y[654] rieni yn

637 Gyneul *S*
638 dyn *S*
639 y brenhin] euhyn *S*
640 ynn llys *S, Tim*
641 or byd a'e gouynno] – *S*
642 ychod *S*
643 kanys tri *J, Tim*
644 + atta6 o hyn neu *S*
645 + yr ha6l6r *S, Tim*
646 did6yll *Tim*
647 did6yll *Tim*
648 + y ia6n di *Tim*
649 ardel6o *Tim*
650 neu gytetiued] – *S, Tim*
651 ne *Q*
652 vo, diffodi] a vai diffodedic *S, Tim*
653 y etiued] gidetued *Tim*
654 nebun o *Tim*

Q230b

Three men who hold land and receive it in a commote or cantref court and they are not entitled to be parties to answer to anyone for their lands in consequence of plaints, nor to be a justice – judge by virtue of land, such as noblemen: namely, a churchman to whom the king gives land through a deed, and that [consisting] of the king's [very] own entitled land. The second is a layman to whom the king gives [land], either in exchange, or as some other favour in a similar way. The third is a man who holds ownership of bond land under the king. The first and the second, they should answer before the main justice if there is anyone who claims against them, and not in a royal court. The third should answer according to the law of the bond township if there is anyone who claims against them, and not in the noble court.

Q231

These are the three kinds of bar to a case: one of them is if it happens that a man demands land of another by plaint and claim, tracing a descending right to any one of his ancestors, or by collateral right because of co-inheritance, although the land had not been derived from true ancestors; and the respondent was able to argue against him that [their] right had parted from them by unchallengeable legal process, and it had also, by unobjectionable law, descended to one of his ancestors from whom he should be able to derive a submerged right down to himself or to a co-inheritor, although an incomer, whether to himself, or to a third party from whom he might obtain the land, so as he should be able to plead in their right; or time to exchange pledges as to judgement.

The second bar is: a respondent being able to argue against a claimant who may assert a right derived from ancestors, or a co-inheritor, or of his own condition, or in whatever other way, that the right was submerged by appropriate pleading and judgement in the person of the one who asserted right on his own account, or to his heir, by finding his ancestors to have had wrong possession, or

gam6eresgynn6r, neu allu o atteb6r kadarnhau perchenogaeth hyn o'e ansa6d
e hun, a geisser y 6neuthur yn gam6resgyn no'r honn a[655] ardel6o[656] ha6l6r,
megys pei damch6einei y dyn erbynya6 perchennogaeth ar tir, sef y6 hynny,
tr6y ystyn argl6yd, a g6edy hynny dyuot nebun[657] yn absen[658] h6nn6 y orsed
ac y erbynnya6 ystyn *a*nallu ar yr vn tir o la6 y gorseda6c, a thr6y hynny eredic
y tir[659] yn y g6eresgyn. Y kyntaf a diga6n y v6r6 y maes pan y mynno o vy6n
vn dyd a bl6ydyn, a chyt k6yno y llall racda6 am y[660] goresgyn h6nn6, nyt
ennill deturyt arna6, canys trech y6 pob goresgyn kymysgedic yn yr ia6n no
g6eresgyn odieithyr ia6n; a bot kyfreith yn deallu bot ansa6d yr hynaf yn ll6r6
perchennogaeth yn ia6naf yny diffoder tr6y gyfreith a barn; a honno yn
argae[69rb.1]digaeth trag6yda6l y kynhelir, megys y rei uchot, am
damch6eina6 y perchenogaeth tr6y dadyl6ryaeth 6yneb yn 6yneb[661] y'r
amdiffynbleit, tr6y anghyfreith[662] yr ha6lbleit,[663] neu gallu dodi yn erbyn
ha6l6r[664] kaeedigaeth oessoed rieni o vy6n vn orsed, na chantref na chym6t vo.
P6y bynnac a vo yn kynnal, na dyn dirgeledic o'r g6aet y tyfo yr ia6n ida6 o
blegyt yr hir odef, nac estra6n a erbynnyo g6edy bo ennilledic y ia6n tr6y
amseroed y teiroes; canys y h6nn6 y mae dirgeledic y gyfreith megys y neb a
hanffo o'r g6aet ny bo gallel profi y vot yn gam6eresgynn6r ar y neb y tyvei
yr ia6n ida6. A'r dadyl6ryaeth honno nyt perthyna6l yn erbyn y cam6resgynn6r
h6nn6 onyt yn y lle y retto vn o'r hen dylyedogyon ar y 6resgyn, gan dy6edut
yn y amdiffyn na damch6einya6d etiue[69va.1]dyaeth ida6 y gan y neb a'e
hardel6o; ac yn y mod h6nn6 amheu y berchennogaeth o g6b6l yn y lle y pallo
ida6 ar6ein ia6n ar kyffelybyon.[665]

  Trydyd argaeedigaeth y6, gallu o atteb6r dodi yn erbyn ha6l6r godef o honna6
e hun, neu ha6l tra bl6ydyn, neu ovyn dylyet kych6ynna6l yn dydeu dydon,
neu ovyn etiuedyaeth[666] o ach ac etryt yn amser kaedic kyfreith,[667] neu dechreu
kyfreith g6edy hanner dyd, prouedic tr6y uot hyspys a'e kyffelybyon. A'r kyfry6
argaeedigaeth honn a'e cheffelyb a el6ir[668] yn argaeedigaeth amseroed; a'r d6y

[655] honn a] v6r6 *S*, voro *Tim*
[656] + k.a6l yn erbyn yr *S, Tim*
[657] nebun] – *Tim*, + arall *S, Tim*
[658] apsen *Q, J*
[659] eredic y tir] redec *S, Tim*
[660] kam *Tim*
[661] + yr ha6lbleid ar *S, Tim*
[662] gyf. a barn *S, Tim*
[663] yr ha6lbleit] – *S, Tim*
[664] – *C*
[665] + de6i brefi y ganhorth6y *S*
[666] tir a dayar *S, Tim*
[667] + am dir a dauar *S;* + am dir *Tim*
[668] gynhelir *S, Tim*

a respondent being able to confirm an older possession on his own account, which may be attempted to be made into a wrong possession [older] than that asserted by the claimant, as if a man happened to receive possession of land, that is, through investiture by a lord, and afterwards someone else comes in his absence to a court and receives inefficient investiture for the same land from the hand of the president, and because of that ploughs the land during that possession. The first can oust him whenever he wishes within a year and a day, and although the other may complain against him concerning that possession, he cannot gain a verdict against him, for every mixed possession with the right is stronger than a possession without right; and that the law considers the condition of the eldest as to ownership to be the most just until it be extinguished by law and judgement; and that held to be an eternal closure, such as those above, since the ownership fell to the defending party by pleading face to face, through the illegality of the claiming party, or being able to advance against a claimant the bar of lives of ancestors in any one court, whether it be of a *cantref* or a commote.

Whoever shall be holding, whether an unrecognized person of the blood to whom the right extended on account of long sufferance, or a stranger who receives it after the right shall have been gained through the periods of the three lives; for to such the law is unrecognized as to such as may be derived of the blood and there might not be any possibility of proving him to whom the right extended of being a wrongful taker of possession. And that pleading is not pertinent against that wrong possessor except where any of the old proprietors shall press for possession, by saying in his defence that the inheritance did not fall to him from whoever claimed it; and in that manner question the ownership entirely where it shall fail him to derive a right upon similarities.

The third bar to a case is a respondent being able to advance against a claimant that the latter allowed him himself [to occupy the land], or a claim beyond a year, or demanded a due of moveable property on the blank days, or demanded landed property by lineage and paternity during the time when the law is closed for land and earth, or commenced legal process after midday, proved by this being well-known and similar cases. And that kind of obstruction and the like are called an

argaeedigaeth uchot[669] tragy6ydolyon ynt a'e kyffelybyon,[670] acha6s eu bot yn teruynu yr ia6n.

Grym argaeedigaeth[671] dehor rac dyn y r6ym ar kedernyt a dotto y orch6eira6 y ymadra6d, megys cof,[672] neu deturyt[673] am[674] tir,[675] neu vechniaeth ar gyfne6it, neu amod6yr ar amot a ardel6er yn v6ynt gyngheinya6l. Sef y6 hynny, ar da kyfredic,[676] gan drossi y dadyl6ryaeth a'y defnyd y dyall barn a[677] chyfreith diledyf. Ym pob lle y dicha6n dyn gouyn ia6n anyana6l o bleit rieni, a'e ennill lle ny aller dodi yn y erbyn, diffodi yr ia6n my6n g6eithret y gyfreith tr6y[678] gad6 amser.

Q232. I21, J143, L143, M137, Bost128, O14, S21, T130, Tim82, Tr14, Y39, €232, LatD18

[74va.15] O tri acha6s ny chyll g6reic y heg6edi kyt ada6o y g6r: o glafri, ac o eisseu kyt, a dryc anadyl.

Q233. I22, J144, L144, M138, Bost129, O15, S22, T131, Tim83, Tr15, Y40, €233

[74va.19] Teir g6eith y keiff g6reic y h6yneb6erth: yn gyntaf[679] 6heugeint, yr eil 6eith punt, y tryded 6eith y dicha6n ada6 y g6r, a mynet[680] a'e holl dylyet genthi, ac os diodef hi dros y tryded 6eith,[681] ny cheiff hi[682] y h6yneb6erth.

Q234. I23, J145, L145, M139, Bost130, O16, S23, T132, Tim84, Tr16, Y41, €234

[74vb.27] Tri ll6 a dyry g6reic y 6r: pan enllipper gyntaf, ll6 [75ra.1] seith 6raged,[683] ac yr eil enllip, ll6 pedeir g6raged ar dec, a'r trydyd enllip, ll6 deg 6raged a deu vgeint, o byd neb ry6 hyspysr6yd ar yr enllip.

---

[669] argaeedigaeth uchot] erell ae kyffelybjon *S, Tim*
[670] a'e kyffelybyon] a hynny o *S, Tim*
[671] + y6 *Tim*
[672] + llys *S, Tim*
[673] + g6lad *S*
[674] + dadyl *S, Tim*
[675] + a dayar *S, Tim*
[676] kych6ynedic *S, Tim*
[677] barn a] – *S, Tim*
[678] tr6y] a hynny y *S;* a hynny gan *Tim*
[679] + y keiff *I, J, L, M, Bost, S, T, Tr, Tim*
[680] dicha6n ada6 y g6r, a mynet] a ada6et y g6r ac aet *I, S*
[681] hi dros y tryded 6eith] dros hynny *I;* aros hynny *S;* hi dros hyny *Y*
[682] hi] dim yn *I, S, Y; – J*
[683] + a dyry *M, Bost*

obstruction of times; and the two above objections and similar ones are perpetual, because they determine the right.

The force of an obstruction is to take from a man the force and the strength he may put to verify his statement, such as record, or a verdict for land, or a surety-ship for an exchange, or contract-men on a contract which is claimed as not being accordant. That is, on moveable property, by turning the pleading and its matter to the understanding of judgement and unbiased law. In every case a man may demand a natural right in respect of ancestors, and gain it where it cannot be shown against him, that the right has been extinguished by an act in law by keeping time.

Q232

For three reasons a woman does not lose her *agweddi* although she leaves her husband: for leprosy, and for want of intercourse, and for bad breath.

Q233

Three times a woman receives her *wynebwerth*: the first time six score, the second time a pound, the third time she may leave her husband, and go with all of her entitlement with her, and if she suffers beyond the third time, she does not receive her *wynebwerth*.

Q234

Three oaths a wife is to give to her husband: when first accused, she is to give the oath of seven women, upon the second accusation, the oaths of fourteen women, upon the third, the oaths of fifty women, if there be any certainty behind the accusation.

Q235

[77ra.30] Teir g6raged ny dyly [77rb.1] eu g6yr ia6n gantunt am y godineb: vn y6 g6reic a dyccer lathrut; kyt g6nel y'r g6r arall a vo da genti, ny dyly 6neuthur ia6n y'r g6r a'e duc lathrut. Eil y6 g6reic a gyscer genti yg karadas ac yn gyhoed hynny; kyt g6nel honno a vo da genti, ny dyly y g6r a gysc6ys genti caffel vn ia6n. Trydyd y6 g6reic l6yn a pherth; ny dyly y gorderch caffel ia6n genti kyt g6nel any6eirdeb o gymryt ohonei orderch arall.

Q236. *I24, J150, L147, M144, Bost133, O26, S24, T137, Tim89, Y42, €235,* LatD65

[86va.7] O tri mod y telir teithi buch: o dec ar hugeint aryant, neu o vuch hesp tec, neu o vla6t.

Q237. *I135, J151, L151, O36, S134, Tim90, Tr37, Y146, €236, LatD151*

[90rb.3] Teir kynnefa6t yssyd: kynnefa6t a erlit kyfreith,[684] kynhalyad6y y6; a chynefa6t a raculaena kyfreith, or byd a6durda6t brenhinyaeth idi,[685] kynhalad6y vyd; kynefa6t a l6g6r[686] kyfreith,[687] ny dylyir y chynal.[688]

Q238. *J156, L156, S153, Tim95, Tr73, Y159, €237,* LatD155

[90rb.15] Teir gossotedigaeth yssyd her6yd Hy6el Da[689] y g6plau kyfreith a'e harueroed yn perffeith, hyt na aller eu cablu o eisseu neu ormoder, neu o peth anheil6ng. Kyntaf y6: o'r kyffelybyon kyffelyp varn a rodir. Eil y6: o d6y gyfreith yrbyn yn erbyn yn ysgrifenedic[690] y dosparth vn peth, yr vn a vo teilygach no'r llall, honno[691] a cynhelir. Trydyd y6: pop ry6 [90va.1] gyfreith yscriuenedic ar ny bo g6rth6yneb idi yn yscriuenedic a dylyir y chad6 hyt pan gyfunont y pendefic a'e 6lat y dileu honno, gan ossot arall a vo teilygach.[692]

---

[684] + a honno yssyd *I, S;* + a honno *LatD*
[685] + a honno heuyd *LatD*
[686] haayr *S;* lat *LatD*
[687] + ac yna *I;* + ac *O, Tr*
[688] ny dylyir y chynal] ac yna y dyly y chymhell *I, S;* a honno ny chymellir *LatD*
[689] Hy6el Da] k. *S*
[690] yn yscrifenedic] – *Tr*
[691] yr vn a vo ... honno] y teilyghaf *Tr, Y*
[692] a vo teilygach] – *J;* + yn y lle *L*

Q235

Three women whose husbands are not entitled to compensation from them for their adultery: one is a woman who is taken in abduction; although she may do for the other man what may please her, she is not obliged to make reparation to the man who took her clandestinely. The second is a woman who is slept with in a love-affair and that is publicly known; although she does that which pleases her, the man who slept with her is not entitled to any right. The third is a woman of bush and brake; the lover is not entitled to right from her although she is unfaithful by her taking another lover.

Q236

In three ways are the attributes of a cow to be paid: by thirty of silver, or by a fair dry cow, or by meal.

Q237

There are three customs: a custom which follows law, it is to be upheld; and a custom which precedes law, if it have royal authority, it is to be upheld; and a custom which corrupts law, it is not to be upheld.

Q238

There are three ordinances according to the law of Hywel Dda to complete the law and its practices perfectly, so that they cannot be condemned for omission, or for superfluity, or for any unworthy thing. The first is: in similar cases a similar judgement is to be given. The second is: of two written laws opposed one against another to determine the same thing, the one which is more worthy than the other, that one shall be maintained. The third is: every kind of written law to which there is no written opposition ought to be preserved until the sovereign and his country agree on annulling that one, and establishing another which is more worthy.

Q239. *I136, J152, L152, O37, S135, Tim91, Tr38, Y147, €238,* LatD152 *[1 2 3 = 3 2 1 J, L, O, Tr]*

[90ra.19] Tri pheth a gatarnha defa6t: a6durda6t, a gallu, ac adu6ynder.

Q240. *I137, J153, L153, O38, S136, Tim92, Tr39, Y148, €239*

[91ra.23] Tri pheth a 6anha[693] kynefa6t: gorthrymder, ac agheugant voned, a drych[694] agreith; a hi a 6rthledeir rac dryc agreith.[695]

Q241. *I146, J154, L154, Tim93, Tr71, Y157, €240,* LatD153

[91rb.8] Teir ran y6 a6durda6t Hy6el Da a'e gyfreitheu: nyt amgen, kyfreith y lys beunydya6l, a chy[f]reith y 6lat, ac aruer kyfreitha6l o pop vn ohonunt.

Q242. *I147, J155, L155, S152, Tim94, Tr72, Y158, €241,* LatD154

[91rb.17] Tri aruer kyfreith yssyd. Kyntaf y6 kynnal dyd kyfreitha6l[696] y dechreu dadyl, megys na6uet dyd Mei neu galan gayaf[697] am dadyl tir[698] tr6y ach ac etryt, neu dyd[699] y att6yn[700] dadyl ebryfegedic, nyt amgen noc o vy6n vn dyd a bl6ydyn or pan dechreuher.

　　Eil aruer y6, kynnal mod kyfreitha6l [91va.1] y dadleu, gan ymhaol val y de6isso g6yr y llys a'r bra6t6yr, ae geir tra geir, ae g6ers tra g6ers; canys g6yr y llys bieu datganu pop dadyl yn gofya6dyr kyn barn; a g6edy hynny y bra6t6yr y[701] varnu ac y datganu[702] y dadyl a'r varn[703] pan *vo* reit. Pop cof llys a phop deturyt g6lat gan t6g tr6yda6 perued y cofa6duron, a th6g[704] y sa6l a duuna6[705] ac 6ynt her6yd eu kyt6ybot. Cof llys a deturyt g6lat vn rym ynt, *ac* nyt am yr vn ry6 perthynant. Cof llys, am yr hyn a vu yg g6yd llys y perthyn.[706] Deturyt g6lat, g6iryoned a dengys ymy6n llys am yr hynn a vu yn a6ssen llys.

　　Trydyd aruer y6 kynhal amser kyfreitha6l y 6neuthur grym a chrynodeb ymy6n dadyl, megys amser y tystu neu y diu6yna6 tystolyaeth

---

[693] wna *J*
[694] dryc *I, J, O*
[695] a hi ... agreith] – *I, S*
[696] – *Tim*
[697] galan gayaf] racuyr *I, Y*
[698] + a ofynher *I;* + a dayar *S,*
[699] na6uetyd *I*
[700] atovyn *J, S, Tim*
[701] bieu *I;* – *S*
[702] + yn gofa6dyr *Tr*
[703] ar varn] – *Tr*
[704] chof *I*
[705] a gyfunho *I;* dyno *Tim;* duhuno *Tr*
[706] cof llys ... y perthyn] kanys llys a perthyn am yr hyn a vu gynt yg6yd llys *I*

Q239

Three things which strengthen custom: competence, and power, and fairness.

Q240

Three things which weaken custom: oppression, and doubtful origin, and bad example; and it is driven out in the face of bad example.

Q241

Three parts is the authority of Hywel Dda and his laws: namely, the law of his daily court, and the law of the country, and the legal practice of each of them.

Q242

There are three practices of law. The first is to hold a lawful day to commence a pleading, such as the ninth day of May or the Calends of Winter for a pleading for land by lineage and paternity, or a day for reopening a disregarded suit, namely within a year and a day from the time it shall be commenced.

The second practice is maintaining a lawful procedure in pleading, by accusing as the men of the court and the justices choose, whether on each point individually, or on each point in turn; for it belongs to the men of the court to summarize every pleading as recorders before judgement; and after that the justices are to judge and to recapitulate the case when necessary. Every record of court and every verdict of country [is to be] accompanied by swearing on every point by the recorders, together with the oath of whoever agrees with them according to their consciences. Record of court and verdict of country are of equal force, but they do not pertain to the same kind of matter. A record of court is concerning what has occurred in the presence of the court. A verdict of the country, it shows within the court the truth of what has happened outside the court.

The third practice is holding a lawful time to give effect and expediency to a pleading, such as a time for testifying or for rejecting defunct testimony, or for

uar[91vb.1]6a6l, neu y lyssu tystolyaeth v6ya6l, neu y al6 g6ybydyeit, neu eu g6rthneu,[707] neu amser y ym6ystla6 am varn.[708]

Triads from the tail of manuscript Q

Q243. S163, Tim105, €242

[92ra.23] Teir vchel llys yssyd Yghymry, nyt amgen, llys Aberfra6, a llys Dinef6r, a llys y Mathrafel.

Q244. S197, €243.

[92vb.24] Tri chyfeiliorn kyfreith yssyd: ha6l anhyspys, a g6at[709] agh6byl, a chof aghytun.[710]

Q245. €244

[99ra.16] Teir gorssed brenhina6l yssyd: vn argl6yd, ac vn escob, ac vn abat, pob vn onadunt a dyly gorssed tr6yda6 e hun.

Q246. J168, Tim161, €245 This triad is faulty in both Q and J. Additions from Tim.

[110ra.22] Tri pheth ny drycheuir arnunt: 6yneb6erth, a[711] sarhaet alltut, [a g6arthryd kelein, kanyd kymeint g6arad6yd 6yneb6arth a sarhaed, ac nyd kymeint sarhaed alltyd a bonhedic breiniol,][712] canyt kymeint y anryded na[713] breint dyn mar6 a dyn by6; 6rth hynny nyt ardrycheuir ar vn o'r tri hynny.[714]

[707] + rac y eu llyssu *I, Tr;* + neu oe llyssu *J;* neu eu llyssu *Tim*
[708] am varn] a barn *Q, I*
[709] atteb *S*
[710] aghyfun *Q*
[711] ar *Q*
[712] ac ar y lyas neu y alanas *Q;* a bonhedic breinhawl *J*
[713] na] *from J;* a hynny a *Q;* nay *Tim*
[714] vn o'r tri hynny] yr un or petheu hynny *J*
[715] + gyfreithawl *S*

objecting to living testimony, or for calling forward knowers, or for rejecting them, or a time for giving pledges for the judgement.

Triads from the tail of manuscript Q

Q243

There are three high courts in Wales, namely, the court of Aberffraw, and the court of Dinefwr, and the court of Mathrafael.

Q244

There are three strayings of law: an unknown claim, and an incomplete denial, and a record in disagreement.

Q245

There are three royal courts: the one of a lord, and the one of a bishop, and the one of an abbot, and each of them is entitled to a court by his own right.

Q246

Three things which are not augmented: *wynebwerth*, and the *sarhaed* of an alien, and the shame of a corpse, as the disgrace of *wynebwerth* is not as great as that of *sarhaed*, and the *sarhaed* of an alien is not as great as that of a privileged noble, and neither the honour or the status of a dead man is as great as that of a living man; and because of that there is no augmentation on any of those three things.

Q247. S202, C246

[125ra.1] Tri ry6 dyn yssyd ny dleir her6yd kyfreith erbynya6 neb na'y 6randa6 y ganhebr6ng k6yneu racdunt ygyfreith gorssed[715] megis my6n dadleu brenhin; ac ny ret kyfreith tremic arnadunt o neb ry6 defnyd nac achos y nyd gal6. Kyntaf y6 g6r a el y lud y brenhin o 6assanaeth tir a gynhaler dan y brenhi*n*, canys pennaf g6assanaeth tir y6 mynet y lud y brenhin 6rth y reit;[716] neu dyn a rodit y g6ystyl y arall 6lat o dyundeb g6lad ac argl6yd, yn gedernyt ar gad6 hed6ch kyfr6ng argl6ydiaetheu a phendeuigyon. Ac 6rth hynny y dlyir, her6yd kyfreith, cad6 pop peth o'r eidia6 h6ynteu yn digynen,[717] megis y bei yna, na da kyffro vei na da digyffro vei; canys yn reit y brenhin a'y 6assanaeth yd oydunt h6ynteu, ac o acha6s hynny y dleir yn dilesteir kynal y hansod h6ynteu o ble[125rb.1]gyt y brenhin hyt pan delont h6ynteu o'r g6assanaeth dlyedus h6nn6. Eil y6 dyn y dam6h6eino ido g6neuthur g6eithreit ar ny allo caffel kymhedi6e egl6ys Du6 hyt pan gaffei rydhau gan y Pab. Os g6edy y darffei ida6 gymryt y fford y'r bererinda6t honno y kyffroit ha6l arna6, ny dlyir g6randa6 yr ha6l6r h6nn6 na chynn6ys y deissyf y g6eithret barn[718] hyt pan vei lithredic vn dyd a bl6ydyn o'r dyd y hadnepit kych6yn y pererin o'r gyghelloryaeth hono;[719] cany dlyir her6yd kyfreith symmvt ansa6d neb a vei[720] vedyant a orffei arna6 geissa6 rydit dedua6l[721] o acha6s g6eithret a 6nelei,[722] o vy6n yr amser y gallei dyuot trachefyn. Trydyd y6 gor6eida6c o gleuyt anyana6l, neu dyrna6t, neu vri6,[723] neu vrath; tystolyaeth medic [125va.1] neu berigla6r a gredir yn y lle h6nn6, gan tyghu na allei y cl6yfedic dyuot 6rth gyfreith yn diberigl.[724] A llyna y tri lle ny dlyir, o bleit argl6yd, gymell bra6d6r y rodi barn ar absendra pleit ygyfreith tremic, na chyn6ys deissif ha6l6r ar vedyant,[725] os y p6nckeu hynn a vydant adnabyddus a chyhoyda6c y gan y bra6d6yr, canys tystolyaeth y kyhoed yssyd gredad6y yn y lleoed hynny her6yd kyfreith gyffredin. A llyna y tri lle y seif dadyl6ryaeth absen dros pleideu y gorseda6c a'r bra6d6yr a dyly y 6aranda6.[726] A llyna y lleoed[727] y dyly argl6yd oedi kyfreith yn dioir,[728] heb 6randa6 deissyf, na llafurya6 bra6d6r y g6eithret kyfreith am de6ededigyon bynkeu.[729]

---

[716] + neu yfyllda6d *S*
[717] gymen *S*
[718] kyfreith *S*
[719] allan *S*
[720] neb a vei] na *S*
[721] du6a6l *S*
[722] a 6nelei] andu6a6l *S*
[723] neu vri6] – *S*
[724] yn diberigl] – *S*
[725] + neb or hei hynny *S*
[726] 6arnda6 *Q*
[727] y gorseda6c … lleoed] – *S*
[728] yn dioir] – *S*
[729] de6ededigyon bynkeu] ynn y lleoed d6ededigion ychod

Q247

There are three kinds of person who are not obliged to receive anyone or hear anyone bringing plaints against them in the law of the session as in the court of a king; and the law of contempt does not apply to them in regard to any issue nor cause on the day of summons. The first is a man who goes in the king's hosting through the service of land which is held under the king, because the main service of land is to go to the king's hosting when necessary; or a person who is given as a hostage to another land by the consent of country and lord, as a security for keeping the peace between lordships and sovereigns. And because of that, according to the law, he is entitled to keep everything in his possession without dispute, as if he were there, whether it is livestock or immovable property; because they were at the need of and in the service of the king, and because of that their condition should be maintained without obstruction on behalf of the king until they return from that duty which they had to do. The second is a man who happens to commit an act so that he cannot receive the sacraments of the church of God until he gets absolution from the Pope. If after setting out on that pilgrimage a claim is brought against him, that claimant is not entitled to be heard nor should his petition be allowed in an action of judgement until one year and a day has passed from the day that pilgrim was ascertained to have left that *cynghelloriaeth*; because it is not right according to the law to disturb, within the time he could return, the condition or possession of one who is forced to seek lawful remission of a deed committed. The third is a man who is bedridden through a natural illness or a blow, or an injury, or a wound; the evidence of a mediciner or a confessor is credible in that case, by swearing that the injured could not come to attend to law without danger. And those are the three places where, on the lord's part, he ought not compel a justice to judge in the absence of a legal party as guilty of contempt, nor accept the petition of a claimant to the possession, if these points are recognized and public among the justices, because public testimony is credible in these places because of common law. And these are the three places where pleading in the absence of a parties is to be heard by the enthroned one and the justices. And those are the cases that a lord ought to suspend law without delay, without listening to the petition, nor is the justice to work on the aforementioned subjects.

Q248. S204, C247

[125vb.11] O tri pheth y kyll dyn y ha6l[730] er daet vo y defnyd:[731] llys kyn amser, a thyst ar vach, a chad6 g6edy g6rthot.

Q249. S186, C248

[125vb.14] Tri chenol yssyd yghyfreith: vn y6 kena6l y cad6 ky6irdeb, eil y6 kena6l y gadarnhau kyfya6nder, trydyd y6 kena6l y eglura6 g6irioned.[732]

Q250. C249

[125vb.20] Tri pheth a dyly offeirat llys y 6neuthur yn y dadleuoed: vn y6 cad6 yn escriuenedic pob dadyl hyt pan vo teruyn arnei, eil y6 dileu pop dadyl a darffo y theruynnu, trydyd y6 bot yn barot pop amser ac yn diued6, 6rth reit y argl6yd yn y 6assanaeth.

Q251. S203, C250 [1 2 3 = 2 1 3 S]

[126rb.24] Tri dyn ysyd a ellir y llyssu o'r vn ry6 ach6ysson: nyt amgen no galanas, a g6reictra, a dirdra: tyst, a g6ybydyat, a lli6at kyfreitha6l.

Q252. C251

[126rb.29] Tri dyn kyn g6r[126va.1]thebhont tr6y 6at, ny thalant reith ossodedic ony byd g6rtht6g yn y herbyn: nyt amgen, mach, ac amod6r, a lli6at.

Q253. S168, C252

[126va.5] Tri pheth ny dyly tavodya6c y dadleu dros dyn arall: vn y6 rodi g6ystyl yn erbyn barn, eil y6 dadleu dros 6arant dyn[733] arall, trydyd y6 dadleu dros dyn am perigl eneit a chorff[734] ac aelodeu.

---

[730] o tri ... ha6l] Tri pheth yssyd y dychon y dyn golli y dadyl ohonynt *S*
[731] + o 6ir a chyfreith sef ynt y tri hynny *S*
[732] + sef ynt y tri hynny argl6yd a mach a bra6d6r teil6g r6g pleideu *S*
[733] – *S*
[734] a chorff] – *S*

Q248

On account of three things a man loses his claim however good the substance of his case: an objection before time, and a witness on a surety, and keeping after a refusal.

Q249

There are three middle men in law: one is a middle man to keep integrity, the second is a middle man to confirm justice, the third is a middle man to explain the truth.

Q250

Three things a court priest ought to do in pleadings: one is to preserve each pleading in writing until it is ended, the second is to delete [the record of] every pleading that is over, the third is to be ready at all times and sober, at the need of the lord of his services.

Q251

There are three men who can be objected to for the same kinds of reason: namely *galanas*-feud, and woman-feud, and land-feud: a witness, and a knower, and a lawful informer.

Q252

There are three men who although they answer through denial, do not give a set compurgation unless there is a counter-oath against them: namely, a surety, and a contract-man, and an informer.

Q253

Three things that a representative should not plead on behalf of another man: one is to give a pledge against a judgement, the second is to plead in spite of another man's warranty, the third is to plead on behalf of a man when there is danger to life and body and limbs.

Q254. S182, €253

[126va.12] Tri ry6 dyn yssyd a dylyir eu mechniaethu o blegyt argl6yd, er na bo k6yn pleit racdunt. Vn y6 dyn a vegytho corff dyn arall, os y dyn a t6g ar greir y vegytho; ac ny dylyir d6yn tyston ar vyg6th. Sef achos y6, or llyssir y tyston, nyt diogelach y dyn rac y b6g6th no chynt. Eil y6 dyn a dy6etto caffel argy6ed ar y gorff, ac a 6rthotto yr ia6n a dlyei y gaffel her6yd kyfreith. Trydyd y6 gorsedd6r a vo my6n g6lat h6y no thri dieu a their nos, heb rodi y 6rogaeth y argl6yd neu vreyr.

S182

Tri dyn a dyly y brenhin[735] neu y s6ydogyon vynu meicheu gantynt [er] diogelr6yd y ba6b o'[e] 6erin ef, rac g6neuthur kam ohonynt, er na bo na ch6yn na chanlyn arnynt gan neb: vn y6 gorssed6r a vynno prys6ylya6 me6n g6lad hep rodi g6rogaeth y'r brenhin nac y vn uchel6r, eil y6 dyn a vygytho arall yn*n* y absen yg6yd yr argl6yd neu u s6ydogion, trydyd y6 dyn a m6rthotto achyfreith yn*n* y llys neu ynn vn o'r tri chyhoed, gan d6edyd y mynei i e6yllys odieithir kanlyn k*yfreith* neu g6yneu.

Q255. €254

[126va.29] Tri pherigl dyn ynt: dyrna6t ym pen [126vb.1] hyt yr [emenhyd, a dyrnaut eg corf hyt er][736] emyscar, a thorri vn o'r pet6ar post.

Q256. [S255], [Tim136], €255, LatD38

[127ra.30] Tri dyn y telir g6eli [127rb.1] tafa6t vdunt: y'r brenhin pan dy6etter geir hagyr 6rtha6, ac y'r bra6d6r pan 6ystler ac ef am y ia6n varn, ac offeiriat yn y egl6ys yn y teir g6yl arbenic, neu yn darllein llythyr rac bron y brenhin, neu yn y 6neuthur.

LatD38

Tri dyn y telir gweli tafawd utunt: arglwyt, a brawdwr, a effeiryad llys.

---

[735] berenhin *S*
[736] *Ior 147/2; Q has eyeskipped*

Q254

There are three men who ought to be compelled on the part of a lord to give surety, despite there being no plaint by a party before them. One is a man who threatens the body of another, if the [threatened] man swears on a relic to the threat; and witnesses should not be taken for the threatening. The reason is, if the witnesses are objected to, the man is not safer from being threatened than before. The second is a man who states that he received an injury to his body, and who refuses the compensation he is entitled to have according to law. The third is a session man who is in a country longer than three days and three nights, without paying homage to the lord or the nobleman.

S182
Three men from whom the king or his officers are entitled to demand sureties for the safety of everyone of his people, lest they should do wrong, although there is neither a plaint nor prosecution against them by anyone: one is a session-man who wishes to live in a land without paying homage to the king or to any nobleman, the second is a man who threatens another in his absence in the presence of the lord or his officers. The third is a man who refuses to adhere to law in the court or in one of the three publicities, by stating that he wishes to follow his own will rather than following law or plaints.

Q255

These are the three dangers of a man: a blow to the head as far as the brain, and a blow to the body as far as the entrails, and breaking one of the four posts.

Q256

Three men to whom a tongue-injury is paid: to the king when an ugly word is said to him, and to the justice when a pledge is exchanged with him for a correct judgement, and to the priest in the church in the three special festivals, or when reading a letter before the king, or producing it.

LatD38
Three men to whom a tongue-injury is paid: a lord, and a justice, and the court priest.

Q257. €256

[127va.12] Tri aghyuarch adeuedic ysyd ny dylyir na dir6y na chaml6r6[737] ymdanunt dieithyr diessi6o y perchenogyon. Vn y6 o deruyd bot da kyt r6g deu dyn a diuetha o'r gorcheit6at y da heb groes, heb 6ahard. Eil y6 or kymer dyn varch dyn arall er bryssya6 y rybudya6 g6lat rac llu gor6lat. Trydyd y6 or kymer dyn varch dyn arall er bryssya6 er kruchu offeirat at glaf rac y vynet heb gvmyn.

Q258. €257, LatD34

[127va.27] Tri lle y telir caml6r6 deudyblyc: vn y6 pan taler g6eli [127vb.1] taua6t y'r brenhin; eil y6 pan dynessao[738] dyn ar yr[739] eneit pan vont[740] yn barnu,[741] heb genat, or byd yr argl6yd yn y lle; trydyd y6 pan 6ssyer dyn yn erbyn arall y odef y holi, a'y dyfot ef a'r k6yn6r rac bron yr argl6yd y'r llys, a chilio o'r k6yn6r o'y g6yn,[742] a'r neb y k6yn6yt racda6[743] yn kynic kymryt kyfreith ida6. Ony byd yr argl6yd yn y llys, vn caml6r a dal. Ac yn oes yr argl6yd h6nn6 ny dylyir[744] y 6randa6.[745]

Q259. S264, Tim145, €258

[127vb.15] Tri chanlyn di6all yssyd: canlyn k6yn hyt ar r6ym,[746] a chanlyn r6ym hyt ar dadyl6ryaeth, a chanlyn dadyl6ryaeth hyt pan gaer[747] barn, a chanlyn barn hyt pan gaer teruyn.

---

[737] chachl6r6 *Q*
[738] nesseao *Q*
[739] ar yr] at *LatD*
[740] pan vont] – *LatD*
[741] + brawd *LatD*
[742] o'y g6yn] or hawl *LatD*
[743] y k6yn6yt racda6] a wyssywyd *LatD*
[744] caffayl *LatD*
[745] + am y gofyn hwnnw *LatD*
[746] ar r6ym] ar 6ym *Q*
[747] dadyl6ryaeth ... pan gaer] – *S, Tim*

Q257

There are three acknowledged surreptions for which neither a *dirwy*-fine nor a *camlwrw* ought to be paid but reparation to the owners. One is if it happens that there are shared goods between two men and the custodian ruins the goods without a cross, without prohibition. The second is if a man takes the horse of another man to hurry to warn a country about the [approach of the] army of a neighbouring country. The third is if a man takes the horse of another man to hurry to seek a priest for a sick person lest he departs without communion.

Q258

Three places where twofold *camlwrw* is paid: one is when a tongue-injury is paid to the king; the second is when a man goes near the justices whilst they are judging, without permission, if the lord is present; the third is when a man is summoned against another to suffer a claim against him, and he and the complainant come before the lord to the court, and the complainant retracts his plaint, and the person against whom complaint was made offers to take it to law. If the lord is not present in the court, he [the complainant] pays one *camlwrw*. And in the time of that lord it ought not be heard.

Q259

There are three faultless pursuits: prosecuting a plaint as far as bond, and prosecuting a bond as far as pleading, and prosecuting pleading until judgement is given, and prosecuting a judgement until a termination is had.

Q260. S200, €259

[127vb.21] Tri dyn yssyd a geiff da kyfroedic a dylyet kyfroedic o var6olaeth perchen yghyfreith etiuedyon, ac ny ellir kymell vn onadunt yn bleit y dalu dylyet[748] ygyfreith etiuedyon: nyt amgen, mab[749] eillt brenhin neu vreyr, yr [128ra.1] h6n a eil6 kyfreith yn alltut[750] prioda6l, yr h6nn a dricyo gyt a'y argl6yd yn disumyt hyt y ped6ryd o pob parth. Eil y6 brenhin yny dam6eino etiuedyaeth ida6 o da y vab eillt a vo mar6 heb etiued o'y gorff. Trydyd y6 yny dam6eino y vreyr discunu ygkyfreith etiued, yn y gyffelyb vod, o da[751] y vab eillt a vo mar6 heb etiued o'y gorff.

Q261. S159, Tim101, €260

[128vb.20] Teir dadyl yssyd aghyn6yssedic ygkyfreith Ho6el. Vn y6 dadyl o pleit ha6l6r a discyno ar 6alla6geir, neu anyspysr6yd, neu lithra6 amser. Eil y6 dadyl o pleit amdiffynn6r o'r kyffelyb vod. Trydyd y6 yn y lle y g6nel dyn ardel6 my6n dadyl a vo aghyn6yssedic [128vb.1] ygkyfreith her6yd anyan dadleuat y dadyl.

Q262. S211, €261

[136ra.16] **Am teir diaspat y6ch aduan.**[752] Teir diaspat y6ch aduan ysyd. Vn y6 dylyeda6c am y tir g6edy bo yg6lat arall hyt ympen y na6fyt ach, a dyuot ohona6 att[753] yr argl6yd dylyeda6c yssyd ar y tir a dylyai,[754] a dodi diaspat y rac y vron am ia6n a'e dylyet, ac gouyn o'r argl6yd y'r henaduryeit a tyghant y ach, canys dylyeda6c bieu d6yn y ach yn y blaen a henaduryeit g6edy ynteu y tygu. Ac onys g6ybydant, a'r dylyeda6c yn [136rb.1] gouyn y'r argl6yd, g6edy pallu y'r henaduryeit tygu y ach, ynteu yn d6yn y ach y'r tir a'r dayar a'r tref y heny6 oheni. Argl6yd a dyly rodi y tir ida6, kyny thygho yr henaduryeit y ach, a g6edy y bo y ry6 dyn h6nn6 y maes o'e 6lat hyt y nauet ach, ac ef o'e dehol ae o alanas ae o var argl6yd ae o 6ystloryaeth, a'r na6uet dyn h6nn6 yn mynet o prioda6r yn amprioda6r; yna kyfreith yn muny[755] y gyn6ys ar y dylyet, sef y6 hynny, kymeint[756] a g6r m6yaf y 6archad6 yn yr oes

---

[748] – *S*
[749] mab mab *Q*, – *S*
[750] eillt *S*
[751] o da] – *S*
[752] Am teir diaspat y6ch aduan] – *S*
[753] ar *Q*
[754] dylyeda6c ... dylyai] – *S*
[755] mynny *S*
[756] *From S*; kyfnyeint *Q*

Q260

There are three men who receive moveable goods and moveable entitlement following the death of an owner in the law of heirs, and not one of them can be forced to be a party to pay what ought to be paid in the law of heirs: namely, a bondsman of a king or a nobleman, the one whom the law calls a proprietary exile, the one who stays with the lord without removal until the fourth [man] on every side. The second is the king when an inheritance falls to him from the goods of his bondsman who dies without an heir of his body. The third is when it happens that a freeman succeeds by the law of inheritance, in the same way, to the goods of a bondsman who dies without an heir of his body.

Q261

There are three pleadings not included in the law of Hywel. One is a pleading on the party of a claimant who lapses on account of a faulty word, or uncertainty, or the passing of time. The second is a pleading on the part of the defendant in a similar way. The third is where a man makes a claim in a pleading which is not included in law because of the nature of pleading in the suit.

Q262

Regarding the three cries above emptiness. There are three cries above emptiness. One is by an entitled person regarding his land after he has been in another country until the end of the ninth generation, and he comes to the entitled lord who is over the land to which he is entitled, and gives a cry before him for his right and entitlement, and the lord asks the elders whether they swear to his lineage, because the entitled person has the right to state his lineage before them and the elders after him swear to it. And unless they know, the entitled man asks the lord, after the elders have failed to swear to his lineage, that he himself should state his lineage to the land and earth and the township he springs from. The lord should give the land to him, although the elders do not swear his lineage, and after the same man has been out of his country until the ninth descendant, and he exiled either because of expulsion or because of *galanas* or because of the anger of the lord or because of hostageship, and that ninth man is going from being a proprietor to being a non-proprietor; then the law insists on including him within his entitlement, that is, as much as the largest possession in the hands of a man at the time he goes to the land, and that is called a cry above emptiness, and a man is not heard from beyond the ninth man. The second is that of a nobleman for his exiles when they leave him without having right done to him. The third is that of a woman for her husband, for the kindred should not take her *dilystod* without her permission after she has taken a husband. A man becomes a proprietor when he

y del ef y'r tir, a honno a el6ir yn diaspat y6ch aduan, ac ny 6erende6ir dyn o'r na6uet dyn allan. Eil y6 vn mab uchel6r am y alltutyon pan ymada6ont ac ef heb 6neuthur ia6n ida6. Trydyd y6 vn 6reic am y g6r, cany dyly kenedyl kymryt dilysta6t heb y chenat g6edy g6rha. Yn y pet6ryd [136va.1] dyn yd a dyn yn prioda6r, y tat a'e hendat a'e orhentat ac ef e hun yn pet6ryd. G6edy del dyn yn prioda6r,[757] ny diffyd y priodolder hyny el yn na6uet dyn.

---

[757] y tat a'e hendat ... yn prioda6r] – *S*

is the fourth man, his father and his grandfather and his great-grandfather and himself as fourth. After he becomes a proprietor, his proprietorship is not extinguished until it goes as far as the ninth man.

Notes

X1–X3

Both triads are found early on in the laws of the court, and they deal with the *sarhaed* of the king and the queen respectively. As they occur in most redactions, including the Latin texts and Ior, they were probably part of the laws of court from an early stage. X3 is found in the falconer's section in the laws of court. Although it does not appear to be a stand-alone triad in *X*, but rather a continuation of a previous statement, it is found as a triad proper in the falconer's section in Bleg. See T. M. Charles-Edwards, M. E. Owen and P. Russell, *The Welsh King and his Court* (Cardiff, 2000).

X4, X5

These triads are found in a section on land law, found early on in *X*.

X6, X7

A pair of triads found in all of the redactions, including Ior; in *X* they are found in the *meiri* and *cyngellorion* section. They occur in the short triad collection found at the end of the laws of court in Ior. See Q61 and Q62.

X8

A triad found as part of the section on cattle, in the value of wild and tame tractate, in Cyfn and Bleg manuscripts. The version in *X* is slightly different.

X9, X10

A triad found in the law of women in the Cyfn and Bleg manuscripts. See D. Jenkins and M. E. Owens (eds), *The Welsh Law of Women* (Cardiff, 1980).

X11, X12

These triads are found in a section of miscellaneous material in *X*, shortly before the triad collection. X11 is found in other Cyfn manuscripts and in two of the Latin manuscripts, but not usually in Bleg. X12 only occurs in *X*, but it is similar to another triad found in *Q* – see Q245.

X13

This triad only occurs in *X* of the Cyfnerth redaction, but it is a triad found in the triad collection in most Bleg manuscripts. The form of the triad is fuller in Bleg, but it also seems that this version in *X* is corrupt: certain verbs and subjects of verbs are missing. See Q8.

X *Triad Collection*

X14. Z10, U14, Mk21, V19, W17. Bleg9, Q19, LatD9. Latin: B12, E5. Ior, 101; DwC, 149, 300

This is a title triad, where the heading is known separately from the contents of the triad. See S. E. Roberts, 'Tri Dygyngoll Cenedl', for a full discussion of this triad.

Tri dygyngoll cenedl is the first triad in the large triad collection found at the end of the Cyfn manuscripts in *V*, *W*, *X*, *Z*, and *Mk*, but not *U*. This probably points to the beginning of a standard collection of triads, rather than indicating any significance in the *dygyngoll* triad being the first in the collection. The Bleg triad is very similar indeed to the Cyfn version, with the order of the first and second case reversed; however, the triad is part of the *galanas* section (*Bleg*, 33. 4–17). Latin D is identical to Bleg and the triad is in Latin with the heading in Welsh (*LTWL*, 335. 15–29). Both Latin B and Latin E have a version of the triad, found in the *galanas* tractate, but it has been confused with a section on *oer-gwymp galanas*, often found with this triad (*LTWL*, 210. 20–30, 450. 8–19).

In Ior, a triadic section including the words *tri dygyngoll* appears in a tractate that is only found in Ior, dealing with the affiliation and rejection of children to a kindred (*Ior*, 101/1–6, *LTMW*, 129). The only link between the two versions of the triad (the Bleg/Cyfn version and the Ior version) is the second limb in Ior. In the *galanas* section in *Col* there are four sentences similar to *damweiniau* (*Col*,

279–82). The last of the four is called *oergwymp galanas*, and the remaining three are similar to the three limbs of the *dygyngoll* triad. The three *damweiniau* are closer in subject and content to the Bleg/Cyfn triad than to the Ior version. The remaining versions of the triad occur in *Damweiniau Colan*, *S* and *K. DwC*, 300–2, appears to be unique: a new idea, not found in any of the other versions of the triad, is presented in the second limb. Both S277 and *Damweiniau Colan*, 149–51, are versions of the same triad, similar to the Ior triad, and the triad shared in the *K* and *S* collection is an extended, fuller version of the Bleg and Cyfn triad.

digingoll: *Dygyngoll* is not found as a compound in *GPC*, but the word *dygyn* means grievous or dire.

mab amheuedic: A doubted son in a kindred; no formal affiliation or denial process has been started. If that son kills someone, *galanas* needs to be paid for the dead by the kindred of the killer, and the triad goes on to state that the kindred of the child ought to pay the *galanas* for the dead man, and that they may then (and only then) deny the killer, or affiliate him to a man from another kindred. This is certainly a case where doubt could arise as to who pays the *galanas*, and the triad prevents the affiliation of a *mab amheuedic* out of a kindred becoming a means by which that kindred might avoid paying *galanas* for the deed of one of their members.

talu galanas oll eithyr keinhyawc a dimei: Someone has been killed, and the kindred of the killer have started to pay *galanas*, but not all of the *galanas* has been paid; because of that, someone from the paying kindred is killed. Nothing is owed for a man killed because the money is not all paid; none of the *galanas* will be returned, which is a dire loss to the kindred, and they do not receive any *galanas* for the second killing, so they have also lost a kinsman. This is the first limb in both Latin B and Latin E.

pan enlliper gwiryon am gelein: An innocent man is accused of homicide, and he does not deny the deed within the appointed time. After that, someone from the innocent man's kindred is killed, as a revenge killing; the *galanas* of this latest dead man is not paid, and the kindred of the innocent man lose a kinsman. This is the third element in Latin B and E, and it is labelled *oergwymp galanas*. *Oergwymp galanas* does occur in the Cyfn redaction, earlier than the triad collection but nevertheless towards the end of the manuscript, in a section discussing *galanas*; in Wade-Evans's list of contents, the section is titled 'Of *galanas*', and is followed directly by what Wade-Evans calls 'Miscellaneous notes', so it could be called an anomalous or floating section on *galanas* within the Cyfn manuscripts (*WML*, 110. 4–11, xc). However, each Cyfn manuscript includes this section. In this final limb, the words *oed kyfureithyawl* are found, and since triad

22, *Tri oed kyfureith*, is immediately after it, these words may link the two triads. It is significant that the triad collection in Bleg begins with a version of X16, whereas the equivalents of X14 and X15 are found in the *galanas* section in Bleg.

X15. *Z11, U15, Mk22, V20, W18. Bleg57, Q20, LatD11*

oed kyfureith: There is a section in Ior dealing with allotted times: if a lord and a kindred are asking for *galanas* and the other kin wants a delay, a fortnight is allowed for each lordship (*Ior*, 107/6; *LTMW*, 147). *E* goes into detail about when each member of the kindred should pay their share (VC III. i. 16; trans. *LTMW*, 148). Bleg also gives a list of allotted times for giving an answer, giving surety or finding truth (*Bleg*, 83. 4–17; *WML*, 115. 7–17), but as the list does not correspond to the times given in this triad, the provisions in this triad are special to *galanas*.

dial kelein: *Kelein* means a corpse. In Bleg, *dial* has the same meaning as in Modern Welsh, revenge, and can mean a revenge killing. This is in contrast to the payment for *galanas*, and *dial* is a possible route if *galanas* has not been paid, or only some of it paid (*Bleg*, 32).

X16. *Z12, U16, Mk23, V21, W19. Bleg44, Q56, LatD71. Latin: A16, B7, E22. Ior, 42/6*

The three triads on the nets of a king, nobleman and a bondsman are always together and usually mark the beginning of a triad collection in Cyfn and Bleg. They are also found in Ior, as the beginning of the only collection of triads in that redaction, following the laws of court. As the three triads on nets refer first to the king's sources of income, they may have been placed at the end of the laws of court as the subject matter is similar to that which went before the triads. In *Mk*, and *Mk* alone, the order of the triads is different: in all other manuscripts, the three triads are in order of rank, with the nobleman before the bondsman.

rwyd: The word net is being used in the figurative sense, and each of the nets is referring either to a collection of men or animals, or a place for them to live (*Bleg*, 223). Each of the items in the triad, apart from the *teulu*, are cases where the owner receives money if an animal is caught in his herd, so the net metaphor is taken further: the people in the triad are netting fourpence.

teulv: Although some of the *anreith*, booty, that the *teulu* acquired was shared amongst the officers of the court, the king had a large share; hence it was a good source of income.

y gre: Wade-Evans translates this as stud; in *Q*, *all6est y veirch* is found, and both mean the same thing (*WML*, 265, Q56). A stud was a very valuable commodity as the court needed horses for battle, hunting and for warfare.

X19. *Z15, U19, Mk26, V24, W22. (Bleg16, Q55, LatD17). Latin: A8, B15, E12. Ior 104/14–17*

This triad is found in all of the Cyfn texts but is not in the later collections although a similar version, *tri rhyw dirwy* is found in the Bleg and Latin collections; the Bleg version, however, has a different extension (Q54). *S* has two versions, one very similar to the triad found here, and the other closer to the *Q* version. Both *X* and *Z* have an expanded heading, quoting the payments for the king's *sarhaed* as set out in the laws of the court.

This is a good example of a triad involving a simple statement and then an extension; the triads in the *X* collection tend to be simple lists of three, but by the time of the *Q* extended collection, the triads are more likely to involve at least a sentence of explanation. The extension to this triad is unusual in that the order of the items in the extension does not follow the order of the heading; it may be that the extension is a later addition.

dirwy: The standard financial penalty of three pounds was originally only applicable to the third element in this triad, but was later extended to cover other offences too (*LTMW*, 336).

treis: This word means a violent deed, and can refer in the lawtexts to particular forms of violence, such as rape and robbery, or to violence in general. Fighting, however, is treated differently from violence, and has its own entry. Most Bleg manuscripts have *tri rhyw dirwy* rather than this heading, and the triad is different. *S* has a version of both this triad and the Bleg triad; S37 has *treis mor6yn* in this section, and rape is what is referred to here. One of the senses in which Irish *díre* was used was for the life price; Dafydd Jenkins suspected that *dirwy* had that sense at one time in Welsh too, and this is reflected by the first element of the triad, where the honour price of the king is owed as payment for the rape of a maiden (M. E. Owen, 'Shame and reparation: woman's place in the kin', *WLW*, 68). The use of *dirwy* for honour price is reflected in the items paid to the king: the *clawr eur* should be the same size as the king's face, thus reflecting *wynebwerth*, but *wynebwerth* later narrowed in scope and by the time of *X* was limited to the laws of women. *Sarhaed*, however, widened in meaning, and *dirwy*, as *sarhaed* spread, was pushed down. Thus the triad is only loosely based on *dirwy* as payment for the king's *sarhaed*.

ymlad kyuadev: In Ior it is stated that there is a *dirwy* for fighting, and fighting is defined too: assault and battery, and blood and wound. The *dirwy* for the three elements of fighting is twelve kine or three pounds (*Ior*, 104/15–16; *LTMW*, 143).

ledrad: *Lledrad* originally referred to a deed done secretly, but came to mean theft, in contrast to robbery, for which the word *trais*, violent wrong-doing, can be used. In *X* and *Z*, the theft is described as *anofeis*, which is explained as meaning *anobaith*, hopeless. In Ior, the amount payable for *dirwy lledrad* is stated: twelve kine or three pounds, and it is payable to the lord (*Ior*, 111/14; *LTMW*, 157).

diwyn dirwy: Stephen J. Williams takes *diwwyn/difwyn* to be an old verbal noun for the verb with the stem *diwyg-*; this assumes that, in *difwyn dirwy*, *dirwy* is an objective genitive depending on *difwyn*, or a loose compound – payment of the *dirwy* (*Bleg*, 43. 31–44. 7). So, *trais* is the offence and *dirwy trais* is the fine or the debt to the king from the *dirwy*. *Difwyn*, then, is actually to pay the fine. This is supported in the evidence found in *Damweiniau Colan* (*DwC*, 223–5).

X20. Z16, Mk27, V25, W23. Bleg52, Q64, LatD78. Latin: A9, B1, E15. Ior, 42/2

In Bleg this triad, like X15–X17, above, forms a group of three triads, including the indispensables of a nobleman and a bondsman. All three triads are also in *Mk* of the Cyfnerth redaction, but the other two are towards the end of the triad collection, not placed with this triad. In *Q* and the Latin texts, each element of the triad has an explanatory sentence showing why the people are indispensable. The version of the triad found in Ior has an extension explaining each of the items in the triad: the priest is needed to bless the king's food, the justice is needed to debate doubtful things and the king's retinue are needed to serve his needs (*Ior*, 42/2).

X21. Z17, Mk28, V26, W24. Bleg55, Q30, LatD81, 92. Latin: A12, B2, E17. Ior, 42/5, 43/8

eurgrawn: A treasure trove or hoard; if a person buries something in another person's land (to hide it) the owner of the land gets four legal pence, as his land was dug without his permission, and also gets whatever was hidden, unless it was an *eurgrawn* (*canys brenhin bieu pop eurgra6n*, as the king owns all treasure troves: *WML*, 60. 17). Ior has *swllt* here (*Ior*, 42/5).

hebawc: The king's falcons were for hunting, and only Cyfn gives them a legal value; they are more valuable than hawks (*WKC*, 264). A mature hunting falcon is worth a pound (*WKC*, 264). The etymology of both *hebawc* and *gwalch* is discussed by Dafydd Jenkins: *hebawc* represents the long-winged falcon, and *gwalch* is the less specific short-winged hawk, meaning a hunting bird in general, so every falcon is a hawk, but not every hawk is a falcon (D. Jenkins, '*Gwalch*: Welsh', *CMCS*, 19 (1990), 63).

leidyr: The king gets all the *dirwy* for a thief.

X22. Z18, Mk29, U56, V27, W25. Bleg56, Q69, LatD82

The triad of tetrads shows the redactors' love of numerical ordering; it is found in Bleg, Cyfn and Latin D, but it does not occur as a triad in Latin A, B or E. However, the three limbs do occur both in Latin B and Latin E, as separate tetrads. In Latin B, the first and second limbs are found in the triad collection, the first tetrad following LatB62, and the second following LatB63 (*LTWL*, 244. 15–17, 22–33). In Latin E the first limb only is found in the triad collection, between the same two triads, in the same position as in Latin B (*LTWL*, 495. 14–15). The other two tetrads are independent sections in both redactions (*LTWL*, 258. 3–8; 455. 35–456. 10, 502. 25–30). The readings of the Bleg and Cyfn versions of this triad are almost identical. Although there are many variant readings for this triad, the differences tend to be small variations in syntax or individual words and there are no major differences in content. The three elements of the triad are dealing with very different subjects: perverting justice, theft and sanctuary.

Theft
taryan: The figurative meaning is found elsewhere in the laws in a section which is quite similar to this limb (*Bleg*, 44. 8; *LTWL*, 353. 20). This limb appears to be a tetrad constructed from a triad by adding the first limb; the section occurs as a triad in Ior (55/13). These are the things which save a man from *rhaith gwlad*. The *rhaith gwlad* system is summed up in *Bleg*, 106. 22–6, and it involves the oath of fifty men holding their land from the king.

geni a meithrin: This phrase is not found elsewhere in Bleg and Cyfn but Ior has a long section on how to accuse someone for theft. The first step is to claim ownership of the thing stolen, *damdwng*. Then there are three defence routes for the accused to take: 'birth and rearing', 'keeping before loss' and 'voucher to warranty' (*Ior*, 114/1; trans. *LTMW*, 161–2). To make a plea by birth and rearing, maintainers must state that the mother of the animal was the claimant's, and that the claimed animal was born and reared with the claimant, and never left him; *Q* adds either through being sold or through being given as a gift. The maintainers must be one man of higher status, and one of lower status than the claimant (*Ior*, 114/4; *LTMW*, 162). In this triad, however, the maintainers are of the same status as the claimant.

gwarant: Voucher to warranty; in the northern texts, such as Ior, the word used is *arwaesaf*. The *gwarant* is a warrantor. In the case of claiming a cow, the claimant states that the cow in the possession of A is his. A claims he got it from B; B acknowledges the truth of A's claim and is then A's warrantor. B claims he got it from C, and C acknowledges the transaction so both A and B have a warrantor and are cleared of suspicion. C cannot repeat the process: he is the 'third hand' and must resort to another defence (*Ior*, 114/15). In the triad in *Q* there is an additional sentence stating that, after the third hand, the item must be defended by law. For another triad on the subject of *gwarant* see *Bleg*, 44. 29–45. 4.

cadw kyn coll: In this case, there are two people swearing; in Ior these are distinguished using *enteu* and *y llall* (*Ior*, 114/5). A, the claimant, claims (*damdwng*) an animal in the possession of B, the defendant, stating the date it passed out of his (A's) possession. B's answer is to say he has *ceidwaid* (because they are attesting to a state of affairs; *ceidwaid* are used in cases of possession and ownership) to show that he had possession of the animal before the period during which it passed out of A's possession (*Ior*, 114/5). So, B's animal is not the same as A's: B had *cadw*, possession of an animal, before A lost his animal, *cyn coll*.

Sanctuary
nawd: Huw Pryce discusses the final limb of this triad at length and states that there were two versions of it: the first is the version found in the Cyfn and Bleg redactions and Latin D (in Welsh) and the second version is found in Latin B and Latin E (Pryce, *Native Law*).

wystler o vod: This is probably a reference to the common practice of taking hostages to guarantee an agreement between two rulers (Pryce, *Native Law*, 175).

cwynossawc: Originally meaning the supper-giver of the king, this is not found in the second version of this paragraph, and this item, according to Pryce, suggests that the triad, or at least the final branch of the triad, was obsolete by the thirteenth century as the duties of the supper-giver, who was obliged to give the king supper for one night, had been commuted (Pryce, *Native Law*, 175; see also *EIWK*, 378–9).

X23. Z19, Mk30, V28, W26. Bleg51, Q63, LatD10. Latin: B28, E35. Col, 283–8

Cf. *WML*, 52. 6. There is a similar triad in *Col*, but it is longer, and only loosely corresponds to this one (*Col*, 286–8). Two of the people in the *Col* triad are found as people who should not be sold in X56, and *Col* states that a *cynllwynwr* and a *bradwr arglwydd* should be executed, and are worse than thieves. The third person who loses his patrimony in *Col*, as in Cyfn, is a person who cannot cope with it (*Col*, 288; *WML*, 52. 15–16).

teispantyle: The origin of this word is uncertain. *Teispan* means blanket, and *gobennydd tyle* seems to mean a type of bedspread; according to a note in *Llyfr Blegywryd* (224), this term is only found in the triads, and the meaning of bed-protector was extended to include the person who defended the kindred (*Bleg*, 224). See also *Breudwyt Ronabwy*, ed. M. Richards (Cardiff, 1948, reprinted 2001), 35.

X24. Z20, Mk31, V29, W27. Bleg58, Q21, LatD83. Latin: E88

There is some provision in the laws on when to be silent during court cases: in the procedure for claiming land set out in Ior, there is a point where *gostec*, silence, needs to be announced, and anyone breaking that silence is punished (*Ior*, 177/6–7). There is no similar provision to be found for suretyship and for the lord in the court, but then detailed procedural information in the lawtexts is largely confined to land law.

X25. Z21, U49, Mk32, V30, W28. Bleg59, Q22, LatD12. Latin: B69, E4

The provisions found in this triad occur as a paragraph in the *galanas* section of Latin B (*LTWL*, 210. 12–18). There are similar provisions in the Anglo-Saxon laws: in Alfred's laws, if someone is killed after being impaled by a spear carried over another's shoulder, the owner of the spear must pay the dead man's *wergeld*, but does not pay the fine (*LEEK*, Alfred, 36).

X26. Z22, Mk33, V31, W29. Bleg60, Q67, LatD84. Latin: B41, E49

gwad kyn deduryt: The *deturyt* is the verdict, the final decision made by the justice or justices (*Bleg*, 17–18). Stephen J. Williams sums up the situation in this limb of the triad: once the justice has heard the case, there is no point in denying further whilst waiting for the judgement (*Bleg*, 226).

chynghaws: *Caws* is from Latin, *causa*; *cynghaws* is someone who shares a case (as an aid) or a case that is shared between the litigants and their helpers. In Bleg and Cyfn, this means the case or the argument, and in Ior it means the person who presents the case; in Bleg and Cyfn, the person who presents the case is called a *tafodiog* in certain circumstances (*LTMW*, 331; *Bleg*, 45. 19–30). Here it is the former meaning: pleading the case. See also Charles-Edwards, '*Cynghawsedd*', 188–98.

X27. Z23, Mk34, V32, W30. Bleg61, Q68, LatD85

The contents of this triad are not found elsewhere in the laws but it is rather obvious: the milk of these animals is not usually used by humans.

X28. Z24, Mk35, V33, W31. Bleg62, Q23, LatD86. Latin: E89

effeiryad teulv: There is also a triad found in the priest of the household's section in Bleg which sets out the priest's duties in legal cases (to delete the terminated cases, and to write down the judgements) and it includes the statement that he must be sober as the king may need him to read or write letters (*Bleg*, 13). According to Latin B, the falconer is another person who is not allowed to be drunk (*LTWL*, 199. 8).

X29. Z25, Mk36, V34, W32. Bleg63, Q70, LatD87. Latin: E37

In ordinary circumstances, *sarhaed* would be paid for a blow unless it was accidental (*Bleg*, 57. 20–8), but although the blows in this triad are deliberate, the circumstances are deemed to be extraordinary and therefore they are allowed. This is not discussed elsewhere in the laws.

X30. Z26, 118. Mk37, U11, V35, W33. Bleg64, Q71. Ior; 86/1–6

A similar triad is found in the Bleg triad collections (*Bleg*, 111. 5), but the wording differs in that the opening sentence of the triad makes it clear that it is a triad about children and inheritance, not a triad about the law of women.

tref eu mam: This phrase is modelled on the form *tref tad*, as a woman in the lawtexts does not have a *tref*; she has no right to land (*Ior*, 86/1). The point is that, in the cases of these three sons, the inheritance passes through the mother's side rather than the father's.

alltud: A woman should not be given in marriage where her sons will not be entitled to patrimony (*Ior*, 86/2). Ior presents a similar triad as what 'the law says' rather than what others say (*Ior*, 86/4–5). If she gave herself to the alien, then her sons would not be entitled to inherit through her (*Ior*, 86/6).

X31. Z27, Mk41, V40, W34. Bleg65, Q24, LatD88. Latin: B35, E43

The law of women is a subject that appears regularly in the triads, and this one is dealing with *sarhaed* payments. Each of the three items found in this triad, a kiss, *cusan*, to finger, *gofysio*, and to copulate, *ymrain* (called a *cyflafan dybryd* in *Ior*,

26/5, or *achaws dybryt* in *Bleg*, 66), are serious offences for which a husband is entitled to *sarhaed* if the wife is willing (Owen, 'Shame and reparation', *WLW*, 53). In this triad, the woman is unwilling, and it is made clear (*idi*) that the woman herself receives the *sarhaed*.

cussan: Only a third of the *sarhaed* is due for a kiss, according to the triad, but according to Bleg, whoever kisses a woman pays a fourth part of her *sarhaed*. The previous sentence in Bleg states that if she is kissed, the husband gets a third of the *sarhaed* unless it occurs during a game called *raffan* (*Bleg*, 66. 30–1).

y ffaluv: The same as *gofysio*, meaning to grope, or to make indecent contact (*WLW*, 203). This is a full *sarhaed* offence according to the triad, but Bleg states that, as with kissing, the offence is only worth a fourth of the *sarhaed*; again, the payment due to her husband for this offence is full *sarhaed* with no augmentation (*Bleg*, 66). In *Col*, three instances where a man does not receive compensation for *gofysio* are given (*Col*, 22).

vod genthi: To be with her, literally, but in the laws it is used to mean 'to have intercourse' (*Ior*, 110/10); here, the extra clause *o'e hanuod* is added, to make it clear that in this case, it is against her will, and her *sarhaed* is augmented by a third. According to Bleg, it is a full *sarhaed* (for the complete act the complete *sarhaed* is paid) or the *sarhaed* is augmented once (*Bleg*, 66). See discussion by Owen, 'Shame and reparation', *WLW*, 50–3. Latin A, Latin B and Latin E state that the *sarhaed* is paid in full for copulation, and a quarter of it is paid for *gofysio* and kissing, but Latin D and Bleg state that for copulation the *sarhaed* is augmented by a half, two-thirds or even doubled (Owen, 'Shame and reparation', *WLW*, 53). See also X32, below.

gwryawc: In *X*, but not in every Cyfn manuscript, there are instructions on how to calculate the *sarhaed*, depending on the status of the woman; if she is married, her *sarhaed* is calculated according to her husband's *sarhaed*. *Z* also adds that if she is a widow, her *sarhaed* reverts to being calculated according to her father's *sarhaed*.

X32. Z29, Mk39, V38, W36. Bleg67, Q73, LatD90. Latin: B24, E30. Col, 29–30; DwC, 243

This is found as part of one of the *damweiniau* in *DwC*, as a reference, but with the limbs given as an aside.

enllip: Cf. Owen, 'Shame and reparation', *WLW*, 52. The first and second limbs are found in *Ior*, 52/7. The other limb in Ior, also found in *DwC*, is seeing both the man and the woman leaving an empty house (*o wacty*).

X33. Z28, Mk38, U20, V36, W35. Bleg66, Q72, LatD89. Latin: B35/B40, E31/E48

Latin E31 and 48 are on a similar subject, but the closest match in Latin E is triad 31 (*LTWL*, 475. 26–8). Latin E48 concerns the three *sarhaed* of a woman (not a kindred, so the heading is different): her husband taking a concubine; being struck without cause; and being raped or having something taken from her violently, *dwyn treis* (*LTWL*, 494. 3–4). In Latin B35 version both the first and second limbs found here appear in Latin, but instead of the ambiguous third limb, we have *adulterari sub viro*, committing adultery with a man (*LTWL*, 242. 22–3). However, the heading also causes some problems in Latin B: *tri seudan gureic*. *Seudan* is uncertain according to *GPC*, but may mean shame; Latin B has the only occurrence of the word.

hyspeilyaw: To despoil, usually used in the sense of taking spoil after battle, and it may also be used figuratively for rape, but this is not a common usage. In the earlier Welsh examples given in *GPC*, *ysbeilio* means to strip a person of their clothes, and this meaning is also found for *despoil* in *OED*. In Latin E31, the phrase used is *spoliare feminam*, again meaning to despoil, and in this case it may mean to steal or snatch something from the woman; this is one of the three ways *sarhaed* is done to the queen in the laws of court (*WKC*, 37; *WML*, 3. 13–16, *Bleg*, 4. 7–10, *Ior*, 3/6). This section may be the equivalent of *dwyn treis* in Latin E48, if *dwyn treis* means to steal something violently rather than to rape the woman.

bot yn trech gan y gwr …: This extension to the triad is not found in the Latin versions, nor is it found in Bleg or Latin D; however, the order of the triad is the same in all the versions except for Latin E31, where the first and second items are reversed. The extra sentence in Cyfn may be based on a text with the same order as that found in Latin E31: the second limb is taking her *llathludd*, raping her, and the third is despoiling her. So, the man prefers despoiling her to having intercourse with her, for example, in the case of the second limb, raping her. However, it is still a mystery why this (especially the contrast between *ysbeilio* and *bod genti*) is a shame to the kindred or to the woman.

X34. Z30, U21, W37. Bleg68, Q25, LatD91

A triad found in the Bleg collection in most manuscripts, but not in all of the Cyfn manuscripts, the triad deals with the incitements to revenge, and is rather abstract. Seeing the three things – wailing relatives, the bier and the grave – would be a reminder of the death of the person. However, in *X* the grave is 'without reparation', suggesting that a formal case of *galanas* has not been held or has been unsuccessful; revenge is the next step – see X15.

X35. Z31, Mk42, V41, W39. Bleg10, Q38.

This triad has several different versions: one in *X*, *W* and *Z*; another in *Mk* and *V*, and another in the tractate on witnesses in Bleg (37. 11–16). Another version occurs in Ior (79/12). Also, *AL*, VII. i. 12 lists five objections, two of which are the same thing; and there is a similar section, listing four objections, in the *arferion cyfraith* in Bleg (128. 11, 21). The Bleg and *Mk* versions have the same content but Bleg gives a few more details on each of the subjects.

llyssv: A list of three reasons for objecting to witnesses is found in the land law section of Ior: they are land-feud, enmity and nearer kin (*Ior*, 79/12, and *LTMW*, 93). In *Col* (527–35) and Latin E (457. 13–20), there is a philosophical discussion on the grounds for objection, and Latin B has the three objections found here as part of a longer list of the *Naw affeith galanas herwyd gwyr Powys* (*LTWL*, 251. 12–20). *Affaith* is here being used in the sense of grounds for/causes of homicide (Owen, 'Shame and reparation', *WLW*, 61–5, and Russell, 'Etymology of *affaith*', 106).

anudon kyhoedoc am ledrad: The triad as found in *X*, *Z* and *W* has a different first item to the other versions: witnesses can be objected to if they have been guilty of perjury in the past. This is also found in the *arferion cyfraith* in Bleg (*Bleg*, 128. 11, 21). The *Mk* version has *tirdra*. Each limb is explained in the Bleg version of this triad: *dadyl am tir yrydunt heb teruynu* is given for this item (*Bleg*, 37. 12–13).

galanas heb ymdiwyn: unpaid or uncompensated *galanas*. It appears to be a feud (-*tra* in the *Mk* version) where killing was the source of the trouble. The word is not common, and may be formed from *galanas* on the example of the previous two limbs of the triad.

bod y vn gan y wreic y gilyd: In the Bleg triad, the more ambiguous *kamarueru o vn ohonunt o wreic y llall*, one misusing the wife of another, is given, and the version in *X*, *W* and *Z* makes it clear that this is sexual intercourse. This item is not found in the original three in the Ior land law section, but the text states that 'some say' that woman-feud, *gwreictra*, is a fourth objection, but the law says that woman-feud derives from enmity or *galanas*-feud and therefore is one of the original three (the third being *kerennyd nes*) in the Ior list (*Ior*, 80/1). The same idea is found in the list in *AL*, VII. i. 12, as *gelynyaeth* (enmity) and *gureyctra* are combined, and a fourth objection is added, where a Welshman can object to an alien or vice versa.

X36. Z32, Mk40, V39, W38. Bleg69, Q31

hawl dyn yn lledrat ac ny chynghein lledrad yndaw: A man may prosecute for theft although these things do not constitute theft; they are not stealing, but they are acts done *yn lledrad*, without permission (*Bleg*, 227). In Ior, this would be *anghyfarch*, but *anghyfarch* does not appear in this context in Bleg or Cyfn (*Cyfraith Hywel*, 63).

adeilad: This is coupled with ploughing. If it is committed on land that is prohibited the punishment for breaking a boundary applies: the building and nine score pence *camlwrw* goes to the lord (*DwC*, 473–5; *LTMW*, 127).

diod coet: The punishment for removing timber without permission is a penny to the owner of the land for the load of two oxen or one horse load, and a *camlwrw* to the lord; if the suspect denies it, then the compurgation on theft falls upon him (*Bleg*, 98). There is a plaint in *Q* dealing with this very subject (*AL*, XII. vi; Roberts, 'Plaints in Mediaeval Welsh Law', 219–61); the claimant made the crime known to the *amhinogeu* (see X76, below), and stated that the crime was one of the three deprivations in law (Q140).

eredic: Ploughing land without permission results in the guilty party paying four pence to the owner of the land and a surreption fee to the king (*Ior*, 95/2; *LTMW*, 126). Furthermore, *Llyfr Damweiniau* states that if there is a dispute for land and the land is prohibited as a result, and someone breaks the prohibition either by ploughing or building, the punishment is the same as for breaking a boundary (*DwC*, 473; *LTMW*, 126).

X37. Z33, Mk43, U7, V42, W40. Bleg70, Q74. Latin: B27, E34

In his discussion of this triad, Pryce states that it was probably composed no earlier than the late twelfth century, and was a response to the reformers' condemnation of Welsh society and their practices regarding illegitimate children (Pryce, *Native Law*, 100).

mab llwyn a pherth: A son of bush and brake is one who is conceived by a woman of bush and brake; this is not an open union and it seems to involve some degree of secrecy (*WLW*, 206). Although this is one of the legal unions found in the *naw kynywedi teithiog* list, the list of unions, it is not a open marriage in any sense, although it is not prostitution (Charles-Edwards, 'Nau Kynywedi Teithiauc', *WLW*, 26–8). The son is not entitled to inherit land because of the (secret) circumstances in which he was conceived. However, in this case the mother goes on to have a legal union, by gift of kin, with the father of the child of bush and brake, and the sons of that legal union are entitled to inherit land through their father. According to Huw Pryce, this section reflects an English law idea which originated in the reign of Henry II, that a son born out of wedlock is not entitled to inherit land, which conflicts with Welsh law which allows a woman of bush and brake to affiliate her child to the father's kindred (Pryce, *Native Law*, 101). The affiliation process as carried out by a woman of bush and brake is found later on in the triad collection (X40).

ysgolheic: A cleric. Pryce states that this limb reflects the desire of the Norman church reformers to enforce clerical celibacy and even refers to canon law (Pryce, *Native Law*, 102). There are similar rules and laws found in other countries from the same period (ibid., 102–3).

mvd: Pryce suggests that this limb has no relation to ecclesiastical law and is probably a later addition to the two other rules; the *U* version of the triad differs from the other version in that the opening phrase refers to three brothers of whom two are not entitled to patrimony, and the other versions refer to three brothers who are denied patrimony (*Native Law*, 104–5). Pryce states that the original 'triad' or phrase only had the first two elements found in this triad, and that the final element discussing the mute may have been added to round the number up to three. It appears that the third limb was borrowed from the large collection of proverbs circulating in some manuscripts, and which occurs as an appendix to some law manuscripts. The poet Gruffudd ap Maredudd also refers to the proverb: see A. Parry Owen, *Gwaith Gruffudd ap Maredudd III*, 4. 34–6n. Inheritance of land is denied to the mute in this triad. The addition stating that no one is entitled to land unless he can answer for it does not occur in *U*. This may be an attempt in the other manuscripts to rectify the confusion (Pryce, *Native Law*, 105). Stating that a mute is denied kingship of a *gwlad* may be a justification of his denial of inheritance, and it is probably linked with the idea that a king should be physically unblemished.

X38. Z34, Mk44, V43, W41. Bleg71, Q75, LatD93. Latin: B62, E66

There is a pair of triads found earlier in the Cyfn manuscripts, as part of a tractate (X6, X7) on a similar subject. There is also a different pair in the additional triad collection in *Q* which also give three bondsmen who become free, and vice versa (Q144 and Q145). The triad in *Q* gives the two known free professions – poetry and smithcraft. The second and third limbs of the triad are also the same as the two of the three things a bondsman cannot teach his son (because he becomes free): Mk14 and Q62.

tayawctref a gyssegrer: This item is not actually a man but a township. According to *Col*, if a church is built in a bond township, once mass is sung there and bodies are buried in the churchyard, the township is free (*Col*, 573). Pryce states that this shows that to some extent, the lawbooks were ready to acknowledge their debt to the churchmen who contributed to and compiled the lawbooks by giving clerics and churches some special privileges and powers (Pryce, *Native Law*, 131).

vn o'r pedeir swyd ar hvgein: All of the officers of the court are freemen according to this triad; the laws of the court state that most of the officers hold their land as freemen (D. Jenkins, 'Proglomena to the Welsh Laws of Court', *WKC*, 19–22; *Bleg*, 12–19). See also P. Russell, '*Swydd, swyddog, swyddwr*: office, officer and official', *WKC*, 281–95.

ysgolheic y dyd y caffo corun: A cleric the day he is tonsured. Clerics are freemen in Welsh law. This freedom was granted to a bondsman who became tonsured even if it was done without the permission of his lord (Pryce, *Native Law*, 131–2).

X39. Z35, Mk45, V44, W42. Bleg72, Q26, LatD13

beichyogi: This can mean pregnancy, or the foetus itself. In this context it is the foetus and the triad is dealing with the payments due if the foetus is lost through cruelty. The ideas expressed in this triad are closer to older European tradition and canon law than to the Ior section on the foetus (97). See M. E. Owen, 'Medics and medicine', *WKC*, 131–2.

X40. Z36, Mk46+47, U51+52, V45+46, W43+44. Tim163+164.
LatD94. Latin: A19, B31, E39. [Q76, Bleg73, LatD95]

Manuscripts *X* and *Z* have one triad whereas all the other Cyfn manuscripts have two triads, one for denying and one for affiliating a son. It appears that *X* and *Z* combined the two triads to make one by reproducing the first triad, and adding the second triad in a shortened form as an appendix to the first triad. This material is found in Ior but not as a triad, and it is fuller (*Ior*, 102; *LTMW*, 137). The three elements in this triad are separated in Ior as there are other pieces of text between them. In the Latin texts, the triad is similar but the wording of the oath is not given. This triad, or the two in the other Cyfn manuscripts, are strictly Cyfn triads and are not found in the Bleg redactions, although a version is found in a Cyfn collection in the tail of *Tim* (Tim163). There are two separate triads on a similar subject, children and inheritance, earlier in this collection (X30 and X37). This triad (or the pair in the other Cyfn manuscripts) seems to correspond in general to part of the section on family and children in *Ior*, 102/9–13, 103; there is no such section in the Cyfn or Bleg redactions.

llawfuaeth: The legal sense of this word seems to mean time of childbirth, and corresponds to the other Welsh word for the same thing, *tymp* (*GPC*, *llawfaeth*). *Maeth* is related to *magu*, rear, and *llawfaeth* is still used in modern Welsh in the sense of hand-rearing a lamb which has no mother; an *oen llywaeth* in north Wales is a bottle-fed lamb. There is confusion in the triad as this word could be referring to breastfeeding or nursing, but if the mother is pregnant, *beichawc*, the child is not yet born; it may be that the scribe is trying to convey the last months of pregnancy when a woman already has milk.

offeiryad: Most of the other Cyfn manuscripts have *periglor*, confessor. See Pryce, *LAL*, 68–9. *U* has *offeirat pl6yf*.

esgor neidyr … y dwc: The final sentence of this element suggests that only by saying this formula is the affiliation a legal one. In the Ior tractate on children, the actual words which ought to be said for affiliating a child are given too, so this is not unusual; however, it is a different phrase altogether in Ior (*Ior*, 100/6; *LTMW*, 132–133). In this limb there seem to be three requirements for affiliating a child: the priest or *periglor* must be present, the timing is important (see *llawfaeth*), and the formula must be quoted.

penkenedyl … a seith law kenedyl: This is the same as the ordinary affiliation of a son, not that of a woman of bush and brake, and could be called the 'standard' way of affiliating a son to a father (*Ior*, 103; *LTMW*, 136–7).

llw dengwyr a deugeint: In Ior this section, i. e. what should happen if there is no *pencenedyl*, is found, but the number of men needed to swear the oath is twenty-one rather than the fifty found here, which is the same as the number of men needed in Powys (*Ior*, 103/4; *LTMW*, 137).

llw dengwyr a deugeint: As for affiliation, fewer men are needed to swear the oath to deny a son in Ior: twenty-one again (*Ior*, 103/4; *LTMW*, 136).

> *X41. Z37, Mk49, U53, V48, W45. Bleg74, Q77, LatD96. Latin: B61, E65*

One of the few gnomic-type triads found in the collection. There is a collection of these triads in Welsh, and also the more mixed Irish collection of triads (e. g. K. Meyer, 'The Triads of Ireland'; Owen, 'Trioed hefut y6 yrei hyn'). There is a very similar Irish triad: three things that make a wise man foolish: quarrelling, anger, drunkenness (Meyer, 'Triads of Ireland', 25).

X42. *Z38, U54, Mk50, V49, W46. Bleg75, Q78, LatD31, 97. Latin: B63, E67*

tafuodyawc: There are two meanings to this word; it can be the man who speaks in court, either for a person incapacitated by defective speech or legal incapacity, or as the representative of a group; on the other hand, it can be a witness whose unsupported evidence is conclusive (*WLW*, 217–18). It is quite clearly the first meaning in this triad.

gvreic: '… in most legal institutions, she, [the woman] like the dumb and the mad, was regarded as a non-person' (Owen, 'Shame and reparation', *WLW*, 40). This was so much the case in Welsh law, it seems, that she had to have someone to speak on her behalf in court.

alltud anghyuyeith: In the Latin texts, the *exul qui nesciat recte loqui Walensice* (*LTWL*, 352. 34–40, 494. 17–19). In *X*, there is an error in this triad: the manuscript reads *alltud ac anghyuyeith*, which gives four items. However, the scribe has underlined (indicating an error) the *ac* written before *alltud*, so he realized his mistake but attempted to delete the wrong conjunction.

chryc annyanawl: In the version of this triad found in Latin D, this man is called the 'raucus, id est *cryc*' (*LTWL*, 354. 19). A *raucus* is someone who is hoarse or has a harsh-sounding voice, but not actually mute; however, despite the Latin explanation, the word *cryg* was more commonly used to describe a stutterer in medieval Welsh. Mutes though would naturally fall under the same category.

X43. Z39, U55, Mk51,V50, W47. Bleg76, Q79, LatD98. Latin: E87

This is one of the many triads on animals in Welsh law. If any of these animals injure another animal, nothing is due for the injury. These are valuable animals for breeding, and their deeds are excused if their females are on heat. There is more information in the *Q* triad which has an extension stating that the behaviour of 'other' animals (the same three are listed) is not compensated if they find the females of their species in heat, and this is the point of the triad. They are also the three special animals worth more than their legal value in another triad (*WML*, 140. 13–16; *LTMW*, 178; Mk95).

X44. Z40, Mk52, V51, W48. Bleg77, Q80, LatD99

knyw hwch: A young sow; it does not have a legal value in the laws until it is a year old (*WML*, 76. 18–19).

bitheiad: From descriptions of a *bytheiad* in poetry, it appears to be a baying dog that hunted by following a scent, used to hunt hinds and foxes (*WKC*, 271–2).

charlwng: A stoat, also found in the *Q* version of this triad; the other Cyfn manuscripts have *broch*, a badger. The justices could not assign a value to the badger as they could not decide whether it was the same as a dog or the same as a sow (*WML*, 80. 2–8). The badger makes more sense because of the above passage and the fact that the stoat's skin has a legal value of twelve pence.

X45. Z41 [Z99], Mk53, V52, W49. Bleg78, Q81, LatD100. Latin: A3, B20, E14. Ior, 147/1

Blood is used to estimate the seriousness of an injury in other triads, Mk71 and Mk127, and Q116, *tri argae gwaet*. A similar triad to the Bleg version is also found in the tail of *S* (S273). Stephen J. Williams notes a Welsh proverb: *Hawdd tynnu gwaed o ben crach* (*Bleg*, 228). For the third element, the Latin texts give the reading *capitis tiniosi/scabiosi* (*LTWL*, 122, 220, 463): this corresponds to *pen crach*, the ambiguous reading of most of the other Cyfn mansucripts, meaning either a scabby head, or the top of a scab. However, if blood flows from any of these three places as a result of an injury made through anger, then payment is due. Blood, according to Cyfn, is worth twenty-four pieces of silver as it is not right for it to be worth as much as God's blood (*WML*, 42. 21–5): Judas Iscariot received thirty pieces of silver.

X46. Z42, 98, U26, Mk54, V53, W50. Bleg79, Q27, LatD14.
Latin: A4, B13, E6. Ior, 118/1; Col, 430

This is the only triad relating to fire in the lawtexts and the section on fire in Cyfn is very short – the *naw affaith* are listed but with no discussion as is found with *galanas* and *lladrad*. This triad appears in every redaction; the *Col* and Latin version are very close to each other, and the *Col* version is very clear: rather than *digyfreith*, *Col*'s wording is *Try than ny diwygyr eu gueythret*, which is a good explanation for *digyfraith* in many of the triads (*Col*, 430).

tan godeith o hanner Mawrth hyd hanner Ebrill: This probably refers to the burning of dead material on moorland; in the extended version of the triad found only in *Z*, the fire is *ynifaith*, on land which is not settled. In both *Col* and *Z*, the fire is only in March.

eneint trefgord: An interesting reference to the bathhouse of a township; in the Bleg and Latin D triad, a kiln replaces the bath, but *Col* and Latin A, B and E have bath: *balnei publici cuiusdam uille* (*Col*, 430; *LTWL*, 123. 18–22, 211. 27–30, 451. 28–32). In Ior, the bathhouse must be seven fathoms (the length of the outstretched arms including the hands) from the houses (*Ior*, 118/1).

geveil trefgord a uo naw cam y wrth y dref: If someone burns a house which then sets the next house on fire, he must pay for the house he set fire to, and let it be paid from house to house (*Ior*, 117/1; *LTMW*, 169). Presumably the smithy here (which would catch fire quite often in the Middle Ages) is far enough from the town so as not to raze the whole place to the ground; the distance given in *Col* is nine cubits (430).

tho o vanadyl arnei neu tywarch: In *Col* a roof may consist of shingles as well as broom or turf (430).

X47. *Z43, U22, Mk55, V54, W51. Bleg80, 86, Q82, 88, LatD101, 107. Latin: A29*

There are two triads in *Q* on this subject which are very similar: Q88 is identical to this one, whereas Q82 has different birds. There is also another similar triad in *X* – X73 is almost the same as this one. This version from *X* is the same as Q82, and the birds are a hawk and a raven or carrion crow. In *Mk* and the other Cyfn manuscripts, and also X73, below, the birds are an eagle, a heron/crane and a raven. They are not listed in the lawtexts as they are wild birds, but the king gets the value of the birds and the owner of the land gets fifty pieces of silver: this is his share as in Welsh law people were entitled to hunt on other people's land (*WKC*, 275–6). The three wild birds in *Mk* are the ones for which the chief falconer receives a gift from the king when his hawk kills one of them (*Ior*, 9/12; *LTMW*, 15; *WKC*, 262–3).

X48. *Z44, Mk56, V55, W52. Bleg81, Q83, LatD102. Latin: A13, B66, E70, 78*

Another of the triads on animals, this relates again to wild animals, but this time animals killed for their fur. The Latin version of this triad is a little different as the values of the skins of the animals are given, and there is no mention of the *amaerwyeu*.

llostlydan: The law lists it under one of the animals whose skin has a value: its skin is worth fifty pence (*WML*, 98. 14–15).

belev: A sable or marten's skin is valued at twenty-four pence (*WML*, 98. 15–16).

charlvnc: The value of the stoat's skin is twelve pence (*WML*, 98. 16–17).

ohonunt wy: Manuscripts *Tr* and *S* have *oc eu dillat* here, *dillat* being their skins, although it looks like eyeskip. The king's clothes are fur-trimmed according to this triad, and the values of different kinds of furs are recognized (*Ior*, 137/6; *WKC*, 276).

X49. Z45, Mk57, V56, W53. Bleg82, Q84, LatD103

damdwng: One can swear ownership, *damdwng*, of something in the law of theft, and sworn appraisal, to swear a value to something, is also *damdwng* (*LTMW*, 333). Bleg states that for every thing that does not have a set legal value, *damdwng* is allowed, so the owner of an animal would swear that an animal was worth the value he put on it (*Bleg*, 93). The second *damdwng* is found in this triad, which excludes certain commodities from such an oath.

gwenyn: Bees do not have a legal value but swarms are valued; in the case of theft, the value of the tree in which the swarm was found, or the land they were on, is paid to the owner of the said tree/land (*Ior*, 135/1–4; *WML* 81. 15–21; *LTMW*, 183–4). Also, in Cyfn, if someone finds a swarm on land and the owner of the land wants it, he pays the finder four pence (*WML*, 81. 15–18). According to Latin E, if someone finds a swarm and shows it to the owner, the finder receives dinner that day and the wax (*LTWL*, 483. 18–19; *Bechbretha*, 198).

aryant: Also found in triad Q191, one cannot swear ownership to silver which is not in a container.

X49a. Z46, U27, Mk58, V57, W54

Text from Z. This is an interesting triad in that it seems to have no legal connection whatsoever. It may be that this triad was remembered by a scribe and inserted into his collection but he added the word *kyfreithawl* to justify its place in the collection of strictly legal triads. The triad is only found in the Cyfn manuscripts, and is in each of the Cyfn manuscripts apart from *X*; however, it is likely that it should have been in the collection at this position but because of the nature of the triad, the scribe of *X* omitted it. The triad is censored in *W*, blackened out, making it illegible, and the word *cont* has not been written out in full in *Z* either. Another justification for returning this triad to the collection in *X* is that, in the triad *Tri hwrd ny diwygir*, X56, *X* has omitted the words *a bonllost ai hymrain vn weith*, 'with his penis and copulates with her once'. The words are found in all of the other Cyfn manuscripts so they were probably deliberately omitted in *X* because of their sexual nature.

attal … gillwng: Only *Z* and *U* give this pair; the other Cyfn manuscripts offer *dill6g ac ell6g*. Wade-Evans translates this pair of words as 'liberate and relax' (*WML*, 275). Both words mean more or less the same thing – to set free, release; loose, untie (*GPC*, *dillwng*, *ellwng*). *Attal*, meaning to prevent, suggests that *dillwng* is the opposite of *ellwng*; *Z* and *U* may have the correct reading as opposed to *Mk* and *V*. It suggests that the creatures have many litters and without difficulty.

X50. Z47, 91, U43, Mk59, V58, W55. Bleg83, Q85, LatD105. Latin: E91

There is another triad on timber which is similar to this one: X67, equivalent to Q97 in the Bleg collection. That triad states that the three timbers a builder may have are a roof-tree and two roof-forks; the owner of the wood has to give them whether he wants to or not. In this triad they are three timbers which anyone may freely take.

X51. Z48, U42, Mk62, V37, W56. Bleg84, Q86, LatD15

This is a good example of a 'title triad', where the triad is created using an old legal term which has an existence independent of the triad itself. There are different versions of this triad in Cyfn and Bleg, but they all have the limbs in the same order and appear to be related. Two other versions have the final two limbs in reverse order, but the version in *AL* IX is not explicitly a triad (*AL*, IX. xx. 6–8, XIV. xliv. 16–22).

chehyryn canhastyr: An obscure term, it also occurs in the Ior tractate on theft (*Ior*, 160/27; *LTMW*, 282). In his introduction to Llanstephan 116, Timothy Lewis suggests receiver for *astr* (*The Laws of Hywel Dda*, ix–x). The two personal names found in *Culhwch ac Olwen* – Cilydd Canhastyr and Canhastyr Canllaw – suggest that the term *astr* is known, but the text is apparently playing on *can(t)*, a hundred, and *can(t)*, with (*CO*, n. on line 190). *GPC*'s entry also gives a possible comparison with Irish *astar*, trouble but also journey. The Welsh and Irish words are probably related, and there may be an etymological gloss embedded in the triad: the literal meaning of the legal phrase may be 'sinew of a hundred journeys', with the meaning of *astyr* as journey being confirmed by the use of *y ffordd y kertho*. The theft, in this triad, travels from hand to hand, so each person in the chain, up to the hundredth person, should pay a *dirwy*.

The issue is of a limit on secondary liability for theft, and the person accused is not the thief but has shared in the stolen goods (*Ior*, 113/7). Ior confines the phrase to liability arising out of sharing the carcass of a dead animal, and the phrase appears to be a metaphor. In the case of a carcass, the sinew may have been understood as a metaphorical rope travelling from one to another, and binding a hundred hands. The hundred hands would be the furthest limit of liability and, as a round number, may express the notion that liability, for practical purposes, extended as far as it could be traced.

ba ford bynnac y del kyfuran ohonaw: Whoever receives a share of the carcass of a stolen animal, even as a gift, is guilty of an abetment. Both the *X* version and that in *Mk* share the metaphor of the road by which a share of the stolen goods may travel, and this may be compared with Ior which talks of the flesh on an animal going 'as far as the hundredth hand' (*Ior*, 113/9, 113/12–16).

o naw affeith lledrad y byd: *X*'s extension to the first limb is more clearly expressed than that in *Mk*; the first limb should be compared with the eighth item in the list of the nine abetments of theft, when someone takes a share of stolen goods (*WML*, 40. 14; *Bleg*, 34. 27; *Ior*, 111/9). The first limb in *X* refers directly to the eighth abetment; in *Mk*, the clause *kanys na6 affeith yssyd ida6* is confusing, as the point is that one of the abetments, the eighth, concerns sharing the stolen goods.

The explanation for the first limb given in the triad in *H* (*AL*, XIV. xliv. 21) is problematic. It distinguishes two categories of people who have received parts of a stolen animal. First, someone who has received the skin, either as part of the original division or subsequently by purchase or gift; if the skin is found in his possession he is *eneit faddeu*, as if he were a hand-having thief, unless he can defend himself. Q191 states, however, that *damdwng* is not possible for meat without the skin. In addition, there are those who have received part of the flesh: if the owner complains to the lord, the defendant must deny or admit his action. If he denies, he has to provide a hundred compurgators, and if this fails (or if he admits) his penalty is a *dirwy* of three pounds. The implication is, therefore, that a far larger body of compurgators is required in such cases than the normal *rhaith* (*Ior*, 111/17–20); and yet the penalty is the same as for an abetment of theft, three pounds, rather than the seven pounds due for theft itself when a *rhaith* fails.

hyd brenhin: This limb is clearer in *Mk*: *p6y bynhac a'e kyllello*. The explanation given above accounts for both the first limb and this limb; the person who cut up the carcass might not be one of the men who shared the meat. The hart of the king in its prime has twelve legal joints and whoever knifes it pays a *camlwrw* for each of its joints (*Bleg*, 51–2; *LTMW*, 184–5). This is an illicit counterpart to a ceremony of high courtly significance (*WKC*, 349–50; *LTMW*, 293).

abo bleid: It is uncertain how this one fits into the triad of liability. The only other reference to *abo bleid*, the dead prey of a wolf, in the lawtexts is in Bleg; whoever takes the prey of another animal without permission must pay an animal similar to it for the theft, and a *camlwrw* to the king; the same procedure is followed if someone knifes someone else's animal (*Bleg*, 90). So in this case, someone has a prior claim over the carcass (presumably having hunted it and intending to return for it, or the landowner who has rights to it) so it is a form of theft: *anghyfarch*, surreption.

X52. *Z49, U28, Mk60, V59, W57. Bleg47, Q59, LatD74. Latin: A21, B3, E18. Ior, 42/9*

This triad is found in most of the law manuscripts, and the version in Ior needs emending: see *LTMW*, 237, n. on 40. 14–19. The horns are valued in Ior (140/13–15; *LTMW*, 192).

chorn buelhin: A buffalo horn is one of the gifts a court justice receives from the poet when he wins a chair (*WML*, 17. 1–2).

y gorn yved: Another reference to drinking horns is that the chief groom gets a hornful of drink (*Ior*, 11/15; *LTMW*, 19).

y penkynyd: If the *pencynydd* swears, he must swear on his horn and his leash (*WML*, 20. 8–10, *WKC*, 272); it is right for his horn to be a buffalo horn (Ior, 15/7; *LTMW*, 22); and he has to show his horns, dogs and leashes to the king annually (Ior, 15/17; *LTMW*, 22–3). According to the lawtexts the *pencynydd*'s horn is valued at a pound (Ior, 15/7; *LTMW*, 22). *X*, *Q* and *W* make it clear that this is his hunting horn.

X53. *Z50, U47, Mk61,V60, W58. Bleg115, Q117, LatD140.*
Latin: A20, B4, E19. Ior, 135/7; DwC, 423

This triad implies that the right to hunt goes with the land on which they made their home, therefore a landowner could hunt any animal on his own land; the king is free to hunt and villeins are excluded, as are ordinary freemen who have not come into their inheritances (*WKC*, 274–5). Another triad on the subject of hunting is found as part of a collection in Latin E25, and in *DwC* and Ior: the three free huntings for any villein (*LTWL*, 469. 20–1; *DwC*, 423; *Ior*, 135/7). This triad lists three types of snares (given in Welsh in Latin E) which a villein may use for hunting: *annel*, snare, *croclath*, springe, and *slepan*, gin. This allows villeins some freedom in hunting, but they were excluded from the hunt (*WKC*, 258).

ywrch: The roebuck is valued as a billygoat in the laws; *X* states this at the end of the triad. This and the other two animals in the triad are solitary and are ejected from their natal territory to find a territory of their own (*WKC*, 275). In the Ior version of this triad a swarm of bees is the item found instead of the *iwrch* (*Ior*, 135/5).

dyfuyrgi: Its skin is valued at twelve pence (*WML*, 98. 13–14).

chadno: One of the animals that the laws states is free for everyone to kill, along with a wolf, as they only do bad deeds (*WML*, 78. 8–11). However, a curt penny is paid for its skin (*WML*, 113. 15–18).

X54. *Z51, Mk63, V61, W59. Bleg85, Q87, LatD106*

Two elements in this triad in *Q* are different.

amod: In the case of an *amod*, a contract, even though the contract has been made unlawfully, it has to be kept (*WML*, 89. 12–13; *Ior*, 69/12).

anghuuureith: *Treis* in some of the other Cyfn manuscripts, and *Defod gyfyawn* in *Q*.

ychenoctid: *angenoctid*. *Angheu/anghen* in *Q*, *agheu* in Bleg (114. 29); it may be that at some point in Bleg, someone miscopied a word containing the element *aghen-* from an earlier manuscript, as the letters *u* and *n* are easily confused. However, both readings make sense, and there is evidence in several sources which supports *anghenoctit*, as paupers are not liable to punishments for theft (*Ior*, 115/18; *Bleg*, 122. 26; Lat D, 356. 37–41; Lat B, 29–30).

X55. *Z52, U23, Mk66, V64, W60. Bleg104, Q106, LatD128. Latin: A26, B42, E50*

hwrd: A blow usually needs to be compensated unless it is accidental (*WML*, 118. 8–9). The three here are special circumstances; in the first and second limbs, violence is allowed. A similar idea is found in X23. The third limb of this triad sets out the punishment for a false virgin, and has been put together with the previous two limbs by a legal conceit. The third limb is very similar to a section of the laws of women (*Ior*, 47/2–5).

govyn o dyn yawn … : In this triad, in a case of *galanas*, if compensation is sought three times and it is not received, and out of anger the party that should pay is killed, that revenge is allowed. It seems that if the legal procedure of payments for *galanas* as set out in the laws does not work, reverting to blood-feud and violence as revenge is acceptable (D. Jenkins, *Cyfraith Hywel*, 72, and X19).

eil yw … : Like the third element, this refers to the law of women. This is a case of a woman losing her husband to another woman, and the Bleg version reads *gwreic wryawc ynn y chywyres*, making it clear by the use of the word *cywyres* that the other woman is a concubine (*Bleg*, 116, 231). If she kills the other woman out of jealousy, with her own hands, then she is not obliged to pay for the injury.

morwyn … a mach ar y morwyndawd: A mature maiden in *Mk* and *V*, within the age of consent. The punishment reflects the shame of a girl who has surety on her virginity but is no longer a virgin (M. E. Owen, 'Shame and reparation', *WLW*, 48). Surety would be given for the payment of *amobr* (*WLW*, 138; *Cyfn*, 73/25).

a'e chaffael yn wreic: This distinction is found in the *Mabinogi*: after she has been raped Goewin says: 'Gwreic wyf i' (*PKM*, 74; C. McAll, 'The normal paradigms of a woman's life in the Irish and Welsh law texts', *WLW*, 15). According to Cyfn, if a girl is given to a man and he states that she is not a virgin, she has to swear as one of five women that she was not a *gwraig*, i. e. still a virgin (*WML*, 93. 10–13). However, a different procedure is given here, as the girl is already sworn to be a virgin – surety has been given on her virginity and it is clear that someone has been lying.

neithyorwyr: The wedding guests, who wait while the couple go away to consummate the marriage. According to Ior, if the man wishes to claim that his new wife is not a virgin, he must rise from the bed without delay and state his claim before the wedding guests with his penis still erect; if he suffers her until the next morning he does not get any of her entitlement (*Ior*, 47/2).

golheuaw kanhwyllev: This is a ceremonial action and is not found in the laws of women.

twyll morwyn: This is a different law from that referring to a woman who purports to be a virgin (Charles-Edwards, '*Nau Kynywedi Teithiauc*', *WLW*, 34). In the law of women in both Cyfn and Ior, if the girl is accused of being a false virgin, she may clear herself by compurgation but there is no mention of that in this triad (*WML*, 93. 10–13; *Ior*, 47/4). In the section on women in Latin A, there is a trial the next morning where her age is considered and, if she is mature, seven relatives swear; if she is definitely not a virgin, as in this triad, she receives the mocking *argyfrau* (*WLW*, 153). The third limb of the triad differs in *Q* in that the details of the sexual act are left out, possibly under the influence of the Norman church. The details of the sexual act are also omitted in *X*, but the rather graphic description of the cutting of the girl's shift is left, which suggests that the full version, as found in all the other Cyfn manuscripts, was also in *X*'s exemplar.

X56. Z53, Mk67, V65, W61. Bleg88, Q90, LatD110

Q makes it clear that these are men whom the king is not entitled to sell – this is referring to the king's right to sell a thief in some circumstances.

lleidyr: *Lleidr cyfaddef* in the other Cyfn manuscripts. In *Q*, this triad states that the thief is adjudged to be hanged, and there is no specified amount with which he must be caught. A man becomes a *lleidr cyfaddef*, an admitted thief whose guilt is as obvious as if he had confessed (*Ior*, 115/2n.), if he is found with the goods in his possession, according to a triad in *DwC*, and if he does not attempt to defend himself with a legal plea (445–8). He is also an admitted thief if his *arwaesaf* fails (*Ior*, 115/1; *LTMW*, 164; *Cyfraith Hywel*, 66). Once the man is an admitted thief, he is at the mercy of the law, and his punishment depends on the value of the stolen goods. He is a sale thief if the goods are worth up to fourpence, and if they are worth more than fourpence, he is an *enaid faddeu* (*Ior*, 115/2, 4; *LTMW*, 164, 165; *Cyfraith Hywel*, 66). As this triad states, if a thief is to be hanged, he cannot be sold as well (cf. *Ior*, 115/4).

chynllwynwr: *Cynllwyn* is often equated with *murdwrn*, English *murdrum*, meaning a secret killing, or a killing where the body is hidden (Owen, '*Cynllwyn*', 347). Double *galanas* has to be paid for a *cynllwyn*, a secret killing, and twelve kine *dirwy*, doubled (*WML*, 46. 16–18; Owen, '*Cynllwyn*', 347). There is no reference to selling a *cynllwynwr* following the procedure for theft.

bradwr arglwyd: This is a person who commits *brad arglwydd*, an offence which seems to be equal to *cynllwyn*. Again he pays double of the *galanas dirwy*, and he loses his patrimony, as stated in X30 (*WML*, 52. 6–7).

X57. Z54, Mk64, V62, W62. Bleg89, Q91, LatD111

righill: The serjeant was one of the officers of the court and has a section in the laws of the court although he was one of the officers by use and custom, not one of the main officials (*Ior*, 34; *LTMW*, 34). His work involved maintenance of order and enforcement of the commands of authority, and this made him un- popular (*LTMW*, 232–3). The office was still known in thirteenth-century Wales, and he was an officer of the lawcourts (Stephenson, *Governance of Gwynedd*, 44).

guaet gwlad: The shout/cry of a country – his duties included summoning in the thirteenth century, and he may have assumed the *gostegwr's* functions by that time (ibid., 45). Both this nickname for the *rhingyll* and the next are alliterative (cf. Owen, 'Y Cyfreithiau (2)', 233). This is very similar to some of the nick- names found in the list of the members of Arthur's court in *Culhwch ac Olwen*.

garw gychwetyl gwas y kynghellawr: The *rhingyll* was linked with the *cynghellor*, and by the thirteenth century, he was answerable to the *cynghellor's* successor, the *rhaglaw* (Stephenson, *Governance of Gwynedd*, 44). This limb of the triad hints at the unpopularity of the *rhingyll* – he is seen as bringer of bad news.

At this point, both the collection in *X* and *Z* are 'interrupted' by tractates, although they are different tractates in the two manuscripts. This does not happen in any of the other Cyfn manuscripts. It is uncertain whether this means that the scribes of *X* and *Z* considered the triad collection as two separate collections; the correspondence in order and content between the Cyfn manuscripts is not as strong after this break. There are three triads found in the tractate here in *X*, two on *mechniaeth*, and one on the *sarhaed* of the king. The two on *mechniaeth* are also found in Bleg, as 'main text'-type triads rather than collection-triads. The third of these triads in *X*, *O teir ffordd y telir gwialen y brenin*, is found in the triad collection in *Mk*, *V* and *W*, but it is in a non-triadic section of text in *X*. It is a triad unique to Cyfnerth.

X60. *Z61, [67], Mk65, V63, W63. Tim 166. Latin: B51, E26*

This triad is not found in Bleg or Ior, and the version in the Latin texts is different. There is some confusion regarding the form of this triad as *Mk* and *V* have different elements, but there is also some confusion in *Z* and *W*. It may be that the triad was not well-known or standard in form.

treis ar wreic: See X19. The king receives his *sarhaed* as payment for the rape of a maiden (*WML*, 2. 23–3. 7 and, for a discussion on rape in Cyfn, *WML*, 97. 19). The rod is the same one found in this triad; in *X*, *Z* and *W*, the description of the payments is given as part of the triad but not in the other Cyfnerth manuscripts. These payments are set out in the laws of the court found at the very beginning of every lawtext. There is also a very similar triad found in *Z* which discusses both the silver rod and the drinking cup – see Z67.

a thorri tangneved y fford: It seems that this aspect of law is not found in any of the lawtexts other than as part of this triad. *Mk*, *V* and *W* offer *am torri na6d fford ar aghena6c diatlam*, which is perhaps a little more detailed and may explain the limb. An *anghenawc* is a needy person, a pauper or beggar; a *diatlam* is a person without a home (*GPC, diadlam*). The *anghenawg diatlam*, the homeless needy person or pauper is found in the list of the *wyth pynfarch* (eight packhorses) of a king, the eight sources of casual income for the king in the laws (*LTMW*, 237), and paupers were part of the king's entourage (*WML*, 3. 23; *Ior*, 3/8; *WKC*, 82). The implication is that the king's protection extends to the *ffordd*: whoever ploughs a *priffordd* should pay a hundred and twenty pence to the king (*WML*, 55. 16–17; *Bleg*, 83. 15–16), and attacking the homeless pauper on the road violates the king's *nawdd*, which means that the king is due a silver rod. It is also connected with the *wyth pynfarch*, as the paupers can be a source of income to the king, in particular if they are injured when they are under his protection.

gynllwyn: A very serious matter indeed, this is also one of the three secrets better concealed, see X65. Some of the manuscripts offer *sarhaed brenin* instead, and the payment is identical to that in the first element of the triad and is found in the laws of the court under the section on the king (*WML*, 2. 23–3. 7). This is the obvious instance where the king receives a silver rod. It may be the case that the reading *sarhaed brenin* is the correct one.

X61. Z62, U34, Mk92, W86. Bleg90, Q92, LatD112. Latin: A38, B34, E42

There does not seem to be any further reference to this triad or the rule found in it in the lawtexts, although it refers to the corn damage section and various payments have to be made by the owners of animals found trespassing on corn.

X62. Z63, Mk131, Bleg91, Q93, LatD113. Latin: A39, B70, E16

This triad implies that the justice is at the king's side apart from during the most intimate conversations: with his priest, wife or mediciner. There is nothing elsewhere in the laws to imply that this may be true, but it certainly elevates the justice to a very high position in relation to the king.

X63. Z64, U36, Mk75, W70. Bleg92, Q94, LatD114. Latin: A40, B36, E44. DwC, 421

This triad is similar, as a list, to Ior 180–4 (needles are not in the list of valued items, but other tools are). The three needles listed here are valued, and their use is given but the amount of detail varies in the redactions. A needle is included in the triad on the three things for which no one should answer – X74.

gwenigawl: The *sarhaed* of a bondswoman is twelve pence, but if she is a *gwenigawl, sef vyd honno, gwreic wrth y notwyd* (*Bleg*, 59. 27), a woman who works with a needle, her *sarhaed* increases to twenty-four pence, reflecting the value of the profession (*Bleg*, 59).

X64. Z76, 96, U10, Mk76, W71. Bleg106, Q108, LatD130. Latin: A36, B64, E68. DwC, 339–42

The triad found in the *damweiniau* is very different from this triad although the heading is the same (*DwC*, 339).

marw tystyolaeth: According to Bleg, in the *arferion cyfraith* it is stated that every testimony is dead testimony (*tystolyaeth marwol*) apart from three (*Bleg*, 127–8). This triad though is about testimony regarding the dead (*Bleg*, n. on 117. 11).

yn gwyd pawb: The people who were present when the dispute was settled were the eyewitnesses.

meibyon ... hwyryon: These were not present to witness the settling of the dispute but the knowledge has been passed down to them – the triad calls them *gwybyddiaid*. However, the *gwybyddiaid* in law are eyewitnesses, who can testify that they saw a person being ejected from his land, for example; it is the *ceidwaid*, maintainers, who maintain someone's claim to land. The *gwybyddiaid* have a triad to themselves, as there are three types of *gwybyddiaid* – see Q42 and also Q43. *Gwybyddiaid* are used mainly in land cases.

amhinogev: *Amhinogion* in some Cyfn manuscripts. Bleg has the elders of the country knowing lineage and descent; their duties are the same as the *amhinogyon*. The original meaning of *aminogeu* is door posts, and the *amhinogyon* are the post setters. In the laws it is a term used to describe a certain type of witness in land cases (*Bleg*, 118). They are described as men from each part of the *tref* who know the borders of the strips of land (*WML*, 54. 21–3).

pentan: Signs of habitation seem to be enough evidence for a claim for land. It is surprising that the *croesfaen*, a stone with a cross on it marking a boundary which is found elsewhere in Cyfn, does not feature in this third limb (*WML*, 55. 14–16).

X65. U31, Mk82, W72. Bleg93, Q95, LatD115. Latin: A41, B37, E45

This is another gnomic triad, and it lists secrets that are best confessed rather than concealed. Two of the men are found in another triad as the men who ought not to be sold by law (see Q90 and X56).

X66. U29, Mk83, W73. Bleg94, Q96, LatD116. Latin: A43, B71, E73

vn troedyawc: One-footed, literally, but the metaphorical meaning is clear – the additional sentence in the *Q* and the *W* versions states that whoever breaks or injures the foot of one of these animals must pay their full legal value. Their feet are equal to their lives.

X67. W16. Bleg95, Q97, LatD67, 117

Found in a miscellaneous section in both *V* and *W*, but in the triad collection in *X*, this section does not appear to actually be a triad in Cyfn as it does not have the customary statement to make it clear that a list of three follows. However, it later appears in the Bleg redaction in triadic form, and may be counted as a triad.

nenbren a dwy nenforch: Both of these items have a legal value: each cruck is worth twenty pence, and a ridge piece is worth forty pence if damaged (*Bleg*, 95.

5–6). Houses could not be roofed without a ridge-piece, the beam laid along the roof, and two crucks, the supporting pieces of the roof structure, which take the weight.

X68. Bleg21. [Q181], 225, Latin: A50, B33, E41

This triad only occurs in *X* of the Cyfn manuscripts, although a version of it occurs in Bleg and the Latin manuscripts. There are different versions of this triad in *Q*, with Q181 being an extended version with different items. This triad, like the Bleg version, deals with cases where the law divides goods equally in two halves.

da a dyccer o anghyfureith y gyfureith: This is the third element in the Bleg version, and in Bleg it is suggested that the item may be an animal. This situation does not appear to be explained elsewhere in the lawtexts.

rwng byw a marw: In Bleg, this is a situation when either a husband or a wife dies, and the living partner receives half the goods (*Bleg*, 61. 5–6). However, after seven years of marriage, if the man leaves the woman without just cause, or divorces her, she would still receive half the goods, although provision is made for these cases (*Bleg*, 61. 1–4, 64. 30–65. 32).

amrysson am dev teruyn: The Bleg version does not give this item – instead, *racdywededic*, aforementioned, is given, and it refers to the previous section of law in Bleg, which deals with a case where two men are arguing about a border. In that case, each man should swear as to where he thinks the border should be, and any remaining land is split in half between them (*Bleg*, 70. 26–71. 1).

X69. Mk84, W74. Bleg96, Q98, LatD118

randy: A shared house, or a *llety*, lodging house (*Bleg*, 229). The reason nothing is received for these things if they are lost is explained in the qualifying sentence – the owner of a knife, a sword and trousers should guard them. There is a similar triad stating the three things which, if found on a road, no one need answer for them – X74.

llawdyr: Trousers – it seems that the compiler of this triad had a sense of humour, and included this item as he could not find anything else to make three. As Fergus Kelly notes, the Irish triads in particular tend to be witty, with a climax or anti-climax in the third item; this triad appears to be similar in style (Kelly, *Three Best Things*, 3).

X70. *U39, Mk86, W75. Bleg98, Q99, LatD120. Latin: A28, B45, E53. DwC, 148*

This is one of two triads on corpses – the other is the next triad, X71 – and the significance of both triads is mysterious. It may be a preoccupation with the sanctity of a corpse, or this triad may have a further link with despoiling or defacing a corpse. *X* has both triads next to each other; as do the Bleg collections. Cf. X71, below.

y llath: Cf. Ior 108/1.

gwan gwth troed yndaw: The other Cyfn manuscripts offer *Ythyer yn y gorwed* rather than shoving it with a foot – the meaning is clearer in *X*. In *Q*, the triad reads *hyny dyg6ydho* here rather than *yn y gorwed*, meaning to shove the corpse until it falls. Several of the Bleg manuscripts have different readings for this item: both *I* and *S* have 'causing it to fall from a standing position'; one of the versions of the triad in *S* has 'to shove the corpse with the foot', similar to *X*; this is also found in Latin A, *calce pulsatur*, and *DwC* (*LTWL*, 128. 18–19; *DwC*, 148).

X71. *Z73, U41, Mk70, W76. Bleg97, Q100, LatD119. Latin: A24, B46, E54*

The *Q* version of the triad is the same as that found in *X*, but *S* has a different version found in the tail of the manuscript. In S276 (see Q100 for the *S* version) the heading matches that in *X*, but the remainder seems to be a combination of this triad and X70: striking a corpse, despoiling it and kicking the corpse whilst asking who it is. For the third element, the redactor has combined the actions found in X70 with the insincere comments found in this triad: the third limb in *S* and *K* has the person asking 'pa gelein y6 honn?' as well as giving the corpse a shove. The extension to the *S/K* triad explains the *sarhaed* payment for every one of the limbs, and is less for the second and third limbs as it is more of an insult to the living than it is to the dead: each of the items is equal to *sarhaed* without augmentation, and others call them *teir sarhaed kelein*, the same as in triad S87. There is some confusion between triads Q99 and Q100 – *M* and *Bost* combine them, probably by accident, to make one triad.

gwarthrud kelein: In X70, which is comparable to this triad, the word *sarhaed* is used; *sarhaed* can mean an insulting injury (as it was deliberate), or the payment for the insulting injury.

X72. Z74, U40, Mk85, W78. Bleg99, Q101, LatD16. Latin: A27, B44, E52

gauael: Distraint (*WML*, 85. 23–5; *Bleg*, 39. 29, 99. 23). The Z variant, *ytavel*, is also found in *Ior*, 152/2, and it corresponds to Irish *athgubá(i)l*; *gafael*, distraint, is not found in Ior. See Binchy, 'Distraint in Irish law', 27–71.

X74. Z65, U33, Mk87, W79. Bleg87, Q89, LatD108. Latin: A30, B60, E64

Cf. X69. The wording and syntax of the heading is different in each of the Cyfn manuscripts.

X75. Mk88, W80. Bleg111, Q113, 255, LatD136. Latin: A32, B48, E56

gweli dauawt: Tongue-wound; the amount paid is the same as that for an injury to a tongue. This is very significant, as the tongue is the symbol of the judge's office. In the lawtexts, the tongue is valued at forty-four pounds, a huge amount, and the explanation for this is that it defends the other parts of the body (*WML*, 42. 5–9; *Ior*, 146/6; *LTMW*, 196). In a triad in Bleg, a word which causes a tongue-wound is one of the *tri geir kylus*, three guilty words (*Bleg*, 119).

brenhin: The king gets a tongue-wound payment when an ugly word is said to him in the version of this triad in *Bleg*, 118. 14–15; cf. *LTWL*, 199. 18–20, 283. 26–28; *WML* 111. 4–7; *Ior* 43/2.

brawdwr: In the section on the court justice in the lawtexts, it is stated that anyone who wishes to accuse the justice of making a false judgement should give a pledge and if he succeeds in proving that the judgement was false, the justice loses his tongue unless he buys it from the king at its legal value (*Ior*, 10/19; *LTMW*, 17). This sentiment is repeated at the beginning of the test book in Ior (VC I. iii, pref.; *LTMW*, 141).

effeiriad: According to the triad, he gets payment for the work he does for the king. When he is saying or singing mass, a harsh word said to him would be equivalent to a harsh word to the king (Christ/God), and then reading a letter to the king is treated in the same way; writing a letter may have been added as it is included in the triad listing the duties he does for the king (*Bleg*, 13; *LTMW*, 12). Furthermore, it is stated that it is possible to cause a tongue-wound to the priest, and that is the one case where an offence against him is not subject to canon law (*Bleg*, 9; *WKC*, 84–5).

X76. *U8, Mk12, V12, W6*

This triad, found after the triad collection, is on the subject of land law, but although it is found in several Cyfn manuscripts, the form of the triad in *X* is different and shorter to the other Cyfn manuscripts. A very similar triad to the version in *Mk* and the other Cyfn manuscripts is found in Bleg, but with a different heading: see Q111.

U3. *V3, W3, Z4*

A triad only found in Cyfn, and even then only in four of the Cyfn manuscripts, it occurs in the short tractate on the value of limbs and injuries.

U9

Although it is only found in *U* of the Cyfn manuscripts, another version of this triad is found in *X*, and two versions of the triad are found in *Q*: Q181 and Q225. The concept of the places where law divides equally in two was a popular one in the triads.

W15. *U12*

This triad is also found in the additional collection in *K* and *S*. See the note on K19.

Mk48. *U44, V47, W95. Tim165*

ll6 g6eilyd: Only appearing in the Cyfn version of this triad, this is a problematic term. In Bleg, the *llw gweilydd* appears in an extension on a triad about *manac*: if a *llw gweilydd* fails for the victim, then it is the only case where *rhaith gwlad* is appropriate for theft without one of the *manageu* (*Bleg*, 124. 22–30). In the notes to *Llyfr Blegywryd* it is explained as *llw ofer*, an oath in vain (*Bleg*, 234). In Ior it is stated that no one may make a *llw gweilydd* for corn damage as it is of no effect even if it is denied (*Ior*, 156/3). If the animals were not caught on the corn, the owner's unsupported oath would clear them, so a *llw gweilydd* was not appropriate as there could be no counter-oath (*LTMW*, 307). The other example of the term is in the law of women in Latin A, but the term is untranslated from Welsh in that text, and no explanation is given (*WLW*, 156; cf. *WLW*, 208–9). Jenkins translates this as 'fore-oath' and explains that it is 'the unsupported oath of a suspect, taken at the instance of the suspector; if the oath is refused, no counter-oath is required from the suspector before further procedure can follow' (*LTMW*, 307, n. on 205. 15); see also J. Lloyd Jones, '*Gweilydd*', 37–8.

Mk69. *U30, W65*

chyffredin g6lat: The use of *cyffredin* as intermediary is found in Mk91. Here, it must mean 'common to', as every *gwlad* has these things, and the people of a *gwlad* are subject to the three things. The version of this triad found in *W* has an explanatory sentence after the triad: *Kanys guys a uyd ar pa6b vdunt*: for every one is under summons to them (*WML*, 134. 21–135. 2). The triad is also found in the tail of *S*: S184.

Mk71. *U46, W67, Z58*

Two similar triads on *argae gwaed* are found in *Mk*: this triad, Mk71, and Mk127, also found as *datsaf gwaed* in Bleg (Q116). Both *argae* and *datsaf gwaed* mean stays of blood but the form *argae* is seen in other contexts too – *argae terfyn*, *argae llys* and *argae damdwng* (*GPC, argae,* and *AL*, V. i. 3, 5). See *WKC*, 124–5.

Mk73. *U32, W68. Tim167*

di6yneb: The meaning of this word is uncertain; Wade-Evans has 'unabashed' and *GPC* has '?that cannot be insulted.' (*GPC, diwyneb*). This triad is given as the only example. The explanation in *GPC* is not satisfactory – a king, the highest status possible for a lord, can be insulted (*WML*, 2. 19–4. 6), as can a priest (*WML*, 8. 21–9. 3, 11. 14–17). Law, on the other hand, is not a person but an institution, which causes further problems. The three elements of the triad have various things in common, the most obvious being that they are rulers or governors.

Mk79. *U25. Latin: E90. Tim168*

In manuscript *U*, this triad is fuller and the heading is clearer.

kerdet fford a heb ford: This sentence is unclear because of the obscurity in the old meaning of *heb*, preserved in *heibio*; *U* has *kerdet ford a dieithyr ford*, and Aneurin Owen took this to mean two different types of roads: an ordinary road, and 'out of the road' (*GC*, III. xxxix. 15). 'Off road' makes better sense as in each of the three cases there is a sense of urgency and the three members of the triad may have to take a short cut; often avoiding the main roads is interpreted as being up to no good. In the Anglo-Saxon laws, it is assumed that a stranger avoiding the highway is a thief, and even states that he is to be put to death (*LEEK*, Wihtred, 28). A Welsh example is the plaint for theft found in *Q*: the thief takes the stolen horse *a cherdet gochelffyrd a gochel priffyrd*, and avoids the main roads (*AL*, XII. x, and see Roberts, 'Plaints in Mediaeval Welsh Law', 259).

effeirat: The priest. Priests have special rights in law anyway, but *U* has more: the priest and his messenger, going to visit the sick. There would be a sense of urgency here.

medyc: *U* again has the messenger of the sick included in the triad.

righyll: The official in the lawtexts; his duties include making summonses, acting as clerk in court and maintaining public order (Rees, *South Wales and the March*, 9; Stephenson, *Governance of Gwynedd*, 44). He is therefore an important character in the context of the law. *U*'s addition here is the *rhingyll* when he is running his lord's errands/upon his lord's commission (*yn negesseu y argl6yd*).

Mk81. U48. Tim169

dial6r: A shadowy character in the laws, the word translates as avenger. These seem to be members of the kindred who share and pay a share of *galanas* (*LTMW*, 335). A similar character is found in the Irish legal glossary *Críth Gablach* (70–2). The *aire échta* should 'avenge the outrages' offered to any members of his *tuath*, although how the function is exercised is unclear.

ardadl6r: Not found elsewhere in the lawtexts, but a similar Irish position occurs in *Críth Gablach*. The *aire coisring* represents his kin in dealings with external authorities, and acts as an automatic surety for their obligations to the king and the church (ibid., 70).

Mk89. W81. Tim170

proui bugeilgi: A *bugeilgi*, literally a shepherd-dog, has certain duties. He has to guard the stock and go before them in the morning, and behind them in the evening – in other words, he is doing a shepherd's work, and according to Ior it is worth the most important beast of the stock he guards (*Ior*, 133/7; *LTMW*, 181–2). Cyfn states his value as an *eidon taladwy*: a steer of current value (*WML*, 34. 24–5). There is also a section in Cyfn which shows how this trial of a herd-dog is to take place: the owner, a neighbour who stands above the door, and another neighbour below the door all have to swear that the dog goes before the animals in the morning and behind them in the evening (*WML*, 34. 25–35. 3; *LTMW*, 290–1).

ha6l6r ... vch pen bed y mach: As with the previous element, there is evidence for this trial in the lawtexts; according to Cyfn, if a surety dies, the plaintiff must come as one of seven men to swear over the surety's grave (*WML*, 87. 4–10). The section has been tidied up in Bleg and it is stated that this procedure only takes place if the grave of the surety is known (if the resting place is not known the procedure takes place over an altar); the lord then takes the place of the surety (*Bleg*, 42).

g6reic bieu profi treis ar 6r: In the law of women the rules are set out on how a woman should accuse a man of rape, *trais*. If a woman accuses a man and he denies, she must take a relic in her right hand and his penis in her left and swear that he raped her; she then loses none of her rights (*WML*, 92. 13–18).

Mk93. w90

t6yll6r: This man is not found in the lawtexts apart from the triads, but the form *twyll* is found in *twyllforwyn*; *twyll* means deception (*WLW*, 220).

Mk94. U37, W92

llibin6r: The only example given in *GPC*, this means a feeble person (*GPC*, *llibiniwr*). *Llibin* occurs in the Four Branches, meaning spiritless, and in the note Williams quotes this triad as an example; *llib*, to make weak, occurs in *Canu Aneirin*, and it is compared with *enllib*, a compound with *llib* and *en-*, the intensifier *an-* (*PKM*, 147–8; *Canu Aneirin*, 385–6).

Mk96

In *Mk*, there is a series of triads only found in manuscript *Mk* from the Cyfn redaction, but some of them are found in *Q*. This particular triad is interesting as it is used as the basis for a passage found in *G* and *F* (*AL*, VIII. iv, v, vi). The section begins with a version of this triad, very similar indeed to the version found in *Mk*, and continues with a prologue to the next section: 'ac or byd y gyghavssed am y tri hynny ual hyn y byd', making it clear that the next three sections are pleadings on the topics found in the triad (*AL*, VIII. iv. 1). Aneurin Owen labelled the sections 'Am lys cyn amser', 'Am tyst ar uach' and 'Am cad6 g6edy g6rthot' respectively; the final two titles were taken from manuscript *F* (*AL*, VIII. iv, v, vi). The three sections in *Ancient Laws* are discussions based around triads, and give further explanation of the topics found in the triad in *Mk*. Compare the way the account of *dadannudd* in Ior begins with a triad and continues with procedural detail.

yr dahet vo y defnyd: However good his *defnydd*, literally material; *defnydyeu* are the things used to support the case, and it can mean people needed to give evidence (*Ior*, 76/15n., 77/3, 4); here it is the argument or evidence used in a legal case. The word is often found in *cynghawsedd* (*AL*, VII. i. 9, 45).

llys kyn amser: An objection (to witnesses) before the time is right means that the person loses his case (*AL*, VIII. iv. 2). Witnesses must be objected to after the witness has brought his testimony, but before he withdraws from the relic; but not when it is stated that the witness is a witness. Cyfn states that anyone who objects to a witness before he gives evidence loses the case (*WML*, 119. 4–6; *AL*, VIII. iv. 3).

thyst ar vach: It is possible to deny a surety (*Bleg*, 41. 9–15) unless there is a witness to someone having surety or someone being a surety for something (*AL*, VIII. i. 4). According to the section in *G*, there is a set compurgation for a surety to deny his suretyship (*AL*, VIII. v. 1–3).

chad6 g6edy g6rthot: Keeping something after it has been refused or denied. In the *cynghawsedd* on this subject, the claimant refuses to have a set time for getting his property back, but the claimant then keeps the *oed* after originally rejecting it (*AL*, VIII. vi. 1–3). When the claimant claims his property back, the debtor is able to appeal to the law by stating that the claimant may not have what he rejected under a pretence (i. e. the *oed*).

Mk97

This triad is found in one other source: in a section only found in *Q*, entitled *Llyfr Kynyr vab Kad6ga6n* (*AL*, X. x. 1–8). The book uses this triad as a basis for the text.

maba6l ieuenctit y dyscu: Kynyr ap Cad6ga6n explains, using the metaphor of weaving a young sapling, that in youth it is easier to absorb information. If a sapling grows to be large, it breaks as it bends. If a man is older, it is more diffi-cult to concentrate, according to Kynyr.

a synh6yr oet y datcanu: The information gathered when young, and kept in the memory, should not be used, according to Kynyr, until the person is *mywn synnwyr ac oetran*, sensible and of age. This is because *deua6t yr ieuanc y6 bot yn an6astat an6adal*, the custom of the young is to be inconstant and unreliable. These two virtues come with age.

Mk99. Latin: *B43, E51*

dinewyt claf6r: *Dinewyt* is the plural of *dinawed* (cf. *Bleg*, 49. 12), so the phrase means bull calves of a leper. In both Latin B and E, the singular *vitulus leprosus*, bull-calf of a leper, is found (*LTWL*, 243. 3–4, 494. 11–12). This implies that a leper may not sell his calves, presumably to prevent the spread of the disease;

Q168 states that lepers are separated from healthy people, and selling anything would bring them into contact with others.

lledrat: If *cyfnewit* is trade, rather than exchange, we may have a reference to selling stolen property. Provisions for this are found in Ior; if the stolen property is found in someone's house, the owner of the house should be despoiled (*Ior*, 112/4–5).

Tri pheth ny at kyfreith: Found as a triad in Cyfn (see X49) and Bleg, these three things are a horse, swine and honey (*Bleg*, 108). This is a rare example of a triad found within a triad; there are not many cases of cross-referencing within the triad collection.

Mk102

Another of the triads on children; this triad is on the situations where the denial of a son cannot happen; it goes with triad X40. In the three cases listed here, the procedures set out in X40 cannot take place.

g6ely kyfreitha6l: The legal bed, so there is no doubt in the eyes of the law about the validity of the parents' relationship. Bringing up a son means that he is acknowledged (*Ior*, 102/4; *LTMW*, 134).

g6erth yr y vagu: In the case of a child of a woman of bush and brake, it is stated in the law that the father of the child is responsible for his upbringing (*WLW*, 168).

kymerir ar osteg neu or dygir yn gyfreitha6l: The son who is affiliated *ar osteg* appears to be the same as a son by clamour, *mab dyolef* in Ior, whose mother has made it known who his father is but has not completed the legal proceedings (*Ior*, 102/1, 2; *LTMW*, 134; *Ior*, 102/1, 4; *LTMW*, 134). However, if the son has been affiliated legally but the father has not denied him by following the legal process outlined in X40, above, he is a son by sufferance; both options appear to be given in this triad.

Mk103. *Z75. Latin: A25, B47, E55*

A similar situation to the three found in this triad is outlined in the *galanas* section in Latin B: a third of the *galanas* falls on the owner of the spear, unless he places the spear properly (and declares that he has done so), *in pace Dei et regis*, in the peace of God and the king (*LTWL*, 210. 12–18). In *Col*, the owner of the weapon pays nothing if he has placed it under the protection of the lord (*Col*,

293). In this triad, if anyone is injured/killed by the weapons placed in the three places given, then the owner does not have to take responsibility as the weapons are again under the protection of either God or the king, or both as in the third element of the triad.

<h2 style="text-align:center">U35. W77</h2>

Only found in two Cyfn manuscripts, and not in any of the other redactions, this may be an old triad as it contains an unusual and archaic term (*gwg*), and it has similar concepts to some other triads: see *Tri hwrdd ny diwygir*, X55, and the triads on injuries and insults which are not compensated. However, the content of this triad is different to the others, but the concept is the same – certain cases in law where revenge or injury is justified.

g6g: Although primarily meaning indignation or anger, including facial expressions, *GPC* notes that this word can mean an injury or offence. It does not occur elsewhere in the laws (*GPC*, *gwg*).

6rth wreic a rodit rith mor6yn: This appears to be the law of a false maiden, *twyllforwyn*, found as the third limb of triad X55.

ki yn y gyrchu: If a dog attacks a man, and the man kills the dog with a weapon, the man does not have to pay anything to the owner of the dog (*WML*, 82. 16–19).

<h2 style="text-align:center">U38. W94</h2>

This triad does not appear to be a specifically legal triad, but is more gnomic in nature, and similar in style to the Irish collection of triads, although a parallel is not found there. Provision for the three items is not found elsewhere in the laws.

<h2 style="text-align:center">W82</h2>

The three items were probably a nuisance to the kindred as they were expensive and a lot of responsibility.

<h2 style="text-align:center">W87</h2>

Another triad which perhaps has more in common with the Irish collection, it is more gnomic in style, and the statements are rather obvious. The style of this triad is also a little different to the majority – it has an air of poetry about it, with its compound words.

argl6yd dau eira6c: A lord who says two different things plays games with people. This concept does not occur elsewhere in the laws.

ygnat camweda6c: Again, not a concept which is found elsewhere in the laws but rather obvious: an unjust justice is not good for a country.

maer cuhudyat: The *maer* was the royal official and, along with the *cynghellor*, was in charge of administration on a local level.

W89

There are several triads on animals in the Cyfnerth redaction, and this triad is very similar to X66, but the animals are different.

eboles tom: The value of a dunghill mare is the same as a cow, which is forty (*Bleg*, 92. 1, 89. 27), but in the list of items all worth the same amount, a deficient (*ymdiuat*) foal is worth four curt pence (*Bleg*, 87. 9–16). Its tail and eyes are worth four curt pennies each (*Bleg*, 92. 1–3).

cath a warchatwo yscuba6r brenhin: The provision for a cat which guards the king's barn is rather odd in the laws. The dead cat ought to be placed on a barn floor with her tail sticking up, and grain must be poured onto the cat until the tip of the tail is hidden, and that is the value (*WML*, 82. 6). However, it is uncertain what relation this has to its eyes and its tail as the value of the eyes and tail is not given in the laws.

Z56

These men lose all of their possessions because of their crimes. This triad is found in Bleg, although not as a triad proper; the first item is found, then the other two are added, but the normal triad heading is not found (*Bleg*, 82. 4–7). The wording of this triad is not the same as that in Bleg but the concepts are the same, and the limbs are in the same order.

fflemawr: Only occurring in Bleg, and only in the section containing the three limbs of this triad, the word appears to mean fugitive.

Q1–Q6

Three triads found in the laws of court, the first three discussing *sarhaed*, Q4 opens the section on *braint* in the laws of court. Q5 is found at the end of the priest's section, and Q6 in the falconer's section. See *WKC*.

Q7, Q8

Not found in the Cyfn laws of court, these triads are found in Bleg in a section following the justice's paragraph in the laws of court. Called *brawdwr a brawd* (justice and justiceship) by Melville Richards, it is a section comprised mainly of triads. In the *OTr*-type Bleg manuscripts, the triads are found towards the end of the manuscript, not long before the main triad collection.

Q9–Q18

In the *L*-type Bleg manuscripts, which contain the laws of court, these triads are one of the several little groups of triads scattered throughout the lawtexts. They are not part of the main triad collection, and are found after the *rhingyll*'s section, as the collection starts off dealing with summonses, part of the *rhingyll*'s duties. In *OTr*-Bleg manuscripts, this group is tagged onto the end of the main triad collection, and is therefore found just before the *arferion cyfraith* section.

Q19

Found as part of the triad collection in most Cyfn manuscripts (see X14), this triad is very similar indeed to that found in Cyfn, with the order of the first and second limbs reversed. In Bleg, *Oergwymp galanas*, the section immediately after the triad, is again identical in subject matter to Cyfnerth, and like the triad, the wording only differs slightly. The main difference between the material found in Cyfn and Bleg is the positioning of the triad. By the time we get to the Bleg manuscripts (and indeed, every Bleg manuscript is identical in this sense) the triad is not found as part of the collection at all, but is part of the *galanas* section of the three columns of law.

Q20–Q26

The redactors of the law manuscripts did not slavishly copy the manuscripts, but were editors to a great extent; *Q* is particularly significant when looking at triads, as some heavy editing can be seen in the three columns of law section. The compiler of the lawbook seems to have started editing the section on the three columns of law by first copying the standard section on *galanas* found in all Bleg manuscripts, starting with the nine abetments, and the explanations after them, then placing additional material directly after it, including these triads, which are usually found in the main Bleg collection. They are not consecutive in the triad collection. Not all of the triads actually relate to *galanas*; some seem to have been copied as they are adjacent to other triads which were being moved. Following the triads, the scribe continues with the three columns section as found in Bleg and, towards the end, adds some relevant *arferion cyfraith* sections, normally found at the end of the manuscript, and some material found only in *Q*.

Q27–Q29

The second of the three columns of law in Bleg is arson; material on this subject is scant in any redaction of the law, and there is only one triad in *Q* directly related to the subject. The redactor of *Q* moved that one triad, Q27, from the triad collection to the arson section. He also added two triads which have a reference to the three columns of law and placed them directly after: Q28, Q29. He appears to have forgotten that he moved these two triads, because when he copied the triad collection, Q28 and Q29 were repeated. See Q121 and Q122.

Q30–Q36

This is the last of the three columns of law: theft. Q30 is not about theft at all, but Q31 is on that subject. Both were moved from the triad collection. The next triads, Q32–Q36, are found as a consecutive group of triads on different types of thieves, situated towards the end of the main triad collection in most Bleg manuscripts. The first three of this group are also found in manuscript *Z*, but there is a hiatus in the manuscript at this point.

Q37, Q38

Q37 is part of the *gwarant* (warranty) section in both branches of the Bleg redaction, although the positioning of the tractate changes. Q39 is part of the *tystion* (witnesses) section found immediately after the theft tractate in both branches. It is found twice in manuscript *I*.

Q39–Q44

Another group of triads moved from the triad collection to a relevant point in the manuscript in *Q*, this group of six, relating to testimony, is found after the nine credible witnesses section, but they are also found in the triad collection as well: Q129–Q134.

Q45–Q54

Found in the *mechniaeth* tractate, these triads are not consecutive but scattered throughout the section. The *mechniaeth* tractate in the Ior redaction starts as a structured section of law but after a while seems to become groups of additional material such as *damweiniau*. This may also be the case with the Bleg section on *mechniaeth*; there are certainly many triads scattered throughout the section, and there are very many triads relating to *mechniaeth* in the triad collection as well. In *Q*, the *mechniaeth* section appears to be a mixture of Bleg and Ior material. For studies on the *mechniaeth* tractate, see *LAL*.

Q48. *S185, Y17*

Also found in *S* and *Y*, this is a triad which is not usually found in Bleg or Ior, and lists the three things which no person may be protected from if they have already acknowledged them. The triad was probably placed in the suretyship section of *Q* as the second item is suretyship.

goruodogaeth: *LAL*, 178. The *gorfodog* is different to other sureties in Welsh law as he guarantees the good conduct of the person he is representing, often for appearance in court (*Ior*, 70). The responsibility is huge, and the bailsman risked total ruin (*Ior*, 70).

goresgyn: This usually means acquisition of land, and it would be lawful, as opposed to *camoresgyn*, wrongful taking of possession (*LTMW*, 254).

Q49. *S164, Y16*

Again found in the tail of *S* and in *Y*, this triad lists the sureties who cannot act on their suretyship with their own oath alone – they need others to swear with them. The first surety became a surety in a public situation, and so there are other people who need to swear; the second surety has been rejected as a surety, so his own oath is not useful as he is not officially a surety.

mach kynnogyn: *Cynnogyn* is the word used in the laws to mean debtor, so this surety is also a debtor, and it appears that someone else needs to swear as well as himself (*LAL*, 106–7).

Q50. *S162, Tim104*

Only otherwise found in the tail of *S* and *Tim*, there is a triad within this triad. The sureties cannot deny their suretyship as it was taken on in a public situation.

tri chyhoed kyfreith: Although this appears to be a triad, no such triad is found in manuscript *Q*, but there are other references to it: Q175 lists the three publicities, and the same three situations are found. S182 (given in this edition as a variant of Q254) also quotes the triad, but does not list the three situations.

Q51, Q52

These two triads are again found in most Bleg manuscripts, as part of the suretyship tractate.

Q53. [J167], Tim119

A version of this triad is found in *J* and *Tim*, but *J* is incomplete and so does not give the full triad, but the first limb only. Q53 is a long triad found in the Ior *mechniaeth* section (*Ior*, 65). The first limb appears to be different in *Tim*.

Q54. S204

Also found in the tail of *S*, this may be an early triad on a general concept in law: three claims which will be lost in any circumstance. This was probably put in the suretyship section of *Q* as the second item has a reference to suretyship: a witness on a surety can never be denied.

Q55

See X19.

Q *Triad Collection*

To avoid repetition, notes are only given for the triads that do not also occur in the Cyfn triad collections.

Q60. Mk128. Latin: A22, B19, E13. Ior, 42/10, 11.

The values of the harps agree in each version of this triad: in the Bleg collections this is one of the first triads following the *tair rhwyd* series, and it is also in the short collection of triads in *Ior* 42/10 (*Bleg*, 108. 8–12). The Bleg triads add a value for the tuning horn (twenty-four pence for that of a king and a *pencerdd*, twelve pence for that of a nobleman). The values also agree with the values for harps and tuning horns given in the equipment lists in Ior (*Ior*, 140/9–11; *LTMW*, 191, 192). According to Cyfn, the *cynghellor* also received a harp (along with a gold ring and a throwboard) from the king when he went into office (*WML*, 29. 10–11).

Q61. X6

Although this triad, which gives the lord the right of pre-emption, and the following are in *Mk*, they are in the main text, not in the triad collection. According to Ior, the bondsman is liable to a *dirwy* if he sells these items without permission (*Ior*, 42/12).

Q62. X7

Both this triad and Q61 concern royal bondsmen, and they are the final pair of triads in the short collection found in Ior.

gofanyaeth: The *gof llys* held his land free in that he was not liable to *gwestfa* or *twnc*; *gwestfa* and *twnc* were the obligations of freemen, so it may be assumed that the other smiths were freemen and therefore owed *gwestfa* or *twnc*.

ny dicha6n eu keithi6a6: The Bleg and Cyfn versions of this triad are more generous than that found in Ior 42/13. In Ior, the lord may take the men back as bondsmen after they have learnt the crafts, apart from the cleric; here, once the crafts are learnt, the men cannot be bound to a lord again. There is a very similar pair of triads later on in the *Q* collection (Q145 and Q146).

Q76

This triad is not found in *X* but is found in most of the Bleg manuscripts.

y neb a dy6etter: Whoever is said to be the father of the child must deny him on oath. This is the procedure found in *Ior*, 100/5–11. Although not a triad, the procedure follows the order of this text.

penkenedyl: This is identical to the section in *Ior*, 102/11. The clause *a seith law kenedyl* is omitted in *Q* though eyeskip.

ony byd penkenedyl: As in *Ior*, 102/12.

deg6yr a deugeint: In Ior the number of men needed to deny the son is twenty-one; in Powys fifty men are required, according to *Ior*, 102/13.

ac velly ...: This next section is not found in Ior, but cf. the *mab dyodef* of 102/4–6.

Q97

This triad is similar to Q85 in that it gives three timbers that any builder can have from the owner of the woods whether the owner is willing or not.

Q102

There are two main problems with this triad: first, what, in this context, are the meanings of *tal* and *geudwng*? The only textual variant of any consequence is *O*'s *g6irt6g* in place of *geud6g*. *Geud6g* is shared by the *L* group of Bleg manuscripts and Latin D, but the other *OTr* group manuscripts do not contain it, so it is probably an *L*-type variant.

The heading, 'there are three kinds of payment to a plaintiff', fits tolerably well with the second and third limbs. The assumption seems to have been made that the plaintiff is either of the two parties in exchange of money or goods: *atwerth* is the return of the sale price to the purchaser, *eturyt* the restoration of the goods to the purchaser. On this basis the *tal* in question is the reversal of a sale. For this use of *at-* compare *Ior*, 123: *atnewit* seems to be the generic term, *atwerth* and *eturyt* the same reversal of an exchange but now seen from each side of a contract of sale. *Attal* was not available in place of *tal*, since it had another sense (*Ior*, 88/4). However, the triad does not make it clear whether the three forms of *tal* are being made as a consequence of the action brought by the plaintiff (and so it would be assumed that the defendant was in the wrong) or that they were made in the past (and thus the plaint would be shown to lack foundation).

A second, more substantial problem arises when we consider the first limb, *geud6g*, false oath. According to the note in *Llyfr Blegywyrd*, 116. 8n., this means that it is proved that the defendant swore a false oath. The presupposition behind this interpretation is that the various payments followed a successful plaint. Even if this is correct, however, it would still be the case that the triad shifts its ground from the reason why a *tal* to the *cwynwr* is appropriate (that the defendant swore a false oath) to the actual payments themselves (*atwerth* and *eturyt*). A further problem is what kind of false oath was in question? One possibility is that one contractual party made the promise forming his side of the contract falsely, namely that he had no intention of delivering his side of the bargain; another that the contract was vitiated because the livestock promised did not have their required *teithi* (*Ior*, 123/1, 127/15, 128/5 etc.). The truth is that the triad does not contain sufficient clues to its own meaning.

Q104. Mk132, U13, Z77. Latin: A35, B65, E69

There are a number of different versions of this triad, and the triad varies in the Cyfn and Bleg; *K* has two versions of the triad, one of which seems to be unique.

The triad as found in the Cyfn versions is short, and each of the versions of the triad in Cyfn and Bleg contains the same elements in one way or another: a woman and marriage, a man and land, and a son.

chargychwyn: Found in compounds such as *carddychwel* and *carllawedrog*, this compound means car starting. *Cargychwyn* means to depart in a formal or ceremonial way, and the vehicle seems to have some significance (*LTMW*, 324). The car would be a *car llusg*, dragged car or cart (*LTMW*, 324).

Q107. Mk68, V66, W64. Latin: A34, B55, E11. DwC, 303

This triad does not seem to be the same in the *Mk* and Bleg versions of it; the Latin texts have the same version as Bleg. S180 is the same as the Cyfn version. The first limb of the Bleg version of the triad is the same as that found in Cyfn, but the remaining items are different – see S180. Similar to the Irish provisions on immunities, the title to the goods stays with the giver; offering surety would transfer the ownership as well as possession (Stacey, 'Ties that bind', 52).

Q109. Mk105. Latin: A44, B38, E46

gellast: The staghound is worth double the value of the *milgi*, greyhound, at all stages of its development (*WKC*, 269–71), and in this triad, if a litter of puppies is stolen, the value of the bitch is paid rather than the value of each pup (*WML*, 34. 6–11).

Q110. Mk126. Latin: A45, B30, E85

Most animals vary in worth depending on their age: these three are an exception, and in the tractate on swine they are called the three special animals (*WML*, 76. 9–11).

baed kenuein: *Cenfaint* is now used as the collective noun for pigs but it was originally used for other litters too. A *baedd cenfain* is a herd boar; it is only found in the triads in Cyfn and it is uncertain why its value does not increase or decrease.

arbenhic y genuein: The principal one of the swine, *arbennic moch* in Cyfn (*WML*, 222). In Latin A and B, *sus maior in grege* is given, the largest sow in the herd, and Latin B adds the Welsh equivalent, *arbennic moch* (*LTWL*, 129. 40–3, 235. 39–236. 3). Latin E does not give a Latin translation, but gives two Welsh options: '*arbennic moch*, id est, *kessewin*', *kessewin* or *cysefin* meaning the principal or main one (*LTWL*, 507. 16–18).

yg kyfeir yr argl6yd: In *Mk*, it is for *gwestfa*, the food render due to the king; it has to be paid twice a year by the bondsmen and the sow has to be a certain size: three fingers in the shoulder and the long ribs and in the ham (*WML*, 56. 19–20; *EIWK*, 370, 391).

Q111

This triad deals with the *gwybyddiaid* (knowers) who are special witnesses for land cases.

de6edir: *GPC* and Melville Richards translate this as 'denied', but there is no evidence in this triad to support that translation.

henuryeit g6lat: The elders of the country are the ones who, according to the lawtexts, know a man's lineage (*WML*, 54. 19–20). Bleg has a section showing how to claim land; the elders should discuss and agree who is telling the truth (*Bleg*, 70. 11, 76. 28–77. 8; *WML*, 57. 18–19, 50. 23–51. 3).

ach ac etryt: See Charles-Edwards, '*Edryd, Edryf, Edfryd, Edrydd*', 117–20. According to Ior a man must show his lineage as far as the stock from which he derives, and if he is a fourth man, he is a proprietor (*Ior*, 85/1–2).

amhinogeu tir: See the note on X64. These are men from each section of the township who know how land was shared between the relatives (*WML*, 54).

meiri a chyghelloryon: These two officers are often grouped together. According to Cyfn, if there is a dispute between two towns of the same status it is the duty of the *meiri*, *cyngellorion* and the *rhingylliaid* to keep or remember the borders and how the land was shared because all borders belong to the king (*WML*, 54–5). The *maer* was the royal official and, along with the *cynghellor*, was in charge of administration of land occupied by husbandmen, on a local level; the status of the *cynghellor* seems to be higher (see *LTMW*, 331–2, 363–4).

Q114. Latin: A33, E77

This triad is not found in the Cyfnerth collections. The first two items are brewed, and would need to be covered for fermentation to take place. There is an alternative version of this triad in *Tim*, a different version to that found in the main triad collection. In that triad, three people are named: the justice, a poet and the mediciner. It is uncertain what this refers to – perhaps their practice of wearing some sort of headcovering? – but it may have been an error for *medyd* (the mead brewer) or something similar which led to the interpretation found in *Tim*.

ker6yn ved: There is a mead brewer in the laws of the court and a mead cellar of which the brewer has possession (*Bleg*, 11. 25, 27. 23; *WML*, 25. 22–6. 2).

braga6t: Made of honey and ale fermented together; shares are given to the offi- cers of the court (*LTMW*, 319). *L*, *J* and *M* have *bra6t* for this limb; Christine James argues that that is a better reading, but she may have been influenced by the alternative triad in *Tim* ('Golygiad o BL Add. 22,356', 248).

chathyl: A song or poem, this triad suggests that the king has the first right to every poem. The court poet has to sing of God and the king, and he is to sing to the queen, quietly (*Ior*, 13/6; *WKC*, 150).

Q115

The three men who keep the status of a court in the absence of the king. The three men are listed together in Cyfn, but the sentiment is not quoted as a triad (*WML*, 27. 19–21)

offeirat teulu: There are references to this triad in the laws of the court (*Bleg*, 12. 27–8, 13. 9–10, cf. Ior 4/10; 6/18; see also *WKC*, 83).

distein: The *distain* increased in importance throughout the twelfth century and by the time of Llywelyn ap Iorwerth he was no longer a domestic servant but the principal administrative and judicial official (Stephenson, *Governance of Gwynedd*, 13). This reference to his holding court status in the absence of the king suggests that the position was gaining importance at this stage.

Q118. Mk72, U45, W66, Z57. Latin: A49, B23, E29. Col, 42–5

chy6ilyd mor6yn: According to Morfydd Owen (*WLW*, 48–9), this triad is trying to rationalize the exchanges of property that occur during marriage in terms of reparation for the shames.

Q119

cowyll: Her morning gift (*WLW*, 196).

argyfreu: This is similar to the English dowry. It becomes part of the matrimonial pool after seven years, so the man must leave her before the seven years are up in this case for the woman to be able to keep her *argyfreu* (*WLW*, 191).

Q120

gol6c: This is a sighting of the crime being committed; the next triad is dedicated to this idea.

Q121

llygadrud kylus: The guilty eyewitness. According to the *affeithiau*, abetments of homicide, a person could be guilty of homicide by seeing (*Bleg*, 30. 6–9). The word *llygadrud* was formed on the model of *llofrudd*, as red-handedness came to mean guilt (*Bleg*, 179). *Llofruddiaeth* originally meant killing by means of a hand (see *LTMW*, 81. 7n.; 95. 8n.), whereas *llygadruddiaeth* means killing by means of eye/sight (*Bleg*, 179). These concepts are only found in Bleg.

Q122

This triad is found in the three columns section of *Q* as well (Q27).

thaua6trudyaeth: See the note on *llygadrud* in the previous triad. In the abetments for homicide, pointing out the person who is to be killed to the killer is an example (*Ior*, 104/4).

Q123

6alla6geir: Faulty, erroneous word. No one may lose his land because of a faulty word, and no pleading is bound to a faulty word (*Bleg*, 45. 31–2, 76. 16–17).

eithyr tri: *Tri chamgwyn kylus* is a triad found in the main text in *Q*: Q218.

Q124

Although this triad's heading is the same as Mk120, the content is different. This, however, is very similar to other triads in the *Mk* collection, triads Mk134 and Mk135.

g6adu: This is the third limb in Mk135. If the defendant denies, the claimant may bring witnesses (*AL*, IX. xxvii. 13).

profi: If it is proved, the case is ended and the guilty party pays; this is found instead of the second limb in Mk135, *adef.*

lyssu tyston: This is a step following denial in *cynghawsedd*: if the defendant denies the accusation put upon him, the claimant may bring witnesses to try and prove his case, and the defendant may then object to the witnesses offered (*AL*, IX. xxvii. 13). According to X35, there are three reasons for objecting to witnesses.

Q125

Cf. Q126–Q128, and the different version in S213.

pra6f ar 6eithret eithyr tri: This is referring to the next triad, Q126.

g6at dros 6aessaf: A denial on a guarantee. It is suggested in *Llyfr Blegywryd*, 232 (note on *gwat dros waessaf*), that the reading should be denial instead of a guarantee, as denial was not enough – it had to be confirmed in the three ways outlined in Q127.

chof g6edy bra6t: Appealing against a judgement because of new evidence is not allowed.

Q126

These are the only three instances where proof is sufficient for a deed – see the previous triad.

llafur: The proof is there on the land. References to this are found in the section on boundary.

torri ffin neu 6neuthur ffin: Breaking a boundary would mean a fine to the king and four pennies to the owner of the land, and the same goes for any work done on the land without permission (*Bleg*, 82. 8–16).

tystolyaeth y bugeil: The shepherd is one of the nine tongued-ones (*Bleg*, 39. 1–3, *WML*, 41. 13–14).

kytleidyr lleidyr a grocker am letrat: Another one of the nine tongued-ones (*Bleg*, 39. 4–9; *WML*, 41. 14–18).

Q127

g6aessaf: This is mentioned in triad Q125, above.

ardel6: The stance taken by the parties (*AL*, VII. i. 10). Instead of denying an accusation, the defendant could claim something else that the accuser would have to prove, or lose his claim (*Bleg*, 232).

6arant neu amdiffyn heb 6arant: The guarantee or defending without a guarantee. See the note *gwarant* for X22.

Q128. Mk133

This triad is discussed briefly by Dafydd Jenkins who suggests it concerns the medieval Welsh version of the appeal today (*Cyfraith Hywel*, 99).

bra6t tremyc: In the triad, it may be a judgement that a justice does not pronounce so that the party may hear it, or if the party is under unjust pressure before the judgement is made, or if an unqualified or underqualified man makes the judgement (*Bleg*, 104. 8–18). For this, whoever loses out may give a pledge on the judgement any time within a year and a day, but not immediately as in the case in this triad (*Bleg*, 103. 19–104. 7).

Q135. Mk113

treis: *Trais* in this context is everything taken in the presence of the owner, against his will: robbery rather than secret theft (*Ior*, 115/15; *LTMW*, 167).

pallo y reith y dyn: If his compurgation fails, he is given a *dirwy* (*Cyfraith Hywel*, 67). The *rhaith* could fail if he could not gather enough men to swear, or if he did not have the right type of men (*Cyfraith Hywel*, 105).

amdiffyn: In this triad, *amddiffyn*, defence, seems to be a general term for things such as witnesses, but not those means of defence in the first or last element of the triad.

Q136. Mk114

Forming a pair with Q135, above, this is a procedural triad, and the following triad, Q137, may be linked to it. It shows how a case for violence, *dadl treis*, fails; the correct procedure may not be followed, or the wrong type of evidence may be given.

o pallu teithi treis: 'Teithi treis yw llef a chorn a chwyn' (*WML*, 80. 25).

tystolyaeth v6ya6l: See X64; all *tystolyaeth* is *mar6* except for three.

Q137. Mk115

The victim of *trais*, violence in general rather than rape specifically, may lose one or more of the three items in this triad: his life, land or goods, or status.

vreint: On the whole someone who has been a victim of violence would not lose his status, so this limb of the triad may be referring to the more specific use of the word *trais*, rape. The loss of virginity would mean that the victim of rape would lose her status and would no longer be a *morwyn* (*Ior*, 54/4–5; *PKM*, 74).

Q138. Mk116

amdiffyn: Defence, which is neither admitting nor denying. This may be an *ardelw*, a further refined legal stance, in the Book of Cynghawsedd, and if an *arddelw* is offered, there is no need for either admission or denial (*AL*, VIII. xi. 16). Legal arguments and manœuvring will follow: there would be conflict of *arddelw*, counter-*arddelw*, and even a further *arddelw* and the justices would decide the case on the evidence and legal argument given by the parties (Charles-Edwards, '*Cynghawsedd*', 196).

6rtheper yn anamserya6l y'r gofyn: In the land law section in Ior the justice questions (*gofyn*) the claimant about various parts of the case and the claimant has to answer (*Ior*, 74/8–10, 76/1, 77/18, 20). The procedure for land is set out in Ior 74–7, and there is a proper time for each step, so an appropriate defence is made at the right time for each step of the case. Objecting to witnesses at the wrong time can cause a man to lose his case (see Mk96).

atteb mal na choller dim y'r ha6l: This and the previous limb are successful defences; although the defendant is being claimed against, he manages to bring the right type of witnesses, and the best evidence, so he does not lose out in spite of the claim, and in the second limb, there cannot be an answer (*Ior*, 77/26–8).

Q140. Mk118

In the plaints in *Q*, an example of this triad is included, and each of the plaints is based on one of the elements in the triad (*AL*, XII. i–x; Roberts, 'Plaints in Mediaeval Welsh Law').

Q142. Mk120

This triad is not the same version as that found in *Mk*.

theruyn kyfreitha6l: *Ha6l* in *Mk*: the three terminations of a claim, or literally, three ways of ending a claim.

Q143. Mk121

Although this triad is also found in *Mk*, it is the triad preceding the hiatus, and half of it is therefore missing in *Mk*.

deturyt g6lat: Verdict of the country, similar to a modern jury. In this triad the three items given must be judged in this way.

Q *Extended Triad Collection*

From now on the triads found as part of the *Q* collection are not normally found in the Bleg manuscripts, and are only found as a collection of triads in *Q*, *C* and *P* (the three manuscripts are very similar and *C* is a copy of *Q*; *P* may also be a copy). William Maurice annotated both *P* and *Q* heavily; in his notes on the triad collection in *P* he marks out triad 144 and states that there are more triads in *P* than in *M* ('Beta'): 'dyma drioedd ychwaneg nag sydd yn Beta'. The triads found below are the 'Trioedd Ychwanegol', the additional triads. Many of the rules found in this extended collection are only found as triads and a similar passage cannot be found in the main text of the laws.

Q144. S270, Y9, Z83

Marking the start of the extended triad collection, this triad is found in several sources, and it is linked with the *holiadon*, but the version of the triad found in *J*, *L*, *S* and *Tim* is slightly different; the limb containing the mad dog appears to have been replaced with the limb concerning any animal, and a rather unusual limb is given as a substitute, where an intruder is killed in the king's chamber.

bonhedic canh6yna6l g6iryon: Cf. *Ior*, 87/4. Their *galanas* is three kine and three score kine, and their *sarhaed* is three kine and sixty pieces of silver (*Ior*, 98/8, 110/14).

dyn a ladho ki kyndeira6c: Cyfn states that there is no compensation for deeds done by rabid dogs as they cannot be controlled (*WML*, 83. 2–4). There is a provision in the *damweiniau* for a person dying of a bite from a mad or rabid man: as with a rabid dog, the kin of the madman do not pay the *galanas* of the dead man (*DwC*, 6).

prenn 6rth y v6r6 y la6r gan y rybudya6: If, however, there was no warning and someone was killed, the *galanas* of the dead man would have to be paid, but not his *sarhaed* as it would be an unintentional killing. A similar passage is found in *Damweiniau Colan*: if the man was warned, the one who felled the tree pays nothing (*DwC*, 246).

dyn a ladho annyueil: Again, provisions for this are found in the *damweiniau*; one person (the owner of the animal) cannot pay *galanas*, and a kindred are not bound to pay for a kin member's animal's deed (*DwC*, 20).

Q145, Q146. S177, Y161, Z84; S178, Y162, Z85

The following two triads are a pair and are found in *S* and *Y*. They are triads discussing freemen and the situations in which bondsmen can become free. There are other triads discussing this subject, in particular, the three crafts a bondsman may not teach his son (Q62). The three items are the same. However, the second triad in this pair makes it clear that once the bondsmen have become freemen, the status only lasts for their lifetime. The sons of these freemen will be bondsmen, so their status is the same as their fathers' original status. In practice, it is unlikely that such crafts were hereditary in many cases. These appear to be the only example of triads which have to travel together in order for the full story to be told.

Q147. S194, Z88

creuyd6r: According to Pryce, *G* includes testimony of a married clergyman as unreliable, and *S* lists a monk, a friar, an anchorite or a hermit who has broken his vows in another section. Pryce also refers to an anomalous section in *Q*: 'the twelve things which corrupt the world'; a married priest is included amongst them (*AL*, X. ix. 1–13; Pryce, *Native Law*, 104).

cam tystolyaeth: In Bleg, *anudon*, false testimony or perjury, is one of the reasons to object to witnesses. It seems that once they have been proved guilty of perjury they will never be believed again (*Bleg*, 37. 14–15; *WML*, 119. 20–2).

Q148. S269, Y8, Z79

In *S*, this triad and the next are found as a set of three, with the *S* version of Q144 as the final in the group. They are also found in a few other manuscripts, including *L*, and are often linked with the *holiadon*. As a pair in *Q*, the two triads are contrasting, dealing with times when only *galanas* is paid and times when only *sarhaed* is paid.

saeth tr6y arall: A similar rule is found in one of the *damweiniau*: if someone throws something at an animal and hits a person, killing him, it is inadvertence so only the *galanas* is paid; if an arrow pierces two people, *sarhaed* is paid for the person it was aimed at (*DwC*, 169–72).

g6en6yn: The answer to why *sarhaed* is not paid for poisoning is in the *damwain* discussed in the previous limb: if there is no battery or assault on the person hurt, there is no disgrace, and therefore no *sarhaed* payment, even though *sarhaed* can mean both injury and insult (*DwC*, 171). In *E*, a poisoner pays double *galanas* or loses his life (*AL*, IV. iii. 12, 13).

ynuyt: According to the *damweiniau* the kin pays *galanas* on behalf of the madman (*DwC*, 2). Another triad states that the kin should look after the madmen and ensure that they do not commit crimes (Q165, below).

Q149. *S268, Y10, Z80*

The reverse of the previous triad, these are the cases where *sarhaed* is paid for the disgrace but no *galanas* is paid, even though the men are killed. Each of the men is worthless in law. The version of this triad in *Q* is very different from that in the other manuscripts.

a'r deu dyn ynt: There does not appear to be a parallel to this statement in the lawtexts. This limb is not found in the version of the triad found in *J, L, S, Tim* and *Y*, and two separate limbs are found instead. The redactor of *Q* may have been referring to the two people listed in each limb, namely the man who is accused of *galanas* but does not deny it, and the man who has paid all of the *galanas* except for a penny. In the other version of the triad there is some overlap between the people mentioned in the first and second limb with the *tri dygyngoll cenedl* triad (X14); the two people listed appear to be the same, but explanation for why *sarhaed* is owed is added in each of the limbs.

Q150. *S210*

Again dealing with *sarhaed*, there are three serious offences for which *sarhaed* is not paid. *Sarhaed* is not paid for an unintentional deed, as demonstrated in Q144, above, but it is also not paid if the person committing the offence is not responsible.

dyrna6t mab kynn y uot yn oet kyfreitha6l: The legal age is 14 in the Welsh laws; before the age of 14, the father is responsible for everything that his son does, and ought to pay for any offence he commits (*Ior*, 98/1). *Sarhaed* is not payable in this case because the son is not responsible.

eidiged kyfreitha6l: This phrase is not found in the rules set out in the lawtexts, but is found in one other triad (X55, Q106), as a blow arising from jealousy (between a wife and a concubine) is not compensated.

anuod: Inadvertence; an inadvertent blow is not compensated (*Bleg*, 57. 26; *WML*, 118. 8–9). This limb echoes the section found in Cyfn and Bleg (*WML*, 118. 8–11; *Bleg*, 57. 26–8).

g6aet a g6eli ac asc6rn t6nn, hagen, a telir or byd: If there is any injury resulting from the blows, then the value of the injury must be paid as set out in the lawtexts (*Bleg*, 56. 1–57. 14).

Q152. Mk90, W84

The three elements of this triad are the things which prevent a man from answering a summons to court. A similar concept is also in early English common law. The three *essoins* found here are found in English law: a broken bridge, bed-sickness, crusade and pilgrimage are all acceptable *essoins* (Pollock and Maitland, *History of English Law*, ii. 562–3).

Q153. S271

The next two triads deal with *amobr* and are again a pair of triads with contrasting themes. *Amobr* is the virginity payment paid to the lord the first time a woman goes to a man.

ebedi6: The general principle is that a man's *ebediw* and his daughter's *amobr* are the same; Bleg suggests this, and this is probably an assumption behind this triad (*Bleg*, 84. 4–8; *LTMW*, 244). *Amobr* is the female payment; women do not pay *ebediw* unless they have a cell (*WML*, 100. 5–6; *WLW*, 175; *LTMW*, 244). *Ebediw* is similar to the English heriot payment, a death duty to the lord (*LTMW*, 340); this triad, however, seems to give up discussing *ebediw* as a contrast to *amobr* after the first element. *Ebediw* is one of the eight packhorses (sources of income) of the king in Ior (43/1). It seems that *ebediw* was originally paid in the form of the return of martial equipment, for example, a horse (*LTMW*, 225). The *ebediwau* of the officers of the court are set out in the lawtexts, and the *ebediw* goes to the king; however, if someone pays some sort of duty or rent for their land they do not pay *ebediw* when they die (*Bleg*, 21. 25–6, 22. 4, 23. 2, 47. 6, 49. 20–50. 11, 76. 18–19).

g6r a diennydho yr argl6yd: Cf. *Ior*, 115/8, *Col*, 394.

a'e uerch a dal amobyr: This element works well: a man who does not pay *ebediw*, and a woman who ought to pay *amobr* (or have it paid for her). The laws of women state that whoever gives a woman to a man pays her *amobr*, and if she gives herself, she pays her own *amobr* (*WLW*, 167).

g6r a dalo gobyr ystyn: There does not seem to be any reference to *ebediw* in this triad. The basic meaning of *gobyr* is fee, and *gobyr ystyn* is basically the same as *amobr* (*WLW*, 203). *Gobr ystyn* is paid for this girl instead of *amobr*.

Q154. z86

Cf. *Ior*, 4/5. According to Dafydd Jenkins, by the thirteenth century the *ebediw* became a money payment related to the man's holding of land; the payment in kind was anomalous (*LTMW*, 225). The *edling* and the *penteulu* paid their *ebediw* in kind because of their close relationship to the king, not because of their office (*LTMW*, 225).

Q155. U60, W88. S272. DwC, 135

This triad is popular and is found amongst the *damweiniau* (*AL*, IV. iv. 34), and in other manuscripts, including some Cyfn manuscripts, but not in *Mk*. It is also found in the collection of gnomic triads, but without the extension (Owen, 'Trioed hefut y6 yrei hynn', triad 29). This triad is very similar in each version. As with *tri dygyngoll cenedl* and *tri chyhyryn canastyr* some phrases in this triad seem to be title phrases, and some of the words have an explanation within the triad.

maen dros iaen: According to the explanation, a lord is *maen dros iaen*, a stone across a piece of ice. This is a complicated metaphor and it occurs in a section on surety in the *damweiniau* (*DwC*, 344). According to Dafydd Jenkins, the explanation is that ice is weaker than stone and does not bear very much weight; the lord is the stone to bear the weight of the weaker ones under him to prevent them being crushed (*LTMW*, 249). However, there may be confusion between two different metaphors here. If the lord is a stone in place of ice, the stone is stronger as it can break ice, a straight comparison. Alternatively, if the lord is a stone over a sheet of ice, he can crush or override those beneath him, which seems more likely in this triad. The lord can secure the rights of a blind man to property which he cannot swear to because he cannot see it (*DwC*, 307; *LTMW*, 249; *AL*, V. ii. 53).

drut: Explained in the extension to the triad, a *drut* is an *ynvyt*, an idiot, and an idiot is one who cannot be compelled to do anything apart from what he wishes to do. Therefore he is a strong man in law. The meaning 'idiot' is not found under *drud* in *GPC*, but the entry does state that the word has an Irish cognate, *drúth*, '*ffŵl*'.

One of the triads dealing with children in the collection in *Q*, this triad is repeated as the last triad in the extended collection in the same manuscript. There are several triads under this subject, possibly because there is no section on children in the main Cyfn or Bleg lawtexts, whereas it is found appended to the laws of country in the Ior texts (*Ior*, 97–103). This triad however is not found in Ior.

gouyn: The scribe of *Q* seems to have got this wrong; the word should actually be *go6yn* according to *Q*'s orthography. The word *gowyn* usually means a fee of some kind (found in the laws of women it can mean *wynebwerth*) and here it is roughly equivalent to *galanas*. This is made clear in the additional sentence which states why the mother's kindred is entitled to the *galanas*.

kenedyl y vam: It is rare for the mother's kindred alone to get a share of *galanas*; the larger share usually goes to the father's kin (*Ior*, 107/2).

mab g6reic vonhedic a rother y alltut: The explanatory statement in the triad explains that the child in question has no father's kindred; they would have to pay the *galanas* if the situation was reversed and the child had killed someone rather than been killed.

mab g6reic ny 6ypo p6y uo y tat: This sentence is a little ambiguous but the fact that *tat* is not mutated after the possessive *y* shows that this is the child; the father of the child is unknown, so he does not have a father's kindred (to his knowledge).

mab g6reic a 6atter o genedyl y tat: The procedure for denying a son (as well as affiliating him) is found as a triad in *Q*; see Q76, Q185 and Q186, and X40. If the son has been denied, he does not have a father's kindred.

g6arthec diuach: Cf. *WLW*, 205; *Ior*, 53/3, 101/5; *Bleg*, 81. 21; *WML*, 62. 15–20.

This triad is discussed fully by P. K. Ford and E. P. Hamp in *BBCS*, 26 (1974–6). They compare Celtic legal idiom with the items in this triad as the word *asswynaw* is found in *Culhwch ac Olwen* meaning more or less the same thing that it does here. The triad in *DwC* has been amended following the text found in V. i. 9, as the heading is different (*DwC*, 159; *LTMW*, 267).

6rogaeth: According to Ford, this is an arrangement where a man enters into a bond relationship with another, and it is a contractual relationship with mutual obligations (Ford and Hamp, 'Welsh *asswynaw*', 148). The obligations are the three items given in this triad.

cletrenn g6aessaf6r: One who gives a pledge, or warrantor (Ford and Hamp, 'Welsh *asswynaw*', 148). *Gwaessaf6r* appears to be based on the same element as *arwaesaf*, voucher to warranty, and *cletrenn* means the compensation or guarantee he gives, so this homage may create an obligation in the lord to warrant the man (*LTMW*, 119. 23n.).

ass6yn6r: One who is obligated to an *aswyn*; *aswyn* is found in *Culhwch ac Olwen* and means a petition for protection or entreaty, so the *asswyn6r* is the temporary tenant (Ford and Hamp, 'Welsh *asswynaw*', 148–9).

atlam6r: One who is obligated to an *adlam*; *adlam* means habitation or refuge so he is a temporary inhabitant in the laws (ibid.; *LTMW*, 119. 23n). The three items in the triad are very similar, according to Ford, in that each of the men have a contractual relationship with someone more powerful; the weaker one invokes the stronger, and if the contract is abrogated the petitioner (weaker one) retreats from the refuge of his protector (the stronger one) and a fine is set (Ford and Hamp, 'Welsh *asswynaw*', 148).

Q158. S212. DwC, 163

This triad also occurs in the *damweiniau* (*DwC*, 163). The first and second items are free for all – flowing water and a stone (but not a millstone, as it has a legal value). There are provisions in the laws for borrowing fire, which would be borrowing from another person's hearth, as there is no need to ask permission for borrowing a naturally occurring fire from an empty tree (*Ior*, 117/7, *Col*, 163) and there is a surreption payment for taking fire without consent (*Ior*, 117/5). If the fire is stolen, there is a *camlwrw* to pay (*Ior*, 120/3).

Q159. Latin: B54, E61. DwC, 253

offeirat: See Pryce, *Native Law*, 148–9.

ygnat: Cf. *Ior*, 10/12, 78/1. He also receives twenty-four pence for testing judges (*Ior*, 10/16).

manag6r: This is the informant and the triad explains that he receives the tenth penny for his information or his work as an informant. This does not seem to appear elsewhere in the laws.

Q160

This triad is setting out the three pleadings that must be heard by a justice or the official who is in his place. This suggests that arbitrators can be called to settle other cases.

kymryt dyn y genedyl neu y 6rthlad o genedyl: The process of affiliating and denying children is found in other triads: Q76, Q185 and Q186, X40, and in the family law section in *Ior*, 100, 103. The only place where it is made clear that the justice should be present for this action is Q186, below.

Q161

There is a similar triad in the collections listing the three men who are entitled to have a *tafodiog*, a representative, in court: X42 and Q78, so this triad is the corresponding one, listing the people who are entitled to represent others in court. The lord is obvious, as is the justice; the fact that the surety is included emphasizes his importance in the laws. Each of them is found in the list of the nine credible witnesses (*Ior*, 56/2, 4, 5).

Q162. Y5

There are two triads earlier on in the *Q* collection contrasting the offences for which either *galanas* or *sarhaed* is paid, but not both: Q147 and Q148. This and the next triad are a similar contrasting pair listing the people who ought pay *galanas* but do not receive a share of it and vice versa.

g6reic: Cf. *Ior*, 106/15.

yscolheic: Both women and clerics pay *galanas* unless they swear that they will never have children (*Col*, 271); they pay on behalf of any children they may have, but do not receive a share (*Ior*, 106/15). It is also stated in Ior that they are not entitled to a share of *galanas* because they are not avengers (*Ior*, 108/5).

dyn a talho keina6c paladyr: If a killer has nothing with which to pay, he gets a shaft penny as assistance from the seventh person onwards (*Ior*, 106/6–9).

Q163. Y6

The explanatory sentence sets out the reasons why each of them gets a share of the *galanas*.

argl6yd: He gets a third of the *galanas* as an enforcing part of every *galanas* that is paid (*Ior*, 106/14, *Col*, 272). A woman who will never have children is also a person who will receive a share but will not pay *galanas* (*Col*, 271).

ygnat: He gets twenty-four pence for judging *galanas* cases and making peace between the kindreds.

righill: He gets four pence for enforcing the collection of *galanas*; this is only found set out as a rule in this triad.

Q164

The justice should not listen to any of these things, as they are all pointless: they are not allowed because they are done at the wrong times. Once he has made his judgement (*brawd*), there should not be any pleading or arguing; it is not possible to object to a judgement or verdict before it has been made, and a denial after the case has finished or after judgement has been proclaimed (*kyfreith*) is also quite pointless.

Q165

There does not seem to be a parallel outside of the triads for the rules found here.

mab ny bo pedeir bl6yd ar dec: The age of consent is 14 in medieval Welsh law (*Ior*, 98/5), and according to this triad the father should keep his son from taking arms before he is 14; if he does not and someone is killed or injured by his son, the father has to pay on his son's behalf. The child may have been allowed to train before the age of 14.

ynvyt kyhoeda6c: A known idiot; it is the kin's duty to keep the idiots from arms, possibly as their kin would have to take responsibility for their actions and pay on their behalf.

Q166. Mk98. DwC, 457

The triad found in *Mk* is a simple triad with no extension, though it is extended in the later versions. However, some complications occur during this process. The triad is found in *Tim*, *J*, *Q* and the *damweiniau* (*DwC*, 457). Of those manuscripts, *Tim* and *DwC* have the same version as that found in *Mk*, but with an extension. *J* does not copy the triad correctly, and seems to eyeskip, missing out the third limb and the first part of the extension, thus creating a meaningless triad (*Coleg yr Iesu LVII*, 137. 31–4). The triad occurs twice in *Q*, both in the extended triad collection (Q166) and in the tail of the manuscript, in a section which is also found in *J*, but the same version is found each time. *Q* appears to have made almost the same eyeskip as *J* but it is doubtful that *Q* was copying *J* directly, although *Q*'s version appears to be an attempt at an emendation of the faulty version as found in *J*; it is unlikely that the scribe of *Q*, in emending *J*, would leave out *bonhedic breiniawl*. The redactor of *Q*, however, may have attempted to correct a faulty original.

6yneb6erth: The earliest word for honour-price, and it is used for *sarhaed* (compensation for insult) in the laws of women, mainly to mean the payment to a man from his wife for a sexual offence (*WLW*, 220). *Q* has the corrupt version, *6yneb6erth ar sarhaet alltut*, but *DwC* seems to separate the two items. The punctuation in Jenkins's edition, however, does not assume that they are separate limbs (*DwC*, 457).

sarhaet alltut: The status of an *alltud*, an alien, was fixed by law and the law states that every man's *galanas* and *sarhaed* are augmented, apart from an alien's (*Bleg*, 58; *WML*, 44. 22–45. 3).

g6arthryd kelein: The shame or disgrace of a corpse. There is a triad discussing the three shames of a corpse: X70, above, and cf. X71.

Q167. S187, S199

Also found in *S*, there are a number of similar triads that are proverbial or gnomic in nature.

breint yny galler y broui: Special privilege until contrary proof is shown.

amot adeuedic: Cf. *WML*, 89. 11–12.

Q168

The following two triads are discussing inheritance and the children who are, in the first triad, not entitled to inheritance, and in the second, the sons whose inheritance is from their mother.

mab offeirat: The extension to the triad explains this further to prevent contradiction. According to Welsh law, any children a cleric of the lower orders has are acceptable (as long as the father recognizes them) but once he enters into the higher orders, as a subdeacon or above, the children are not acceptable. The redactors are careful in the terminology they use; *ysgolheic*, cleric, is someone who is not ordained; *offeirat*, priest, is someone in the order of priesthood; this distinction is found in Q74, above.

mab claf6r: Just as a leper should not beget a son, so also leprosy of a husband entitled the wife to a divorce (*Ior*, 45/4).

mab g6r a dalei tref y tat yn 6aetir: Cf. *Ior*, 87/2, 8, 9.

Q169. Latin: B25. Ior 53/5, 86/5

There is a triad dealing with the same material earlier on in the triad collection (Q71). Two of the items are the same, but the second limb found in this triad is not found in Q71. This triad is also longer than Q71 and gives an explanation for each of the limbs. The triad also occurs in Ior, twice; in 53/5 it is a simple triad with no extension, and 86/5 lacks the traditional heading for a triad – it begins with *e keureyth eyssyoes a dyweyt*. The triad is also in Latin B, written in Latin (*LTWL*, 225. 42–226. 4), but the emphasis is on the fact that the son will not otherwise have any *hereditas*. Each limb of this triad is dealing with aliens and the children they beget with Welshwomen; the difference in each item is how and why the child is begotten.

Q170. Col, 599, Ior 83/10; see also Q193

gorssed: This can mean many things in medieval Welsh but in *Q* it generally means court; there is a long triad on *gorsed dygunull* in *Q* (Q219, in the tail of *Q*). Two of the three are churchmen and the law of the church, or canon law, is often recognized in Welsh law as being a separate law (Pryce, *Native Law*, 215–16). The triad found in *Col* 599 and Ior 83/10 are very similar to the one in *Q*, but are simpler, with no extension.

Q171. z90

The following triads (to Q175) are on surety and gages, and some of the ideas expressed in the triads are found in the lawtexts. Often, they are found in the Ior surety tractate, which is a large section, and *Ior* 62 is on gages, but some of them are general ideas and have no parallels outside of the triad collection. The surety tractate in each of the lawtexts is interesting in that it usually contains a number of triads at relevant points, and *damweiniau* are also features of the tractate. The longest triad in this extended collection, triad Q196, relates to surety, and sections from the Cyfn surety tractate, not found elsewhere in *Q*, are appended to it.

g6anas g6ystyl: 'The means of conveyance or depository' of a gage (*Bleg*, 110. 15–21; cf. *PKM*, 200). According to the surety tractate, the gage should be a third more in value than the payment (*Ior*, 62/1–3).

lla6, a breich, ac ysg6yd: The person who takes the gage is to take it in his hand and put it on his shoulder, and then put it where it is to be kept, and if he does more than that, he loses the gage (*AL*, VIII. xi. 5). A gage is a third more than the debt (*Ior*, 62/2). Therefore, if the gaged item cannot be led or carried by one person – it may be too heavy, or too large – then it is a case where a large thing is being gaged for a small debt.

Q172

See *Ior*, 62, for gages.

Q173

vn a dycco ha6l6r y ar y mach or na mynnei 6assanaethu y vechni: See *Ior*. 66/1–5.

Q174

See *Ior*, 77/35.

mach o'r argl6yd: See *Ior*, 66/3, 4. This may be an attempt to stretch two items into three; in the preceding triads, one limb is given to the lord or his assistant, but here the lord and his assistants are separated to make two separate limbs.

Q176. Latin: *B53, E60. Ior, 51/11; Col, 6; DwC, 177–9*

This triad is one of the few triads from the extended collection that is not included in Book X of Ancient Laws, but it is found in the *damweiniau*, and also in the Ior tractate on women (*DwC*, 177–9; *Ior*, 51/11). There is also some overlap between *Q* and the separate collection found in *S* and *K* at this point, up to Q192.

y lle y kyscer genti: The version of this triad in the *damweiniau* adds that she should stay there for the sake of getting used to her new husband and his bed (*DwC*, 177).

y edrych a vu gyfreitha6l yd ysgar6ys y g6r a hi: There is some dittography in the *Q* version as these words are found in the next limb of *Q* as well. They clearly belong in the second limb, where they are found in *DwC*, not the first limb as found in *Q*.

lle yd yscaro a'e g6r: She should stay for nine days to see whether the separation was lawful; the same sentiment is found in Ior (*Ior*, 51/11). It is stated there that the woman should stay for nine days in the house, and then she may leave with all the belongings going before her (*Ior*, 51/11). This is also found in another triad as *tri chargychwyn* (see Q104); and she may not return afterwards.

Q177

chyghyauo6c: The form of the word found in *GPC* is *cynghafog*, a compound word from *cyngaf*, burdock, and *-og*, meaning thick branches. The meaning was further extended to mean complexities, although the only medieval example given is the *Q* version of this triad (*GPC*, q. v. *cynghafog*, 2).

Q178

This triad is very similar to X66 and Q96, above (*tri anifail untroediog*). The same animals are found in this triad and X66, but this triad has an explanation that is not found in *X*.

budyr: See *Ior*, 131/4–5. For a triad on the useless milks, see X27 and Q68. If a clean animal is found dead on another's land, the finder gets a quarter of the animal, but he only receives a penny for an unclean animal (*Ior*, 137/1–2).

annolo: Null and void (*Ior*, 75/6, 76/8, 77/8, 100/1).

Q179

mab gan y dat ac ef ar y vreint: This is also one of the blows that are not compensated; Q70, above. Once the son is over 14 years old he has his own status and any blow would have to be compensated. Cf. *Ior*, 98/1, 5.

g6reic gan y g6r am vn o'r tri acha6s kyfreitha6l: The three cases are given in the next triad, Q180, and these triads are another pair which need to be read together.

g6r gan y argl6yd: Also mentioned in the triad on the three blows not compensated (Q70), there the blow is during a day of battle; here no such situation is given.

Q180

maedu: To beat. These three cases are the legal cases where a man may beat his wife without having to pay *sarhaed*. Cf. *Ior*, 51/3; *Bleg*, 61. 14–19; Owen, 'Shame and reparation', *WLW*, 52; *DwC*, 411.

vna6 meuyl ar y uaryf: *DwC*, 411. However, the other option available to her husband is to strike her three blows with a rod as long as a man's forearm and as thick as a long finger, and he may strike her on any part of her body but her head (*Bleg*, 61. 16–17). This limb is included in the Ior version of the triad (*Ior*, 51/3), and other shameful words she may say to him are given in a triad (Owen, 'Shame and reparation', *WLW*, 52). The beard was significant in many cultures, and viewed as a symbol of virility, authority, wisdom and strength (Pickering, *Cassell Dictionary of Folklore*, 27, q. v. beard).

am gyfulauann arna6: This is a serious offence of some sort. Instead of this limb, giving something which she ought not to give is found in *Ior*, 51/3.

Q181. *Latin: A50, B33, E41*

There are several versions of this triad: the one found in land law in Bleg, Q225, which is similar to X68, and this version, which is closer to U9.

dylyet a mach arnaw, ac ada6 o'r kynogyn y 6lat: This is not found in Bleg or Cyfn, but Ior has a section where this item is set out in the surety tractate, and it refers to a version of this triad (64/1–2).

amrysson am teruynu ar 6yr: Ior again has this limb set out, naming it as one of the three; if the men are equal in rank and have the same entitlement to land, the land should be divided equally (*Ior*, 95/3).

ynys r6g y d6y auon: The only provision for this in the lawtexts apart from this triad is *DwC*, 232.

kyhyded: According to this triad, 'equality' is every pleading that is followed equally long and equally well. However, there are references to *keureyth kyhyded*, and that law is to divide equally (*Ior*, 77/31, 79/9, 80/2, 85/4; *Col*, 537; *DwC*, 26, 310).

Q182. W96. DwC, 162

This triad also occurs in *W* and *DwC*.

ouer groes: A cross was often used to mark boundaries. The idea of using a cross for such purposes probably originated with church lands but was expanded to include secular and privately owned lands. Pryce refers to a fine which was payable both to the lord and to the church when someone violated the rules regarding crosses: a *dirwy croes* occurs in an arbitration of 1252, the text of which is preserved in the 'Record of Caernarfon' but not in the lawtexts (Pryce, *Native Law*, 220). However, it suggests that the link between the church and using crosses in legal actions was still remembered. A cross was taken from the lord and placed in the land and, since bishops or abbots could be landowners, a cross could also be obtained from them (*AL*, XIV. xli. 30). Generally, the cross was a symbol of disputed lands being claimed (R. R. Davies, 'Twilight of Welsh law 1284–1536', 158). In the Welsh legal texts, however, the references to crosses are more widespread:

> Pawb a fo dylyet iddaw mewn peth a eill roi croes yn y peth yny ddosparther.

> Every body who may have a right to a thing, can place a cross in that thing, until it shall be settled. (*AL*, XIV. xli. 2)

In the lawtexts, a cross is placed on the land by the claimant, and the defendant is required to ask for legal action (*AL*, IV. iv. 1). A cross should be taken from the lord at all times, except one – in the case of a *priodor*, a rightful owner, claiming the land of his father used by another (*AL*, IX. xvii. 1). Placing a cross in Welsh law therefore prohibits use of land claimed to be unlawful and induces legal action (see Roberts, 'Legal practice in fifteenth-century Brycheiniog', 307–23).

croes a 6ahardo ll6ybyr a lyccro y yt: This is a difficult sentence, but it seems that what the scribe is trying to express is either a cross which obstructs a path to corn or which may damage the corn. *W* has a cross which is placed in a path through corn (*WML*, 143), and *DwC* has a cross on a path to protect/keep corn (*DwC*, 162).

ny hebryger a ll6: Someone must swear an oath that they will take legal action if they place a cross in something. In the *damweiniau, croes ar dyeprug a llu* is the wording, which seems to be the same as the *Q* reading (*DwC*, 162). *W*, however, does not have this limb; in its place, the case is that of a cross which a man places on an altar – the church may not interfere with it (*WML*, 143).

Q184

Q183 and Q184 appear to be a pair, not just because they are on similar topics but also because Q184 appears to refer back to Q183.

y neb a vo rodyat arnei: This is stated clearly in the tractate on women: whoever gives a woman to a man must pay her *amobr* (*Ior*, 48/1).

a hitheu e hun: See *Ior*, 58/1.

a'r vn a dy6edassam ni vchot: This appears to be referring back to the householder in a case of abduction in Q183.

Q185

One of a pair of triads on affiliation of children along with Q186, below. Normally, one triad is found for affiliation and another for rejection or denial; here, the pair of triads is concerned with who affiliates the child, the way in which he is affiliated, who accepts the child into the kindred and the way in which this is done. The process of affiliating a child to a kindred is found as a triad in the Cyfn collection, X40, which should be compared with this triad.

dygyat: The actual person who does the affiliation; cf. *cymeryat* in Q186. However, *kymeryat* occurs in *Ior*, 102/10, with a reference to a triad where it means the ways of accepting a child into a kindred. The same meaning is not found for *dygyat* in *Ior*.

y vam arna6 ar y llog6yd: A similar provision is found in Mk46 (see X40), but *lla6uaeth* is found rather than *llog6yd*. *Llog6yd* is in *GPC* but it is uncertain what it means; it may mean deathbed. If so, it may be difficult for the mother to follow the correct procedure as set out in *Ior*, 100/2.

Q186

chymeryat: The reverse of *dygyat*, the person or group who accept the child into the kindred.

a'r g6yr hynny nyt oes nodyat arnunt: This section is not found in Ior. The men needed to accept a son do not have to be anyone special, but they should not be entitled to share land with the son if he were to be affiliated (this is because they could reject him for their own personal gain).

or darffei vot mab ar ardel6 tat yn vab diodef: In Ior 102/4 a *mab dioddef* is a child affiliated by the mother and neither accepted nor denied by the father for a year and a day; here, however, *dioddef* refers to a failure on the part of the father to deny someone supposed to be his child when no affiliation has taken place.

Q187. *S215*

A triad dealing with execution, this is referring to theft, as theft is the main crime for which execution is the punishment in Welsh law.

yscolheic coruna6c: The triad states that he reverts to being a layman again; *DwC*, 372, explains that the reason he is not executed is that, if he has lost his status, he has been punished and it is not right to punish a person twice for the same crime. However, elsewhere *Llyfr y Damweiniau* does not treat a cleric any differently from anyone else; it is stated that, if he commits a crime, he must pay compensation and the church may do what it wishes with him (Pryce, *Native Law*, 134).

mab hyt tra uo ar vreint y tat: If a son commits a crime before he is 14 years old his father ought to be responsible (*Ior*, 98/1).

dyn agkyfieithus: There is some confusion in *Q* so the triad has been amended from *K*, and occurs in *S* and *Tim*; rather than *anghyuieith*, *Q* has *agkyfreithus*, unlawful, which is probably a miscopying for a word which occurs commonly in the laws, *anghyfreith*. Then, in the following line, there appears to be an attempt to make the error make sense: rather than *yni wypynt*, *Q* has *yny b6ynt*, until they are. There is another example of *Q* attempting to make sense from a confused passage in Q166 and Mk98. The *dyn agkyfieithus* is a foreigner who falls from a ship and lands in Wales; he does not speak the language and does not know the law of the land. Until he knows the law of the land the only punishment is that he repays the loser (*Col*, 406). However, according to Q78, he is entitled to have a representative to speak on his behalf in court. *DwC*, 8, states that nothing the foreigners (and the deaf) say in pleadings is used, as they do not understand what is said to them.

Q188. z72, s189

The three items in this triad are also found in another triad in the collection: Q194, below, *tri thlos kenedyl*.

Q189

These are also three of the four things which save a man from compurgation of the country for theft (Q69, above) and they are the three *arddelw* for an animal (*Ior*, 114/1).

Q191

None of the items here is found in the lawtexts apart from in this triad, but they are all quite self-explanatory.

or collei y dyn anyueil by6: The triad, as an extra paragraph, explains that if the man does not find his animal where he thought it would be, he cannot claim meat as a man cannot swear ownership to something which he cannot see (the man lost an animal, not meat, and the recognizable features are lost). There are provisions regarding stolen meat in the triad *tri chyhyryn canastyr* (X51, Q86).

yt ar y galaf: There is no compensation for corn damage after the corn has been removed from the field (cf. *Ior*, 155/4–5).

Q192

Another triad on gages, this triad would fit in with the group on gages and sureties found earlier on in the collection: (Q170–Q174). It may be a later addition which was not put with the other triads on the same topic.

telyn: There is a triad on harps: Q60, one of the first triads following the *tair rhwyd* series, and it is also in the short collection of triads in *Ior*, 42/10; (*Bleg*, 108. 8–12). The Bleg triads give a value for the tuning horn (twenty-four pence for that of a king and a *pencerdd*, twelve pence for that of a nobleman). The values also agree with the values for harps and tuning horns given in the equipment lists in Ior (*Ior*, 140/9–11; *LTMW*, 191, 192).

Q194. Latin: B29, E36, 82, [92]. Ior 88/2; Col, 617; DwC, 145–6. S275:
See also LTWL, 133. 1–3, 387. 3–6.

This is very similar to Q187. A version of this triad is found in the *damweiniau*, and in Ior, and these are the three precious things of a kindred (*DwC*, 145–6; *Ior*, 88/2). The *Q* triad states that the three items should not be shared but their fruits should; this is the same as in Q187. There is a version of the triad in Latin B29 and Latin E36 and 92 (*LTWL*, 231. 29–30, 482. 34–5, 509. 25–6); there is a non-triadic version in Latin D, but the items are not the same (*LTWL*, 387. 3–6). The cauldron, coulter and axe found in the similar triad, Latin E82, also occur in Latin A and Ior as the three things for which the smith receives payment if any special work is done (*LTWL*, 504. 16–7, 133. 1–3; *Ior*, 39/2; *LTMW*, 234).

melyn: Bleg states that a millstone is worth twenty-four pence, and the mill is worth a hundred and twenty, and all that is inside should be subject to *damdwng*, sworn appraisal (*Bleg*, 96. 2–4). *S*, however, states that a mill is worth a pound in its addition (see the variant reading).

choret: The weir is worth a pound in both *DwC* and *S* (*DwC*, 146).

pherllann: In *damweiniau*, every apple tree in the orchard has its own legal value; otherwise no legal value is given for an orchard (*DwC*, 147). *S* similarly states that every apple tree has a value, but there is some ambiguity regarding what the abbreviation *k* stands for. In *S*, *k* can represent *keinha6c* or *kyfreith*; James has expanded it here as *kyfreith* (James, 'Golygiad o BL Add. 22,356', 171).

Q195

This does not seem to be a triad but a section of the law (*Ior*, 88/3). There appears to be a copying error in *Q*, as the copier has mistaken *tir*, as found in the Ior version, for *tri*. The opposite of this mistake, *tri* for *tir*, is made in *J* in Q126, and *M* in Q137. Another significant point is that the previous triad, Q194, occurs in both Ior and *Col*, and is immediately preceded by this section in both versions of the law (*Col*, 617, 618).

Q196. DwC, 462–468

This also occurs in *Damweiniau Colan*, but the opening sentence is wrongly written as *halauc uechni* (*DwC*, 462; *LTMW*, 73–4, 251).

deua6t bala6c vechni y6: This triad is based on the metaphor of a buckle or a binding of some sort; the contract does not hold fast because one side of the bargain has not been kept, and as with a buckle, if the contract is tested it does not hold. This triad is not set out in most Bleg manuscripts, but there is a reference to it in the surety section; it is stated there that if one hand is wanting from the binding ceremony of the surety, then that is called a buckle surety (*Bleg*, 40. 9–14).

kyntaf y6 ohonunt: This is a case where a man (A) buys something from another (B) and A seeks a surety. B willingly gives the surety, and A goes to the surety, but A and the surety do not bind hands; they reach towards each other but their hands do not touch. This means that the contract is not binding: the ceremony of binding hands has to be carried out according to the lawtexts and all three hands need to come together when making a contract (*Bleg*, 40. 6–9; *LAL*, 19, 57).

eil y6 ohonunt: A very similar case to the previous one in the triad, here it is A who asks for a surety, and B says he will give it but does not touch the hand of the surety. So, the first and second situations in the triad are opposing situations: in the first case, the buyer does not bind hands with the surety, and in the second it is the seller and the surety who do not bind hands.

trydyd y6: This third case is a little different. The proctor (C) for the buyer, A, takes surety for the goods in the absence of A from the seller or debtor, B. There are three people present but the actual person involved in the contract, B, is not present; his representative is there. Bleg notes an exception to the rule of having the three hands coming together; that is, if a man becomes surety (*mach kynnogyn*, a paying surety) for himself or another (*Bleg*, 40. 11–12). However, this would not work in Gwynedd, where they rejected the *mach kynnogyn*.

sef achos y gel6ir y rei hynny yn teir bala6c: This final paragraph in the triad explains the metaphor used; if a buckle is pulled the wrong way, it releases, and if the sureties given here are pulled the wrong way, they too release; the contracts do not bind. This paragraph is the end of the triad as found in *Damweiniau Colan* and in *S*.

There now follows a long section on surety; it appears to be part of the previous triad, but as most versions of the triad do not contain this extra section, it must have been appended to the surety triad in *Q* as it is a convenient place to add more material on surety. The material is not triadic in form or organization, but it deals with the surety and is actually parts of the surety section in the Cyfn lawbooks. The section is edited, translated and discussed fully by Morfydd Owen in *Laywers and Laymen* (*LAL*: *Cyfn* 10–18, 23–30, 48–51, 186 and 187, 188 and 189, 192, 193). However, the final line in the section, stating that the lord will be surety on all unsuretied goods is not found in the Cyfn section; the principle is stated in *Ior*, 66/3.

Q197

This is a triad on animals that is not found in Cyfn, although Cyfn includes many triads on animals. These are the three animals whose value increases in one day. The reason their value increases is given in the triad: they change hands, and the animals are more valuable depending on who owns them, whether a king, an *uchelwr* or a bondsman. In another triad these are the three noble dogs (*WKC*, 272; *AL*, XIV. vi. 4; cf. *Bleg*, 97. 27–32, which does not mention the bondsman).

milgi: The greyhound had a special status which was lost if it was found without its collar (*WKC*, 268). There are many notes in the lawtexts on greyhounds. A king's greyhound is worth eight legal pence, and a nobleman's greyhound is worth four legal pence according to Bleg; their collars differ in value too (*Bleg*, 97. 27–32). Every greyhound breeder or keeper was to give four legal pence to the *pencynydd* when he entered the job (*Bleg*, 20. 16–19). According to the laws, the value of the greyhound in each of its stages was half that of the law for the king's staghound (*Bleg*, 53. 9–11).

gellgi: The staghound is worth double the value of the *milgi*, greyhound, at all stages of its development (*WKC*, 269–71). Bleg describes the staghound as the one dog whose value increases from four pence (when it is a bondsman's dog) to a pound (when a king's dog) in one day – a loose reference to this triad, although it is stated that only one dog has this feature (*Bleg*, 53. 15–18).

chol6yn: A lapdog; however, according to Ior, the nobleman's *colwyn* is worth more than his staghound; it is quasi-*sarhaed* if it is injured (*Ior*, 133/5; *LTMW*, 290). According to the lawtexts, all of the bondsman's dogs are worth the same (fourpence) except for the herd dog (*Bleg*, 53. 27–54. 3; *Ior*, 133/5).

Q198

Another triad on the value of animals, this deals with animals whose injury is the same value as their lives. This is also very similar to Q96 and Q178; the same animals are given in those triads and a sentence of explanation states that if their foot is injured, their legal value must be paid. In this triad, however, any injury has the same value as their lives. What is certain is that these three animals are the most valuable animals in the laws, and each is a hunting animal.

Q199

The third of a group of triads on animals, this triad is not found in the Cyfn collection. The animals given here reach their full value in one year; most animals in the lawtexts increase in value until they are fully grown (this usually takes more than a year; in the case of cattle, they are not fully grown for two years).

kosta6c tom: This is a dog, a dunghill cur, which has the same value whoever owns it (*Bleg*, 54. 3–4). It is also listed under the section *pethau unwerth*, things valued at four pence (*Bleg*, 87. 9–16). Its value increases from a penny (when its eyes are closed) to four pence when it is free or fully grown (*Bleg*, 53. 23–7).

dauat a gafar: In the laws both sheep and goats are listed together. The paragraph for sheep is much shorter than for the other animals so it seems that sheep (and goats) were not the most popular animals in medieval Wales. A lamb goes from a penny (when it is suckling) to four legal pence in August; goats have the same value (*Bleg*, 93. 1–10). According to modern-day sheep farmers, this section is very accurate: if a mountain lamb is born in March, it will be fully grown and ready for the market by August or September, by which time it will have its eight teeth; it is fully grown in five days less than five months.

Q200

o keinia6c hyt ym pedeir: The trained justice gets four pence from every case which pays that much, and he gets his payment from the one the value was adjudged to (*Bleg*, 16. 13–15). This rule is not applicable to the justice by virtue of land: he has to work for free, as the work is part of his ownership of land (*Bleg*, 99. 9–11). He is bound to judge freely to the officers of the court (*Ior*, 10/13).

Q202. *S10*

This sentence is not actually a triad, and is found in the *sarhaed, galanas a gwerth* section of Bleg manuscripts (*Bleg*, 59. 10–11). It seems to have been mistaken for a triad by the redactor of *Q*.

Q204

This triad is a version of one found earlier in the collection (Q173). The only difference is that there is an extra limb in this version; in Q173, the final limb here, *mach o'r argl6yd neu y 6assanaeth6yr*, is treated as two limbs. Here, the second limb is the additional one.

Q205. *S254*

This triad is almost identical to Q61, above – only the extension is different. In this triad the two options are given: what some lawyers think, and what the law says. According to the law, if the bondsman sold the items they are not returned but, if he did wrong, the lord may punish the deed. In Q61, it is stated that, if the lord refuses to exercise his right of pre-emption, he may sell them to whoever he wishes.

Q206

See Q156.

End of Q *Triad Collection*

Q207

In both branches of the Bleg redaction, this triad is found in a section on *rhaith gwlad a dedfryd gwlad* (*Bleg*, 106–7). This is similar to the final triad in the *Mk* collection, Mk135, but no extension is found in the *Mk* triad. Each item of this triad gives the options available to someone during a legal case: to admit, deny or defend, while further details are given on procedure in the extension.

Q208–Q213

These triads are a section on *swydd a braint brawdwr*, on the subject of the justice and his duties.

Q214. *J169*

Triads Q214-Q219 form part of the material which the redactor of *Q* has appended to the section. Several of them also occur in other later manuscripts, such as *S*, *Tim* and *J*, and several of the shorter triads also occur in *Z*. This particular triad is also found in *J*, as the last item in the manuscript, and is in a different hand to the remainder of *J*. It is a later addition in *J*. The triad is on a general topic – the justice should listen to evidence and listen to the litigants before judging. A justice by virtue of land would not have had formal training, and such a triad may have been necessary as a guideline.

Q215. S175

Also found in *S*, the triad lists the three pleadings which a justice is not allowed to judge – the first has witnesses to prove the matter, the second is the king's business, and the third is to state that a man is entitled to *dadannudd*: it seems that, if a man is actually entitled to *dadannudd*, there is no need for a justice to judge it as it is already lawful. Q215 and Q216 may be Ior material.

Q216. S156, Tim98

The triad is also found in *J*, as triadic material but not set out as a triad: the section starts with *deall tremyc barn*, lists three cases of *tremyg cyndrychol* (see the triad in *S* and *Tim*) numbering the second and third items, and then presents *tremyg absen*, listing two items, numbering the second only (*Coleg yr Iesu LVII*, 127). The triad in *S* and *Tim* give the opposite of the triad in *Q*, but both triads are on the subject of contempt in court – in the *Q* triad, the three cases happen before the time is right for the claimant, and so he is absent; in *S* and *Tim* the judgements also happen at the wrong time.

Q217. S154, Tim96

This triad is one of three long triads found in this section of the tail of *Q*, and each of the three explains complex procedural matters – pertaining to the justice and his duties – in a triadic form. It could be said that each of the three triads are a tractate, and they appear to be later developments in Welsh law. They are listed as sections of law rather than as individual triads in Christine James's edition, suggesting that they are legal explanations or essays set out in the triadic form rather than actual triads. Each of the following triads, including the extended triads, deals with the administration of law and the justice's office.

Q218. S161, Tim103, LatD32

Found in the later Bleg manuscripts, but also in Latin D, there are two versions of this triad – the *Q* version being slightly different to that found in the other manuscripts, although the differences are largely labelling: the triad in *Q* gives situations, whereas the triad in the other manuscripts gives the three complainants, in the same three situations as those in *Q*. Both triads list the punishments as well. The three wrong plaints are to do with giving pledges against a judgement (i. e. accusing a justice of making a wrong judgement), but in each case the case fails. In the first instance, written authority is found for the judgement, in the second, the pledge is not given by the man who received the judgement personally, and the third pledge is given by a man who is not entitled to give pledges against judgements. The punishments for the three cases are high: *camlwrw* for the second two, and the value of the tongue for the first.

Q219. S155, Tim97

See Q217.

Q220–Q231

These are found in the land law tractate. Q220–Q224 are a short collection of triads in all Bleg manuscripts. They were seen as a fixed collection from an early date, and some are found in the Cyfnerth manuscripts.

Q229, Q230. J164, J165

These two triads form part of the additional land law material in *Q*, and are both taken from Ior. They are also found in the Ior tail of *J*.

Q231. J166, S157, Tim99

Another extended triad, similar in style to Q217 and Q219.

Q230a, Q230b

These triads are taken from $\mathcal{E}$, as the middle leaf of a quire was lost when *Q* was rebound. They are part of the additional material on land law, and only Q230b occurs in other sources – it is in *S* and *Tim*. Both of the triads appear to be later material.

Q232–Q235

Not a consecutive group of triads, they are found in the laws of women in Bleg. See *WLW*.

Q235

Again additional material in *Q*, not found in any other law manuscript. On the subject of sexual offences, the men of the three women listed would not receive compensation for adultery. The word *gwr* (husband) is used, but the three situations are not lawful marital unions – the first is abduction, the second is a publicly known love-affair and the third is a woman of bush and brake – but the three situations were legally recognized sexual unions according to the list of nine unions found as *naw cynyweddi teithiog* (see Charles-Edwards, *WLW*, 23–39), and the triad makes it clear that the men who do not receive compensation are the ones who are taking part in the three unions. It is uncertain why they would want compensation – perhaps the women have moved on to another union in each case.

Q236

See X8.

Q237–Q242

Q237, Q239 and Q240 are found together as a section called *cynefodau* in all other Bleg manuscripts, but seem to have been separated by another triad in *Q*. In L-type Bleg, this section is found following the value of animals, and there is only one other section between it and *arferion cyfraith*. Q238, Q240 and Q241 are found in the closing sections of Bleg manuscripts, on the practices of law.

Triads From the Tail of Manuscript Q

Several triads are found in the tail of *Q*, as well as *damweiniau*, sections of law taken from other redactions, such as the Ior, and sections which are not found in any other source. Some of the triads listed below are found in manuscript *S*, three in manuscript *Tim*, two in Latin D, and only one in manuscript *J*.

Q243. S163, Tim105

Marking the beginning of the tail in *Q*, as it is not found in most other Bleg manuscripts, this triad may have been placed here as it is loosely related to the subject discussed previously. It is a short triad listing the three high courts in Wales: Aberffraw, Dinefwr and Mathrafal. In *S*, this section is found towards the beginning of the tail, between two sections on *mechniaeth*.

Q244

Only occurring elsewhere in *S*, this triad is found just before the beginning of the book of *damweiniau* in the tail of *Q*. It is another general triad on things which are and are not allowed in law.

Q245

See X12.

Q246. J168, Tim161

In *J*, it is in the tail of the manuscript, but it is not found in Ior. See Q166.

Q247

Only appearing in *Q*, this triad lists situations where a legal case cannot be brought against someone, and in each case the person is indisposed – either taking part in a war, on pilgrimage, or suffering from a mortal wound or illness. In these three special cases, carrying on with the case is suspended, presumably until the men are able to return and deal with the claim against them.

Q248. S204

Q248–Q250 are consecutive in *Q*, but they do not appear to be related to each other or to the material surrounding them, and two of them occur elsewhere in *Q*. For this triad, see Q54.

Q249. S186

The only one of the group of three which does not occur elsewhere in the manuscript, the triad gives a concept not found elsewhere in Welsh law, that of the middle man. Although *cena6l* can literally mean centre or middle, it does appear to refer to a person in this case.

Q250

A version of this triad occurs earlier on in *Q* – see Q5.

Q251. *S203*

Appearing as a consecutive group of five, some of the following triads occur in the tail of *S*, but are not consecutive there. Most of these triads are on the subject of court procedure. This triad contains another triad – it lists the three witnesses who can be objected to, but also has a reference to the triad giving the three situations for objecting to witnesses, found in most Cyfnerth manuscripts, and also in Bleg – see Q38, and also Q190.

Q252

This triad is only found in *Q*, and is self-explanatory. The *lli6at* appears to be the same as the *manag6r*, see Q159. There are no other references to the contract-man in the triads.

Q253. *S168*

Another triad on aspects of court procedure which are not permitted, this lists the three things which a representative in court is not allowed to argue – it appears that the person has to be present himself. The third limb may be an addition, as it does not fit in as well with the subject of the triad – rather than being a legal case which the representative would not be permitted to argue, it is a situation where someone is dying, and it is uncertain why a representative would not be allowed to act in that case, as the person could not appear in court himself.

Q254. *S182*

There are two versions of this triad, although the concept and the content is largely the same in both *S* and *Q*. The three men are dangerous or refusing to adhere to law, and need someone to act on their behalf to guarantee their good conduct even though there is no legal case against them.

Q255

This triad occurs in Ior, in the section on the value of limbs and injuries.

Q256. *[S255], LatinD38. Z101*

One of the two triads found in the tail of *Q* which appear in Latin D. See X75.

Q257

Q257–Q260 are another consecutive group, and again, these triads do not appear to be related in subject. This triad is one of the few triads on surreption, *anghyfarch*, a situation where someone takes an item (often an animal) without the owner's permission, but it is not a case of theft; rather, it is borrowing without consent. In this triad, the surreption is acknowledged, but there is no punishment as, in the second two limbs, the surreption happened to deal with an emergency situation. The first limb is different, and does not appear to fit in with the rest of the triad.

Q258. LatinD34

The *camlwrw* was a serious fine payable to the king or the lord, and a double *camlwrw* would only be paid in very serious circumstances. In this triad, the first two limbs set out such serious situations: a tongue-wound to the king, or interfering with justices as they are doing their work. The third limb does not fit in as it gives a situation where only one *camlwrw* is paid. There is a series of triads on *camlwrw* in Z, where the situations for one *camlwrw*, twofold and threefold *camlwrw* are set out. See Z111–Z113.

Q259. S264, Tim144

Also found in *S* and *Tim*, this triad seems to give four faultless pursuits in law rather than three. It gives the steps in the legal process from the starting point, a plaint, until termination is reached.

Q260. S200

The reference in this triad to the law of heirs is mysterious, as there is no such section in the Welsh lawbooks, but it seems that the three situations given in this triad are where someone unusual – not a family member or a son – inherits goods on another man's death, although the first limb of the triad is rather unclear.

Q261. S159, Tim101

Found in both *S* and *Tim*, this triad lists the three cases which are not included in the Welsh law. It is not in a section of similar material.

Appearing in both *S* and *Q* this is the only triad in manuscript *Q* to have a title in red: *am teir diaspat y6ch adneu* is written on the line before the triad. It is followed by several sections with titles but none of the sections which follow are triads. This is the final triad in the manuscript, and it is a land law triad. The concept is found in other manuscripts but it is only found as a triad in the two manuscripts listed.

diaspat y6ch aduan: In Ior, the phrase is 'dyaspat uuch Annuuen', *annwfn* being the underworld in Welsh mythology (*Ior*, 85. 7, and note; see also *LTMW*, 263). The saying is found in several different forms in the Welsh law manuscripts – apart from *annwfn* and similar forms, there is also *adnau* and *aduan* (*Col*, 582n.). The section in Ior is also found in *Col* and the tail of *J*, and it is the first, and fullest, limb found in this triad – the cry of a man whose status changes from being a proprietor to land to being a non-proprietor, and losing ownership of the family land. It is likely that this triad was formed around the first limb, as the first limb is detailed and long, whereas the second and third limbs are only a sentence each. Also, there is a short extension to the triad, following the third limb, on the same topic – proprietorship. The second and third limb of the triad are also Ior concepts, but not a great deal of detail is found on either topic in Ior, and there is no section for the final two limbs comparable to the section on the first limb of this triad in Ior.

Appendix 1. Triads in the additional collection in *K* and *S*

These are the triads which do not also occur in the extended triad collection in *Q*. Corrections from *S*.

K15. S220 [128]

Tair craith gogyuarch ynt:[1] craith ar 6ynep, ac ar la6, ac ar troet. Am y gyntaf, g6erth g6aet a g6eli a gogyuarch teir g6aith; am yr ail, g6erth g6aet a g6eli a gogyuarch d6y 6eith; am y tryted, g6erth g6aet a g6eli a gogyuarch un 6eith. Sef achos i ragora cosp yn[2] y kyntaf yn u6y noc yn[3] yr ail, ac yn[4] yr ail yn[5] u6y noc yn[6] y dryded, cans amlycaf ac u[r]dedicaf y6'r graith ar 6ynep nac ar la6, ac ar la6 noc ar droet; 6rth hynny, i drycheif yr honn rac y llall.

K19. S224 [129]

Tri argae t*e*ruyn: braint, a chyng6archad6, a phriodolt*e*r. Sef ual i mae hynny:[7] breinioc a argae rac amreinioc i deruyn, cani dyly amreinioc t*e*ruynu ar[8] dyn a braint ida6; a heuyt p*r*ioda6r a argae rac amp*r*ioda6r,[9] kani [130] dyly t*e*ruynu arno; ac i gita hynny, hen 6archad6 a argae[10] rac un a uo iav noc ef. Cyt b6ynt deu p*r*iodor o gymreint,[11] a chyt y6 g6archad6, ac un ry6 p*r*iodorion, ac na

---

[1]   − *S*
[2]   am *S*
[3]   am *S*
[4]   am *S*
[5]   am *S*
[6]   am *S*
[7]   + braint *S*
[8]   + dor *S*
[9]   a argae rac amprioda6r] − *S*
[10] + tervyn *S*
[11] ogymerieid *S*

Translation of the triads in the additional collection in *K* and *S*

K15

These are the three conspicuous scars: a scar on the face, and on a hand, and on a foot. For the first, three times the value of blood and wound and noticeability; for the second, twice the value of blood and wound and noticeability; and for the third, one times the value of blood and wound and noticeability. The reason the punishment for the first is greater than for the second, and the second greater than for the third, because a scar on the face is more obvious and unconcealed that on a hand, and that on a hand [more] than that on a foot; because of that, one is augmented more than the other.

K19

Three stays of a boundary: status, and priority of occupation, and proprietorship. This is how that is: a person of status may enclose his boundary against a person without status, as a person without status is not entitled to fix a boundary against a person who has status; and also a proprietor may enclose against a non-proprietor, as he [the latter] is not entitled to fix a boundary against him; and in the same way, an old occupation may enclose against one which is more recent than it.

6ypo henadurieit y 6lat y ia6n ter*u*yn rydynt, rannu deu hann*er* a dylyir her6yd
k*yfreith* cyhyded.

K20. *S225* [130]

Dadl am dir a daear
Tri datleu am tir ni dlyir aros un amser m6y no'i gilyd amdanunt: tir llann, a thir
a uynner i ter*u*ynu, a rannu tir.

K27. [133]

Tri mach ni dlyir eu g6adu: mach ar obyr yngnat, a mach ar k*yfreith*, a mach i'r
argl6yd neu i 6assanaeth6yr.

K28. [133]

Tri lle o rodir mach yn duhun ni dlyir i 6adu: kyoedogr6yd pl6yf, a gorsed k*yfreithi*ol, neu rac bronn argl6yd, 6rth uot y tri lle hynny yn tri kyoedogr6yd
k*yfreithi*ol, ac nat oes dim a 6neler ynghyoedogr6yd y dlyir i 6adu.

K34. [134]

Tri phriot g6r: i uarch, a'i arueu, a'i 6ynep6erth gan i 6raic.

K39. *S240* [135]

Tri aryf k*yfreithi*ol ysyd:[12] kledyf, a g6ae6, a b6a a xii saeth. G6erth kledyf
[g6einsyth], xxiiii; o byd breulif, xvi; o byd g6ynsaid[13] [deudec keinha6c].
G6erth pop un o rai[14] ereill, xi[15] k*einioc*.

[12] – *S*
[13] g6einsyth *K*, grymsaid *S*
[14] dau *S*
[15] pedeir *S*

Should they both be proprietors of equal status, and their occupation equally long, and they are the same kind of proprietors, and the elders of the country do not properly know how to set the boundary between them, it ought to be divided in half according to the law of equality.

K20.

A case for land and earth
Three land cases which are not entitled to have any delay for them more than the other: church land, and land upon which there is a wish to fix a boundary, and dividing land.

K27

Three sureties which should not be denied: a surety for the justice's fee, and a surety on law, and a surety [given] to the lord or his servants.

K28

Three places where if surety is given promptly it ought not to be denied: in the publicity of a parish, and a lawful session, or before a lord, as those three places are the three lawful public places, and nothing done publicly ought to be denied.

K34

Three unclaimable things of a man: his horse, and his arms, and his *wynebwerth* from his wife.

K39

There are three legal weapons: a sword, and a spear, and a bow with twelve arrows. The value of a white-bladed sword, twenty-four [pence]; if it is ground on the stone, sixteen [pence]; if it is straight-bladed, twelve pence. The value of every other one, eleven pence.

K41. S242 [135]

Tri ysgyuaetheu[16] milgi: ysgyuarnoc, a i6rch, a ll6ynoc. Sef achos i gel6ir y rai hynny yn ysgyuaetheu[17] milgi, cans y cyntaf a'i cyuoto bieufyd, oni bai[18] un peth, kyuaruot k6n[19] argl6yd a'r ll6dyn a gyuotei g6n map uchel6r; pa g6n bynac a gyuotei un o'r tri hynny[20] a'i ysgyuaetheu[21] o uilgi, ef [a'e] bieuyd.

---

[16] assgavaeth *S*
[17] asgavaetheu *S*
[18] oni bai] onyd *S*
[19] + y brenhin neu g6n yr *S*
[20] enifeil *S*
[21] asgafaethe *S*

K41

Three preys of a greyhound: a hare, and a roebuck, and a fox. This is the reason those three are called the preys of a greyhound, because the first one who raises it owns it, apart from one case, when the hounds of a king meet with an animal raised by the hounds of a nobleman; whichever hounds raised one of those three and it becomes a greyhound's prey, he owns it.

Notes

K15

This triad is not found in *Q* or the main Bleg collection, but a short version of it does occur in *U*, *V*, *W* and *Z* (Cyfn), and also in Ior, as part of the value of limbs tractate (*Ior*, 147. 10–13). The version found here and that in the Cyfn manuscripts give the same scars: on a hand, a foot and on the face, but all the Cyfn manuscripts also specify that the scar is on the right hand. This distinction is not made in the version given here, and the distinction is not made in the tractate on the value of limbs in Bleg (*Bleg*, 56. 21–8). The values for the scars are the same in Ior and Cyfn, but in this version from *K*, the reader has to work out the value given in the extension. The extension also explains why the first scar, that on the face, is the most expensive – it is most visible. In Bleg, a broken front tooth is the same value as a scar on the face, as it is disfiguring (*Bleg*, 56. 21–2).

gogyuarch: Conspicuous or visible. In Welsh law injuries had to be paid for according to their worth, but scars which were not on show did not have a value in Bleg. Ior states that hidden scars are worth four pence (*Ior*, 147. 10).

K19

This triad is also found in Latin E, twice in the tail of *S* (S173 and S274, both short versions), towards the beginning of the triad collection in manuscript *U*, and in the main text of manuscripts *W* (on a section on dividing land). The Cyfn version is similar to the one found here, without the extension, but the Latin E version has different limbs.

argae teruyn: *Argae* can mean 'stay'; see Mk71 for *argae gwaed*. However, here it seems to be the verb, 'to enclose'. The three limbs give three different statuses of landowners, who are able to enclose land and set their borders as, in each limb, they have a right to do so due to being of higher status. The final section of the extension is also found in another triad: see Q181.

K20

Only found in this collection in *S* and *K*, the three cases for land listed in this triad need to be settled without delay. It is not made clear why there ought not to be delay in these cases.

llann: According to some of the lawbooks, there was no need to wait for the appointed time for land cases if the land involved was church land (Pryce, *Native Law*, 207). The provisions behind this triad are all found in Ior, in the land law tractate: the reason church land can be dealt with at any time is because it is not of 'our' law, that is, it is a different law to *Cyfraith Hywel* (*Ior*, 81/13).

teruynu: Setting boundaries is allowed to be dealt with in the legal way at any time, rather than during the set periods for land law (*Ior*, 81/12).

rannu tir: Similar to the previous triad, the laws for dividing land are discussed in Q181 as well as elsewhere in the laws. It is stated that dividing land can happen at any time, including the times when law is closed for land (*Ior*, 81/15).

K27, K28

This triad and the following are examples of the numerous triads on surety, and list cases where a person cannot deny that a surety has been given. In the scenarios listed in both triads, the sureties have either been given by people of high status, or have been given publicly and therefore cannot be denied.

K34

This triad is not found elsewhere, although it is similar to the triad on the three things which the king is not entitled to sell. One would expect a matching triad on the three unclaimable things of a woman, but none is given in this collection. There is, however, a triad on the three privy things of a woman given in *S*; they are her *cowyll* (similar to morning gift), compensation for her disgrace, and her *sarhaed*.

K39

This triad is not found anywhere else. In Bleg, in the list of the value of goods, these are the only weapons mentioned, although a knife occurs after the bow and arrows (but it may not have been classed as a weapon even though it could be used in that way) and a shield is also found (*Bleg*, 98. 11–19). Only two swords are offered in the list in Bleg and the values are a little different, and this triad seems to match the Ior version of the tractate more closely (*Ior*, 141. 18–21). However, two of the swords are confused in the manuscripts – unsurprising as their names are very similar. The first of the three swords is just called a sword, *kledyf*, in *S* and *K*, but it is clear from Ior that there are three different swords: *gweinsyth*, *gwynsaid* and *breulif*. The value of the first sword in *S* and *K* is given as twenty-four pence, and in Ior, that would be the *gweinsyth* (straight-bladed) sword. However, the third sword named in *K* is *gweinsyth*, but the value of a *gwynsaid* (white-bladed) sword as found in Ior is given. In *S*, the third sword is called *grymsaid*, which may be an attempt at *gwynsaid*, white-bladed. In any event, the value is the same as that given for a white-bladed sword in Ior.

K41

This triad is only found in *S* and *K*.

ysgyuaetheu: The preys. This triad is referring to three special preys, as the first person whose dogs catches one of these three animals in the hunt is allowed to keep the animal. This is different to the other hunting laws found in the Welsh lawtexts.

Appendix 2. Triads from the Latin texts

These triads are found in the Latin texts, and do not appear to have corresponding Welsh triads in the Welsh manuscripts.

Latin A

LatA31. B50, E58 [*LTWL*, 128. 25–7; 243. 19–20, 494. 27–8]

Tribus de causis non potest corpus malefactoris redimi: pro latrocinio, si fuerit confessus; proditione domini sui, id est, *brat*; homine furtim occiso.

LatA37. B49, E57 [*LTWL*, 129. 18–9; 243. 15–6, 494. 24]

Tri agcheuarch gwr: equus et arma, et quicquid redditur ei de terra sua, et ea que in *wynebwerth* habebit.

LatA42. B32, E40 [*LTWL*, 129. 31–2; 242. 15–7, 493. 22–4]

Tres homines non sunt occidendi: scilicet, rex, sacerdos, et *kerdaur*. Et ideo *galanas* eis secundum leges non est constitutum.

Latin B

LatB14. E7 [*LTWL*, 216. 26–9; 458. 26–7]

Tres manus oportet convenire ad constituendum quem fideiussorem: scilicet, manus dantis, fideiussoris, et accipentis.

Translation of the triads from the Latin texts

Latin A

LatA31

In three cases the body of a wrongdoer cannot be redeemed: for theft, if he confessed to it; for betrayal of his lord, that is, *brad* [betrayal]; for killing a man by stealth.

LatA37

The three unassailables of a man: his horse and his arms, and having his land returned to him, and that which he has as his *wynebwerth*.

LatA42

Three men must not be killed: namely a king, a priest and a *cerddor* [poet]. And accordingly no *galanas* has been settled for them under the laws.

Latin B

LatB14

There are three hands that should come together to establish a surety: namely, the hand of the creditor, of the surety and of the debtor.

LatB52. E59 [*LTWL*, 243. 23–5; 494. 29–31]

Tres sunt qui debent habere *guirawt* de curia: scilicet, faber curie, preco, *trulliat.* Mensura potus est plenitudo vasorum de cervisia, dimidium de *bragaut,* tercia pars de medone.

LatB57. [*LTWL*, 243. 39]

Teir gorsaf unben: geueil, erhyl, kennadyl.

LatB58. E62 [*LTWL*, 244. 1–3; 495. 1–2]

Tria animalia debet *costauc tom* habere pre leporariis et molosis, si ceperit prius ante ipsos: id est, lepus, capreus, et vulpis.

LatB59. E63, 83 [*LTWL*, 244. 4–5; 495. 3–4, 504. 27]

Tri argay teruin: scilicet, amnis a monte usque ad mare; et molina; et eclesia, vel *pentan.*

LatB72. E84 [*LTWL*, 259. 24–7; 507. 7–9]

Tres sunt qui dicuntur *tri tremyg argluyd*, et pro quolibet redduntur novies viginti denarii: videlicet, crucem suam frangere; placitum contra ius relinquere; et nuntium suum verberare.

Latin E

LatE25. [*LTWL*, 469. 30–1]

Tres sunt libere venaciones villano: videlicet, *croclach, slepan, annel.*

LatB52

There are three who ought to have *gwirawd* [liquor] from the court: namely the smith of the court, the *rhingyll*, the *trulliad*. The amount of the drink is containers full of beer, half of *bragaut* [bragget], a third part of mead.

LatB57

Three stoppings of a ruler: a smithy, a hunt, pleadings.

LatB58

There are three animals which a dunghill cur ought to have in preference to the greyhounds and hound dogs, if it catches them before those [hounds]: they are, a hare, a wild goat, and a fox.

LatB59

Tri argae teruin [the three stays of a boundary]: namely, a river from a mountain to the sea; and a mill; and a church, or *pentan* [hearthstone].

LatB72

There are three [things] which are called *tri tremyg arglwydd* [the three contempts of a lord], and for each of them nine score pence are paid: namely, to break his cross; to abandon a legal hearing contrary to justice; and to beat his messenger.

Latin E

LatE25

There are three free huntings for a villain: *croclach* [springe], *slepan* [gin], *annel* [snare].

LatE72. [*LTWL*, 502. 17–23]

Tres sunt qui, si iniuriam invenerunt, nullum ius habebunt: videlicet, *maer y bisweil* inter coquinam et aulam inventus et a ministris regis iniuriatus; hostiarius ultra longitudinem sue virge extra ostium inventus dum rex in aula sedet; tercius, qui citacionem fecerit super *maer*, et in illa citacione iniuriam passus erit. Quartus, preco sedens presente rege in placito; qui non habet pro qualibet iniuria nisi cribrum avene et testam ovi.

LatE74. [*LTWL*, 502. 31–40]

Tria sunt forefacta regis. Forefactum duorum hominum vel plurium qui bellum faciunt donec utriusque querela venerit ad curiam. Secundum est cum aliquis femine vim facit, si femina suum iudicium faciat. Quilibet istorum reddet iii vaccas. Tercium, latro si rem furari calumpniatur, et res in manu eius manifeste non habetur. Ipse debet affirmare se esse salvum iuramento xii virorum, scilicet, *guercheitweit*. Et si illorum iuramentum ei deficiat, tamen de suo ore salvus est. Talis deficiente iuramento reddet xii vaccas. Si autem unum istorum trium *yn llys neu yn llan* fuerit, pro quolibet xxiiii vacce reddantur.

LatE79. [*LTWL*, 504. 4–7]

In tribus locis debet rex persequi vulnus lingue, licet ille cui iniuria facta est nichil inveniat: in curia vel placito regis; in ecclesia coram sacerdote et plebe; in cimiterio coram populo.

LatE81. [*LTWL*, 504. 14–5]

Tria sunt pro quibus non debetur refugium in nullo si non negantur: videlicet, *goruodogaeth, mechniaeth, goreskyn.*

LatE72

These are the three who, if they meet with *sarhaed*, they shall have no legal remedy: namely, *maer y biswail* if he is found between the kitchen and the hall and *sarhaed* is done to him by the officers of the king; a doorkeeper found further out from the door than the length of his stick whilst the king is seated in the hall; the third, the person who makes a summons to the *maer*, and in that summons he suffers *sarhaed*. Fourth, the *rhingyll* seated in the presence of the king during a legal hearing; he does not receive anything for whatever *sarhaed* apart from a sieve of oats and the shell of an egg.

LatE74

These are the three forfeitures of the king. The forfeiture of two men or more if they wage war until the complaint of each come to the court. The second is if someone takes a woman by force, if the woman brings her own lawsuit. Anyone of those shall pay three kine. The third, a thief if he is accused of stealing something, and the thing is not clearly seen to be in his hand. He should confirm that he is innocent by the oath of twelve men, namely, *gwarcheidwaid*. And if the oath of these fails him, nevertheless he is saved by his own mouth. Such a person, whom the oath fails, shall pay twelve kine. If any of those three should occur in court or in church-enclosure, twenty-four kine should be paid for them.

LatE79

In three places the king ought to prosecute tongue-wound, although he to whom the *sarhaed* was done discovers nothing: in the court or the session of the king; in the church in the presence of the priest and the people; in the cemetery in the presence of the people.

LatE81

There are three things for which refuge is not owed in any place, unless they are denied: namely, *goruodogaeth* [bailsmanship], *mechniaeth* [suretyship], *goresgyn* [conquest].

Latin D: triads that are not in Q or Bleg

LatD32. [354. 23–34]

Tres sunt rei conquestores a rege propter querelas suas puniendi. Primus est qui det pignus contra iudicium quod per aliud, id est, *gwrthwystyl*, et auctoritatem scriptam de legibus contra ipsum poterit confirmari; ille precio lingue sue debet puniri. Secundus, qui det pignus contra iudicium quod super aliquem alium quam seipsum detur; ille suo *camlwrw* debet puniri. Tercius est, si quis careat dignitate impignorandi, ut sacerdos vel alius; licitum est ei contradicere iudicio per auctoritatem de legibus. Et si sic contradicat, et auctoritas ei fallat, *camlwrw* amittat. Nemo autem per iudicium litigiosum amittet plus quam *camlwrw* ubi non sit impignoracio vadio contra vadium.

LatD33. [354. 35–41]

Tres sunt querimonie in quibus calumpnia verbo ad verbum non pertinet, id est, *geir tra geir*, sed ostendi. Prima est querela de terra, quia super eam veritas per *dedwryd gwlad* debet procedere. Secunda, de *galanas*, quia responsum de *galanas* gentibus occisi debet dari, et non uni soli. Tercia, de iudicio quod per auctoritatem legis contradicetur, quia super hoc veritas de libro legis debet ostendi et recipi utrum sit rectum vel non rectum.

LatD143. [382. 26–32]

Tria solum sunt iudicia in lege constituta, et nullum iudicium est tenendum nec audiendum in curia preter illa. Primum est iudicium iudicis curie regis cotidiane. Secundum est iudicium iudicis *swytawc* commoti vel cantredi. Tercium est iudicium curie in qua non sit iudex *swytawc*, sed iudices per dignitatem curie. Nullius eorum autem solius iudicium est tenendum, sed unius solius eorum est referre iudicium commune ipsorum omnium.

Latin D: translation

LatD32

There are three complainants who should be punished by the king for their disputes. The first is he who should give a pledge in relation to a judgement which can be confirmed against him through another pledge, that is, *gwrthwystl*, and the written authority of the law; that person should be punished to the value of his own tongue. The second is the one who should give a pledge in relation to a judgement which may be given concerning someone other than himself; that person should be punished to the value of his own *camlwrw*. The third is, if someone should lack the status to give a pledge, such as a priest or someone else; it is permitted for him speak against the judgement by the authority of the law. And if he does speak against it thus, and the authority should fail him, he should lose his *camlwrw*. But no one will lose more than his *camlwrw* through a contested judgement when the giving of a pledge is not a pledge against a pledge.

LatD33

These are the three disputes in which an accusation does not belong to a word [referring] to word, that is, *geir tra geir*, but should be shown. The first is a case for land, because concerning this proof ought to proceed through verdict of the country. The second, concerning *galanas*, because an answer ought to be given about *galanas* to the kindreds of the one killed, and not to one person alone. The third, concerning a judgement which is contradicted by the authority of law, because the proof of this ought to be shown according to a lawbook and accepted whether it is right or not.

LatD143

These are only three judgements established in law, and no judgement is to be maintained or heard in a court apart from them. The first is the judgement of a judge of the daily court of the king (*ynad llys beunyddiol*). The second is the judgement of an *ynad swyddog* of a commote or a *cantref*. The third is the judgement of the court in which there is not an *ynad swyddog*, but justices by the status of the court. The judgement of one alone is not to be maintained, but it belongs to one of them on his own to declare the common judgement of them all.

Appendix 3. Additional triads
from other law manuscripts

Additional triads from S *that do not occur in* Q

S150. [1220–3]

Tri lle y dyly g6reic atteb heb y g6r. Vn y6 o lofrydiaeth kelein a lado hi o 6eithret lla6 a throet, eil y6 o ledrat a 6nel hi heb y g6r, trydyd y6 o anianolder tir a dayar.

S151. [1224]

Tri dyn ny allant ych6anecau anssa6d y neb ar dir: g6agla6, a gorcheid6at, a chamoressgyn6r; sef acha6s, am nad oes berchnogaeth dilis gantynt eu hunein.

S160. *Tim102* [1368–71, *AL*, XI. i. 8]

Tri ry6 6archeid6ad yssyd ar dir her6yd k*yfreith*:[1] vn[2] y6[3] argl6yd a vyd g6archeid6ad ar dir a disgynno yn y la6 o var6olaeth perchena6c[4] hynny del yr ia6n dlyeda6c y ofyn; eil y6 kidettifed a 6archatt6o dlyed y gidettifedion hyn*n*y delont y gymeryd y hen ia6n[5] a dylyed, me[g]is brodyr[6] neu gefender6 neu gyferder6, kans y rei hynny yssyd gid ettifedion; trydyd y6 dyn y rodo

[1] + nyd amgen *Tim*
[2] + o nodynt *Tim*
[3] − *Tim*
[4] y perchen *Tim*
[5] y hen ia6n] y hia6n *Tim*
[6] bra6d *Tim*

Translation of the additional triads
from other law manuscripts

Translation of the additional triads from S *that do not occur in* Q

S150

Three cases where a woman is entitled to answer without her husband. One is for the killing of a corpse which she herself kills by an act of hand and foot, the second is for a theft which she commits without her husband, the third is for hereditary ownership of land and earth.

S151

Three men who cannot increase anyone's state regarding land: an empty-hand (a man who has completely alienated his ownership of land), and a guardian, and an usurper; this is the reason, because they do not have valid ownership of their own.

S160

There are three kinds of guardians of land according to law: one is a lord who is the guardian of land which falls to his hand through the death of the owner until the true entitled person comes to claim it; the second is a co-heir who guards the entitlement of his co-heirs until they come to take up the old right and entitlement, such as brothers or first-cousins or second-cousins, because those ones are

perchena6c tir g6archeid6adaeth yda6[7] o'e dir[8] dr6y amod[9] gaffel y dir a'e vreint pan*n* y mynno drachefen.

S165. [1414, *AL*, XI. i. 15]

Tri pheth nys dycha6n mach y gaffel dros pleid ystrona6l: vn y6 amdiffyn o r6ym, eil[10] y6 oed dyd kof, trydyd datleu yghyf*reith* y bleid nis dyly.

S168. [1421–3]

Tri pheth ni dyly tafodia6c y datyleu dros neb vn arall: vn y6 rodi g6ystyl yn erbyn barn, eil y6 dadleu dros 6arant arall, trydyd y6 datleu dros dyn ymherigl eneid ac aelodeu.

S169. [1424–7, *AL*, XI. i. 18]

Tri ch6yn gorychel yssyd: vn y6 k6yn am dir o ach ac edryd, eil y6 k6yn y ym6ystla6 a barn, trydyd y6 k6yn galanas.

S171. [1434–7, *AL*, XI. i. 19]

Tri ry6 perchnogaeth yssyd ar dir her6yd kyfreith: vn y6 estyn hep oresgyn, eil y6 goresgyn hep estynn, trydyd y[6] goresgyn ac ystyn.

S172. J161, L156 [1438–41]

O deir fford yd a kogeil ymreint paladr: vn y6 o'e[11] odef, kanys godef a dyr pob kyga6s; eil y6 o eisseu ettifed k*yfreith*a6l o 6r; trydyd y6 o[12] brynu,[13] kans y dryded ettifediaeth k*yfreith*a6l y6.

---

⁷ − *Tim*
⁸ + yda6 *Tim*
⁹ + ovod ar y *Tim*
¹⁰ eeil *S*
¹¹ tr6y *J, L*
¹² tr6y y *J, L*
¹³ + yr da *J, L*

co-heirs; the third is a man to whom the owner of land gives guardianship of his land on the condition that he gets his land and his privilege back when he wishes it.

S165

Three things a surety cannot get on behalf of a foreign party: one is a defence by virtue of a bond, the second is an appointed day for recording, the third is to plead in law for a party he is not entitled to [plead for].

S168

Three things a representative is not entitled to plead on the behalf of anyone else: one is giving a pledge against a judgement, the second is pleading on the behalf of another warrantor, the third is pleading on behalf of a man [who is] in danger of life and limbs.

S169

There are three supreme plaints: one is a plaint for land by kin and descent, the second is a plaint involving giving a pledge against a judgement, the third is a plaint of *galanas*.

S171

There are three possessions on land according to law: one is handing over without possession, the second is possession without handing over, the third is possession and handing over.

S172

In three ways a distaff acquires the privilege of a shaft: one is by its being suffered, because sufferance overrides every plea; the second is by a man lacking a lawful heir; the third is through purchase, because it is the third lawful inheritance.

S173. [1442]

Tri argeu tervyn yssyd: ry6, a braint, a chyg6archad6.

S174. *Y82, 156* [1,443, *AL*, XI. i. 20] *Triad is identical in both versions in Y*

Tri aela6d a dylu g6neuthur ja6n[14] dros dyn a'e gymryd[15] er[16] na bo argl6yd odef[17] ida6: tad, a bra6d hynnaf, a ch6egr6n.

S179. [1497, *AL*, XI. iii. 5]

Tri dyn ni ellir kanlyn k6yneu vnic racdynt: manach hep y abad, a g6reic hep y g6r priod, a mab dioedran hep y dad neu geid6ad tra dylyo vod drosto.

S181. [1513, *AL*, XI. iii. 8]

Tri dyn a gyneil tir yn*n* llys y brenhin ac a'e herbyn gan y brenhin os her6yd ia6n ettifediaeth y disgyn ydynt y tir, ac ny dylyant 6neuthur y'r argl6yd vn o'r tri ry6 6assanaeth yssyd ar dir euth*ur* talu y rent a'e 6estva ida6: 6reic 6ed6, a mab dioedran, ac ysgolheic r6ymedic 6rth yrdeu kysegredic. Sef acha6s y6'r 6reic a'r mab, o eisseu a6dyrda6d, syn6yr a phersonda6d, ac ysgolheic am nad oes 6erth ar y dafa6d yghyf*reith*, ac na dycha6n neb varnu euthur dan perigl g6erth y dafa6d.

S184. [1523, *AL*, XI. iii. 10]

Tri chyffredin g6lad yssyd: kyman, a dadleu, a egl6ys.

S188. [1609]

Tri ph6gk yssyd ia6n y g6ady yn*n* y sarhaed: na 6nathoed na sarhaed na mefel, [n]ac yda6, nac o'e argl6yd, nac o'e genedyl; sef acha6s y g6edir y'r argl6yd, rac y dir6y; sef acha6s y g6edir y'r genedyl, rac y dial ohonynt, kans g6arad6yd

---

[14] + a'e gymryt *Y*
[15] a'e gymryd] – *Y;* + dros dyn *Y*
[16] – *Y*
[17] adef *Y*

S173

There are three stays of a boundary: kind [of person], and status, and established possession.

S174

Three members who are entitled to make satisfaction for a man and take it although he has no lord by sufferance: a father, and an eldest brother, and a father-in-law.

S179

Three men before whom no single plaints can be brought: a monk without his abbot, and a woman without her lawful husband, and an underage son without his father or a guardian while he ought to be responsible for him.

S181

Three men who hold land in the court of the king and who receive it from the king if the land falls to them because of just entitlement, and they are not entitled to do to the lord one of the three kinds of service that there is on land except paying him his rent and his *gwestfa*: a widow woman, and an underage son, and a cleric bound to holy orders. This is the reason for the woman and the son, because of lack of authority, sense and [legal] personality, and a cleric because there is no value to his tongue in law, and that no one may judge except under the danger of the value of his tongue.

S184

There are three things common to a country: a battle-hosting, and pleadings, and a church.

S188

There are three subjects which it is right to deny as *sarhaed*: that neither *sarhaed* nor a shame was committed, neither against him, nor against his lord, nor against his kindred; this is the reason they are denied in relation to a lord, for fear of the

y6 y'r genedyl sarhau eu kar, ac ony thelir, neu ony 6edir, k*yfreith*a6l y dial; o telir ida6 ynteu y sarhaed, neu or g6edir, di6rad6yd vyd y genedyl, a'r lle ni bo g6rad6yd ni byd ha6l.

S190. *Tim109* [1658, *AL*, XI. iii. 24]

Tri pheth ni ellir yn*n* absen: tysty, a g6ranty, a threissa6.

S191. *Tim110* [1659–62, *AL*, XI. iii. 25]

Tri godef yssyd yn*n* kidgerded a chyf*reith* hyd ar amser, ac nyd ynt gorgyfy6ch a chyf*reith*, ac ni dylir[18] m6yniant ohonynt her6yd kyf*reith*,[19] sef y6 hynny, dangos yr ach6ysson:[20] vn y6 godef o dyn orthrymder gan[21] s6yda6c argl6yd yn[22] g6neuth*ur* aghyf*reith* arna6 yn*n* lle k*yfreith*; a h6nn6 a eil6 k*yfreith* yn*n* a*n*reith odef. Eil y6 godef o dyn dyn kebyd neu agidna6s a vei yn kyg6archad6 s6yd, neu didysk dida; a'r heni a eil6 k*yfreith* yn anheil6g odef, a her6yd k*yfreith*[23] ni dylir m6ynant o vn godef anheil6g, namyn y diffr6ytha6.[24] Trydyd y6 godef o dyn y argl6yd y gymell ar y afles[25] yg6yd y llys; a h6nn6 a eil6 k*yfreith* yn d6yll aniana6l yg6yd yr ygneid6yr, a h6nn6 a dylir y adver her6yd a d6eid k*yfreith*,[26] val y haduerir treis, kans kosbad6y y6 llys y brenhin y rodi kygor y neb pryd nas gofyno, ac er yr aghyf*reith* honno, ymod6ared a 6n*n*a k*yfreith* ida6 pan*n* y gofyno.

S192. *Tim111* [1663–5, *AL*, XI. iii. 26]

Tri ch6yn a diffyd pob k6yn pan gyfarffont yn y llys: vn y6 y kyntaf a gaffer g6ssanaeth yn*n* y llys arna6, eil y6 k6yn dlyeda6c, trydyd y6 k6yn gorthrymder.

---

[18] + kaffel *Tim*
[19] + ho; *Tim*
[20] + penaf *Tim*
[21] y *Tim*
[22] − *Tim*
[23] + ho; *Tim*
[24] + a dylir *Tim*
[25] ar y afles] − *Tim*
[26] + ho6el *Tim*

dirwy-fine; this is the reason they are denied the kindred, lest they avenge it, as it is a disgrace to the kindred that their kin is insulted, and if it is not paid, or not denied, it is lawful to avenge it; if his *sarhaed* is paid to him, or if it is denied, it is not disgrace to the kindred, and where there is no disgrace there is no claim.

S190

Three things which cannot be done in absence: testifying, and guaranteeing, and violence.

S191

Three sufferances accompany the law for a period, and they are not higher than law, and they should not be enjoyed according to law, that is, showing the causes: one is a man suffering oppression from the officer of a lord committing an illegality against him instead of law; and the law calls that suffering confiscation of goods. The second is a person suffering a miserly or uncongenial man who has established possession of an office, or an unlearned man with no goods; and those the law calls unworthy sufferings, and according to law there should be no profit from an unworthy suffering, but he should be deprived of the fruits [of office]. The third is a man suffering a lord who forces him to his disadvantage in the presence of the court; and that the law calls natural deceit in the presence of the justices, and that ought to be restored according to what the laws says, as violence is restored, because the court of a king is punishable for giving counsel to anyone when he does not ask for it, and because of that illegality, the law will give him relief when he asks for it.

S192

Three plaints which extinguish every plaint when they meet in the court: one is the first in relation to which service is obtained in the court, the second is the plaint of an entitled person, the third is a plaint of oppression.

S193. Tim112 [1667, *AL*, XI. iii. 27]

Tri pheth ni byd dilis yghy*freith*: t6yll, a cholissi6n, a cham varn, odieith*u*r llithro amseroed.

S195. Tim114 [1669–71, *AL*, XI. iii. 29]

Tri pheth nid atteb k*yfreith* dilys drostynt: vn y6 barnu yn drygar6c, eil y6 ysgy[m]uno dyn kyn atteb, trydyd y6 krogi dyn am bedeir ke*inha6c* k*yfreith*[27] ac ni ellir ont krogi am gan pynt.

S196. Tim115 [1672–4, *AL*, XI. iii. 30]

Tri aghid6ybod k*yfreith* yssyd: vn y6 d6yn tervyn yn g6byll kyn ymofyn g6ir, eil y6 barnu ar dra6s agen, trydyd y6 kymell dyn ar y afles.

S198. Tim116 [1677–9, *AL*, XI. iii. 31]

Tri aghy*freith* yssyd: vn y6 gofed[28] ia6n y arall yn lle k*yfreith,* eil y6 d6y*n* enifeil yn vn o'r teir gafael ryd m6y no'r deuparth a'r trayan, trydyd y6[29] d6yn tervyn y dyn m6y no messyr y ha6l.

S201. [1836, *AL*, XI. iv. 8]

Tri dyn a saif tafodya6c absen drosdynt: vn y6 dyn a vo me6n pererinda6d tya Ryfein neu a bed Krist, a dyn a vo klaf gor6eida6c o vri6 neu vrath neu glefyd aniana6l arall hyd na alleu dyfod nac ar varch nac ar draed, a dyn a vo me6n kaethi6ed karchar; a hefyd dyn a vo me6n llyd argl6yd, kans penaf g6ass[an]aeth tir y6 me6n llyd o reid[30] neu yfyllda6d, a h6nn6 yssyd pe[d]6ryd acha6s. De6i Brefi!

S206. [1903–5, *AL*, XI. iv. 19]

Tri g6reidyn aniana6l yssyd y'r vn geir k*yfreith*: g6irioned, kid6ybod, a dysk. Ony chyflad y rei hynny, ni cheiff k*yfreith* y hen*n*6. G6irioned y6 g6reidyn baran;

---

[27] bedeir ke*ina6c* k*yfreith*] deir ar dec *Tim*
[28] godef *Tim*
[29] – *Tim*
[30] rif *S, but amended in the margin of the manuscript.*

S193

Three things which are not valid in law: deceit, and collusion, and a wrong judgement, except through the slipping of time.

S195

Three things for which valid law does not answer: one is judging mercifully, the second is a man is excommunicated before he answers, the third is hanging a man for four legal pence and one can only be hanged for a hundred pounds.

S196

There are three disregards of law: one is to fix a boundary completely before seeking the truth, the second is to judge over a breach, the third is to compel a man to evil.

S198

There are three illegalities: one is suffering [giving] compensation to another instead of law, the second is to bring an animal from one of the three free distraints more than two parts and a third, the third is to fix a boundary for a man which is more than the measure of his claim.

S201

Three men for whom a representative may stand on their behalf when absent: one is a man who is on pilgrimage to Rome or the grave of Christ, and a man who is ill in bed due to an injury or a wound or another natural illness so that he could not come either on horseback or by foot, and a man who is incarcerated in prison; and also a man who is in the hosting of a lord, because the main service on land is to be in a host either through need or duty, and that is a fourth reason. Dewi Brefi!

S206

There are three natural roots to the same word of law: truth, conscience, and learning. Unless those ones coincide, law does not get its name. Truth is the root of judgement; conscience is the root of equal division; learning is the root of

kid6ybod y6 g6reidyn kyfraniad; dysk y6 g6reidyn kynhebrygiad dadyl; a'e
herbynyad anhervynad6y y6 bop kyga6s ni th*e*rvyner dr6y y g6reideu hynny.

S207. [1906, *AL*, XI. iv. 20]

Teir perchnogaeth yssyd ar dir hyt ar amser ac a vydant gargych6yn, ac oessoed
yssyd ydynt: oes deilad ar dir dyn arall, vn dyd a bl6ydyn a thri ni6arna6d
na6d; oes ystynol, hyd pan rodo y vreint a'e ansa6d o'e la6; oes g6rthrifiad, hyt
pan y kymhello yr argl6yd y wellhay y vreint a'e ansa6d; ac os g6rthyd,
kaeedic vyd k*yfreith* ryda6 ac ef ynn vn o'r modyon y mae y dylyeda6c golli
y dir; sef y6 g6rthrifiad,[31] yttifed kyssefin y gaffel dadanyd.

S208. [1907–11, *AL*, XI. iv. 21]

Tri goresgyn yssyd ni dylir kaffel m6y[n]ant o honynt: vn y6 goresgyn o anvod,
eil y6 goresgyn hep 6ybod, trydyd y6 goresgyn y bo ymr6ym a phoen arna6 er
hyd y bo yndo, megis obligassion neu esgrifen arall. Ny chyll dyleda6c y dir
er myned rifedi o dynyon dros ben na6ved ach, pei gallei 6irio vod llef treisic
yn ol ar yr amseroed k*yfreith*a6l, kans nid a ha6l yn ll6r6 g6yd6aled yn erbyn
dlyeda6c nes tervynny yr ach6ysson ychod.

S209. [1925–6]

Tri lle yssyd her6yd k*yfreith* y dyly datl gynhenys y thervyny tr6y dedryd g6lad
yn erbyn haerllygr6yd kyfr6g ettifedion o amryfaelyon deilygda6d neu vreint.
Vn y6 dadl o gidettifedion, yr h6nn a dyg6yd dr6y dylyed ananol: kyntaf y6 o
derfydd geni mab y 6reic o'e g6r priod, a geni mab arall o'e gorderch, a g6edy
mar6olaeth y g6r briod dyfod y mab anedua6l gida'r defua6l y dadleu yr
argl6yd y ofyn ran o'r ettifediaeth o acha6s y eni ynn y g6ely k*yfreith*a6l a
veuthrin vn dyd a bl6ydyn ac ach6aneg ar allu y tad k*yfreith*a6l, k*yfreith* a
d6eid er yr ach6ysson hynny na dyly gaffel dim ony dycha6n d6edyd y vod
yn*n* vab o gorff y neb y tyf6ys grym yr ettifediaeth o'e blegid, kans k*yfreith* a
de6eid na dyly neb dlyed aniana6l onyd vn a hanffo o gorff y neb y tyfo y
dyled o'e blegid, neu y neb a vo nesaf y'r neb a vo mar6 hep ettifed o'e gorff.[32]

---

[31] g6rthgrifiad *S*
[32] 'dilewyd nifer o eiriau ar ddiwedd brawddeg 1,926, ac nid eir ymlaen i orffen y triad'. C. James.

conducting a pleading; and each case which is not terminated through those roots is an acceptance which should not be concluded.

S207

There are three possessions of land for a period and they are [cases of] car-starting, and they have terms: the period of a building on another man's land, one day and a year and three protection days; the period of an invested person, until he conveys his privilege and his condition by his hand; the period of a *gwrthrifiad*, until he compels the lord to improve his privilege and his condition; and if he refuses, the law is closed between him and him [the lord] and it is one of the ways an entitled man loses his land; this is what a *gwrthrifiad* is, an eldest son to receive *dadannudd*.

S208

There are three occupations that no advantage should be gained by them: one is occupation through unwillingness, the second is occupation without knowledge, the third is occupation in which he is subject to compulsion and penalty however long it has been there, such as an obligation or some other written document. The entitled person does not lose his land even though a number of [generations of] men have passed in excess of the ninth generation, if he could prove that a cry of one who has suffered violence was previously uttered at the legal periods, because a claim does not follow the path of obstruction against an entitled person until the issues [raised] above are settled.

S209

There are three places according to law where a contentious pleading ought to be terminated by compurgation of the country against impudence between heirs through various worthinesses or privileges. One is a pleading by co-heirs, that which was brought by a natural entitlement: the first is if it happens that a son is born to a woman from her lawful husband, and another son is born from his concubine, and after the death of her lawful husband the illegitimate son comes with the legitimate to the pleadings of the lord to claim part of the entitlement because he was born in the lawful bed and was nurtured for one year and a day and more to the ability of the lawful father; the law says that despite those reasons he is not entitled to have anything unless he is able to say that he is a son of the body of the person from whom the strength of the inheritance originated, because the law says that no one is entitled to natural entitlement except one who derives from the body of the person from whom the strength of the entitlement came, or whoever is nearest to the person who died without an heir of this body.

S213. [1959, *AL*, XI. iv. 25]

Tri pheth ni ch[yg]ein: hocked me6n ll6, esgys yghyffes, ac ymdired y hir einoes.

S214. [1962–3]

Tri dyn ny dyliyr y klady yghysegyr: lleidir a dienydyer am ledrad, a brad6r argl6yd, a ffyrnig6r a dienydier am y ffyrnicr6yd. Sef y6 ffyrnicr6yd: myrna6 dyn, a llad dyn a g6en6yn, a dif6yna6 da ida6 ef y hyn ac y'rr perchena6c.

S *and* K *additional triad collection:* S *numbers 216–263*

S265. *Tim145* [2131–4, *AL*, XI. iv. 26]

Tri dyn her6yd k*yfreith* ni safant 6rth a 6nelont. Vn y6 dyn med6, eil y6 mab kyn*n* y y bedeir bl6yd ar dec, trydyd y6 dyn a gymheller o'e anvod.

S266. *Tim146* [2135–8, *AL*, XI. iv. 27]

Tri breint yssyd y gyghella6r: breint kastell, a braint amdiffynbleid, a braint dyn disg*yfreith*. Sef achos ymae breint kastell ido ef: karcharu a dycho*n* pan y myno. Sef achos y mae breint amdiffyn*n*bleid ydo:[33] am orvod arno atteb y orthrymder. Sef achos y mae braint dyn disg*yfreith* ido ef: am nad oes y neb dasgy arno.

S267. *Tim147* [2139, *AL*, XI. iv. 28]

Tri dyn ni adm6ynheir dim o'r a d6etton me6n llys: dall, a med6, a bydar; sef achos y6, am nad g6neuthuredic dim o'r a 6nelont yghyf*reith*.

S274. *Tim154* [2175–6]

Tri argae tervyn: breint, a prodolder, a chyg6archad6. Ni eill dyn a vo is y rad noc vn o rhei hynny dervyny arnadynt h6ynteu.

---

[33] – *Tim*

S213

Three things which are not permissible: cheating in an oath, and excuse in a confession, and trusting to long life.

S214

Three men who are not entitled to be buried in consecrated ground: a thief who is executed for theft, and a traitor to the lord, and a furious man who is executed for his fury. This is what fury is: secretly murdering a man, and killing a man with poison, and spoiling goods [so that they are useless] to him and to the owner.

S *and* K *additional triad collection:* S *numbers 216–263*

S265

Three men according to law who do not stand by that which they have done. One is a drunk, the second is a son before his fourteenth year, the third is a man who is compelled against his will.

S266

A *cynghellor* has three statuses: the status of a castle, and the status of a defending party, and the status of an unrestrained man. This is the reason he has the status of a castle: he can imprison [people] when he wishes. This is the reason he has the status of a defending party: because he has to answer to oppression. This is the reason he has the status of an unrestrained man: because no one can set a task against him.

S267

Three men none of whose statements in court can be enjoyed: a blind man, and a drunk, and a deaf man; this is the reason, because in law anything they do is not [effectively] accomplished.

S274

The three stays of a boundary: status, and privilege, and prior ownership. A man who is ranked lower than one of those is not entitled to fix a boundary against them.

S278. [2188]

Tri phrifieu g6reic y6: y cho6yll, a'e g6arthryd, a'e sarhaed.

S279. *Tim156* [2219–22]

Tri dyn y traeana y brenhin ac h6ynt: y vrenhines, a'r penteyly, a'r penkynyd.

Additional triads from Tim *that do not occur in* Q

Tim160

Tri lle y dyly argl6yd erlid g6eli tafa6d, kany chaffo y dyn y de6etter 6rtha6 ja6n: vn y6 o nadynt, p6y bynac a ymgeinio a'y gilyd ynatleu, neu em myn6ent, neu yn egl6ys, neu yn llys.

Tim172

Tri dyn y telir galanas udynt ac ny thalant h6y [Hiatus here]

Tim173

Tri dyn a dyly bod ynn tafodia6c apsen dros glaf o vri6 neu vrath neu glefyd anianol, a tros garcharor: nid amgen, effeiriad, medic, a phortha6r; a bra6d6r a saif dros dyn a el y lyd ne pererinda6d, o byd cadnabydys eu my*n*ed.

Additional triads from Y *that do not occur in* Q

Y155

O teir fford ny ellir g6adu mab o genedyl: vn y6 or ganet yn y g6ely kyfreithaul a'e vagu vn dyd a bl6ydyn o da y dat. Eil y6 or rodir g6erth yr y vagu kyn bo mab ll6yn a fferth. Trydyd y6 or kymerir ar ostec neu or dygir yn gyfreitha6l.

S278

These are the three privy things of a woman: her *cowyll*, and [compensation for] her disgrace, and her *sarhaed*.

S279

Three men with whom the king shares a third: the queen, and the chief of the kindred, and the chief huntsman.

Translation of the additional triads from Tim *that do not occur in* Q

Tim160

Three places where a lord is entitled to prosecute a tongue-wound, although the man to whom it be said does not get redress: one of them is, whoever insults the other in pleadings, or in a cemetery, or in a church, or in the court.

Tim172

Three men to whom *galanas* is paid and they do not pay. [Hiatus here].

Tim173

Three men who are entitled to be a representative on behalf of an absent person who is ill because of an injury or a natural disease, and on behalf of a prisoner: namely, a priest, and a mediciner, and a porter; and a justice stands on behalf of a man who goes to hostings or on pilgrimage, if it is acknowledged that they went.

Translation of the additional triads from Y *that do not occur in* Q

Y155

In three ways a son cannot be denied from a kindred: one is if he is born in the lawful bed and reared for one year and a day on the goods of the father. The second is if value for rearing him is given although he may be a son of bush and brake. The third is if he is affiliated by word of mouth or if he is affiliated lawfully.

Y160

Tri dyn y mae caeth kyfreith vdunt pob amser: dall, a bydar, a mut.

Triads from the 'tail' of Z that are not found in other Cyfnerth manuscripts

Z66. [43rb]

O dair fforđ y dyly dyn vod yn enaidvadde: o ladrad barnedic i groc, ac o vrad arglwydd, ac o lađ dyn yn lladrad.

Z78. [55ra]

Tair agweddi k*yfreith*iawl: agweddi merch brenin, xxiiij o bvnoedd, a'i chowill viiij bvnt; agweddi merch vchelwr tair pvnt, a'i chowill pvnt; agweddi merch mab aillt, cxx đ a ffvnt, a'i chowill cxx đ.

Z81. [55va]

Tri dyn a ddyly talv galanas ac ni ddyly i gaffel: gwraic, ac yscolhaic, a llowruđ.

Z87. [55vb]

Tri dyn a ddyly le yn y llys vddvn heb vod ev kefyn ar y pared: y pengwasdrawd, a'r penkynyđ, a'r troydiawc.

Z89. [57ra]

Tri achaws y kyll [57rb] dyn dref i dad: o brad arglwydd, a mvrn, a rrybyddio kyrch kohoyddawc gorwlad ydd el arglwydd iddaw a'i ddiffryd.

Z93. [57rb]

Tri anogonyon kyfraith: gad[a]w praw y'r amddiffynwr, a cheidwaid i'r hawlwr, ac esdrawn yn talv galanas.

Y160

Three men to whom law is refused at all times: a blind man, and a deaf man, and a mute.

Translation of the triads from the 'tail' of Z that are not found in other Cyfnerth manuscripts

Z66

In three ways a man should be condemned to death: for a theft for which he is adjudged to execution, and for betrayal of the lord, and for killing a man by stealth.

Z78

There are three lawful *agweddiau*: the *agweddi* of the daughter of a king, twenty-four pounds, and her *cowyll* 9 pounds; the *agweddi* of the daughter of a nobleman three pounds, and her *cowyll* a pound; the *agweddi* of the daughter of a bondsman, 120*d* and a pound, and her *cowyll* 120*d*.

Z81

Three persons who are should pay *galanas* but are not entitled to receive it: a woman, and a cleric, and a homicide.

Z87

Three men who are entitled to have a place in the court without having their backs to the wall: the chief groom, and the chief huntsman, and the footholder.

Z89

Three reasons a man loses his patrimony: for treason of the lord, and murder, and giving warning about a major raid to a bordering country on which a lord goes and there be defence against it.

Z93

The three instigators of law: allowing proof for the defendant, and guardians for the claimant, and a foreigner paying *galanas*.

Z94. [57rb]

Tri argay tir: ty ac aylwyd, ac ar ac eredic a chlawdd kyva heb i droi; ni ddyleir dangos ar dor hyny.

Z100. [73r]

Tair ffordd y llyssir ynad: i vod yn gyngaws gynt am y dadyl hono, neu gymrvd gobyr yn erbyn y ddadyl hono, neu roddi dysc i vn o'r pleidie gwedi i dyvod i'r mays; ac o gyrrir arno vn o'r tri hynny ni ellir praw arno onid i lw o hvn i wadv.

Z102. [79ra]

Tair ffordd y dylir dienyddv dyn: am ladrad o adde o honaw e hun, ac o ballu i arddelw iddaw, ac o'i daly ar foadraeth o gwatta ef i ffo.

Z103. [79va]

Tri ffeth y sydd vn vraint a lladrad yn llaw: i gayl ar i gefyn neu yn i vwrw i wrthaw, i[34] gayl dan vn to ac vn klo ac ef, ac i gayl gar y vron yn i vwrw.

Z109. [86ra]

Tri modd y bydd kamlwrw: vn yw am anaddawt a wneler yn erbyn y brenin, a hwnnw a ddamweinia o lawer modd. Ail yw gwnethur peth kamgyleus anghyvyreithiawl yn erbyn brenin yn i lys neu oddige i lys. Trydydd yw gwneuthur peth yn erbyn i wyr nev y denantiait i wlat yn anghyvreithlon ac y perthyn kamlwrw amdanunt.

Z110. [86va]

Tri ryw gamlwrw y sydd: kamlwrw vn dyblic, a chamlwrw dav dyblic, a chamlwrw tridyblic.

---

[34] di *Z*

Z94

Three stays of land: a house and a hearth, and tillage and ploughing and a whole dyke [which has] not turned over: they ought not to be shown on the basis of that.

Z100

Three ways a justice is objected to: for being a *cyngaws* in that case previously, or for taking a fee against that case, or by giving learned advice to one of the parties after coming to the field; and if he is charged with one of those three cases there is no proof in relation to him except his own oath to deny it.

Z102

Three ways [for three reasons] a man ought to be hanged: for a theft if he admits to it himself, and for his warranty failing him, and for his being caught whilst escaping if he denies escaping.

Z103

Three things that are of the same value as theft in hand: finding it on his back, or throwing it away from him [after] it is found under the same roof and lock as him, and finding it in front of him when he throws it.

Z109

In three ways there is *camlwrw*: one is for harm (?) which is committed against the king, and that happens in many ways. The second is doing something which is guilty and illegal against the king in his court or apart from his court. The third is committing something against his men or the tenants of his country unlawfully and to which *camlwrw* pertains.

Z110

There are three kinds of *camlwrw*: a onefold *camlwrw*, and a twofold *camlwrw*, and a threefold *camlwrw*.

Z111. [86va]

Tri modd y kollir kamlwrw vn dyblic: o vethlu yr howlw yn holi, nev na chyl[l] hynno; nev o vethlv yr amddiffyn i amddiff*ynnwr* o dremygv y dadylav hep esgussot drostaw k*yfreith*iawl yn y llys; y trydyđ drwy varn k*yfreith*.

Z112. [86va]

Tri modd y bydd [86vb] kamlwrw dav ddyblic: vn yw pan daler gweli tavot y arglwydd, ail yw pan ddinesao dyn ar yr yngynat yn barnv a bydd y brenin yn y lle, trydydd yw pan wyssier dyn yn erbyn arall yn gaddav i holi a'i ddyvot ef a'r cwynwr rac bron y brenin y'r llys ac yna kiliaw o'r kwynwr rac bron.

Z113. [86vb]

Tri modd y bydd kamlwrw tri dybylic: vn yw am y tair affaith diwaetha o affeithiau galanas o ffalla yr yvraith yr affeithwyr, sef yw, lle gomeddo [87ra] amddiffynwr gwibiawdyr a mach drosdaw ar ddyvot a'i wyssiaw deir gwaith o blygit y breni*n* heb ysgvssod k*yfreith* drostaw yn y dadylev. Tryddydd ar hawlwr gwibiawdyr a mach drostaw ar galyn i ddadyl a'i alw deir gwaith ymop vn o'r tri dadylav camlwrw am bob vn y'r arglwydd a'i adel ef yn rrydd o'i hawl o bylegid na ddoeth ef i'r dadylev kyntaf.

Z114. [87ra]

Tri dyn ni dyly kamlwrw arnvnt: arglwydd, a'r neb a vo trosto yn holi, ac ynat, kanys gwell yngynadiaeth no dim prysenawl, [87rb] a mab llai no ffedeir blwydd ar ddec o oet kanys kosb y tat y sydd arno.

Z115. [87rb]

Tri dyn a dal abediw hep dir: bonheddic kanhwynawl, a gwr kyvarwyssawc, a map pedeir blwydd ar ddec. Y mab aill[t] a ddyly bod yn arddelw o hynny allan a'i abediw yw dros yr arddelw.

Z111

In three ways a onefold *camlwrw* is lost: by the claimant making an error in the course of his claim, or [in other words] he does not lose that claim; or if the defendant makes an error in his defence by contemptuous absence from the pleadings without having anyone to excuse him lawfully in the court; the third [a *camlwrw*] by lawful judgement.

Z112

In three ways is there a twofold *camlwrw*: one is when a tongue-wound is paid to the lord, the second is when a man draws near to the justice judging and the king is at hand, the third is when a man is summoned against another who promises to make a claim against him, and he comes with the plaintiff before the king to the court and then the plaintiff retreats from his presence.

Z113

In three ways is there a threefold *camlwrw*: one is for the final three abetments of homicide if their compurgation fails to the abettors, that is, where a defendant denies a vagabond and a surety on his behalf for his coming and being summoned three times before the king without a lawful excuse for him in the case. The third is against a vagabond claimant with a surety on his behalf to follow his case and he is called three times in every one of the three pleadings a *camlwrw* for each one to the lord and let him be free of his claim because he did not come to the first case.

Z114

Three men who ought not to be subject to a *camlwrw*: a lord, and whoever is on his behalf in the claim; and a justice, because justiceship is better than anything of this present world; and a son who is less than fourteen years of age, because he is subject to the punishment of his father.

Z115

Three men who pay *ebediw* without land: an innate nobleman, and a man with a gift [from his lord], and a son who is fourteen years of age. The *mab aillt* ought to be claiming (the status of someone aged) from those (years) on and his *ebediw* is for his confirmation.

Z116. [87rb]

Tri ffeth nit rait praw arnvnt: nid rait praw ar addef, namyn i dystv; nit rrait praw ar ddiddim i vot yn [87va] ddiddim, namyn provet y llall nat ddiddim ef; try[dy]dd ar vyrawt eithyr tystiolaeth ynat i bwy y barnawdd hi.

Z119. [97vb]

Tri argay dangos: rrandir, a braint, ac adeilad, gani ellir dangos tervyn ar dor y rrai hynny, ac na ellir dwyn randir yn nangos.

Z120. [98rb]

Tri lle y dyly dyn vesur i hawl gan amddiffynwr hep hawl hep atep o hon*n*o. Vn yw o gomedd ygwyl kyffreithiawl, kyffaddav vydd yr hawl am omedd y gwys. Ni vernir hagen yn vessvr hawl i neb ar absen, hyt yn oet y trydydd gwys, ac ni ddylyff tystiaw na ddel amddiffynwr i'r maes na galw am vyrawt y hyt y [98va] trydydd gwys. A'r tri gwys hynny a ddyleir i gwnevthvr yn gyffyreithiawl hagen a'i galw velly. Ail yw yn y dydd koll kaffel: nit oes esgvsot kyvyreithiawl eithyr na wypo ynat i varn, ac o dodir angav yn esgus drosdo ni rrymia, kanit esgus k*yfreithawl* ac ni rrymia. A chyvadde vydd messur yr hawl arnaw ac ar i dda mal pe byw vai, os bydd iddaw. Oni ddaw yr amddiffynwr ynydd koll kaffel gossodedic o ben ynat wedi rwymo pleidiev barn er messur i hawl arnaw, kani ddyl kyvyraith nis gwnel. Trydydd yw lle y kais [98vb] howlwr vesur i hawl ar y talawdur marw neu [*rest of page is blank*]

Z116

Three things which do not need proof on them: there is no need for proof on an admission, except to testify; there is no need for proof on a have-not that he is a have-not, but let the other prove that he is not a have-not; the third on a judgement apart from the testimony of the justice to whom he judged it.

Z119

Three stays of showing: shareland, and status, and building, because a boundary cannot be shown on the basis of those three and shareland cannot be established in a demonstration.

Z120

Three places a man ought to measure his claim by the defendant without a claim or an answer in respect of it. One is if he denies a lawful delay, the claim will be admitted because the summons was denied. No one, however, will be judged to measure the extent of their claim for anybody in absence, until the third summons, and they are not entitled to testify that the defendant did not come to the field nor call for judgement until the third summons. And those three summons ought to be made lawfully, however, and called as such. The second is in the day of loss or gain; there is no lawful excuse except that the justice does not know his judgement, and if death is given as an excuse on his behalf, it does not bind, because it is not a lawful excuse and it does not bind. And the measure of the claim will be admitted for him and for his goods, as if he were alive, if he have any. If the defendant does not come in the day of loss and gain set by the mouth of a justice after binding the parties to judgement despite measuring his claim against him, because he who may not abide by the law is not entitled to it. The third is where the claimant asks for the measure of his claim against the dead debtor or [rest of page is blank].

The Conspectuses

The conspectuses list the triads in the order in which they occur in the first manuscript listed, with correspondence from other manuscripts.

The triad collections are marked using numbers in bold, to distinguish the triad collection in the main manuscript from the other triads.

Where a triad is in square brackets, the correspondence is not exact. However, where square brackets are used for another purpose, this is noted at the top of the conspectus. Any other points will be noted at the top of the conspectus.

Conspectus 1. The Triads in X
Conspectus 2. The Triads from the Other Cyfnerth Manuscripts
Conspectus 3. The Mk Triads
Conspectus 4. The Triads in Z
Conspectus 5. Triads in Published Sources
Conspectus 6a. The Triads in Q showing OTr-type Bleg Manuscripts
Conspectus 6b. The Triads in Q showing L-type Bleg Manuscripts
Conspectus 7. The Latin D Triads
Conspectus 8. The K and S Triad Collection
Conspectus 9. The Latin A Triads
Conspectus 10. The Latin B Triads
Conspectus 11. The Latin E Triads

Conspectus 1. The Triads in X

All Cyfn manuscripts are listed here, but the base manuscript is X. For additional triads in other Cyfn manuscripts, see Conspectus 2. Bold numbers mark the triad collection in X. Italics mark the three triads in Llyfr Cynog, which interrupt the triad collection.

X – Keywords	X	Fo.	Z	Fo.
Tri dyn a wnant sarhaed y'r brenhin	1	166r	1	1rb
O dri mod y sarheir y brenhines	2	166v	2	1va
Tri gwassanaeth a wna y brenhin y'r hebogyd	3	174r	3	4vb
Tri datahn6d tir y syd	4	188r		
Teir gweith y rennir [tir]	5	188v	5	12va
Tri pheth ny werth taeawc	6	190r	68	49ra
Teir keluydyt ny dysc taeawc	7	190r	69	49ra
O teir mod y telir teithi buwch	8	192r	70	49rb
O dri achaws ny chyll gwreic y hagwedi	9	202r	6	25ra
Tri pheth ny dygir y ar wreic kyd gatter hi	10	202r	7	25ra
Teir aelwyd a dyly wneuthur yawn	11	207v	55, 60	37vb, 39rb
Teir gosgord brenhinawl ysyd	12	207v		
Tri ame6 brawd ysyd	13	207v		
Tri digingoll kenedyl ynt	**14**	208r	10	32vb
Tri oed kyfureith y dial kelein	**15**	208v	11	33ra
Teir rwyd brenhin yw	**16**	208v	12	33rb
Teir rwyd breyr ynt	**17**	209r	13	33rb
Teir rwyd taeawc ynt	**18**	209r	14	33rb
Teir dirwy brenhin ynt	**19**	209r	15	33va
Tri anhepcor brenhin ynt	**20**	209v	16	33va
Tri pheth ny chyfran brenhin a nep	**21**	209v	17	35vb
Tri phedwar ysyd	**22**	209v	18	35vb
Teir kyfulauan, os gwna dyn yn y wlad	**23**	210r	19	34(ii)rb
Tri thauedawc gosgord yssyd	**24**	210v	20	34(ii)rb
Teir gwanas gwaew kyureithyawl ysyd	**25**	210v	21	34(ii)rb
Tri ouer ymadrawd a dywedir yn dadle6	**26**	210v	22	34(ii)va
Tri ouer laeth yssyd	**27**	211r	23	34(ii)va
Teir sarhaed ny diwygir os keffir drwy uedawd	**28**	211r	24	34(ii)va
Teir paluawd ny diwygir	**29**	211r	25	34(ii)va
Teir gwraged ny dyliir datle6 ac eu hetuied am tref eu mam	**30**	211r	26, 118	34(ii)va
Teir sarhaed gwreic ynt	**31**	211r	27	34(ii)vb
Tri chadarn enllip gwreic ynt	**32**	211v	29	35ra
Tri chewilyd kenedyl ynt	**33**	211v	28	35ra
Tri chyffro dial ynt	**34**	211v	30	35ra
Teir fford yssyd y lyss6v tystyon	**35**	212r	31	35rb
Tri peth a hawl dyn yn lledrat ac ny chynghein lledrad	**36**	212r	32	35rb
Tri meib yn tri broder vn mam vn dat	**37**	212r	33	35rb
Tri dyn a gynnyd ev breint yn vn dyd	**38**	212v	34	35va
Tri gwerth kyfureith beichyogi gwreic	**39**	212v	35	35vb

U	p.	Mk	p.	V	Fo.	W	Fo.	Bleg	p.	WML
1	3	1	2	1	1v	1	34r	1	3	2
2	5	2	3	2	2v	2	34v	3	4	3
								6	13	
5	85	8	43	4	22v	4	59r	27	79	48
6	90	9	45	5	23v	5	59v	23	75	49
		13	53	13	28r	7	62r	49	108	57, 59
		14	53	14	28v	8	62r	50	108	58, 59
4	81	15	62	15	31r	9	67v	30	88	71
		18	80			12	78v	18	64	92
		19	80			13	79r	117	119	93
		74	115			69	102r			135
								8	18	
14	106	21	102	19	40v	17	95r	9	33	122
15	107	22	103	20	40v	18	95r	57	109	122
16	108	23	103	21	41r	19	95v	44	107	123
17	108	25	104	22	41r	20	95v	45	107	123
18	108	24	104	23	41r	21	95v	46	108	123
19	109	26	104	24	41r	22	96r	16	42	123
		27	105	25	41v	23	96r	52	108	124
		28	105	26	41v	24	96r	55	108	124
56	119	29	105	27	41v	25	96r	56	109	124
		30	106	28	42r	26	97r	51	108	125
		31	106	29	42r	27	97r	58	110	125
49	116	32	106	30	42r	28	97r	59	110	125
		33	107	31	42r	29	97v	60	110	126
		34	107	32	42v	30	97v	61	110	126
		35	107	33	42v	31	97v	62	110	126
		36	107	34	42v	32	97v	63	111	126
11	105	37	107	35	42v	33	97v	64	111	126
		41	108	40	43r	34	98r	65	111	127
		39	108	38	43r	36	98r	67	111	127
20	109	38	107	36	42v	35	98r	66	111	126
21	109					37	98v	68	111	303
		42	108	41	43r	39	98v	10	37	127
		40	108	39	43r	38	98v	69	112	127
7	92	43	108	42	43r	40	98v	70	112	127
		44	109	43	43v	41	99r	71	112	128
		45	109	44	43v	42	99r	72	112	128

X – Keywords	*X*	Fo.	*Z*	Fo.
Teir ford y dygir mab ac y diwedir	**40**	212v	36	35vb
Teir gormes doeth ynt	**41**	213v	37	36rb
Tri dyn a dyly tafuodyawc drostun yn dadle6	**42**	213v	38	36rb
Tri llwdyn digyfureith y gweithred yssyd	**43**	213v	39	36rb
Tri llwdyn nyd oes gwerth kyfureith arnunt	**44**	213v	40	36rb
Tri gwaed kyfureith ysyd	**45**	213v	41	36rb
Tri than digyfureith ysyd	**46**	213v	42, 98	36rb, 67ra
Tri edyn a dyly brenhin e6 gwerth	**47**	213v	43	36va
Tri phryf a dyly brenhin ev gwerth	**48**	213v	44	36va
Tri pheth ny ad kyfureith y e6 damdwng	**49**	214r	45	36va
Tair k[ont] kyfreithiawl y sydd	**49a**	214r	46	36va
Tri phren ysy ryd e6 llad y mewn forest	**50**	214r	47, 91	36vb
Tri chehyryn canhastyr yssyd	**51**	214r	48	36vb
Tri chorn buelhin y brenhin	**52**	214r	49	37ra
Tri hely ryd yssyd ymhob gwlad	**53**	214r	50	37ra
Tri pheth a dyrr ar gyfureith	**54**	214r	51	37ra
Tri hwrd ny diwygir	**55**	214r	52	37ra
Tri dyn ny dyly brenhin eu gwerthu	**56**	214v	53	37rb
Tri henw righill yssyd	**57**	214v	54	37rb
Tri lle yd ymdiueichya mach gan gyfureith	**58**	216r	9	28ra
O teir fford y differis mach a chynnogyn	**59**	216v		
O teir ford y telir gwialen y brenhin	**60**	217r	61	39vb
Tri ergyd ny thelir dim amdanunt	**61**	217v	62	39ra
Tri chyfwrch dirgel a dyly y brenhin y gaffael	**62**	217v	63	39ra
Teir nodwyd gyfureithyawl yssyd	**63**	217v	64	39ra
Teir marw tystyolaeth yssyd	**64**	217v	76	54ra
Teir kyfurinach yssyd gwell ev hade6	**65**	218r		
Tri aniueil vn troedyawc yssyd	**66**	218r		
Pob adeilwr maestir a dyly caffael tri ph[r]en	**67**	218r		
Tri lle y ran kyfureith	**68**	218v		
Tri pheth ny thelir kyd koller yn y randy	**69**	218v		
Teir sarhaed kelein yw	**70**	218v		
Teir gwarthrud kelein yw	**71**	218v	73	53vb
Teir gauael nyd atuerir	**72**	218v	74	53vb
Tri edyn ar dyr dyn arall heb ganyad	**73**	218v		
Tri peth or keffir ar ford ryd ynt y'r neb a'y caffo	**74**	218v	65	39rb
Tri dyn a dyly gweli dauawt	**75**	219r		
Tri gwybyteid yssyd am dir	**76**	221v		

U	p.	Mk	p.	V	Fo.	W	Fo.	Bleg	p.	WML
51	117	46	110	45	44r	43	99v	[73]	113	129
53	118	49	111	48	44v	45	100r	74	113	130
54	119	50	111	49	44v	46	100r	75	113	130
55	119	51	111	50	44v	47	100r	76	113	130
		52	111	51	44v	48	100r	77	113	130
		53	112	52	44v	49	100r	78	114	130
26	112	54	112	53	44v	50	100r	79	114	130
22	109	55	112	54	44v	51	100r	80, 86	114	130
		56	112	55	45r	52	100v	81	114	131
		57	112	56	45r	53	100v	82	114	131
27	112	58	112	57	45r	54	100v			131
43	115	59	112	58	45r	55	100v	83	114	
42	115	62	113	37	45r	56	100v	84	114	127
28	112	60	113	59	45r	57	100v	47	108	131
47	116	61	113	60	45r	58	101r	115	119	131, 133
		63	113	61	45r	59	101r	85	114	131, 133
23	110	66	113	64	45v	60	101r	104	116	131, 133
		67	114	65	45v	61	101v	88	115	132, 134
		64	113	62	45r	62	101v	89	115	131, 134
		16	73	16	35r	10	73v			85
		17	74	17	35r	11	73v	12	40	85
		65	113	63	45v	63	101v			
34	113	92	118			86	101r	90	115	139
		131	126					91	115	
36	114	75	115			70	102r	92	115	135
10	103	76	115			71	102v	106	117	136
31	113	82	117			72	103r	93	115	137
29	112	83	117			73	103r	94	115	137
						16	91r	95	115	117
								21	71	
		84	117			74	103r	96	115	137
39	114	86	117			75	103r	98	115	137
41	115	70	114			76	103r	97	116	137
40	114	85	117			78	103r	99	116	137
33	113	87	117			79	103v	87		138
		88	117			80	103v	111	118	138
8	93	12	49	12	28r	6	60v			54

Conspectus 2. The Triads from the other Cyfnerth manuscripts

Keywords	Z	Fo.	U
O tri mod y kedernheir g6ys			
Tri ouerwys a ellir eu g6adu			
Tri dyn ny dylyir eu g6yssa6			
Tri ry6 wadu yssyd			
Tri ry6 t6g yssyd			
Teir etiuedyaeth kyfreitha6l			
Tri ry6 prit yssyd ar tir			
Tri ll6 a dyry g6reic y 6r	8	25rb	
O teir fford y g6edir mab o genedyl			52
Tri lle ny dyly dyn rodi ll6 g6eilyd			44
Teir cont kyfreitha6l	46	36va	27
Tri phren ryd yn fforest brenhin	47, 91	36vb, 57rb	43
O teir fford y telir g6yalen aryant y'r brenhin	61, [67]	39vb, 43rb	
Tri da dilis diuach yssyd			
Tri chyffredin g6lat			30
Tri argae g6aet	58	38ra	46
Teir g6arthrud mor6yn	57	37vb	45
Tri di6yneb g6lat yssyd			32
Tri pheth a gadarnha deua6t			
Tri pheth a wanha defa6t			
Tri dyn yssyd ryd udunt kerdet fford			25
Tri pheth a geid6 cof ac a seif yn lle tyston			
Tri anhebcor kenedyl			48
Tri lle yg kyfreith Hywel y mae pra6f			
Tri pheth a dyffer dyn rac gwys dadleu			
Tri chyffredin kenedyl			
Tri dyn kas kenedyl			
Tri mefyluethyant gwr			37
Tri aneueil yssyd u6y g6erth eu teithi			
Tri pheth a dyly dyn colli y dadyl			
Tri gr6ndwal doethinab			
Tri pheth ny drycheif y neb			
Teir kyfnewit a doant trachefyn			
Teir mefyl6ryaeth mach			
O teir ffordd y telir amobyr			58
O teir ffordd ny ellir g6adu mab o genedyl			
Tri gorsaf aryf yssyd	75	54ra	
O tri achaws y gossodet kyfreith			
Tri thorllwyth vn werth ac eu mam			
Teir tystolyaeth dilis yssyd			
Tri lle y perthyn cof llys			
Teir tystolyaeth marwa6l yssyd			
Teir tystolyaeth yssyd ar eir			
Tri g6ahan yssyd r6g g6ybydyeit a thyston			
O teir ffordd y mae cadarnach g6ybydyeit			

p.	V	Fo.	W	Fo.	Mk	p.	WML p.
					3	24	
					4	24	
					5	25	
					6	25	
					7	26	
	7	25r			10	46	53
	6	25r			11	48	53
			14	79r	20	80	
118	46	44r	44	99v	47	110	129
115	47	44v	95	105v	48	111	130
112	57	45r	54		58	112	131
115	58	45r	55		59	112	131
	63	45r	63		65	113	131, 134
	66	45v	64	101v	68	114	132, 134
113			65	101v	69	114	134
116			67	102r	71	115	135
115			66	102r	72	115	135
113			68	102r	73	115	135
					77	116	
					78	116	
111					79	116	
					80	116	
116					81	117	
			81	103v	89	117	138
			84	103v	90	118	138
			91	104v	91	118	140
			90	104v	93	118	140
114			92	104v	94	118	140
			93	104v	95	118	140
					96	118	
					97	118	
					98	119	
					99	119	
					100	119	
133					101	119	
					102	119	
					103	119	
					104	120	
					105	120	
					106	120	
					107	120	
					108	121	
					109	121	
					110	121	
					111	122	

Keywords	*Z*	Fo.	*U*
Tri ryw vanac yssyd			
O tri mod y telir dir6y treis			
O tri mod y kyll dadyl treis			
Vn o tri pheth a gyll y neb a treisser			
Tri ry6 amdiffyn yssyd			
Tri pheth nyt reit attep y neb ohonunt			
Tri ry6 diebryt yssyd			
O tri mod y kae kyfreith r6g ha6l6r			
Tri theruyn ha6l yssyd			
Teir dadyl a dylyant eu barnu (Hiatus in Mk)			
O tri mod yd holir tir a dayar			
Tri chamwerescyn yssyd			
Tri ry6 vreint yssyd			
Tri phriodolder yssyd y pop dyn			
Tri llydyn o'r genuein ny drycheif			
Tri argae g6aet yssyd			61
Teir telyn kyfreitha6l			
Tri anhepcor brehyr			
Tri anhepcor taya6c			
Tri charrgychwyn heb attychwel	77	54ra	13
Tri chof g6edy bra6t yssyd			
Tri pheth a dyly bra6t6r y datganu			
Tri ry6 atteb yssyd yn dadleu			
Tri ry6 prit yssyd ar tir			
Tri ry6 varn tremyc yssyd			
Teir creith gogyuarch yssyd ar dyn	4	11rb	3
Tri argae teruyn yssyd			12
Pob adeil6r maestir a dyly caffel tri phren			
Tri chyffro dial	30	35ra	21
Tri g6g ny diwygir			35
Teir pla kenedyl			
Tri pheth a tyrr ar amot			
Tri dyn y telir galanas udunt ac ny thalant	59	38ra	24
Tri dyn a wna gulat yn tla6t			
Tri chadarn byt			60
Tri aniueil yssyd un werth eu llosgyrneu			
Tri chyuanhed g6lat			38
Teir ouer groes yssyd			
Tri mach hagen yssyd ac ny cheiff vn			
Tri lle y rann kyfreith			9
Tri anyueil a a o pedeir keina6c y punt yn un			50
Teir gorssed breinha6l yssyd			57
Teir merchet ny dylyir amobyr udunt			59
Tri pheth ni chyngain hawl ladrad arnvnt	32	35rb	
Tri dyn a ddylant vod yn anrraith odde	56	37vb	

p.	V	Fo.	W	Fo.	Mk	p.	WML p.
					112	122	
					113	123	
					114	123	
					115	123	
					116	123	
					117	124	
					118	124	
					119	124	
					120	124	
					121	124	
	8	25r			122	124	53
	9	25r			123	124	53
	10	25v			124	124	54
	11	25v			125	125	54
					126	125	
151					127	125	
					128	126	
					129	126	
					130	126	
106					132	126	
					133	126	
					134	127	
					135	127	
					136	136	
					137	137	
52	3	19v	3	57r			42
106			15	91v			
			16	91r			117
109			37	98r			303
113			77	103r			137
			82	103v			138
			83	103v			138
111			85	104r			139
			87	104r			139
150			88	104r			139
			89	104r			139
114			94	104v			140
			96	106r			143
	18	35v					86
94							
117							
127							
133							

Conspectus 3. The *Mk* triads

Mk – Keywords	no.	p.	*X*	Fo.	*WML*
Tri dyn a wna sarhaed y'r brenhin	1	2	1	166r	2
O tri mod y serheir y vrenhines	2	3	2	166v	3
O tri mod y kedernheir g6ys	3	24			
Teir ouerwys a ellir eu g6adu	4	24			
Tri dyn ny dylyir eu g6yssa6	5	25			
Tri ry6 wadu yssyd	6	25			
Tri ry6 t6g yssyd	7	26			
Tri ry6 datanhud tir yssyd	8	43	4	188r	48
Teir gweith y rennir tir r6g brodoryon	9	45	5	188v	49
Teir etiuedyaeth kyfreitha6l	10	46			53
Tri ry6 prit yssyd ar tir	11	48			53
Tri g6ybydyeit yssyd am tir	12	49	76	218v	54
Tri pheth ny werth taya6c heb ganhat	13	53	6	190r	57, 59
Teir keluydyt ny dysc taya6c y vab	14	53	7	190r	58, 59
O tri mod y telir teithi buch	15	62	8	192r	71
O teir fford yd ymdiueicha mach	16	73	58	214v	85
O teir fford y differir mach a chynnogyn	17	74	59	216r	85
O tri achaws ny chyll g6reic y heg6edi	18	80	9	202r	92
Tri pheth ny chyll g6reic kyt gatter am y cham	19	80	10	202r	93
Tri ll6 a dyry g6reic y 6r	20	80			
Tri dygyngoll kenedyl	**21**	102	14	208r	122
Tri oet kyfreith y dial kelein	**22**	103	15	208v	122
Teir r6yt brenhin ynt	**23**	103	16	208v	123
Teir r6yt taya6c ynt	**24**	104	18	209r	123
Teir r6yt breyr ynt	**25**	104	17	209r	123
Teir dir6y brenhin ynt	**26**	104	19	209r	123
Tri anhebcor brenhin ynt	**27**	105	20	209v	124
Tri pheth ny chyfran brenhin a neb	**28**	105	21	209v	124
Tri phetwar yssyd	**29**	105	22	209v	124
Teir kyflauan os g6na dyn yn y wlat	**30**	106	23	210r	125
Tri thaweda6c gorsed	**31**	106	24	210v	125
Tri g6anas g6ay6 kyfreitha6l yn dadleu	**32**	106	25	210v	125
Tri ofer ymadra6d	**33**	107	26	210v	126
Tri ofer llaeth yssyd	**34**	107	27	211r	126
Teir sarhaet ny diwygir or keffir tr6y vedda6t	**35**	107	28	211r	126
Teir palua6t ny dywygir	**36**	107	29	211r	126
Teir g6raged ny dylyir dadleu ac eu hetiued	**37**	107	30	211r	126
Tri chewilyd kenedyl ynt	**38**	107	33	211v	126
Tri chadarn enllip g6reic	**39**	108	32	211v	127
Tri pheth a ha6l dyn yn lledrat	**40**	108	36	212r	127
Teir sarhaet g6reic ynt	**41**	108	31	211r	127
O teir fford y llyssir tyston	**42**	108	35	212r	127
Tri meib yn tri broder vn vam vn tat	**43**	108	37	212r	127
Tri dyn a gynnyd eu breint	**44**	109	38	212v	128
Tri g6erth kyfreith beichogi g6reic	**45**	109	39	212v	128
O teir fford y dygir mab y tat	**46**	110	40	212v	129
O teir fford y g6edir mab o genedyl	**47**	110			129
Tri lle ny dyly dyn rodi ll6 g6eilyd	**48**	111			130

Mk – Keywords	no.	p.	X	Fo.	WML
Teir gormes doeth ynt	49	111	41	213v	130
Tri dyn a dyly tauodya6c yn llys	50	111	42	213v	130
Tri llydyn digyfreith eu g6eithret	51	111	43	213v	130
Tri llydyn nyt oes werth kyfreith arnunt	52	111	44	213v	130
Tri gwaet digyfreith yssyd	53	112	45	213v	130
Tri than digyfreith yssyd	54	112	46	213v	130
Tri edyn y dyly y brenhin eu g6erth	55	112	47	213v	130
Tri phryf y dyly y brenhin eu g6erth	56	112	48	213v	131
Tri pheth ny at kyfreith eu damd6g	57	112	49	214r	131
Teir cont kyfreitha6l	58	112	49a		131
Tri phren ryd yn fforest brenhin	59	112			131
Tri chorn buelyn y brenhin	60	113	52	214r	131
Teir hela ryd yssyd ym pop g6lat	61	113	53	214r	131, 133
Tri cheheryn canhastyr yssyd	62	113	51	214r	127
Tri pheth a tyrr ar gyfreith	63	113	54	214r	131, 133
Tri en6 righyll yssyd	64	113	57	214v	131, 134
O teir fford y telir g6yalen aryant y'r brenhin	65	113			131, 134
Tri h6rd ny diwygir	66	113	55	214r	131, 133
Tri dyn ny dylyir eu g6erthu o gyfreith	67	114	56	214r	132, 134
Tri da dilis diuach yssyd	68	114			132, 134
Tri chyffredin g6lat	69	114			134
Teir g6arthrud kelein	70	114	71	218v	137
Tri argae g6aet	71	115			135
Teir g6arthrud mor6yn	72	115			135
Tri di6yneb g6lat yssyd	73	115			135
Teir ael6yt a dyly g6neuthur ia6n	74	115	11	207v	135
Teir notwyd kyfreitha6l yssyd	75	115	63	217v	135
Teir mar6 tystolyaeth yssyd	76	115	64	217v	136
Tri pheth a gadarnha deua6t	77	116			
Tri pheth a wanha defa6t	78	116			
Tri dyn yssyd ryd udunt kerdet fford	79	116			
Tri pheth a geid6 cof ac a seif yn lle tyston	80	116			
Tri anhebcor kenedyl	81	117			
Teir kyfrinach yssyd well eu hadef noc eu kelu	82	117	65	217v	137
Tri aneueil vn troedawc yssyd	83	117	66	217v	137
Tri pheth ny thelir kyn coller yn ranty	84	117	69	218r	137
Tair gauael nyt atuerir	85	117	72	218v	137
Teir sarhaet kelein	86	117	70	218v	137
Tri pheth nyt reit atteb y eu perchenna6c	87	117	74	218v	138
Tri dyn y telir g6eli taua6t udunt	88	117	75	218v	138
Tri lle yg kyfreith Hywel y mae pra6f	89	117			138
Tri pheth a differ dyn rac gwys dadleu	90	118			138
Tri chyffredin kenedyl	91	118			140
Tri ergyt ny diwygir	92	118	61	216v	139
Tri dyn kas kenedyl	93	118			140
Tri mefyluethyant gwr	94	118			140
Tri aneueil yssyd u6y g6erth eu teithi	95	118			140
Tri pheth a dyly dyn colli y dadyl	96	118			
Tri gr6ndwal doethinab	97	118			
Tri pheth ny drycheif y neb	98	119			

Mk – Keywords	no.	p.	*X*	Fo.	*WML*
Teir kyfnewit a doant trachefyn	**99**	119			
Teir mefyl6ryaeth mach	**100**	119			
O teir ffordd y telir amobyr	**101**	119			
O teir ffordd ny ellir g6adu mab o genedyl	**102**	119			
Tri gorsaf aryf yssyd	**103**	119			
O tri achaws y gossodet kyfreith	**104**	120			
Tri thorllwyth vn werth ac eu mam	**105**	120			
Teir tystolyaeth dilis yssyd	**106**	120			
Tri lle y perthyn cof llys	**107**	120			
Teir tystolyaeth marwa6l yssyd	**108**	121			
Teir tystolyaeth yssyd ar eir	**109**	121			
Tri g6ahan yssyd r6g g6ybydyeit a thyston	**110**	121			
O teir ffordd y mae cadarnach g6ybydyeit	**111**	122			
Tri ryw vanac yssyd	**112**	122			
O tri mod y telir dir6y treis	**113**	123			
O tri mod y kyll dadyl treis	**114**	123			
Vn o tri pheth a gyll y neb a treisser	**115**	123			
Tri ry6 amdiffyn yssyd	**116**	123			
Tri pheth nyt reit attep y neb ohonunt	**117**	124			
Tri ry6 diebryt yssyd	**118**	124			
O tri mod y kae kyfreith r6g ha6l6r	**119**	124			
Tri theruyn ha6l yssyd	**120**	124			
Teir dadyl a dylyant eu barnu (Hiatus in Mk)	**121**	124			
O tri mod yd holir tir a dayar	**122**	124			53
Tri chamwerescyn yssyd	**123**	124			53
Tri ry6 vreint yssyd	**124**	124			54
Tri phriodolder yssyd y pop dyn	**125**	125			54
Tri llydyn o'r genuein ny drycheif	**126**	125			
Tri argae g6aet yssyd	**127**	125			
Teir telyn kyfreitha6l	**128**	126			
Tri anhepcor brehyr	**129**	126			
Tri anhepcor taya6c	**130**	126			
Tri chyfr6ch dirgel a dyly y brenhin eu kaffel	**131**	126	62	217v	
Tri charrgychwyn heb attychwel	**132**	126			
Tri chof g6edy bra6t yssyd	**133**	126			
Tri pheth a dyly bra6t6r y datganu	**134**	127			
Tri ry6 atteb yssyd yn dadleu	**135**	127			
Tri ry6 prit yssyd ar tir	136	136			
Tri ry6 varn tremyc yssyd	137	137			

Conspectus 4. The Triads in Z

Z – Keywords	No.	Fo.
Tri dyn a wna syrhaed i'r brenin	1	1rb
O dri mod i syrheir y vrenhines	2	1va
Tri gwysanaeth a wna y brenin i'r hebogud	3	4vb
Tair kraith gogyvarch ysyd	4	11rb
Tair gwaith y rennir tir	5	12va
O dri achaws ni chyll gwraic i hagweddi kyd adawo i gwr	6	25ra
Tri pheth ni ddygyr rrac gwraic	7	25ra
Tri llw a ddyry gwraic	8	25rb
Tri lle ydd ymddi6acha mach gan kyfraith	9	28ra
Tri dygyngoll kenedl	10	32vb
Tri oed kyfraith i ddial kelain	11	33ra
Tair rrwyd brenin	12	33rb
Tair rrwyd bryr	13	33rb
Tair rrwyd taiawc	14	33rb
Tair dirwy brenin	15	33va
Tri anhepcor brenin	16	33va
Tri pheth ni chyfran brenin	17	35vb
Tri phedwar y sydd	18	35vb
Tair kyflavan o'r a wnel dyn yn i wlad	19	34(ii)rb
Tri thawedawc gorsedd	20	34(ii)rb
Tair gwanas kyfreithiawl y syd i wayw	21	34(ii)rb
Tri over ymadrawd	22	34(ii)va
Tri over laeth	23	34(ii)va
Tair syrhaed ni ddiwygir	24	34(ii)va
Tair palwawd ni ddiwygir	25	34(ii)va
Tair gwraged ni ddadle6ir ac ev hytived	26	34(ii)va
Tair syrhaed gwraic	27	34(ii)vb
Tri chywilid kenedl	28	35ra
Tri chadarn enllib gwraic	29	35ra
Tri chyffro dial ynt	30	35ra
Tair fford y llyssir tystion	31	35rb
Tri pheth ni chyngain hawl ladrad arnvnt	32	35rb
Tri mab yn dri broder 6n vam 6n dad	33	35rb
Tri dyn a gynyd ev breint yn vn dyd	34	35va
Tri gwerth kyfraith beichiogi	35	35vb
O dair fford y dygir mab ac y dywedir	36	35vb
Tair gormes doeth	37	36rb
Tri dyn a ddyly tavodiawc drostvnd	38	36rb
Tri llwdwn digyfraith ev gwaith	39	36rb
Tri llwdwn nid oes werth kyfraith arnaddvnt	40	36rb
Tri gwaed digyfraith syd	41	36rb
Tri than ni ddywygir	42	36rb
Tri edyn a ddyly brenin e6 gwerth	43	36va
Tri ffryf a ddyly brenin ev gwerth	44	36va
Tri pheth ni ad kyfraith ev damdwng	45	36va
Tair k[ont] (censored in W, Z)	46	36va
Tri phren y syd rydd i llad	47	36vb
Tri chyhyr[y]n kanastr	48	36vb

Z – Keywords	No.	Fo.
Tri chorn bvelin brenin	**49**	37ra
Tair hely rryd ysyd ymhob gwlad	**50**	37ra
Tri ffeth a dyr kyfraith	**51**	37ra
Tri hwrd ny ddiwygir	**52**	37ra
Tri dyn ni ddyly brenin i gwerth6	**53**	37rb
Tri enw rringill y sydd	**54**	37rb
Tair aylwyd a ddyly gwnethvr iawn	**55**	37vb
Tri dyn a ddylant vod yn anrraithodde	**56**	37vb
Tri gwarthrud morwyn	**57**	37vb
Tri argay gwaed	**58**	38ra
Tri dyn y telir galanas 6ddvnt	**59**	38ra
Tair aelwyd a ddyly gwneuthur bodd	60	39rb
O dair fford y telir gwialen ariant	61	39vb
Tri ergid ni thelir dim	62	39ra
Tair kyfrinach a ddyly y brenin i gaffal	63	39ra
Tair nodwydd kyfreithiawl	64	39ra
Tri pheth or ceffir ar fford	65	39rb
O dair fford y dyly dyn vod yn enaidvadde	66	43rb
O dair fford y telir gw[i]alen ariant a phiol	67	43rb
Tri pheth ni werth tayawc	68	49ra
Tair kel6yddyd ni ddysc mab taiawg	69	49ra
O dri modd y telir teithi buwch	70	49rb
Tri adeilad a ddylant vod yn gyffredin y rrwng	71	50rb
Tri ffeth ni ddyly ev perchenawc i rranv	72	50rb
Tri gwarthrvdd kenedl	73	53vb
Tri ytavel nid atverir	74	53vb
Tair gorsedd arf	75	54ra
Tair marwdysdioleth y sydd	76	54ra
Tri chargychwyn heb attychwel	77	54ra
Tair agweddi kyfreithiawl	78	55ra
Tri dyn a ddyly galanas	79	55rb
Tri dyn a ddyly syrhaed	80	55va
Tri dyn a ddyly rran galanas	81	55va
Tri dyn a ddyly talv galanas	82	55va
Tri dyn bonheddic gwirion	83	55va
Tri maib kayth o rydd	84	55vb
Tri maib rrydd o gayth	85	55vb
Tair merched ni ddyly i tad dalv i hebediw	86	55vb
Tri dyn a ddyly le yn y llys	87	55vb
Tri dyn nid gair ev gair	88	57ra
Tri achaws y cyll dyn dref i dad	89	57ra
Tri gwanas gwystl	90	57rb
Tri phren y sydd rydd i ambriodawr	91	57rb
Tri anifail a a yn ev gwerth yn ev blwydd	92	57rb
Tri anogonyon kyfraith	93	57rb
Tri argay tir	94	57rb
Tri lleidyr kamlyrvs	95	58vb
Tri lleidyr dirwyvs	96	58vb
Tri lleidyr gwerth	97	58vb
Tri than ni ddiwygir	98	67ra

Z – Keywords	No.	Fo.
Tri gwaed y sydd ni thelir eu gwerth	99	69va
Tair ffordd y llyssir ynad	100	73rb
Eithyr tri dyn a ddyly tavawd drosdunt ym hob lle	101	73va
Tair ffordd y dylir dienyddv dyn	102	79ra
Tri ffeth y sydd vn vraint a lladrad yn llaw	103	79va
Tri ryw vyrowdyr y sydd ynghymrry	104	85ra
Tri achos y gellir gwrthod browdwr	105	85rb
Tri ffeth ni ddyly lliaws o vyrwdwyr i wneuthur	106	85va
Tri devnydd hawl yssyd	107	85va
Tri gwallowgair y sydd	108	85va
Tri modd y bydd kamlwrw	109	86ra
Tri ryw gamlwrw y sydd	110	86va
Tri modd y kollir kamlwrw vn dyblic	111	86va
Tri modd y bydd kamlwrw dav ddyblic	112	86vb
Tri modd y bydd kamlwrw tri dybylic	113	86vb
Tri dyn ni dyly kamlwrw arnvnt	114	87ra
Tri dyn a dal abediw hep dir	115	87rb
Tri ffeth nit rait praw arnvnt	116	87rb
Tri rryw ddadanvdd ysydd	117	90vb
Tair merched ni ddyleir dadle	118	93rb
Tri argay dangos	119	97vb
Tri lle y dyly dyn vesur i hawl gan amddiffynwr	120	98rb

Conspectus 5.   Triads in published sources

Bold numbers indicate triads found in collections in Latin D. *Q* numbers in square brackets
indicate triads moved from the triad collection to relevant points in the text.

Keywords – Llyfr Blegywryd	no.	p.	Dim.	*J*
Teir sarhaet brenhin	1	3	I. ii. 2	1
Tri ryw sarhaet yssyd	2	3	I. ii. 3	2
O tri mod y serheir y vrenhines	3	4	I. iii. 1	3
Tri ryw dyn yssyd	4	5	I. v. 8	4
Tri ryw wassannaeth yssyd	5	13	I. xii. 9	5
Tri gwassannaeth a dyly y brenhin	6	13	I. xiii. 2	6
Tri pheth a berthynn wrth vrawdwr	7	17	I. xiv. 22	7
Tri amheu braut yssyd	8	18	I. xiv. 24	8
Tri dygyngoll kenedyl ynt	9	33	II. i. 33	19
Tri achaws yssyd y lyssu tyston	10	37	II. iv. 3	20
O teir fford y byd ryd mach	11	40	II. v. 4	21
O teir fford yd oedir mach a	12	40	II. vi. 10	22
Teir mefylwryaeth mach yssyd	13	40	II. vi. 11	23
Tri lle yd ymdiueicha mach	14	42	II. vi. 24	24
Tri pheth ny henynt o vechni	15	42	II. vi. 25	25
Tri ryw dirwy yssyd	16	42	II. vii. 1	26
Tri pheth a dyly gwarant diball	17	44	II. ix. 2	142
O tri achaws ny chyll gwreic	18	64	II. xviii. 21	143
Teir gweith y keiff gwreic	19	64	II. xviii. 22	144
Tri llw a dyry gwreic y wr	20	64	II. xviii. 25	145
Tri lle y ran kyfreith yn deu hanher	21	71	II. xx. 6	146
Teir etiuedyaeth kyfreithawl	22	74	II. xii. 6	147
Teir gweith y renhir yr vn tref	23	75	II. xxiii. 2	148
Tri ryw prit yssyd ar tir	24	78	II. xxiii. 23	149
O tri mod yd holir tir	25	78	II. viii. 105	130
Tri chamwerescyn yssyd	26	78	II. viii. 106	131
O tri mod y dosperthir dadyl datanhud	27	79	II. viii. 107	132
Tri ryw vreint yssyd	28	79	II. viii. 108	133
Tri phriodolder yssyd	29	80	II. viii. 109	134
O tri mod y telir teithi buch	30	88	II. xxvi. xix	150
Tri ryw vrawtwyr yssyd yg Kymry	31	98	II. viii. 110	135
Tri dyn ny allant ymwystlaw	32	102	II. viii. 124	136
Tri pheth a dyly pob brawdwr	33	103	II. viii. 125	137
Tri ryw varn tremyc yssyd	34	104	II. viii. 127	138
Tri dyn yssyd ny digawn	35	104	II. viii. 128	139
Teir fford y gellir gwrthot brawdwr	36	104	II. viii. 129	140
O teir fford y dosperthir brawt	37	105	I. xxx. 8	15
Tri pheth a dyly brawdwr eu datganu	38	105	I. xxx. 10	17
O tri mod y kyll brawdwr gamlwrw	39	106	I. xxx. 11	18
Tri gwrtheb yssyd	40	106	II. viii. 133	141
Teir kynefawt yssyd	41	107	II. xxxvi. 1	151

p.	Lat D	p.	Q	fo.	X	fo.
2	1	317	1	1va	1	166r
2	2	317	2	1vb		
3	3	317	3	2ra	2	166v
4	4	318	4	2rb		
9	5	323	5	4vb		
10			6	4vb	3	174r
12	6	325	7	6ra		
13	7	326	8	6rb	13	207v
25	9	335	19	11va	14	208r
28			38	22va	35	212r
30	68	368	45	24va		
31	69	368	46	24vb	59	216v
31	**70**	368	47	24vb		
32	**121**	373	51	26va		
32	**122**	373	52	26va		
32	17	337	55	32vb	19	209r
50	**30**	353	37	16vb		
63	18	343	232	74va	9	202r
63			233	74va		
63			234	74vb		
68			225	57va	69	218v
70	149	386	226	58vb		
70			227	59ra	5	188v
72			228	60va		
44	144	384	220	56vb		
44	145	385	221	56vb		
44	146	385	222	56vb	4	188r
44	147	385	223	57rb		
44	148	385	224	57rb		
78	65	358	236	86va	8	192r
45	**23**, [143]	349, 382	208	46vb		
47	**24**	351	209	48va		
48	**25**	352	210	48va		
48	**26**	352	211	49ra		
48	**27**	352	212	49ra		
49	**28**	352	213	49rb		
22			15	9vb		
22			17	10ra		
22			18	10ra		
141	**29**	353	207	45vb		
85	**151**	394	237	90rb		

Keywords – Llyfr Blegywryd	no.	p.	Dim.	*J*
Tri pheth a gadarnha kynefawt	42	107	II. xxxvi. 2	152
Tri pheth a wanha kynefawt	43	107	II. xxxvi. 3	153
Teir rwyt brenhin ynt	**44**	107	II. viii. 1	27
Teir rwyt breyr ynt	**45**	107	II. viii. 2	28
Teir rwyt tayawc ynt	**46**	108	II. viii. 3	29
Tri chorn buelyn y brenhin	**47**	108	II. viii. 4	30
Teir telyn kyfreithawl	**48**	108	II. viii. 5	31
Tri pheth nyt ryd i vilaen	**49**	108	II. viii. 6	32
Teir keluydyt ny eill tayawc	**50**	108	II. viii. 7	33
Teir kyflafan os gwna dyn	**51**	108	II. viii. 8	34
Tri anhebcor brenhin ynt	**52**	108	II. viii. 9	35
Tri anhebcor breyr ynt	**53**	108	II. viii. 10	36
Tri anhebcor tayawc ynt	**54**	109	II. viii. 11	37
Tri pheth ny chyfran brenhin a neb	**55**	109	II. viii. 12	38
Tri phetwar yssyd	**56**	109	II. viii. 13	39
Tri oet kyfraith y dial kelein	**57**	109	II. viii. 14	40
Tri thawedawc gorsed	**58**	110	II. viii. 15	41
Tri gwanas gwayw kyfreithawl	**59**	110	II. viii. 16	42
Tri ouer ymadrawd	**60**	110	II. viii. 17	43
Tri ouer llaeth	**61**	110	II. viii. 18	44
Teir sarhaet ny diwygir	**62**	110	II. viii. 19	45
Teir paluawt ny diwygir	**63**	111	II. viii. 20	46
Teir gwragedd a dyly eu meibon	**64**	111	II. viii. 21	47
Teir sarhaet gwraic ynt	**65**	111	II. viii. 22	48
Tri chewilyd kenedyl ynt	**66**	111	II. viii. 23	49
Tri chadarn enllib gwreic ynt	**67**	111	II. viii. 24	50
Tri chyffro dial ynt	**68**	111	II. viii. 25	51
Tri pheth a hawl dyn yn lletrat	**69**	112	II. viii. 26	52
Tri meib yssyd ny dylyant	**70**	112	II. viii. 27	53
Tri dyn a gynnyd eu braint yn vn dyd	**71**	112	II. viii. 28	54
Tri gwerth kyfraith beichogi gwreic	**72**	112	II. viii. 29	55
O tri mod y gwedir kysswynnplant	**73**	113	II. viii. 30	56
Teir gormes doeth ynt	**74**	113	II. viii. 31	57
Tri dyn a dyly tauotyawc yn llys	**75**	113	II. viii. 32	58
Tri llydyn digeureith	**76**	113	II. viii. 33	59
Tri llydyn nyt oes werth kyureith	**77**	113	II. viii. 34	60
Tri gwaet digyureith	**78**	114	II. viii. 35	61
Tri than digyureith	**79**	114	II. viii. 36	62
Tri edyn a dyly y brenhin	**80**	114	II. viii. 37	63
Tri phryf a dyly y brenhin	**81**	114	II. viii. 38	64
Tri pheth ny at kyfraith eu damdwg	**82**	114	II. viii. 39	65
Tri phren yssyd ryd yn fforest	**83**	114	II. viii. 40	66
Tri chehyryn canhastyr	**84**	114	II. viii. 41	67
Tri pheth a tyrr ar gyfreith	**85**	114	II. viii. 42	68
Tri edyn ny dylyir eu llad	**86**	114	II. viii. 43	69

p.	Lat D	p.	Q	fo.	X	fo.
85	152	394	239	91ra		
85			240	91ra		
33	**71**	369	**56**	33rb	16	208v
33	**72**	370	**57**	33rb	17	209r
33	**73**	370	**58**	33rb	18	209r
33	**74**	370	**59**	33rb	58	216r
33	**75**	370	**60**	33va		
33	**76**	370	**61**	33va	6	190r
33	**77**	370	**62**	33va	7	190r
33	**10**	335	**63**	33va	23	210r
33	**78**	370	**64**	33vb	20	209v
33	**79**	370	**65**	33vb		
33	**80**	370	**66**	33vb		
33	**81, 92**	370, 371	**[30]**	16rb	21	209v
34	**82**	370	**69**	34ra	22	209v
34	**11**	335	**[20]**	12ra	15	208v
34	**83**	371	**[21]**	12ra	24	210v
34	**12**	336	**[22]**	12rb	25	210v
35	**84**	371	**67**	33vb	26	210v
35	**85**	371	**68**	33vb	27	211r
35	**86**	371	**[23]**	12rb	28	211r
35	**87**	371	**70**	34ra	29	211r
35			**71**	34rb	30	211r
35	**88**	371	**[24]**	12rb	31	211r
35	**89**	371	**72**	34rb	33	211v
35	**90**	371	**73**	ꞏ34rb	32	211v
35	**91**	371	**[25]**	12rb	34	211v
35			**[31]**	16rb	36	212r
35			**74**	34rb	37	212r
36	**93**	371	**75**	34va	38	212v
36	**13**	336	**[26]**	12va	39	212v
36	**104**	372	**76**	34va		
36	**96**	372	**77**	34vb	41	213v
36	**31, 97**	354, 372	**78**	34vb	42	213v
36	**98**	372	**79**	34vb	43	213v
37	**99**	372	**80**	35ra	44	213v
37	**100**	372	**81**	35ra	45	213v
37	**14**	336	**[27]**	15ra	46	213v
37	**101**	372	**82**	35ra	47	213v
37	**102**	372	**83**	35ra	48	213v
37	**103**	372	**84**	35ra	49	214r
37	**105**	373	**85**	35rb	50	214r
37	**15**	337	**86**	35rb	51	214r
37	**106**	373	**87**	35rb	54	214r
37	**107**	373	**88**	35rb	48	213v

Keywords – Llyfr Blegywryd	no.	p.	Dim.	J
Tri pheth or keffir ar fford	87	115	II. viii. 44	70
Tri dyn ny dyly brenhin eu gwerthu	88	115	II. viii. 45	71
Tri eno righill yssyd	89	115	II. viii. 46	72
Tri ergyt ny thelir dim ymdannunt	90	115	II. viii. 47	73
Tri chyfurwch dirgel	91	115	II. viii. 48	74
Teir nottwyd kyureithawl	92	115	II. viii. 49	75
Teir kyfrinach yssyd well eu hadef	93	115	II. viii. 50	76
Tri annyueil vntroedawc yssyd	94	115	II. viii. 51	77
Tri phrenn a dyly pob adeilwr maestir	95	115	II. viii. 52	78
Tri pheth ny thelir kyn coller	96	115	II. viii. 53	79
Teir sarhaet kelein ynt	97	116	II. viii. 55	81
Teir gwarthrut kelein ynt	98	116	II. viii. 54	80
Teir gauael nyt atuerir	99	116	II. viii. 56	82
Tri ryw tal yssyd i gwynwr	100	116	II. viii. 57	83
Tri ymdillwng o rwym hawl yssyd	101	116	II. viii. 58	84
Tri chargychwyn heb attychwel	102	116	II. viii. 59	85
O tri achaws y gossodet kyfreith	103	116	II. viii. 60	86
Tri hwrd ny diwygir	104	116	II. viii. 61	87
Tri da nyt reit mach arnunt	105	117	II. viii. 62	88
Teir marw tystolyaeth	106	117	II. viii. 63	89
Tri thorllwyth vn werth	107	117	II. viii. 64	90
Tri llydyn vn werth	108	117	II. viii. 65	91
Teir fford y dywedir gwybydyeit	109	118	II. viii. 66	92
Tri pheth a geidw cof	110	118	II. viii. 67	93
Tri dyn y telir gwely tauot	111	118	II. viii. 68	94
Tri chowyllawc llys	112	118	II. viii. 69	95
Tri dyn a geidw breint llys	113	118	II. viii. 70	96
Tri datssaf gwaet yssyd	114	118	II. viii. 71	97
Tri hela ryd yssyd	115	119	II. viii. 72	98
Tri chewilyd morwyn yssyd	116	119	II. viii. 73	99
Tri pheth ny ellir eu dwyn rac gwreic	117	119	II. viii. 74	100
Tri defnyd hawl yssyd	118	119	II. viii. 75	101
Tri golwc a dygir yg kyfreith	119	119	II. viii. 76	102
Tri geir kylus yssyd	120	119	II. viii. 77	103
Tri ryw wallawgeir yssyd	121	119	II. viii. 78	104
Tri theruyn hawl yssyd	122	120	II. viii. 79	105
Tri pheth ny chygein yg kyfreith	123	120	II. viii. 80	106
Tri gweithret yssyd ar prawf	124	120	II. viii. 81	107
Tri gwaessaf yssyd	125	120	II. viii. 82	108
Tri chof gwedy brawt yssyd	126	120	II. viii. 83	109
Teir tystolyaeth dilis yssyd	127	120	II. viii. 84	110
Tri lle y tywys cof llys	128	121	II. viii. 85	111
Teir tystolyaeth marwawl yssyd	129	121	II. viii. 86	112
Tri gwahan yssyd	130	121	II. viii. 87	113
Teir fford y mae kadarnach	131	121	II. viii. 88	114

p.	Lat D	p.	*Q*	fo.	*X*	fo.
37	**108**	373	**89**	35rb	74	218v
37	**110**	373	**90**	35rb	56	214v
37	**111**	373	**91**	35va	57	214v
37	**112**	373	**92**	35va	61	217v
38	**113**	373	**93**	35va	62	217v
38	**114**	373	**94**	35va	63	217v
38	**115**	373	**95**	35va	65	218r
38	**116**	373	**96**	35va	66	218r
38	**67, 117**	364, 373	**97**	35vb	67	218r
38	**118**	373	**98**	35vb	69	218v
38	**120**	373	**99**	35vb	70	218v
38	**119**	373	**100**	35vb	71	218v
38	**16**	337	**101**	35vb	72	218v
38	**123**	374	**102**	35vb		
38	**124**	374	**103**	35vb		
38	**125, 133**	374, 375	**104**	35vb		
38	**127**	374	**105**	36ra		
38	**128**	374	**106**	36ra	55	214r
39	**129**	374	**107**	36rb		
39	**130**	374	**108**	36rb	64	217v
39	**131**	375	**109**	36va		
39	**132**	375	**110**	36va		
39	**134**	375	**111**	36va		
40	**135**	375	**112**	36vb		
40	**136**	375	**113**	36vb		
40	**137**	376	**114**	36vb		
40	**138**	376	**115**	36vb		
40	**109, 139**	373, 376	**116**	36vb		
40	**140**	376	**117**	37ra	53	214r
40	**19, 141**	346, 376	**118**	37ra		
40	**142**	376	**119**	37ra	10	202r
40	**35**	355	**120**	37rb		
40	**36**	355	**121**	37rb		
40	**37**	355	**122**	37rb		
41	**39**	355	**123**	37rb		
41	**40**	355	**124**	37va		
41	**41**	355	**125**	37va		
41	**42**	355	**126**	37va		
41	**43**	355	**127**	37va		
41	**44**	355	**128**	37va		
41	**45**	355	**129**	37vb		
41	**46**	355	**130**	37vb		
41	**47**	355	**131**	37vb		
42	**48**	356	**132**	38ra		
42	**49**	356	**133**	38ra		

Keywords – Llyfr Blegywryd	no.	p.	Dim.	J
Teir tystolyaeth yssyd ar eir	**132**	122	II. viii. 89	115
Tri lleidyr camlyryus yssyd	**133**	122	II. viii. 90	116
Tri lleidyr dirwyus yssyd	**134**	122	II. viii. 91	117
Tri lleidyr gwerth yssyd	**135**	122	II. viii. 92	118
Tri lleidyr crogadwy yssyd	**136**	122	II. viii. 93	119
Tri lleidyr a dieinc o letrat kyfadef	**137**	122	II. viii. 94	120
O tri mod y telir dirwy treis	**138**	123	II. viii. 97	121
O tri mod y kyll dadyl treis	**139**	123	II. viii. 98	122
Vn o tri a gyll	**140**	123	II. viii. 98	123
Tri ryw amdiffyn yssyd	**141**	123	II. viii. 99	124
Tri pheth nyt reit atteb y neb	**142**	123	II. viii. 100	125
Tri ryw diebryt yssyd	**143**	123	II. viii. 101	126
O tri mod y cae kyfreith	**144**	124	II. viii. 102	127
Tri theruyn kyfreithawl	**145**	124	II. viii. 103	128
Teir dadyl a dylyant eu iachau	**146**	124	II. viii. 104	129
Tri ryw vanac yssyd	147	124	I. xxx. 9	16
O tri mod y kedernheir gwys	148	125	I. xxx. 1	9
Teir gwys a ellir eu gwadu	149	125	I. xxx. 2	10
Tri dyn ny dylyir eu gwyssyaw	150	125	I. xxx. 3	11
Tri ryw wadu yssyd	151	125	I. xxx. 4	12
Tri mach yssyd ny cheiff vn ohonunt	152	126	I. xxx. 5	13
Tri ryw twg yssyd	153	126	I. xxx. 7	14
Teir ran yw awdurdawt Hywel Da	154	126	II. xxxvi. 5	154
Tri aruer kyfreith yssyd	155	127	III. i. 1	155
Teir gossodedigaeth yssyd	156	129	III. i. 13	156

p.	Lat D	p.	Q	fo.	X	fo.
42	**50**	356	**134**	38rb		
42	**51**	356	**[32]**	16rb		
42	**52**	356	**[33]**	16rb		
42	**53**	356	**[34]**	16rb		
42	**54**	356	**[35]**	16va		
43	**55**	356	**[36]**	16va		
43	**56**	357	**135**	38rb		
43	**57**	357	**136**	38va		
43	**58**	357	**137**	38va		
43	**59**	357	**138**	38va		
43	**60**	357	**139**	38vb		
43	**61**	357	**140**	38vb		
43	**62**	357	**141**	38vb		
43	**63**	357	**142**	38vb		
44	**64**	357	**143**	38vb		
22			16	9vb		
20	20	348	9	9rb		
20	21	349	10	9rb		
20	22	349	11	9rb		
20	8	335	12	9rb		
21			13, 49	9va, 25va		
21			14	9vb		
86	153	394	241	91rb		
86	154	394	242	91rb		
87	155	395	238	90rb		

Conspectus 6a. The Triads in Q, showing OTr-type Bleg Manuscripts

Where the text is underlined, the triads are given in the expected position in Bleg. These triads do not, however, occur in that position in Q. Where the text is given in italic they are in the correct position in Q, but are found in the triad collection in most other Bleg manuscripts. The text in bold shows the triad collection. Where * is given for Latin D, the triads have been moved in that manuscript

Keywords – Q	Q	fo.	J	p.	L	fo.	M	p.	N	fo.	R	p.	T	fo.	Tim	p.	Bost	p.	Lat D	p.
Teir sarhaet brenhin	1	1va	1	4	1	4v	1	4			1	3	1	1r			1	4	1	317
Tri ry6 sarhaet yssyd	2	1vb	2	4	2	4v	2	4			2	3	2	1v			2	4	2	317
O tri mod y serheir y vrenhines	3	2ra	3	5	3	5v	3	5			3	4	3	1v			3	5	3	317
Tri ry6 dyn yssyd	4	2rb	4	7	4	6r	4	6			4	5	4	2r			4	7	4	318
Tri ry6 6assanaeth a 6na	5	4vb	5	17	5	11r	5	18			5	14	5	6v					5	323
Tri g6assanaeth a 6na y brenhin	6	4vb	6	17	6	11v	6	18			6	14								
Tri pheth a perthyn y vra6d6r	7	6ra	7	23	7	14r	7	24	1	5r	7	19					5	22	6	325
Tri amheu bra6t yssyd	8	6rb	8	24	8	14v	8	25	2	5v	8	19					6	23	7	326
O tri modd y kedernheir	9	9rb	9	38	9	20v			3	7r	9	21	6						20	348
Tri g6ys a ellir eu g6adu	10	9rb	10	38	10	20v			4	7v	10	21	7	9v					21	349
Tri dyn ny dylyir eu g6ysya6	11	9rb	11	39	11	20v			5	8r	11	32		9v					22	349
Tri ry6 6adu yssyd	12	9rb	12	39	12	20v			6	8r	12	32								
Tri mach yssyd ny cheiff	13	9va	13	40	13	21r	9	37	7	8v	13	33			106	61			8	335
Tri ry6 t6g yssyd	14	9vb	14	42	14	21r	10	37	8	8v	14	33								
O teir fford y dosperthir	15	9vb	15	42	15	21v	11	37	9	9r	15	33								
Tri ry6 vanac yssyd	16	9vb	16	42	16	21v	12	38	10	9r	16	34								
Tri pheth a dyly bra6d6r	17	10ra	17	43	17	22r	13	39	11	10r	17	34								
O tri mod y kyll bra6d6r	18	10ra	18	44	18	22r	14	39	12	10r	18	34								
Tri dygyngoll kenedyl	19	11va	19	50	19	25r	15	46	13	13v	19	40								
Tri oet kyfraith y dial	20	12ra																	9	335
Tri tha6eda6c gorsed	21	12ra																		
Tri g6anas g6ay6	22	12rb																		
Teir sarhaet ny di6gir	23	12rb																		
Teir sarhaet g6reic ynt	24	12rb																		
Tri chyffro dial yssyd	25	12rb																		
Tri g6erth kyfreith beichogi	26	12va																		
Tri than digyfreith	27	15ra																	13	336
Tri gol6c a dygir	28	15rb																		

See the triad collection, below, for these cross-references

Rows 29–36 (Tri geir kylus yssyd … Tri lleidyr a dieinc): *See the triad collection, below, for these cross-references.*

No.	Triad	Fol.	(a)	(b)	(c)	Fol.	(d)	(e)	(f)	Fol.	(g)	(h)	Fol.	(i)	(j)	(k)	(l)	(m)	Page
29	Tri geir kylus yssyd	15rb																	
30	Tri pheth ny chyfran	16rb																	
31	Tri pheth a ha6l dyn yn	16rb																	
32	Tri lleidyr camlyryus yssyd	16rb																	
33	Tri lleidyr dir6yus yssyd	16rb																	
34	Tri lleidyr g6erth yssyd	16rb																	
35	Tri lleidyr crogad6y yssyd	16va																	
36	Tri lleidyr a dieinc	16va																	
37	Tri pheth a dyly g6arant diball	16vb	142	105	142	49v	104	136	20				30r	81	11	127	95	30	353
38	Tri acha6s yssyd y lyssu tyston	22va	20	56	20	27v	41	16	45							7	49		
39	Teir tystolyaeth dilys	23rb				17v	14		129										
40	Tri lle y ty6ys cof llys	23va																	
41	Teir tystolyaeth mar6a6l	23va																	
42	Tri g6ahan yssyd	23va																	
43	Teir fford y mae kadarnach	23vb																	
44	Teir tystvolaeth yssyd	23vb																	
45	Teir fford ybyd ryd mach	24va	21	60	21	29r	55	17	15	19r	48	8	10r			8	52	68	368
46	O teir fford yd oedir mach	24vb	22	61	22	30r	55	18	16	19v	49	9	10v			9	53	69	368
47	Teir mefe6lryaeth mach yssyd	24vb	23	61	23	30	56	19	17	20r	49	10	10v			10	53	70	368
48	Tri pheth ny dylyir na6d racdun	25va																	
49	Tri mach yssyd ny cheiff	25va																	
50	Tri lle yssyd or or rodir meicheu	26ra	24	63	24	31r	59	20	18					104	60				
51	Tri lle yd ymdiueicha mach	26va	25	63	25	31r	59	21	19	21v	51	11	12r			11	56	121	373
52	Tri pheth ny henynt o vechni	26va	167	277						22r	51	12	12r	119	69	12	56	122	373
53	Teir ouer vechni yssyd	28rb	277																
54	Tri pheth y kyll dyn	31rb																	
55	Tri ry6 dir6y yssyd	32vb	26	63	26	31r	60	22	20	22r	51	13	10r	128	79	13	56	17	337
56	Teir r6yt brenhin ynt	33rb	27	65	27	32r	62	23	21	23r	53	14	13r					71	369
57	Teir r6yt breyr ynt	33rb	28	65	28	32r	62	24	22	23v	53	15	13r			14	59	72	370
58	Teir r6yt taya6c ynt	33rb	29	66	29	32r	62	25	23	23v	53	16	13r			15	59	73	370
59	Tri chorn buelyn	33rb	30	66	30	32r	62	26	24	23v	53	17	13r			16	59	74	370
60	Teir telyn kyfreitha6l	33va	31	66	31	32v	62	27	25	23v	54	18	13r			17	59	75	370
61	Tri pheth nyt ryd y vilaen	33va	32	66	32	32v	63	28	26	24r	54	19	13r			18	59	76	370
62	Teir keluydyt ny eill	33va	33	66	33	32v	63	29	27	24r	54	20	13v	134	80	19	59	77	370
63	Teir kyflauan os g6na	33va	34	67	34	32v	63	30	28	24r	54	21	13v			20	59	10	335

Keywords	Q	fo.	J	p.	L	fo.	M	p.	N	fo.	R	p.	T	fo.	Tim	p.	Bost	p.	Lat D	p.
Tri anhepcor brenin	64	33vb	35	67	35	33r	31	63	29	24v	35	54	22	13v			21	60	78	370
Tri anhepcor breyr	65	33vb	36	67	36	33r	32	64	30	24v	36	55	23	13v			22	60	79	370
Tri anhepccor taya6c	66	33vb	37	67	37	33r	33	64	31	24v	37	55	24	13v			23	60	80	370
(Tri pheth ny chyfran brenin)	*	*	38	67	38	33r	34	64	32	24v	38	55	25	13v			24	60	81, 92	370, 371
(Tri oet kyfreith y dial)	*	*	40	69	40	33v	36	65	34	25v	40	56	27	14r			26	62	*	
(Tri thawedog gorsedd)	*	*	41	69	41	34r	37	66	35	25r	41	56	28	14v			27	62	83	371
(Tri gwanas gwayw)	*	*	42	69	42	34r	38	66	36	26r	42	56	29	14v			28	62	*	
Tri ofer ymadra6d	67	33vb	43	70	43	34r	39	67	37	26v	43	57	30	14v			29	63	84	371
Tri over llaeth	68	33vb	44	70	44	34r	40	67	38	26v	44	57	31	15r			30	63	85	371
Tri phetfoar yssyd	69	34ra	39	67	39	33r	35	64	33	26v	39	57	26	15r			25	60	82	370
(Tri sarhaet ny ddiwygir)	*	*	45	70	45	34r	41	67	39	24v	45	55	32	13v			31	63	*	
Teir palua6t ny di6ygir	70	34ra	46	70	46	34v	42	67	40	26v	46	57	33	15r			32	63	87	371
Teir g6raged a dyly	71	34rb	47	70	47	34v	43	67	41	27r	47	57	34	15r			33	63		
Teir sarhaet gwreic	*	*	48	71	48	34v	44	68	42	27r	48	58	35	15r			34	64	*	
Tri che6y(li)d kenedyl ynt	72	34rb	49	71	49	34v	45	68	43	27r	49	58	36	15v			35	64	89	371
Tri chadam enllip g6reic	73	34rb	50	71	50	34v	46	68	44	27r	50	58	37	15v			36	64	90	371
(Tri chyffro dial yssyd)	*	*	51	71	51	35r	47	69	45	27v	51	58	38	15v			37	64	*	
(Tri pheth a hawl dyn yn lledrad)	*	*	52	72	52	35r	48	69	46	27v	52	58	39	15v			38	64	*	
Tri meib yssyd ny dylyant	74	34rb	53	72	53	35r	49	69	47	27v	53	58	40	15v			39	65	*	
Tri dyn a gymryd eu breint	75	34va	54	72	54	35v	50	69	48	28r	54	59	41	16r			40	66	93	371
(Tri gwerth cyfraith beichiogi)	*	*	55	73	55	35v	51	70	49	28v	55	59	42	16r			41	66	13	336
O tri mod y g6edir	76	34va	56	73	56	35v	52	70	50	28v	56	60	43	16v			42	66	104	372
Teir gormes doeth ynt	77	34vb	57	74	57	36r	53	71	51	29r	57	60	44	16v			43	67	96	372
Tri dyn a dyly tauodya6c	78	34vb	58	74	58	36r	54	71	52	29r	58	60	45	16v			44	67	31, 97	354, 372
Tri ll6dyn digyfreith	79	34vb	59	74	59	36r	55	71	53	29r	59	61	46	16v			45	67	98	372
Tri ll6dyn nyt oes 6erth	80	35ra	60	75	60	36r	56	72	54	29v	60	61	47	17r			46	67	99	372
Tri g6aet digyfreith	81	35ra	61	75	61	36r	57	72	55	29v	61	61	48	17r			47	67	100	372
(Tri than digyfraith)	*	*	62	75	62	36v	58	72	56	29v	62	61	49	17r	1	1	48	67	*	
Tri edyn y dyly y brenhin	82	35ra	63	75	63	36v	59	72	57	30r	63	61	50	17r	2	1	49	68	101	372
Tri phryf y dyly	83	35ra	64	75	64	36v	60	72	58	30r	64	61	51	17r	3	1	50	68	102	372
Tri pheth ny at kyfreith	84	35ra	65	76	65	36v	61	72	59	30r	65	62	53	17r	4	1	51	68	103	372
Tri phren yssyd ryd	85	35rb	66	76	66	36v	62	72	60	30r	66	62	52	17r	5	1	52	68	105	373

86	Tri chehyryn canastyr	35rb	67	76	36v	63	61	30r	67	62	54	17v	6	1	53	68	15	337
87	Tri pheth a tyrr	35rb	68	76	37r	64	62	30v	68	62	55	17v	7	1	54	68	106	373
88	Tri edyn ny dylyir	35rb	69	76	37r	65	63	30v	69	62	56	17v	8	2	55	69	107	373
89	Tri pheth or keffir	35rb	70	76	37r	66	64	30v	70	62	57	17v	9, 138	2,81	56	69	108	373
90	Tri dyn ny dyly y brenhin	35rb	71	76	37r	67	65	30v	71	62	58	17v	10	2	57	69	110	373
91	Tri en6 righyll yssyd	35va	72	77	37r	68	66	30v	72	62	59	17v	11	2	58	69	111	373
92	Tri ergyt ny thelir	35va	73	77	37r	69	67	30v	73	62	60	17v	12	2	59	69	112	373
93	Tri chyfr6ch dirgel	35va	74	77	37r	70	68	31r	74	63	61	17v	13	2	60	69	113	373
94	Teir not6yd kyfreitha6l	35va	75	77	37r	71	69	31r	75	63	62	17v	14	2	61	69	114	373
95	Teir kyfrinach yssyd	35va	76	77	37v	72	70	31r	76	63	63	18r	15	2	62	69	115	373
96	Tri aneueil un troeda6c	35va	77	77	37v	73	71	31r	77	63	64	18r	16	2	63	70	116	373
97	Tri phren a dyly pop	35vb	78	77	37v	74	72	31r	78	63	65	18r	17	2	64	70	67, 364, 373
98	Tri pheth ny thelir	35vb	79	78	37v	75	73	31v	79	63	66	18r	18	2	65	70	118	373
99	Teir sarhaet kelein	35vb	80	78	37v		74	31v	80	63	67	18r	19	2			119	373
100	Teir g6arthrud kelein	35vb	81	78	37v	76	75	31v	81	63	68	18r	20	2	66	70	120	373
101	Teir gauael nyt atuerir	35vb	82	78	37v	77	76	31v	82	63	69	18r	21	2	67	70	16	337
102	Tri ry6 tal yssyd	35vb	83	78	37v	78	77	31v	83	63	70	18r	22	2	68	70	123	374
103	Tri ymdill6g	35vb	84	78	37v		78	31v	84	63	71	18r	23	2	69	70	124	374
104	Tri chargych6yn	35vb	85	78	37v	79	79	31v	85	64	72	18r	24, 126	2,78	70	70	125, 133	374, 375
105	O tri acha6s y gossodet	36ra	86	78	38r	80	80	32r	86	64	73	18v	25	2	71	71	127	374
106	Tri h6rd ny di6ygir	36ra	87	79	38r	81	81	32r	87	64	74	18v	26	2A	72	71	128	374
107	Tri da nyt reit mach	36rb	88	79	38v	82	82	32v			75	18v	27, 124	2A,78	73	71	129	374
108	Teir mar6 tystolyaeth	36rb	89	80	38v	83	83	32v			76	19r	28, 140	2A,82	74	72	130	374
109	Tri thorll6yth vn 6erth	36va	90	80	38v	84	84	33r			77	19r	29	2A	75	72	131	375
110	Tri ll6dyn vn 6erth	36va	91	80	39r	85	85	33v			78	19r	30	2A	[76]	73	132	375
111	Teir ff6rd y de6edir	36va	92	81	39r	86	86	33v			79	19v	31	2A	[77]	73	134	375
112	Tri pheth a geid6 cof	36vb	94	81	39r	87	87	33v			80	19v	32	3	[78]	73	135	375
113	Y tri dyn y telir	36vb	93	81	39r	88	88	33v			81	19v	33	3	[79]	73	136	375
114	Tri chofyllá6c llys	36vb	95	81	39r	89	89	34r			82	19v	34, 159	3,92	[80]	73	137	376
115	Tri dyn a geid6	36vb	96	82	39v	90	90	34r			83	19v	35	3	[81]	74	138	376
116	Tri argae g6aet yssyd	36vb	97	82	39v	91	91	34r			84	19v	36	3	[82]	74	109, 139	373, 376
117	Teir hela ryd yssyd	37ra	98	82	39v	92	92	34v			85	20r	37	3	[83]	74	140	376
118	Tri chy6ilyd mor6yn	37ra	99	82	39v	93	93	34v			86	20r	38	3	[84]	74	19, 141	346, 376
119	Tri pheth ny ellir	37ra	100	83	40r	94	94	34v			87	20r	39	3	85	74	142	376
120	Tri defnyd ha6l	37rb	101	83	40r	95	95	35r			88	20r	40	3	86	74	35	355

Keywords	Q	fo.	J	p.	L	fo.	M	p.	N	fo.	R	p.	T	fo.	Tim	p.	Bost	p.	Lat D	p.
Tri gol6c a dygir	121	37rb	102	83	102	40r	96	80	96	35r			89	20r	41	3	87	75	36	355
Tri geir kylus	122	37rb	103	83	103	40r	97	80	97	35r			90	20r	42	3	88	75	37	355
Tri ry6 6alla6geir	123	37rb	104	83	104	40r	98	80	98	35v			91	20r	43	3	89	75	39	355
Tri theruyn ha6l	124	37va	105	84	105	40r	100	81	99	35v			92	20r	44	3A	90	75	40	355
Tri pheth ny chygein	125	37va	106	84	106	40r	99	81	100	35v			93	20r	45	3A	91	76	41	355
Tri g6cithret yssyd	126	37va	107	84	107	40v	101	81	101	35v			94	20r	46	3A	92	76	42	355
Tri g6aessaf yssyd	127	37va	108	84	108	40v	102	81	102	36r			95	21r	47	3A	93	76	43	355
Tri chof g6edy bra6t	128	37va	109	84	109	40v	103	81	103	36r			96	21r	48	3A	94	76	44	355
Teir tystolyaeth dilis	129	37vb	110	85	110	40v	104	82	104	36r			97	21r	49	3A	95	77	45	355
Tri lle y ty6ys cof llys	130	37vb	111	85	111	41r	105	82	105	36r			98	21r	50	3A	96	77	46	355
Teir tystolyaeth mar6a6l	131	37vb	112	85	112	41r	106	82	106	36v			99	21r	51	3A	97	77	47	355
Tri g6ahan yssyd	132	38ra	113	85	113	41r	107	83	107	36v			100	21v	52	3A	98	78	48	356
Teir fford y mae kadarnach	133	38ra	114	86	114	41v	108	83	108	37r			101	21v	53	4	99	78	49	356
Teir tystolyaeth yssyd	134	38rb	115	87	115	41v	109	84	109	37v			102	22r	54	4	100	79	50	356
(Tri lleidyr camlyrus)	*	*	116	87	116	41v	110	84	110	37v			103	22r	55	4	101	79	51	356
(Tri lleidyr dirwyus)	*	*	117	87	117	42r	111	84	111	37v			104	22r	56	4	102	79	52	356
(Tri lleidyr gwerth)	*	*	118	87	118	42r	112	84	112	38r			105	22r	57	4	103	79	53	356
(Tri lleidyr crogadwy)	*	*	119	87	119	42r	113	85	113	38r			106	22r	58	4	104	79	54	356
(Tri lleidyr a dieinc o ledrat)	*	*	120	88	120	42r	114	85	114	38r			107	22v	59	4	105	79	55	356
O tri mod y telir dir6y	135	38rb	121	88	121	42r	115	85	115	38v			108	22v	60	4	106	80	56	357
O tri mod y kyll	136	38va	122	88	122	42v	116	86	116	38v			109	22v	61	4	107	80	57	357
Vn o'r tri a gyll y neb a treisser	137	38va	123	88	123	42v	117	86	117	39r			110	22v	62	5	108	80	58	357
Tri ry6 amdiffyn	138	38va	124	89	124	42v	118	86	118	39r			111	22v	63	5	109	80	59	357
Tri pheth nyt reit	139	38vb	125	89	125	42v	119	86	119	39r			112	23r	64	5	110	80	60	357
Tri ry6 diebryt	140	38vb	126	89	126	42v	120	87	120	39r			113	23r	65	5	111	81	61	357
O tri mod y kae	141	38vb	127	89	127	43r	121	87	121	39v			114	23r	66	5	112	81	62	357
Tri theruyn kyfreitha6l	142	38vb	128	90	128	43r	122	87	122	39v			115	23r	67	5	113	81	63	357
Teir dadyl a dylyant	143	38vb	129	90	129	43r	123	87	123	39v			116	23r	68	5	114	81	64	357
Tri dyn bonhedic	144	39ra	159, 162	186, 219	159	85r									151	85	136	177		
Tri meib ryd o gaeth	145	39ra																		
Tri meib caeth o ryd	146	39ra																		
Tri dyn nyt geir	147	39ra	163	220											113	65	135			
Tri dyn a dylyant alanas	148	39ra	158	186	158	84v									150	85	135	177		

Keywords	*Q*	fo.	*J*	p.	*L*	fo.	*M*	p.	*N*	fo.	*R*	p.	*T*	fo.	Tim	p.	Bost	p.	Lat D	p.
Teir ouer groes	**182**	42rb													129	79				
Tri mod y telir amobyr	**183**	42rb													130	79				
Tri dyn a dyly talu amobyr	**184**	42va													131	79				
Tri dygyat a vyd ar vab	**185**	42va													132	79				
Tri chymeryat a vyd ar vab	**186**	42va													133	79				
Tri dyn a dieinc rac dihenyd	**187**	43ra													137	81				
Tri pheth ny dylyir eu rannv	**188**	43rb													108	64				
Tri pheth a r6g dyn a daly	**189**	43rb													142	83				
Tri llyssyat yssyd ar tir	**190**	43rb													141	82				
Tri pheth ny dylyir eu damt6g	**191**	43rb													143	83				
Tri g6ystyl ny dyg6ydant	**192**	43va													144	83				
Tri gorsseda6c a allant	**193**	43vb																		
Tri thlos kenedyl	**194**	43vb													156	88				
Tri corfflamn ny dylyir	**195**	43vb																		
Teir bala6c vechni y6	**196a**	43vb													162	96				
Y neb a vo mach dros dyn	**196b**	44va																		
Tri amueil a drycheif	**197**	45ra																		
Tri pheth yssyd gymeint	**198**	45ra																		
Tri amueil a a g6erth	**199**	45ra																		
Tri lle y dyly ynat kym6t	**200**	45ra																		
Tri lle y gallei dyn	**201**	45rb																		
Teir g6eith y drycheif	**202**	45rb																		
Tri pheth nyt reit mach	**203**	45rb													124	78				
Tri meich ny dylyir eu g6adu	**204**	45va																		
Tri pheth ny dyly taya6c	**205**	45va													135	80				
Tri dyn a dyly kenedyl y vam	**206**	45va																		
Tri g6rtheb yssyd	**207**	45vb	141	103	141	48v	135	102					128	28v	80	10	126	93	29	353
Tri ry6 vra6d6yr yssyd	**208**	46vb	135	92	135	44r	129	90					122	24v	74	7	120	83	23, [143]	349, 382
Tri dyn ny allant ym6ystla6	**209**	48va	136	99	136	47r	130	97					123	27r	75	8	121	89	24	351
Tri pheth a dyly pop bra6t6r	**210**	48va	137	99	137	47r	131	98					124	27r	76	9	122	90	25	352
Tri ry6 varn tremyc	**211**	49ra	138	101	138	47v	132	99					125	27v	77	9	123	91	26	352
Tri dyn yssyd ny dicha6n	**212**	49ra	139	101	139	48r	133	100					126	28r	78	9	124	91	27	352
Teir fford y gellir g6rthneu	**213**	49rb	140	102	140	48r	134	101					127	28r	79	9	125	92	28	352

Triad												
Tri pheth a dyly bra6t6r	214	49va	169	303								
Teir dadyl nyt oes oet y vra6t6r	215	50ra					98	53				
Tri ry6 tremyc absen yssyd	216	50va					96	49				
Tri ry6 gamdosparth yssyd	217	50vb										
Tri chamg6yn kelus	218	52va					103	59			32	354
Teir gorsed dygunull	219	54vb					97	51				
O tri mod yd holir tir	220	56vb	130	90	117	23v	69	5	115	82	144	384
Tri chamoresgyn yssyd	221	56vb	131	90	118	23v	70	5	116	82	145	385
O tri mod y dosperthir	222	56vb	132	91	119	23v	71	7	117	82	146	385
Tri ry6 vreint yssyd	223	57rb	133	92	120	24r	72	7	118	83	147	385
Tri phriodolder yssyd	224	57rb	134	92	121	24r	73	7	119	83	126, 148	374, 386
Tri lle y rann kyfreith	225	57va	146	142	133	45r	85	27				
Teir etiuedyaeth kyfreitha6l	226	58vb	147	147	134	47r	86	28	131	136	149	385
Teir g6eith y rennir yr vn tref	227	59ra	148	148	135	47v87, [139]	3, 81					
Tri ry6 prit yssyd ar tir	228	60va	149	152	136	49v	88	31	132	138		
Tri ry6 datannud	229	66va	164	239			125, 174	78, 120				
Teir g6ragedd her6yd	230	67rb	165	241								
Tri lle her6yd kyfreith ny pherth	230a											
Tri dyn a gyneil tir ac ae herbyn	230b						100	57				
							99	53				
Tri ry6 argaedigaeth	231	68vb	166	258	130	40v	82	22	128	122	18	343
O tri acha6s ny chyll g6reic	232	74va	143	132	131	41r	83	23	129	122		
Teir g6eith y keiff g6reic	233	74va	144	132	132	41r	84	23	130	123		
Tri ll6 a dyry g6reic y 6r	234	74vb	145	133								
Teir g6ragedd ny dyly eu g6yr	235	77ra										
O tri mod y telir teithi buch	236	86va	150	163	137	54v	89	35	133	154	65	358
Teir kynnefa6t yssyd	237	90rb	151	177			90	42			151	394
Teir gossotedigaeth yssyd	238	90rb	156	181			95	47			155	395
Tri pheth a gatarnha	239	91ra	152	177			91	42			152	394
Tri pheth a 6anha	240	91ra	153	177			92	42				
Teir rann y6 a6durda6t	241	91rb	154	177			93	42			153	394
Tri aruer kyfreith yssyd	242	91rb	155	178			94	45			154	394
Teir vchel llys yssyd	243	92ra					105	61				

Keywords	Q	fo.	J	p.	L	fo.	M	p.	N	fo.	R	p.	T	fo.	Tim	p.	Bost	p.	Lat D	p.
Tri chyfeiliorn cyfraith	244	92vb																		
Teir gorssed brenhina6l yssyd	245	99ra																		
Tri pheth ny drycheuir	246	110ra	168	284											161	96				
Tri ry6 dyn yssyd ny dleir	247	125ra																		
O tri pheth y kyll dyn y ha6l	248	125vb																		
Tri chenol yssyd ynghyfreith	249	125vb																		
Tri pheth a dyly offeirat	250	125vb																		
Tri dyn ysyd a ellir y llyssu	251	126rb																		
Tri dyn kyn g6rthebhont	252	126rb																		
Tri pheth ny dyly tavodya6c	253	126va																		
Tri ry6 dyn yssyd a dylyir	254	126va																		
Tri pherigl dyn ynt	255	126va																		
Tri dyn y telir g6eli taua6t udynt	256	127ra														136	80			38	355
Tri anghyuarch adeuedic ysyd	257	127va																		
Tri lle y telir caml6r6 deudyblyc	258	127va																	34	354
Tri chanlyn di6all yssyd	259	127vb														145	85				
Tri dyn yssyd a geiff da kyfroedic	260	127vb																		
Teir dadyl yssyd aghyn6yssedic	261	128vb														101	58				
Am teir diaspat y6ch aduan	262	136ra																		

Conspectus 6b. The Triads in Q, showing L-type Bleg Manuscripts

Where the text is underlined, the triads are given in the expected position in Bleg. These triads do not, however, occur in that position in Q. Where the text is given in italic they are in the correct position in Q, but are found in the triad collection in most other Bleg manuscripts. The text in bold shows the triad collection.

Keywords	Q	fo.	C	p.	P	fo.	Bleg	p.	O	p.	Tr	fo.	I	fo.	S	fo.	Y	fo.
Teir sarhaet brenhin	1	1va	1	2	1	1v	1	3	1	4	1	2v	1	2v	1	5r		
Tri ry6 sarhaet yssyd	2	1vb	2	2	2	1v	2	3	2	4	2	2v	2	2v	2, 221	5r, 109r		
O tri mod y serheir y vrenhines	3	2ra	3	3	3	2r	3	4	3	5	3	3r	3	3r	3	5v		
Tri ry6 dyn yssyd	4	2rb	4	3	4	2v	4	5	4	7	4	4r	4	3v	4	5v		
Tri ry6 6assanaeth a 6na	5	4vb	5	8	5	5r	5	13							170	76r		
Tri g6assanaeth a 6na y brenhin	6	4vb	6	9	6	5r	6	13										
Tri pheth a perthyn y vra6d6r	7	6ra	7	9	7	6v	7	17			25	52v	25	51r	25	41r	27	57v
Tri amheu bra6t yssyd	8	6rb	8	12	8	6v	8	18			26	53r	26	5*v	26	41v	28	58r
O tri mod y kedernheir	9	9rb	9	17	9	10r	148	125			65	63r	140	67v	139	57r	149	106r
Tri g6ys a ellir eu g6adu	10	9rb	10	17	10	10r	149	125			66	63v	141	67v	140	57v	150	106r
Tri dyn ny dylyir eu g6ysya6	11	9rb	11	18	11	10r	150	125			67	63v	142	68r	141	58r	151	106v
Tri ry6 6adu yssyd	12	9rb	12	18	12	10r	151	125			68	63v	143	68r	142	58r	152	106v
Tri mach yssyd ny cheiff	13	9va	13	18	13	10r	152	126			69	64r	144	68r	143	58r		
Tri ry6 t6g yssyd	14	9vb	14	18	14	10v	153	126			70	64r	145	68r	144	58v	153	107r
O teir fford y dosperthir	15	9vb	15	19	15	10v	37	105	32	120	33	64r	28, 138	53v, 67r	28	44r	35	64r
Tri ry6 vanac yssyd	16	9vb	16	19	16	10v	147	124			64	58v	139	67r	138	57r	11	32v
Tri pheth a dyly bra6d6r	17	10ra	17	19	17	10v	38	105	33	120	34	63v			137	57r	37	23r
O tri mod y kyll bra6d6r	18	10ra	18	19	18	11r	39	106	34	120	35	58v						
Tri dygyngoll kenedyl	19	11va	19	22	19	11r	9	33	5	12	5	59r	5		6r5, 216, 277	7v, 108r, 121r	4	28v
Tri oet kyfraith y dial	20	12ra	20	23	20	12v												
Tri tha6eda6c gorsed	21	12ra	21	23	21	13r												
Tri g6anas g6ay6	22	12rb	22	23	22	13r												
Teir sarhaet ny di6gir	23	12rb	23	23	23	13r												
Teir sarhaet g6reic ynt	24	12rb	24	23	24	13r												
Tri chyffro dial yssyd	25	12rb	25	23	25	13r												
Tri g6erth kyfreith beichogi	26	12va	26	23	26	13v												
Tri than digyfreith	27	15ra	27	29	27	16r												
Tri gol6c a dygir	28	15rb	28	30	28	16v												

(Rows 20–28 bracketed:) See the triad collection, below, for these cross-references

Keywords	Q	fo.	€	p.	P	p.	fo.	Bleg	p.	O	p.	Tr	fo.	I	fo.	S	fo.	Y	fo.
Tri geir kyhus yssyd	29	15rb	29	30	29	29	16v												
Tri pheth ny chyfran	30	16rb	30	32	30	30	17r												
Tri pheth a ha6l dyn yn	31	16rb	31	32	31	31	17v												
Tri lleidyr camlyryus yssyd	32	16rb	32	32	32	32	17v	See the triad collection, below, for these cross-references											
Tri lleidyr dir6yus yssyd	33	16rb	33	32	33	33	17v												
Tri lleidyr g6erth yssyd	34	16rb	34	32	34	34	17v												
Tri lleidyr crogad6y yssyd	35	16va	35	32	35	35	17v												
Tri lleidyr a dieinc	36	16va	36	32	36	36	18r												
Tri pheth a dyly g6arant diball	37	16vb	37	33	37	37	18r	17	44	13	29	13	16v	35	56v	35	46v		
Tri acha6s yssyd y lyssu tyston	38	22va	38	48	38	38	29v	10	37	6	19	6	9r10, 20		18r, 30v	20	25r		
Teir tystolyaeth dilys	39	23rb	39	50	39	39	25r	[127]	120										
Tri lle y ty6ys cof llys	40	23va	40	50	40	40	25r	[128]	121										
Teir tystolyaeth mar6a6l	41	23va	41	50	41	41	25v	[129]	121										
Tri g6ahan yssyd	42	23va	42	51	42	42	25v	[130]	121										
Teir fford y mae kadarnach	43	23vb	43	51	43	43	25v	[131]	121										
Teir tystyolaeth yssyd	44	23vb	44	51	44	44	25v	[132]	122										
Teir fford ybyd ryd mach	45	24va	45	53	45	45	26v	11	40	7	22	7	13r	6	10r			12	35r
O teir fford yd oedir mach	46	24vb	46	54	46	46	26v	12	40	8	24	8	13r	7	10v			13	35v
Teir mefel6ryaeth mach yssyd	47	24vb	47	55	47	47	26v	13	40	9	24	9	13r						
Tri pheth ny dylyir na6d racdun	48	25va	48	56	48	48	27v									185	80r	17	39v
Tri mach yssyd ny cheiff	49	25va	49	57	49	49	28r	152	126							164	73r	16	39r
Tri lle yssyd or or rodir meicheu	50	26ra	50	58	50	50	28v									162	72r		
Tri lle yd ymdiueicha mach	51	26va	51	58	51	51	28v	14	42	10	26	10	15v	8	12r	8	11v	14	37r
Tri pheth ny henynt o vechni	52	26va	52	63	52	52	28v	15	42	11	27	11	15v	9	12v	9	11v	15	37r
Tri ouer vechni yssyd	53	28rb	53	71	53	53	30r									204	102r		
Tri pheth y kyll dyn	54	31rb	54	75	54	54	33r												
Tri ry6 dir6y yssyd	55	32vb	55	76	55	55	37v	16	42	12	27	12	15v	37	57v	37, 247	47v, 113r	44	90v
Teir r6yt brenhin ynt	56	33rb	56	76	56	56	35r	44	107	39	123	40	60r	38	58r	38, 235	48r, 111v	45	90v
Teir r6yt breyr ynt	57	33rb	57	77	57	57	35r	45	107	40	123	41	60r	39	58r	39, 236	48r, 112r	46	91r
Teir r6yt taya6c ynt	58	33rb	58	77	58	58	35r	46	108	41	123	42	60r	40	58r	40, 237	48r, 112r	47	91r
Tri chorn buelyn	59	33rb	59	77	59	59	35r	47	108	42	123	43	60r	41	58r	41	48r	48	91r
Teir telyn kyfreitha6l	60	33va	60	77	60	60	35r	48	108	43	123	44	60v	42	58r	42	48r	49	91r

No.	Incipit																
61	Tri pheth nyt ryd y vilaen	33va	61	77	61	35r	49	108	44	123	45	60v	43	58r	43	48v	50	91v
62	Teir keluydyt ny eill	33va	62	77	62	35r	50	108	45	124	46	60v	44	58v	44, 253	48v, 113r	51	91v
63	Teir kyflauan os góna	33va	63	77	63	35r	51	108	46	124	47	60v	45	58v	45, 222	48v, 109r	52	91v
64	Tri anhepcor brenhin	33vb	64	77	64	35r	52	108	47	124			46	58v	46	48v	53	91v
65	Tri anhepcor breyr	33vb	65	78	65	35r	53	108	48	124			47	58v	47	48v	54	92r
66	Tri anhepccor taya6c	33vb	66	78	66	35r	54	109	49	124			48	58v	48	48v	55	92r
	(Tri pheth ny chyfran brenin)	*	*	*	*	*	55	109	50	125			49	58v	49	48v	56	92r
	(Tri oet kyfreith y dial)	*	*	*	*	*	57	109	52	126			36	57v	36	47v	43	90r
	(Tri thawedog gorsedd)	*	*	*	*	*	58	110	53	126			51	59r	50, 239	48v	58	92v
	(Tri gwanas gwayw)	*	*	*	*	*	59	110					52	59v	51	49r	59	92v
67	Tri ofer ymadra6d	33vb	67	78	67	35r	60	110					53	59v	52	49r	60	93r
68	Tri over llaeth	33vb	68	78	68	35r	61	110					54	59v	53	49v		
69	Tri phet6ar yssyd	34ra	69	78	69	35v	56	109	51	124			50	58v	49	48v	57	92r
	(Tri sarhaet ny ddiwygir)	*	*	*	*	*	62	110					55	59v	54	49r	61	93r
70	Teir palua6t ny difygir	34ra	70	79	70	35v	63	111					56	59v	55	49v	62	93r
71	Teir g6raged a dyly	34rb	71	79	71	35v	64	111	106	147			57	60r	56	49v	63	93v
	Teir sarhaet gwreic	*	*	*	*	*	65	111					58	60r	57	49v	64	93v
72	Tri che6y(li)d kenedyl ynt	34rb	72	79	72	35v	66	111	54	129			60	60r	59	50r	65	93v
73	Tri chadarn enllip g6reic	34rb	73	79	73	35v	67	111	55	129			61	60r	60	50r	66	93v
	(Tri chyffro dial yssyd)	*	*	*	*	*	68	111	56	129			62	60r	61	50r	67	94r
	(Tri pheth a hawl dyn yn lledrad)	*	*	*	*	*	69	112	57, 99	129, 147			63	60r	62	50r	68	94r
74	Tri meib yssyd ny dylyant	34rb	74	79	74	36r	70	112	58	130			64	60v	63, 166, 205	50v, 74v, 102r	69	94r
75	Tri dyn a gynnyd eu breint	34va	75	80	75	36r	71	112	59	130			59	60v	58	50r	70	94v
	(Tri gwerth cyfraith beichiogi)	*	*	*	*	*	72	112					65	60v	64	50v	71	94v
76	O tri mod y g6edir	34va	76	80	76	36r	73	113					66	61r	65	50v	72	95r
77	Teir gormes doeth ynt	34vb	77	80	77	36r	74	113					67	61r	66	51r	73	95r
78	Tri dyn a dyly tauodya6c	34vb	78	81	78	36v	75	113					68	61r	67	51r	74	95r
79	Tri llf6dyn digyfreith	34vb	79	81	79	36v	76	113					69	61r	68	51r	75	95v
80	Tri llf6dyn nyt oes 6erth	35ra	80	81	80	36v	77	113					70	61v	69	51r	76	95v
81	Tri g6aet digyfreith	35ra	81	81	81	36v	78	114					71	61v	70, 219	51v, 109r	77	95v
	(Tri than digyfraith)	*	*	*	*	*	79	114					72	61v	71	51v	78	95v
82	Tri edyn y dyly y brenhin	35ra	82	81	82	36v	80	114	60	133			73	61v	72	51v	79	95v
83	Tri phryf y dyly	35ra	83	81	83	36v	81	114	61	133			74	61v	73	51v	80	96r
84	Tri pheth ny at kyfreith	35ra	84	81	84	36v	82	114	62	133			75	61v	74	51v	81	96r
85	Tri phren yssyd ryd	35rb	85	81	85	36v	83	114					76	61v	75	51v	83	96r

Keywords	Q	fo.	€	p.	P	fo.	Bleg	p.	O	p.	Tr	fo.	I	fo.	S	fo.	Y	fo.
Tri chehyryn canastyr	86	35rb	86	81	86	36v	84	114	63	133			77	62r	76	51v	84	96r
Tri pheth a tyrr	87	35rb	87	82	87	36v	85	114	64	133			78	62r	77	51v	85	96v
Tri edyn ny dylyir	88	35rb	88	82	88	36v	86	114	65	133			79	62r	78	52r	86	96v
Tri pheth or keffir	89	35rb	89	82	89	36v	87	115					80	62r	79, 257	52r, 115r	87	96v
Tri dyn ny dyly y brenhin	90	35rb	90	82	90	36v	88	115					81	62r	80, 176	52r, 78r	88	96v
Tri en6 righyll yssyd	91	35va	91	82	91	37r	89	115					82	62r	81	52r	89	96v
Tri ergyt ny thelir	92	35va	92	82	92	37r	90	115					83	62r	82	52r	90	96v
Tri chyfr6ch dirgel	93	35va	93	82	93	37r	91	115					84	62r	83	52r	91	97r
Teir not6yd kyfreitha6l	94	35va	94	82	94	37r	92	115					85	62r	84	52r	92	97r
Teir kyfrinach yssyd	95	35va	95	82	95	37r	93	115					86	62r	85	52r	93	97r
Tri aneueil um troeda6c	96	35va	96	82	96	37r	94	115					89	62v	88	52v	94	97r
Tri phren a dyly pop	97	35vb	97	82	97	37r	95	115					90	62v	89	52v	95	97r
Tri pheth ny thelir	98	35vb	98	83	98	37r	96	115	66	134			91	62v	90	52v	96	97v
Teir sarhaet kelein	99	35vb	99	83	99	37r	97	116	67	134			87	62v	86	52r	97	97v
Teir g6arthrud kelein	100	35vb	100	83	100	37r	98	116	68	134			88	62v	87, 217, 276	52r, 108v, 111r	98	97v
Teir gauael nyt atuerir	101	35vb	101	83	101	37r	99	116	69	134			92	62v	91	52v	99	97v
Tri ry6 tal yssyd	102	35vb	102	83	102	37r	100	116	70	134			93	62v	92	52v	100	97v
Tri ymdill6g	103	35vb	103	83	103	37r	101	116	71	134			94	62v	93	52v	101	97v
Tri chargych6yn	104	35vb	104	83	104	37r	102	116	72	134			95	62v	94, 233	52v, 111v	102	97v
O tri acha6s y gossodet	105	36ra	105	83	105	37r	103	116	73	134			96	62v	95	52v	103	98r
Tri h6rd ny di6ygir	106	36ra	106	83	106	37v	104	116					98	63r	97	52v	104	98r
Tri da nyt reit mach	107	36rb	107	84	107	37v	105	117					97	63r	96, 180, 231	52v, 111r	105	98v
Teir mar6 tystolyaeth	108	36rb	108	84	108	37v	106	117					99	63r	98, 259	53r, 115v	106	98v
Tri thorll6yth vn 6erth	109	36va	109	85	109	37v	107	117					100	63v	99	53v	107	99r
Tri ll6dyn vn 6erth	110	36va	110	85	110	37v	108	117					101	63v	100	53v	108	99r
Teir fford y de6edir	111	36va	111	85	111	37v	109	118					103	63v	101	53v	109	99v
Tri pheth a geid6 cof	112	36vb	112	85	112	38r	110	118					102	63v	102	53v	110	99v
Y tri dyn y telir	113	36vb	113	85	113	38r	111	118					104	63v	103	53v	111	99v
Tri cho6ylla6c llys	114	36vb	114	85	114	38r	112	118					105	64r	104	53v	112	100r
Tri dyn a geid6	115	36vb	115	85	115	38r	113	118					106	64r	105	53v	113	100r
Tri argae g6aet yssyd	116	36vb	116	85	116	38r	114	118					109	64r	108, 218	54r, 109r	114	100r
Teir hela ryd yssyd	117	37ra	117	86	117	38r	115	119					107	64r	106, 241	54r, 112v	115	100v
Tri chy6ilyd mor6yn	118	37ra	118	86	118	38r	116	119	74	139			108	64r	107	54r	116	100v

#	Triad																	
119	Tri pheth ny ellir	37ra	119	86	119	38r	117	119	119	75	139			110	109	54r	117	100v
120	Tri defnyd ha6l	37rb	120	86	120	38v	118	119	119	76,100	139,147			111	110	54r	118	100v
121	Tri gol6c a dygir	37rb	121	86	121	38v	119	119	119	77,101	139,147			112	111	54r	119	101r
122	Tri geir kylus	37rb	122	86	122	38v	120	119	120	78,103	139,147			113	112	54v	120	101r
123	Tri ry6 6alla6geir	37rb	123	87	123	38v	121	120	120	79	139			114	113	54v	121	101r
124	Tri theruyn ha6l	37va	124	87	124	38v	122	120	120	80	140			115	114	54v	122	101r
125	Tri pheth ny chygein	37va	125	87	125	38v	123	120	120	81	140			116	115	54v	123	101v
126	Tri g6eithret yssyd	37va	126	87	126	38v	124	120	120	82	140			117	116	54v	124	101v
127	Tri g6aessaf yssyd	37va	127	87	127	38v	125	120	120	83,104	140,148			118	117	54v	125	101v
128	Tri chof g6edy bra6t	37va	128	88	128	38v	126	120	121	84,105	141,147			119	118	55r	126	101v
129	Teir tystolyaeth dilis	37vb	129	88	129	38v	127	120	121	85	141			121	120	55r	128	102r
130	Tri lle y ty6ys cof llys	37vb	130	88	130	38r	128	121	121	86	141			120	119	55r	127	102r
131	Teir tystolyaeth marf6a6l	37vb	131	88	131	38r	129	121	121	87	141			122	121	55r	129	102r
132	Tri g6ahan yssyd	38ra	132	89	132	38r	130	121	121	88	142			123	122	55r	130	102r
133	Teir fford y mae kadarnach	38ra	133	89	133	38r	131	121	122	89	142	48	61r	124	123	55v	131	102r
134	Teir tystolyaeth yssyd	38rb	134	89	134	38r	132	122	123	90	143	49	61r	125	124	55v		
	(Tri lleidyr camlyrus)	*	*	*	*	*						50	61r	146	145	58v	141	105r
	(Tri lleidyr dirwyus)	*	*	*	*	*						51	61r	147	146	58v	142	105r
	(Tri lleidyr gwerth)	*	*	*	*	*						52	61r	148	147	58v	143	105r
	(Tri lleidyr crogadwy)	*	*	*	*	*						53	61v	149	148	58v	144	105r
	(Tri lleidyr a dieinc o ledrat)	*	*	*	*	*						54	61v	150	149	58v	145	105r
135	O tri mod y telir dir6y	38rb	135	89	135	38r	133	123	124	91	143	55	61v	126	125	56r	132	103v
136	O tri mod y kyll	38va	136	89	136	39v	134	123	124	92	143	56	61v	127	126	56r	133	103v
137	Vn o'r tri a gyll y neb a treisser	38va	137	89	137	39v	135	123	124	93	143	57	62r	128	127	56r	134	103v
138	Tri ry6 amdiffyn	38va	138	90	138	39v	136	123		94	144	58	62r	129	128	56r	135	103v
139	Tri pheth nyt reit	38vb	139	90	139	39v	137	123		95	144	59	62r	130	129	56v	136	103v
140	Tri ry6 diebryt	38vb	140	90	140	39v	138	124		96	144	60	62r	131	130	56v	137	104v
141	O tri mod y kae	38vb	141	90	141	39v	139	124		97	144	61	62v	132	131	56v	138	104v
142	Tri theruyn kyfreitha6l	38vb	142	90	142	39v	140	124		98	144	62	62v	133	132	56v	139	104v
143	Teir dadyl a dylyant	38vb	143	90	143	39v	141					63	62v	134	133	56v	140	104v
144	Tri dyn bonhedic	39ra	144	91	144	40r	142								270	118v	9	29r
145	Tri meib ryd o gaeth	39ra	145	91	145	40r	143								177	78v	161	114r
146	Tri meib caeth o ryd	39ra	146	91	146	40r	144								178	78v	162	114r
147	Tri dyn nyt geir	39ra	147	91	147	40r	145								194	87v		
148	Tri dyn a dylyant alanas	39ra	148	91	148	40r	146								269	118v	8	29r

Keywords	Q	fo.	C	p.	P	fo.	Bleg	p.	O	p.	Tr	fo.	I	fo.	S	fo.	Y	fo.
Tri dyn a dylyant sarhaet	149	39ra	149	91	149	40r									268	118r	10	29v
Teir kyflauan nid oes	150	39ra	150	91	150	40r									210	105v		
Tri chyfredin kenedyl	151	39rb	151	91	151	40r												
Tri pheth a differ dyn	152	39rb	152	91	152	40r												
Teir merchet a dylyant	153	39rb	153	91	153	40r									271	118v		
Teir merchet ny dylyir	154	39rb	154	92	154	40r												
Tri chadarn byt ynt	155	39va	155	92	155	40r									272	120v		
Tri dyn a dyly kenedyl	156	39va	156	92	156	40v											7	29r
Tri ry6 6rogaeth yssyd	157	39vb	157	92	157	40v									167	74v		
Tri pheth a dyly pop dyn	158	39vb	158	92	158	40v									212	106r		
Tri dyn y degemir	159	39vb	159	93	159	40v												
Tri dadleu ny dylyir	160	39vb	160	93	160	40v												
Tri thauodya6c argl6yd	161	40ra	161	93	161	40v											5	28v
Tri dyn a dylyant talu galanas	162	40ra	162	93	162	40v											6	28v
Tri dyn a gaffant ramn o alanas	163	40ra	163	93	163	40v												
Tri pheth ny dyly ygnat	164	40ra	164	93	164	41r												
Tri dyn a dylyir eu cad6 rac arueu	165	40rb	165	93	165	41r												
Tri pheth ny drycheuir	166	40rb	166	94	166	41r												
Tri pheth yssyd uch no chyfreith	167	40va	167	94	167	41r									187, 199	83v, 88r		
Tri meib ny dylyant tref tat	168	40va	168	94	168	41r									223	109v		
Teir g6ragedd a dyly eu meibon	169	40va	169	95	169	41r									226	110r		
Teir gorssed gyfreitha6l	170	41ra	170	96	170	41v									227	110v		
Tri g6anas g6ystyl ynt	171	41ra	171	96	171	41v									228	110v		
Tri g6ystyl gogymreint	172	41rb	172	96	172	41v									229	110v		
Tri g6ystyl nyt reit meicheu	173	41rb	173	96	173	41v									230	110v		
Tri meich ny dylyir eu g6adu	174	41va	174	97	174	42r												
Tri lle y rodir mach	175	41va	175	97	175	42r												
Tri gorsaf g6reic ynt	176	41va	176	97	176	42r									234	111v		
Tri chyghyana6c kyfreith	177	41vb	177	97	177	42r									238	112r		
Tri aneueil yssyd	178	41vb	178	97	178	42r									243	112v		
Teir sarhaet ny di6ygir	179	41vb	179	98	179	42r									244	112v		
Tri achos y dyly g6r maedu	180	41vb	180	98	180	42r									245	112v		

Keywords	Q	fo.	€	p.	P	fo.	Bleg	p.	O	p.	Tr	fo.	I	fo.	S	fo.	Y	fo.
Teir dadyl nyt oes oet y vra6t6r	215	50ra	215	116											175	76v		
Tri ry6 tremyc absen yssyd	216	50va	216	118											156	66r		
Tri ry6 gamdosparth yssyd	217	50vb	217	118											154	62v		
Tri chamg6yn kelus	218	52va	218	121											161	71v		
Teir gorsed dygunull	219	54vb	219	125											155	64r		
O tri mod yd holir tir	220	56vb	220	129			25	78	21	79	20	39v	15	24v	15	20r	22	49r
Tri chamoresgyn yssyd	221	56vb	221	129			26	78	22	79	21	40v	16	24v	16	20r	23	49v
O tri mod y dosperthir	222	56vb	222	129			27	79	23	79	22	40v	17	25r	17	20r	24	49v
Tri ry6 vreint yssyd	223	57rb	223	129			28	79	24	80	23	40v	18	25v	18	20v	25	50r
Tri phriodolder yssyd	224	57rb	224	129			29	80	25	80	24	40v	19	25v	19	20v	26	50r
Tri lle y ram kyfreith	225	57va	225	130			21	71	17	67			11	19v	11	16r	18	43v
Teir etiuedyaeth kyfreitha6l	226	58vb	226	132			22	74	18	72	17	36r	12	21r	12	17v	19	45v
Teir g6eith y remir yr vn tref	227	59ra	227	133			23	75	19	73	18	37v	13	22r	13, [258]	18r, 115r	20	46v
Tri ry6 prit yssyd ar tir	228	60va	228	135			24	78	20	78	19	39v	14	24r	14	19v	21	48v
Tri ry6 datanmud	229	66va	229	144											232	111r		
Teir g6ragedd her6yd	230	67rb	230	145														
Tri lle her6yd kyfreith ny pherth	230a		230a	147														
Tri dyn a gyneil tir ac ae herbyn	230b		230b	148														
Tri ry6 argaedigaeth	231	68vb	231	150											158	68r		
O tri acha6s ny chyll g6reic	232	74va	232	159			19	64	14	56	14	30v	21	35r	157	67r	39	70r
Teir g6eith y keiff g6reic	233	74va	233	159			20	64	15	56	15	30v	22	35r	21	28r	40	70r
Tri ll6 a dyry g6reic y 6r	234	74vb	234	159					16	57	16	31r	23	35v	22	28r	41	70r
Teir g6ragedd ny dyly eu g6yr	235	77ra													23	28v		
O tri mod y telir teithi buch	236	86va	235	173					26	92			24	41v	24	33v	42	80v
Teir kynnefa6t yssyd	237	90rb	236	179			41	107	36	122	37	59v	135	67r	134	56v	146	105v
Teir gossotedigaeth yssyd	238	90rb	237	180			156	129			73	66v			153	61v	159	109v
Tri pheth a gatarnha	239	91ra	238	181			42	107	37	122	38	60r	136	67r	135	56v	147	106r

Tri pheth a 6anha	240	91ra	239	181	43	107	38	122	39	60r	137	67r	136	56v	148	106r
Teir rann y6 a6durda6t	241	91rb	240	181	154	126			71	64v	146	69r			157	107v
Tri aruer kyfreith yssyd	242	91rb	241	181	155	127			72	64v	147	69r	152	59r	158	107v
Teir vchel llys yssyd	243	92ra	242	182									163	72v		
Tri chyfeiliorn cyfraith	244	92vb	243	184									197	88r		
Teir gorssed brenhina6l yssyd	245	99ra	244	194												
Tri pheth ny drycheuir	246	110ra	245	194									202	97v		
Tri ry6 dyn yssyd ny dleir	247	125ra	246	246									204	102r		
O tri pheth y kyll dyn y ha6l	248	125vb	247	248									186	83v		
Tri chenol yssyd ynghyfreith	249	125vb	248	248												
Tri pheth a dyly offeirat	250	125vb	249	248									203	99r		
Tri dyn yssyd a ellir y llyssu	251	126rb	250	249												
Tri dyn kyn g6rthebhont	252	126rb	251	249									168	74v		
Tri pheth ny dyly tavodya6c	253	126va	252	249									182	79v		
Tri ry6 dyn yssyd a dylyir	254	126va	253	250												
Tri pherigl dyn ynt	255	126va	254	250									255	114v		
Tri dyn y telir g6eli taua6t udynt	256	127ra	255	251												
Tri anghyuarch adeuedic yssyd	257	127va	256	252												
Tri lle y telir caml6r6 deudyblyc	258	127va	257	252												
Tri chanlyn di6all yssyd	259	127vb	258	252									264	117v		
Tri dyn yssyd a geiff da kyfroedic	260	127vb	259	253									200	96v		
Teir dadyl yssyd aghyn6yssedic	261	128vb	260	254									159	70r		
Am teir diaspat y6ch aduan	262	136ra	261	269									211	105v		

Conspectus 7. The Latin D triads

Q numbers in square brackets indicate triads moved from the main collection. Italic text indicates triads which occur in Welsh in Latin D. Keywords are from Latin D, or Bleg if they are in Latin in Latin D.

Latin D	no.	p.	Q	fo.	Bleg	p.	Lat A	p.	Lat B	p.	Lat E	p.
Teir sarhaet brenhin	1	317	1	1va	1	3						
Tri ryw sarhaet yssyd	2	317	2	1vb	2	3	7	126	10	207	1	436
O tri mod y serheir y vrenhines	3	317	3	2ra	3	4	1	110			2	436
Tri ryw dyn yssyd	4	318	4	2rb	4	5			11	207	3	437
Tri ryw wassannaeth	5	323	5	4vb	5	13						
Tri pheth a berthynn wrth frawdwr	6	325	7	6ra	7	17						
Tri ammeu brawd yssyt	7	326	8	6rb	8	18						
Tri ryw wadu yssyd	8	335	12	9rb	151	125						
Tria sunt que dicuntur tri digyngoll kenetyl	9	335	19	11va	9	33			12	210	5	450
Teir kyulauan a wna dyn en y wlad	10	335	63	33va	51	108			28	231	35	482
Tri oed kyureith y dial kelein	11	335	[20]	12ra	57	109						
Tri gwanas gwaew kyureithawl	12	336	[22]	12rb	59	110			69	257	4	449
Tri gwerth kyureithawl beichogi gureic yw	13	336	[26]	12va	72	112						
Tri than digyureith	14	336	[27]	15ra	79	114	4	123	13	211	6	451
Tri chyhyryn canastyr	15	337	86	35rb	84	114						
Teir gauael nyd aduerir	16	337	101	35vb	99	116	27	128	44	243	52	493
Tri ryw dirwy yssyd	17	337	55	32vb	16	42	8	126	15	217	12	461
O tri achaws ny chyll gwreic	18	343	232	74va	18	64	47	145	21	222	27	471
O tri chewilyd morwyn	19	346	118	37ra	116	119	49	146	23	223	29	472
O tri modd y kedernheir gwys	20	348	9	9rb	148	125						
Tri gwys a ellir eu gwadu	21	349	10	9rb	149	125						
Tri dyn ny dylyir eu gwyssyaw	22	349	11	9rb	150	125						
Tri ryw vrawtwyr yssyd yg Kymry	23	349	208	46vb	31	98						
Tri dyn ny allant ymwystlaw	24	351	209	48va	32	102						
Tri pheth a dyly pob brawdwr y warandaw	25	352	210	48va	33	103						
Tri ryw varn tremyc	26	352	211	49ra	34	104						
Tri dyn yssyd ny digawn	27	352	212	49ra	35	104						
Teir fford y gellir gwrthot brawdwr	28	352	213	49rb	36	104						

Entry	No.											
Tri gwrtheb yssyd	29	353	207	45vb	40	106						
Tri pheth a dyly gwarant diball	30	353	37	16vb	17	44			63	244	67	495
Tri dyn a dyly tauotyawc	31	354	78	34vb	75	113						
Tres sunt rei conquestores a rege propter querelas	32	354										
Tres sunt querimonie in quibus calumpnia verbo	33	354										
Tri lle y telir camlwrw deudyblyc	34	354	258	127va								
Tri defnyt hawl yssyt	35	355	120	37rb	118	119						
Tri gollwg a dygir yg kyureith	36	355	121	37rb	119	119						
Tri geir kylus yssyt	37	355	122	37rb	120	119						
Tri dyn y telir gweli tafawd utunt	38	355	256	127ra								
Tri gwallawgeir yssyt	39	355	123	37rb	121	119						
Tri theruyn hawl yssyt	40	355	124	37va	122	120						
Tri pheth ny gygein yg kyureith	41	355	125	37va	123	120						
Tri gweithred yssyt ar praw	42	355	126	37va	124	120						
Tri gwaessaf yssyt	43	355	127	37va	125	120						
Tri chof wedy brawd yssyt	44	355	128	37va	126	120						
Teir tystolyaeth dilys yssyt	45	355	129	37vb	127	120						
Tri lle y thywys cof llys	46	355	130	37vb	128	121						
Teir tystolyaeth marwawl yssyt	47	355	131	37vb	129	121						
Tri gwahan yssyt y rwg gwybtyeid a tystyon	48	356	132	38ra	130	121		126				
Teir fort y may cadarnach gwybyteid no tystyon	49	356	133	38ra	131	121		126				
Teir tystolyaeth yssyt ar eir	50	356	134	38rb	132	122		126				
Tri lleidyr camlyrus yssyt	51	356	[32]	16rb	133	122						
Tri lleidyr dirwyus yssyt	52	356	[33]	16rb	134	122						
Tri lleidyr gwerth yssyt	53	356	[34]	16rb	135	122						
Tri lleidyr crocgadwy yssyt	54	356	[35]	16va	136	122						
Tri lleidyr a dieinc o ledrad kyfatef	55	356	[36]	16va	137	122						
O tri modd y telir dirwy treis	56	357	135	38rb	138	123	16		7	205	22	469
O tri modd y cyll dadyl treis	57	357	136	38va	139	123	17		8	205	23	469
Vn o tri a gyll	58	357	137	38va	140	123	18		9	205	24	469
Tri ryw amdiffyn	59	357	138	38va	141	123						
Tri pheth nyt reit atteb y neb ohonynt	60	357	139	38vb	142	123			60	244	64	495
Tri ryw diebryt yssyd	61	357	140	38vb	143	123						
O tri modd y cae kyfreith rwng hawlwr	62	357	141	38vb	144	124						
Tri theruyn kyfreithawl	63	357	142	38vb	145	124						

Latin D	no.	p.	Q	fo.	Bleg	p.	Lat A	p.	Lat B	p.	Lat E	p.
Teir dadyl a dylyant eu iachau	64	357	143	38vb	146	124						
O dri mod y telir teithi buch	65	358	236	86va	30	88						
Tri anifail digyureith	66	362	79	34vb								
Tri fren a dyly pob adeiladwr maestir	67	364	97	35vb	95	115						
O teir ffordd y byd ryd mach	68	368	45	24va	11	40	5	125	16	217	9	459
O teir ffordd yd oedir mach	69	368	46	24vb	12	40	6	125	18	218	10	460
Teir meuelwryaeth mach	70	368	47	24vb	13	40			17, 57	218, 243		
Teir rwyt brenhin	71	369	56	33rb	44	107	16	126	7	205	22	469
Teir rwyt breyr	72	370	57	33rb	45	107	17	126	8	205	23	469
Teir rwyt tayawc	73	370	58	33rb	46	108	18	126	9	205	24	469
Tri chorn buelyn y brenhin	74	370	59	33rb	47	108	21	127	3	200	18	465
Teir telyn kyfreithawl	75	370	60	33va	48	108	22	128	19	218	13	461
Tri pheth nyt ryd i vilaen eu gwerthu	76	370	61	33va	49	108	14	126	5	205	20	468
Teir keluydyt ny eill tayawc	77	370	62	33va	50	108	15	126	6	205	21	469
Tri anhebcor brenhin	78	370	64	33vb	52	108	9	126	1	199	15	464
Tri anhebcor breyr	79	370	65	33vb	53	108	10	126			75	503
Tri anhebcor tayawc	80	370	66	33vb	54	109	11	126			76	503
Tri pheth ny chyfran brenhin a neb	81	370	[30]	16rb	55	109	12	126	2	199	17	465
Tri phedwar yssyt	82	370	69	34ra	56	109						
Tri tawedawc gorset	83	371	[21]	12ra	58	110					88	509
Tri ouer ymadrawd	84	371	67	33vb	60	110			41	242	49	493
Tri ouer llaeth	85	371	68	33vb	61	110						
Teir saraed ny diwgyr or ceffir	86	371	[23]	12rb	62	110					89	509
Teir paluawd ny diwygir	87	371	70	34ra	63	111					37	483
Teir saraed gwreic ynt	88	371	[24]	12rb	65	111			35	242	43	493
Tri chewilyt kenetyl ynt	89	371	72	34rb	66	111			35/40	242	31/48	475/493
Tri chadarn enllip gwraic ynt	90	371	73	34rb	67	111			24	224	30	473
Tri cyffro dial yssyt	91	371	[25]	12rb	68	111						
Tri pheth ny chyfran brenhin a neb	92	371	[30]	16rb	55	109	12	126	2	199	17	465
Tri dyn a guyd eu breint yn un dyt	93	371	75	34va	71	112			62	244	66	495
O teir fort y dygir mab ac y diwedir	94	372	[76]	34va	[73]	113						
Teir fort y diwedir mab o genetyl	95	372	[76]	34va	[73]	113	19	127	31	241	39	493
Teir gormes doeth ynt	96	372	77	34vb	74	113			61	244	65	495

No.												Triad
97	372	78	34vb	75	113			63	244	67	495	*Tri dyn a dyly tauodyawc*
98	372	79	34vb	76	113					87	509	*Tri llwtyn digyfreith*
99	372	80	35ra	77	113							*Tri llwtyn nyd oes kyureithawl werth arnunt*
100	372	81	35ra	78	114	3	122	20	220	14	463	*Tri gwaed digyureith yssyt*
101	372	82	35ra	80	114	29	128					*Tri etyn a dyly brenhin eu gwerth*
102	372	83	35ra	81	114	13	126	66	250	70, 78	500, 503	*Tri phryf a dyly brenhin pa du bynnac*
103	372	84	35ra	82	114							*Tri pheth ny ad kyureith eu damdwng*
104	372	76	34va	73	113	19	127					*O tri mod y gwedir kysswynnplant o*
105	373	85	35rb	83	114					91	509	*Tri phren yssyt ryt eu llat yn forest*
106	373	87	35rb	85	114							*Tri pheth a tyrr ar gyureith*
107	373	88	35rb	86	114							*Tri etyn ny dylyir eu llat hep gannyad*
108	373	89	35rb	87	115	30	128	60	244	64	495	*Tri pheth, or keffir ar fort, nyd reid roti attep*
109	373	116	36vb	114	118	2	122	68	257	38	492	*Tri argae gwaed yssyt*
110	373	90	35rb	88	115							*Tri dyn ny dyly brenhin eu gwerthu*
111	373	91	35va	89	115							*Tri enw righyll yssyt*
112	373	92	35va	90	115	38	129	34	242	42	493	*Tri ergyd ny thelir dim amdanunt*
113	373	93	35va	91	115	39	129	70	257	16	465	*Tri chyfrwch dirgeledic*
114	373	94	35va	92	115	40	129	36	242	44	493	*Teir nodwyt kyureithawl yssyt*
115	373	95	35va	93	115	41	129	37	242	45	493	*Teir kyfrinach yssyt well eu adef noc eu kelu*
116	373	96	35va	94	115	43	129	71	257	73	502	*Tri anyueil untroydawc yssyt*
117	373	97	35vb	95	115							*Tri pren a dyly pob adeilwr maestir y gaffael*
118	373	98	35vb	96	115							*Tri peth ny thelir kyd coller yn randy*
119	373	99	35vb	97	116	24	128	45	243	53	493	*Teir saraed kelein ynt*
120	373	100	35vb	98	116	24	128	46	243	54	493	*Teir gwarthrut kelein yw*
121	373	51	26va	14	42							*Tri lle yd ymdiueicha mach kyuatef am dylyed*
122	373	52	26va	15	42							*Tri peth ny hanunt o mychni*
123	374	102	35vb	100	116							*Tri ryw tal yssyt y cwynnawdyr*
124	374	103	35vb	101	116							*Tri ymdillung o rwym hawl yssyt*
125	374	104		102	116	35	128	65	247	69	496	*Tri charrychwyn heb attychwel*
126	374	224	57rb		116							*Tri phriodolder yssyd y bob dyn*
127	374	105	36ra	103	116							*O tri achaws y gossodet kyfreith*
128	374	106	36ra	104	116	26	128	42	242	50	493	*Tri hwrth ny diwgir*
129	374	107	36rb	105	117	34	128	55	243	11	460	*Tri da nyd reid mach arnunt*
130	374	108	36rb	106	117	36	129	64	246	68	496	*Tair marw tystolyaeth*
131	375	109	36va	107	117	44	129	38	242	46	493	*Tri thorllwyth vn werth*

Latin D	no.	p.	Q	fo.	Bleg	p.	Lat A	p.	Lat B	p.	Lat E	p.
Tri llydyn vn werth	**132**	375	110	36va	108	117	45	129	30	235	85	507
Tri charrgychwyn hep attychwel	**133**	375	104	35vb	102	116	35	128	65	247	69	496
Teir fford y dywedir gwybydyeit	**134**	375	111	36va	109	118						
Tri pheth a geidw cof	**135**	375	112	36vb	110	118	23	128				
Tri dyn y telir gwely tauot idynt	**136**	375	113	36vb	111	118	32	128	48	243	56	493
Tri chowyllawc llys	**137**	376	114	36vb	112	118	33	128				
Tri dyn a geidw breint llys	**138**	376	115	36vb	113	118						
Tri datssaf gwaet yssyd	**139**	376	116	36vb	114	119	2	122	68	257	38	492
Tri hela ryd yssyd	**140**	376	117	37ra	115	119	20	127	4	203	19	467
Tri chewilyd morwyn	**141**	376	118	37ra	116	119	49	146	23	223	29	472
Tri pheth ny ellir eu dwyn rac gwreic	**142**	376	119	37ra	117	119	48	145	22	222	28	471
Tria solum sunt iudicia in lege constituta	143	382	208	46vb	31	98						
O tri mod yd holir tir	144	384	220	56vb	25	78						
Tri chamwerescyn yssyd	145	385	221	56vb	26	78						
O tri modd y dosperthir dadyl dadanhud	146	385	222	56vb	27	79					32	477
Tri ryw vreint yssyd	147	385	223	57rb	28	79						
Tri phriodolder yssyd	148	385	224	57rb	29	80						
Teir etiuedyaeth kyfreithiawl	149	386	226	58vb	22	74						
Tri dyn amreith otef	150	389										
Teir kynneuawd yssyt	151	394	237	90rb	41	107						
Tri pheth a gadarnha kynefawd	152	394	239	91ra	42	107						
Teir ran yw awdurdawt Hywel Da	153	394	241	91rb	154	126						
Tri aruer kyfreith	154	394	242	91rb	155	127						
Teir gossodedigaeth yssyd	155	395	238	90rb	156	129						

Conspectus 8. The *K* and *S* Triad Collection

Numbers in bold indicate triads found in the additional collection in Q.

K collection / S – 'Trioedd IV'	*K*	p.	*S*	fo.	Tim	p.	*Q*	fo.
Tri anhepgor brenin	8	126					64	33vb
Tri anhepgor g6rda	9	126					65	33vb
Tri anhepcor tayoc	10	126					66	33vb
Tri dygyngoll cenetyl	11	126	216	108r			19	11va
Tri g6arthrud kelein	12	127	217	108v			100	35vb
Tri g6aet argae ynt	13	128	218	109r			116	36vb
Tri g6aet ni di6ygir	14	128	219	109r			81	35ra
Tair craith gogyuarch ynt	15	128	220	109r				
O dri mod i serheir pop dyn	16	128	221	109r			2	1vb
Tri anhepcor brenin	17	129	222	109r			64	33vb
Tri meip ni dyly tref tat	18	129	223	109v			**168**	40va
Tri argae teruyn	19	129	224	109v				
Tri datleu am tir ni dlyir aros un amser	20	130	225	110r				
Teir g6raged a dyly i meibion uam6ys	21	130	226	110r			**169**	40va
Tair gorssed yssyd yn kyfreithiol	22	131	227	110v	120	77	**170**	41ra
Tri g6anas g6ystyl	23	131	228	110v	121	77	**171**	41ra
Tri g6ystyl nit rait meichieu ar dilysr6yd	24	132	230	110v	123	77	**173**	41rb
Tri g6ystyl gogymreint ysyd	25	132	229	111r	122	77	**172**	41rb
Tri pheth nit rait mach ar dilysr6yd trostunt	26	132	231	111r	124	78	107	36rb
Tri mach ni dlyir eu g6adu	27	133						
Tri lle o rodir mach yn duhun	28	133						
Tri ry6 dadanyd yssyd			232	111r	125	78	229	48va
Tri kargych6yn hep atch6edyl	29	133	233	111v	126	78	104	35vb
Tri gorsaf g6raic	30	133	234	111v	[127]	78	**176**	41va
Teir r6yt brenin	31	134	235	111v			56	33rb
Tair r6yt map uchel6r	32	134	236	112r			57	33rb
Tair r6yt map aillt	33	134	237	112r			58	33rb
Tri phriot g6r	34	134						
Tri chorn gogy6erth	35	134	41	48r			59	33rb
Tair telyn kyureithol	36	134	42	48r			60	33va
Tri chynghauoc kyfreith	37	134	238	112r			**177**	41vb
Tri ta6edoc gorsed	38	135	239	112r			21	12ra
Tri aryf kyfreithiol ysyd	39	135	240	112r				
Tri hely ryd ysyd	40	135	241	112v			117	37ra
Tri ysgyuaetheu milgi	41	135	242	112v				
Tri aniueil yssyd gymeint g6erth eu troet	42	135	243	112v			178	41vb
Tri eniueil y syd kymint g6erth eu torll6yth	43	136						
Tair sarhaet ysyd ac ni di6ygir	44	136	244	112v			**179**	41vb
Tri achos i dyly g6r maedu i 6raic	45	136	245	112v			**180**	41vb
Tri lle i rann kyfreith yn deuhanner	46	136	246	113r			**181**	42ra

Tri ry6 dir6y ysyd	47	137	247	113r	128	79	55	32vb
Tair ouer groes yssyd	48	138	248	113r	129	79	**182**	42rb
Tri mod i dlyir amobyr i 6raic	49	138	249	113r	130	79	**183**	42rb
Tri dyn a dyly talu amobyr	50	138	250	113v	131	79	**184**	42va
Tri dygiat a uyd ar uap	51	138	251	113v	132	79	**185**	42va
Tri cymeriat a uyd ar uap	52	139	252	113v	133	79	**186**	42va
Tair keluydyt ni dyly map tayoc i dyscu	53	140	253	114r	134	80	62	33va
Tri pheth ni dyly taeoc eu g6erthu o byd ar i hel6	54	140	254	114v	135	80	205	45va
Tri dyn i telir g6eli tauot udunt	55	141	255	114v	136	80	256	127ra
Tri dyn a dieingk rac dihenyd am letrat kyuadef	56	141	256	114v	137	81	**187**	43ra
Tri douot yssyd ryd i dyn eu kymryt ar y fford	57	141	257	115r	138	81	89	35rb
Tri phrif raniat a uyd ar tir	58	142	258	115r	139	81	[227]	59ra
Tri peth ni dlyir eu rannu namyn her6yd i ffr6ytheu	59	142	189	87r	108	64	**188**	43rb
Teir mar6 dystoliath yssyd	60	142	259	115v	140	82	[108]	36rb
Tri llyssiat yssyd ar tyst	61	143	260	116r	141	82	**190**	43rb
Tri peth a a r6ng dyn a daly a damd6ng	62	144	261	116r	142	83	**189**	43rb
Tri ffeth ni dlyir eu damt6ng	63	144	262	116r	143	83	**191**	43rb
Tri g6ystyl ni dig6yd	64	145	263	116v	144	83	**192**	43va

Conspectus 9. The Latin A Triads

Keywords: Latin A	no..	p.	Lat B	Lat E	X	fo.	Q	fo.
O tri mod y serheir y vrenhines	1	110		2	2		3	2ra
Try argay gwayth	2	122	68	38			116	36vb
Tri gwaet digyureith	3	122	20	14	45	213v	81	35ra
Tri than digyureith	4	123	13	6	46	213v	27	15ra
O teir fford y differir	5	125	18	10	20	209v	46	24vb
Teyr meuyllwryayth yssyt ymmechniayth	6	125	17	8			47	24vb
Tri ryw sarhaet yssyd	7	126	10	1			2	1vb
Teir dirwy brenhin ynt	8	126	15	12	19	209r	55	32vb
Try anhepcor breenhyn	9	126	1	15			64	33vb
Try anhepcor mab hucchelur	10	126		75			65	33vb
Try anhepcor tayauc	11	126		76			66	33vb
Tri pheth ny chyfran brenhin	12	126	2	17	21	209v	30	16rb
Tri phryf y dyly y brenhin eu gwerth	13	126	66	70, 78	48	213v	83	35ra
Tri pheth ny werth tayawc	14	126	5	20	6	190r	61	33va
Teir keluydyt ny dysc tayawc	15	126	6	21	7	190r	62	33va
Teir rwyt brenhin	16	126	7	22	16	208v	56	33rb
Teyr rwyth mab hucchelur	17	126	8	23	17	209r	57	33rb
Teyr rwyth tayauc	18	126	9	24	18	209r	58	33rb
O teir fford y gwedir mab o genedyl	19	127	31	39	40	212v	76	34va
Teir hela ryd yssyd	20	127	4	19	53	214r	117	37ra
Tri chorn buelyn y brenhin	21	127	3	18	52	214r	59	33rb
Teir telyn kyfreithawl	22	128	19	13			60	33va
Tri pheth a geidw cof	23	128					112	36vb
Teyr gwarth keleyn	24	128	46	54	71	218v	100	35vb
Teyr gorset araf	25	128	47	55				
Try gwth ne dywegyr	26	128	42	50	55	214r	106	36ra
Teyr gauayl nyt datuerir o kefreyt	27	128	44	52	72	218v	101	35vb
Teyr sayrhaed keleyn	28	128	45	53	70	218v	99	35vb
Tri edyn y dyly y brenhin eu gwerth	29	128			47	213v	82, 88	35ra, 35rb
Tri pheth nyt reit atteb y eu perchennawc	30	128	60	64	74	218v	89	35rb
Tri achos ni dyly talu gwerth celain	31	128	50	58				
Try thauodyayc yssyt yaun talu gwely	32	128	48	56	75	218v	113, 255	36vb, 126va
Try cowyllyauc llys	33	128		77			114	36vb
Tri da dilis diuach yssyd	34	128	55	11			107, 203	36rb, 45rb
Try charr kewyn heb dat dewel	35	128	65	69			104	35vb
Teyr maru testolyayth	36	129	64	68	64	217v	108	36rb
Try agcheuarch gwr	37	129	49	57				
Tri ergyt ny diwygir	38	129	34	42	61	217r	92	35va
Tri chyfrwch dirgel	39	129	70	16	62	217v	93	35va
Teir notwyd kyfreithawl	40	129	36	44	63	217v	94	35va
Teyr kyfrynach	41	129	37	45	65	217v	95	35va

Tri dyn ni ddylid eu lladd	**42**	129	32	40				
Tri aneueail vn troedawc	**43**	129	71	73	66	218r	96	35va
Tri thorllwyth vn werth ac eu mam	**44**	129	38	46			109	36va
Tri llydyn o'r genuein	**45**	129	30	85			110	36va
Teir gwerth y rennir tir	46	132	26	33	5	188v	227	59ra
O tri achaws ny chyll gwreic	47	145	21	27	9	202r	232	74va
Tri pheth ny chyll gwreic	48	145	22	28	10	202r	119	37ra
Teir gwarthrud morwyn	49	146	23	29			118	37ra
Tri lle y rann kyfreith	50	158	33	41	68	218r	181	42ra

Conspectus 10. The Latin B Triads

Keywords: Latin B	no.	p.	A	E	X	fo.	Q	fo.
Tri anhepcor brenhin	1	199	9	15	20	209v	64	33vb
Tri pheth ny chyfran brenhin	2	199	12	17	21	209v	30	16rb
Tri chorn buelyn	3	200	21	18	52	214r	59	33rb
Teir hela ryd	4	203	20	19	53	214r	117	37ra
Tri pheth ny werth tayawc	5	205	14	20	6	190r	61	33va
Teir keluydyt ny dysc tayawc	6	205	15	21	7	190r	62	33va
Teir rwyt brenhin	7	205	16	22	16	208v	56	33rb
Teir rwyt breyr	8	205	17	23	17	209r	57	33rb
Teir rwyt tayawc	9	205	18	24	18	209r	58	33rb
Tri ryw sarhaet yssyd	10	207	7	1			2	1vb
Tri ryw dyn yssyd	11	207		3			4	2rb
Trichoet kenedyl	12	210		5	14	208r	19	11va
Tri than digyureith	13	211	4	6			27	15ra
Tair llaw (mach a chynnogyn)	14	216		7	46	213v		
Teir dirwy brenhin ynt	15	217	8	12	19	209r	55	32vb
O tri modd y bydd rhydd mach	16	217		9			45	24va
Teir meuylwryaith yssid y uechniaith	17	218	6	8			47	24vb
O teir fford y differir	18	218	5	10			46	24vb
Teir telyn kyfreithawl	19	218	22	13			60	33va
Tri gwaet digyfreith	20	220	3	14	45	213v	81	35ra
O tri achaws ny chyll gwreic	21	222	47	27	9	202r	232	74va
Tri pheth ny chyll gwreic kyt gatter	22	222	48	28	10	202r	119	37ra
Teir gwarthrud morwyn	23	223	49	29			118	37ra
Tri lle y rhoddir dedfryd/Tri chadarn enllip	24	224		30	32	211v	73	34rb
Teir gwragedd a dyly eu meibon	25	225					169	40va
Teir gwerth y rennir tir	26	227	46	33	5	188v	227	59ra
Tri meib yn tri broder vn vam vn tat	27	231		34	37	212r	74	34rb
Teyr kyulauan	28	231		35	22	209v	63	33va
Tri adeilad sydd rhwng brodyr	29	231		36, [92]			194	43vb
Tri llydyn o'r genuein	30	235	45	85			110	36va
O teir fford y gwedir mab o genedyl	31	241	19	39	40	212v	76	34va
Tri dyn ny dylyir eu lladd	**32**	242	42	40				
O tri lle y rhan cyfraith	**33**	242	50	41	68	218r	181	42ra
Tri ergyt ny diwygir	**34**	242	38	42	61	217r	92	35va
Tri seudan gureic	**35**	242		43	31, 33	211r, 211v	24	12rb
Teir notwyd kyfreithawl	**36**	242	40	44	63	217v	94	35va
Teir kyfrinach	**37**	242	41	45	65	217v	95	35va
Tri thorllwyth vn werth ac eu mam	**38**	242	44	46			109	36va
Tri chywilydd gwraig	**39**	242		47				
Teir sarhaet gwreic	**40**	242		31, 48	33	211v	72	34rb
Tri ofer ymadrawd	**41**	242		49	26	210v	67	33vb
Tri gwth ny diwygir	**42**	242	26	50	55	214r	106	36ra

424

CONSPECTUSES

Keywords – Latin B	no.	p.	A	E	X	fo.	Q	fo.
Teir newit a doant tracheuyn	43	243		51				
Teir gauail	44	243	27	52	72	218v	101	35vb
Teir sarhaet kelein	45	243	28	53	70	218v	99	35vb
Teir guarchaet kelein	46	243	24	54	71	218v	100	35vb
Teir gorsed arah	47	243	25	55				
Tri tauodyauc	48	243	32	56	75	218v	113, 255	36vb, 126va
Tri anghyuarch gwr	49	243	37	57				
Tri achaws ni dyly talu gwerth celain	50	243	31	58				
O teir fford y telir gwyalen aryant	51	243		26	60	216v		
Tri dyn a dyly gwirawd	52	243		59				
Teir gorsaf gureic	53	243		60			176	41va
Tri dyn y degemir	54	243		61			159	39vb
Tri da dilis diuach yssyd	55	243	34	11			107, 203	36rb, 45rb
Teir gorsaf unben	56	243						
Teir meuylwriath mechniaith yssyd	57	243	6	8			47	24vb
Tri anifail costawg tom	58	244		62				
Tri argaey teruin	59	244		63, 83				
Tri pheth nyt reit atteb	60	244	30	64	74	218v	89	35rb
Teir gormes doeth	61	244		65	41	213v	77	34vb
Tri dyn a gynnyd eu breint	62	244		66	38	212v	75	34va
Tri dyn a dyly tauodyawc	63	244		67	62	217v	78	34vb
Teir marw tystolyaeth	64	246	36	68	64	217v	108	36rb
Tri karkychwyn gep attychwel	65	247	35	69			104	35vb
Tri phryf y dyly y brenhin	66	247	13	70, 78	48	213v	83	35ra
Teir ayluyt	67	250		71	11	207v		
Tri argai gwaet	68	257	2	38			116	36vb
Tri gwanas gwayw	69	257		4	25	210v	22	12rb
Tri chyfrwch dirgel	70	257	39	16	62	217v	93	35va
Tri aneueil vn troedawc	71	257	43	73	66	218r	96	35va
Tri tremyc argluyd	72	259		84				

Conspectus 11. The Latin E Triads

Keywords: Latin E	no.	p.	Lat A	Lat B	X	fo.	Q	fo.
Tri ryw sarhaet	1	436	7	10			2	1vb
O tri mod y serheir y vrenhines	2	436	1		2	166v	3	2ra
Tri ryw dyn yssyd	3	437		11			4	2rb
Tri gwanas gwayw	4	449		69	25	210v	22	12rb
Tri dyngyn gollet kenedyl	5	450		12	14	208r	19	11va
Tri than digyureith	6	451	4	13	46	213v	27	15ra
Tair llaw [mach a chynnogyn]	7	458		14				
Teir meuylwryaeth yssyd y uechni	8	459	6	17, 57			47	24vb
Teir fford y byd ryd mach	9	459		16			45	24va
O teir fford y differir	10	460	5	18			46	24vb
Tri da dilis diuach	11	460	34	55			107, 203	36rb, 45rb
Teir dirwy brenhin	12	461	8	15	19	209r	55	32vb
Teir telyn kyfreithawl	13	461	22	19			60	33va
Tri gwaet digyfreith	14	463	3	20	45	213v	81	35ra
Tri anhepcor brennin	15	464	9	1	20	209v	64	33vb
Tri chyfrwch dirgel	16	465	39	70	62	217v	93	35va
Tri pheth ny chyfran brenhin	17	465	12	2	21	209v	30	16rb
Tri chorn buelyn	18	465	21	3	52	214r	59	33rb
Teir hela ryd	19	467	20	4	53	214r	117	37ra
Tri pheth ny werth tayawc	20	468	14	5	6	190r	84	35ra
Teir keluydyt ny dysc tayawc	21	469	15	6	7	190r	62	33va
Teir rwyt brenhin	22	469	16	7	16	208v	56	33rb
Teir rwyt breyr	23	469	17	8	17	209r	57	33rb
Teir rwyt tayawc	24	469	18	9	18	209r	58	33rb
Tair hela rhydd yssyd i filaen	25	469						
O teir fford y telir gwyalen aryant	26	470		51	60	216v		
O tri achaws ny chyll gwreic y hegwedi	27	471	47	21	9	202r	232	74va
Tri pheth ny chyll gwreic	28	471	48	22	10	202r	119	37ra
Teir gwarthrud morwyn	29	472	49	23			118	37ra
Tri lle y rhoddir dedfryd/Tri chadarn enllip	30	473		24	32	211v	73	34rb
Tri chewliyd kenedyl	31	475		40	33	211v	72	34rb
Tri ryw datanhud	32	477			4	174r	229	66va
Teir gweith y rennir tir	33	478	46	26	5	188v	227	59ra
Tri meib yn tri broder vn vam vn tat	34	482		27	37	212r	74	34rb
Teir kyflauan	35	482		28	23	210r	63	33va
Tri thlos kenedyl	36	482		29			194	43vb
Teir paluawt ny diwygir	37	483			29	211r	70	34ra
Tri argai sanguinis	38	492	2	68			116	36vb
O teir fford y gwedir mab	39	493	19	31	40	212v	76	34va
Tri dyn ny dylyir eu lladd	**40**	493	42	32				
Tri lle y rann kyfreith	**41**	493	50	33	68	218r	181	42ra

Keywords: Latin E	no.	p.	Lat A	Lat B	X	fo.	Q	fo.
Tri ergyt ny diwygir	**42**	493	38	34	61	217r	92	35va
Tri seudan gureic	**43**	493		35	31	211r	24	12rb
Teir notwyd kyfreithawl	**44**	493	40	36	63	217v	94	35va
Teir kyfrinach	**45**	493	41	37	65	217v	95	35va
Tri thorllwyth vn werth	**46**	493	44	38			109	36va
Tri chywilyd gwreic	**47**	493		39				
Teir sarhaet gwreic	**48**	493		40	33	211v	72	34rb
Tri ofer ymadrawd	**49**	493		41	26	210v	67	33vb
Tri guth ny duwegir	**50**	493	26	42	55	214r	106	36ra
Teir newit a doant tracheuyn	**51**	493		43				
Teir gauael	**52**	493	27	44	72	218v	101	35vb
Teir sarhaet kelein	**53**	493	28	45	70	218v	99	35vb
Teir guarchaet kelein	**54**	493	24	46	71	218v	100	35vb
Teir gorsaf aryf	**55**	493	25	47				
Tri tauodiauc	**56**	493	32	48	75	218v	113, 255	36vb, 126va
Tri aghyuarch gwr	**57**	493	37	49				
Tri achaws ni dyly talu gwerth celain	**58**	493	31	50				
Tri dyn a dyly gwirawd yn llys	**59**	493		52				
Teir gorsaf gureic	**60**	493		53			176	41va
Tri dyn y degemir	**61**	493		54			159	39vb
Tri anifail costawg tom	62	495		58				
Tri argai teruin	63	495		59				
Tri pheth nyt reit atteb	**64**	495	30	60	74	218v	89	35rb
Teir gormes sapientis	**65**	495		61	41	213v	77	34vb
Tri dyn a gynnyd eu breint	**66**	495		62	38	212v	75	34va
Tri dyn a dyly tauodyawc	**67**	495		63	42	213v	78	34vb
Teir marw tystolyaeth	68	496	36	64	64	217v	108	36rb
Tri kychwin hep attechuel	69	496	35	65			104	35vb
Tri phryf y dyly y brenhin	70	500	13	66	48	213v	83	35ra
Tair aylwyt	71	501		67	11	207v		
Tri dyn a serheir ni dylir cyfraith	72	501						
Tri aneueil vn troedawc	73	502	43	71	66	218r	96	35va
Tria sunt forefacta regis	74	502						
Tri anhepcor breyr	75	503	10				65	33vb
Tri anhepcor tayawc	76	503	11				66	33vb
Tri cowylliauc llys	77	503	33				114	36vb
Tri phryf y dyly y frenhines	78	503			48	213v	83	35ra
Tri lle y dyly y brenin gweli tafod	79	504						
Teir ouer vechni	80	504					53	28rb
Tria sunt pro quibus non debetur refugium	81	504						
Tri tlus kenedyl	82	504					194	43vb
Tri argai teruyn	83	504		59				
Tri tremyc arglwyd	84	507		72				
Tri llydyn o'r genuein	85	507	45	30			110	36va
Tair ofer groes	86	508					182	42rb

Keywords: Latin E	no.	p.	Lat A	Lat B	X	fo.	Q	fo.
Tri llydyn digyfreith	87	509			43	213v	79	34vb
Tri tawedauc gorsed	88	509			24	210v	21	12ra
Tri breinniauc os kefir yn uedw	89	509			28	211r	23	12rb
Tri dyn yssyd ryd udunt kerdet	90	509						
Tri phren yssid ryd eu llad	91	509			50	214r	85	35rb
Tri thlos kenedyl	92	509		[29]			194	43vb

List of Triads in this Edition

This is a complete list of the triads which are found in this edition. The triad keywords are given first, in modern Welsh. The number of the main edition of the triad, including the location of the note on the triad, is then given. The second reference is to corresponding triads from other collections, and the note will be found under the first number listed unless noted otherwise. If the triad number is given in square brackets, the triad is a variant which is given in full. The triads are listed in the order of the English alphabet.

Triad heading	Number	Other edition
Am dair diasbad uwch adfan	Q262	
O dair ffordd ni ellir gwadu mab o genedl	Mk102	Y155
O dair ffordd y differir mach a chynnogn	X59	
O dair ffordd y dosberthir brawd gyngaws	Q15	
O dair ffordd y dyly dyn fod yn enaidfaddau	Z66	
O dair ffordd y telir gwialen arian i'r brenin	X60	[Mk65]
O dair ffordd ydd â cogail ym mraint paladr	S172	
O dair ffordd ydd oedir mach a chynnogn	Q46	
O dair modd y telir teithi buwch fawr	X8	Q236
O dri achos ni chyll gwraig ei hagweddi cyd gadawo hi ei gŵr	Q232	X9
O dri achos y gosoded cyfraith	Q105	
O dri modd y cadarnheir gwys	Q9	
O dri modd y cau cyfraith rhwng hawlwr ac amddiffynnwr	Q141	
O dri modd y cyll brawdwr gamlwrw	Q18	
O dri modd y cyll dadl trais y braint mwyaf	Q136	
O dri modd y gwedir cyswynblant o genedl	Q76	
O dri modd y sarheir y frenhines	X2	Q3
O dri modd y telir dirwy trais	Q135	
O dri modd ydd holir tir	Q220	

Triad heading	Number	Other edition
O dri pheth y cyll dyn ei hawl er daed fo ei ddefnydd	Q248	
Pob adeilwr maestir a ddyly gaffael tri phren	X67	
Tair aelwyd a ddyly wneuthur iawn dros ddyn ni bo arglwydd oddef iddo	X11	[Z60]
Tair agweddi gyfreithiol	Z78	
Tair balog fechni y sydd	Q196	
Tair celfyddyd ni eill taeog eu dysgu i'w fab heb ganiad ei arglwydd	Q62	X7
Tair cont gyfreithiol y sydd	X49a	
Tair craith gogyfarch y sydd ar ddyn	U3	
Tair craith gogyfarch ŷnt	K15	
Tair cyflafan nid oes sarhaed amdanynt	Q150	
Tair cyflafan, os gwna dyn yn ei wlad	X23	Q63
Tair cyfnewid a ddoant drachefn	Mk99	
Tair cyfrinach a ddyly y brenin eu caffael	X65	[Z76], Q95
Tair cynefod y sydd	Q237	
Tair dadl a ddylyant eu iacháu ac eu barnu	Q143	
Tair dadl nid oes oed i frawdwr am eu barnu	Q215	
Tair dadl y sydd anghynwysedig yng nghyfraith Hywel	Q261	
Tair dirwy brenin ŷnt	X19	[U19], Q55, [S37]
Tair etifeddiaeth gyfreithiol y sydd	Q226	
Tair ffordd y bydd rhydd mach am ddylyed cyfaddef	Q45	
Tair ffordd y diwedir gwybyddiaid am dir	Q111	
Tair ffordd y dygir mab ac y'i diwedir [y]	X40	[Mk46, Mk47]
Tair ffordd y dylyir dienyddu dyn	Z102	
Tair ffordd y gellir gwrthnau brawdwr teilwng	Q213	
Tair ffordd y llysir ynad	Z100	
Tair ffordd y mae cadarnach gwybyddiaid na thystion	Q43	Q133
Tair ffordd y sydd i lysu tystion	X35	[Mk42], Q190
Tair gafael nid adferir	X72	Q101
Tair gormes ddoeth ŷnt	X41	Q77
Tair gorsedd dygynull	Q219	
Tair gorsedd frenhinol y sydd	Q245	
Tair gorsedd gyfreithiol y sydd	Q170	
Tair gosgordd brenhinol y sydd	X12	Q193
Tair gosodedigaeth y sydd	Q238	
Tair gwaith y caiff gwraig ei hwynebwerth	Q233	
Tair gwaith y drychaif ar sarhaed gŵr	Q202	
Tair gwaith y rhennir tir	X5	Q227
Tair gwanas gwayw cyfreithiol y sydd	X25	

Triad heading	Number	Other edition
Tair gwarthrudd celain yw	X71	Q100, [S276]
Tair gwragedd a ddyly eu meibion dir o famwys	Q169	Q71
Tair gwragedd herwydd cyfraith a ddyly eu meibion eu dylyed o famwys	Q230	
Tair gwragedd ni ddyly eu gwŷr iawn ganddynt	Q235	
Tair gwragedd ni ddylyir dadlau ag eu hetifedd am dref eu mam	X30	[Z118]
Tair gwys a ellir eu gwadu cyn amser tyston	Q10	
Tair marwdystiolaeth y sydd a allant sefyll yn y dadlau yn dda	X64	Q108
Tair meflwriaeth mach y sydd	Q47	
Tair merched a ddylyant dalu amobrau	Q153	
Tair merched ni ddylyir amobrau iddynt	Q154	
Tair nodwydd gyfreithiol y sydd	X63	Q94
Tair ofer fechni y sydd	Q53	
Tair ofer groes y sydd	Q182	
Tair palfod ni ddiwygir	X29	Q70
Tair perchnogaeth y sydd ar dir	S207	
Tair pla cenedl	W82	
Tair rhan yw awdurdod Hywel Dda a'i gyfreithiau	Q241	
Tair rhwyd brenin yw	X16	Q56
Tair rhwyd brëyr ŷnt	X17	Q57, note on X16
Tair rhwyd taeog ŷnt	X18	Q58, note on X16
Tair sarhaed celain yw	X70	Q99
Tair sarhaed gwraig ŷnt	X31	
Tair sarhaed gwraig ŷnt	Q24	
Tair sarhaed ni ddiwygir	Q179	
Tair sarhaed ni ddiwygir os ceffir drwy fedd-dod	X28	Q23
Tair telyn gyfreithiol y sydd	Q60	
Tair tystiolaeth ddilys y sydd	Q39	Q129
Tair tystiolaeth farwol y sydd	Q41	Q131
Tair tystiolaeth y sydd ar air, ac ni ddygir i grair	Q44	Q134
Tair uchel lys y sydd yng Nghymru	Q243	
Tri achos y cyll dyn dref ei dad	Z89	
Tri achos y dyly gŵr faeddu ei wraig	Q180	
Tri achos y sydd i lysu tystion	Q38	
Tri aelod a ddyly wneuthur iawn dros ddyn a'i gymryd	S174	
Tri amau brawd y sydd	X13	Q8
Tri anghydwybod cyfraith y sydd	S196	
Tri anghyfarch addefedig y sydd	Q257	
Tri anghyfraith y sydd	S198	
Tri anhepgor brenin ŷnt	X20	Q64
Tri anhepgor brëyr	Q65	See X20

Triad heading	Number	Other edition
Tri anhepgor cenedl	Mk81	
Tri anhepgor taeog	Q66	See X20
Tri anifail a â gwerth cyfraith cyn eu blwydd	Q199	
Tri anifail a ddrychaif eu gwerth dair gwaith yn un dydd	Q197	
Tri anifail untroediog y sydd	X66	Q96
Tri anifail y sydd gymaint gwerth ei droed pob un ohonynt â'i enaid	Q178	
Tri anifail y sydd unwerth eu llosgyrnau a'u llygaid a'u henaid	W89	
Tri anogonion cyfraith	Z93	
Tri arf cyfreithiol y sydd	K39	
Tri arfer cyfraith y sydd	Q242	
Tri argae dangos	Z119	
Tri argae gwaed	Mk71	Q116, [LatD109]
Tri argae terfyn	K19	W15, S173, S274
Tri argae tir	Z94	
Tri braint y sydd i gynghellor	S266	
Tri chadarn byd ŷnt	Q155	
Tri chadarn enllib gwraig ŷnt	X32	Q73
Tri chamgwyn cylus y sydd yng nghyfraith	Q218	[S161]
Tri chamoresgyn y sydd	Q221	
Tri chanlyn diwall y sydd	Q259	
Tri chanol y sydd yng nghyfraith	Q249	
Tri chargychwyn heb atychwel	Q104	
Tri chof wedi brawd y sydd	Q128	
Tri chorfflan ni ddylyir eu rhannu herwydd tyddynau	Q195	
Tri chorn buelin y brenin	X52	Q59
Tri chowyllog llys y sydd	Q114	[Tim159]
Tri chwyn a ddiffydd bob cwyn	S192	
Tri chŵyn goruchel y sydd	S169	
Tri chyfannedd gwlad	U38	
Tri chyfeiliorn cyfraith y sydd	Q244	
Tri chyffredin cenedl ŷnt	Q151	
Tri chyffredin gwlad	Mk69	S184
Tri chyffro dial ŷnt	X34	Q25
Tri chyfrwch dirgel a ddyly y brenin ei gaffael	X62	[Mk131, Z63], Q93
Tri chyhyryn canastr y sydd	X51	[Mk62, U42], Q86
Tri chymeriad a fydd ar fab	Q186	
Tri chynghafog cyfraith	Q177	
Tri chywilydd cenedl ŷnt ac o achos gwraig y maent oll tri	X33	Q72
Tri chywilydd morwyn y sydd	Q118	

Triad heading	Number	Other edition
Tri da nid rhaid mach arnynt	Q107	[S180]
Tri dadanudd tir y sydd	X4	Q222
Tri dadlau am dir ni ddylyir aros un amser mwy na'i gilydd	K20	
Tri dadlau ni ddylyir eu gwneuthur namyn rhag bron ynad	Q160	
Tri defnydd hawl y sydd	Q120	
Tri diwyneb gwlad y sydd ac ni ellir bod hebddynt	Mk73	
Tri dygiad a fydd ar fab	Q185	
Tri dygngoll cenedl ŷnt	X14	Q19, [S277]
Tri dyn a dâl ebediw heb dir	Z115	
Tri dyn a ddiainc rhag dihenydd cyfaddef	Q187	
Tri dyn a ddyly cenedl y fam eu gowyn, heb genedl y tad	Q156	Q206
Tri dyn a ddyly dalu amobr	Q184	
Tri dyn a ddyly dalu galanas ac ni ddyly ei gaffael	Z81	
Tri dyn a ddyly fod yn dafodiog absen dros glaf	Tim173	
Tri dyn a ddyly gweli dafod	X75	Q113
Tri dyn a ddyly le yn y llys iddynt heb fod eu cefn ar y pared	Z87	
Tri dyn a ddyly tafodiog drostynt yn nadlau	X42	Q78
Tri dyn a ddylyant alanas ac ni ddylyant sarhaed	Q148	
Tri dyn a ddylyant dalu galanas ac ni ddylyant ran o alanas	Q162	
Tri dyn a ddylyant fod yn anrhaith oddef	Z56	
Tri dyn a ddylyant sarhaed ac ni ddylyant alanas	Q149	[J157]
Tri dyn a ddylyir eu cadw rhag arfau	Q165	
Tri dyn a gaffant ran o alanas ac nis talant	Q163	
Tri dyn a geidw braint llys yn absen y brenin	Q115	
Tri dyn a gynnail dir yn llys y brenin	S181	
Tri dyn a gynnal dir ac a'i herbyn	Q230b	
Tri dyn a gynnydd eu braint yn un dydd	X38	Q75
Tri dyn a saif tafodiog absen drostynt	S201	
Tri dyn a wna gwlad yn dlawd	W87	
Tri dyn a wnant sarhad i'r brenin	X1	Q1
Tri dyn bonheddig canhwynol gwirion	Q144	[J159]
Tri dyn cas cenedl	Mk93	
Tri dyn cyn gwrthebont trwy wad, ni thalant raith osodedig	Q252	
Tri dyn herwydd cyfraith ni safant wrth a wnelont	S265	
Tri dyn ni admwynheir dim o'r a ddyweton mewn llys	S267	
Tri dyn ni allant ychwanegu ansawdd i neb ar dir	S151	
Tri dyn ni allant ymwystlo	Q209	[S183]

Triad heading	Number	Other edition
Tri dyn ni ddyly brenin eu gwerthu	X56	Q90
Tri dyn ni ddyly camlwrw arnynt	Z114	
Tri dyn ni ddylyir eu claddu yng nghysegr	S214	
Tri dyn ni ddylyir eu gwysio	Q11	
Tri dyn ni ellir canlyn cwynau unig rhagddynt	S179	
Tri dyn nid gair eu gair ar neb nac ar ddim	Q147	
Tri dyn y degymir iddynt	Q159	
Tri dyn y mae caeth cyfraith iddynt bob amser	Y160	
Tri dyn y sydd a ellir eu llysu o'r un rhyw achosion	Q251	
Tri dyn y sydd a gaiff dda cyffroëdig	Q260	
Tri dyn y sydd ni ddichon un ohonynt fod yn frawdwr teilwng	Q212	
Tri dyn y sydd rydd iddynt gerdded ffordd a heb ffordd	Mk79	
Tri dyn y telir galanas iddynt ac ni thalant hwy	Tim172	
Tri dyn y telir gweli tafod iddynt	Q256	[LatD38]
Tri dyn y traeana y brenin â hwynt	S279	
Tri edn a ddyly brenin eu gwerth pa le bynnag y'u lladder	X47	Q82
Tri edn ar dir dyn arall heb ganiad	X73	Q88
Tri enw rhingyll y sydd	X57	Q91
Tri ergyd ni thelir dim amdanynt	X61	Q92
Tri gair cylus y sydd	Q122	Q29
Tri goddef y sydd yn cydgerdded â chyfraith	S191	
Tri golwg a ddygir yng nghyfraith	Q121	Q28
Tri goresgyn y sydd ni ddylyir caffael mwyniant ohonynt	S208	
Tri gorsaf arf y sydd	Mk103	[Z75]
Tri gorsaf gwraig ŷnt	Q176	
Tri grwndwal doethineb	Mk97	
Tri gwaed cyfraith y sydd	X45	Q81
Tri gwaesaf y sydd	Q127	
Tri gwahan y sydd rhwng gwybyddiaid a thystion	Q42	Q132
Tri gwanas gwayw cyfreithiol yn nadlau y sydd	Q22	
Tri gwanas gwystl ŷnt	Q171	
Tri gwasanaeth a wna y brenin i'r hebogydd	X3	Q6
Tri gweithred y sydd ar brawf	Q126	
Tri gwerth cyfraith beichiogi gwraig	X39	Q26
Tri gwg ni ddiwygir	U35	
Tri gwreiddyn anianol y sydd i'r un gair cyfraith	S206	
Tri gwrtheb y sydd	Q207	
Tri gwybyddiaid y sydd am dir	X76	[Mk12]
Tri gwystl gogymraint ŷnt	Q172	

Triad heading	Number	Other edition
Tri gwystl ni ddigwyddant fyth	Q192	
Tri gwystl nid rhaid meichiau ar eu dilysrwydd	Q173	
Tri hely rhydd y sydd ym mhob gwlad	X53	Q117
Tri hwrdd ni ddiwygir	X55	Q106
Tri lle herwydd cyfraith ni pherthyn i ŵr dyfod fod yn blaid	Q230a	
Tri lle ni ddyly dyn roddi llw gweilydd	Mk48	
Tri lle o roddir mach yn dduhun ni ddylyir ei wadu	K28	
Tri lle y dyly arglwydd erlid gweli tafod	Tim160	
Tri lle y dyly dyn fesur ei hawl gan amddiffynnwr	Z120	
Tri lle y dyly gwraig ateb heb ei gŵr	S150	
Tri lle y dyly ynad cwmwd farnu yn rhad	Q200	
Tri lle y gallai dyn wneuthur cywerthyd deg punt o golled i arall	Q201	
Tri lle y rhan cyfraith	X68	Q225
Tri lle y rhan cyfraith	U9	[Z5], note on Q181
Tri lle y rhan cyfraith yn ddau hanner	Q225	Note on X68
Tri lle y sydd herwydd cyfraith y dyly dadl gynhennus ei therfynu	S209	
Tri lle y sydd o rhoddir meichiau, ni ellir eu gwadu	Q50	Q175, K27
Tri lle y telir camlwrw deuddyblyg	Q258	
Tri lle y tywys cof llys	Q40	Q130
Tri lle ydd ymddifeichia mach	X58	Q51
Tri lle yng nghyfraith Hywel y mae prawf	Mk89	
Tri lleidr a ddiainc o ledrad cyfaddef	Q36	
Tri lleidr camlyryus y sydd	Q32	
Tri lleidr crogadwy y sydd	Q35	
Tri lleidr dirwyus y sydd	Q33	
Tri lleidr gwerth y sydd	Q34	
Tri llw a ddyry gwraig i ŵr	Q234	
Tri llwdn digyfraith eu gweithred y sydd	X43	Q79
Tri llwdn nid oes gwerth cyfraith arnynt	X44	Q80
Tri llwdn unwerth y sydd	Q110	
Tri mach y sydd ni chaiff un ohonynt ddwyn ei fechni ar ei lw	Q49	Q13
Tri maib caeth o rydd	Q146	
Tri maib ni ddylyant dref tad	Q168	
Tri maib rhydd o gaeth	Q145	
Tri maib yn dri brodyr un fam un dad	X37	Q74 [S166, S205]
Tri maich ni ddylyir eu gwadu	Q174	
Tri maich ni ddylyir eu gwadu	Q204	

Triad heading	Number	Other edition
Tri meflfethiant gŵr	Mk94	
Tri modd y bydd camlwrw	Z109	
Tri modd y bydd camlwrw deuddyblyg	Z112	
Tri modd y bydd camlwrw tridyblyg	Z113	
Tri modd y collir camlwrw undyblyg	Z111	
Tri modd y telir amobr i wraig	Q183	[Y154], see Q184
Tri oed cyfraith i ddial celain	X15	Q20
Tri ofer laeth y sydd	X27	Q68
Tri ofer ymadrodd a ddywedir yn nadlau ac ni ffynnant	X26	Q67
Tri phedwar y sydd	X22	Q69
Tri pherygl dyn ŷnt	Q255	
Tri pheth a â rhwng dyn a daly a damdwng	Q189	
Tri pheth a berthyn i frawdwr	Q7	
Tri pheth a ddiffer ddyn rhag gwys dadlau	Q152	
Tri pheth a ddyly brawdwr eu datganu pan farno	Q17	
Tri pheth a ddyly brawdwr o fraint tir ei wneuthur cyn barno dim	Q214	
Tri pheth a ddyly dyn golli ei ddadl, er daed fo ei ddefnydd	Mk96	
Tri pheth a ddyly gwarant diball eu gwneuthur	Q37	
Tri pheth a ddyly offeiriad llys ei wneuthur yn y dadleuoedd	Q250	
Tri pheth a ddyly pob brawdwr ei wrando i gan y cynhennwr	Q210	
Tri pheth a ddyly pob dyn ei gymryd heb ganiad arall	Q158	
Tri pheth a dyr ar gyfraith	X54	Q87
Tri pheth a gadarnha defod	Q239	
Tri pheth a geidw gof ac a saif yn lle tystion	Q112	
Tri pheth a hawl dyn yn lledrad ac ni chyngain lledrad ynddo	X36	Q31
Tri pheth a wanha cynefod	Q240	
Tri pheth ni ad cyfraith eu damdwng	X49	Q84
Tri pheth ni bydd dilys yng nghyfraith	S193	
Tri pheth ni chyfran brenin â neb	X21	Q30
Tri pheth ni chyngain yng nghyfraith	Q125	S213
Tri pheth ni ddrychefir arnynt	Q166	Q246
Tri pheth ni ddyly tafodiog eu dadlau dros ddyn arall	Q253	S168
Tri pheth ni ddyly ynad eu gwrando rhag ei fron	Q164	
Tri pheth ni ddylyir eu damdwng	Q191	

Triad heading	Number	Other edition
Tri pheth ni ddylyir eu rhannu namyn herwydd eu ffrwythau	Q188	
Tri pheth ni ddylyir nawdd rhagddynt o byddant addefedig	Q48	
Tri pheth ni ellir eu dwyn rhag gwraig cyd gwahaner â hi am ei cham	Q119	X10
Tri pheth ni ellir yn absen	S190	
Tri pheth ni henynt o fechni	Q52	
Tri pheth ni thelir cyd coller yn y rhandy	X69	Q98
Tri pheth nid ateb cyfraith ddilys drostynt	S195	
Tri pheth nid rhaid ateb i neb ohonynt	Q139	
Tri pheth nid rhaid mach ar ddilysrwydd drostynt	Q203	
Tri pheth nid rhaid prawf arnynt	Z116	
Tri pheth nid rhydd i filaen eu gwerthu heb gennad ei arglwydd	Q61	Q205, X6
Tri pheth nis dichon mach ei gaffael dros blaid estronol	S165	
Tri pheth or ceffir ar ffordd rhydd ŷnt i'r neb a'u caffo	X74	Q89
Tri pheth y cyll dyn ei hawl, er daed fo ei ddefnydd	Q54	
Tri pheth y sydd gymaint gwerth eu hanaf ag eu henaid	Q198	
Tri pheth y sydd un fraint â lladrad yn llaw	Z103	
Tri pheth y sydd uwch na chyfraith	Q167	[S199]
Tri phren a ddyly pob adeilwr maestir	Q97	
Tri phren y sydd rydd eu lladd i mewn fforest	X50	[Z91], Q85
Tri phrifiau gwraig ŷnt	S278	
Tri phriod gŵr	K34	
Tri phriodolder y sydd	Q224	
Tri phryf a ddyly brenin eu gwerth pa le bynnag y'u lladder	X48	Q83
Tri phwnc y sydd iawn eu gwadu	S188	
Tri rhyw amddiffyn y sydd	Q138	
Tri rhyw argaeëdigaeth dadl ŷnt	Q231	
Tri rhyw berchnogaeth y sydd ar dir	S171	
Tri rhyw brid y sydd ar dir	Q228	
Tri rhyw dâl y sydd i gwynwr	Q102	
Tri rhyw ddadanudd y sydd	Q229	
Tri rhyw ddiebryd y sydd	Q140	
Tri rhyw ddyn y sydd	Q4	
Tri rhyw ddyn y sydd a ddylyir eu mechniaethau oblegid arglwydd	Q254	[S182]
Tri rhyw ddyn y sydd ni ddylyir herwydd cyfraith erbynio neb	Q247	

Triad heading	Number	Other edition
Tri rhyw dremyg absen y sydd	Q216	[S156]
Tri rhyw dwng y sydd	Q14	
Tri rhyw fanag y sydd	Q16	
Tri rhyw farn tremyg y sydd	Q211	
Tri rhyw fraint y sydd	Q223	
Tri rhyw frawdwr y sydd yng Nghymru	Q208	
Tri rhyw gamddosbarth y sydd	Q217	
Tri rhyw gamlwrw y sydd	Z110	
Tri rhyw sarhaed y sydd i bob gŵr gwreigiog	Q2	
Tri rhyw wadu y sydd	Q12	
Tri rhyw wallawgair y sydd	Q123	
Tri rhyw warcheidwad y sydd ar dir herwydd cyfraith	S160	
Tri rhyw wasanaeth a wna offeiriad llys yn y dadleuoedd	Q5	
Tri rhyw wrogaeth y sydd	Q157	
Tri thafodiog	Q161	
Tri thân digyfraith y sydd	X46	[Z98], Q27
Tri thawedog gosgordd y sydd	X24	Q21
Tri therfyn cyfreithiol y sydd	Q142	
Tri therfyn hawl y sydd	Q124	
Tri thlos cenedl ŷnt	Q194	
Tri thorllwyth unwerth ag eu mam y sydd	Q109	
Tri ymddillwng o rwym hawl y sydd	Q103	
Tri ysgyfaethau milgi	K41	
Un o'r tri a gyll y neb a dreiser	Q137	

Latin Triads

In tribus festis debet distein ministrate in cibo et potu vii viris	LatB54	
In tribus locis debet rex persequi vulnus lingue	LatE79	
Tair gorsaf unben	LatB57	
Tres homines non sunt occidendi	LatA42	
Tres manus oportet convenire ad constituendum quem fideiussorem	LatB14	
Tres sunt libere venaciones villano	LatE25	
Tres sunt querimonie in quibus calumpnia verbo ad verbum	LatD33	
Tres sunt qui debent habere guirawt de curia	LatB52	
Tres sunt qui dicuntur tri tremyg argluyd	LatB73	
Tres sunt qui, si iniuriam invenerunt, nullum ius habebunt	LatE73	
Tres sunt rei conquestores a rege propter querelas suas puniendi	LatD32	

Triad heading	Number	Other edition
Tri anghyfarch gŵr	LatA37	
Tri argae terfyn	LatB60	
Tria animalia debet costauc tom habere pre leporariis et molosis	LatB59	
Tria solum sunt iudicia in lege constituta	LatD143	
Tria sunt forefacta regis	LatE74	
Tria sunt pro quibus non debetur refugium	LatE81	
Tribus de causis non potest corpus malefactoris redimi	LatA31	

Glossary

The following is a list of terms commonly used, and several of them are left in Welsh in the translation. A fuller discussion on some of the legal concepts discussed briefly here may be found in the notes on the triads.

agweddi: One of the several technical terms connected with marriage and unions, the *agweddi* was a specific, prearranged, sum taken from the matrimonial property which the woman received in the case of a justified separation from her husband in the first seven years of the union. After seven years, she received half of their common goods. The *agweddi* was measured according to the woman's natal status.

amobr: A virginity payment due to the lord when a woman was given in marriage, or when she had intercourse with a man for the first time.

argyfreu: A 'dowry' given to by the woman's kin to the married couple.

camlwrw: A fine payable to the king or the lord – three cows or 15s.

camweresgyn: literally 'wrongful taking of possession', alleging that someone had wrongfully taken possession of another person's land was one of the actions for land. *Goresgyn* means possession of land or taking possession of land.

cantref: The largest administrative unit in medieval Wales, the term means 'a hundred townships', similar to the English hundred. *Cantrefi* were divided into smaller units, the commotes.

cyngaws: The person who shares a case with a principal, so a pleader.

cynghellor: the main officer in local administration, he worked with, but was superior to, the *maer*.

dadannudd: literally 'uncovering the hearth'. This was another way of claiming land: the claimant would be a son claiming his patrimony. There are three actions for *dadannudd* in the lawtexts.

damweiniau: And also *Llyfr Damweiniau*, 'the book of cases', a Gwynedd text closely related to Ior. The *damweiniau* are a series of statements giving a possible legal situation and the legal judgement on the situation. They occur in collections of sentences beginning with *o derfydd*, 'if it happens'.

dirwy: The major fine of twelve cows or £3 due to the king or the lord.

ebediw: A death-duty, payable on succession to land, similar to the Anglo-Saxon heriot.

edling: The heir-apparent in the Welsh laws of court. The word is borrowed from Anglo-Saxon ætheling.

galanas: Literally 'enmity', it can be used to refer to homicide in general, or more commonly the payment for homicide or the life-price of a person. *Galanas* is one of the three columns of law, and the concept of life-price/honour-price is central to medieval Welsh law.

gwarcheidwaid: The one who has *gwarchadw*, possession or occupation of land, but usually that person does not hold the fullest right to land, *priodolder*, proprietorship.

gwestfa: The food-render owed to the king from the freemen.

holiadon: A collection of question-and-answer sentences found in some of the later lawbooks. The term *holiadon*, interrogatories, is not found in the lawbooks but was probably first used by Aneurin Owen in *Ancient Laws*.

lledrad: Theft, but *gweithred lledrad* can mean a stealth act. The basic concept of theft in the Welsh laws was something taken by stealth, and in contrast to something taken violently – *trais*.

Llyfr Cynghawsedd: The Book of Pleading, a thirteenth-century Gwynedd text, giving model examples of pleading in court.

Llyfr Prawf: The test book, or the justices' test book, one of the three main sections of *Llyfr Iorwerth*. The test book could be said to contain the core subjects of Welsh law which each jurist needed to know, and the basic contents were the three columns of law, and the value of wild and tame.

maer: A royal official responsible for local administration, along with the *cynghellor*.

maer y biswail: Dung *maer*. He had a similar function to the *maer* but in relation to the free tenants. He himself was unfree, and his title suggests that his office was the object of some contempt.

mechniaeth: Suretyship, or the law of contract. If a person was selling an animal to another person, an exchange needed to take place, and the *mach*, the surety, would be a third party called to witness the contract (including a ceremonial joining of hands) and also to ensure that the money was paid and that the animal was handed over. Some sureties would be expected to compel the debtor to pay, and others would be expected to pay on behalf of a defaulting debtor.

prid: Purchase, usually of land, but the term came to mean a gage or pledge of land, which was recovered on repayment of the debt which it secured.

rhaith: compurgation. *Rhaith gwlad*, compurgation of the country, is similar to a modern jury.

rhingyll: The serjeant. One of the officers of the court, his work involved maintenance of order and enforcement of the commands of authority, including summoning.

sarhaed: This can mean an insult, but usually refers to the compensation to a person for an injury to their honour. Every person had a *sarhaed* or fixed insult-price (honour-price), set according to status, which was payable for every deliberate injury.

three columns of law: Criminal law. The three columns of law were a large section of the Welsh lawtexts with a triadic form. The three columns are *galanas* or homicide, theft and arson.

wynebwerth: Literally face-value, *wynebwerth* is the oldest term for honour-price used in the law, and is interchangeable with *sarhaed*. The term *wynebwerth* is mainly found in the law of women, and the usage was narrowed to mean compensation for a sexual offence within marriage.

Bibliography

Primary Sources

Ancient Laws and Institutes of Wales, ed. A. Owen (London, 1841).

Bechbretha: An Old Irish Law-Tract on Bee-Keeping, ed. T. M. Charles-Edwards and F. Kelly (Dublin, 1983).

Breudwyt Ronabwy, ed. M. Richards (Cardiff, 2001).

Canu Aneirin, ed. I. Williams (Cardiff, 1961).

The Chirk Codex of the Welsh Laws, ed. J. G. Evans (Llanbedrog, 1921).

Corpus Iuris Hibernenici, ed. D. Binchy (Dublin, 1978).

Crith Gablach, ed. D. Binchy (Dublin, 1979).

Culhwch ac Olwen, ed. R. Bromwich and D. Simon Evans (Cardiff, 1997).

Cyfranc Lludd a Llefelys, ed. B. F. Roberts (Dublin, 1975).

Cyfreithjeu Hywel Dda ac Ereill seu Leges Wallicae Ecclesiasticae & Civiles Hoeli Boni et Alconium Wallicae Principium, ed. W. Wotton and W. Moses (London, 1730).

Cyfreithiau Hywel Dda yn ôl Llawysgrif Coleg yr Iesu LVII, ed. M. Richards, 2nd edn (Cardiff, 1990).

Damweiniau Colan, ed. D. Jenkins (Aberystwyth, 1973).

Geiriadur Prifysgol Cymru, ed. R. J. Thomas *et al.* (Cardiff, 1952–2002).

Gramadegau'r Penceirddiaid, ed. G. J. Williams and E. I. Jones (Cardiff, 1934).

Gwaith Gruffudd ap Maredudd III, ed. A. Parry Owen (Aberystwyth, 2007).

Gwaith Meilyr Brydydd a'i Ddisgynyddion, ed. J. E. Caerwyn Williams, P. Lynch and R. G. Gruffydd (Cardiff, 1994).

The Latin Texts of the Welsh Laws, ed. H. D. Emanuel (Cardiff, 1967).

The Laws of the Earliest English Kings, ed. F. L. Attenborough (Cambridge, 1922).

The Laws of Howel Dda: A Facsimile Reprint of Llanstephan MS 116 in the National Library of Wales, Aberystwyth, ed. T. Lewis (London, 1912).

The Laws of Hywel Dda, ed. M. Richards (Liverpool, 1954).

Llyfr Blegywryd, ed. S. J. Williams and J. E. Powell (Cardiff, 1942).

Llyfr Colan, ed. D. Jenkins (Cardiff, 1963).
Llyfr Cynog, ed. A. Rh. Wiliam (Pamffledi Cyfraith Hywel, 1990).
Llyfr Iorwerth, ed. A. Rh. Wiliam (Cardiff, 1960).
Pedeir Keinc y Mabinogi, ed. I. Williams (Cardiff, 1951).
'The triads of Ireland', ed. K. Meyer, *Royal Irish Academy Todd Lecture Series*, 13 (Dublin, 1906).
Trioedd Ynys Prydein: The Welsh Triads, ed. R. Bromwich, 2nd edn (Cardiff, 1978).
Welsh Medieval Law, ed. A. W. Wade-Evans (Oxford, 1909).

Secondary Literature

Aberystwyth Studies X: The Hywel Dda Millenary Volume (Aberystwyth, 1928).
The Welsh History Review Special Number: The Welsh Laws (Cardiff, 1963).
Beverley Smith, Ll., '"Cannwyll Dibwyll a Dosbarth": Gwŷr Cyfraith Ceredigion yn yr Oesoedd Canol Diweddar', *Ceredigion Antiquaries*, 3 (1986), 229–53.
——, 'Disputes and settlements in medieval Wales: the role of arbitration', *English Historical Review*, 106/421 (1991), 835–60.
Binchy, D. A., 'Distraint in Irish law', *Celtica*, 10 (1973), 27–71.
Brynmor-Jones, D., 'Foreign elements in Welsh law', *THSC* (1916–17), 1–51.
Bromwich, R., 'The historical triads: with special reference to Peniarth MS. 16', *BBCS*, 12 (1946), 1–15.
——, 'William Camden and *Trioedd Ynys Prydain*', *BBCS*, 23 (1968), 14–17.
——, '*Trioedd Ynys Prydain*: The Myvyrian "Third Series"', *THSC* (1968 + 1969), 229–338, 127–256.
——, '*Trioedd Ynys Prydain*' in *Welsh Literature and Scholarship* (Cardiff, Darlith Goffa G. J. Williams, 1969).
Carruthers, M., *The Book of Memory* (Cambridge, 1990).
Celtic Law Papers: Introductory to Welsh Medieval Law and Government, vol. 42, *Studies Presented to the International Commission for the History of Representatives and Parliamentary Institutions* (Aberystwyth, 1971).
Charles-Edwards, T. M., '*Edryd, Edryf, Edfryd, Edrydd*', *BBCS*, 23 (1969), 117–20.
——, '*Cynghawsedd*: counting and pleading in medieval Welsh law', *BBCS*, 33 (1984), 188–98.
——, *The Welsh Laws* (Cardiff, 1989).
——, *Early Irish and Welsh Kinship* (Oxford, 1993).
——, Owen, M. E., and Russell, P. (eds), *The Welsh King and his Court* (Cardiff, 2000).
——, Owen, M. E., and Walters, D. B. (eds), *Lawyers and Laymen* (Cardiff, 1980).

——, and Russell, P. (eds), Tair Colofn Cyfraith. *The Three Columns of Law in Medieval Wales: Homicide, Theft, and Fire* (Cardiff, 2007).

Cule, J., 'The court mediciner and medicine in the laws of Wales', *Journal of the History of Medicine and Allied Sciences*, 21 (1966), 213–36.

Davies, R. R., 'The twilight of Welsh law 1284–1536', *History*, 51 (1966), 143–64.

——, 'The survival of the blood feud in medieval Wales', *History*, 54 (1969), 338–57.

——, 'The law of the March', *WHR*, 5 (1970–1), 1–30.

Dillon, M., 'The semantic history of Irish *Gal* "Valour; Steam"', *Celtica*, 8 (1968), 196–200.

Emanuel, H. D., 'Llyfr Blegywryd a Llawysgrif Rawlinson 821', *BBCS*, 29 (1962–4), 23–8.

Evans, J. G., *Report on Manuscripts in the Welsh Language*, vols 1–4 (London, Historical Manuscripts Commission, 1898–1910).

Ford, P. K., and Hamp, E. P., 'Welsh *asswynaw* and Celtic legal idiom', *BBCS*, 26 (1974–5), 147–60.

Gruffydd, R. G., 'Cywyddau Triawdaidd Dafydd ap Gwilym', in J. E. Caerwyn Williams (ed.), *Ysgrifau Beirniadol*, 13 (1985), 167–77.

——, 'A glimpse of medieval court procedure in a poem by Dafydd ap Gwilym', in C. Richmond and I. Harvey (eds), *Recognitions: Essays Presented to Edmund Fryde* (Aberystwyth, 1996), 165–76.

Hamp, E. P., 'On the justification of ordering in TYP', *Studia Celtica*, 16/17 (1981/2), 104–9.

Hopper, V. F., *Medieval Number Symbolism* (Cambridge, 1906).

Huws, D., *The Medieval Codex with Reference to the Welsh Laws* (Pamffledi Hywel Dda, 1980).

——, *Peniarth 28: Darluniau o Lyfr Cyfraith Hywel Dda* (Aberystwyth, 1988).

——, *Medieval Welsh Manuscripts* (Cardiff, 2000).

James, C., 'Golygiad o BL Add. 22,356 o Gyfraith Hywel Ynghŷd ag Astudiaeth Gymharol Ohono â Llanstephan 116' (University of Wales Aberystwyth Ph.D. thesis, 1984).

——, 'Llyfr Cyfraith o Ddyffryn Teifi: Disgrifiad o BL. Add. 22, 356', *NLWJ*, 27 (1991–2), 383–404.

——, 'Tradition and innovation in some later medieval Welsh lawbooks', *BBCS*, 40 (1993), 148–56.

——, 'Ysgrifydd Anhysbys: Proffil Personol', in J. E. Caerwyn Williams (ed.), *Ysgrifau Beirniadol*, 23 (Denbigh, 1997), 44–72.

Jenkins, D., 'Deddfgrawn William Maurice', *NLWJ*, 2 (1941–2), 33–6.

——, 'Llawysgrif Goll Llanforda o Gyfreithiau Hywel Dda', *BBCS*, 14 (1950–2), 89–104.

——, 'Iorwerth ap Madog: Gŵr Cyfraith o'r Drydedd Ganrif ar Ddeg', *NLWJ*, 8 (1953–4), 164–70.

——, 'A lawyer looks at Welsh land law', *THSC* (1967), 220–46.

——, *Cyfraith Hywel* (Llandysul, 1976).

——, '*Cynghellor* and chancellor', *BBCS*, 27 (1976–7), 115–18.

——, 'The significance of the law of Hywel', *THSC* (1977), 54–76.

——, *The Law of Hywel Dda* (Llandysul, 1986).

——, 'Pencerdd a Bardd Teulu', in J. E. C. Williams (ed.), *Ysgrifau Beirniadol*, 14 (Denbigh, 1988), 19–44.

——, '*Gwalch*: Welsh', *CMCS*, 19 (1990), 53–67.

——, and Owen, M. E. (eds.), *The Welsh Law of Women* (Cardiff, 1980).

Jones, R. M., 'Tri Mewn Llenyddiaeth', *Llên Cymru* 14 (1981–2), 92–110.

Jones Pierce, T., 'The law of Wales: the last phase', in J. B. Smith (ed.), *Medieval Welsh Society: Selected Essays by T. Jones Pierce* (Cardiff, 1972), 369–89.

Kelly, F., *A Guide to Early Irish Law* (Dublin, 1988).

——, *The Three Best Things* (Belfast, 1993).

——, 'Thinking in threes: the triad in early Irish literature', *Proceedings of the British Academy*, 125 (2003 lectures), 1–18.

Linnard, W., *Trees in the Law of Hywel* (Pamffledi Cyfraith Hywel, 1979).

——, 'The Nine Huntings: a re-examination of *Y Naw Helwriaeth*', *BBCS*, 31 (1984), 119–32.

Lloyd, N., and Owen, M. E. (eds), *Drych yr Oesoedd Canol* (Cardiff, 1986).

Lloyd Jones, J., 'Gweilydd' *BBCS*, 11 (1941), 37–8.

Matonis, A., 'Problems relating to the composition of the Welsh bardic grammars', in A. Matonis and D. F. Melia (eds), *Celtic Language, Celtic Culture: A Festschrift for Eric P. Hamp* (California, 1990), 3–94.

Maund, K., *The Welsh Kings: The Medieval Rulers of Wales* (Stroud, 2000).

Owen, M. E., '*Cynllwyn* a *Dynyorn*', *BBCS*, 22 (1966–8), 346–50.

——, 'Y Trioedd Arbennig', *BBCS*, 24 (1972), 434–50.

——, 'Y Cyfreithiau (1): Natur y Testunau', in G. Bowen (ed.), *Y Traddodiad Rhyddiaith yn yr Oesau Canol* (Llandysul, 1974), 196–218.

——, 'Y Cyfreithiau (2): Ansawdd y Rhyddiaith', in G. Bowen (ed.), *Y Traddodiad Rhyddiaith yn yr Oesau Canol* (Llandysul, 1974), 220–44.

——, 'Trioedd hefut y6 yrei hynn', in J. E. Caerwyn Williams (ed.), *Ysgrifau Beirniadol*, 14 (1988), 87–114.

——, 'Gwŷr Dysg yr Oesoedd Canol', in J. E. Caerwyn Williams (ed.), *Ysgrifau Beirniadol*, 17 (Denbigh, 1990), 42–62.

Parry, T., 'Statud Gruffudd ap Cynan', *BBCS*, 5 (1929–31), 25–33.

Pickering, D., *The Cassell Dictionary of Folklore* (London, 1999).

Pollock, F., and Maitland, F., *The History of English Law Before the Time of Edward I*, 2 vols (Cambridge, 1895).

Powell, J. E., 'Floating sections in the law of Hywel', *BBCS*, 9 (1937–9), 27–34.

Pryce, H., 'The prologues to the Welsh lawbooks', *BBCS*, 33 (1986), 151–82.

——, *Native Law and the Church in Medieval Wales* (Oxford, 1993).

——, 'Lawbooks and literacy in medieval Wales', *Speculum*, 75 (2000), 29–67.

——, 'The context and purpose of the earliest Welsh lawbooks', *CMCS*, 39 (2000), 39–63.

Rees, W., *South Wales and the March 1284–1415* (Oxford, 1924).

Roberts, S. E., 'Legal practice in fifteenth-century Brycheiniog', *Studia Celtica*, 35 (2001), 307–23.

——, 'Creu trefn o anhrefn: gwaith copïydd testun cyfreithiol', *NLWJ*, 32 (2002), 397–420.

——, 'Addysg broffesiynol yng Nghymru yn yr oesoedd canol: y beirdd a'r cyfreithwyr', *Llên Cymru*, 26 (2003), 1–17.

——, 'Tri Dygyngoll Cenedl: the development of a triad', *Studia Celtica*, 37 (2003), 163–82.

——, 'Plaints in mediaeval Welsh law', *Journal of Celtic Studies*, 4 (2005), 219–61.

Rowlands, E. I., 'Bardic lore and education', *BBCS*, 32 (1985), 143–55.

Russell, P., 'The etymology of *affaith* "abetment"', *BBCS*, 38 (1991).

——, 'Scribal (in)competence in thirteenth-century north Wales: the orthography of the Black Book of Chirk (Peniarth MS. 29)', *BBCS*, 29 (1995), 129–76.

——, *Vita Griffini Filii Conani: The Medieval Latin Life of Gruffudd ap Cynan* (Cardiff, 2005).

Sorabji, R., *Aristotle on Memory* (London, 1972).

Stacey, R. C., *The Road to Judgement: From Custom to Court in Medieval Ireland and Wales* (Philadelphia, 1994).

——, 'Ties that bind: immunities in Irish and Welsh law', *CMCS*, 20 (1990), 39–57.

——, 'Learning to plead in medieval Welsh law', *Studia Celtica* 38 (2004), 107–23.

Stephenson, D., *Thirteenth Century Welsh Law Courts: Some Notes on Procedure and Personnel* (Pamffledi Cyfraith Hywel, 1980).

——, *The Governance of Gwynedd*, Studies in Welsh History, 5 (Cardiff, 1984).

Walters, D. B., '*Meddiant* and *goresgyn*', *BBCS*, 31 (1984), 112–18.

Wiliam, A. Rh., 'Y Deddfgronau Cymraeg', *NLWJ*, 8 (1953), 97–103.

Williams, J. E. Caerwyn, *Traddodiad Llenyddol Iwerddon* (Cardiff, 1958).

——, 'Beirdd y Tywysogion: Arolwg', *Llên Cymru*, 11 (1970–1), 3–94.

Index to the Triads

The Index is a guide to the subjects found in the triads, and triad numbers are given. Key words are in the order of the English alphabet. Terms found in the glossary are left in Welsh.

Index to the notes